PEARSON ALWAYS LEARNING

Compiled by Dr. Craig Edwards

Introduction to Literature
Discovering Theme through Form

Indiana Wesleyan University
ENG 243

ISBN 10: 1-323-42189-0
ISBN 13: 978-1-323-42189-5

GENERAL EDITOR

John Bryant, *Hofstra University*

ASSOCIATE EDITOR

David Shields, *University of South Carolina*

PERIOD EDITORS

John Bryant, *Hofstra University*
Jacquelyn McLendon, *The College of William and Mary*
Cristanne Miller, *University at Buffalo, The State University of New York*
Robin Schulze, *Pennsylvania State University*
David Shields, *University of South Carolina*

COPYRIGHT ACKNOWLEDGMENTS

Table of Contents

Workshop I: Faith and Other Relationships

Workshop 2: What Constitutes a Well-lived Life?

Workshop 3: The Individual Versus the Community

Workshop 4: The Scales of Justice and Mercy

Workshop 5: The Quest for Hope and Redemption

Additional Stories

Workshop 1: Faith and Other Relationships

Active Reading of Literature

Does the following scenario sound familiar to you?

> Sitting in your Introduction to Literature course, you wonder what you might possibly be able to say about the story assigned for today's class. Another student, in response to a question by your instructor, offers an interpretation of the main character's behavior. "How did she *come up* with that?" you wonder. "I read the same story and *nothing* like that even occurred to me. I guess some people just have it and some don't."

Don't be too sure of that. Many people share a relatively common misperception about understanding literature—that some people can read a story, a novel, a play, or a poem once and understand all of its subtle nuances. Not so. In fact, critics, instructors, and experienced students of literature formulate insightful observations not because of some genetic literary superiority but because of the *way they read* a literary work. Those critics, instructors, and students engage in what is called **active reading**, an activity in which they engage with the work rather than simply passively taking in what the author has written. Most of us do a good deal of **passive reading** every day: We scan newspaper or magazine articles; we read letters, notes, e-mails; we browse Web sites. But there is a significant difference between this type of reading and the type necessary to appreciate fully a work of literature. Perhaps an analogy to listening would help explain the difference. Although people are surrounded by music much of the time, they don't always *listen* to it. When the radio is on in the background—in the cafeteria, in the car, at the gym, at home—people rarely really pay attention to the music. They are aware of it, but they don't appreciate it fully. Even when people are dancing, they focus on little more than the rhythm of the music. But when you have just bought your favorite artist's new CD, or when a friend has burned an exciting new mix for you, or when you are settling in at a live concert, you pay attention. You hear the melodies; you listen to the lyrics; you distinguish between instruments and voices. It is at times such as these that you truly appreciate the music. The same holds true for reading: There is a time to treat reading as a chore, or as a type of background music, and there is a time to truly pay attention to it. In order to appreciate what literature can reveal about humanity, its history, and its prospects, it is necessary to take the time to explore or analyze works of literature.

"Easy for you to say," you may be thinking. Actually, it *is* easy for experienced readers of literature to say—after all, they have developed an aptitude for analysis. But this appreciation is not something reserved for the literary scholar. Active reading can be learned, and it can benefit even the most skeptical reader.

Reading Actively

What happens when you read actively? Put simply, you become engaged in a conversation with the author—a conversation that expands when you discuss the literary work in class, read articles about the work, and eventually write a paper about it. These larger conversations, however, begin privately, between the reader and the writer. Since you, the reader, are just feeling your way around the material, you cannot expect to take much meaning from it at first. You and the author do not know each other yet. You might consider the analogy of a couple's first meeting on a blind date, or of college roommates meeting for the first time. You converse, and you understand each other's words, but you do not yet know that your roommate is a very reticent, low-key person whose "It's all right" is the equivalent of your "Wow, this is fabulous!" You only get to know those things after paying close attention to the other person's way of speaking, to his or her "style." You do much the same thing with the literature you read. Some writers are like the first roommate—their prose is clipped, sparse, and seemingly not very demonstrative. Consider, for example, this passage from Bobbie Ann Mason's story "Shiloh":

> Leroy is a truckdriver. He injured his leg in a highway accident four months ago, and his physical therapy, which involves weights and a pulley, prompted Norma Jean to try building herself up. Now she is attending a body-building class. Leroy has been collecting temporary disability since his tractor-trailer jackknifed in Missouri, badly twisting his left leg in its socket. He has a steel pin in his hip. He will probably not be able to drive his rig again.

Others write with an abundant, complex, and rich style, as in this passage from William Faulkner's "A Rose for Emily":

> They rose when she entered—a small, fat woman in black, with a thin old chain descending to her waist and vanishing into her belt, leaning on an ebony cane with a tarnished gold head. Her skeleton was small and spare; perhaps that was why what would have been merely plumpness in another was obesity in her. She looked bloated, like a body long submerged in motionless water, and of that pallid hue. Her eyes, lost in the fatty ridges of her face, looked like two small pieces of coal pressed into a lump of dough as they moved from one face to another while the visitors stated their errand.

You are not always aware of such differences when you first encounter an author. And even if you have already read something by a given author, you cannot know his or her characters, the situation of a story or play, or the theme of a poem until you have lived with them for a while. That roommate whom you were sure you would never understand may well become your best friend by the end of the semester; the blind dates who seemed completely inscrutable to each other may end up spending the rest of their lives together.

In both cases, continuing the conversation makes it possible for the parties to understand each other better. So the moral of *this* story is: Look at the mystery of a literary work as a challenge, an adventure of sorts. Getting to know a story, a play, or a poem can be enjoyable in much the same way that getting to know another person is—if you take the time and put in the effort.

The first thing to do when you set out to read a literary work actively is to leave yourself enough time to truly engage with the work. Consider Kate Chopin's "The Story of an Hour" (reproduced at the end of this chapter), for example. This brief story would not take more than ten or fifteen minutes to read passively. But such a reading would at best clue you in to the basic plot of the story. If you are to get a sense of the flavor of Chopin's language, the significance of her imagery, or the inner workings of Mrs. Mallard's mind, you have to slow down and become engaged with the story. This chapter will introduce you to some of the strategies that will help you to enter into a conversation of sorts with a writer, focusing on you and the literary work. There are two stages involved in active reading: **preliminary reading** and **annotating the text**. The following outline provides a glimpse of what will be covered in the remainder of the chapter.

Preliminary Reading
    Reviewing Prior Knowledge
    Asking Questions

Annotating the Text
    Commenting on Language
    Making Note of Familiar Passages
    Commenting on Imagery and Theme
    Making Note of Difficult Passages

Preliminary Reading

Even before you begin reading, you can prepare yourself to get the most out of a work of literature. The first steps to take in active reading might be more accurately called **preliminary reading: reviewing prior knowledge** and **asking questions**.

Reviewing Prior Knowledge

What is prior knowledge? Quite simply, it refers to what you may already know that is relevant to the literary work you are reading. Perhaps you have read something before by this author, or heard the author's name in another class. Perhaps you are familiar with the *genre* (play, poem, short story, novel, essay) or with the setting of the work. In addition to considering what you already know, you may also want to begin thinking about any relevance a literary work may have to your own experience. Often in an introductory literature class, the instructor will briefly lecture about the writer and the context in which a literary work was produced; in an anthology such as this, headnotes provide biographical and other contextual information on the writer; an instructor might also provide a link to an electronic source such as *Dictionary of Literary Biography.* Such resources can be invaluable in helping you enter into conversation with the writer. Consider, for example, the headnote for Kate Chopin (at the end of this chapter). In it you learn that Kate Chopin wrote at the turn of the twentieth century, that she grew up in a household dominated by strong women, and that her best work, *The Awakening*, caused a scandal that all but ended her publishing career. Perhaps you recall a history class in which you learned about American cultural values during that period, perhaps you too come from a home in which women played a dominant role, or perhaps you have read *The Awakening* in another course. When your instructor introduces the story by talking about the sense of freedom that creeps up on Mrs. Mallard after she is told of her husband's death, perhaps you think about what you have come to know about rigidly prescribed sex roles in the late nineteenth century. All of these pieces of information constitute *prior knowledge*, and taken together, they can help you to navigate your way through the story. No matter how marginally relevant prior knowledge seems at first, it can come in handy by making the material you are about to read more familiar to you. Your recollections from the history class and your knowledge of turn-of-the-twentieth-century sex roles, for example can help you understand Mrs. Mallard's sense of married life as a sort of prison. Your own experience with strong women might prepare you for Chopin's characterization of Mrs. Mallard. And your familiarity with *The Awakening* can prepare you for Mrs. Mallard's rather shocking response to the news of her husband's death. Regardless of the extent of your general knowledge or the nature of your personal experience, drawing on prior knowledge offers you a unique perspective from which to consider the story.

Asking Questions

Many students have been afraid, at one time or another, that their questions might sound stupid to others—especially to an instructor. Granted, it is sometimes difficult to ask a question in front of an entire class, but when you are in the privacy of your own reading space, who cares how stupid the question seems to be? Nobody is there to hear it but you, and most "stupid" questions are not stupid at all. In fact, you should be asking questions throughout your reading process, and beyond it in your discussions of a literary work. However, the initial questions you ask can help you make sense of what you are reading. One of the first and most common questions readers have about literary works is, "Why this title?" (In fact, that question is particularly relevant with regard to Chopin's story, since a well-received film version of it was retitled "The Joy that Kills.") When you think about the original title, "The Story of an Hour," you might ask yourself why the time frame of an hour is so significant. With this question in mind, you will be more likely to appreciate the profound significance of this one hour in Mrs. Mallard's life—in one sense, she lives her entire life in that hour. This single question at the beginning of your reading can lead you to a clearer understanding of an apparently significant theme in the story.

More academically oriented questions can lead you to do a little research even before reading a literary work. Often research is considered an activity that occurs well after reading, writing responses, and discussing a work—an expansion, if you will, of the initial conversation between reader and writer. Occasionally, however, you might find yourself interested enough to do a little preliminary research. For example, say you want to learn more about the author before reading the work. Although it is not necessary to have biographical information before reading a text, it is often interesting to get an idea of the mind behind the material. That is why this anthology includes headnotes on each writer. If you consider engaging with a text as a conversation between you and the writer, then it might seem natural to explore the writer's world more closely before reading. Often two parties engaged in conversation try to find out something about one another; in this case, as a reader you might want to know more about the writer with whom you are engaged in this form of conversation. The headnotes provided are obviously a starting point, but you can also explore Web sites such as the *Dictionary of Literary Biography* to discover more about the author. Biographical information will not necessarily unlock all of the mysteries found in a literary work. However, in much the same way that people discussing any subject sometimes like to know a little about their partners in conversation, readers sometimes feel more comfortable if they know something about the author before they begin to read. Learning about the strong female role models in Chopin's life, for example, will probably make Mrs. Mallard's brief experience with freedom more understandable, while the knowledge that Chopin herself was very happy in her marriage will strike a discordant note. Taken together, these two pieces of information should cause you to look more closely at Chopin's characterization of Mrs. Mallard. Thus preliminary questions not only provide you with an interesting perspective from which to read, but encourage you to pay keener attention to the text as well.

Annotating the Text

Whether you have made extensive prereading notes or simply jotted down a few questions, the next steps in active reading will truly be active, engaging you in that conversation with the author that has been promised throughout the first part of this chapter. As you begin to read more closely, you will begin **annotating** the text: underlining significant words, phrases, and passages, as well as writing observations and questions in the margins. Sometimes you will find yourself underlining brief passages that simply grab you. If a passage is compelling enough for you to underline it, then it is probably worth remembering, and it can help you to understand the work better. You might also find your pen drawn to sections that make you think, perhaps a segment in which the writer seems to present in excessive detail a scene that at first appears irrelevant. For example, in "The Story of an Hour" Chopin provides the following lengthy description of what Mrs. Mallard sees from her window as she takes in the news of her husband's death.

> She could see in the open square before her house the tops of trees that were all aquiver with the new spring life. The delicious breath of rain was in the air. In the street below a peddler was crying his wares. The notes of a distant song which some one was singing reached her faintly, and countless sparrows were twittering in the eaves.
>
> There were patches of blue sky showing here and there through the clouds that had met and piled one above the other in the west facing her window.

You might wonder why Chopin takes such care with a description of a scene wholly unrelated to the train accident, the news that Mrs. Mallard has received, and her response to that news. You might underline a few of the more vivid images in the description and write in the margin something like "significance of scene?" Later, when you have finished your close reading of the story, you will be able to put that annotation together with others to get a sense of how they fit and contribute to an understanding of the story.

As you read you will find other reasons for underlining passages or making notes in the margins. Perhaps a description in a play reminds you of a religious image, for example, or a name in a novel sounds like it comes from a famous Greek myth. Perhaps a certain phrase recurs several times in a poem, or a character in a story has a distinctive way of speaking. Or perhaps you come across a passage that intrigues you—you are not quite sure of what it means or what to make of it. When you encounter such references or uses of language, it is well worth making note of them. At first you might be uncertain about what to annotate, but rest assured, the more you engage in active reading, the more comfortable you will become with how and when to annotate a text. As you discuss your annotations with fellow students, you will also discover that each reader responds differently to a text.

A word of caution: Underlining significant passages is fine so long as you do not overdo it. When you begin to discuss the literary work, and especially when you begin to write a formal paper about it, you do not want to look at pages and pages filled from top to bottom with underlined passages. If you underline too much, you defeat the purpose of the exercise. Remember, underlining should be reserved for *selected* important words and passages.

Now that you are familiar with the how-to, what are some of the things to look for when annotating a selection? Again, what you choose to annotate depends on your experience, your familiarity with the author or the genre, and your personal response to the literature. If you pursue the study of literature further, your critical perspective will also influence the nature of your annotations. What follows is a discussion of some common types of annotation that you might find helpful as you become accustomed to reading actively. The following outline lists the areas that will be covered:

Commenting on Language
Images
Descriptions
Repetition
Similes and Metaphors

Making Note of Familiar Passages
Cross-References
Reminders of Your Own Experience
References to Myths, Religion, or Classical Figures

Commenting on Characterizations
Personalities of Characters
Dialogue

Making Note of Difficult Passages
Intriguing Passages

In the following discussion you will encounter examples from a number of different literary works that might not appear in your anthology. Do not be concerned if you are not familiar with many of them; it is not necessary to understand the entire work in order to appreciate, for example, an author's use of language. In fact, it is only through careful attention to language, dialogue, and references *as you read* that you can come to a fuller understanding of a literary work. (At the end of the chapter you will find a few sample annotations of "The Story of an Hour" for you to compare with your own annotations.)

Commenting on Language

Frequently, when readers are engrossed in a literary work, they pay little conscious attention to the language used by the writer. But in fact, it is precisely that language that makes the work so engrossing. Think for a moment: Do you know people who always tell a great story, or others who can bore and confuse you with even the most exciting material? Anyone who has heard the same story from two different sources understands how important language is to the tale. Naturally, then, one of the first things you will find yourself looking at as you annotate a text is how the author presents the material. The following examples illustrate various uses of language and should give you an idea of what to look for as you make note of significant passages.

Images

You might be familiar with F. Scott Fitzgerald's *The Great Gatsby*. The last line of that book creates a very powerful image: "And so we beat on, boats against the current, borne back ceaselessly into the past." Some of you might also be familiar with William Butler Yeats's poem "The Second Coming," which ends with the question "And what rough beast, its hour come round at last, / Slouches toward Bethlehem to be born?"

Each of these passages focuses on an *image*, a picture created by the writer to help the reader understand what he is saying. Some readers find that Fitzgerald's image suggests a world-weary frustration with life. Even without having read the novel, someone who thinks about these lines can feel the drag of the current (the past) on the boats (people trying desperately to move beyond the past). Similarly, reading Yeats's last lines creates a picture in some readers' minds: A "rough beast" is surely something to fear, especially since the poet tells us that its time (to rule the world?) has come "at last." Even without considering the cryptic reference to Bethlehem, the town of Jesus of Nazareth's birth, the image is disquieting. It is through an understanding of images like these—an understanding that arises not from the intellect but from the emotions—that readers begin to make sense of the larger work.

Descriptions

One of the most powerful tools a writer has at her or his disposal is *description*; the mark of a skilled writer is the ability to convey a sense of place so that the reader can fully experience it. In *Incidents in the Life of a Slave Girl*, Harriet Jacobs describes the tiny attic space in which she hid from her master for almost seven years.

The garret was only nine feet long and seven wide. The highest part was three feet high, and sloped down abruptly to the loose board floor. There was no admission for either light or air. . . . To this hole I was conveyed as soon as I entered the house. The air was stifling; the darkness total. A bed had been spread on the floor. I could sleep quite comfortably on one side; but the slope was so sudden that I could not turn on the other without hitting the roof. The rats and mice ran over my bed; but I was wary, and I slept such sleep as the wretched may, when a tempest has passed over them.

Note that there is no flowery language used in this description; the garret is described in the simplest and most ordinary terms. But that is precisely what makes the scene so compelling—to think that this hole, as Jacobs calls it, was her dwelling place for almost seven years. No amount of inflated prose extracted from the pages of a thesaurus could come close to this matter-of-fact, photographic account of Jacobs's prison.

Sometimes, however, it is appropriate to use more lavish language to describe a scene. Consider Elizabeth Barrett Browning's apocalyptic vision in "The Cry of the Human."

> The plague runs festering through the town,
>   And never a bell is tolling,
> And corpses, jostled 'neath the moon,
>   Nod to the dead-cart's rolling;
> The young child calleth for the cup,
>   The strong man brings it weeping,
> The mother from her babe looks up,
>   And shrieks away its sleeping.
> Be pitiful, O God!

Barrett Browning's language is certainly less ordinary than Jacobs's. Each writer is describing a fearsome place, but the approach is quite different in the poem. The fact that Barrett Browning chooses language that cries out with emotion tells the reader that her purpose is different from Jacobs's. There has to be a *reason* why Jacobs does not choose to use the kind of language Barrett Browning uses; as readers continue to annotate, write about, and discuss the two works, these reasons will become clearer. But the first step toward understanding is simply making note of the fact that the writer has used a particular type of description—an underlined passage, with the marginal note "vivid language," is enough to remind the reader that the description is worth remembering.

Repetition

The importance of repetition in verse is indisputable. From the song-games children play to the music adults listen to, the refrain plays an important role in conveying meaning. In speeches, repetition is particularly effective. Many of you are probably familiar with one of the most famous phrases in modern American history, the "I have a dream" refrain from Martin Luther King, Jr.'s speech at the 1963 March on Washington.

Even in fiction, repetition can take on the role of a refrain. Consider, for example, the first paragraphs of Leslie Marmon Silko's short story "Yellow Woman." At the opening of the story the narrator, having awakened on a riverbank before her lover, mounts a horse, observing that the animal "felt warm underneath me." Then as she talks to her mysterious lover, she remembers the previous night and "his warmth around me." Later, as they embrace, she reflects on the way he feels, "warm, damp, his body beside me." At the end of the section, when the lover finally brings the narrator to his house, he asks her to "come inside where it's warm." If you read this section of the short story closely, you cannot help but make a mental note of the repetition of the word "warm." Clearly, that sensation is important to the narrator. Simply making note of this refrain, either by underlining the repeated words or by writing a margin note, will inform your reading of the rest of the story.

Similes and Metaphors

Perhaps the most powerful tools of language that the writer can use are similes and metaphors. Sometimes referred to as *figurative language*, similes and metaphors allow the writer to use a familiar image to help explain something that might not be familiar to the reader, or to convey a particular impression. In Nadine Gordimer's novel *A Sport of Nature*, for example, the following simile appears: "He talked about 'his book' as a companion and a leg-iron by which he had been shackled a long time, dragging it around the world with him." Comparing a book that a person is writing to the image of a companion is something most of us can understand. But comparing the book to a legiron is something else again. Some readers will sense that the task of writing serves to imprison this character.

Metaphors, unlike similes, actually present an equation without using the words "like" or "as." The main character in James Joyce's "The Dead" uses a metaphor to convey how he responds to the sound of a song. "To follow the voice, without looking at the singer's face, was to feel and share the excitement of swift and secure flight." Clearly the song in this instance has a profound effect on Gabriel; he feels himself take wing as he listens.

Both metaphors and similes help readers understand what writers and their characters want to convey. As readers make note of these figures of speech, they can begin to put the figures together with other elements of the literary work to make its meaning clearer.

Making Note of Familiar Passages

One of the reasons why literature provides pleasure for so many readers is the sense of familiarity if offers. As readers enter the world created by the writer, they become familiar with language, settings, characters, and action. Sometimes they find material that relates to their own lives, and sometimes they discover references to other works they have read—particularly classics, myths, or religious texts. This familiarity not only provides pleasure, but it also helps readers make meaning of literary works.

Cross-References

Dictionaries, encyclopedias, and other reference books make frequent use of **cross-references**, references in one part of the book to related material in another part. For example, in an encyclopedia entry on "World Series" you might find the cross-reference "See also 'Baseball.' " In a literary work, the writer frequently makes reference to other parts of the work. The reference might be in the form of dialogue, with different characters saying almost the same thing at different times. Or a writer might use similar terms or images to describe different settings or characters. It is up to the reader to make note of those cross-references. As you read a literary work, you will become aware gradually of references to other parts of the selection. In August Wilson's *Joe Turner's Come and Gone*, for example, characters continually make reference to travel and roads: In the first scene a character talks of men "working on the road gang with the sweat glistening on them." Later in that same scene a newcomer tells where he has come from: "Come from all over. Which ever way the road take us that's the way we go." Toward the end of the scene a woman tells of her lost love, who "was born in Alabama then . . .come to West Texas and find me and we come here . . .[Then] he started walking down the road and ain't never come back." This story is followed closely by a young man's asking her to be his companion: "You wanna go along the road a little ways with me?" When considered together, these and numerous other references to roads, wandering, and travel lead some readers to discover a *theme* of instability and searching in the play. A reader who has underlined such references and made margin notes of pages where cross-references appear will be able to recognize the pattern that emerges.

Reminders of Your Own Experience

Often readers find themselves drawn to works that reflect their own experience. Literature is an exploration of the human condition; therefore it is only natural that readers find characters, settings, or concepts that remind them of their own experience. For example, someone reading John Donne's

"The Good Morrow" might recall that feeling brought on by first deep love;

> I wonder, by my troth, what thou and I
> Did till we loved?
> . . .
> If ever any beauty I did see,
> Which I desired, and got, 'twas but a dream of thee.

Many people reading this poem will have experienced deep love at least once, and many will sympathize with Donne's wondering what he and his lover did all their lives until they met, as well as sharing his belief that all other beauty is "but a dream of" the only true beauty, his love.

References to Myths, Religion, or Classical Figures

At times readers recognize references to myths, religion, or classical figures in literature. Since most writers are themselves avid readers, such references abound in poetry, drama, and fiction. Consider, for example, Thomas Pynchon's novel *The Crying of Lot 49*. Pynchon's main character, Mrs. Oedipa Maas, must solve the riddle of the estate left by real estate mogul Pierce Inverarity. The names in the novel call attention to themselves; would any reader know real people by those names? This is a fairly clear indication that the names are significant. Many readers will recognize that "Oedipa" is the feminine form of "Oedipus." The fact that Oedipa must solve a riddle of sorts recalls *Oedipus Rex*, the ancient Greek play by Sophocles in which Oedipus must solve the riddle of the sphinx. A reader familiar with the Oedipus story will be able to make use of the reference in coming to terms with the novel.

References to religion also abound in literature. Regardless of the writer's affiliation, he or she can draw on religious images familiar in the culture. In her poem "I dreaded that first Robin," for example, Emily Dickinson calls the bird "The Queen of Calvary." Many readers will recognize the reference to the hill on which Jesus of Nazareth was executed. That reference underscores the dread the speaker feels in the first line, calling up a vivid image of pain, suffering, and death.

In Robert Bolt's play *A Man for All Seasons* a particular reference to a classical figure is found. The "man for all seasons" is Thomas More, the great humanist and Chancellor of England under King Henry VIII. When Henry insists that More sign an oath declaring the king to be the head of the Church of England, More cannot bring himself to comply — even though his refusal means certain death. When told that he has been dubbed "the English Socrates," More replies, "Socrates! I've no taste for hemlock, Your

Excellency, if that's what you require." This scene calls to mind quite specifically the ancient Greek philosopher's suicide after being condemned for his teachings. The reference not only emphasizes Thomas More's intense desire to avoid martyrdom, but it also reinforces the greatness of his character. After all, few people in history are as widely known and respected as Socrates.

Perhaps a reader is not familiar with all of the references cited here. They assume some knowledge of the concept of romantic love, of classical mythology, of the New Testament of the Bible, and of ancient Greek philosophers. Every reader encounters unfamiliar references on occasion. Sometimes a literary work is grounded in a culture unfamiliar to you, or sometimes you find references to classic works of your own culture that you have yet to read. Most literary works, however, can be understood without a thorough knowledge of all references; furthermore, many college texts (such as this one) provide annotations to acquaint readers with unfamiliar references. And as you continue your education, you will become better acquainted with your own and other cultures. Regardless, you will always find many references to some familiar material in your reading, and paying close attention to those references can enhance your appreciation of a literary work.

Commenting on Characterizations

Readers come to know characters in literary works in much the same way that they come to know others in real life. The character's own words and actions are often revealing, as is what others (in literature, narrators and/or authors) say about the character.

Descriptions of Characters

In Margaret Atwood's *Cat's Eye*, the young girl narrating the story describes her only friend in school, Carol. The passage reads like one half of a conversation in which one person is describing to another her initial impressions of a third person.

> She tells me her hair is honey-blond, that her haircut is called a pageboy, that she has to go to the hairdresser's every two months to get it done. . . . Carol and her younger sister have matching outfits for Sundays: fitted brown tweed coats with velvet collars, round brown velvet hats with an elastic under the chin to hold them on. They have brown gloves and little brown purses. She tells me all this.

This description reveals to readers a little girl caught up in appearance, probably well-to-do, and perhaps a bit of a snob. (Of course, the narrator also reveals something about herself as she describes Carol: There is more than a touch of envy in the lines.) A reader might underline or bracket this passage and make a margin note referring to both Carol's character and the narrator's envy.

Dialogue

Often a character is best understood through his or her own words. In real life, initial impressions are often formed to a great extent through conversation. It is possible to tell where a person comes from, her social class, education, likes, and dislikes simply by listening to her in conversation. Characters in literature provide readers with the same opportunity. In drama readers expect to become acquainted with characters through their words, since plays are almost exclusively dialogue. But fiction writers also use dialogue to allow their characters' personalities to emerge. Eudora Welty does precisely this in her story "Petrified Man." In the following conversation, the beautician Leota and her customer Mrs. Fletcher are discussing how they met their husbands. Mrs. Fletcher says, "I met Mr. Fletcher, or rather he met me, in a rental library." Leota responds, "Honey, me an' Fred, we met in a rumble seat eight months ago and we was practically on what you might call the way to the altar inside of half an hour."

Mrs. Fletcher's reference to her husband as "Mr. Fletcher," (implying that it is not ladylike for a woman to introduce herself to a man), and her reference to the rental library reveal a woman who prides herself on propriety. Leota, on the other hand, calls Mrs. Fletcher "honey," calls her husband by his first name, uses nonstandard English ("me an' Fred," "we was"), and jokingly intimates that she and Fred engaged in sex in the back seat of a car on their first date. Leota is clearly not one to worry about proper behavior; in fact she seems to revel in her earthiness. Each of these women is characterized without the author's ever having commented on her; the women themselves reveal their personalities. Noting these personality characteristics in the margins of the text allows readers to recall the basis on which they have made judgments about the two women.

You should be aware that characterization is not confined to fiction and drama. Often a poem reveals character as well. In Countee Cullen's "Incident," for example, the narrator relates the story of his first visit to Baltimore as a child. Smiling at white child, he is shocked when the other child responds by sticking his tongue out and saying, "Nigger." The poem ends with the narrator's lament that of everything that happened during his six-month stay in the city, "That's all that I remember." The innocence of the narrator and the ignorant hatred of the white child contribute significantly to the meaning of the poem.

Making Note of Difficult Passages

At one time or another every reader encounters confusing or intriguing passages in a literary work. Sometimes it is only after several readings and a good deal of conversation that readers can make meaning of such passages. Simply making note of them by underlining and perhaps putting a question mark in the margin is all you need to do initially. Often you will come to a clearer understanding of the passage as you continue to read. If not, you can address the issue as you write about the work and discuss your responses to it with classmates.

Intriguing Passages

Poetry often presents readers with intriguing passages. Because of the need to say so much in so little space, and the need to pay close attention to rhythms as well as to meaning, poetry can be difficult to understand on first reading. But it is precisely that difficulty that makes reading poetry so rewarding—in poetry, perhaps more so than in any other genre, the reader is aware of the interaction, the conversation, between writer and audience. A case in point is Gerard Manley Hopkins's "I wake and feel the fell of dark." The last two stanzas of this poem read as follows:

> I am gall, I am heartburn. God's most deep decree
> Bitter would have me taste: my taste was me;
> Bones built in me, flesh filled, blood brimmed the curse.
> Selfyeast of spirit a dull dough sours. I see
> The lost are like this, and their scourge to be
> As I am mine, their sweating selves; but worse.

Why would the speaker describe himself as "gall" and "heartburn"? Is he tasting something or is he talking about what he tastes like? What is "self-yeast" and why does the "dull dough" sour? And what does sweating have to do with anything else in these lines? All of these questions seem unanswerable at first, but in fact, began to address them, you would begin to make meaning of the poem. Simply making note of the lines as you annotate will call your attention to them later as you write about the poem and discuss it in class.

Conclusions

When you begin doing prereading activities and reading actively, perhaps all that you will do is follow the steps outlined in this chapter. That's all right; frequently it is only later, after reflection, that you begin to put some of these annotations together to make meaning of the literary work. You will also develop your own style of making notes and annotating, using symbols and code words that have evolved as you feel more and more comfortable reading literature. In fact, once you become accustomed to reading actively, you might find yourself unable to pick up a literary work without a pen in your hand. You can also find yourself willingly—sometimes eagerly—rereading lines, passages, and even entire sections of a work. When that happens, you will know that you have taken your place in the initial conversation that leads to making meaning of a text.

Sample Annotations

KATE CHOPIN
[1851–1904]

Born in St. Louis to an Irish immigrant father and a French Creole mother, KATE CHOPIN enjoyed a life of wealth and privilege. During her early years she was <u>influenced heavily by a number of strong women</u>; after her father's death in 1855, Kate was reared by her mother, grandmother, and great-grandmother. Although her upbringing was conventional according to genteel Southern standards, she exhibited an <u>independent spirit</u> at an early age, preferring her books and writing tablet to dancing with shallow young men. Regardless of her tastes, at nineteen she wed a Louisiana businessman, Oscar Chopin, to whom she was <u>happily married</u> for twelve years before his untimely death. A young widow with six children, Chopin returned to St. Louis and began writing. Her first stories were published in 1889, followed by a novel, At Fault, in 1890.

Chopin gained national attention with the publication in 1894 of Bayou Folk, a collection of stories that featured settings and characters culled from her years in Louisiana among French Creoles. Soon she was being compared to other <u>"local color" writers</u>—writers who focus on the cultures and customs of specific areas of the country—such as Sarah Orne Jewett and Hamlin Garland. Critics also recognized the influence of French writer Guy de Maupassant, as well as Americans Nathaniel Hawthorne and Walt Whitman, in Chopin's work. In 1897 a second collection, A Night in Acadie, was greeted with equal enthusiasm by readers and critics alike. Both turned on the author in 1899, however, when her novel The Awakening was published. Exploring the sexual and social rebellion of protagonist Edna Pointellier, a young wife and mother, <u>the novel challenged existing moral standards</u> and shocked the public. Chopin was accused of fostering immoral behavior with her uncritical depiction of Edna, who chooses suicide *rather than succumb to the rigid requirements of marriage and motherhood in turn-of-the-century New Orleans. Reception of the novel was so harsh that Chopin's publisher cancelled publication of her next volume of short stories,* A Voice and a Vocation, *in 1899.*

Chopin was devastated by the negative response to The Awakening, *which she considered (as do many contemporary critics) her best work. Although she had published twenty poems, almost a hundred short stories—including children's stories, two novels, a play, and several critical essays—in a ten-year period, she wrote very little after 1900. When she died of a brain hemorrhage at age 53, her contributions to American literature were almost forgotten. Her reputation was revived in 1969 with the publication of* The Complete Works of Kate Chopin, *edited by Per Seyersted. Late twentieth-century critics recognized the <u>existential quality of Chopin's work,</u> as well as her courageous <u>social criticism,</u> particularly with regard to women's lives. <u>Chopin's women,</u> from the peasant Calixta in "The Storm" to the middle-class Mrs. Mallard in "The Story of an Hour," <u>exhibit an independence and vitality rarely found in late nineteenth century female characters.</u> Chopin's prose is considered as vividly poetic as that of Hawthorne, and her characters as complex as those of Henry James. In the past several decades she has been recognized as one of the most significant writers in the American canon.*

Edna

The Story of <u>an Hour</u>

one hour?

KATE CHOPIN

KNOWING THAT MRS. MALLARD was afflicted with a heart trouble, great care was taken to break to her as gently as possible the news of her husband's death.

It was her sister Josephine who told her, in broken sentences, veiled hints that revealed in half concealing. Her husband's friend Richards was there, too, near her. It was he who had been in the newspaper office when intelligence of the railroad disaster was received, with Brently Mallard's name leading the list of "killed." He had only taken the time to assure himself of its truth by a second telegram, and had hastened to forestall any less careful, less tender friend in bearing the sad message.

She did not hear the story as many women have heard the same, with a paralyzed inability to accept its significance. She wept at once, with sudden, wild abandonment, in her sister's arms. When the storm of grief had spent itself she went away to her room alone. She would have no one follow her.

There stood, facing the open window, a comfortable, roomy armchair. Into this she sank, pressed down by a physical exhaustion that haunted her body and seemed to reach into her soul.

She could see in the open square before her house the <u>tops of trees</u> that were all <u>aquiver with the new spring life.</u> The delicious <u>breath of rain</u> was in the air. In the street below a peddler was crying his wares. The notes of a distant song which someone was singing reached her faintly, and <u>countless sparrows</u> were twittering in the eaves.

There were <u>patches of blue sky</u> showing here and there <u>through the clouds</u> that had met and piled above the other <u>in the west</u> facing her window.

She sat with her head thrown back upon the cushion of the chair, quite motionless, except when a sob came up into

detailed description of nature significance of scene?

"elixir of life life"

19

her throat and shook her, as a child who has cried itself to sleep continues to sob in its dreams.

strong woman

She was <u>young,</u> with a fair, calm face, whose lines bespoke <u>repression and</u> even a certain <u>strength.</u> But now there was a dull stare in her eyes, whose gaze was fixed away off yonder on one of those patches of blue sky. It was not a glance of reflection, but rather indicated a suspension of intelligent thought.

image - animal?

There was something coming to her and she was waiting for it, fearfully. What was it? She did not know; it was too subtle and elusive to name. But she felt it, <u>creeping out of the sky, reaching toward</u> her through the sounds, the scents, the color that filled the air.

Now her bosom rose and fell tumultuously. She was beginning to recognize this thing that was approaching to possess her, and she was striving to beat it back with her will—as powerless as her two white slender hands would have been.

When she abandoned herself a little whispered word escaped her slightly parted lips. She said it over and over under her breath: "Free, free, free!" The vacant stare and the look of terror that had followed it went from her eyes. They stayed keen and bright. Her pulses beat fast, and the coursing blood warmed and relaxed every inch of her body.

dissonance:
monstrous

joy
"joy that kills"

She did not stop to ask if it were or were not a <u>monstrous joy</u> that held her. A clear and exalted perception enabled her to dismiss the suggestion as trivial.

She knew that she would weep again when she saw the kind, tender hands folded in death; the face that had never looked save with love upon her, fixed and gray and dead. But she saw beyond that bitter moment a long procession of years to come that would belong to her absolutely. And she opened and spread her arms out to them in welcome.

There would be no one to live for her during those coming years; she would live for herself. There would be <u>no powerful will bending her</u> in that blind persistence with which men and women believe they have a right to impose a private will upon a fellow-creature. A <u>kind intention or a cruel intention made the act seem no less a crime as</u> she looked upon it in that brief moment of illumination.

important - loved him

And yet <u>she had loved him</u>—sometimes. Often she had not. What did it matter! What could love, the unsolved mystery, count for in face of this possession of self-assertion which she suddenly recognized as the strongest impulse of her being!

"Free! Body and soul free!" she kept whispering.

Josephine was kneeling before the closed door with her lips to the keyhole, imploring for admission. "Louise, open the door! I beg; open the door—you will make yourself ill. What are you doing, Louise? For heaven's sake open the door."

description of nature ¶ₛ 5,6

"Go away. I am not making myself ill." No; <u>she was drinking in a very elixir of life through that open window.</u>

Her fancy was running riot along those days ahead of her. <u>Spring days, and summer days,</u> and <u>all sorts of days</u> that would be her own. She breathed a quick prayer that <u>life might be long.</u> It was only yesterday she had thought with a shudder that <u>life might be long.</u>

*days...
days...
days*

She arose at length and opened the door to her sister's importunities. There was a feverish triumph in her eyes, and she carried herself unwittingly <u>like a goddess of Victory.</u> She clasped her sister's waist, and together they descended the stairs. Richards stood waiting for them at the bottom.

classical image

Someone was opening the front door with a latchkey. It was Brently Mallard who entered, a little travel-stained, composedly carrying his gripsack and umbrella. He had been far from the scene of accident, and did not even know there had been one. He stood amazed at Josephine's piercing cry; at Richards' quick motion to screen him from the view of his wife.

*dissonance:
"joy that kills"
|
"monstrous
joy"*

But Richards was <u>too late.</u>

When the doctors came they said she had died of heart disease—<u>of joy that kills.</u>

John Donne
[1573–1631]

The son of a wealthy London merchant and a noblewoman, a relative of Sir Thomas More, JOHN DONNE began life with great advantage. He attended both Cambridge and Oxford and studied law. His father's death when he was nearing twenty left him a wealthy and independent young man. Donne is a fascinating study for he displays many features of the early modern period that coincide with the writing of Shakespeare's plays. He was both a wild young man about town, and a serious religious writer who struggled with the conflicts between his early Catholicism and the Anglicanism that blew in on the winds of change, dominating England throughout the first decade of the 1600s. By the time he was twenty, he had finished the poems in his Divine Poems as well as the first three poems in his Satires. By 1594 he wandered through Europe and by 1596 and 1597, he had served as a soldier in Cadiz and traveled to the Azores. In addition, his travels to Italy and Spain introduced him to the excitement of the literary and artistic Renaissance that swept through the south of Europe. Upon his return to London, he secretly married the daughter of Sir George Moore, lord lieutenant of the Tower of London, an act for which he was thrown in prison by his outraged father-in-law. Sir Francis Wooley rescued him and provided a home for the couple. The poetry he wrote to his wife is among the most treasured of personal writing from husband to wife. He finished his Satires and The Progress of the Soul during this time (1601). He also wrote a defense of suicide, Biathanatos, which was not published until after his death.

Donne then embarked on a mental and spiritual struggle that brought him to take holy orders in the Anglican Church in 1611. He wrote prose against Catholicism, Pseudo-Martyr (1610) and Ignatius His Conclave (1611), as well as his great mystical treatise, The Anatomy of the World. He was a favorite preacher of King James I and was appointed the Dean of St. Paul's Cathedral in 1621, a post he held until his death. His collected poems were printed in 1633, but his prose works, including his Letters and more than 150 Sermons were published in assorted venues from 1633 to 1651.

Donne displayed a range of intellectual and poetic talents as well as a multitude of personal faces. Thus he is remembered and admired as one of the great poets and thinkers of his own era and of the twentieth century as well. Donne has been appreciated for his conceits, his satire, his profound mysticism, and his political insight. Few poets have been so complete and so essentially paradoxical as John Donne.

Batter my heart, three-personed God, for You

JOHN DONNE

Batter my heart, three-personed God, for You
As yet but knock, breathe, shine, and seek to mend.
That I may rise and stand, o'erthrow me, and bend
Your force to break, blow, burn, and make me new.
I, like an usurped town to another due,   5
Labor to admit You, but Oh! to no end.
Reason, Your viceroy in me, me should defend,
But is captived, and proves weak or untrue.
Yet dearly I love You, and would be lovèd fain,
But am betrothed unto Your enemy;   10
Divorce me, untie or break that knot again;
Take me to You, imprison me, for I,
Except You enthrall me, never shall be free,
Nor ever chaste, except You ravish me.

[C. 1610]

Published 1635 in *Poems*.

GWENDOLYN ELIZABETH BROOKS
[1917–2000]

In 1950, Gwendolyn Elizabeth Brooks won a Pulitzer Prize for her poetry collection Annie Allen *(1949). As the first African American to win a Pulitzer, Brooks both established her own reputation as a skilled poet and helped to pioneer the serious scholarly consideration of "black" belles-lettres. Publishing her first collection,* A Street in Bronzeville *(1945), nearly two decades after the "vogue" of the Harlem Renaissance literary movement, Brooks was determined to show that the kind of poetry she wrote—poetry depicting the concerns, lives, and culture of African Americans—was "good," even if not modeled on the work of white poets such as Ezra Pound. From her earliest work throughout a career that spanned over sixty years, Brooks's poetry and prose focused primarily on ordinary black people because she firmly believed that "what was common could also be a flower." This belief motivated the development of what the poet herself would come to call a "G. B. voice," a voice that she sustained throughout her career and one that influenced generations of younger black poets.*

Born in Topeka, Kansas, on June 7, 1917, Brooks began very early searching for and developing her own poetic voice, in large part due to the encouragement of her parents. David Anderson Brooks and Keziah Corine (Wims) Brooks both valued learning and passed their attitude on to Brooks and her brother, Raymond, who was sixteen months her junior. David Brooks had attended Fisk University for a year but finally had to drop out, foregoing his plans to pursue a medical career. Keziah Brooks, having graduated from Emporia State Normal School, taught fifth grade at Monroe School in Topeka Kansas, where she had been born and raised. To encourage their daughter's interest in writing, David Brooks provided her with a desk and Keziah Brooks saw to it that she had time away from household chores to write. Indeed, her mother predicted that Brooks would become a "lady Paul Laurence Dunbar." Just as important in her development, she later explained, was the warmth and love of the Brooks household. According to Brooks, her family was "poor but happy," a sentiment she used to describe her early married life with Henry Lowington Blakeley II, whom she married in 1939 and with whom she had two children: Henry III, born in 1940, and Nora, born in 1951.

No doubt in large part owing to the devotion and support of her parents, Brooks began to share her poetry outside her household at an early age. When she was eleven years old, a local paper, Hyde Parker, published several of her poems. At thirteen, she was published in American Childhood. By the time she was sixteen years old, her poems were being published weekly in the "Lights and Shadows" column of the Chicago Defender. Also at age sixteen, probably at the urging of her mother, Brooks sent some of her poems to James Weldom Johnson, a prominent Harlem Renaissance figure, who wrote her in response, telling her that she had talent and advising her to read the modern poets. However, when she later met Johnson in person, he did not remember having written to her. It was a different story with Langston Hughes. Hughes, also a well-known Harlem Renaissance figure, spoke on an occasion at the church the Brooks family attended and her mother gave him "a whole pack of [Gwendolyn's] stuff," which he read on the spot. He encouraged her to keep writing. Some years later, Brooks became well enough acquainted with Hughes to entertain him in her home. Hughes's positive attitudes about race and about the word "black," as well as his belief in the importance of writing about the ordinary aspects of black life were great influences on her poetry and poetic career. Although, according to Brooks herself, her earliest poetry was of the lofty type, she realized that it was best to write from her own milieu. Thus, most of her writing fit her description of her novella, Maud Martha (1953), in that it was taken from real life and "twisted... highlighted or dulled, dressed up or down." The people Brooks knew or heard stories of as she was growing up, mostly family members, became the subjects of her poetry.

Despite Brook's undeniable talent, the early attention her poetry had received, and her graduation from Wilson Junior College in 1936, "at first the only work the poet could find was that of a domestic," according to D. H. Mellen, who has written extensively on Brooks. This was not her first experience with the negative effects of having dark skin and it would not be her last. Important, however, was that she made poems from this negative experience. The light skin versus dark skin theme, which critics commonly called the "black and tan motif," runs throughout much of the early work in poems such as "the ballad of chocolate Mabbie," "The Anniad," "Jessie Mitchell's Mother," and more. Other experiences influenced her writing, for example, her "four 'horrible' months as secretary to a spiritual adviser who sold lucky numbers and 'magic potions'," especially recognizable in the work she initially conceived of as a novel but that eventually became the book-length poem In the Mecca (1968).

Brooks's poetry reflects her responses to the world in which she lived, beginning with the impact of poverty, oppression, and war on the lives of black people in A Street in Bronzeville (1945). Especially remarkable is her use of the sonnet form to write about reflections on World War II by some of the men who fought in it. Her use of conventional forms such as the sonnet was the basis of some criticism regarding her so-called "dual commitment," or the *white style and black content of her poetry. Brooks indeed appropriated conventional forms, but her use of them for unconventional subjects provides the foundation for her masterful handling of the irony that so pervades her poetry. In* A Street in Bronzeville, *her sonnet sequence, "Gay Chaps at the Bar," for example, describes the thoughts and feelings of black servicemen, their chaotic lives, and their futile attempts to achieve order. They were once "gay chaps at the bar," but they "return from the front crying and trembling." Brooks certainly was not the first poet to use the sonnet for socio-political commentary rather than expressions of love, nor was she the first to use the form for black subject matter. What distinguishes her sonnets are their technical complexity—as with most of her poetry. They are variants on, sometimes parodies of, the traditional Petrarchan and Shakespearean forms, often defying scansion. Other poems in the collection describe the poor occupants of the "kitchenette building," who are "Grayed in and gray," or "the old marrieds," who are constrained to be silent in the "crowding darkness" of their lives. She depicts sympathetically "chocolate Mabbie," who is doomed to loneliness because of her dark skin, and "Satin-Legs Smith," whose aspirations surpass his possibilities.*

Brooks also appropriates a traditional form for "The Anniad," the mock-heroic poem that is central to Annie Allen. *The title alludes to Homer's* The Iliad *and Vergil's* The Aeneid *and uses the conventions of the epic for commonplace characters, events, and situations. In many of the poems in these collections and such famous collections as* The Bean Eaters *(1960), —which, as Mellon describes rightly, "sounds the righteous thunder of the Civil Rights Movement," —themes center on the harsh reality of the cramped physical and emotional space of the poor as well as larger issues of violence and racism. The famous case of Emmet Till, the fourteen-year-old boy who was killed in a violent hate crime, as one of the many examples, is poeticized in "A Bronzeville Mother Loiters in Mississippi. Meanwhile a Mississippi Mother Burns Bacon" and "The Last Quatrain of the Ballad of Emmet Till," poems that have caused some to accuse Brooks of "forsaking lyricism for polemics."*

The three above-mentioned collections, her autobiographical bildungsroman Maud Martha, *and her book-length poem* In the Mecca, *represent the bulk of her poetry published during the first twenty-five years of her poetic career. She also wrote reviews for Chicago's* Daily News, Sun Times, *and* Tribune, *as well as for* Black World *(then the* Negro Digest), *the* New York Times, *and the* New York Herald Tribune. *She taught poetry throughout her career at numerous colleges and universities, including Columbia College, Elmhurst College, Northeastern Illinois State College (now Northwestern Illinois University), the University of Wisconsin–Madison, and briefly at the City College of New York. In 1968, she succeeded Carl Sandburg as Poet Laureate of Illinois.*

Brooks's decision to use black publishers at this point in her career marked a significant change. Harper & Row had been her publisher since 1945, but from the publication of Riot in 1969, with the exception of The World of Gwendolyn Brooks (1971 by Harper), the bulk of her work was published by Broadside Press and Third World Press until the 1980s when she began publishing under her own imprint, The David Company. Her poetry did not circulate as widely once she moved from Harper, but the change coincided with, or perhaps was a direct result of, one of the great influences on her career, indeed on her life—the Black Arts movement. This influence of the "contemporary young black voice of the 1960s" marks a change from her integrationist views, although she did not move entirely to the opposite extreme of separatism. Indeed, the pro-black and feminist themes that had always dominated her poetry were still predominant but expressed, perhaps, more urgently. The calm and rational, albeit ironic, tones of her earlier poetry had all but disappeared by the time she wrote In the Mecca, representing what she called her "newish voice."

In fact, many critics cite the 1967 Second Black Writers' Conference at Fisk University, where she became acquainted with many of these younger poets, as a major turning point in her approach to poetry. however, as David Perkins has rightly pointed out in A History of Modern Poetry, Brooks wrote about black urban life "because it was what she naturally knew, what roused her emotion. She had continued to be the same type of poet. Her poems are personal responses to particular events." To say that she is the "same type of poet" means that she has remained true to her stated desire "to write poems that will somehow successfully 'call' . . . all black people; black people in taverns, black people in alleys, black people in gutters, schools, offices, factories, prisons, the consulate . . . black people in pulpits, black people in mines, on farms, on thrones." Some of the best expressions of this desire in her later poetry are the poems in To Disembark (1981) and Children Coming Home (1991).

In 1996 Brooks published her second autobiography, Report From Part Two, twenty-four years after her first, Report from Part One. Both books also depart from convention with their lack of a linear, chronological narrative structure. They include reminiscences of her life, interviews, photographs, sketches of poems, and other writings. Part Two, in addition, contains introductions of well-known poets appearing as speakers at the Library of Congress when Brooks was its Poetry Consultant (1985–86). The most striking aspect of both of her autobiographies is their orality, drawing them closer to the poetic quality of the rest of her writing.

Brooks wrote poetry and traveled to various writers conferences throughout the rest of her life. She sustained a career in which she continually received an abundance of fellowships, grants, and other awards and honors: the Guggenheim (1946, 1947); grants from The American Academy of Arts and Letters and the National Institute of Arts and Letters; the Shelley Memorial Award; the Ainsfield-Wolf Award; the Kuumba Liberation Award; the Frost Medal from the Poetry Society of America; a National Book Award nomination for In the

Mecca; *the National Endowment for the Arts Lifetime Achievement Award; and numerous honorary degrees. A cultural center at Western Illinois University and a junior high school in Harvey, Illinois, have been named after her.*

Gwendolyn Brooks died at the age of eighty-three at her home in Chicago, Illinois. Her last contribution to the world of poetry is an anthology titled In Montgomery: New and Other Poems, *published posthumously by Third World Press, containing poems previously published in* Children Coming Home, *as well as new and recent poems.*

For Further Reading

Primary Works

A Street in Bronzeville (New York: Harper & Brothers, 1945); *Annie Allen* (New York: Harper & Brothers, 1949); *Bronzeville Boys and Girls* (New York: Harper & Brothers, 1956); *The Bean Eaters* (New York: Harper & Row, 1960); *Selected Poems* (New York: Harper & Row, 1963); *The Wall: For Edward Christmas* (Detroit: Broadside Press, 1967); *In the Mecca* (New York: Harper & Row, 1968); *Riot* (Detroit: Broadside Press, 1969); *Family Pictures* (Detroit: Broadside Press, 1970); *Aloneness* (Detroit: Broadside Press, 1971); *Jump Bad: A New Chicago Anthology* (Detroit: Broadside Press, 1971); *The World of Gwendolyn Brooks* (New York: Harper & Row, 1971); *The Tiger Wore White Gloves* (Chicago: Third World Press, 1974); *Beckonings* (Detroit: Broadside Press, 1975); *Primer for Blacks* (Chicago: Black Position Press, 1980); *To Disembark* (Chicago: Third World Press, 1981); *The Near-Johannesburg Boy and Other Poems* (Chicago: The David Company, 1986); *Blacks* (Chicago: The David Company, 1987); *Gottschalk and the Grande Tarantelle* (Chicago: The David Company, 1988); *Winnie* (Chicago: The David Company, 1988); *Children Coming Home* (Chicago: The David Company, 1991); *In Montgomery: New and Other Poems* (Chicago: Third World Press, 2002). **Prose:** *Maud Martha* (New York: Harper & Brothers, 1953); *The Black Position,* annual vol., ed. Brooks (Detroit: Broadside Press, 1971–); *Report from Part One* (Detroit: Broadside Press, 1972); *A Capsule Course in Black Poetry Writing* (Detroit: Broadside Press, 1975); *Young Poet's Primer* (Chicago: Brooks Press, 1980); *Report from Part Two* (Chicago: Third World Press, 1996).

Secondary Works

Bloom, Harold, ed. *Gwendolyn Brooks* (Philadelphia: Chelsea House Publishers, 2000); Bolden, B. J. *Urban Rage in Bronzeville: Social Commentary in the Poetry of Gwendolyn Brooks, 1945–1960* (Chicago: Third World Press, 1999); Christian, Barbara. *Black Feminist Criticism: Perspectives on Black Women Writers* (New York: Pergamon Press, 1985); Kent, George E. *A Life of Gwendolyn Brooks* (Lexington: University Press of Kentucky, 1990); Melhem, D. H. *Gwendolyn Brooks: Her Poetry and the Heroic Voice* (Lexington: University Press of

Kentucky, 1987); Mootry, Maria K. and Gary Smith, eds. *A Life Distilled: Gwendolyn Brooks, Her Poetry and Fiction* (Urbana and Chicago: University of Illinois Press, 1987); Shaw, Harry B. *Gwendolyn Brooks* (Boston: Twayne, 1980); Spillers, Hortense J. "Gwendolyn the Terrible: Propositions on Eleven Poems," in *Shakespeare's Sisters: Feminist Essay on Women Poets,* ed. Sandra M. Gilbert and Susan Gubar (Bloomington: Indiana University Press, 1979); Washington, Mary Helen. "'Taming All That Anger Down': Rage and Silence in Gwendolyn Brooks' Maud Martha," in *Black Literature and Literary Theory,* ed. Henry Louis Gates, Jr. (New York: Methuen, 1984); Wright, Stephen Caldwell, ed., *On Gwendolyn Brooks: Reliant Contemplation* (Ann Arbor: University of Michigan Press, 1996).

We Real Cool

GWENDOLYN ELIZABETH BROOKS

The Pool Players.
Seven at the Golden Shovel.[1]

We real cool. We
Left school. We

Lurk late. We
Strike straight. We

Sing sin. We   5
Thin gin. We

Jazz June.[2] We
Die soon.

[1960]

---

[1]a pool hall in Chicago.
[2]enjoying popular music and the summer of youth.

EDNA ST. VINCENT MILLAY
[1892–1950]

The poet and critic Allan Tate once referred to Edna St. Vincent Millay as "not an intellect, but a sensibility." Both condemned and applauded as a poet of sentiment rather than sense, sensuality rather than depth, personality rather than profundity, Millay seems doomed to attract attention for her life rather than her art. Yet, rather than read Millay as a victim of her own bohemian excesses, it is more useful to remember her as a powerful presence in a world not yet comfortable with women determined to make spectacles of themselves. The very notion of spectacle played an important part in early twentieth century female activism. The theater of the early twentieth century was often the only place where a woman could be rewarded for her transgressions. Theatricality, for Millay, was not merely a literary concept. While a student at Vassar, Millay both penned plays and acted in them; the theater formed the organizing basis of her college experience. When she moved to New York City after her graduation in 1917, Millay set her sights on Broadway. Her poems sustained her intellectually, but her dream was the stage — the performance space that offered a complete melding of art and personality. Her introduction to the modern world of Greenwich Village bohemia came not through her poetry, but through her desire to act. In the fall of 1917, Millay appeared on the doorstep of 137 MacDougal Street, the recently established winter home of the avant-garde theater troupe, the Provincetown Players — the creative home of Susan Glaspell, Eugene O'Neill, John Reed, and Jig Cook. She came to audition for a part in a play by Floyd Dell, the writer who would become one of her many lovers. Only when Dell read the name on her call-back sheet did he realize that she was the Edna Millay, the one who had burst onto the literary scene at the tender age of nineteen with the long, visionary poem "Renascence." Millay came to the Village, not as a poet, but as a performer.

Indeed, recent reassessments of Millay's verses picture them as the speaking parts of the roles that Millay chose to play: the imp, the cynic, the disappointed romantic, the happy bohemian, the elegiac troubadour, the love goddess. At times, Millay speaks as a New Woman, championing her right to live fast, die young, and leave a nice looking corpse, as in "First Fig":

My candle burns at both ends;
  It will not last the night;
But ah, my foes, and oh, my friends—
  It gives a lovely light!

Poetry: A Magazine of Verse, *June 1918*

At other times, Millay speaks as a passive observer of her own fate, imagining the aftermath of the rush of experience as a kind of curse, as in "Ebb":

I know what my heart is like
  Since your love died:
It is like a hollow ledge
Holding a little pool
  Left there by the tide,
  A little tepid pool,
Drying inward from the edge.

Second April *(1921)*

Both poems depict self-extinction in very different ways. Critics also credit Millay with pushing the boundaries of "proper" poetic subject matter in her frankly sexual verses and reinvigorating the sonnet with her colloquial undercutting of the conventions of the form.

Born in 1892, Millay was raised in Maine by an iconoclastic, independent, divorced mother. Millay began writing verse while in high school in Camden and, in 1912, entered her first long poem, "Renascence," in a poetry contest run by publisher Mitchell Kennerley to fill the pages of his Lyric Year *anthology. While the poem did not win a prize, it set off a firestorm of controversy in its failure. Readers of the anthology loved the poem and wrote in droves to complain about the judging. Millay became a literary celebrity and, as the result of the attention, secured a sponsor who paid for her college education. Kennerley also agreed to publish a volume of her verse. Millay's first book of poems,* Renascence and Other Poems, *appeared in 1918, the year after she graduated from Vassar.*

After college Millay moved to New York City. Once established as a poet, actress, and playwright with the Provincetown crew, she began to publish poems in a variety of venues, including Ainslee's; *the* Dial; *the* Yale Review; *the* Smart Set; Poetry: A Magazine of Verse; *and with the coaxing of another of her Village lovers, Edmund Wilson,* Vanity Fair. *In April of 1920, a group of twenty of Millay's sonnets appeared in Reedy's* Mirror, *staking her special claim to that verse form. By late 1919, Millay had collected enough poems to complete a second volume for Kennerley, titled* Second April. *The book's* appearance was delayed, however, and in the summer of 1920, she made the fateful decision to publish a set of "light verses" as a separate chapbook under the imprint of a Greenwich Village book shop owned by Frank Shay. A Few Figs from Thistles appeared in November 1920, and Millay once again found herself a literary celebrity. Her set of witty, often biting, rhymes depicting the devil-may-care spirit of her bohemian world struck a chord with her contemporaries. She was hailed as "the spokesman for the New Woman" and her "First Fig" (quoted above) became an anthem of "rebellious 'flaming' youth."

Penning the anthem of a generation, however, proved a mixed blessing for Millay. Her popular status carried with it certain pressures. Those inclined to favor her more "serious" poetry were dismayed by the flippant tone of A Few Figs from Thistles. Those enamored of A Few Figs were disappointed when her subsequent volume (Second April finally appeared in 1921) did not deliver similar fare. Millay further complicated the issue of her audiences with the 1922 pamphlet release of a long, sentimental poem titled "The Ballad of the Harp-Weaver," spoken from the perspective of a small boy. The poem captured a wide popular audience and helped to secure Millay the first Pulitzer Prize ever awarded a female author in 1923, but it infuriated many of her modernist peers. John Gould Fletcher dismissed the language of the poem as "the verbal utterance of a primer . . . used to deal out an idea which is wishy-washy to the point of intellectual feebleness." Millay then bundled her poem together with a mature and masterful set of sonnets, including her experimental narrative sonnet sequence, "Sonnets from an Ungrafted Tree," to form her fourth book, The Harp Weaver and Other Poems (1923). Throughout her career, Millay refused to limit herself to one voice or one audience. Her desire to play to a variety of houses often baffled her readers.

In 1923, she surprised her bohemian friends by getting married and leaving the Village for a quiet farm in the Berkshires. For the remainder of the 1920s, Millay wrote the libretto for The King's Henchman, an opera by American composer Deems Taylor that was performed at the Metropolitan Opera in early 1927. That same year she protested the executions of Sacco and Vanzetti, the immigrant anarchists who many believed were wrongly convicted of murder because of their political beliefs. Several of her most political poems, penned in response to the executions, made their way into her 1928 volume, The Buck in the Snow. Filled with contemplative verses that address broad moral and ethical questions about the state of mankind, the book left many readers cold. Edmund Wilson referred to the poems as "studied," a sign of his own unwillingness to accept Millay's poetry as anything other than an emotional experience. In 1931, however, Millay again fanned the flames of her own literary celebrity with the release of Fatal Interview, a narrative set of sonnets that tells the story of a passionate extra-marital affair. Rather than discuss the poems, her readers set to work trying to discover the identity of Millay's secret lover.

The late 1930s and 1940s were not particularly kind to Millay, although she kept publishing even as her health and reputation waned. Disturbed by the rise of fascism and the prospect, soon realized, of World War II, Millay wrote a series of books of poems that expressed her anxieties: Wine from These Grapes *(1934), which included the extended sonnet sequence "Epitaph for the Race of Man";* Huntsman, What Quarry *(1939);* Make Bright the Arrows: 1940 Notebook *(1940), which included her long, didactic poem in favor of an American entry into World War II; "There Are No Islands Any More"; and* The Murder of Lidice *(1942), her long verse elegy to the Czech village exterminated by the Nazis in 1942. Plagued by the lingering effects of a serious back injury, Millay died in 1950 at the age of fifty-eight.*

The versions of the Millay poems printed in The Pearson Custom Library *issue from* The Collected Poems of Edna St. Vincent Millay, *edited by Norma Millay (New York: Harper Brothers, 1956).*

For Further Reading

Primary Works

Renascence and Other Poems (New York: Kennerley, 1917); *A Few Figs from Thistles* (New York: Shay, 1920); *Aria da Capo,* a play (New York: Kennerley, 1921); *Second April* (New York: Kennerley, 1921); *The Lamp and the Bell,* a play (New York: Shay, 1921); *Two Slatterns and a King,* a play (Cincinnati: Kidd, 1921); *The Ballad of the Harp-Weaver* (New York: Shay, 1922); *The Harp-Weaver and Other Poems* (New York & London: Harper, 1923; London: Secker, 1924); *Poems* (London: Secker, 1923); *Renascence* (New York: Anderson Galleries, 1924); *Distressing Dialogues,* as Nancy Boyd, journalistic prose (New York & London: Harper, 1924); *Three Plays* (New York & London: Harper, 1926; London: Cape, 1927); *The King's Henchman* libretto by Millay, music by Deems Taylor, an opera (New York & Birmingham, U.K.: Fischer, 1926); *The King's Henchman: A Play in Three Acts* (New York & London: Harper, 1927; London: Cape, 1927); *Edna St. Vincent Millay,* Hughes Mearns, ed. (New York: Simon & Schuster, 1927); *Fear,* reprint of an article first published in *Outlook* after the executions of Sacco and Vanzetti (New York: Sacco-Vanzetti National League, 1927); *The Buck in the Snow and Other Poems* (New York & London: Harper, 1928); *Edna St. Vincent Millay's Poems Selected for Young People* (New York & London: Harper, 1929); *Fatal Interview, Sonnets* (New York & London: Harper, 1931; London: Hamilton, 1931); *The Princess Marries the Page: A Play in One Act* (New York & London: Harper, 1932; London: Hamilton, 1932); *Wine from These Grapes* (New York & London: Harper, 1934; London: Hamilton, 1934); *Vacation Song* (Hanover, N.H.: Baker Library Press, 1936); Charles Baudelaire, *Flowers of Evil,* trans. by Millay and George Dillon, with an introduction and a biography by Millay (New York & London: Harper, 1936; London: Hamilton, 1936); *Conversation at Midnight* (New York & London: Harper, 1937; London: Hamilton, 1937); *Huntsman, What Quarry?* (New York & London: Harper;

1939; London: Hamilton, 1939); "There Are No Islands Any More" (New York & London: Harper, 1940); *Make Bright the Arrows: 1940 Notebook* (New York & London: Harper, 1940; London: Hamilton, 1941); *Collected Sonnets* (New York & London: Harper, 1941); *The Murder of Lidice* (New York & London: Harper, 1942); *Collected Lyrics* (New York & London: Harper, 1943); *Second April and The Buck in the Snow* (New York: Harper, 1950); *Mine the Harvest*, Norma Millay, ed. (New York: Harper, 1954; London: Hamilton, 1954); *Collected Poems*, Norma Millay, ed. (New York: Harper, 1956; London: Hamilton, 1957).

Secondary Works

Elizabeth Atkins. *Edna St. Vincent Millay and Her Times* (Chicago: University of Chicago Press, 1936); Norman Brittin. *Edna St. Vincent Millay* (New York: Twain, 1967); Anne Cheney. *Millay in Greenwich Village* (Tuscaloosa: University of Alabama Press, 1975); Suzanne Clark. *Sentimental Modernism: Women Writers and the Revolution of the Word* (Bloomington: Indiana University Press, 1991); Debra Fried. "Andromeda Unbound: Gender and Genre in Millay's Sonnets," in *Twentieth Century Literature* 32, 1 (Spring 1986): 1–22; Jean Gould. *The Poet and Her Book: A Biography of Edna St. Vincent Millay* (New York: Dodd, Mead and Co., 1969); Nina Miller. *Making Love Modern: The Intimate Public Worlds of New York's Literary Women* (New York: Oxford University Press, 1999).

[Oh, oh, you will be sorry for that word!]

EDNA ST. VINCENT MILLAY

Oh, oh, you will be sorry for that word!
Give back my book and take my kiss instead.
Was it my enemy or my friend I heard,
"What a big book for such a little head!"
Come, I will show you now my newest hat,   5
And you may watch me purse my mouth and prink!
Oh, I shall love you still, and all of that.
I never again shall tell you what I think.
I shall be sweet and crafty, soft and sly;
You will not catch me reading any more: 10
I shall be called a wife to pattern by;
And some day when you knock and push the door,
Some sane day, not too bright and not too stormy,
I shall be gone, and you may whistle for me.

[1922]

"Oh, oh, you will be sorry" first appeared in *Vanity Fair* in April 1922. Millay first collected the poem in *The Harp Weaver and Other Poems* (1923).

NATHANIEL HAWTHORNE
[1804–1864]

Deeply rooted in New England culture, Nathaniel Hawthorne was among the first American writers to draw on the history, scenery, characters, and values of a particular region to create distinctive and lasting works of fiction. A dedicated, professional writer with high literary ambitions, Hawthorne spent twenty–five years developing his craft before he reached fame with his first novel, The Scarlet Letter *(1850). Since this his reputation has never flagged, and he is regarded as one of the most influential and accomplished American writers of the nineteenth century.*

Hawthorne was born in Salem, Massachusetts, on July 4, 1804, the descendant of six generations of New England Hathornes (he changed the spelling to ensure correct pronunciation). His ancestors included William Hathorne, famous for his persecutions of Quakers in seventeenth century Boston; John Hathorne, one of the judges at the Salem witchcraft trials in 1692; and a grandfather and father who were ship captains, a common vocation in Salem. When his father died on a voyage in 1808, Hawthorne moved with his mother and two sisters into the Salem home of the Mannings, his maternal grandparents. He made several childhood visits to the family house in Raymond, Maine, near Lake Sebago, and long remembered his days fishing, hunting, and running wild in the woods. He obtained a good education from private tutors and in a few years of local schooling, and from 1821 to 1825 attended Bowdoin College in Brunswick, Maine. Among his fellow students were Franklin Pierce, later fourteenth president of the United States, and Henry Wadsworth Longfellow, eventually one of America's most popular poets.

After graduating, Hawthorne returned to the Manning household in Salem and began writing fiction. His first publication, Fanshawe *(1828), a short romantic novel based on his college days, failed to sell, and he later destroyed all the copies he could find. He had more success with short tales and sketches, and during the 1830s contributed over sixty short pieces to such publications as his local newspaper, the* Salem Gazette, *the* New-England Magazine, *and* The Token, *an annual giftbook. Only some of his early works* were stories in the modern sense. Many were historical narratives, descriptions of local manners and customs, moralistic fables, gothic fantasy pieces, and travel sketches based on his extensive journeys through New England. "Mrs. Hutchinson" (1830), for example, reveals Hawthorne's command of early New England history and its inherent drama and psychological complexity. Yet the piece also presents a compelling portrait of a strong-willed, independent women who might foreshadow the aspiring women of his present day. New England, in Hawthorne's hands, provided materials not only for understanding the American past, but also for representing the American present. By reading widely in the Salem Athenaeum Library and keenly observing his neighbors and countrymen, Hawthorne found ample resources for plots, situations, and characters he could turn into fiction of unusual power and scope.

Yet Hawthorne was not just interested in the Puritan past, nor was he a Puritan himself. He read history to dramatize and criticize it, to bring it alive and give it wider relevance, and to help Americans understand how, from humble beginnings, they had arrived at nationhood. In "My Kinsman Major Molineux" (1832), national history and individual psychology converge in a tale resonant with the symbolism one finds in dreams, hallucinations, fantasies, and fears. Young Robin Molineux's visit to the provincial capital, presumably Boston, simultaneously records an adolescent's initiation into political rebellion and the terrors of maturity. Robin's perplexing night-journey exposes him to mobs like those that preceded the American Revolution even as it separates him from home and family. He must find his own way through this political and moral labyrinth and confront life on his own, a liberated but anxious youth embarking on the difficult road toward individual freedom.

Hawthorne's best-known tale, "Young Goodman Brown" (1835), directly asks whether Brown has "only dreamed a wild dream of a witch meeting?" "Be it so, if you will," the narrator replies, offering readers multiple choices that deliberately create ambiguity. The point is not to play parlor games with serious historical events, in this case the Salem witchcraft trials, but to force readers to consider more than one view of historical events and their effect on individuals. Brown's experience probes into the relationship between personal and institutional religious beliefs; gender roles; illusion and reality; family traits; sexuality; the effects of the wilderness; and ultimately the nature and source of good and evil themselves. No one, with the possible exception of Philadelphia novelist Charles Brockden Brown, had used American materials for such powerful symbolic dramas of the self, or marshaled them into such elegantly constructed, tightly wound narratives. With such tales, Hawthorne was laying the foundation for the modern short story.

Similarly, "The Minister's Black Veil" (1836) studies the effect of religious dogmatism on both community and individual psychology. On the one hand, Father Hooper becomes a powerful preacher because of his sense of sin; on the other, he dies alone, separated from his parishioners, his fellow minister, and *his fiancee's love. The mysterious veil focuses meaning around a central symbol and multiplies it depending on the perspective of the beholder. It is a source of both strength and weakness, an avenue into understanding sin and evidence of sinfulness, a way to communicate spiritual insight and a barrier to communication, an ironic symbol that invites the reader to consider why people view such a simple object in so many opposing ways. Such considerations contribute to readers' understanding of the story as well as themselves.*

Although Hawthorne initially published anonymously, making him, as he said in 1851, "the obscurest man in American letters," his first collection of stories brought him fame if not profit. Twice-Told Tales *(1837) included eighteen works previously published in newspapers, magazines, and annuals, and received favorable reviews from some of the leading journals in New England. He published a second, expanded edition in 1842, adding seventeen tales, and a third edition in 1851. While he still could not support himself solely through his writing, he had established himself as one of America's leading writers of tales. In 1837 he began courting Sophia Peabody, daughter of a prominent Salem family and sister of Elizabeth Peabody, an intellectual who ran a famous bookstore in Boston. With marriage in view, he accepted the job of coal measurer in the Boston Custom House in 1839, the first of several government appointments in his career. While there he wrote four collections of children's stories, three of them published by Elizabeth Peabody, and began a long and emotional correspondence with Sophia. In another attempt at gaining financial independence, he joined Brook Farm in early 1841, a gathering of New England intellectuals who hoped to create a utopian socialist farming community on the outskirts of Boston. Hawthorne, ever skeptical of idealist projects, left after six months.*

In 1842 Hawthorne married Sophia and couple moved to the small village of Concord, Massachusetts, into a house known as the "Old Manse," the former residence of several Concord clergymen. Neighbors included Ralph Waldo Emerson, Henry David Thoreau, Margaret Fuller, William Ellery Channing, and Bronson Alcott, all writers associated with transcendentalism, the new secular gospel of spiritual self-reliance and Nature's essential goodness. Hawthorne valued their company, but remained skeptical of their idealism and optimism. He "admired Emerson as a poet of deep beauty and austere tenderness," he wrote in an 1846 preface, "but sought nothing from him as a philosopher," and found many of Concord's residents to be "simply bores of a very intense water." Nevertheless, these were the happiest years of his life, years that witnessed the birth of his first daughter, Una, in 1844, and saw an important turn in his writing away from the New England past and toward more contemporary issues such as women's rights, transcendentalism, scientific progress, industrialization, and the place of art in an increasingly commercial and capitalist economy. He published almost exclusively in The United States Magazine and Democratic Review, *a periodical of social and* political commentary, and widened his reach by placing scattered pieces in The Pioneer, a short-lived but distinguished journal edited by James Russell Lowell, Graham's Magazine, a widely distributed periodical published in Philadelphia, and Godey's Magazine, perhaps the most popular magazine of the day. In 1846 he published another collection of tales, Moses from an Old Manse, emphasizing his most recent productions.

"The Birth-Mark" (1843) demonstrates Hawthorne's move away from regional themes and characters. Devoid of the historical particulars that mark his earlier stories, this tale seems more like science fiction than historical fable, taking place as it does in a nonspecific, symbolic realm of scientific inquiry and marital anxiety. Aylmer's quest to "perfect" his wife might represent any human wish to reshape nature into forms of personal desire, a Faustian goal that takes Aylmer out of history into the realm of obsessive psychology. Similarly, "The Artist of the Beautiful" (1844) allegorizes one man's quest for artistic perfection, a quest that separates him from humanity yet results in the creation of a marvelous object that seems to transcend the material world. In these tales Hawthorne interrogates the role of the artist in society, and opposes artistic to material creativity in a contest with ambiguous results. "Rappaccini's Daughter" (1844), Hawthorne's only tale set outside America, focuses on a love relationship entangled with patriarchal lust for scientific achievement. Intermixing the passions of the two loves (Giovanni Guasconti and Beatrice) with the rationalism of the head (Rappacini) leads to the terrifying psychological insight that love and hate can be two sides of the same emotion, and that passion, however essential to the human condition, can destroy as well as create. In all three of these stories, Hawthorne uses a central symbol—birthmark, butterfly, garden—to create unity without sacrificing complexity in tales with multiple interpretive possibilities.

In April 1846, with a second child, his son Julian, now in the family, Hawthorne accepted a political appointment as Surveyor of Customs at Salem, a position obtained through his associations with the Democratic Party. For the next three years he wrote almost nothing, his imagination having become, as he said, "a tarnished mirror." It probably didn't help that he and his family had taken up housekeeping with his mother and sisters. In 1849, after the Whigs won the election of 1848, Hawthorne was dismissed, and once more found himself without a stable income. His mother died in July 1849, an event that reinvigorated his imagination and led him to write The Scarlet Letter (1850), his first novel and the work that would finally win him the combination of popular and literary success he had always desired.

The Scarlet Letter, set in seventeenth century Boston, draws once more on Hawthorne's historical knowledge, yet infuses it with Concord transcendentalism and the political and social upheaval of the American 1840s. Hester Prynne, unwed mother of Pearl, is one of the strongest female characters in American fiction, a combination of Ann Hutchinson and contemporary feminists. Her refusal to name Pearl's father or leave the community challenges male religious and social authority. She and Pearl stand as living reproaches to Arthur Dimmesdale, the guilt-ridden Puritan minister who fathers Pearl and then disowns her. Dimmesdale combines the hypocrisy of Young Goodman Brown with the idealism of Father Hooper and the sexual yearnings of Giovanni Gausconti. In Roger Chillingworth, Hester's elderly husband, Hawthorne paints a villain of unsurpassed evil, another man of science whose materialism denies him full humanity. Secrecy, concealment, and deception fuel the plot of this compact novel whose central symbol, the scarlet "A," radiates the dilemma of personal freedom confronting social authority. The Christian press roundly condemned the book for its frank themes of ministerial adultery, illegitimacy, religious hypocrisy, and sexual passion, yet its popularity gave Hawthorne his widest audience so far and encouraged him to continue his career as a novelist instead of a teller of tales.

After the gloomy theme of The Scarlet Letter, Hawthorne consciously set out to write a cheerier novel in The House of the Seven Gables (1851). Although the narrative begins in the Puritan past, it quickly moves into the busy, present-day life of Salem. Hepzibah and Clifford Pyncheon, an elderly sister and brother, are living isolated lives in the family mansion. With the help of Phoebe Pyncheon, a fresh young cousin who comes to live with them, and Holgrave, a young lodger, they gradually come into the sunshine of the present. Judge Jaffray Pyncheon, the family patriarch, symbolizes the evil of the Puritan past, and with his death Hepzibah and Clifford can finally leave the oppressive house, and Phoebe and Holgrave can marry. The House of the Seven Gables, along with The Wonder-Book (1851), a retelling of classical myths for children, and The Snow-Image (1851), a final collection of tales, demonstrated Hawthorne's ability to reach ever wider audiences and finally succeed in the literary marketplace.

The Blithedale Romance (1852) concluded an extraordinary three-year outburst of creativity, and continued Hawthorne's move toward contemporary topics by drawing on his experiences at Brook Farm. Best read as topical satire, incorporating his skepticism toward reformers and idealists of all stripes, the novel describes life in a socialist community through the eyes of Miles Coverdale, one of Hawthorne's rare first-person narrators. A vain, self-deceptive poet of little talent and less human sympathy, Coverdale discovers in others the shortcomings he fails to see in himself, allowing Hawthorne to expose both his narrator and the utopian community he describes to ironic authorial ridicule. Zenobia, the transcendental heroine; Hollingsworth, the prison reformer; and even Priscilla, the sentimental waif, all come in for Coverdale's criticism. Wary readers understand Coverdale's self-delusions, his unreliability, and lack of warmth, and realize that Hawthorne once more writes about the forces that blunt genuine human feeling and make love difficult.

With the birth of his third child, Rose, in 1851, and the financial success of his novels and story collections, Hawthorne purchased a large home in Concord in

1852, the first place he could truly call his own. He published a campaign biography of Franklin Pierce, and in 1853 produced a second volume of myths for children, Tanglewood Tales. *The Pierce biography led to Hawthorne's appointment as U.S. consul in Liverpool, England, a position he held from 1853 to 1857. A remunerative but tedious job, the consulship gave him little time for imaginative writing but allowed him to save $30,000, enough to spend two years in Italy and a year in England before returning to the United States in 1860.*

While abroad he began his final published novel, The Marble Faun *(1860). This story of two couples caught in a web of intrigue among the expatriate artists of Rome and Florence drew heavily on Hawthorne's voluminous Italian travel notebooks, and painstakingly described the landscapes, architecture, statues, and paintings the author had observed in Italy. The title character Donatello, a young Italian nobleman who reminds his friends of Praxiteles' statue of a faun, falls in love with Miriam, a mysterious sculptress with a secret past. The Americans Kenyon and Hilda, a sculptor and a copyist, observe the budding relationship with fascination and eventually fall in love themselves. The backdrop of Italian history and art dominates these personal relationships and gives the novel a sprawling, digressive structure unlike Hawthorne's earlier, tightly organized works. His longest novel,* The Marble Faun *creates varied symbols from Old World materials and characters and addresses a wide range of moral and aesthetic issues.*

Hawthorne produced comparatively little in his last four years. "Chiefly About War Matters" (1862), an essay on the Civil War, reveals Hawthorne's growing distaste for the rise of the commonplace in American life, even while recognizing that a certain rudeness may be the price of egalitarianism. Our Old Home *(1863) draws heavily on his English notebooks for a series of essays on contemporary English life that combine travelogue with social and political commentary to reveal the author's mixed nostalgia, admiration, and disdain for England. Hawthorne tried to complete four additional novels between 1860 and 1864, but his imaginative powers seem to have evaporated, perhaps due to undiagnosed illness. He died in 1864 on a journey to New Hampshire with his old friend Franklin Pierce, and was buried in Sleepy Hollow Cemetery in Concord.*

For most of his life, Hawthorne remained an outsider, perhaps the vantage point from which, like Miles Coverdale, he could best view American history and values. By the time of his death, Americans recognized his central place in the new nation's literature, and honored his memory with posthumous publications of his notebooks, letters, travel journals, unfinished romances, and numerous handsomely bound editions of his complete works. As a fabricator of searching, carefully wrought allegories of the American mind and the human heart, Hawthorne has few peers, and exercised influence on writers from Herman Melville and Henry James, through William Faulkner, Eudora Welty, Flannery O'Connor, John Updike, and even foreign writers such as Jorge Luis Borges. Truly, Hawthorne is an American writer for the world whose works repay close reading and lifelong scrutiny as they mirror the dilemmas not only of his own time, but of today.

For Further Reading

Primary Works

Fanshawe (1828); *Twice-Told Tales* (1837, 1842, 1851); *Grandfather's Chair: A History for Youth* (1841); *Famous Old People: Being the Second Epoch of Grandfather's Chair* (1841); *Liberty Tree: With the Last Words of Grandfather's Chair* (1841); *Biographical Stories for Children* (1842); *Mosses from an Old Manse* (1846a); *The Scarlet Letter, a Romance* (1850); *The House of the Seven Gables, a Romance* (1851); *The Snow-Image, and Other Twice-told Tales* (1851); *The Blithedale Romance* (1852); *Life of Franklin Pierce* (1852); *Tanglewood Tales for Girls and Boys: Being a Second Wonder-book* (1853); *The Marble Faun; or The Romance of Monte Beni* (1860); *Our Old Home: A Series of English Sketches* (1863); *Passages from the American Note-Books of Nathaniel Hawthorne* (1868); *Passages from the English Note-Books of Nathaniel Hawthorne* (1870); *Passages from the French and Italian Note-Books of Nathaniel Hawthorne* (1872); *Septimius Felton; or The Elixir of Life* (1872); *The Dolliver Romance and other Pieces* (1876); *Doctor Grimshawe's Secret: A Romance* (1883); *Twenty Days with Julian and Little Bunny: A Diary* (1904); *Hawthorne as Editor: Selections from His Writings in The American Magazine of Useful and Entertaining Knowledge,* edited by Arlin Turner (Baton Rouge: Louisiana State University Press, 1941); *The Centenary Edition of the Works of Nathaniel Hawthorne,* 23 volumes, ed. William Charvat et al. (Columbus: Ohio State University Press, 1962–94).

Biographies

Julian Hawthorne, *Nathaniel Hawthorne and His Wife: A Biography* (Boston: James R. Osgood, 1885); Henry James, *Hawthorne* (London, 1879); Edward C. Wagenknecht, *Nathaniel Hawthorne: Man and Writer* (New York: Oxford University Press, 1961); Beatrice Ricks, Joseph D. Adams, and Jack O. Hazling, *Nathaniel Hawthorne: A Reference Bibliography, 1900–1971* (Boston: G. K. Hall, 1972): Lea Newman, Bertani Vozar, *A Reader's Guide to the Short Stories of Nathaniel Hawthorne* (Boston: G. K. Hall, 1979); James R. Mellow, *Nathaniel Hawthorne in His Times* (Boston: Houghton Mifflin, 1980); Arlin Turner, *Nathaniel Hawthorne: A Biography* (New York: Oxford University Press, 1980); Robert L. Gale, *A Hawthorne Encyclopedia* (Westport, Conn.: Greenwood Press, 1988); Gary Scharnhorst, *Nathaniel Hawthorne: An Annotated Bibliography of Comment and Criticism Before 1900* (Metuchen, N.J.: Scarecrow Press, 1988); Edwin Haviland Miller, *Salem Is My Dwelling Place: A Life of Nathaniel Hawthorne* (Iowa City: University of Iowa Press, 1991); John L. Idol, Jr. and Buford Jones, eds., *Nathaniel Hawthorne: The Contemporary Reviews* (New York: Cambridge University Press, 1994).

Secondary Works

Hyatt Waggoner, HawthorneA: A Critical Study (Cambridge, Mass.: Harvard University Press, 1955); Roy R. Male, *Hawthorne's Tragic Vision* (Austin: University of Texas Press, 1957); Millicent Bell, *Hawthorne's View of the Artist* (Albany: State University of New York Press, 1962); Richard Harter Fogle, *Hawthorne's Fiction: The Light and the Dark,* revised edition (Norman: University of Oklahoma Press, 1964); Neal F. Doubleday, *Hawthorne's Early Tales: A Critical Study* (Durham, N.C.: Duke University Press, 1972); Nina Baym, *The Shape of Hawthorne's Career* (Ithaca, N.Y.: Cornell University Press, 1976); Edgar A. Dryden, *Nathaniel Hawthorne: The Poetics of Enchantment (Ithaca:* Cornell University Press, 1977); Rita K. Gollin, *Nathaniel Hawthorne and the Truth of Dreams* (Baton Rouge: Louisiana State University Press, 1979); Claudia D. Johnson, *The Productive Tension in Hawthorne's Art* (Tuscaloosa: University of Alabama Press, 1981); Terence Martin, *Nathaniel Hawthorne,* rev. edition (Boston: Twayne, 1983); Michael J. Colacurcio, *The Province of Piety: Moral History in Hawthorne's Early Fiction* (Cambridge, Mass.: Harvard University Press, 1984); Gloria C. Erlich, *Family Themes and Hawthorne's Fiction: The Tenacious Web* (New Brunswick, N.J.: Rutgers University Press, 1984); Richard Brodhead, *The School of Hawthorne* (New York: Oxford University Press, (1986); Frederick Newberry, *Hawthorne's Divided Loyalties: England and America in His Works* (Teaneck, N.J.: Fairleigh Dickinson University Press, 1987); Kenneth Marc Harris, *Hypocrisy and Self-Deception in Hawthorne's Fiction* (Charlottesville: University Press of Virginia, 1988); Gordon Hutner, *Secrets and Sympathy: Forms of Disclosure in Hawthorne's Novels* (Athens: University of Georgia Press, 1988); Edwin H. Cady and Louis J. Budd, eds., *On Hawthorne: The Best from American Literature* (Durham, N.C.: Duke University Press, 1990); Frederick Crews, *The Sins of the Fathers: Hawthorne's Psychological Themes,* with a new afterword (Berkeley: University of California Press, 1989); Sacvan Bercovitch, *The Office of The Scarlet Letter* (Baltimore: Johns Hopkins University Press, 1991); Joel Pfister, *The Production of Personal Life: Class, Gender, and the Psychological in Hawthorne's Fiction* (Stanford, Calif.: Stanford University Press, 1991); Charles Swann, *Nathaniel Hawthorne, Tradition and Revolution* (Cambridge: Cambridge University Press, 1991); Laura Laffrado, *Hawthorne's Literature for Children* (Athens: University of Georgia Press, 1992); Richard H. Millingtion, *Practicing Romance: Narrative Form and Cultural Engagement in Hawthorne's Fiction* (Princeton, N.J.: Princeton University Press, 1992); T. Walter Herbert, *Dearest Beloved: The Hawthornes and the Making of the Middle-Class Family* (Berkely: University of California Press, 1993); Alison Easton, *The Making of the Hawthorne Subject* (Columbia: University of Missouri Press, 1996). Margaret B. Moore, *The Salem World of Nathaniel Hawthorne* (Columbia: University of Missouri Press, 1998); John L. Idol, Jr. and Melinda M. Ponder, eds., *Hawthorne and Women: Engendering and Expanding the Hawthorne Tradition* (Amherst: University of Massachusetts Press, 1999).

Young Goodman Brown[*]

NATHANIEL HAWTHORNE

Young Goodman Brown came forth, at sunset, into the street of Salem village, but put his head back, after crossing the threshold, to exchange a parting kiss with his young wife.[1] And Faith, as the wife was aptly named, thrust her own pretty head into the street, letting the wind play with the pink ribbons of her cap, while she called to Goodman Brown.

"Dearest heart," whispered she, softly and rather sadly, when her lips were close to his ear, "pr'y thee, put off your journey until sunrise, and sleep in your own bed to-night. A lone woman is troubled with such dreams and such thoughts, that she's afeard of herself, sometimes. Pray, tarry with me this night, dear husband, of all nights in the year!"

"My love and my Faith," replied young Goodman Brown, "of all nights in the year, this one night must I tarry away from thee. My journey, as thou callest it, forth and back again, must needs be done 'twixt now and sunrise. What, my sweet, pretty wife, dost thou doubt me already, and we but three months married!"

"Then, God bless you!" said Faith, with the pink ribbons, "and may you find all well when you come back."

"Amen!" cried Goodman Brown. "Say thy prayers, dear Faith, and go to bed at dusk, and no harm will come to thee."

So they parted; and the young man pursued his way, until, being about to turn the corner by the meeting-house, he looked back, and saw the head of Faith still peeping after him, with a melancholy air, in spite of her pink ribbons.

"Poor little Faith!" thought he, for his heart smote him. "What a wretch am I, to leave her on such an errand! She talks of dreams, too. Methought, as she spoke, there was trouble in her face, as if a dream had warned her what work is to be done to-night. But, no, no! 'twould kill her to think it. Well;

---

[*]First published in the *New England Magazine* (April 1835); collected in *Mosses from an Old Manse* (1846). This text is from volume 10 of *The Centenary Edition of the Works of Nathaniel Hawthorne* (1974).

[1]"Goodman" and "Goodwife" (or "Goody") were terms of polite address for ordinary men and women. Salem village, the present Danvers, was a few miles north of Salem, Massachusetts, site of the witchcraft trials of 1692.

she's a blessed angel on earth; and after this one night, I'll cling to her skirts and follow her to Heaven."

With this excellent resolve for the future, Goodman Brown felt himself justified in making more haste on his present evil purpose. He had taken a dreary road, darkened by all the gloomiest trees of the forest, which barely stood aside to let the narrow path creep through, and closed immediately behind. It was all as lonely as could be; and there is this peculiarity in such a solitude, that the traveller knows not who may be concealed by the innumerable trunks and the thick boughs overhead; so that, with lonely footsteps, he may yet be passing through an unseen multitude.

"There may be a devilish Indian behind every tree," said Goodman Brown, to himself; and he glanced fearfully behind him, as he added, "What if the devil himself should be at my very elbow!"

His head being turned back, he passed a crook of the road, and looking forward again, beheld the figure of a man, in grave and decent attire, seated at the foot of an old tree. He arose, at Goodman Brown's approach, and walked onward, side by side with him.

"You are late, Goodman Brown," said he. "The clock of the Old South[2] was striking as I came through Boston; and that is full fifteen minutes agone."

"Faith kept me back awhile," replied the young man, with a tremor in his voice, caused by the sudden appearance of his companion, though not wholly unexpected.

It was now deep dusk in the forest, and deepest in that part of it where these two were journeying. As nearly as could be discerned, the second traveller was about fifty years old, apparently in the same rank of life as Goodman Brown, and bearing a considerable resemblance to him, though perhaps more in expression than features. Still, they might have been taken for father and son. And yet, though the elder person was as simply clad as the younger, and as simple in manner too, he had an indescribable air of one who knew the world, and would not have felt abashed at the governor's dinner-table, or in King William's court,[3] were it possible that his affairs should call him thither. But the only thing about him, that could be fixed upon as remarkable, was his staff, which bore the likeness of a great black snake, so curiously wrought, that it might almost be seen to twist and wriggle itself, like a living serpent. This, of course, must have been an ocular deception, assisted by the uncertain light.

"Come, Goodman Brown!" cried his fellow-traveller, "this is a dull pace for the beginning of a journey. Take my staff, if you are so soon weary."

---

[2]church about sixteen miles from Salem village.
[3]William III (1650–1702) ruled England jointly with his wife, Queen Mary II (1662–1694), from 1689–1702.

"Friend," said the other, exchanging his slow pace for a full stop, "having kept covenant by meeting thee here, it is my purpose now to return whence I came. I have scruples, touching the matter thou wot'st of."[4]

"Sayest thou so?" replied he of the serpent, smiling apart. "Let us walk on, nevertheless, reasoning as we go, and if I convince thee not, thou shalt turn back. We are but a little way in the forest, yet."

"Too far, too far!" exclaimed the goodman, unconsciously resuming his walk. "My father never went into the woods on such an errand, nor his father before him. We have been a race of honest men and good Christians, since the days of the martyrs.[5] And shall I be the first of the name of Brown, that ever took this path, and kept—"

"Such company, thou wouldst say," observed the elder person, interpreting his pause. "Well said, Goodman Brown! I have been as well acquainted with your family as with ever a one among the Puritans; and that's no trifle to say. I helped your grandfather, the constable, when he lashed the Quaker woman so smartly through the streets of Salem. And it was I that brought your father a pitch-pine knot, kindled at my own hearth, to set fire to an Indian village, in King Philip's war.[6] They were my good friends, both; and many a pleasant walk have we had along this path, and returned merrily after midnight. I would fain be friends with you, for their sake."

"If it be as thou sayest," replied Goodman Brown, I marvel they never spoke of these matters. Or, verily, I marvel not, seeing that the least rumor of the sort would have driven them from New-England. We are a people of prayer, and good works, to boot, and abide no such wickedness."

"Wickedness or not," said the traveller with the twisted staff, "I have a very general acquaintance here in New-England. The deacons of many a church have drunk the communion wine with me; the selectmen, of divers towns, make me their chairman; and a majority of the Great and General Court[7] are firm supporters of my interest. The governor and I, too—but these are state-secrets."

"Can this be so!" cried Goodman Brown, with a stare of amazement at his undisturbed companion. "Howbeit, I have nothing to do with the governor and council; they have their own ways, and are no rule for a simple husbandman,[8] like me. But, were I to go on with thee, how should I meet the eye

---

[4]knowest of

[5]Almost three hundred Protestants were executed under the reign of Mary I (1516–1558), also known as Mary Tudor and "Bloody Mary," the Roman Catholic queen of England from 1553–58.

[6]A 1661 Massachusetts law required that disobedient Quakers be stripped to the waist, led through the streets, and whipped. King Philip's War was named for Metacom, also known as King Philip, a Wampanoag chief who led several New England Indian tribes in a war against the English from 1675–76.

[7]colonial legislature

[8]usually a farmer, but here any man of ordinary means.

of that good old man, our minister, at Salem village? Oh, his voice would make me tremble, both Sabbath-day and lecture-day!"[9]

Thus far, the elder traveller had listened with due gravity, but now burst into a fit of irrepressible mirth, shaking himself so violently, that his snake-like staff actually seemed to wriggle in sympathy.

"Ha! ha! ha!" shouted he, again and again; then composing himself, "Well, go on, Goodman Brown, go on; but pr'y thee, don't kill me with laughing!"

"Well, then, to end the matter at once," said Goodman Brown, considerably nettled, "there is my wife, Faith. It would break her dear little heart; and I'd rather break my own!"

"Nay, if that be the case," answered the other, "e'en go thy ways, Goodman Brown. I would not, for twenty old women like the one hobbling before us, that Faith should come to any harm."

As he spoke, he pointed his staff at a female figure on the path, in whom Goodman Brown recognized a very pious and exemplary dame, who had taught him his catechism, in youth, and was still his moral and spiritual adviser, jointly with the minister and Deacon Gookin.[10]

"A marvel, truly, that Goody Cloyse[11] should be so far in the wilderness, at night-fall!" said he. "But, with your leave, friend, I shall take a cut through the woods, until we have left this Christian woman behind. Bring a stranger to you, she might ask whom I was consorting with, and whither I was going."

"Be it so," said his fellow-traveller. "Betake you to the woods, and let me keep the path."

Accordingly, the young man turned aside, but took care to watch his companion, who advanced softly along the road, until he had come within a staff's length of the old dame. She, meanwhile, was making the best of her way, with singular speed for so aged a woman, and mumbling some indistinct words, a prayer, doubtless, as she went. The traveller put forth his staff, and touched her withered neck with what seemed the serpent's tail.

"The devil!" screamed the pious old lady.

"Then Goody Cloyse knows her old friend?" observed the traveller, confronting her, and leaning on his writhing stick.

"Ah, forsooth, and is it your worship, indeed?" cried the good dame. "Yea, truly is it, and in the very image of my old gossip, Goodman Brown, the grandfather of the silly fellow that now is. But—would your worship believe it?—my broomstick hath strangely disappeared, stolen, as I suspect,

---

[9] a midweek day for sermons.

[10] perhaps Daniel Gookin (1612–1687), Massachusetts official, but never a church deacon.

[11] Sarah Cloyse, sentenced to death for witchcraft in 1692, but never executed.

by that unhanged witch, Goody Cory, and that, too, when I was all anointed with the juice of smallage and cinque-foil and wolf's-bane—"[12]

"Mingled with fine wheat and the fat of a new-born babe," said the shape of old Goodman Brown.

"Ah, your worship knows the receipt," cried the old lady, cackling aloud. "So, as I was saying, being all ready for the meeting, and no horse to ride on, I made up my mind to foot it; for they tell me, there is a nice young man to be taken into communion to-night. But now your good worship will lend me your arm, and we shall be there in a twinkling."

"That can hardly be," answered her friend. I may not spare you my arm, Goody Cloyse, but here is my staff, if you will."

So saying, he threw it down at her feet, where, perhaps, it assumed life, being one of the rods which its owner had formerly lent to the Egyptian Magi.[13] Of this fact, however, Goodman Brown could not take cognizance. He had cast up his eyes in astonishment, and looking down again, beheld neither Goody Cloyse nor the serpentine staff, but his fellow-traveller alone, who waited for him as calmly as if nothing had happened.

"That old woman taught me my catechism!" said the young man; and there was a world of meaning in this simple comment.

They continued to walk onward, while the elder traveller exhorted his companion to make good speed and persevere in the path, discoursing so aptly, that his arguments seemed rather to spring up in the bosom of his auditor, than to be suggested by himself. As they went, he plucked a branch of maple, to serve for a walking-stick, and began to strip it of the twigs and little boughs, which were wet with evening dew. The moment his fingers touched them, they became strangely withered and dried up, as with a week's sunshine. Thus the pair proceeded, at a good free pace, until suddenly, in a gloomy hollow of the road, Goodman Brown sat himself down on the stump of a tree, and refused to go any farther.

"Friend," said he, stubbornly, "my mind is made up. Not another step will I budge on this errand. What if a wretched old woman do choose to go to the devil, when I thought she was going to Heaven! Is that any reason why I should quit my dear Faith, and go after her?"

"You will think better of this, by-and-by," said his acquaintance, composedly. "Sit here and rest yourself awhile; and when you feel like moving again, there is my staff to help you along."

Without more words, he threw his companion the maple stick, and was as speedily out of sight, as if he had vanished into the deepening gloom. The young man sat a few moments, by the road-side, applauding himself greatly,

---

[12]Martha Cory was hanged for witchcraft in 1692; smallage, cinquefoil, and wolf's-bane are wild plants with supposed magical powers.

[13]Exodus 7:9–12 describes Egyptian priests turning their rods into serpents.

and thinking with how clear a conscience he should meet the minister, in his morning-walk, nor shrink from the eye of good old Deacon Gookin. And what calm sleep would be his, that very night, which was to have been spent so wickedly, but purely and sweetly now, in the arms of Faith! Amidst these pleasant and praiseworthy meditations, Goodman Brown heard the tramp of horses along the road, and deemed it advisable to conceal himself within the verge of the forest, conscious of the guilty purpose that had brought him thither, though now so happily turned from it.

On came the hoof-tramps and the voices of the riders, two grave old voices, conversing soberly as they drew near. These mingled sounds appeared to pass along the road, within a few yards of the young man's hiding-place; but owing, doubtless, to the depth of the gloom, at that particular spot, neither the travellers nor their steeds were visible. Though their figures brushed the small boughs by the way-side, it could not be seen that they intercepted, even for a moment, the faint gleam from the strip of bright sky, athwart which they must have passed. Goodman Brown alternately crouched and stood on tip-toe, pulling aside the branches, and thrusting forth his head as far as he durst, without discerning so much as a shadow. It vexed him the more, because he could have sworn, were such a thing possible, that he recognized the voices of the minister and Deacon Gookin, jogging along quietly, as they were wont to do, when bound to some ordination or ecclesiastical council. While yet within hearing, one of the riders stopped to pluck a switch.

"Of the two, reverend Sir," said the voice like the deacon's, "I had rather miss an ordination-dinner than to-night's meeting. They tell me that some of our community are to be here from Falmouth and beyond, and others from Connecticut and Rhode-Island; besides several of the Indian powows,[14] who, after their fashion, know almost as much deviltry as the best of us. Moreover, there is a goodly young woman to be taken into communion."

"Mighty well, Deacon Gookin!" replied the solemn old tones of the minister. "Spur up, or we shall be late. Nothing can be done, you know, until I get on the ground."

The hoofs clattered again, and the voices, talking so strangely in the empty air, passed on through the forest, where no church had ever been gathered, nor solitary Christian prayed. Whither, then, could these holy men be journeying, so deep into the heathen wilderness? Young Goodman Brown caught hold of a tree, for support, being ready to sink down on the ground, faint and overburthened with the heavy sickness of his heart. He looked up to the sky, doubting whether there really was a Heaven above him. Yet, there was the blue arch, and the stars brightening in it.

---

[14]Falmouth is a village on southern Cape Cod, about seventy miles from Salem; powows, usually spelled powwow, are medicine men.

"With Heaven above, and Faith below, I will yet stand firm against the devil!" cried Goodman Brown.

While he still gazed upward, into the deep arch of the firmament, and had lifted his hands to pray, a cloud, though no wind was stirring, hurried across the zenith, and hid the brightening stars. The blue sky was still visible, except directly overhead, where this black mass of cloud was sweeping swiftly northward. Aloft in the air, as if from the depths of the cloud, came a confused and doubtful sound of voices. Once, the listener fancied that he could distinguish the accents of town's-people of his own, men and women, both pious and ungodly, many of whom he had met at the communion-table, and had seen others rioting at the tavern. The next moment, so indistinct were the sounds, he doubted whether he had heard aught but the murmur of the old forest, whispering without a wind. Then came a stronger swell of those familiar tones, heard daily in the sunshine, at Salem village, but never, until now, from a cloud of night. There was one voice, of a young woman, uttering lamentations, yet with an uncertain sorrow, and entreating for some favor, which, perhaps, it would grieve her to obtain. And all the unseen multitude, both saints and sinners, seemed to encourage her onward.

"Faith!" shouted Goodman Brown, in a voice of agony and desperation; and the echoes of the forest mocked him, crying—"Faith! Faith!" as if bewildered wretches were seeking her, all through the wilderness.

The cry of grief, rage, and terror, was yet piercing the night, when the unhappy husband held his breath for a response. There was a scream, drowned immediately in a louder murmur of voices, fading into far-off laughter, as the dark cloud swept away, leaving the clear and silent sky above Goodman Brown. But something fluttered lightly down through the air, and caught on the branch of a tree. The young man seized it, and beheld a pink ribbon.

"My Faith is gone!" cried he, after one stupefied moment. "There is no good on earth; and sin is but a name. Come, devil! for to thee is this world given."

And maddened with despair, so that he laughed loud and long, did Goodman Brown grasp his staff and set forth again, at such a rate, that he seemed to fly along the forest-path, rather than to walk or run. The road grew wilder and drearier, and more faintly traced, and vanished at length, leaving him in the heart of the dark wilderness, still rushing onward, with the instinct that guides mortal man to evil. The whole forest was peopled with frightful sounds; the creaking of the trees, the howling of wild beasts, and the yell of Indians; while, sometimes, the wind tolled like a distant church-bell, and sometimes gave a broad roar around the traveller, as if all Nature were laughing him to scorn. But he was himself the chief horror of the scene, and shrank not from its other horrors.

"Ha! ha! ha!" roared Goodman Brown, when the wind laughed at him. "Let us hear which will laugh loudest! Think not to frighten me with your deviltry! Come witch, come wizard, come Indian powow, come devil himself! and here comes Goodman Brown. You may as well fear him as he fear you!"

In truth, all through the haunted forest, there could be nothing more frightful than the figure of Goodman Brown. On he flew, among the black pines, brandishing his staff with frenzied gestures, now giving vent to an inspiration of horrid blasphemy, and now shouting forth such laughter, as set all the echoes of the forest laughing like demons around him. The fiend in his own shape is less hideous, than when he rages in the breast of man. Thus sped the demoniac on his course, until, quivering among the trees, he saw a red light before him, as when the felled trunks and branches of a clearing have been set on fire, and throw up their lurid blaze against the sky, at the hour of midnight. He paused, in a lull of the tempest that had driven him onward, and heard the swell of what seemed a hymn, rolling solemnly from a distance, with the weight of many voices. He knew the tune; it was a familiar one in the choir of the village meeting-house. The verse died heavily away, and was lengthened by a chorus, not of human voices, but of all the sounds of the benighted wilderness, pealing in awful harmony together. Goodman Brown cried out; and his cry was lost to his own ear, by its unison with the cry of the desert.

In the interval of silence, he stole forward, until the light glared full upon his eyes. At one extremity of an open space, hemmed in by the dark wall of the forest, arose a rock, bearing some rude, natural resemblance either to an altar or a pulpit, and surrounded by four blazing pines, their tops aflame, their stems untouched, like candles at an evening meeting. The mass of foliage, that had overgrown the summit of the rock, was all on fire, blazing high into the night, and fitfully illuminating the whole field. Each pendent twig and leafy festoon was in a blaze. As the red light arose and fell, a numerous congregation alternately shone forth, then disappeared in shadow, and again grew, as it were, out of the darkness, peopling the heart of the solitary woods at once.

"A grave and dark-clad company!" quoth Goodman Brown.

In truth, they were such. Among them, quivering to-and-fro, between gloom and splendor, appeared faces that would be seen, next day, at the council-board of the province, and others which, Sabbath after Sabbath, looked devoutly heavenward, and benignantly over the crowded pews, from the holiest pulpits in the land. Some affirm, that the lady of the governor was there. At least, there were high dames well known to her, and wives of honored husbands, and widows, a great multitude, and ancient maidens, all of excellent repute, and fair young girls, who trembled, lest their mothers should espy them. Either the sudden gleams of light, flashing over the obscure field, bedazzled Goodman Brown, or he recognized a score of the churchmembers of Salem village, famous for their especial sanctity. Good old Deacon Gookin had arrived, and waited at the skirts of that venerable saint, his revered pastor. But, irreverently consorting with these grave, reputable, and pious people, these elders of the church, these chaste dames and dewy virgins, there were men of dissolute lives and women of spotted fame, wretches given over to all mean and filthy vice, and suspected even of horrid crimes. It was strange to see, that the good shrank not from the wicked, nor were the sinners abashed by the saints. Scattered, also, among their pale-faced enemies, were the Indian priests, or powows, who had often scared their native forest with more hideous incantations than any known to English witchcraft.

"But, where is Faith?" thought Goodman Brown; and, as hope came into his heart, he trembled.

Another verse of the hymn arose, a slow and mournful strain, such as the pious love, but joined to words which expressed all that our nature can conceive of sin, and darkly hinted at far more. Unfathomable to mere mortals is the lore of fiends. Verse after verse was sung, and still the chorus of the desert swelled between, like the deepest tone of a mighty organ. And, with the final peal of that dreadful anthem, there came a sound, as if the roaring wind, the rushing streams, the howling beasts, and every other voice of the unconverted wilderness, were mingling and according with the voice of guilty man, in homage to the prince of all. The four blazing pines threw up a loftier flame, and obscurely discovered shapes and visages of horror on the smoke-wreaths, above the impious assembly. At the same moment, the fire on the rock shot redly forth, and formed a glowing arch above its base, where now appeared a figure. With reverence be it spoken, the figure bore no slight similitude, both in garb and manner, to some grave divine of the New-England churches.

"Bring forth the converts!" cried a voice, that echoed through the field and rolled into the forest.

At the word, Goodman Brown stept forth from the shadow of the trees, and approached the congregation, with whom he felt a loathful brotherhood, by the sympathy of all that was wicked in his heart. He could have well nigh sworn, that the shape of his own dead father beckoned him to advance, looking downward from a smoke-wreath, while a woman, with dim features of despair, threw out her hand to warn him back. Was it his mother? But he had no power to retreat one step, nor to resist, even in thought, when the minister and good old Deacon Gookin seized his arms, and led him to the blazing rock. Thither came also the slender form of a veiled female, led between Goody Cloyse, that pious teacher of the catechism, and Martha Carrier,[15] who had received the devil's promise to be queen of hell. A rampant hag was she! And there stood the proselytes, beneath the canopy of fire.

"Welcome, my children," said the dark figure, "to the communion of your race! Ye have found, thus young, your nature and your destiny. My children, look behind you!"

---

[15]Martha Carrier was hanged as a witch in 1692.

They turned; and flashing forth, as it were, in a sheet of flame, the fiend-worshippers were seen; the smile of welcome gleamed darkly on every visage.

"There," resumed the sable form, "are all whom ye have reverenced from youth. Ye deemed them holier than yourselves, and shrank from your own sin, contrasting it with their lives of righteousness, and prayerful aspirations heavenward. Yet, here are they all, in my worshipping assembly! This night it shall be granted you to know their secret deeds; how hoary-bearded elders of the church have whispered wanton words to the young maids of their households; how many a woman, eager for widow's weeds, has given her husband a drink at bedtime, and let him sleep his last sleep in her bosom; how beardless youths have made haste to inherit their fathers' wealth; and how fair damsels—blush not, sweet ones!—have dug little graves in the garden, and bidden me, the sole guest, to an infant's funeral. By the sympathy of your human hearts for sin, ye shall scent out all the places—whether in church, bed-chamber, street, field, or forest—where crime has been committed, and shall exult to behold the whole earth one stain of guilt, one mighty blood-spot. Far more than this! It shall be yours to penetrate, in every bosom, the deep mystery of sin, the fountain of all wicked arts, and which inexhaustibly supplies more evil impulses than human power—than my power, at its utmost!—can make manifest in deeds. And now, my children, look upon each other."

They did so; and, by the blaze of the hell-kindled torches, the wretched man beheld his Faith, and the wife her husband, trembling before that unhallowed altar.

"Lo! there ye stand, my children," said the figure, in a deep and solemn tone, almost sad, with its despairing awfulness, as if his once angelic nature could yet mourn for our miserable race. "Depending upon one another's hearts, ye had still hoped, that virtue were not all a dream. Now are ye undeceived! Evil is the nature of mankind. Evil must be your only happiness. Welcome, again, my children, to the communion of your race!"

"Welcome!" repeated the fiend-worshippers, in one cry of despair and triumph.

And there they stood, the only pair, as it seemed, who were yet hesitating on the verge of wickedness, in this dark world. A basin was hollowed, naturally, in the rock. Did it contain water, reddened by the lurid light? or was it blood? or, perchance, a liquid flame? Herein did the Shape of Evil dip his hand, and prepare to lay the mark of baptism upon their foreheads, that they might be partakers of the mystery of sin, more conscious of the secret guilt of others, both in deed and thought, than they could now be of their own. The husband cast one look at his pale wife, and Faith at him. What polluted wretches would the next glance shew them to each other, shuddering alike at what they disclosed and what they saw!

"Faith! Faith!" cried the husband. "Look up to Heaven, and resist the Wicked One!"

Whether Faith obeyed, he knew not. Hardly had he spoken, when he found himself amid calm night and solitude, listening to a roar of the wind, which died heavily away through the forest. He staggered against the rock and felt it chill and damp, while a hanging twig, that had been all on fire, besprinkled his cheek with the coldest dew.

The next morning, young Goodman Brown came slowly into the street of Salem village, staring around him like a bewildered man. The good old minister was taking a walk along the grave-yard, to get an appetite for breakfast and meditate his sermon, and bestowed a blessing, as he passed, on Goodman Brown. He shrank from the venerable saint, as if to avoid an anathema. Old Deacon Gookin was at domestic worship, and the holy words of his prayer were heard through the open window. "What God doth the wizard pray to?" quoth Goodman Brown. Goody Cloyse, that excellent old Christian, stood in the early sunshine, at her own lattice, catechising a little girl, who had brought her a pint of morning's milk. Goodman Brown snatched away the child, as from the grasp of the fiend himself. Turning the corner by the meeting-house, he spied the head of Faith, with the pink ribbons, gazing anxiously forth, and bursting into such joy at sight of him, that she skipt along the street, and almost kissed her husband before the whole village. But, Goodman Brown looked sternly and sadly into her face, and passed on without a greeting.

Had Goodman Brown fallen asleep in the forest, and only dreamed a wild dream of a witch-meeting?

Be it so, if you will. But, alas! it was a dream of evil omen for young Goodman Brown. A stern, a sad, a darkly meditative, a distrustful, if not a desperate man, did he become, from the night of that fearful dream. On the Sabbath-day, when the congregation were singing a holy psalm, he could not listen, because an anthem of sin rushed loudly upon his ear, and drowned all the blessed strain. When the minister spoke from the pulpit, with power and fervid eloquence, and, with his hand on the open Bible, of the sacred truths of our religion, and of saint-like lives and triumphant deaths, and of future bliss or misery unutterable, then did Goodman Brown turn pale, dreading, lest the roof should thunder down upon the gray blasphemer and his hearers. Often, awakening suddenly at midnight, he shrank from the bosom of Faith, and at morning or eventide, when the family knelt down at prayer, he scowled, and muttered to himself, and gazed sternly at his wife, and turned away. And when he had lived long, and was borne to his grave, a hoary corpse, followed by Faith, an aged woman, and children and grand-children, a goodly procession, besides neighbors, not a few, they carved no hopeful verse upon his tomb-stone; for his dying hour was gloom.

[1835]

Workshop 2: What Constitutes a Well-lived Life?

CHARLOTTE PERKINS GILMAN
[1860–1935]

Charlotte Perkins Gilman is among the most radical of nineteenth century feminists. She offers a model ahead of, and, in certain ways, critical of main trends in contemporary feminism. Widely known in her own lifetime as a lecturer, activist, and essayist, Gilman also wrote fiction and poetry. These writings were continuous with her other writings, in that polemic remained her main rhetorical mode, whatever the genre. In the nineteenth century, her poetry directly addressed and engaged in the broad concerns of American life. During her years as sole editor and writer for her journal, The Forerunner, *she also published a great deal of fiction in serial form, including three utopian novels that reconceive society in feminist terms:* Herland, With Her in Ourland, *and* Moving the Mountain.

Charlotte Perkins Gilman's life was as polemical as her work. She was born into the Beecher family, daughter to the nephew of Harriet and Catherine Beecher. Her father, Frederick Perkins, unofficially abandoned his family when Charlotte was two, leaving her mother to manage an irregular and destitute household, with constant moves—first among Beecher relatives and then (after Charlotte's mother divorced her father) through a series of makeshift domestic arrangements. At an early age Charlotte pledged herself to personal independence, including a desire to work and to remain single, with the Beecher heritage of service a central commitment. These plans were interrupted by her acquiescence, after two years of ambivalence, to marriage with Charles Stetson. The consequences of this decision are recorded in Gilman's autobiographical story, "The Yellow Wallpaper," which recounts her breakdown after the birth of her daughter, her subsequent "rest cure" for hysteria with the famous Dr. Weir Mitchell (which included total bed rest, spoon feeding with crème, and absolutely no intellectual effort), and her near descent into insanity. In a last effort to save her mind and self, Gilman left for a visit to her girlhood friend, Grace Channing, in California. The almost immediate lifting of her depression with distance from her husband was a fact neither she nor he could fail to notice. Gilman's subsequent divorce, and entrusting of her child to her ex-husband and his newly married (at Gilman's encouragement) wife, the self-same friend Grace Channing, caused her great and painful scandal for many years. Gilman eventually was happily remarried to her cousin, Houghton Gilman. She lived with him until his death, in 1934, followed fifteen months later by her own death in 1935 by suicide, in response to her advanced state of breast cancer. Characteristically, she left a suicide note-treatise in support of the right of euthanasia for the suffering, which has been reprinted as the conclusion to her autobiography, The Living of Charlotte Perkins Gilman.

After her divorce, Gilman's life of constant traveling, lecturing, and writing was as far removed as possible from domestic restriction. Her own experience of domesticity as imprisonment impelled her into activist feminism, specifically critical of the domestic womanhood of nineteenth-century ideology. For example, her widely famous work Women and Economics *attacks women's economic dependence as unnatural and wasteful, and as encouraging debility in women. As this analysis suggests, while supporting suffrage in association with Susan Anthony and Elizabeth Cady Stanton, Gilman committed her own greatest energies toward a much wider revolution than the focus on electoral politics, which she felt could not alone restructure society. Her proposals concerning universal day care, the pooling of kitchen and laundry services to release women from repetitious and inefficient domestic labor, and education reform remain radical, even today. While committed to ideals of equality, Gilman was also critical of the increasingly unrestrained self-interest of contemporary liberalism and identified instead with a form of utopian socialism. Associated at various times with Jane Addams's Hull House experiment, Gilman promoted attention to material support, educational opportunity, restructuring of gender roles, and general social welfare. Hers is a vision of community as the arena in which each individual finds his and her truest nature and fulfillment. She speaks for a range of feminist values that extend beyond (although by no means repudiate) the demand for equal opportunity and personal realization, values of service to society that restores individual endeavor to a greater communal and cultural world.*

Gilman's poetry ranges from the humorous, to children's verse, to the didactic. Her fiction has recently seen a resurrection from literary obscurity. Much of her writing, however, remains uncollected from The Forerunner, *the journal she initiated when other journals refused to publish her work as too radical. In general, her writing is subordinate to her ideological mission, and can be programmatic. Yet, at times she succeeds in capturing the rhetoric and viewpoints of the discourses of the world, framing and exposing them with the self-consciousness and command of accomplished art.*

Shira Wolosky
Hebrew University of Jerusalem

For Further Reading

Primary Works

"The Yellow Wall-Paper" (1892); *Women and Economics* (1898); *In This Our World* (1893); *Forerunner*, vols. 1–7 (1909–1916); *The Home: Its Work and Influence* (1903); *The Man-Made World* (1911); *Moving the Mountain* (1911); *The Living of Charlotte Perkins Gilman: An Autobiography* (1935); *"Herland" and Selected Stories of Charlotte Perkins Gilman* (1992); *"The Yellow Wall-Paper" and Selected Stories of Charlotte Perkins Gilman*, ed. Denise D. Knight (1992); *The Diaries of Charlotte Perkins Gilman*, 2 vols., ed. Denise Knight (1994); *The Later Poetry of Charlotte Gilman*, ed. Denise Knight (1996); *Charlotte Perkins Gilman's Utopian Novels*, ed. Minna Doskow (1999); *The Charlotte Perkins Gilman Reader*, ed. Ann J. Lane (1999).

Secondary Works

Mary A. Hill. *Charlotte Perkins Gilman: The Making of a Radical Feminist 1860–1896* (1980); Gary Scharnhorst. *Charlotte Perkins Gilman* (1985); Sheryl Meyering. *Charlotte Perkins Gilman, The Woman and Her Work* (1989); Ann Lane. *To Herland and Beyond: The Life and Work of Charlotte Perkins Gilman* (1990); Joanne Karpinski, ed. *Critical Essays on Charlotte Perkins Gilman* (1992); Catherine Golden, ed. *The Captive Imagination: A Casebook on "The Yellow Wallpaper"* (1992); Carol Farley Kessler. *Charlotte Perkins Gilman, Her Progress Toward Utopia with Selected Writings* (1994); Val Gough and Jill Rudd. *A Very Different Story: Essays on the Fiction of Charlotte Perkins Gilman* (1998); Jill Rudd and Val Gough. *Charlotte Perkins Gilman: Optimist Reformer* (1999); Catherine Golden. *The Mixed Legacy of Charlotte Perkins Gilman* (2000).

The Yellow Wall-Paper

CHARLOTTE PERKINS GILMAN

It is very seldom that mere ordinary people like John and myself secure ancestral halls for the summer.

A colonial mansion, a hereditary estate, I would say a haunted house, and reach the height of romantic felicity—but that would be asking too much of fate!

Still I will proudly declare that there is something queer about it.

Else, why should it be let so cheaply? And why have stood so long untenanted?

John laughs at me, of course, but one expects that in marriage.

John is practical in the extreme. He has no patience with faith, an intense horror of superstition, and he scoffs openly at any talk of things not to be felt and seen and put down in figures.

John is a physician, and *perhaps*—(I would not say it to a living soul, of course, but this is dead paper and a great relief to my mind—) *perhaps* that is one reason I do not get well faster.

You see he does not believe I am sick!

And what can one do?

If a physician of high standing, and one's own husband, assures friends and relatives that there is really nothing the matter with one but temporary nervous depression—a slight hysterical tendency[1]—what is one to do?

My brother is also a physician, and also of high standing, and he says the same thing.

So I take phosphates or phosphites—whichever it is, and tonics, and journeys, and air, and exercise, and am absolutely forbidden to "work" until I am well again.

Personally, I disagree with their ideas.

Personally, I believe that congenial work, with excitement and change, would do me good.

But what is one to do?

First published in *New England Magazine* January 1892.

[1]At the end of the nineteenth century, this was a catch-all category for women's nervous disorders or strong emotional responses, ranging from anger to depression to anxiety to nervousness.

I did write for a while in spite of them; but it *does* exhaust me a good deal—having to be so sly about it, or else meet with heavy opposition.

I sometimes fancy that in my condition if I had less opposition and more society and stimulus—but John says the very worst thing I can do is to think about my condition, and I confess it always makes me feel bad.

So I will let it alone and talk about the house.

The most beautiful place! It is quite alone, standing well back from the road, quite three miles from the village. It makes me think of English places that you read about, for there are hedges and walls and gates that lock, and lots of separate little houses for the gardeners and people.

There is a *delicious* garden! I never saw such a garden—large and shady, full of box-bordered paths, and lined with long grape-covered arbors with seats under them.

There were greenhouses, too, but they are all broken now.

There was some legal trouble, I believe, something about the heirs and coheirs; anyhow, the place has been empty for years.

That spoils my ghostliness, I am afraid, but I don't care—there is something strange about the house—I can feel it.

I even said so to John one moonlight evening, but he said what I felt was a *draught,* and shut the window.

I get unreasonably angry with John sometimes. I'm sure I never used to be so sensitive. I think it is due to this nervous condition.

But John says if I feel so, I shall neglect proper self-control; so I take pains to control myself—before him, at least, and that makes me very tired.

I don't like our room a bit. I wanted one downstairs that opened on the piazza and had roses all over the window, and such pretty old-fashioned chintz hangings! but John would not hear of it.

He said there was only one window and not room for two beds, and no near room for him if he took another.

He is very careful and loving, and hardly lets me stir without special direction.

I have a schedule prescription for each hour in the day; he takes all care from me, and so I feel basely ungrateful not to value it more.

He said we came here solely on my account, that I was to have perfect rest and all the air I could get. "Your exercise depends on your strength, my dear," said he, "and your food somewhat on your appetite; but air you can absorb all the time." So we took the nursery at the top of the house.

It is a big, airy room, the whole floor nearly, with windows that look all ways, and air and sunshine galore. It was nursery first and then playroom and gymnasium, I should judge; for the windows are barred for little children, and there are rings and things in the walls.

The paint and paper look as if a boys' school had used it. It is stripped off—the paper—in great patches all around the head of my bed, about as far as I can reach, and in a great place on the other side of the room low down. I never saw a worse paper in my life.

One of those sprawling flamboyant patterns committing every artistic sin.

It is dull enough to confuse the eye in following, pronounced enough to constantly irritate and provoke study, and when you follow the lame uncertain curves for a little distance they suddenly commit suicide—plunge off at outrageous angles, destroy themselves in unheard of contradictions.

The color is repellant, almost revolting; a smouldering unclean yellow, strangely faded by the slow-turning sunlight.

It is a dull yet lurid orange in some places, a sickly sulphur tint in others.

No wonder the children hated it! I should hate it myself if I had to live in this room long.

There comes John, and I must put this away,—he hates to have me write a word.

We have been here two weeks, and I haven't felt like writing before, since that first day.

I am sitting by the window now, up in this atrocious nursery, and there is nothing to hinder my writing as much as I please, save lack of strength.

John is away all day, and even some nights when his cases are serious.

I am glad my case is not serious!

But these nervous troubles are dreadfully depressing.

John does not know how much I really suffer. He knows there is no *reason* to suffer, and that satisfies him.

Of course it is only nervousness. It does weigh on me so not to do my duty in any way!

I meant to be such a help to John, such a real rest and comfort, and here I am a comparative burden already!

Nobody would believe what an effort it is to do what little I am able,—to dress and entertain, and order things.

It is fortunate Mary is so good with the baby. Such a dear baby!

And yet I *cannot* be with him, it makes me so nervous.

I suppose John never was nervous in his life. He laughs at me so about this wall-paper!

At first he meant to repaper the room, but afterwards he said that I was letting it get the better of me, and that nothing was worse for a nervous patient than to give way to such fancies.

He said that after the wall-paper was changed it would be the heavy bedstead, and then the barred windows, and then that gate at the head of the stairs, and so on.

"You know the place is doing you good," he said, "and really, dear, I don't care to renovate the house just for a three months' rental."

"Then do let us go downstairs," I said, "there are such pretty rooms there."

Then he took me in his arms and called me a blessed little goose, and said he would go down cellar, if I wished, and have it whitewashed into the bargain.

But he is right enough about the beds and windows and things.

It is an airy and comfortable room as any one need wish, and, of course, I would not be so silly as to make him uncomfortable just for a whim.

I'm really getting quite fond of the big room, all but that horrid paper.

Out of one window I can see the garden, those mysterious deep-shaded arbors, the riotous old-fashioned flowers, and bushes and gnarly trees.

Out of another I get a lovely view of the bay and a little private wharf belonging to the estate. There is a beautiful shaded lane that runs down there from the house. I always fancy I see people walking in these numerous paths and arbors, but John has cautioned me not to give way to fancy in the least. He says that with my imaginative power and habit of story-making, a nervous weakness like mine is sure to lead to all manner of excited fancies, and that I ought to use my will and good sense to check the tendency. So I try.

I think sometimes that if I were only well enough to write a little it would relieve the press of ideas and rest me.

But I find I get pretty tired when I try.

It is so discouraging not to have any advice and companionship about my work. When I get really well, John says we will ask cousin Henry and Julia down for a long visit; but he says he would as soon put fireworks in my pillow-case as to let me have those stimulating people about now.

I wish I could get well faster.

But I must not think about that. This paper looks to me as if it *knew* what a vicious influence it had!

There is a recurrent spot where the pattern lolls like a broken neck and two bulbous eyes stare at you upside down.

I get positively angry with the impertinence of it and the everlastingness. Up and down and sideways they crawl, and those absurd, unblinking eyes are everywhere. There is one place where two breadths didn't match, and the eyes go all up and down the line, one a little higher than the other.

I never saw so much expression in an inanimate thing before, and we all know how much expression they have! I used to lie awake as a child and get more entertainment and terror out of blank walls and plain furniture than most children could find in a toy-store.

I remember what a kindly wink the knobs of our big, old bureau used to have, and there was one chair that always seemed like a strong friend.

I used to feel that if any of the other things looked too fierce I could always hop into that chair and be safe.

The furniture in this room is no worse than inharmonious, however, for we had to bring it all from downstairs. I suppose when this was used as a playroom they had to take the nursery things out, and no wonder! I never saw such ravages as the children have made here.

The wall-paper, as I said before, is torn off in spots, and it sticketh closer than a brother—they must have had perseverance as well as hatred.

Then the floor is scratched and gouged and splintered, the plaster itself is dug out here and there, and this great heavy bed which is all we found in the room, looks as if it had been through the wars.

But I don't mind it a bit—only the paper.

There comes John's sister. Such a dear girl as she is, and so careful of me! I must not let her find me writing.

She is a perfect and enthusiastic housekeeper, and hopes for no better profession. I verily believe she thinks it is the writing which made me sick!

But I can write when she is out, and see her a long way off from these windows.

There is one that commands the road, a lovely shaded winding road, and one that just looks off over the country. A lovely country, too, full of great elms and velvet meadows.

This wall-paper has a kind of subpattern in a different shade, a particularly irritating one, for you can only see it in certain lights, and not clearly then.

But in the places where it isn't faded and where the sun is just so—I can see a strange, provoking, formless sort of figure, that seems to skulk about behind that silly and conspicuous front design.

There's sister on the stairs!

Well, the Fourth of July is over! The people are all gone and I am tired out. John thought it might do me good to see a little company, so we just had mother and Nellie and the children down for a week.

Of course I didn't do a thing. Jennie sees to everything now.

But it tired me all the same.

John says if I don't pick up faster he shall send me to Weir Mitchell[2] in the fall.

But I don't want to go there at all. I had a friend who was in his hands once, and she says he is just like John and my brother, only more so!

Besides, it is such an undertaking to go so far.

I don't feel as if it was worth while to turn my hand over for anything, and I'm getting dreadfully fretful and querulous.

I cry at nothing, and cry most of the time.

Of course I don't when John is here, or anybody else, but when I am alone.

And I am alone a good deal just now. John is kept in town very often by serious cases, and Jennie is good and lets me alone when I want her to.

---

[2]Dr. S. Weir Mitchell (1829–1914), Gilman's own physician, briefly, and famous for his "rest cure" for "hysteria," very much like what the speaker's husband prescribes.

So I walk a little in the garden or down that lovely lane, sit on the porch under the roses, and lie down up here a good deal.

I'm getting really fond of the room in spite of the wall-paper. Perhaps *because* of the wall-paper.

It dwells in my mind so!

I lie here on this great immovable bed—it is nailed down, I believe—and follow that pattern about by the hour. It is as good as gymnastics, I assure you. I start, we'll say, at the bottom, down in the corner over there where it has not been touched, and I determine for the thousandth time that I *will* follow that pointless pattern to some sort of a conclusion.

I know a little of the principle of design, and I know this thing was not arranged on any laws of radiation, or alternation, or repetition, or symmetry, or anything else that I ever heard of.

It is repeated, of course, by the breadths, but not otherwise.

Looked at in one way each breadth stands alone, the bloated curves and flourishes—a kind of "debased Romanesque" with *delirium tremens*[3]—go waddling up and down in isolated columns of fatuity.

But, on the other hand, they connect diagonally, and the sprawling outlines run off in great slanting waves of optic horror, like a lot of wallowing seaweeds in full chase.

The whole thing goes horizontally, too, at least it seems so, and I exhaust myself in trying to distinguish the order of its going in that direction.

They have used a horizontal breadth for a frieze, and that adds wonderfully to the confusion.

There is one end of the room where it is almost intact, and there, when the crosslights fade and the low sun shines directly upon it, I can almost fancy radiation after all,—the interminable grotesques seem to form around a common centre and rush off in headlong plunges of equal distraction.

It makes me tired to follow it. I will take a nap I guess.

I don't know why I should write this.

I don't want to.

I don't feel able.

And I know John would think it absurd. But I *must* say what I feel and think in some way—it is such a relief!

But the effort is getting to be greater than the relief.

Half the time now I am awfully lazy, and lie down ever so much.

John says I mustn't lose my strength, and has me take cod liver oil and lots of tonics and things, to say nothing of ale and wine and rare meat.

---

[3]Highly ornamented style of architecture; *delirium tremens* is an acute delirium caused by alcohol poisoning—literally "trembling" delirium.

Dear John! He loves me very dearly, and hates to have me sick. I tried to have a real earnest reasonable talk with him the other day, and tell him how I wish he would let me go and make a visit to Cousin Henry and Julia.

But he said I wasn't able to go, nor able to stand it after I got there; and I did not make out a very good case for myself, for I was crying before I had finished.

It is getting to be a great effort for me to think straight. Just this nervous weakness I suppose.

And dear John gathered me up in his arms, and just carried me upstairs and laid me on the bed, and sat by me and read to me till it tired my head.

He said I was his darling and his comfort and all he had, and that I must take care of myself for his sake, and keep well.

He says no one but myself can help me out of it, that I must use my will and self-control and not let any silly fancies run away with me.

There's one comfort, the baby is well and happy, and does not have to occupy this nursery with the horrid wall-paper.

If we had not used it, that blessed child would have! What a fortunate escape! Why, I wouldn't have a child of mine, an impressionable little thing, live in such a room for worlds.

I never thought of it before, but it is lucky that John kept me here after all, I can stand it so much easier than a baby, you see.

Of course I never mention it to them any more—I am too wise,—but I keep watch of it all the same.

There are things in that paper that nobody knows but me, or ever will.

Behind that outside pattern the dim shapes get clearer every day.

It is always the same shape, only very numerous.

And it is like a woman stooping down and creeping about behind that pattern. I don't like it a bit. I wonder—I begin to think—I wish John would take me away from here!

It is so hard to talk with John about my case, because he is so wise, and because he loves me so.

But I tried it last night.

It was moonlight. The moon shines in all around just as the sun does.

I hate to see it sometimes, it creeps so slowly, and always comes in by one window or another.

John was asleep and I hated to waken him, so I kept still and watched the moonlight on that undulating wall-paper till I felt creepy.

The faint figure behind seemed to shake the pattern, just as if she wanted to get out.

I got up softly and went to feel and see if the paper *did* move, and when I came back John was awake.

"What is it, little girl?" he said. "Don't go walking about like that—you'll get cold."

I thought it was a good time to talk, so I told him that I really was not gaining here, and that I wished he would take me away.

"Why, darling!" said he, "our lease will be up in three weeks, and I can't see how to leave before.

"The repairs are not done at home, and I cannot possibly leave town just now. Of course if you were in any danger, I could and would, but you really are better, dear, whether you can see it or not. I am a doctor, dear, and I know. You are gaining flesh and color, your appetite is better, I feel really much easier about you."

"I don't weigh a bit more," said I, "nor as much; and my appetite may be better in the evening when you are here, but it is worse in the morning when you are away!"

"Bless her little heart!" said he with a big hug, "she shall be as sick as she pleases! But now let's improve the shining hours[4] by going to sleep, and talk about it in the morning!"

"And you won't go away?" I asked gloomily.

"Why, how can I, dear? It is only three weeks more and then we will take a nice little trip of a few days while Jennie is getting the house ready. Really dear you are better!"

"Better in body perhaps—" I began, and stopped short, for he sat up straight and looked at me with such a stern, reproachful look that I could not say another word.

"My darling," said he, "I beg of you, for my sake and for our child's sake, as well as for your own, that you will never for one instant let that idea enter your mind! There is nothing so dangerous, so fascinating, to a temperament like yours. It is a false and foolish fancy. Can you not trust me as a physician when I tell you so?"

So of course I said no more on that score, and we went to sleep before long. He thought I was asleep first, but I wasn't, and lay there for hours trying to decide whether that front pattern and the back pattern really did move together or separately.

On a pattern like this, by daylight, there is a lack of sequence, a defiance of law, that is a constant irritant to a normal mind.

The color is hideous enough, and unreliable enough, and infuriating enough, but the pattern is torturing.

You think you have mastered it, but just as you get well underway in following, it turns a back-somersault and there you are. It slaps you in the face, knocks you down, and tramples upon you. It is like a bad dream.

---

[4]Allusion to lines from a 1715 hymn by Isaac Watts, "Against Idleness and Mischief": "How doth the little busy bee / Improve each shining hour, / And gather honey all the day / From every opening flower!"

The outside pattern is a florid arabesque, reminding one of a fungus. If you can imagine a toadstool in joints, an interminable string of toadstools, budding and sprouting in endless convolutions—why, that is something like it.

That is, sometimes!

There is one marked peculiarity about this paper, a thing nobody seems to notice but myself, and that is that it changes as the light changes.

When the sun shoots in through the east window—I always watch for that first long, straight ray—it changes so quickly that I never can quite believe it.

That is why I watch it always.

By moonlight—the moon shines in all night when there is a moon—I wouldn't know it was the same paper.

At night in any kind of light, in twilight, candlelight, lamplight, and worst of all by moonlight, it becomes bars! The outside pattern I mean, and the woman behind it is as plain as can be.

I didn't realize for a long time what the thing was that showed behind, that dim sub-pattern, but now I am quite sure it is a woman.

By daylight she is subdued, quiet. I fancy it is the pattern that keeps her so still. It is so puzzling. It keeps me quiet by the hour.

I lie down ever so much now. John says it is good for me, and to sleep all I can.

Indeed he started the habit by making me lie down for an hour after each meal.

It is a very bad habit I am convinced, for you see I don't sleep.

And that cultivates deceit, for I don't tell them I'm awake—O no!

The fact is I am getting a little afraid of John.

He seems very queer sometimes, and even Jennie has an inexplicable look.

It strikes me occasionally, just as a scientific hypothesis,—that perhaps it is the paper!

I have watched John when he did not know I was looking, and come into the room suddenly on the most innocent excuses, and I've caught him several times *looking at the paper*! And Jennie too. I caught Jennie with her hand on it once.

She didn't know I was in the room, and when I asked her in a quiet, a very quiet voice, with the most restrained manner possible, what she was doing with the paper—she turned around as if she had been caught stealing, and looked quite angry—asked me why I should frighten her so!

Then she said that the paper stained everything it touched, that she had found yellow smooches on all my clothes and John's, and she wished we would be more careful!

Did not that sound innocent? But I know she was studying that pattern, and I am determined that nobody shall find it out but myself!

Life is very much more exciting now than it used to be. You see I have something more to expect, to look forward to, to watch. I really do eat better, and am more quiet than I was.

John is so pleased to see me improve! He laughed a little the other day, and said I seemed to be flourishing in spite of my wall-paper.

I turned it off with a laugh. I had no intention of telling him it was *because* of the wall-paper—he would make fun of me. He might even want to take me away.

I don't want to leave now until I have found it out. There is a week more, and I think that will be enough.

I'm feeling ever so much better! I don't sleep much at night, for it is so interesting to watch developments; but I sleep a good deal in the daytime.

In the daytime it is tiresome and perplexing.

There are always new shoots on the fungus, and new shades of yellow all over it. I cannot keep count of them, though I have tried conscientiously.

It is the strangest yellow, that wall-paper! It makes me think of all the yellow things I ever saw—not beautiful ones like buttercups, but old foul, bad yellow things.

But there is something else about that paper—the smell! I noticed it the moment we came into the room, but with so much air and sun it was not bad. Now we have had a week of fog and rain, and whether the windows are open or not, the smell is here.

It creeps all over the house.

I find it hovering in the dining-room, skulking in the parlor, hiding in the hall, lying in wait for me on the stairs.

It gets into my hair.

Even when I go to ride, if I turn my head suddenly and surprise it—there is that smell!

Such a peculiar odor, too! I have spent hours in trying to analyze it, to find what it smelled like.

It is not bad—at first, and very gentle, but quite the subtlest, most enduring odor I ever met.

In this damp weather it is awful, I wake up in the night and find it hanging over me.

It used to disturb me at first. I thought seriously of burning the house—to reach the smell.

But now I am used to it. The only thing I can think of that it is like is the *color* of the paper! A yellow smell.

There is a very funny mark on this wall, low down, near the mopboard. A streak that runs round the room. It goes behind every piece of furniture, except the bed, a long, straight, even *smooch,* as if it had been rubbed over and over.

I wonder how it was done and who did it, and what they did it for. Round and round and round — round and round and round — it makes me dizzy!

I really have discovered something at last.

Through watching so much at night, when it changes so, I have finally found out.

The front pattern *does* move — and no wonder! The woman behind shakes it!

Sometimes I think there are a great many women behind, and sometimes only one, and she crawls around fast, and her crawling shakes it all over.

Then in the very bright spots she keeps still, and in the very shady spots she just takes hold of the bars and shakes them hard.

And she is all the time trying to climb through. But nobody could climb through that pattern — it strangles so; I think that is why it has so many heads.

They get through, and then the pattern strangles them off and turns them upside down, and makes their eyes white!

If those heads were covered or taken off it would not be half so bad.

I think that woman gets out in the daytime!

And I'll tell you why — privately — I've seen her!

I can see her out of every one of my windows!

It is the same woman, I know, for she is always creeping, and most women do not creep by daylight.

I see her in that long shaded lane, creeping up and down. I see her in those dark grape arbors, creeping all around the garden.

I see her on that long road under the trees, creeping along, and when a carriage comes she hides under the blackberry vines.

I don't blame her a bit. It must be very humiliating to be caught creeping by daylight!

I always lock the door when I creep by daylight. I can't do it at night, for I know John would suspect something at once.

And John is so queer now, that I don't want to irritate him. I wish he would take another room! Besides, I don't want anybody to get that woman out at night but myself.

I often wonder if I could see her out of all the windows at once.

But, turn as fast as I can, I can only see out of one at one time.

And though I always see her, she *may* be able to creep faster than I can turn!

I have watched her sometimes away off in the open country, creeping as fast as a cloud shadow in a high wind.

If only that top pattern could be gotten off from the under one! I mean to try it, little by little.

I have found out another funny thing, but I shan't tell it this time! It does not do to trust people too much.

There are only two more days to get this paper off, and I believe John is beginning to notice. I don't like the look in his eyes.

And I heard him ask Jennie a lot of professional questions about me. She had a very good report to give.

She said I slept a good deal in the daytime.

John knows I don't sleep very well at night, for all I'm so quiet!

He asked me all sorts of questions, too, and pretended to be very loving and kind.

As if I couldn't see through him!

Still, I don't wonder he acts so, sleeping under this paper for three months.

It only interests me, but I feel sure John and Jennie are secretly affected by it.

Hurrah! This is the last day, but it is enough. John is to stay in town over night, and won't be out until this evening.

Jennie wanted to sleep with me—the sly thing! but I told her I should undoubtedly rest better for a night all alone.

That was clever, for really I wasn't alone a bit! As soon as it was moonlight and that poor thing began to crawl and shake the pattern, I got up and ran to help her.

I pulled and she shook, I shook and she pulled, and before morning we had peeled off yards of that paper.

A strip about as high as my head and half around the room.

And then when the sun came and that awful pattern began to laugh at me, I declared I would finish it to-day!

We go away to-morrow, and they are moving all my furniture down again to leave things as they were before.

Jennie looked at the wall in amazement, but I told her merrily that I did it out of pure spite at the vicious thing.

She laughed and said she wouldn't mind doing it herself, but I must not get tired.

How she betrayed herself that time!

But I am here, and no person touches this paper but me,—not *alive*!

She tried to get me out of the room—it was too patent! But I said it was so quiet and empty and clean now that I believed I would lie down again and sleep all I could; and not to wake me even for dinner—I would call when I woke.

So now she is gone, and the servants are gone, and the things are gone, and there is nothing left but that great bedstead nailed down, with the canvas mattress we found on it.

We shall sleep downstairs to-night, and take the boat home to-morrow.

I quite enjoy the room, now it is bare again.

How those children did tear about here!

This bedstead is fairly gnawed!

But I must get to work.

I have locked the door and thrown the key down into the front path.

I don't want to go out, and I don't want to have anybody come in, till John comes.

I want to astonish him.

I've got a rope up here that even Jennie did not find. If that woman does get out, and tries to get away, I can tie her!

But I forgot I could not reach far without anything to stand on!

This bed will *not* move!

I tried to lift and push it until I was lame, and then I got so angry I bit off a little piece at one corner—but it hurt my teeth.

Then I peeled off all the paper I could reach standing on the floor. It sticks horribly and the pattern just enjoys it! All those strangled heads and bulbous eyes and waddling fungus growths just shriek with derision!

I am getting angry enough to do something desperate. To jump out of the window would be admirable exercise, but the bars are too strong even to try.

Besides I wouldn't do it. Of course not. I know well enough that a step like that is improper and might be misconstrued.

I don't like to *look* out of the windows even—there are so many of those creeping women, and they creep so fast.

I wonder if they all come out of that wall-paper as I did?

But I am securely fastened now by my well-hidden rope—you don't get *me* out in the road there!

I suppose I shall have to get back behind the pattern when it comes night, and that is hard!

It is so pleasant to be out in this great room and creep around as I please!

I don't want to go outside. I won't, even if Jennie asks me to.

For outside you have to creep on the ground, and everything is green instead of yellow.

But here I can creep smoothly on the floor, and my shoulder just fits in that long smooch around the wall, so I cannot lose my way.

Why there's John at the door!

It is no use, young man, you can't open it!

How he does call and pound!

Now he's crying for an axe.

It would be a shame to break down that beautiful door!

"John dear!" said I in the gentlest voice, "the key is down by the front steps, under a plantain leaf!"

That silenced him for a few moments.

Then he said—very quietly indeed, "Open the door, my darling!"

"I can't," said I. "The key is down by the front door under a plantain leaf!"

And then I said it again, several times, very gently and slowly, and said it so often that he had to go and see, and he got it of course, and came in. He stopped short by the door.

"What is the matter?" he cried. "For God's sake, what are you doing!"

I kept on creeping just the same, but I looked at him over my shoulder.

"I've got out at last," said I, "in spite of you and Jane.[5] And I've pulled off most of the paper, so you can't put me back!"

Now why should that man have fainted? But he did, and right across my path by the wall, so that I had to creep over him every time!

[1892]

---

[5]John's sister; Jennie is a nickname for Jane.

WILLA CATHER
[1873–1947]

Willa Cather was born in Back Creek Valley, Virginia, in 1873 to a cultivated and prominent family in a small rural community. Her father, Charles, was a sheep farmer who styled himself a country gentleman. When Charles's parents and brother moved west to Nebraska in 1883, Cather's father followed suit and transplanted his family to Red Cloud, a bustling prairie town with stores, hotels, banks, saloons, and an opera house, where he opened a small real estate and loan office. The trade of the shaded hills of Virginia for the vast, windy expanses of Nebraska profoundly affected Cather's life and art. Transported from a conservative, established eastern town with, as Cather put it, "a definitely arranged backdrop," to the more fluid immigrant West, Cather experienced her world as one of greater possibilities, particularly in regard to her gender. During her high school years in Red Cloud, Cather cut her hair short and experimented with a male persona. Determined to assert her independence, she indicated her rejection of traditional domestic life early on.

After graduating from high school, Cather enrolled at the University of Nebraska with the initial goal of becoming a doctor. Early in her college career, however, she shifted her focus to writing and became involved with several campus publications. While still a student, she contributed a regular column on the arts to the Nebraska State Journal *and placed articles in the* Lincoln Courier. *Her features and reviews earned her a state and national reputation as a journalist and, after her graduation in 1895, she secured a job as the managing editor of* Home Monthly, *a woman's magazine designed to compete with the* Ladies Home Journal. *By the time Cather moved east to Pittsburgh to assume her new position, she had published nine short stories. Her tenure as editor, however, proved prolific for her journalistic writing, but not for her fiction. When the magazine changed owners, Cather left the* Home Journal *and, after a brief stint writing for the Pittsburgh* Leader, *took a job teaching English and Latin to high school students. For the next five years (1901–06), Cather devoted herself to her students, her fiction, and Isabelle McClung, the daughter of a prominent Pittsburgh judge with whom Cather lived until she moved to New York. During her years as a teacher,*

Cather published thirteen short stories as well as her first collection of short fiction, The Troll Garden (1905).

In 1906, S. S. McClure, the publisher of The Troll Garden, hired Cather onto the staff of his new popular New York magazine, McClure's. She quickly worked her way from staff writer to managing editor. The magazine proved a success, but Cather became increasingly convinced that if she was to produce truly fine fiction, she must devote herself full-time to her art. In 1911, she took a leave of absence from McClure's and completed her first novel, Alexander's Bridge. McClure, ever Cather's champion, serialized the book in his magazine and published it in volume form in 1912. Cather the journalist finally became Cather the novelist.

Over the next twelve years, Cather, reflecting on her prairie experience from the mature vantage point of the New York apartment that she shared for the rest of her life with Edith Lewis, wrote five highly acclaimed novels: O, Pioneers (1913), The Song of the Lark (1915), My Ántonia (1918), One of Ours (1922), A Lost Lady (1923), and The Professor's House (1925). Cather's WWI novel, One of Ours, garnered her the coveted Pulitzer Prize. In 1927, Cather capped her period of intense creativity with the novel that many critics deem her masterwork, Death Comes for the Archbishop, a book that expressed her deep attraction to the deserts and ruins of the American Southwest, a region she visited many times throughout her life. In 1931, Cather published her saga of Canadian immigration, Shadows on the Rock. She then solidified her status as a literary icon a year later with the publication of her elegant collection of short fiction, Obscure Destinies, which contained three interrelated stories: "Neighbour Rosicky," "Old Mrs. Harris," and "Two Friends." During the remaining fourteen years of her life, Cather published only two additional novels. Obscure Destinies marked the height of both her fame and her literary powers.

Even though Cather spent a relatively short period of her life in Red Cloud, she never lost the feeling that certain landscapes, like the prairie, the desert, and the basin and range, made certain ways of being possible. Cather's most beloved characters are those who have profound relationships with particular places that inspire special, fragile forms of human community.

The texts in The Pearson Custom Library of American Literature issue from three sources. The text of "Paul's Case" comes from Willa Cather: Early Novels and Stories (New York: Library of America, 1987), which reprints the version of the story printed in The Troll Garden (1905). The texts of "Neighbour Rosicky" and "Old Mrs. Harris" issue from the University of Nebraska scholarly edition of Obscure Destinies (Lincoln: University of Nebraska Press, 1998). The texts follow the editorial principle of final authorial intention and incorporates all substantive changes that Cather made to the stories throughout her lifetime. As such, the versions presented differ from those that first appeared in periodicals. The text of "Tom Outland's Story" issues from Willa

Cather: Later Novels *(New York: Library of America, 1990), which reprints the 1925 Alfred Knopf edition of* The Professor's House.

For Further Reading

Primary Works

April Twilights (Boston: Badger, 1903); *The Troll Garden* (New York: McClure, Phillips, 1905); *Alexander's Bridge* (Boston & New York: Houghton Mifflin, 1912); republished as *Alexander's Bridges* (London: Heinemann, 1912); *O Pioneers!* (Boston & New York: Houghton Mifflin, 1913; London: Heinemann, 1913); *The Song of the Lark* (Boston & New York: Houghton Mifflin, 1915; London: Murray, 1916); revised as volume 2 of *The Novels and Stories of Willa Cather* (Boston: Houghton Mifflin, 1937); *My Ántonia* (Boston & New York: Houghton Mifflin, 1918; London: Heinemann, 1919); *Youth and the Bright Medusa* (New York: Knopf, 1920; London: Heinemann, 1921); *One of Ours* (New York: Knopf, 1922; London: Heinemann, 1923); *April Twilights and Other Poems* (New York: Knopf, 1923; London: Heinemann, 1924; enlarged edition, New York: Knopf, 1933); abridged in volume 3 of *The Novels and Stories of Willa Cather* (Boston: Houghton Mifflin, 1937); *A Lost Lady* (New York: Knopf, 1923; London: Heinemann, 1924); *The Professor's House* (New York: Knopf, 1925; London: Heinemann, 1925); *My Mortal Enemy* (New York: Knopf, 1926; London: Heinemann, 1928); *Death Comes for the Archbishop* (New York: Knopf, 1927; London: Heinemann, 1927); *Shadows on the Rock* (New York: Knopf, 1931; London, Toronto, Melbourne & Sydney: Cassell, 1932); *Obscure Destinies* (New York: Knopf, 1932; London, Toronto, Melbourne & Sydney: Cassell, 1932); *Lucy Gayheart* (New York: Knopf, 1935; London, Toronto, Melbourne & Sydney: Cassell, 1935); *Not Under Forty* (New York: Knopf, 1936; London, Toronto, Melbourne & Sydney: Cassell, 1936); *Sapphira and the Slave Girl* (New York: Knopf, 1940; London, Toronto, Melbourne & Sydney: Cassell, 1941); *The Old Beauty and Others* (New York: Knopf, 1948; London: Cassell, 1956).

Secondary Works

Harold Bloom, ed., *Willa Cather* (Philadelphia: Chelsea House, 2000); Johnathan Goldberg, *Willa Cather and Others* (Duke: Duke University Press, 2001); David Harrell, *From Mesa Verde to The Professor's House* (Albuquerque: New Mexico University Press, 1992); Sheryl Meyering, *A Reader's Guide to the Short Stories of Willa Cather* (New York: Macmillan, 1994); Sharon O'Brien, *Willa Cather: The Emerging Voice* (New York: Oxford University Press, 1987).

Neighbour Rosicky[*]

WILLA CATHER

I

When Doctor Burleigh told neighbour Rosicky he had a bad heart, Rosicky protested.

"So? No, I guess my heart was always pretty good. I got a little asthma, maybe. Just a awful short breath when I was pitchin' hay last summer, dat's all."

"Well now, Rosicky, if you know more about it than I do, what did you come to me for? It's your heart that makes you short of breath, I tell you. You're sixty-five years old, and you've always worked hard, and your heart's tired. You've got to be careful from now on, and you can't do heavy work any more. You've got five boys at home to do it for you."

The old farmer looked up at the Doctor with a gleam of amusement in his queer triangular-shaped eyes. His eyes were large and lively, but the lids were caught up in the middle in a curious way, so that they formed a triangle. He did not look like a sick man. His brown face was creased but not wrinkled, he had a ruddy colour in his smooth-shaven cheeks and in his lips, under his long brown moustache. His hair was thin and ragged around his ears, but very little grey. His forehead, naturally high and crossed by deep parallel lines, now ran all the way up to his pointed crown. Rosicky's face had the habit of looking interested,—suggested a contented disposition and a reflective quality that was gay rather than grave. This gave him a certain detachment, the easy manner of an onlooker and observer.

"Well, I guess you ain't got no pills fur a bad heart, Doctor Ed. I guess the only thing is fur me to git me a new one."

Doctor Burleigh swung round in his desk-chair and frowned at the old farmer. "I think if I were you I'd take a little care of the old one, Rosicky."

Rosicky shrugged. "Maybe I don't know how. I expect you mean fur me not to drink my coffee no more."

"I wouldn't, in your place. But you'll do as you choose about that. I've never yet been able to separate a Bohemian from his coffee or his pipe. I've

[*]"Neighbor Rosicky" first appeared serialized in the April and May 1930 issues of *Woman's Home Companion.* Cather first collected the story in *Obscure Destinies* (1932).

quit trying. But the sure thing is you've got to cut out farm work. You can feed the stock and do chores about the barn, but you can't do anything in the fields that makes you short of breath."

"How about shelling corn?"

"Of course not!"

Rosicky considered with puckered brows.

"I can't make my heart go no longer'n it wants to, can I, Doctor Ed?"

"I think it's good for five or six years yet, maybe more, if you'll take the strain off it. Sit around the house and help Mary. If I had a good wife like yours, I'd want to stay around the house."

His patient chuckled. "It ain't no place fur a man. I don't like no old man hanging round the kitchen too much. An' my wife, she's a awful hard worker her own self."

"That's it; you can help her a little. My Lord, Rosicky, you are one of the few men I know who has a family he can get some comfort out of; happy dispositions, never quarrel among themselves, and they treat you right. I want to see you live a few years and enjoy them."

"Oh, they're good kids, all right," Rosicky assented.

The Doctor wrote him a prescription and asked him how his oldest son, Rudolph, who had married in the spring, was getting on. Rudolph had struck out for himself, on rented land. "And how's Polly? I was afraid Mary mightn't like an American daughter-in-law, but it seems to be working out all right."

"Yes, she's a fine girl. Dat widder woman bring her daughters up very nice. Polly got lots of spunk, an' she got some style, too. Da's nice, for young folks to have some style." Rosicky inclined his head gallantly. His voice and his twinkly smile were an affectionate compliment to his daughter-in-law.

"It looks like a storm, and you'd better be getting home before it comes. In town in the car?" Doctor Burleigh rose.

"No, I'm in de wagon. When you got five boys, you ain't got much chance to ride round in de Ford. I ain't much for cars, noway."

'Well, it's a good road out to your place; but I don't want you bumping around in a wagon much. And never again on a hay-rake, remember!"

Rosicky placed the Doctor's fee delicately behind the desk-telephone, looking the other way, as if this were an absent-minded gesture. He put on his plush cap and his corduroy jacket with a sheepskin collar, and went out.

The Doctor picked up his stethoscope and frowned at it as if he were seriously annoyed with the instrument. He wished it had been telling tales about some other man's heart, some old man who didn't look the Doctor in the eye so knowingly, or hold out such a warm brown hand when he said good-bye. Doctor Burleigh had been a poor boy in the country before he went away to medical school; he had known Rosicky almost ever since he could remember, and he had a deep affection for Mrs. Rosicky.

Only last winter he had had such a good breakfast at Rosicky's, and that when he needed it. He had been out all night on a long, hard confinement case at Tom Marshall's,—a big rich farm where there was plenty of stock and plenty of feed and a great deal of expensive farm machinery of the newest model, and no comfort whatever. The woman had too many children and too much work, and she was no manager. When the baby was born at last, and handed over to the assisting neighbour woman, and the mother was properly attended to, Burleigh refused any breakfast in that slovenly house, and drove his buggy—the snow was too deep for a car—eight miles to Antón Rosicky's place. He didn't know another farm-house where a man could get such a warm welcome, and such good strong coffee with rich cream. No wonder the old chap didn't want to give up his coffee!

He had driven in just when the boys had come back from the barn and were washing up for breakfast. The long table, covered with a bright oilcloth, was set out with dishes waiting for them, and the warm kitchen was full of the smell of coffee and hot biscuit and sausage. Five big handsome boys, running from twenty to twelve, all with what Burleigh called natural good manners,—they hadn't a bit of the painful self-consciousness he himself had to struggle with when he was a lad. One ran to put his horse away, another helped him off with his fur coat and hung it up, and Josephine, the youngest child and the only daughter, quickly set another place under her mother's direction.

With Mary, to feed creatures was the natural expression of affection,—her chickens, the calves, her big hungry boys. It was a rare pleasure to feed a young man whom she seldom saw and of whom she was as proud as if he belonged to her. Some country housekeepers would have stopped to spread a white cloth over the oilcloth, to change the thick cups and plates for their best china, and the wooden-handled knives for plated ones. But not Mary.

"You must take us as you find us, Doctor Ed. I'd be glad to put out my good things for you if you was expected, but I'm glad to get you any way at all."

He knew she was glad,—she threw back her head and spoke out as if she were announcing him to the whole prairie. Rosicky hadn't said anything at all; he merely smiled his twinkling smile, put some more coal on the fire, and went into his own room to pour the Doctor a little drink in a medicine glass. When they were all seated, he watched his wife's face from his end of the table and spoke to her in Czech. Then, with the instinct of politeness which seldom failed him, he turned to the Doctor and said slyly: "I was just tellin' her not to ask you no questions about Mrs. Marshall till you eat some breakfast. My wife, she's terrible fur to ask questions."

The boys laughed, and so did Mary. She watched the Doctor devour her biscuit and sausage, too much excited to eat anything herself. She drank her coffee and sat taking in everything about her visitor. She had known him when he was a poor country boy, and was boastfully proud of his success, always saying: "What do people go to Omaha for, to see a doctor, when we got the best one in the State right here?" If Mary liked people at all, she felt physical pleasure in the sight of them, personal exultation in any good fortune that came to them. Burleigh didn't know many women like that, but he knew she was like that.

When his hunger was satisfied, he did, of course, have to tell them about Mrs. Marshall, and he noticed what a friendly interest the boys took in the matter.

Rudolph, the oldest one (he was still living at home then), said: "The last time I was over there, she was lifting them big heavy milk-cans, and I knew she oughtn't to be doing it."

"Yes, Rudolph told me about that when he come home, and I said it wasn't right," Mary put in warmly. "It was all right for me to do them things up to the last, for I was terrible strong, but that woman's weakly. And do you think she'll be able to nurse it, Ed?" She sometimes forgot to give him the title she was so proud of. "And to think of your being up all night and then not able to get a decent breakfast! I don't know what's the matter with such people."

"Why, Mother," said one of the boys, "if Doctor Ed had got breakfast there, we wouldn't have him here. So you ought to be glad."

"He knows I'm glad to have him, John, any time. But I'm sorry for that poor woman, how bad she'll feel the Doctor had to go away in the cold without his breakfast."

"I wish I'd been in practice when these were getting born." The Doctor looked down the row of close-clipped heads. "I missed some good breakfasts by not being."

The boys began to laugh at their mother because she flushed so red, but she stood her ground and threw up her head. "I don't care, you wouldn't have got away from this house without breakfast. No doctor ever did. I'd have had something ready fixed that Anton could warm up for you."

The boys laughed harder than ever, and exclaimed at her: "I'll bet you would!" "She would, that!"

"Father, did you get breakfast for the doctor when we were born?"

"Yes, and he used to bring me my breakfast, too, mighty nice. I was always awful hungry!" Mary admitted with a guilty laugh.

While the boys were getting the Doctor's horse, he went to the window to examine the house plants. "What do you do to your geraniums to keep them blooming all winter, Mary? I never pass this house that from the road I don't see your windows full of flowers."

She snapped off a dark red one, and a ruffled new green leaf, and put them in his buttonhole. "There, that looks better. You look too solemn for a young man, Ed. Why don't you git married? I'm worried about you. Settin' at breakfast, I looked at you real hard, and I seen you've got some grey hairs already."

"Oh, yes! They're coming. Maybe they'd come faster if I married."

"Don't talk so. You'll ruin your health eating at the hotel. I could send your wife a nice loaf of nut bread, if you only had one. I don't like to see a young man getting grey. I'll tell you something, Ed; you make some strong black tea and keep it handy in a bowl, and every morning just brush it into your hair, an' it'll keep the grey from showin' much. That's the way I do!"

Sometimes the Doctor heard the gossipers in the drug-store wondering why Rosicky didn't get on faster. He was industrious, and so were his boys, but they were rather free and easy, weren't pushers, and they didn't always show good judgment. They were comfortable, they were out of debt, but they didn't get much ahead. Maybe, Doctor Burleigh reflected, people as generous and warm-hearted and affectionate as the Rosickys never got ahead much; maybe you couldn't enjoy your life and put it into the bank, too.

II

When Rosicky left Doctor Burleigh's office he went into the farm-implement store to light his pipe and put on his glasses and read over the list Mary had given him. Then he went into the general merchandise place next door and stood about until the pretty girl with the plucked eyebrows, who always waited on him, was free. Those eyebrows, two thin India-ink strokes, amused him, because he remembered how they used to be. Rosicky always prolonged his shopping by a little joking; the girl knew the old fellow admired her, and she liked to chaff with him.

"Seems to me about every other week you buy ticking,[1] Mr. Rosicky, and always the best quality," she remarked as she measured off the heavy bolt with red stripes.

"You see, my wife is always makin' goose-fedder pillows, an' de thin stuff don't hold in dem little down-fedders."

"You must have lots of pillows at your house."

"Sure. She makes quilts of dem, too. We sleeps easy. Now she's makin' a fedder quilt for my son's wife. You know Polly, that married my Rudolph. How much my bill, Miss Pearl?"

"Eight eighty-five."

"Chust make it nine, and put in some candy fur de women."

"As usual. I never did see a man buy so much candy for his wife. First thing you know, she'll be getting too fat."

---

[1] a strong linen or cotton fabric used for upholstering.

"I'd like dat. I ain't much fur all dem slim women like what de style is now."

"That's one for me, I suppose, Mr. Bohunk!"[2] Pearl sniffed and elevated her India-ink strokes.

When Rosicky went out to his wagon, it was beginning to snow,—the first snow of the season, and he was glad to see it. He rattled out of town and along the highway through a wonderfully rich stretch of country, the finest farms in the county. He admired this High Prairie, as it was called, and always liked to drive through it. His own place lay in a rougher territory, where there was some clay in the soil and it was not so productive. When he bought his land, he hadn't the money to buy on High Prairie; so he told his boys, when they grumbled, that if their land hadn't some clay in it, they wouldn't own it at all. All the same, he enjoyed looking at these fine farms, as he enjoyed looking at a prize bull.

After he had gone eight miles, he came to the graveyard, which lay just at the edge of his own hay-land. There he stopped his horses and sat still on his wagon seat, looking about at the snowfall. Over yonder on the hill he could see his own house, crouching low, with the clump of orchard behind and the windmill before, and all down the gentle hill-slope the rows of pale gold cornstalks stood out against the white field. The snow was falling over the cornfield and the pasture and the hay-land, steadily, with very little wind,—a nice dry snow. The graveyard had only a light wire fence about it and was all overgrown with long red grass. The fine snow, settling into this red grass and upon the few little evergreens and the headstones, looked very pretty.

It was a nice graveyard, Rosicky reflected, sort of snug and homelike, not cramped or mournful,—a big sweep all round it. A man could lie down in the long grass and see the complete arch of the sky over him, hear the wagons go by; in summer the mowing-machine rattled right up to the wire fence. And it was so near home. Over there across the cornstalks his own roof and windmill looked so good to him that he promised himself to mind the Doctor and take care of himself. He was awful fond of his place, he admitted. He wasn't anxious to leave it. And it was a comfort to think that he would never have to go farther than the edge of his own hayfield. The snow, falling over his barnyard and the graveyard, seemed to draw things together like. And they were all old neighbours in the graveyard, most of them friends; there was nothing to feel awkward or embarrassed about. Embarrassment was the most disagreeable feeling Rosicky knew. He didn't often have it,—only with certain people whom he didn't understand at all.

Well, it was a nice snowstorm; a fine sight to see the snow falling so quietly and graciously over so much open country. On his cap and shoulders, on the horses' backs and manes, light, delicate, mysterious it fell; and with it a dry cool fragrance was released into the air. It meant rest for vegetation and

---

[2] slang for a laborer from east-central Europe; Bo(hemian) + alteration of Hung(arian).

men and beasts, for the ground itself; a season of long nights for sleep, leisurely breakfasts, peace by the fire. This and much more went through Rosicky's mind, but he merely told himself that winter was coming, clucked to his horses, and drove on.

When he reached home, John, the youngest boy, ran out to put away his team for him, and he met Mary coming up from the outside cellar with her apron full of carrots. They went into the house together. On the table, covered with oilcloth figured with clusters of blue grapes, a place was set, and he smelled hot coffee-cake of some kind. Anton never lunched in town; he thought that extravagant, and anyhow he didn't like the food. So Mary always had something ready for him when he got home.

After he was settled in his chair, stirring his coffee in a big cup, Mary took out of the oven a pan of *kolache*[3] stuffed with apricots, examined them anxiously to see whether they had got too dry, put them beside his plate, and then sat down opposite him.

Rosicky asked her in Czech if she wasn't going to have any coffee.

She replied in English, as being somehow the right language for transacting business: "Now what did Doctor Ed say, Anton? You tell me just what."

"He said I was to tell you some compliments, but I forgot 'em." Rosicky's eyes twinkled.

"About you, I mean. What did he say about your asthma?"

"He says I ain't got no asthma." Rosicky took one of the little rolls in his broad brown fingers. The thickened nail of his right thumb told the story of his past.

"Well, what is the matter? And don't try to put me off."

"He don't say nothing much, only I'm a little older, and my heart ain't so good like it used to be."

Mary started and brushed her hair back from her temples with both hands as if she were a little out of her mind. From the way she glared, she might have been in a rage with him.

"He says there's something the matter with your heart? Doctor Ed says so?"

"Now don't yell at me like I was a hog in de garden, Mary. You know I always did like to hear a woman talk soft. He didn't say anything de matter wid my heart, only it ain't so young like it used to be, an' he tell me not to pitch hay or run de corn-sheller."

Mary wanted to jump up, but she sat still. She admired the way he never under any circumstances raised his voice or spoke roughly. He was city-bred, and she was country-bred; she often said she wanted her boys to have their papa's nice ways.

---

[3] a traditional Czech pastry filled with fruit.

"You never have no pain there, do you? It's your breathing and your stomach that's been wrong. I wouldn't believe nobody but Doctor Ed about it. I guess I'll go see him myself. Didn't he give you no advice?"

"Chust to take it easy like, an' stay round de house dis winter. I guess you got some carpenter work for me to do. I kin make some new shelves for you, and I want dis long time to build a closet in de boys' room and make dem two little fellers keep dere clo'es hung up."

Rosicky drank his coffee from time to time, while he considered. His moustache was of the soft long variety and came down over his mouth like the teeth of a buggy-rake over a bundle of hay. Each time he put down his cup, he ran his blue handkerchief over his lips. When he took a drink of water, he managed very neatly with the back of his hand.

Mary sat watching him intently, trying to find any change in his face. It is hard to see anyone who has become like your own body to you. Yes, his hair had got thin, and his high forehead had deep lines running from left to right. But his neck, always clean shaved except in the busiest seasons, was not loose or baggy. It was burned a dark reddish brown, and there were deep creases in it, but it looked firm and full of blood. His cheeks had a good colour. On either side of his mouth there was a half-moon down the length of his cheek, not wrinkles, but two lines that had come there from his habitual expression. He was shorter and broader than when she married him; his back had grown broad and curved, a good deal like the shell of an old turtle, and his arms and legs were short.

He was fifteen years older than Mary, but she had hardly ever thought about it before. He was her man, and the kind of man she liked. She was rough, and he was gentle,—city-bred, as she always said. They had been shipmates on a rough voyage and had stood by each other in trying times. Life had gone well with them because, at bottom, they had the same ideas about life. They agreed, without discussion, as to what was most important and what was secondary. They didn't often exchange opinions, even in Czech,—it was as if they had thought the same thought together. A good deal had to be sacrificed and thrown overboard in a hard life like theirs, and they had never disagreed as to the things that could go. It had been a hard life, and a soft life, too. There wasn't anything brutal in the short, broad-backed man with the three-cornered eyes and the forehead that went on to the top of his skull. He was a city man, a gentle man, and though he had married a rough farm girl, he had never touched her without gentleness.

They had been at one accord not to hurry through life, not to be always skimping and saving. They saw their neighbours buy more land and feed more stock than they did, without discontent. Once when the creamery agent came to the Rosickys to persuade them to sell him their cream, he told them how much money the Fasslers, their nearest neighbours, had made on their cream last year.

"Yes," said Mary, "and look at them Fassler children! Pale, pinched little things, they look like skimmed milk. I'd rather put some colour into my children's faces than put money into the bank."

The agent shrugged and turned to Anton.

"I guess we'll do like she says," said Rosicky.

III

Mary very soon got into town to see Doctor Ed, and then she had a talk with her boys and set a guard over Rosicky. Even John, the youngest, had his father on his mind. If Rosicky went to throw hay down from the loft, one of the boys ran up the ladder and took the fork from him. He sometimes complained that though he was getting to be an old man, he wasn't an old woman yet.

That winter he stayed in the house in the afternoons and carpentered, or sat in the chair between the window full of plants and the wooden bench where the two pails of drinking-water stood. This spot was called "Father's corner," though it was not a corner at all. He had a shelf there, where he kept his Bohemian papers and his pipes and tobacco, and his shears and needles and thread and tailor's thimble. Having been a tailor in his youth, he couldn't bear to see a woman patching at his clothes, or at the boys'. He liked tailoring, and always patched all the overalls and jackets and work shirts. Occasionally he made over a pair of pants one of the older boys had outgrown, for the little fellow.

While he sewed, he let his mind run back over his life. He had a good deal to remember, really; life in three countries. The only part of his youth he didn't like to remember was the two years he had spent in London, in Cheapside, working for a German tailor who was wretchedly poor. Those days, when he was nearly always hungry, when his clothes were dropping off him for dirt, and the sound of a strange language kept him in continual bewilderment, had left a sore spot in his mind that wouldn't bear touching.

He was twenty when he landed at Castle Garden in New York, and he had a protector who got him work in a tailor shop in Vesey Street, down near the Washington Market. He looked upon that part of his life as very happy. He became a good workman, he was industrious, and his wages were increased from time to time. He minded his own business and envied nobody's good fortune. He went to night school and learned to read English. He often did overtime work and was well paid for it, but somehow he never saved anything. He couldn't refuse a loan to a friend, and he was self-indulgent. He liked a good dinner, and a little went for beer, a little for tobacco; a good deal went to the girls. He often stood through an opera on Saturday nights; he could get standing-room for a dollar. Those were the great days of opera in New York, and it gave a fellow something to think about for the rest of the week. Rosicky had a quick ear, and a childish love of all the stage splendour; the scenery, the costumes, the ballet. He usually went with a chum, and after the performance they had beer and maybe some oysters somewhere. It was a fine life; for the first five years or so it satisfied him completely. He was never hungry or cold or dirty, and everything amused him: a fire, a dog fight, a parade, a storm, a ferry ride. He thought New York the finest, richest, friendliest city in the world.

Moreover, he had what he called a happy home life. Very near the tailor shop was a small furniture-factory, where an old Austrian, Loeffler, employed a few skilled men and made unusual furniture, most of it to order, for the rich German housewives up-town. The top floor of Loeffler's five-storey factory was a loft, where he kept his choice lumber and stored the odd pieces of furniture left on his hands. One of the young workmen he employed was a Czech, and he and Rosicky became fast friends. They persuaded Loeffler to let them have a sleeping-room in one corner of the loft. They bought good beds and bedding and had their pick of the furniture kept up there. The loft was low-pitched, but light and airy, full of windows, and good-smelling by reason of the fine lumber put up there to season. Old Loeffler used to go down to the docks and buy wood from South America and the East from the sea captains. The young men were as foolish about their house as a bridal pair. Zichec, the young cabinet-maker, devised every sort of convenience, and Rosicky kept their clothes in order. At night and on Sundays, when the quiver of machinery underneath was still, it was the quietest place in the world, and on summer nights all the sea winds blew in. Zichec often practised on his flute in the evening. They were both fond of music and went to the opera together. Rosicky thought he wanted to live like that for ever.

But as the years passed, all alike, he began to get a little restless. When spring came round, he would begin to feel fretted, and he got to drinking. He was likely to drink too much of a Saturday night. On Sunday he was languid and heavy, getting over his spree. On Monday he plunged into work again. So he never had time to figure out what ailed him, though he knew something did. When the grass turned green in Park Place, and the lilac hedge at the back of Trinity churchyard put out its blossoms, he was tormented by a longing to run away. That was why he drank too much; to get a temporary illusion of freedom and wide horizons.

Rosicky, the old Rosicky, could remember as if it were yesterday the day when the young Rosicky found out what was the matter with him. It was on a Fourth of July afternoon, and he was sitting in Park Place in the sun. The lower part of New York was empty. Wall Street, Liberty Street, Broadway, all empty. So much stone and asphalt with nothing going on, so many empty windows. The emptiness was intense, like the stillness in a great factory when the machinery stops and the belts and bands cease running. It was too great a change, it took all the strength out of one. Those blank buildings, without the stream of life pouring through them, were like empty jails. It struck young Rosicky that this was the trouble with big cities; they built you in from the earth itself, cemented you away from any contact with the ground. You lived in an unnatural world, like the fish in an aquarium, who were probably much more comfortable than they ever were in the sea.

On that very day he began to think seriously about the articles he had read in the Bohemian papers, describing prosperous Czech farming communities in the West. He believed he would like to go out there as a farm hand; it was hardly possible that he could ever have land of his own. His people had always been workmen; his father and grandfather had worked in shops. His mother's parents had lived in the country, but they rented their farm and had a hard time to get along. Nobody in his family had ever owned any land,— that belonged to a different station of life altogether. Anton's mother died when he was little, and he was sent into the country to her parents. He stayed with them until he was twelve, and formed those ties with the earth and the farm animals and growing things which are never made at all unless they are made early. After his grandfather died, he went back to live with his father and stepmother, but she was very hard on him, and his father helped him to get passage to London.

After that Fourth of July day in Park Place, the desire to return to the country never left him. To work on another man's farm would be all he asked; to see the sun rise and set and to plant things and watch them grow. He was a very simple man. He was like a tree that has not many roots, but one tap-root that goes down deep. He subscribed for a Bohemian paper printed in Chicago, then for one printed in Omaha. His mind got farther and farther west. He began to save a little money to buy his liberty. When he was thirty-five, there was a great meeting in New York of Bohemian athletic societies, and Rosicky left the tailor shop and went home with the Omaha delegates to try his fortune in another part of the world.

IV

Perhaps the fact that his own youth was well over before he began to have a family was one reason why Rosicky was so fond of his boys. He had almost a grandfather's indulgence for them. He had never had to worry about any of them—except, just now, a little about Rudolph.

On Saturday night the boys always piled into the Ford, took little Josephine, and went to town to the moving-picture show. One Saturday morning they were talking at the breakfast table about starting early that evening, so that they would have an hour or so to see the Christmas things in the stores before the show began. Rosicky looked down the table.

"I hope you boys ain't disappointed, but I want you to let me have de car tonight. Maybe some of you can go in with de neighbours."

Their faces fell. They worked hard all week, and they were still like children. A new jack-knife or a box of candy pleased the older one as much as the little fellow.

"If you and Mother are going to town," Frank said, "maybe you could take a couple of us along with you, anyway."

"No, I want to take de car down to Rudolph's, and let him an' Polly go in to de show. She don't git into town enough, an' I'm afraid she's gettin' lonesome, an' he can't afford no car yet."

That settled it. The boys were a good deal dashed. Their father took another piece of apple-cake and went on: "Maybe next Saturday night de two little fellers can go along wid dem. "

"Oh, is Rudolph going to have the car every Saturday night?"

Rosicky did not reply at once; then he began to speak seriously: "Listen, boys; Polly ain't lookin' so good. I don't like to see nobody lookin' sad. It comes hard fur a town girl to be a farmer's wife. I don't want no trouble to start in Rudolph's family. When it starts, it ain't so easy to stop. An American girl don't git used to our ways all at once. I like to tell Polly she and Rudolph can have the car every Saturday night till after New Year's, if it's all right with you boys."

"Sure it's all right, Papa," Mary cut in. "And it's good you thought about that. Town girls is used to more than country girls. I lay awake nights, scared she'll make Rudolph discontented with the farm."

The boys put as good a face on it as they could. They surely looked forward to their Saturday nights in town. That evening Rosicky drove the car the half-mile down to Rudolph's new, bare little house.

Polly was in a short-sleeved gingham dress, clearing away the supper dishes. She was a trim, slim little thing, with blue eyes and shingled yellow hair, and her eyebrows were reduced to a mere brush-stroke, like Miss Pearl's.

"Good evening, Mr. Rosicky. Rudolph's at the barn, I guess." She never called him father, or Mary mother. She was sensitive about having married a foreigner. She never in the world would have done it if Rudolph hadn't been such a handsome, persuasive fellow and such a gallant lover. He had graduated in her class in the high school in town, and their friendship began in the ninth grade.

Rosicky went in, though he wasn't exactly asked. "My boys ain't goin' to town tonight, an' I brought de car over fur you two to go in to de picture show."

Polly, carrying dishes to the sink, looked over her shoulder at him. "Thank you. But I'm late with my work tonight, and pretty tired. Maybe Rudolph would like to go in with you."

"Oh, I don't go to de shows! I'm too old-fashioned. You won't feel so tired after you ride in de air a ways. It's a nice clear night, an' it ain't cold. You go an' fix yourself up, Polly, an' I'll wash de dishes an' leave everything nice fur you."

Polly blushed and tossed her bob. "I couldn't let you do that, Mr. Rosicky. I wouldn't think of it."

Rosicky said nothing. He found a bib apron on a nail behind the kitchen door. He slipped it over his head and then took Polly by her two elbows and pushed her gently toward the door of her own room. "I washed up de kitchen many times for my wife, when de babies was sick or somethin'. You go an' make yourself look nice. I like you to look prettier'n any of dem town girls when you go in. De young folks must have some fun, an' I'm goin' to look out fur you, Polly."

That kind, reassuring grip on her elbows, the old man's funny bright eyes, made Polly want to drop her head on his shoulder for a second. She restrained herself, but she lingered in his grasp at the door of her room, murmuring tearfully: "You always lived in the city when you were young, didn't you? Don't you ever get lonesome out here?"

As she turned round to him, her hand fell naturally into his, and he stood holding it and smiling into her face with his peculiar, knowing, indulgent smile without a shadow of reproach in it. "Dem big cities is all right fur de rich, but dey is terrible hard fur de poor."

"I don't know. Sometimes I think I'd like to take a chance. You lived in New York, didn't you?"

"An' London. Da's bigger still. I learned my trade dere. Here's Rudolph comin', you better hurry."

"Will you tell me about London some time?"

"Maybe. Only I ain't no talker, Polly. Run an' dress yourself up."

The bedroom door closed behind her, and Rudolph came in from the outside, looking anxious. He had seen the car and was sorry any of his family should come just then. Supper hadn't been a very pleasant occasion. Halting in the doorway, he saw his father in a kitchen apron, carrying dishes to the sink. He flushed crimson and something flashed in his eye. Rosicky held up a warning finger.

"I brought de car over fur you an' Polly to go to de picture show, an' I made her let me finish here so you won't be late. You go put on a clean shirt, quick!"

"But don't the boys want the car, Father?"

"Not tonight dey don't." Rosicky fumbled under his apron and found his pants pocket. He took out a silver dollar and said in a hurried whisper: "You go an' buy dat girl some ice cream an' candy tonight, like you was courtin'. She's awful good friends wid me."

Rudolph was very short of cash, but he took the money as if it hurt him. There had been a crop failure all over the county. He had more than once been sorry he'd married this year.

In a few minutes the young people came out, looking clean and a little stiff. Rosicky hurried them off, and then he took his own time with the dishes. He scoured the pots and pans and put away the milk and swept the kitchen. He put some coal in the stove and shut off the draughts, so the place would be warm for them when they got home late at night. Then he sat down and had a pipe and listened to the clock tick.

Generally speaking, marrying an American girl was certainly a risk. A Czech should marry a Czech. It was lucky that Polly was the daughter of a poor widow woman; Rudolph was proud, and if she had a prosperous family to throw up at him, they could never make it go. Polly was one of four sisters, and they all worked; one was book-keeper in the bank, one taught music, and Polly and her younger sister had been clerks, like Miss Pearl. All four of them were musical, had pretty voices, and sang in the Methodist choir, which the eldest sister directed.

Polly missed the sociability of a store position. She missed the choir, and the company of her sisters. She didn't dislike housework, but she disliked so much of it. Rosicky was a little anxious about this pair. He was afraid Polly would grow so discontented that Rudy would quit the farm and take a factory job in Omaha. He had worked for a winter up there, two years ago, to get money to marry on. He had done very well, and they would always take him back at the stockyards. But to Rosicky that meant the end of everything for his son. To be a landless man was to be a wage-earner, a slave, all your life; to have nothing, to be nothing.

Rosicky thought he would come over and do a little carpentering for Polly after the New Year. He guessed she needed jollying. Rudolph was a serious sort of chap, serious in love and serious about his work.

Rosicky shook out his pipe and walked home across the fields. Ahead of him the lamplight shone from his kitchen windows. Suppose he were still in a tailor shop on Vesey Street, with a bunch of pale, narrow-chested sons working on machines, all coming home tired and sullen to eat supper in a kitchen that was a parlour also; with another crowded, angry family quarrelling just across the dumb-waiter shaft, and squeaking pulleys at the windows where dirty washings hung on dirty lines above a court full of old brooms and mops and ash-cans. . . .

He stopped by the windmill to look up at the frosty winter stars and draw a long breath before he went inside. That kitchen with the shining windows was dear to him; but the sleeping fields and bright stars and the noble darkness were dearer still.

V

On the day before Christmas the weather set in very cold; no snow, but a bitter, biting wind that whistled and sang over the flat land and lashed one's face like fine wires. There was baking going on in the Rosicky kitchen all day, and Rosicky sat inside, making over a coat that Albert had outgrown into an over-coat for John. Mary had a big red geranium in bloom for Christmas, and a row of Jerusalem cherry trees, full of berries. It was the first year she had ever grown these; Doctor Ed brought her the seeds from Omaha when he went to some medical convention. They reminded Rosicky of plants he had seen in England; and all afternoon, as he stitched, he sat thinking about those two years in London, which his mind usually shrank from even after all this while.

He was a lad of eighteen when he dropped down into London, with no money and no connexions except the address of a cousin who was supposed to be working at a confectioner's. When he went to the pastry shop, however, he found that the cousin had gone to America. Anton tramped the streets for several days, sleeping in doorways and on the Embankment, until he was in utter despair. He knew no English, and the sound of the strange language all about him confused him. By chance he met a poor German tailor who had learned his trade in Vienna, and could speak a little Czech. This tailor, Lif-schnitz, kept a repair shop in a Cheapside basement, underneath a cobbler. He didn't much need an apprentice, but he was sorry for the boy and took him in for no wages but his keep and what he could pick up. The pickings were supposed to be coppers given you when you took work home to a cus-tomer. But most of the customers called for their clothes themselves, and the coppers that came Anton's way were very few. He had, however, a place to sleep. The tailor's family lived upstairs in three rooms; a kitchen, a bedroom, where Lifschnitz and his wife and five children slept, and a living-room. Two corners of this living-room were curtained off for lodgers; in one Rosicky slept on an old horsehair sofa, with a feather quilt to wrap himself in. The other corner was rented to a wretched, dirty boy, who was studying the vio-lin. He actually practised there. Rosicky was dirty, too. There was no way to be anything else. Mrs. Lifschnitz got the water she cooked and washed with from a pump in a brick court, four flights down. There were bugs in the place, and multitudes of fleas, though the poor woman did the best she could. Rosicky knew she often went empty to give another potato or a spoonful of dripping to the two hungry, sad-eyed boys who lodged with her. He used to think he would never get out of there, never get a clean shirt to his back again. What would he do, he wondered, when his clothes actually dropped to pieces and the worn cloth wouldn't hold patches any longer?

It was still early when the old farmer put aside his sewing and his recollec-tions. The sky had been a dark grey all day, with not a gleam of sun, and the light failed at four o'clock. He went to shave and change his shirt while the turkey was roasting. Rudolph and Polly were coming over for supper.

After supper they sat round in the kitchen, and the younger boys were saying how sorry they were it hadn't snowed. Everybody was sorry. They wanted a deep snow that would lie long and keep the wheat warm, and leave the ground soaked when it melted.

"Yes, sir!" Rudolph broke out fiercely; "if we have another dry year like last year, there's going to be hard times in this country."

Rosicky filled his pipe. "You boys don't know what hard times is. You don't owe nobody, you got plenty to eat an' keep warm, an' plenty water to keep clean. When you got them, you can't have it very hard."

Rudolph frowned, opened and shut his big right hand, and dropped it clenched upon his knee. "I've got to have a good deal more than that, Father, or I'll quit this farming gamble. I can always make good wages railroading, or at the packing house, and be sure of my money."

"Maybe so," his father answered dryly.

Mary, who had just come in from the pantry and was wiping her hands on the roller towel, thought Rudy and his father were getting too serious. She brought her darning-basket and sat down in the middle of the group.

"I ain't much afraid of hard times, Rudy," she said heartily. 'We've had a plenty, but we've always come through. Your father wouldn't never take nothing very hard, not even hard times. I got a mind to tell you a story on him. Maybe you boys can't hardly remember the year we had that terrible hot wind, that burned everything up on the Fourth of July? All the corn an' the gardens. An' that was in the days when we didn't have alfalfa yet,—I guess it wasn't invented.

"Well, that very day your father was out cultivatin' corn, and I was here in the kitchen makin' plum preserves. We had bushels of plums that year. I noticed it was terrible hot, but it's always hot in the kitchen when you're pre-servin', an' I was too busy with my plums to mind. Anton come in from the field about three o'clock, an' I asked him what was the matter.

"'Nothin',' he says, 'but it's pretty hot, an' I think I won't work no more today.' He stood round for a few minutes, an' then he says: 'Ain't you near through? I want you should git up a nice supper for us tonight. It's Fourth of July.'

"I told him to git along, that I was right in the middle of preservin', but the plums would taste good on hot biscuit. 'I'm goin' to have fried chicken, too,' he says, and he went off an' killed a couple. You three oldest boys was little fellers, playin' round outside, real hot an' sweaty, an' your father took you to the horse tank down by the windmill an' took off your clothes an' put you in. Them two box-elder trees was little then, but they made shade over the tank. Then he took off all his own clothes, an' got in with you. While he was playin' in the water with you, the Methodist preacher drove into our place to say how all the neighbours was goin' to meet at the schoolhouse that night, to pray for rain. He drove right to the windmill, of course, and there was your father and you three with no clothes on. I was in the kitchen door, an' I had to laugh, for the preacher acted like he ain't never seen a naked man before. He surely was embarrassed, an' your father couldn't git to his clothes; they was all hangin' up on the windmill to let the sweat dry out of 'em. So he laid in the tank where he was, an' put one of you boys on top of him to cover him up a little, an' talked to the preacher.

"When you got through playin' in the water, he put clean clothes on you and a clean shirt on himself, an' by that time I'd begun to get supper. He says: 'It's too hot in here to eat comfortable. Let's have a picnic in the orchard. We'll eat our supper behind the mulberry hedge, under them linden trees.'

"So he carried our supper down, an' a bottle of my wild-grape wine, an' everything tasted good, I can tell you. The wind got cooler as the sun was goin' down, and it turned out pleasant, only I noticed how the leaves was curled up on the linden trees. That made me think, an' I asked your father if that hot wind all day hadn't been terrible hard on the gardens an' the corn.

"'Corn,' he says, 'there ain't no corn.'

"'What you talkin' about?' I said. 'Ain't we got forty acres?'

"'We ain't got an ear,' he says, 'nor nobody else ain't got none. All the corn in this country was cooked by three o'clock today, like you'd roasted it in an oven.'

"'You mean you won't get no crop at all?' I asked him. I couldn't believe it, after he'd worked so hard.

"'No crop this year,' he says. 'That's why we're havin' a picnic. We might as well enjoy what we got.'

"An' that's how your father behaved, when all the neighbours was so discouraged they couldn't look you in the face. An' we enjoyed ourselves that year, poor as we was, an' our neighbours wasn't a bit better off for bein' miserable. Some of 'em grieved till they got poor digestions and couldn't relish what they did have."

The younger boys said they thought their father had the best of it. But Rudolph was thinking that, all the same, the neighbours had managed to get ahead more, in the fifteen years since that time. There must be something wrong about his father's way of doing things. He wished he knew what was going on in the back of Polly's mind. He knew she liked his father, but he knew, too, that she was afraid of something. When his mother sent over coffee-cake or prune tarts or a loaf of fresh bread, Polly seemed to regard them with a certain suspicion. When she observed to him that his brothers had nice manners, her tone implied that it was remarkable they should have. With his mother she was stiff and on her guard. Mary's hearty frankness and gusts of good humour irritated her. Polly was afraid of being unusual or conspicuous in any way, of being "ordinary," as she said!

When Mary had finished her story, Rosicky laid aside his pipe.

"You boys like me to tell you about some of dem hard times I been through in London?" Warmly encouraged, he sat rubbing his forehead along the deep creases. It was bothersome to tell a long story in English (he nearly always talked to the boys in Czech), but he wanted Polly to hear this one.

"Well, you know about dat tailor shop I worked in in London? I had one Christmas dere I ain't never forgot. Times was awful bad before Christmas; de boss ain't got much work, an' have it awful hard to pay his rent. It ain't so much fun, bein' poor in a big city like London, I'll say! All de windows is full of good t'ings to eat, an' all de pushcarts in de streets is full, an' you smell 'em all de time, an' you ain't got no money,—not a damn bit. I didn't mind de cold so much, though I didn't have no overcoat, chust a short jacket I'd outgrowed so it wouldn't meet on me, an' my hands was chapped raw. But I always had a good appetite, like you all know, an' de sight of dem pork pies in de windows was awful fur me!

"Day before Christmas was terrible foggy dat year, an' dat fog gits into your bones and makes you all damp like. Mrs. Lifschnitz didn't give us nothin' but a little bread an' drippin' for supper, because she was savin' to try for to give us a good dinner on Christmas Day. After supper de boss say I can go an' enjoy myself, so I went into de streets to listen to de Christmas singers. Dey sing old songs an' make very nice music, an' I run round after dem a good ways, till I got awful hungry. I t'ink maybe if I go home, I can sleep till morning an' forgit my belly.

"I went into my corner real quiet, and roll up in my fedder quilt. But I ain't got my head down, till I smell somet'ing good. Seem like it git stronger an' stronger, an' I can't git to sleep noway. I can't understand dat smell. Dere was a gas light in a hall across de court, dat always shine in at my window a little. I got up an' look round. I got a little wooden box in my corner fur a stool, 'cause I ain't got no chair. I picks up dat box, and under it dere is a roast goose on a platter! I can't believe my eyes. I carry it to de window where de light comes in, an' touch it and smell it to find out, an' den I taste it to be sure. I say, I will eat chust one little bite of dat goose, so I can go to sleep, and tomorrow I won't eat none at all. But I tell you, boys, when I stop, one half of dat goose was gone!"

The narrator bowed his head, and the boys shouted. But little Josephine slipped behind his chair and kissed him on the neck beneath his ear.

"Poor little Papa, I don't want him to be hungry!"

"Da's long ago, child. I ain't never been hungry since I had your mudder to cook fur me."

"Go on and tell us the rest, please," said Polly.

"Well, when I come to realize what I done, of course, I felt terrible. I felt better in de stomach, but very bad in de heart. I set on my bed wid dat platter on my knees, an' it all come to me; how hard dat poor woman save to buy dat goose, and how she get some neighbour to cook it dat got more fire, an' how she put it in my corner to keep it away from dem hungry children. Dere was a old carpet hung up to shut my corner off, an' de children wasn't allowed to go in dere. An' I know she put it in my corner because she trust me more'n she did de violin boy. I can't stand it to face her after I spoil de Christmas. So I put on my shoes and go out into de city. I tell myself I better throw myself in de river; but I guess I ain't dat kind of a boy.

"It was after twelve o'clock, an' terrible cold, an' I start out to walk about London all night. I walk along de river awhile, but dere was lots of drunks all along; men, and women too. I chust move along to keep away from de police. I git onto de Strand, an' den over to New Oxford Street, where dere was a big German restaurant on de ground floor, wid big windows all fixed up fine, an' I could see de people havin' parties inside. While I was lookin' in, two men and two ladies come out, laughin' and talkin' and feelin' happy about all dey been eatin' an' drinkin', and dey was speakin' Czech,—not like de Austrians, but like de home folks talk it.

"I guess I went crazy, an' I done what I ain't never done before nor since. I went right up to dem gay people an' begun to beg dem: 'Fellow-countrymen, for God's sake give me money enough to buy a goose!'

"Dey laugh, of course, but de ladies speak awful kind to me, an' dey take me back into de restaurant and give me hot coffee and cakes, an' make me tell all about how I happened to come to London, an' what I was doin' dere. Dey take my name and where I work down on paper, an' both of dem ladies give me ten shillings.

"De big market at Covent Garden ain't very far away, an' by dat time it was open. I go dere an' buy a big goose an' some pork pies, an' potatoes and onions, an' cakes an' oranges fur de children,—all I could carry! When I git home, everybody is still asleep. I pile all I bought on de kitchen table, an' go in an' lay down on my bed, an' I ain't waken up till I hear dat woman scream when she come out into her kitchen. My goodness, but she was surprise! She laugh an' cry at de same time, an' hug me and waken all de children. She ain't stop fur no breakfast; she git de Christmas dinner ready dat morning, and we all sit down an' eat all we can hold. I ain't never seen dat violin boy have all he can hold before.

"Two three days after dat, de two men come to hunt me up, an' dey ask my boss, and he give me a good report an' tell dem I was a steady boy all right. One of dem Bohemians was very smart an' run a Bohemian newspaper in New York, an' de odder was a rich man, in de importing business, an' dey been travelling togedder. Dey told me how t'ings was easier in New York, an' offered to pay my passage when dey was goin' home soon on a boat. My boss say to me: 'You go. You ain't got no chance here, an' I like to see you git ahead, fur you always been a good boy to my woman, and fur dat fine Christmas dinner you give us all.' An' da's how I got to New York."

That night when Rudolph and Polly, arm in arm, were running home across the fields with the bitter wind at their backs, his heart leaped for joy when she said she thought they might have his family come over for supper on New Year's Eve. "Let's get up a nice supper, and not let your mother help at all; make her be company for once."

"That would be lovely of you, Polly," he said humbly. He was a very simple, modest boy, and he, too, felt vaguely that Polly and her sisters were more experienced and worldly than his people.

VI

The winter turned out badly for farmers. It was bitterly cold, and after the first light snows before Christmas there was no snow at all,—and no rain. March was as bitter as February. On those days when the wind fairly punished the country, Rosicky sat by his window. In the fall he and the boys had put in a big wheat planting, and now the seed had frozen in the ground. All that land would have to be ploughed up and planted over again, planted in corn. It had happened before, but he was younger then, and he never worried about what had to be. He was sure of himself and of Mary; he knew they could bear what they had to bear, that they would always pull through somehow. But he was not so sure about the young ones, and he felt troubled because Rudolph and Polly were having such a hard start.

Sitting beside his flowering window while the panes rattled and the wind blew in under the door, Rosicky gave himself to reflection as he had not done since those Sundays in the loft of the furniture-factory in New York, long ago. Then he was trying to find what he wanted in life for himself; now he was trying to find what he wanted for his boys, and why it was he so hungered to feel sure they would be here, working this very land, after he was gone.

They would have to work hard on the farm, and probably they would never do much more than make a living. But if he could think of them as staying here on the land, he wouldn't have to fear any great unkindness for them. Hardships, certainly; it was a hardship to have the wheat freeze in the ground when seed was so high; and to have to sell your stock because you had no feed. But there would be other years when everything came along right, and you caught up. And what you had was your own. You didn't have to choose between bosses and strikers, and go wrong either way. You didn't have to do with dishonest and cruel people. They were the only things in his experience he had found terrifying and horrible; the look in the eyes of a dishonest and crafty man, of a scheming and rapacious woman.

In the country, if you had a mean neighbour, you could keep off his land and make him keep off yours. But in the city, all the foulness and misery and brutality of your neighbours was part of your life. The worst things he had come upon in his journey through the world were human,—depraved and poisonous specimens of man. To this day he could recall certain terrible faces in the London streets. There were mean people everywhere, to be sure, even in their own country town here. But they weren't tempered, hardened, sharpened, like the treacherous people in cities who live by grinding or cheating or poisoning their fellow-men. He had helped to bury two of his fellow-workmen in the tailoring trade, and he was distrustful of the organized industries that see one out of the world in big cities. Here, if you were sick, you had Doctor Ed to look after you; and if you died, fat Mr. Haycock, the kindest man in the world, buried you.

It seemed to Rosicky that for good, honest boys like his, the worst they could do on the farm was better than the best they would be likely to do in the city. If he'd had a mean boy, now, one who was crooked and sharp and tried to put anything over on his brothers, then town would be the place for him. But he had no such boy. As for Rudolph, the discontented one, he would give the shirt off his back to anyone who touched his heart. What Rosicky really hoped for his boys was that they could get through the world without ever knowing much about the cruelty of human beings. "Their mother and me ain't prepared them for that," he sometimes said to himself.

These thoughts brought him back to a grateful consideration of his own case. What an escape he had had, to be sure! He, too, in his time, had had to take money for repair work from the hand of a hungry child who let it go so wistfully; because it was money due his boss. And now, in all these years, he had never had to take a cent from anyone in bitter need,—never had to look at the face of a woman become like a wolf's from struggle and famine. When he thought of these things, Rosicky would put on his cap and jacket and slip down to the barn and give his work-horses a little extra oats, letting them eat it out of his hand in their slobbery fashion. It was his way of expressing what he felt, and made him chuckle with pleasure.

The spring came warm, with blue skies,—but dry, dry as a bone. The boys began ploughing up the wheat-fields to plant them over in corn. Rosicky would stand at the fence corner and watch them, and the earth was so dry it blew up in clouds of brown dust that hid the horses and the sulky plough and the driver. It was a bad outlook.

The big alfalfa-field that lay between the home place and Rudolph's came up green, but Rosicky was worried because during that open windy winter a great many Russian thistle plants had blown in there and lodged. He kept asking the boys to rake them out; he was afraid their seed would root and "take the alfalfa." Rudolph said that was nonsense. The boys were working so hard planting corn, their father felt he couldn't insist about the thistles, but he set great store by that big alfalfa-field. It was a feed you could depend on,—and there was some deeper reason, vague, but strong. The peculiar green of that clover woke early memories in old Rosicky, went back to something in his childhood in the old world. When he was a little boy, he had played in fields of that strong blue-green colour.

One morning, when Rudolph had gone to town in the car, leaving a work-team idle in his barn, Rosicky went over to his son's place, put the horses to the buggy-rake, and set about quietly raking up those thistles. He behaved with guilty caution, and rather enjoyed stealing a march on Doctor Ed, who was just then taking his first vacation in seven years of practice and was attending a clinic in Chicago. Rosicky got the thistles raked up, but did not stop to burn them. That would take some time, and his breath was pretty short, so he thought he had better get the horses back to the barn.

He got them into the barn and to their stalls, but the pain had come on so sharp in his chest that he didn't try to take the harness off. He started for the house, bending lower with every step. The cramp in his chest was shutting him up like a jack-knife. When he reached the windmill, he swayed and caught at the ladder. He saw Polly coming down the hill, running with the swiftness of a slim greyhound. In a flash she had her shoulder under his armpit.

"Lean on me, Father, hard! Don't be afraid. We can get to the house all right."

Somehow they did, though Rosicky became blind with pain; he could keep on his legs, but he couldn't steer his course. The next thing he was conscious of was lying on Polly's bed, and Polly bending over him wringing out bath towels in hot water and putting them on his chest. She stopped only to throw coal into the stove, and she kept the tea-kettle and the black pot going. She put these hot applications on him for nearly an hour, she told him afterwards, and all that time he was drawn up stiff and blue, with the sweat pouring off him.

As the pain gradually loosed its grip, the stiffness went out of his jaws, the black circles round his eyes disappeared, and a little of his natural colour came back. When his daughter-in-law buttoned his shirt over his chest at last, he sighed.

"Da's fine, de way I feel now, Polly. It was a awful bad spell, an' I was so sorry it all come on you like it did."

Polly was flushed and excited. "Is the pain really gone? Can I leave you long enough to telephone over to your place?"

Rosicky's eyelids fluttered. "Don't telephone, Polly. It ain't no use to scare my wife. It's nice and quiet here, an' if I ain't too much trouble to you, just let me lay still till I feel like myself. I ain't got no pain now. It's nice here."

Polly bent over him and wiped the moisture from his face. "Oh, I'm so glad it's over!" she broke out impulsively. "It just broke my heart to see you suffer so, Father."

Rosicky motioned her to sit down on the chair where the tea-kettle had been, and looked up at her with that lively affectionate gleam in his eyes. "You was awful good to me, I won't never forget dat. I hate it to be sick on you like dis. Down at de barn I say to myself, dat young girl ain't had much experience in sickness, I don't want to scare her, an' maybe she's got a baby comin' or somet'ing."

Polly took his hand. He was looking at her so intently and affectionately and confidingly; his eyes seemed to caress her face, to regard it with pleasure. She frowned with her funny streaks of eyebrows, and then smiled back at him.

"I guess maybe there is something of that kind going to happen. But I haven't told anyone yet, not my mother or Rudolph. You'll be the first to know."

His hand pressed hers. She noticed that it was warm again. The twinkle in his yellow-brown eyes seemed to come nearer.

"I like mighty well to see dat little child, Polly," was all he said. Then he closed his eyes and lay half-smiling. But Polly sat still, thinking hard. She had a sudden feeling that nobody in the world, not her mother, not Rudolph, or anyone, really loved her as much as old Rosicky did. It perplexed her. She sat frowning and trying to puzzle it out. It was as if Rosicky had a special gift for loving people, something that was like an ear for music or an eye for colour. It was quiet, unobtrusive; it was merely there. You saw it in his eyes,—perhaps that was why they were merry. You felt it in his hands, too. After he dropped off to sleep, she sat holding his warm, broad, flexible brown hand. She had never seen another in the least like it. She wondered if it wasn't a kind of gypsy hand, it was so alive and quick and light in its communications,—very strange in a farmer. Nearly all the farmers she knew had huge lumps of fists, like mauls, or they were knotty and bony and uncomfortable-looking, with stiff fingers. But Rosicky's was like quicksilver, flexible, muscular, about the colour of a pale cigar, with deep, deep creases across the palm. It wasn't nervous, it wasn't a stupid lump; it was a warm brown human hand, with some cleverness in it, a great deal of generosity, and something else which Polly could only call "gypsy-like,"—something nimble and lively and sure, in the way that animals are.

Polly remembered that hour long afterwards; it had been like an awakening to her. It seemed to her that she had never learned so much about life from anything as from old Rosicky's hand. It brought her to herself; it communicated some direct and untranslatable message.

When she heard Rudolph coming in the car, she ran out to meet him.

"Oh, Rudy, your father's been awful sick! He raked up those thistles he's been worrying about, and afterwards he could hardly get to the house. He suffered so I was afraid he was going to die."

Rudolph jumped to the ground. "Where is he now?"

"On the bed. He's asleep. I was terribly scared, because, you know, I'm so fond of your father." She slipped her arm through his and they went into the house. That afternoon they took Rosicky home and put him to bed, though he protested that he was quite well again.

The next morning he got up and dressed and sat down to breakfast with his family. He told Mary that his coffee tasted better than usual to him, and he warned the boys not to bear any tales to Doctor Ed when he got home. After breakfast he sat down by his window to do some patching and asked Mary to thread several needles for him before she went to feed her chickens,—her eyes were better than his, and her hands steadier. He lit his pipe and took up John's overalls. Mary had been watching him anxiously all morning, and as she went out of the door with her bucket of scraps, she saw that he was smiling. He was thinking, indeed, about Polly, and how he might never have known what a tender heart she had if he hadn't got sick over there. Girls nowadays didn't wear their heart on their sleeve. But now he knew Polly would make a fine woman after the foolishness wore off. Either a woman had that sweetness at her heart or she hadn't. You couldn't always tell by the look of them; but if they had that, everything came out right in the end.

After he had taken a few stitches, the cramp began in his chest, like yesterday. He put his pipe cautiously down on the window-sill and bent over to ease the pull. No use,—he had better try to get to his bed if he could. He rose and groped his way across the familiar floor, which was rising and falling like the deck of a ship. At the door he fell. When Mary came in, she found him lying there, and the moment she touched him she knew that he was gone.

Doctor Ed was away when Rosicky died, and for the first few weeks after he got home he was hard driven. Every day he said to himself that he must get out to see that family that had lost their father. One soft, warm moonlight night in early summer he started for the farm. His mind was on other things, and not until his road ran by the graveyard did he realize that Rosicky wasn't over there on the hill where the red lamplight shone, but here, in the moonlight. He stopped his car, shut off the engine, and sat there for a while.

A sudden hush had fallen on his soul. Everything here seemed strangely moving and significant, though signifying what, he did not know. Close by the wire fence stood Rosicky's mowing-machine, where one of the boys had been cutting hay that afternoon; his own work-horses had been going up and down there. The new-cut hay perfumed all the night air. The moonlight silvered the long, billowy grass that grew over the graves and hid the fence; the few little evergreens stood out black in it, like shadows in a pool. The sky was very blue and soft, the stars rather faint because the moon was full.

For the first time it struck Doctor Ed that this was really a beautiful graveyard. He thought of city cemeteries; acres of shrubbery and heavy stone, so arranged and lonely and unlike anything in the living world. Cities of the dead, indeed; cities of the forgotten, of the "put away." But this was open and free, this little square of long grass which the wind for ever stirred. Nothing but the sky overhead, and the many-coloured fields running on until they met that sky. The horses worked here in summer; the neighbours passed on their way to town; and over yonder, in the cornfield, Rosicky's own cattle would be eating fodder as winter came on. Nothing could be more undeathlike than this place; nothing could be more right for a man who had helped to do the work of great cities and had always longed for the open country and had got to it at last. Rosicky's life seemed to him complete and beautiful.

[New York, 1928]

BERNARD MALAMUD
[1914–1986]

To read the fiction of Bernard Malamud is to enter a Jewish milieu populated by characters whose attitudes and rhythms of speech belong to a world of the not-so-distant past. Tailors, marriage brokers, grocers, and rabbis frequently figure in his novels and short stories, their modes of expression rendered in Malamud's mother tongue—a New York street idiom of Old World Yiddishisms that he heard growing up in Brooklyn. Not limited in setting to New York, his fiction, which blends realism and allegory, tragedy and comedy, myth and magic, is consistent in presenting an embattled hero, usually a Jew, engaged in a quest for the meaning of life. The search often entails a struggle for self-acceptance, love, and happiness that requires the hero to transform himself, through painful experience and suffering, into a different person and more of a human being, capable of loving another person completely. In this transformation, the seeker becomes emblematic of all individuals who yearn to find self-understanding and meaning. Malamud's portrayal of Jews whose aspirations reflect the human condition underscores at once his use of the particular to communicate the universal and his importance as a major twentieth century author and leading American-Jewish writer. His work, above all, made possible the introduction of ethnic characters and their unique dialect into America's literary mainstream.

Born in Brooklyn, New York, on April 26, 1914, Malamud was the son of Russian-Jewish immigrants who ran a neighborhood grocery store. He attended Brooklyn's Erasmus Hall High School from 1928 to 1932 and wrote fiction for its literary magazine, the Erasmian. *After graduation, he went to the City College of New York and received a bachelor of arts four years later in 1936. Malamud's career then took an academic turn. Earning his master's degree in English from Columbia University in 1942 helped him land teaching jobs in the New York public schools over the next several years. His literary reputation started to grow as soon as his short stories—the first of which was "Benefit Performance" in 1943—began to appear in magazines. In 1949, he moved his wife of four years and their young son to the West after he accepted an instructorship in English at Oregon State University, where he taught literature and composition for more than a decade. The move coincided with a period of creativity that produced* some of his finest work. Following the publication of his first novel, The Natural (1952), Malamud's next book, The Assistant (1957), won the Daroff Award of the Jewish Book Council and the Rosenthal Award of the National Institute of Letters in 1958. That same year his first collection of short stories, The Magic Barrel, received the National Book Award. With the notoriety that came from critical recognition, he got the chance to return to the East when Bennington College in Vermont offered him a teaching position on its faculty in 1961. He divided his time between New York City and Vermont over the next twenty-five years and went on to write six more novels and two additional collections of short stories before he died on March 18, 1986.

Among Malamud's major works that first helped establish his reputation, The Natural is perhaps the most popular. A mixture of allegory and myth, the story tells of the rise to stardom of Roy Hobbs, who leads his ball club in a bid for a pennant and a chance to compete in the World Series. Malamud examines the moral implications of ambition so voracious that its fulfillment will demand of Hobbs nothing less than his betrayal of the people dearest to him. The Assistant departs from the author's first novel in its affirmative view of the transformation that takes place in the story, which centers on the relationship between a Jewish grocer and a young Italian-American who works as his helper. The proprietor suffers for the guilt that the young man feels for violating the trust invested in him; the assistant learns from the grocer's anguish, transforms himself into a good person and becomes, in the end, a Jew. Malamud's interest in the drama of the individual's growth into awareness informs The Fixer (1966), winner of a Pulitzer Prize and the National Book Award based on a true story of blood libel. Set in czarist Russia early in the twentieth century, it is a harrowing parable of anti-Semitism that depicts the persecution of a man falsely accused of and then jailed for a murder he did not commit. The prisoner undergoes persistent and intense questioning by government officials hoping to extract his confession, yet grows in strength during the ordeal until he comes to understand himself better as a man and a Jew.

Sandwiched around The Fixer are novels that show Malamud's willingness to explore diverse subject matter and try his hand at new genres. A New Life (1961) is a satiric novel about academic life that relates the experiences of an Easterner whose move out West to teach English at a college and taste freedom amid new surroundings culminates in his spiritual awakening. The Tenants (1971) confronts the thorny issue of race as reflected in the tense relationship between a black and a Jewish writer, sole residents of a dilapidated tenement house, who must learn to accept each other if they are to co-exist. In Dubin's Lives (1979), published in the twilight of his career, Malamud presents the story of a crisis that develops in the life of an aging writer when his desire for a younger woman threatens his long-time marriage. After a time, the number of lies he has to tell to keep the affair going makes him realize that he needs to be honest with himself and return to the *life he shares with his wife. A post-nuclear setting provides the backdrop for the conflict in Malamud's final novel,* God's Grace *(1982), between the last man on earth and the tribe of literate apes over which he presides as patriarch. At stake is the survival of the race, which hinges on whether the protagonist will accept the apes as his equal or allow his ego to stand in the way of letting them determine their own future.*

The sense many of Malamud's characters make of their entangled lives emphasizes the instructive value of his novels. No less instructive, his short fiction, by contrast, is narrower in setting. The stories contained in The Magic Barrel, Idiot's First *(1963), and to a lesser extent,* Rembrandt's Hat *(1973), display impoverished New York Jews, like the hero in the story printed here, struggling to find meaning and achieve happiness.*

Andrew Stambule
Hofstra University

For Further Reading

Primary Works

The Natural (1952); *The Assistant* (1957); *The Magic Barrel* (1958); *A New Life* (1961); *Idiot's First* (1963); *The Fixer* (1966); *A Malamud Reader* (1967); *Pictures of Fidelman: An Exhibition* (1969), *The Tenants* (1971); *Rembrandt's Hat* (1973); *Dubin's Lives* (1979); *God's Grace* (1982); *The Stories of Bernard Malamud* (1983); *The People and Uncollected Stories* (1989); *The Complete Stories* (1997).

Secondary Works

Sidney Richman, *Bernard Malamud* (1967); Glenn Meeter, *Bernard Malamud and Philip Roth: A Critical Essay* (1968); Leslie A. Field and Joyce W. Field, eds., *Bernard Malamud and the Critics* (1970); Rita Kosofsky, *Bernard Malamud: An Annotated Checklist* (1970); Sandy Cohen, *Bernard Malamud and the Trial by Love* (1974); Robert Ducharme, *Art and Ideas in the Novels of Bernard Malamud* (1974); Field and Field, *Bernard Malamud: A Collection of Critical Essays* (1975); Richard Astro and Jackson Benson, eds., *The Fiction of Bernard Malamud* (1977); Bates Hoffer, ed., "Malamud's Magic Barrel," in *Linguistics in Literature*, 2 (Fall 1977); Daniel Walden, ed. "Bernard Malamud: Reinterpretations," in *Studies in American Jewish Literature*, 4 (Spring 1978); Evelyn Avery, *Rebels and Victims: The Fiction of Richard Wright and Bernard Malamud* (1979); Sheldon J. Hershinow, *Bernard Malamud* (1980); Iska Alter, *The Good Man's Dilemma, Social Criticism in the Fiction of Bernard Malamud* (1981); Jeffrey Helterman, *Understanding Bernard Malamud* (1985); Harold Bloom, ed., *Bernard Malamud* (1986); Joel Salzberg, ed., *Critical Essays on Bernard Malamud* (1987); Kathleen Ochshorn, *The Heart's Essential Landscape, Bernard Malamud's Hero* (1990);

Kosofsky, *Bernard Malamud: A Descriptive Bibliography* (1991); Lawrence Lasher, *Conversations with Bernard Malamud* (1991); Edward A. Abramson, *Bernard Malamud Revisited* (1993); Alan Cheuse and Nicholas Delbanco, eds., *Talking Horse, Bernard Malamud on Life and Work* (1996).

Gimpel the Fool

TRANSLATED BY SAUL BELLOW

1

I am Gimpel the fool. I don't think myself a fool. On the contrary. But that's what folks call me. They gave me the name while I was still in school. I had seven names in all: imbecile, donkey, flax-head, dope, glump, ninny, and fool. The last name stuck. What did my foolishness consist of? I was easy to take in. They said, "Gimpel, you know the rabbi's wife has been brought to childbed?" So I skipped school. Well, it turned out to be a lie. How was I supposed to know? She hadn't had a big belly. But I never looked at her belly. Was that really so foolish? The gang laughed and hee-hawed, stomped and danced and chanted a good-night prayer. And instead of the raisins they give when a woman's lying in, they stuffed my hand full of goat turds. I was no weakling. If I slapped someone he'd see all the way to Cracow. But I'm really not a slugger by nature. I think to myself: Let it pass. So they take advantage of me.

I was coming home from school and heard a dog barking. I'm not afraid of dogs, but of course I never want to start up with them. One of them may be mad, and if he bites there's not a Tartar in the world who can help you. So I made tracks. Then I looked around and saw the whole market place wild with laughter. It was no dog at all but Wolf-Leib the Thief. How was I supposed to know it was he? It sounded like a howling bitch.

When the pranksters and leg-pullers found that I was easy to fool, every one of them tried his luck with me. "Gimpel, the Czar is coming to Frampol; Gimpel, the moon fell down in Turbeen; Gimpel, little Hodel Furpiece found a treasure behind the bathhouse." And I like a golem° believed everyone. In the first place, everything is possible, as it is written in the Wisdom of the Fathers. I've forgotten just how. Second, I had to believe when the whole town came down on me! If I ever dared to say, "Ah, you're kidding!" there was trouble. People got angry. "What do you mean! You want to call everyone a liar?" What was I to do? I believed them, and I hope at least that did them some good.

I was an orphan. My grandfather who brought me up was already bent toward

___
golem: simpleton

the grave. So they turned me over to a baker, and what a time they gave me there! Every woman or girl who came to bake a batch of noodles had to fool me at least once. "Gimpel, there's a fair in heaven; Gimpel, the rabbi gave birth to a calf in the seventh month; Gimpel, a cow flew over the roof and laid brass eggs." A student from the yeshiva came once to buy a roll, and he said, "You, Gimpel, while you stand here scraping with your baker's shovel the Messiah has come. The dead have arisen." "What do you mean?" I said. "I heard no one blowing the ram's horn!" He said, "Are you deaf?" And all began to cry, "We heard it, we heard!" Then in came Rietze the Candle-dipper and called out in her hoarse voice, "Gimpel, your father and mother have stood up from the grave. They're looking for you."

To tell the truth, I knew very well that nothing of the sort had happened, but all the same, as folks were talking, I threw on my wool vest and went out. Maybe something had happened. What did I stand to lose by looking? Well, what a cat music went up! And then I took a vow to believe nothing more. But that was no go either. They confused me so that I didn't know the big end from the small.

I went to the rabbi to get some advice. He said, "It is written, better to be a fool all your days than for one hour to be evil. You are not a fool. They are the fools. For he who causes his neighbor to feel shame loses Paradise himself." Nevertheless the rabbi's daughter took me in. As I left the rabbinical court she said, "Have you kissed the wall yet?" I said, "No; what for?" She answered, "It's the law; you've got to do it after every visit." Well, there didn't seem to be any harm in it. And she burst out laughing. It was a fine trick. She put one over on me, all right.

I wanted to go off to another town, but then everyone got busy matchmaking, and they were after me so they nearly tore my coat tails off. They talked at me and talked until I got water on the ear. She was no chaste maiden, but they told me she was virgin pure. She had a limp, and they said it was deliberate, from coyness. She had a bastard, and they told me the child was her little brother. I cried, "You're wasting your time. I'll never marry that whore." But they said indignantly, "What a way to talk! Aren't you ashamed of yourself? We can take you to the rabbi and have you fined for giving her a bad name." I saw then that I wouldn't escape them so easily and I thought: They're set on making me their butt. But when you're married the husband's the master, and if that's all right with her it's agreeable to me too. Besides, you can't pass through life unscathed, nor expect to.

I went to her clay house, which was built on the sand, and the whole gang, hollering and chorusing, came after me. They acted like bear-baiters. When we came to the well they stopped all the same. They were afraid to start anything with Elka. Her mouth would open as if it were on a hinge, and she had a fierce tongue. I entered the house. Lines were strung from wall to wall and clothes were drying. Barefoot she stood by the tub, doing the wash. She was dressed in a worn hand-me-down gown of plush. She had her hair put up in braids and pinned across her head. It took my breath away, almost, the reek of it all.

Evidently she knew who I was. She took a look at me and said, "Look who's here! He's come, the drip. Grab a seat."

I told her all; I denied nothing. "Tell me the truth," I said, "are you really a virgin, and is that mischievous Yechiel actually your little brother? Don't be deceitful with me, for I'm an orphan."

"I'm an orphan myself," she answered, "and whoever tries to twist you up, may the end of his nose take a twist. But don't let them think they can take advantage of me. I want a dowry of fifty guilders, and let them take up a collection besides. Otherwise they can kiss my you-know-what." She was very plainspoken. I said, "It's the bride and not the groom who gives a dowry." Then she said, "Don't bargain with me. Either a flat 'yes' or a flat 'no'—Go back where you came from."

I thought: No bread will ever be baked from *this* dough. But ours is not a poor town. They consented to everything and proceeded with the wedding. It so happened that there was a dysentery epidemic at the time. The ceremony was held at the cemetery gates, near the little corpse-washing hut. The fellows got drunk. While the marriage contract was being drawn up I heard the most pious high rabbi ask, "Is the bride a widow or a divorced woman?" And the sexton's wife answered for her, "Both a widow and divorced." It was a black moment for me. But what was I to do, run away from under the marriage canopy?

There was singing and dancing. An old granny danced opposite me, hugging a braided white *chalah*. The master of revels made a "God 'a mercy" in memory of the bride's parents. The schoolboys threw burrs, as on Tishe b'Av fast day. There were a lot of gifts after the sermon: a noodle board, a kneading trough, a bucket, brooms, ladles, household articles galore. Then I took a look and saw two strapping young men carrying a crib. "What do we need this for?" I asked. So they said, "Don't rack your brains about it. It's all right, it'll come in handy." I realized I was going to be rooked. Take it another way though, what did I stand to lose? I reflected: I'll see what comes of it. A whole town can't go altogether crazy.

2

At night I came where my wife lay, but she wouldn't let me in. "Say, look here, is this what they married us for?" I said. And she said, "My monthly has come." "But yesterday they took you to the ritual bath, and that's afterward, isn't it supposed to be?" "Today isn't yesterday," said she, "and yesterday's not today. You can beat it if you don't like it." In short, I waited.

Not four months later she was in childbed. The townsfolk hid their laughter with their knuckles. But what could I do? She suffered intolerable pains and clawed at the walls. "Gimpel," she cried, "I'm going. Forgive me!" The house filled with women. They were boiling pans of water. The screams rose to the welkin.°

The thing to do was to go to the House of Prayer to repeat Psalms, and that was what I did.

The townsfolk liked that, all right. I stood in a corner saying Psalms and prayers, and they shook their heads at me. "Pray, pray!" they told me. "Prayer never made any woman pregnant." One of the congregation put a straw to my mouth and said, "Hay for the cows." There was something to that too, by God!

She gave birth to a boy. Friday at the synagogue the sexton stood up before the Ark, pounded on the reading table, and announced, "The wealthy Reb Gimpel invites the congregation to a feast in honor of the birth of a son." The whole House of Prayer

welkin: the sky

rang with laughter. My face was flaming. But there was nothing I could do. After all, I *was* the one responsible for the circumcision honors and rituals.

Half the town came running. You couldn't wedge another soul in. Women brought peppered chick-peas, and there was a keg of beer from the tavern. I ate and drank as much as anyone, and they all congratulated me. Then there was a circumcision, and I named the boy after my father, may he rest in peace. When all were gone and I was left with my wife alone, she thrust her head through the bed-curtain and called me to her.

"Gimpel," said she, "why are you silent? Has your ship gone and sunk?"

"What shall I say?" I answered. "A fine thing you've done to me! If my mother had known of it she'd have died a second time."

She said, "Are you crazy, or what?"

"How can you make such a fool," I said, "of one who should be the lord and master?"

"What's the matter with you?" she said. "What have you taken it into your head to imagine?"

I saw that I must speak bluntly and openly. "Do you think this is the way to use an orphan?" I said. "You have borne a bastard."

She answered, "Drive this foolishness out of your head. The child is yours."

"How can he be mine?" I argued. "He was born seventeen weeks after the wedding."

She told me then that he was premature. I said, "Isn't he a little too premature?" She said, she had had a grandmother who carried just as short a time and she resembled this grandmother of hers as one drop of water does another. She swore to it with such oaths that you would have believed a peasant at the fair if he had used them. To tell the plain truth, I didn't believe her; but when I talked it over next day with the schoolmaster he told me that the very same thing had happened to Adam and Eve. Two they went up to bed, and four they descended.

"There isn't a woman in the world who is not the granddaughter of Eve," he said.

That was how it was; they argued me dumb. But then, who really knows how such things are?

I began to forget my sorrow. I loved the child madly, and he loved me too. As soon as he saw me he'd wave his little hands and want me to pick him up, and when he was colicky I was the only one who could pacify him. I bought him a little bone teething ring and a little gilded cap. He was forever catching the evil eye from someone, and then I had to run to get one of those abracadabras for him that would get him out of it. I worked like an ox. You know how expenses go up when there's an infant in the house. I don't want to lie about it; I didn't dislike Elka either, for that matter. She swore at me and cursed, and I couldn't get enough of her. What strength she had! One of her looks could rob you of the power of speech. And her orations! Pitch and sulphur, that's what they were full of, and yet somehow also full of charm. I adored her every word. She gave me bloody wounds though.

In the evening I brought her a white loaf as well as a dark one, and also poppyseed rolls I baked myself. I thieved because of her and swiped everything I could lay my hands on: macaroons, raisins, almonds, cakes. I hope I may be forgiven for stealing from the Saturday pots the women left to warm in the baker's oven. I would take out scraps of meat, a chunk of pudding, a chicken leg or head, a piece of tripe, whatever I could nip quickly. She ate and became fat and handsome.

I had to sleep away from home all during the week, at the bakery. On Friday nights when I got home she always made an excuse of some sort. Either she had heartburn, or a stitch in the side, or hiccups, or headaches. You know what women's excuses are. I had a bitter time of it. It was rough. To add to it, this little brother of hers, the bastard, was growing bigger. He'd put lumps on me, and when I wanted to hit back she'd open her mouth and curse so powerfully I saw a green haze floating before my eyes. Ten times a day she threatened to divorce me. Another man in my place would have taken French leave and disappeared. But I'm the type that bears it and says nothing. What's one to do? Shoulders are from God, and burdens too.

One night there was a calamity in the bakery; the oven burst, and we almost had a fire. There was nothing to do but go home, so I went home. Let me, I thought, also taste the joy of sleeping in bed in mid-week. I didn't want to wake the sleeping mite and tiptoed into the house. Coming in, it seemed to me that I heard not the snoring of one but, as it were, a double snore, one a thin enough snore and the other like the snoring of a slaughtered ox. Oh, I didn't like that! I didn't like it at all. I went up to the bed, and things suddenly turned black. Next to Elka lay a man's form. Another in my place would have made an uproar, and enough noise to rouse the whole town, but the thought occurred to me that I might wake the child. A little thing like that—why frighten a little swallow, I thought. All right then, I went back to the bakery and stretched out on a sack of flour and till morning I never shut an eye. I shivered as if I had had malaria. "Enough of being a donkey," I said to myself. "Gimpel isn't going to be a sucker all his life. There's a limit even to the foolishness of a fool like Gimpel."

In the morning I went to the rabbi to get advice, and it made a great commotion in the town. They sent the beadle for Elka right away. She came, carrying the child. And what do you think she did? She denied it, denied everything, bone and stone!" "He's out of his head," she said. "I know nothing of dreams or divinations." They yelled at her, warned her, hammered on the table, but she stuck to her guns: it was a false accusation, she said.

The butchers and the horse-traders took her part. One of the lads from the slaughterhouse came by and said to me, "We've got our eye on you, you're a marked man." Meanwhile the child started to bear down and soiled itself. In the rabbinical court there was an Ark of the Covenant, and they couldn't allow that, so they sent Elka away.

I said to the rabbi, "What shall I do?"

"You must divorce her at once," said he.

"And what if she refuses?" I asked.

He said, "You must serve the divorce. That's all you'll have to do."

I said, "Well, all right, Rabbi. Let me think about it."

"There's nothing to think about," said he. "You mustn't remain under the same roof with her."

"And if I want to see the child?" I asked.

"Let her go, the harlot," said he, "and her brood of bastards with her."

The verdict he gave was that I mustn't even cross her threshold—never again, as long as I should live.

During the day it didn't bother me so much. I thought: It was bound to happen, the abscess had to burst. But at night when I stretched out upon the sacks I felt it all very bitterly. A longing took me, for her and for the child. I wanted to be angry, but that's my misfortune exactly, I don't have it in me to be really angry. In the first place—this was how my thoughts went—there's bound to be a slip sometimes. You can't live without errors. Probably that lad who was with her led her on and gave her presents and what not, and women are often long on hair and short on sense, and so he got around her. And then since she denies it so, maybe I was only seeing things? Hallucinations do happen. You see a figure or a mannikin or something, but when you come up closer it's nothing, there's not a thing there. And if that's so, I'm doing her an injustice. And when I got so far in my thoughts I started to weep. I sobbed so that I wet the flour where I lay. In the morning I went to the rabbi and told him that I had made a mistake. The rabbi wrote on with his quill, and he said that if that were so he would have to reconsider the whole case. Until he had finished I wasn't to go near my wife, but I might send her bread and money by messenger.

3

Nine months passed before all the rabbis could come to an agreement. Letters went back and forth. I hadn't realized that there could be so much erudition about a matter like this.

Meanwhile Elka gave birth to still another child, a girl this time. On the Sabbath I went to the synagogue and invoked a blessing on her. They called me up to the Torah, and I named the child for my mother-in-law—may she rest in peace. The louts and loudmouths of the town who came into the bakery gave me a going over. All Frampol refreshed its spirits because of my trouble and grief. However, I resolved that I would always believe what I was told. What's the good of *not* believing? Today it's your wife you don't believe; tomorrow it's God Himself you won't take stock in.

By an apprentice who was her neighbor I sent her daily a corn or a wheat loaf, or a piece of pastry, rolls or bagels, or, when I got the chance, a slab of pudding, a slice of honeycake, or wedding strudel—whatever came my way. The apprentice was a goodhearted lad, and more than once he added something on his own. He had formerly annoyed me a lot, plucking my nose and digging me in the ribs, but when he started to be a visitor to my house he became kind and friendly. "Hey, you, Gimpel," he said to me, "you have a very decent little wife and two fine kids. You don't deserve them."

"But the things people say about her," I said.

"Well, they have long tongues," he said, "and nothing to do with them but babble. Ignore it as you ignore the cold of last winter."

One day the rabbi sent for me and said, "Are you certain, Gimpel, that you were wrong about your wife?"

I said, "I'm certain."

"Why, but look here! You yourself saw it."

"It must have been a shadow," I said.

"The shadow of what?"

"Just one of the beams, I think."

"You can go home then. You owe thanks to the Yanover rabbi. He found an obscure reference in Maimonides that favored you."

I seized the rabbi's hand and kissed it.

I wanted to run home immediately. It's no small thing to be separated for so long a time from wife and child. Then I reflected: I'd better go back to work now, and go home in the evening. I said nothing to anyone, although as far as my heart was concerned it was like one of the Holy Days. The women teased and twitted me as they did every day, but my thought was: Go on, with your loose talk. The truth is out, like the oil upon the water. Maimonides says it's right, and therefore it is right!

At night, when I had covered the dough to let it rise, I took my share of bread and a little sack of flour and started homeward. The moon was full and the stars were glistening, something to terrify the soul. I hurried onward, and before me darted a long shadow. It was winter, and a fresh snow had fallen. I had a mind to sing, but it was growing late and I didn't want to wake the householders. Then I felt like whistling, but I remembered that you don't whistle at night because it brings the demons out. So I was silent and walked as fast as I could.

Dogs in the Christian yards barked at me when I passed, but I thought: Bark your teeth out! What are you but mere dogs? Whereas I am a man, the husband of a fine wife, the father of promising children.

As I approached the house my heart started to pound as though it were the heart of a criminal. I felt no fear, but my heart went thump! thump! Well, no drawing back. I quietly lifted the latch and went in. Elka was asleep. I looked at the infant's cradle. The shutter was closed, but the moon forced its way through the cracks. I saw the newborn child's face and loved it as soon as I saw it—immediately—each tiny bone.

Then I came nearer to the bed. And what did I see but the apprentice lying there beside Elka. The moon went out all at once. It was utterly black, and I trembled. My teeth chattered. The bread fell from my hands, and my wife waked and said, "Who is that, ah?"

I muttered, "It's me."

"Gimpel?" she asked. "How come you're here? I thought it was forbidden."

"The rabbi said," I answered and shook as with a fever.

"Listen to me, Gimpel," she said, "go out to the shed and see if the goat's all right. It seems she's been sick." I have forgotten to say that we had a goat. When I heard she was unwell I went into the yard. The nannygoat was a good little creature. I had a nearly human feeling for her.

With hesitant steps I went up to the shed and opened the door. The goat stood there on her four feet. I felt her everywhere, drew her by the horns, examined her udders, and found nothing wrong. She had probably eaten too much bark. "Good night, little goat," I said. "Keep well." And the little beast answered with a "Maa" as though to thank me for the good will.

I went back. The apprentice had vanished.

"Where," I asked, "is the lad?"

"What lad?" my wife answered.

"What do you mean?" I said. "The apprentice. You were sleeping with him."

"The things I have dreamed this night and the night before," she said, "may they come true and lay you low, body and soul! An evil spirit has taken root in you and dazzles your sight." She screamed out, "You hateful creature! You moon calf! You spook! You uncouth man! Get out, or I'll scream all Frampol out of bed!"

Before I could move, her brother sprang out from behind the oven and struck me a blow on the back of the head. I thought he had broken my neck. I felt that something about me was deeply wrong, and I said, "Don't make a scandal. All that's needed now is that people should accuse me of raising spooks and *dybbuks.*°" For that was what she had meant. "No one will touch bread of my baking."

In short, I somehow calmed her.

"Well," she said, "that's enough. Lie down, and be shattered by wheels."

Next morning I called the apprentice aside. "Listen here, brother!" I said. And so on and so forth. "What do you say?" He stared at me as though I had dropped from the roof or something.

"I swear," he said, "you'd better go to an herb doctor or some healer. I'm afraid you have a screw loose, but I'll hush it up for you." And that's how the thing stood.

To make a long story short, I lived twenty years with my wife. She bore me six children, four daughters and two sons. All kinds of things happened, but I neither saw nor heard. I believed, and that's all. The rabbi recently said to me, "Belief in itself is beneficial. It is written that a good man lives by his faith."

Suddenly my wife took sick. It began with a trifle, a little growth upon the breast. But she evidently was not destined to live long; she had no years. I spent a fortune on her. I have forgotten to say that by this time I had a bakery of my own and in Frampol was considered to be something of a rich man. Daily the healer came, and every witch doctor in the neighborhood was brought. They decided to use leeches, and after that to try cupping. They even called a doctor from Lublin, but it was too late. Before she died she called me to her bed and said, "Forgive me, Gimpel."

I said, "What is there to forgive? You have been a good and faithful wife."

"Woe, Gimpel!" she said. "It was ugly how I deceived you all these years. I want to go clean to my Maker, and so I have to tell you that the children are not yours."

If I had been clouted on the head with a piece of wood it couldn't have bewildered me more.

"Whose are they?" I asked.

"I don't know," she said. "There were a lot . . . but they're not yours." And as she spoke she tossed her head to the side, her eyes turned glassy, and it was all up with Elka. On her whitened lips there remained a smile.

I imagined that, dead as she was, she was saying, "I deceived Gimpel. That was the meaning of my brief life."

4

One night, when the period of mourning was done, as I lay dreaming on the flour sacks, there came the Spirit of Evil himself and said to me, "Gimpel, why do you sleep?"

I said, "What should I be doing? Eating *kreplach*?"

"The whole world deceives you," he said, "and you ought to deceive the world in your turn."

"How can I deceive the world?" I asked him.

He answered, "You might accumulate a bucket of urine every day and at night pour it into the dough. Let the sages of Frampol eat filth."

dybbuks: demons or souls of the dead that enter the bodies of the living to take possession of them

"What about the judgment in the world to come?" I said.

"There is no world to come," he said. "They've sold you a bill of goods and talked you into believing you carried a cat in your belly. What nonsense!"

"Well, then," I said, "and is there a God?"

He answered, "There is no God either."

"What," I said, "*is* there, then?"

"A thick mire."

He stood before my eyes with a goatish beard and horn, long-toothed, and with a tail. Hearing such words, I wanted to snatch him by the tail, but I tumbled from the flour sacks and nearly broke a rib. Then it happened that I had to answer the call of nature, and, passing, I saw the risen dough, which seemed to say to me, "Do it!" In brief, I let myself be persuaded.

At dawn the apprentice came. We kneaded the bread, scattered caraway seeds on it, and set it to bake. Then the apprentice went away, and I was left sitting in the little trench by the oven, on a pile of rags. Well, Gimpel, I thought, you've revenged yourself on them for all the shame they've put on you. Outside the frost glittered, but it was warm beside the oven. The flames heated my face. I bent my head and fell into a doze.

I saw in a dream, at once, Elka in her shroud. She called to me, "What have you done, Gimpel?"

I said to her, "It's all your fault," and started to cry.

"You fool!" she said. "You fool! Because I was false is everything false too? I never deceived anyone but myself. I'm paying for it all, Gimpel. They spare you nothing here."

I looked at her face. It was black; I was startled and waked, and remained sitting dumb. I sensed that everything hung in the balance. A false step now and I'd lose Eternal Life. But God gave me His help. I seized the long shovel and took out the loaves, carried them into the yard, and started to dig a hole in the frozen earth.

My apprentice came back as I was doing it. "What are you doing, boss?" he said, and grew pale as a corpse.

"I know what I'm doing," I said, and I buried it all before his very eyes.

Then I went home, took my hoard from its hiding place, and divided it among the children. "I saw your mother tonight," I said. "She's turning black, poor thing."

They were so astounded they couldn't speak a word.

"Be well," I said, "and forget that such a one as Gimpel ever existed." I put on my short coat, a pair of boots, took the bag that held my prayer shawl in one hand, my stock in the other, and kissed the *mezzuzah*. When people saw me in the street they were greatly surprised.

"Where are you going?" they said.

I answered, "Into the world." And so I departed from Frampol.

I wandered over the land, and good people did not neglect me. After many years I became old and white; I heard a great deal, many lies and falsehoods, but the longer I lived the more I understood that there were really no lies. Whatever doesn't really happen is dreamed at night. It happens to one if it doesn't happen to another, tomorrow if not today, or a century hence if not next year. What difference can it make? Often I heard tales of which I said, "Now this is a thing that cannot happen." But before a year had elapsed I heard that it actually had come to pass somewhere.

Going from place to place, eating at strange tables, it often happens that I spin yarns—improbable things that could never have happened—about devils, magicians, windmills, and the like. The children run after me, calling, "Grandfather, tell us a story." Sometimes they ask for particular stories, and I try to please them. A fat young boy once said to me, "Grandfather, it's the same story you told us before." The little rogue, he was right.

So it is with dreams too. It is many years since I left Frampol, but as soon as I shut my eyes I am there again. And whom do you think I see? Elka. She is standing by the washtub, as at our first encounter, but her face is shining and her eyes are as radiant as the eyes of a saint, and she speaks outlandish words to me, strange things. When I wake I have forgotten it all. But while the dream lasts I am comforted. She answers all my queries, and what comes out is that all is right. I weep and implore, "Let me be with you." And she consoles me and tells me to be patient. The time is nearer than it is far. Sometimes she strokes and kisses me and weeps upon my face. When I awaken I feel her lips and taste the salt of her tears.

No doubt the world is entirely an imaginary world, but it is only once removed from the true world. At the door of the hovel where I lie, there stands the plank on which the dead are taken away. The gravedigger Jew has his spade ready. The grave waits and the worms are hungry; the shrouds are prepared—I carry them in my beggar's sack. Another *shnorrer*° is waiting to inherit my bed of straw. When the time comes I will go joyfully. Whatever may be there, it will be real, without complication, without ridicule, without deception. God be praised: there even Gimpel cannot be deceived.

[1953]

---

shnorrer: a beggar; sponger

Workshop 3: The Individual Versus the Community

HERMAN MELVILLE
[1819–1891]

Common knowledge has it that Melville wrote America's great epic of the sea—Moby-Dick *(1851)—a story told by the wanderer Ishmael about a monomaniacal captain's vengeful pursuit of a seemingly omnipotent white whale. But in fact, Melville's literary contribution goes well beyond his "Whale." He created haunting tales concerning labor and alienation ("Bartleby"), slavery and race ("Benito Cereno"), as well as gender and sexuality ("The Paradise of Bachelors and the Tartarus of Maids"). And though few people knew it in his day, or know it even today, he was an exceptional poet. Also, late in life, he continued to experiment, creating innovative works, such as* Billy Budd *(1924), that combined both prose and poetry. The common misconception is that Melville's talent lies in one book only, the one about a whale, but it is time now for some uncommon knowledge about one of America's greatest writers.*

The central "uncommon fact" is that despite his current reputation, Melville lived most of his creative life in obscurity. Unlike Irving and Poe, Emerson and Whitman, or Hawthorne, James, and Twain, all of whom enjoyed robust professional lives and posthumous popularity, Melville flashed briefly then vanished. He burst onto the literary scene in 1846 with a series of sea adventures, virtually one a year starting with Typee *(1846) and culminating with* Moby-Dick, *but just as quickly fell from grace. In 1852 his psychological novel of incest and murder,* Pierre; or, The Ambiguities, *scandalized the few who read it, and by 1857 his dark comedy,* The Confidence-Man, *amused no one. In 1860 his first projected volume of verse failed to secure a publisher, and in 1866 his Civil War poems,* Battle-Pieces and Aspects of the War, *were savaged. From this point on Melville's career as an author was over. Even so, he continued to write, sometimes relishing his obscurity, sometimes seeking resurrection. Thus, a second uncommon fact about Melville concerns his modern revival. In the early 1920s,* Billy Budd *and numerous unpublished poems were discovered in manuscript and published along with the rest of Melville's complete works, and a revival of interest in him ensued. Melville's most appreciative readers were finally coming around but the writer was thirty years in the grave.*

Born to a prosperous New York merchant family, Herman Melville had every reason to expect great things. But economic reversals in the turbulent, early republic and the incautious business practices of his father, Allan, forced the family to relocate to Albany, New York, where in 1832 Allan succumbed to a brain fever that left him raving. Herman was twelve, and the loss etched itself into the fabric of his personality and writing. Quiet at first, he grew to be a genially argumentative adolescent itching to travel and write. He worked as a clerk and country schoolmaster but could not take it and in 1839 shipped aboard the merchant ship St. Lawrence for Liverpool and back. Soon after he walked, rode, sailed, and steamed his way West to Galena, Illinois, and back via the Mississippi and Ohio Rivers. Still without money or prospects, he signed on the whaler Acushnet in 1841 for the South Pacific, and after eighteen months at sea but only three ports of call, he jumped ship on the Marquesan island of Nuku Hiva. Running inland with a friend, he landed in the remote valley of Taipivai and spent a month living with its reputed cannibal inhabitants, the Taipis. Making his way back to the sea, he boarded another whaler, was incarcerated in Tahiti on the charge of mutiny, bummed his way to Hawaii, and joined the U.S. Navy aboard the frigate United States. Not surprisingly, his wayward defiance of authority abruptly halted. Melville kept his nose clean, but regaled fellow shipmates with his ribald island adventures. By the time he reached home in 1844, he was entertaining friends and family with cleaner stories, which he was urged to write up. And in doing so he created Typee (1846).

Melville's first book explores the baffling world of primal island life and questions western assumptions about the difference between "savagery" and "civilization." It was an immediate success. However, readers were not sure whether the book was a factual travelogue or a fictional romance, or whether this common sailor Herman Melville was not in fact an impostor. Further notoriety came when members of America's religious press, angered by Melville's sexy prose and attacks on America's Pacific imperialism and Christianity's missionaries, led Melville's American publisher John Wiley to insist on expurgations of Typee. Later on, Melville's British publisher Richard Bentley also censored Moby-Dick to rid it of its attacks on God and crown.

Melville had no qualms about riding the wave of Typee's notoriety and immediately published Omoo (1847), a bumptious sequel relating more island-hopping adventures. But the writing process deepened Melville. Accused of fabricating fictions, Melville composed Mardi and a Voyage (1849) to show readers what a fiction really could be. The result was a daring "Romance" that explored sexuality, politics, mind, and metaphysics as a fictional sailor chased after fictional women in an allegorical archipelago of South Pacific islands representative of America's imperialist and racist politics. The fiction failed.

Mardi's depth of psychology and symbolism were more than readers could chew, but Melville rebounded with two "jobs" to help sustain his growing *family:* Redburn *(1849) and* White-Jacket *(1850). Both brought Melville back to his semi-autobiographical and factual style, but with significant fictionalizations added.* Redburn *expands on the 1839 trip to Liverpool; it is Melville's bildungsroman about the growth of a naïve youth exposed to raw life on deck, the ravages of capitalism, poverty, and immigration, as well as the vaguely homoerotic antics of the British dandy Harry Bolton.* White-Jacket *surveys Navy life aboard a Man-of-War, and its publication played a role in the outlawing of flogging in the American fleet. Both books reassured readers of Melville's ability to connect with readers.*

Living now in a New York City townhouse crowded with relatives and children, Melville sailed for Europe to absorb London and the Continent. He read voraciously and collected new ideas; on his return he began a book about whaling. Moby-Dick *was a year and a half in the making. During the process Melville moved to Arrowhead, his Berkshire farm, where he brought in crops, met Nathaniel Hawthorne, and composed a novel (dedicated to Hawthorne) that pulled together all that he had learned from his past work: The* Typee *an plunge into primal worlds, the* Mardi *an experiments in narrative voice, and the deep thinking symbolism of* White-Jacket*. He had once told his editor Evert A. Duyckinck that he loved "all men who dive"; he was speaking of Emerson: not simply the transcendentalist who presumes the spiritual "oneness" of the universe, but the pragmatic idealist who desires transcendence and yet knows it cannot happen. This emotional and philosophical conflict is at the heart of the reader's understanding of the novel's mystic and mythic whale, both Ishmael's poetic vision of it and angry Ahab's destructive defiance. In fact, the fear both characters face is that there is no ideal or God; the universe is a Nothing.*

Moby-Dick *is a bracing read for its dramatic conflicts, vivid action, and chilling descriptions of the sea, but challenging for its political and philosophical digressions, both comic and serious, on whales and whaling practice. The novel is about not only alienated men in the capitalistic venture of whaling but also the search for spiritual repose despite human hunger for an absent God and for psychological stability despite the inherent orphan status of humanity. Melville told Hawthorne that he had written a "wicked book" but in getting it out, he felt as "spotless as the lamb," as though his own doubt and anger finally found full expression. But he also knew that the book would be tough to sell, for he also told Hawthorne that he was simply not capable of writing the easy, sentimental fictions that readers wanted; he could not write this "other way"; writing made him dive. Predictably, reviewers who admired the poetry of Melville's prose nevertheless were confused by the challenging depths of Ishmael's and Ahab's conflicting voices. They had trouble diving.*

Melville responded with Pierre *(1852), an angry fiction concerning a young writer and idealistic lover who abandons his fiancée to cohabit incestuously* with his half-sister, the secret illegitimate child of one of his deceased father's pre-marital indiscretions. But this did not bother readers so much as the novel's erratic narrator, the swirling prose, and irreligious view that there is no difference between virtue and vice. One reviewer flatly declared Pierre "a bad book!" and Melville's career was suddenly in peril.

To recuperate, Melville turned to the magazines. From 1853 to 1856 he contributed over a dozen tales and sketches to Putnam's and Harper's. The writing in such works as "Bartleby," "Benito Cereno," and "The Paradise of Bachelors and the Tartarus of Maids" is straightforward, genial, and professional. But in all cases, Melville was able to curb sentimentalism by infusing subtle ironies into the voices of his speakers who never seem as fully aware as his readers are of the poverty, alienation, racism, or sexism staring them in the face. During this period of artistic regeneration, Melville also published his revolutionary war novel, Israel Potter (1855), and his most radical experiment in distant third-person narration, The Confidence-Man (1857).

Exhausted by this output and frustrated by minimal returns in reputation and royalties, Melville again set sail for Europe where Hawthorne, now residing in England, observed that his "honest and courageous" friend persists "in wandering to and fro over these deserts" and that he "can neither believe, nor be comfortable in his unbelief." This time Melville's destination was the Mediterranean and Holy Land, where he would immerse himself in art works, architecture, the austere desert landscape of Egypt and Palestine, and the odd layering of modern life on western culture's most ancient ground. As Hawthorne might have predicted, Melville came no closer to settling his conflict between "belief" and "unbelief," but he returned home rejuvenated artistically; he returned home a poet.

Certainly the most uncommon fact to learn about Melville is that he had been a poet all along (inserting poems into prose works such as Mardi), and in the latter half of his life he made himself into an innovative versifier from lyric to epic. Melville began thinking of himself as a serious poet even before 1860 when his first collection of poems (now unlocated) failed to gain a publisher. He eventually published four volumes of poems throughout his life— Battle-Pieces (1866); Clarel (1876); John Marr (1888); and Timoleon (1891); and left another volume, Weeds & Wildings, and numerous "prose & poem" pieces in manuscript after his death. While lecturing on travel, the South Seas, and Roman statuary, he studied poetry and wrote poems both caustic and pastoral, mostly set in his Berkshire environs. When Melville first failed to attract a publisher for his first collection or to gain a job in Lincoln's new administration, he continued to study and like the rest of the nation followed the unfolding tragedy of Civil War. A year after Appomattox he had created over seventy hard-as-rock poems, such as "The Portent," "The College Colonel," and "A Utilitarian View of the Monitor's Fight," about heroism in the North and South, carnage, fratricide, the machines of war, innocence and fear, and *reconciliation. Reviewers derided* Battle-Pieces *(1866) for its unusual rhythms and rhymes, but Americans bent on "reconstruction" with a vengeance had no patience for Melville's compassion for losers. The book did not sell. But worse was coming.*

In 1867 Melville gave up publishing to become a U.S. Customs Inspector in New York City. Angry and morose, he drank too much, driving his wife to consider a separation. Melville in midlife crisis also had a son, Malcolm, who was confronting his own adolescent crises; it was a recipe for disaster that many survive, but for the Melvilles it culminated in young Malcolm's suicide.

Nine years later Melville came up with the poem Clarel: A Poem and Pilgrimage in the Holy Land *(1876), about a young divinity student in Jerusalem who falls for Ruth, daughter of a converted Zionist who is murdered. While Ruth is in mourning, Clarel joins a group of pilgrims and tourists on a ten-day jaunt to the Dead Sea, Bethlehem, and back. This modern epic of 18,000 four-beat lines (longer than Milton's* Paradise Lost*) includes a score of characters and a range of topics including Protestantism, Catholicism, Judaism, Islam, science, Darwinism, atheism, democracy, revolution, and the Civil War, as well as Clarel's struggle with belief and his sexuality. Published in a limited edition, the "metrical affair" received minimal attention, but Melville continued to write, revise, and re-assemble scores of shorter but no less ambitious poetic works.*

After his retirement in 1884, Melville contemplated several poetic projects. The first to be published was the slim volume John Marr and Other Sailors *(1888), which offers four long reminiscences of former sea mates (real and imagined) and several shorter works (including "The Maldive Shark" and "The Berg") about the unyielding "inhuman sea." In 1891, the year of his death, he published* Timoleon, *which includes "After the Pleasure Party" (a startling monologue about sexuality from the point of view of a female astronomer) and numerous poems about art and travel (including "Art," "Monody," and "Milan Cathedral") drawn from Melville's 1857 trip abroad.*

During these later years Melville also experimented with what may be called "prose and poem" pieces, which combine short prose sketches that introduce or surround a poem. Chief among these is The Burgundy Club *that features sketches of two genial gentlemen who deliver poems on the art of the Picturesque ("At the Hostelry") and an episode during the Italian risorgimento ("Naples in the Time of Bomba"), respectively. But these and others like them were never published in Melville's lifetime; they were preserved among Melville's papers and not printed until 1924.*

The greatest of these prose and poem pieces is Billy Budd. *This novella began as nothing more than a poem with a brief prose introduction about a young sailor accused of mutiny and condemned to die. In this early version, Billy is guilty, but as Melville revised, he added the characters of Claggart and Vere and made Billy into an innocent martyr. In time the little poem grew into the tragic prose work as it is known today. Also among Melville's unpublished works was a volume of poems titled* Weeds and Wildings, *which includes "Rip Van Winkle's Lilac" (Melville's prose and poem retelling of Irving's classic) and the sensual Rose Poems ("Amoroso" and "Rose Window") concerning love, death, and transcendence.*

Melville failed to make a living as a writer, but he never gave up writing. He often wrote beyond the grasp of the readers of his day, and today's readers still must play catch-up with his modern voice and ideas. His fictions continue to delight and astound; only now is his poetry coming into favor. Melville is a challenge to read; he can anger, baffle, and excite. Plot seems incidental; his sentences digress, but they are worth pursuing. His poetic line is short, craggy, and like Dickinson, elliptical and syntactically fragmented, but his poems are a hard, rough stone of meaning to crack. Despite these challenges, Melville's writing has endured the decades of neglect. Melville's persistence lies in his ability to create innovative narratives that go to the heart of the irresolvable problems of existence, democracy, race, gender, and sexuality. He was perhaps America's first modern writer.

The poetry that appears in The Pearson Custom Library *is from the forthcoming Northwestern-Newberry editions of Melville's* Published Poems *and* Billy Budd, Sailor and Other Late Manuscripts.

For Further Reading

Primary Works

Typee: A Peep at Polynesian Life (1846); *Omoo: A Narrative of Adventures in the South Seas* (1847); *Mardi and a Voyage Thither* (1849); *Redburn: His First Voyage* (1849); *White-Jacket, or The World in a Man-of-War* (1850); *Moby-Dick, or The Whale* (1851); *Pierre, or The Ambiguities* (1852); *Israel Potter: His Fifty Years of Exile* (1855); *The Piazza Tales* (1856); *The Confidence-Man: His Masquerade* (1857); *Clarel: A Poem and Pilgrimage in the Holy Land* (1876); *John Marr and Other Sailors* (1888); *Timoleon, Etc.* (1891); *The Works of Herman Melville* (London: Constable, 1922–24); *The Writings of Herman Melville*, ed. Harrison Hayford, Hershel Parker, and G. Thomas Tanselle (Evanston and Chicago: Northwestern University Press and The Newberry Library, 1968); Hayford, Harrison and Merton M. Sealts, Jr., eds. *Billy Budd, Sailor: An Inside Narrative by Herman Melville* (Chicago: University of Chicago Press, 1962); Ryan, Robert C. "Weeds and Wildings Chiefly: With a Rose or Two," by Herman Melville, Ph.D. diss., (Northwestern University, 1967).

Biography and Research

Bryant, John, ed. *A Companion to Melville Studies* (Westport, Conn.: Greenwood Press, 1986); Garner, Stanton. *The Civil War World of Herman Melville*

(Lawrence: University Press of Kansas, 1993); Higgins, Brian and Hershel Parker, eds. *Herman Melville: The Contemporary Reviews* (New York: Cambridge University Press, 1995); Higgins, Brian. *Herman Melville: A Reference Guide, 1931–1960; Reference Guide to Literature* (Boston: G.K. Hall, 1987); Howard, Leon. *Herman Melville: A Biography* (Berkeley: University of California Press, 1951); Leyda, Jay. *The Melville Log*, 2 vols. (New York: Harcourt, Brace, 1951, reprint with supplement, New York: Gordian Press, 1969); Madison, Mary K. *Melville's Sources* (Evanston, Ill.: Northwestern University Press, 1987); Newman, Lea Bertani Vozar. *A Reader's Guide to the Short Stories of Herman Melville* (Boston: G.K. Hall, 1986); Parker, Hershel. *Herman Melville: A Biography* (Baltimore: Johns Hopkins University Press, 1996); Robertson-Lorant, Laurie. *Melville: A Biography* (New York: Clarkson Potter Publishers, 1996); Sealts, Merton M., Jr. *Melville's Reading* (Columbia: University of South Carolina Press, 1988).

Secondary Works

Anderson, Charles R. *Melville in the South Seas* (New York: Columbia University, 1939); Berthoff, Warner. *The Example of Melville* (Princeton, N.J.: Princeton University Press, 1962); Bryant, John and Robert Milder, eds. *Melville's Evermoving Dawn: Centennial Essays* (Kent, Ohio: Kent State University Press, 1997); Bryant, John. *Melville & Repose: The Rhetoric of Humor in the American Renaissance* (New York: Oxford, 1993); Karcher, Carolyn L. *Shadow over the Promised Land: Slavery, Race, and Violence in Melville's America* (Baton Rouge: Louisiana State University Press, 1980); Levine, Robert S. *A Cambridge Companion to Herman Melville* (New York: Cambridge University Press, 1998); Martin, Robert K. *Hero, Captain, and Stranger: Male Friendship, Social Critique, and Literary Form in the Sea Novels of Herman Melville* (Chapel Hill: University of North Carolina Press, 1986); Parker, Hershel. *Reading Billy Budd* (Evanston, Ill: Northwestern University Press, 1990); Post-Lauria, Sheila. *Correspondent Colorings: Melville in the Marketplace* (Amherst: University of Massachusetts Press, 1996); Rogin, Michael Paul. *Subversive Geneology: The Politics and Art of Herman Melville* (New York: Alfred A. Knopf, 1983); Shurr, William H. *The Mystery of Iniquity: Melville as Poet, 1857–1891* (Lexington: University Press of Kentucky, 1972); Stein, William Bysshe *The Poetry of Melville's Later Years: Time, History, Myth, and Religion* (Albany: State University of New York Press, 1970).

SUSAN GLASPELL
[1876–1948]

She was popular with audiences and critics during her lifetime, and in 1931, the second woman ever to win a Pulitzer Prize. Yet Susan Glaspell is frequently recognized only as the author of the much-anthologized one-act play Trifles *and as "midwife" to the talents of the Provincetown Players and their most celebrated playwright, Eugene O'Neill. Glaspell was, not surprisingly, much more complex than this reputation suggests. She was a journalist who wrote fiction, and a playwright who acted onstage. She was a staunch feminist anxious about disrupting patriarchal norms, as evidenced by her false claims to have legally married her long-time lover, Norman Matson. She was a critical success who was simultaneously labeled both "sentimental" and "satiric." And while heralded mainly for her playwriting, Glaspell was also the editor of Cook's poetry, a prolific author of children's stories, novels, and a memoir; and, as the cofounder of the Provincetown Players, one of the most important figures in early twentieth century theater.*

Born in 1876, Glaspell was the middle child and only daughter of middle-class parents. She grew up the small, Midwestern town of Davenport, Iowa—the same city that produced the socialist intellectuals Floyd Dell and George Cram Cook—and graduated from Drake University in Des Moines in 1899. Interested in journalism from an early age, Glaspell used her college newspaper experience to land a job as a statehouse and legislative reporter for the Des Moines Daily News, *the newspaper for which she also wrote a column titled "The News Girl." Glaspell briefly attended graduate school in English at the University of Chicago, only to return to Davenport in order to begin full-time writing. She was immediately successful in this endeavor, publishing short stories in* Ladies' Home Journal, Youth's Companion, Munsey's, Harper's, *and other popular magazines. In 1909, she published her first novel, a romance titled* The Glory of the Conquered, *which became a bestseller. From the start, Glaspell consistently received strong praise for her work from both critics and readers and, perhaps even more impressive, managed to support herself and her family with income derived strictly from her fiction writing.*

After her married lover George Cram (Jig) Cook divorced his wife, Glaspell married him in 1913. Together, they became deeply involved in the cultural and artistic avant-garde centered in New York's Greenwich Village. There, Glaspell joined the Liberal Club, a venue in which radical political and literary figures gathered. She also helped support The Masses, a socialist journal published by George Eastman and her Davenport friend Floyd Dell, and The Washington Square Players, a vanguard of anti-commercial theater in New York. An active participant in this exciting bohemian milieu, Glaspell nonetheless critiqued in her work many of the political and social interests of that world. Her play Suppressed Desires (1915) satirizes the contemporary passion for all things Freudian; Close the Book (1917), social pretensions; The Verge (1921), the belief in a Nietzschean life force. She was, as the critic Linda Ben-Zvi correctly notes, "that special kind of ideological writer: one wary of ideology."

Despite her bounteous fiction writing and her social activism, Glaspell is most famous for her work as a playwright and for her status as one of the founding members of the Provincetown Players. The Provincetown Players were a small group of artists, including Edna St. Vincent Millay and John Reed, committed to the communal production of experimental drama. In part, this company worked to reject the popular commercial theater that thrived on Broadway, but it nonetheless pleased audiences well enough to survive for eight years and to serve as the genesis of a national little theater movement. The company staged plays both at Provincetown's Wharf Theater and at the MacDougal Street Play-wright's Theatre (now known as the Provincetown Playhouse). Glaspell not only wrote many plays for the company, but also directed and ably performed in a number of its productions. During a visit to New York, Jacques Copeau, the French actor, director, and critic, saw her appear onstage in the role of Ann Harding from her play Inheritors and celebrated her as a "truly great actress."

Trifles, a one-act play depicting the investigation of a small-town murder, is Glaspell's most famous and most studied work. Glaspell wrote the play in only ten days, basing it on a murder investigation and trial she had reported on for the Des Moines Daily News in 1901. The play opened at the Province-town Players' Wharf Theater on August 8, 1916, with Glaspell taking the role of Mrs. Hale and Cook performing the role of Mr. Hale. A staple of American professional and community theaters, the play also found international suc-cess. In 1919, a production was staged in London at King's Hall; in 1927, the Dublin Drama League performed Trifles (along with O'Neill's The Emperor Jones) at the Abbey Theater; and in 1930 Glaspell oversaw a production of the work at the People's Theater in London. A year after the American pre-miere of Trifles, Glaspell rewrote the play as a short story entitled, "A Jury of Her Peers" (1917). Both works, by demonstrating how two women solve a murder case simply by looking at the domestic "trifles" men overlook, ask that her readers look critically at ways of seeing, and ask how patriarchy influences how people perceive the world around them.

In 1922, Cook determined to fulfill his ambition to become a classical scholar (though some have argued that he was jealous of O'Neill's increasing popular and critical success) and Glaspell followed him to Greece, where they lived until his death in 1924. Glaspell chronicled their lives in Delphi in her biography of Cook, The Road to the Temple *(1927). Upon her return to the States following Cook's death, Glaspell shared a common-law marriage with Norman Matson, an author most famous for writing the novel that inspired the television show "Bewitched." As she had done with Cook, Glaspell collaborated with her partner, writing a play titled* The Comic Artist *(1928) with Matson. The play was not a success, nor was their romantic partnership; she and Matson parted ways four years later.*

In 1931, Glaspell became the second woman ever to win a Pulitzer Prize, for her three-act play Alison's House *(1930), which was inspired by the life of the poet Emily Dickinson. It was the last play she completed. Her creative productivity did not wane, however, as she published seven novels between 1928 and 1945. Most of these novels were set in the American Midwest, where Glaspell was born, and explored the tension for individuals between traditional regional values and modern ways of living. Toward the end of her life, Glaspell synthesized two important aspects of her identity—her Midwestern roots and her passion for American theater—when she became Director of the Midwest Play Bureau of the Federal Theater Project (1936–38). Glaspell died of viral pneumonia on July 7, 1948, leaving behind her a legacy of undervalued work that demands deeper exploration.*

The text presented here issues from C. W. E. Bigsby's edition of Plays by Susan Glaspell. *(Cambridge: Cambridge University Press, 1987).*

Paige Reynolds
College of the Holy Cross

For Further Reading

Primary Works

Plays

Suppressed Desires, written with Jig Cook (1915); *Trifles* (1916); *The People* (1917); *Close the Book* (1917); *The Outside* (1917); *Woman's Honor* (1918); *Tickless Time*, written with Jig Cook (1918); *Bernice* (1919); *Inheritors* (1921); *The Verge* (1921); *Chains of Dew* (1922); *The Comic Artist*, written with Norman Matson (1928); *Alison's House* (1930); *Plays by Susan Glaspell*, ed. C. W. E. Bigsby. Additional textual notes by Christine Dymkowski. Cambridge: Cambridge University Press, 1987. (Contains *Trifles, The Outside, The Verge, Inheritors*).

Short Stories

Lifted Masks and Other Works, ed. Eric S. Rabkin (Ann Arbor: University of Michigan Press, 1993. [short story collection]

Novels

The Glory of the Conquered (1909); *The Visioning* (1911).; *Fidelity* (1915); *Brook Evans* (1928); *Fugitive's Return* (1929); *Ambrose Holt and Family* (1931); *The Morning Is Near Us* (1939); *Cherished and Shared of Old* (1940); *Norma Ashe* (1942); *Judd Rankin's Daughter* (1945).

Biography

The Road to the Temple (1927).

Secondary Works

Ben-Zvi, Linda, ed., *Susan Glaspell: Essays on Her Theater and Fiction* (Ann Arbor: University of Michigan Press, 1995); C. W. E. Bigsby, Introduction, *Plays by Susan Glaspell,* ed. C. W. E. Bigsby (Cambridge: Cambridge University Press, 1987); Makowsky, Veronica, *Susan Glaspell's Century of American Women* (New York: Oxford University Press, 1993); Papke, Mary E., *Susan Glaspell: A Research and Production Sourcebook* (Westport, Conn.: Greenwood Press, 1993); Sarlós, Robert Károly, *Jig Cook and the Provincetown Players: Theater in Ferment* (Amherst: University of Massachusetts Press, 1982); Waterman, Arthur. *Susan Glaspell* (Boston: Twayne, 1966).

Film Adaptations

Trifles. Dir. Martha Moran (Phoenix/BFA, 1979); *A Jury of Her Peers.* Dir. Sally Heckel (Textfilm, 1982).

Trifles[*]

SUSAN GLASPELL

SCENE *The kitchen is the now abandoned farmhouse of John Wright, a gloomy kitchen, and left without having been put in order—unwashed pans under the sink, a loaf of bread outside the bread-box, a dish-towel on the table—other signs of incompleted work. At the rear the outer door opens and the Sheriff comes in followed by the County Attorney and Hale. The Sheriff and Hale are men in middle life, the County Attorney is a young man; all are much bundled up and go at once to the stove. They are followed by the two women—the Sheriff's wife first; she is a slight wiry woman, a thin nervous face. Mrs Hale is larger and would ordinarily be called more comfortable looking, but she is disturbed now and looks fearfully about as she enters. The women have come in slowly, and stand close together near the door.*

County Attorney *(rubbing his hands).* This feels good. Come up to the fire, ladies.

Mrs Peters *(after taking a step forward).* I'm not—cold.

Sheriff *(unbuttoning his overcoat and stepping away from the stove as if to mark the beginning of official business).* Now, Mr Hale, before we move things about, you explain to Mr Henderson just what you saw when you came here yesterday morning.

County Attorney.   By the way, has anything been moved? Are things just as you left them yesterday?

Sheriff *(looking about).* It's just the same. When it dropped below zero last night I thought I'd better send Frank out this morning to make a fire for us—no use getting pneumonia with a big case on, but I told him not to touch anything except the stove—and you know Frank.

---

[*]*Trifles* premiered at the Wharf Theater, Provincetown, Massachusetts, on August 8, 1916, under the direction of George Cram Cook. First performed by the Provincetown Players at the Wharf Theatre, Provincetown, Mass., August 8, 1916, with the following cast:

George Henderson (County Attorney)	Robert Rogers
Henry Peters (Sheriff)	Robert Conville
Lewis Hale, A neighboring farmer	George Cram Cook
Mrs Peters	Alice Hall
Mrs Hale	Susan Glaspell

County Attorney. Somebody should have been left here yesterday.

Sheriff. Oh—yesterday. When I had to send Frank to Morris Center for that man who went crazy—I want you to know I had my hands full yesterday. I knew you could get back from Omaha by today and as long as I went over everything here myself—

County Attorney. Well, Mr Hale, tell just what happened when you came here yesterday morning.

Hale. Harry and I had started to town with a load of potatoes. We came along the road from my place and as I got here I said, 'I'm going to see if I can't get John Wright to go in with me on a party telephone.' I spoke to Wright about it once before and he put me off, saying folks talked too much anyway, and all he asked was peace and quiet—I guess you know about how much he talked himself; but I thought maybe if I went to the house and talked about it before his wife, though I said to Harry that I didn't know as what his wife wanted made much difference to John—

County Attorney. Let's talk about that later, Mr Hale. I do want to talk about that, but tell now just what happened when you got to the house.

Hale. I didn't hear or see anything; I knocked at the door, and still it was all quiet inside. I knew they must be up, it was past eight o'clock. So I knocked again, and I thought I heard somebody say, 'Come in.' I wasn't sure, I'm not sure yet, but I opened the door—this door *(indicating the door by which the two women are still standing)* and there in that rocker— *(pointing to it)* sat Mrs Wright.

(They all look at the rocker.)

County Attorney. What—was she doing?

Hale. She was rockin' back and forth. She had her apron in her hand and was kind of—pleating it.

County Attorney. And how did she—look?

Hale. Well, she looked queer.

County Attorney. How do you mean—queer?

Hale. Well, as if she didn't know what she was going to do next. And kind of done up.

County Attorney. How did she seem to feel about your coming?

Hale. Why, I don't think she minded—one way or other. She didn't pay much attention. I said, 'How do, Mrs Wright it's cold, ain't it?' And she said, 'Is it?'—and went on kind of pleating at her apron. Well, I was surprised; she didn't ask me to come up to the stove, or to set down, but just sat there, not even looking at me, so I said, 'I want to see John.' And then she—laughed. I guess you would call it a laugh. I thought of Harry and the team outside, so I said a little sharp: 'Can't I see John?' 'No', she says, kind o' dull like. 'Ain't he home?' says I. 'Yes', says she, 'he's home'.

'Then why can't I see him?' I asked her, out of patience. ''Cause he's dead', says she. *'Dead?'* says I. She just nodded her head, not getting a bit excited, but rockin' back and forth. 'Why—where is he?' says I, not knowing what to say. She just pointed upstairs—like that *(himself pointing to the room above)* I got up, with the idea of going up there. I walked from there to here—then I says, 'Why, what did he die of?' 'He died of a rope round his neck', says she, and just went on pleatin' at her apron. Well, I went out and called Harry. I thought I might—need help. We went upstairs and there he was lyin'—

County Attorney. I think I'd rather have you go into that upstairs, where you can point it all out. Just go on now with the rest of the story.

Hale. Well, my first thought was to get that rope off. It looked . . . *(stops, his face twitches)* . . . but Harry, he went up to him, and he said, 'No, he's dead all right, and we'd better not touch anything.' So we went back down stairs. She was still sitting that same way. 'Has anybody been notified?' I asked. 'No', says she unconcerned. 'Who did this, Mrs Wright?' said Harry. He said it business-like—and she stopped pleatin' of her apron. 'I don't know', she says. 'You don't *know?*' says Harry. 'No', says she. 'Weren't you sleepin' in the bed with him?' says Harry. 'Yes', says she, 'but I was on the inside'. 'Somebody slipped a rope round his neck and strangled him and you didn't wake up?' says Harry. 'I didn't wake up', she said after him. We must 'a looked as if we didn't see how that could be, for after a minute she said, 'I sleep sound'. Harry was going to ask her more questions but I said maybe we ought to let her tell her story first to the coroner, or the sheriff, so Harry went fast as he could to Rivers' place, where there's a telephone.

County Attorney. And what did Mrs Wright do when she knew that you had gone for the coroner?

Hale. She moved from that chair to this one over here *(pointing to a small chair in the corner)* and just sat there with her hands held together and looking down. I got a feeling that I ought to make some conversation, so I said I had come in to see if John wanted to put in a telephone, and at that she started to laugh, and then she stopped and looked at me—scared. *(the County Attorney, who has had his notebook our, makes a note)* I dunno, maybe it wasn't scared. I wouldn't like to say it was. Soon Harry got back, and then Dr Lloyd came, and you, Mr Peters, and so I guess that's all I know that you don't.

County Attorney *(looking around)*. I guess we'll go upstairs first—and then out to the barn and around there. *(to the Sheriff)* You're convinced that there was nothing important here—nothing that would point to any motive.

Sheriff. Nothing here but kitchen things.

(The County Attorney, after again looking around the kitchen, opens the door of a cupboard closet. He gets up on a chair and looks on a shelf. Pulls his hand away, sticky.)

County Attorney.   Here's a nice mess.

(The women draw nearer.)

Mrs Peters *(to the other woman)*. Oh, her fruit; it did freeze. *(to the Lawyer)* She worried about that when it turned so cold. She said the fire'd go out and her jars would break.
Sheriff.   Well, can you beat the women! Held for murder and worryin' about her preserves.
County Attorney.   I guess before we're through she may have something more serious than preserves to worry about.
Hale.   Well, women are used to worrying over trifles.

(The two women move a little closer together.)

County Attorney *(with the gallantry of a young politician)*. And yet, for all their worries, what would we do without the ladies? *(the women do not unbend. He goes to the sink, takes a dipperful of water from the pail and pouring it into a basin, washes his hands. Starts to wipe them on the roller-towel, turns it for a cleaner place)* Dirty towels! *(kicks his foot against the pans under the sink)* Not much of a housekeeper, would you say, ladies?
Mrs Hale *(stiffly)*. There's a great deal of work to be done on a farm.
County Attorney.   To be sure. And yet *(with a little bow to her)* I know there are some Dickson county farmhouses which do not have such roller towels.

(He gives it a pull to expose its length again.)

Mrs Hale.   Those towels get dirty awful quick. Men's hands aren't always as clean as they might be.
County Attorney.   Ah, loyal to your sex, I see. But you and Mrs Wright were neighbors. I suppose you were friends, too.
Mrs Hale *(shaking her head)*. I've not seen much of her of late years. I've not been in this house—it's more than a year.
County Attorney.   And why was that? You didn't like her?
Mrs Hale.   I liked her all well enough. Farmers' wives have their hands full, Mr Henderson. And then—
County Attorney.   Yes—?
Mrs Hale *(looking about)*. It never seemed a very cheerful place.

County Attorney. No—it's not cheerful. I shouldn't say she had the home-making instinct.

Mrs Hale. Well, I don't know as Wright had, either.

County Attorney. You mean that they didn't get on very well?

Mrs Hale. No, I don't mean anything. But I don't think a place'd be any cheerfuller for John Wright's being in it.

County Attorney. I'd like to talk more of that a little later. I want to get the lay of things upstairs now.

(He goes to the left, where three steps lead to a stair door.)

Sheriff. I suppose anything Mrs Peters does'll be all right. She was to take in some clothes for her, you know, and a few little things. We left in such a hurry yesterday.

County Attorney. Yes, but I would like to see what you take, Mrs Peters, and keep an eye out for anything that might be of use to us.

Mrs Peters. Yes, Mr Henderson.

(The women listen to the men's steps on the stairs, then look about the kitchen.)

Mrs Hale. I'd hate to have men coming into my kitchen, snooping around and criticising.

(She arranges the pans under sink which the Lawyer had shoved out of place.)

Mrs Peters. Of course it's no more than their duty.

Mrs Hale. Duty's all right, but I guess that deputy sheriff that came out to make the fire might have got a little of this on. *(gives the roller towel a pull)* Wish I'd thought of that sooner. Seems mean to talk about her for not having things slicked up when she had to come away in such a hurry.

Mrs Peters (who has gone to a small table in the left rear corner of the room, and lifted one end of a towel that covers a pan). She had bread set.

(Stands still.)

Mrs Hale (eyes fixed on a loaf of bread beside the bread-box, which is on a low shelf at the other side of the room. Moves slowly toward it). She was going to put this in there. *(picks up loaf, then abruptly drops it. In a manner of returning to familiar things)* It's a shame about her fruit. I wonder if it's all gone. *(gets up on the chair and looks)* I think there's some here that's all right, Mrs Peters. Yes—here; *(holding it toward the window)* this is cherries, too. *(looking again)* I declare I believe that's the only one. *(gets down, bottle in her hand. Goes to the sink and wipes it off on the outside)*

She'll feel awful bad after all her hard work in the hot weather. I remember the afternoon I put up my cherries last summer.

(*She puts the bottle on the big kitchen table, center of the room. With a sigh, is about to sit down in the rocking-chair. Before she is seated realizes what chair it is; with a slow look at it, steps back. The chair which she has touched rocks back and forth.*)

Mrs Peters. Well, I must get those things from the front room closet. (*she goes to the door at the right, but after looking into the other room, steps back*) You coming with me, Mrs Hale? You could help me carry them.

(*They go in the other room; reappear, Mrs Peters carrying a dress and skirt, Mrs Hale following with a pair of shoes.*)

Mrs Peters. My, it's cold in there.

(*She puts the clothes on the big table, and hurries to the stove.*)

Mrs Hale (examining the skirt). Wright was close. I think maybe that's why she kept so much to herself. She didn't even belong to the Ladies Aid. I suppose she felt she couldn't do her part, and then you don't enjoy things when you feel shabby. She used to wear pretty clothes and be lively, when she was Minnie Foster, one of the town girls singing in the choir. But that—oh, that was thirty years ago. This all you was to take in?
Mrs Peters. She said she wanted an apron. Funny thing to want, for there isn't much to get you dirty in jail, goodness knows. But I suppose just to make her feel more natural. She said they was in the top drawer in this cupboard. Yes, here. And then her little shawl that always hung behind the door. (*opens stair door and looks*) Yes, here it is.

(*Quickly shuts door leading upstairs.*)

Mrs Hale (abruptly moving toward her). Mrs Peters?
Mrs Peters. Yes, Mrs Hale?
Mrs Hale. Do you think she did it?
Mrs Peters (in a frightened voice). Oh, I don't know.
Mrs Hale. Well, I don't think she did. Asking for an apron and her little shawl. Worrying about her fruit.
Mrs Peters (starts to speak, glances up, where footsteps are heard in the room above. In a low voice). Mr Peters says it looks bad for her. Mr Henderson is awful sarcastic in a speech and he'll make fun of her sayin' she didn't wake up.

Mrs Hale. Well, I guess John Wright didn't wake when they was slipping that rope under his neck.

Mrs Peters. No, it's strange. It must have been done awful crafty and still. They say it was such a—funny way to kill a man, rigging it all up like that.

Mrs Hale. That's just what Mr Hale said. There was a gun in the house. He says that's what he can't understand.

Mrs Peters. Mr Henderson said coming out that what was needed for the case was a motive; something to show anger, or—sudden feeling.

Mrs Hale (who is standing by the table). Well, I don't see any signs of anger around here. *(she puts her hand on the dish towel which lies on the table, stands looking down at table, one half of which is clean, the other half messy)* It's wiped to here. *(makes a move as if to finish work, then turns and looks at loaf of bread outside the breadbox. Drops towel. In that voice of coming back to familiar things.)* Wonder how they are finding things upstairs. I hope she had it a little more red-up[1] up there. You know, it seems kind of *sneaking.* Locking her up in town and then coming out here and trying to get her own house to turn against her!

Mrs Peters. But Mrs Hale, the law is the law.

Mrs Hale. I s'pose 'tis. *(unbuttoning her coat)* Better loosen up your things, Mrs Peters. You won't feel them when you go out.

(Mrs Peters takes off her fur tippet,[2] goes to hang it on hook at back of room, stands looking at the under part of the small corner table.)

Mrs Peters. She was piecing a quilt.

(She brings the large sewing basket and they look at the bright pieces.)

Mrs Hale. It's log cabin pattern. Pretty, isn't it? I wonder if she was goin' to quilt it or just knot it?

(Footsteps have been heard coming down the stairs. The Sheriff enters followed by Hale and the County Attorney.)

Sheriff. They wonder if she was going to quilt it or just knot it!

(The men laugh, the women look abashed.)

---

[1]red up: tidied up.

[2]tippet: covering for the shoulders, like a cape or scarf.

County Attorney (rubbing his hands over the stove). Frank's fire didn't do much up there, did it? Well, let's go out to the barn and get that cleared up.

(The men go outside.)

Mrs Hale (resentfully). I don't know as there's anything so strange, our takin' up our time with little things while we're waiting for them to get the evidence. *(she sits down at the big table smoothing out a block with decision)* I don't see as it's anything to laugh about.

Mrs Peters (apologetically). Of course they've got awful important things on their minds.

(Pulls up a chair and joins Mrs Hale at the table.)

Mrs Hale (examining another block). Mrs Peters, look at this one. Here, this is the one she was working on, and look at the sewing! All the rest of it has been so nice and even. And look at this! It's all over the place! Why, it looks as if she didn't know what she was about!

(After she has said this they look at each other, then start to glance back at the door. After an instant Mrs Hale has pulled at a knot and ripped the sewing.)

Mrs Peters. Oh, what are you doing, Mrs Hale?

Mrs Hale (mildly). Just pulling out a stitch or two that's not sewed very good. *(threading a needle)* Bad sewing always made me fidgety.

Mrs Peters (nervously). I don't think we ought to touch things.

Mrs Hale. I'll just finish up this end. *(suddenly stopping and leaning forward)* Mrs Peters?

Mrs Peters. Yes, Mrs Hale?

Mrs Hale. What do you suppose she was so nervous about?

Mrs Peters. Oh—I don't know. I don't know as she was nervous. I sometimes sew awful queer when I'm just tired. *(Mrs Hale starts to say something, looks at Mrs Peters, then goes on sewing)* Well I must get these things wrapped up. They may be through sooner than we think. *(putting apron and other things together)* I wonder where I can find a piece of paper, and string.

Mrs Hale. In that cupboard, maybe.

Mrs Peters (looking in cupboard). Why, here's a bird-cage. *(holds it up)* Did she have a bird, Mrs Hale?

Mrs Hale. Why, I don't know whether she did or not—I've not been here for so long. There was a man around last year selling canaries cheap, but I don't know as she took one; maybe she did. She used to sing real pretty herself.

Mrs Peters (*glancing around*). Seems funny to think of a bird here. But she must have had one, or why would she have a cage? I wonder what happened to it.

Mrs Hale.   I s'pose maybe the cat got it.

Mrs Peters.   No, she didn't have a cat. She's got that feeling some people have about cats—being afraid of them. My cat got in her room and she was real upset and asked me to take it out.

Mrs Hale.   My sister Bessie was like that. Queer, ain't it?

Mrs Peters (*examining the cage*). Why, look at this door. It's broke. One hinge is pulled apart.

Mrs Hale (*looking too*). Looks as if someone must have been rough with it.

Mrs Peters.   Why, yes.

(She brings the cage forward and puts it on the table.)

Mrs Hale.   I wish if they're going to find any evidence they'd be about it. I don't like this place.

Mrs Peters.   But I'm awful glad you came with me, Mrs Hale. It would be lonesome for me sitting here alone.

Mrs Hale.   It would, wouldn't it? (*dropping her sewing*) But I tell you what I do wish, Mrs Peters. I wish I had come over sometimes when she was here. I—(*looking around the room*)—wish I had.

Mrs Peters.   But of course you were awful busy, Mrs Hale—your house and your children.

Mrs Hale.   I could've come. I stayed away because it weren't cheerful—and that's why I ought to have come. I—I've never liked this place. Maybe because it's down in a hollow and you don't see the road. I dunno what it is, but it's a lonesome place and always was. I wish I had come over to see Minnie Foster sometimes. I can see now—(*shakes her head*)

Mrs Peters.   Well, you mustn't reproach yourself, Mrs Hale. Somehow we just don't see how it is with other folks until—something comes up.

Mrs Hale.   Not having children makes less work—but it makes a quiet house, and Wright out to work all day, and no company when he did come in. Did you know John Wright, Mrs Peters?

Mrs Peters.   Not to know him; I've seen him in town. They say he was a good man.

Mrs Hale.   Yes—good; he didn't drink, and kept his word as well as most, I guess, and paid his debts. But he was a hard man, Mrs Peters. Just to pass the time of day with him—(*shivers*) Like a raw wind that gets to the bone. (*pauses, her eye falling on the cage*) I should think she would 'a wanted a bird. But what do you suppose went with it?

Mrs Peters.   I don't know, unless it got sick and died.

(She reaches over and swings the broken door, swings it again, both women watch it.)

Mrs Hale. You weren't raised round here, were you? *(Mrs Peters shakes her head)* You didn't know—her?

Mrs Peters. Not till they brought her yesterday.

Mrs Hale. She—come to think of it, she was kind of like a bird herself—real sweet and pretty, but kind of timid and—fluttery. How—she—did—change. *(silence; then as if struck by a happy thought and relieved to get back to everyday things)* Tell you what, Mrs Peters, why don't you take the quilt in with you? It might take up her mind.

Mrs Peters. Why, I think that's a real nice idea, Mrs Hale. There couldn't possibly be any objection to it, could there? Now, just what would I take? I wonder if her patches are in here—and her things.

(They look in the sewing basket.)

Mrs Hale. Here's some red. I expect this has got sewing things in it. *(brings out a fancy box)* What a pretty box. Looks like something somebody would give you. Maybe her scissors are in here. *(Opens box. Suddenly puts her hand to her nose)* Why—*(Mrs Peters bends nearer, then turns her face away)* There's something wrapped up in this piece of silk.

Mrs Peters. Why, this isn't her scissors.

Mrs Hale (lifting the silk). Oh, Mrs Peters—it's—

(Mrs Peters bends closer.)

Mrs Peters. It's the bird.

Mrs Hale (jumping up). But, Mrs Peters—look at it! It's neck! Look at its neck! It's all—other side *to.*

Mrs Peters. Somebody—wrung—its—neck.

(Their eyes meet. A look of growing comprehension, of horror. Steps are heard outside. Mrs Hale slips box under quilt pieces, and sinks into her chair. Enter Sheriff and County Attorney. Mrs Peters rises.)

County Attorney (as one turning from serious things to little pleasantries). Well ladies, have you decided whether she was going to quilt it or knot it?

Mrs Peters. We think she was going to—knot it.

County Attorney. Well, that's interesting, I'm sure. *(seeing the birdcage)* Has the bird flown?

Mrs Hale (putting more quilt pieces over the box). We think the—cat got it.

County Attorney (preoccupied). Is there a cat?

(Mrs Hale glances in a quick covert way at Mrs Peters.)

Mrs Peters.   Well, not *now.* They're superstitious, you know. They leave.

County Attorney *(to Sheriff Peters, continuing an interrupted conversation).* No sign at all of anyone having come from the outside. Their own rope. Now let's go up again and go over it piece by piece. *(they start upstairs)* It would have to have been someone who knew just the—

(Mrs Peters sits down. The two women sit there not looking at one another, but as if peering into something and at the same time holding back. When they talk now it is in the manner of feeling their way over strange ground, as if afraid of what they are saying, but as if they can not help saying it.)

Mrs Hale.   She liked the bird. She was going to bury it in that pretty box.

Mrs Peters *(in a whisper).* When I was a girl—my kitten—there was a boy took a hatchet, and before my eyes—and before I could get there—*(covers her face an instant)* If they hadn't held me back I would have—*(catches herself, looks upstairs where steps are heard, falters weakly)*—hurt him.

Mrs Hale *(with a slow look around her).* I wonder how it would seem never to have had any children around. *(pause)* No, Wright wouldn't like the bird—a thing that sang. She used to sing. He killed that, too.

Mrs Peters *(moving uneasily).* We don't know who killed the bird.

Mrs Hale.   I knew John Wright.

Mrs Peters.   It was an awful thing was done in this house that night, Mrs Hale. Killing a man while he slept, slipping a rope around his neck that choked the life out of him.

Mrs Hale.   His neck. Choked the life out of him.

(Her hand goes out and rests on the bird-cage.)

Mrs Peters *(with rising voice).* We don't know who killed him. We don't know.

Mrs Hale *(her own feeling not interrupted).* If there'd been years and years of nothing, then a bird to sing to you, it would be awful—still, after the bird was still.

Mrs Peters *(something within her speaking).* I know what stillness is. When we homesteaded in Dakota, and my first baby died—after he was two years old, and me with no other then—

Mrs Hale *(moving).* How soon do you suppose they'll be through, looking for the evidence?

Mrs Peters.   I know what stillness is. *(pulling herself back).* The law has got to punish crime, Mrs Hale.

Mrs Hale (not as if answering that). I wish you'd seen Minnie Foster when she wore a white dress with blue ribbons and stood up there in the choir and sang. *(a look around the room)* Oh, I *wish* I'd come over here once in a while! That was a crime! That was a crime! Who's going to punish that?

Mrs Peters (looking upstairs). We mustn't—take on.

Mrs Hale. I might have known she needed help! I know how things can be—for women. I tell you, it's queer, Mrs Peters. We live close together and we live far apart. We all go through the same things—it's all just a different kind of the same thing. *(brushes her eyes, noticing the bottle of fruit, reaches out for it)* If I was you, I wouldn't tell her her fruit was gone. Tell her it ain't. Tell her it's all right. Take this in to prove it to her. She—she may never know whether it was broke or not.

Mrs Peters (takes the bottle, looks about for something to wrap it in; takes petticoat from the clothes brought from the other room, very nervously begins winding this around the bottle. In a false voice). My, it's a good thing the men couldn't hear us. Wouldn't they just laugh! Getting all stirred up over a little thing like a—dead canary. As if that could have anything to do with—with—wouldn't they laugh!

(The men are heard coming down stairs.)

Mrs Hale (under her breath). Maybe they would—maybe they wouldn't.

County Attorney. No, Peters, it's all perfectly clear except a reason for doing it. But you know juries when it comes to women. If there was some definite thing. Something to show—something to make a story about—a thing that would connect up with this strange way of doing it—

(The women's eyes meet for an instant. Enter Hale from outer door.)

Hale. Well, I've got the team around. Pretty cold out there.

County Attorney. I'm going to stay here a while by myself. *(to the Sheriff)* You can send Frank out for me, can't you? I want to go over everything. I'm not satisfied that we can't do better.

Sheriff. Do you want to see what Mrs Peters is going to take in?

(The Lawyer goes to the table, picks up the apron, laughs.)

County Attorney. Oh, I guess they're not very dangerous things the ladies have picked out. *(Moves a few things about, disturbing the quilt pieces which cover the box. Steps back)* No, Mrs Peters doesn't need supervising. For that matter, a sheriff's wife is married to the law. Ever think of it that way, Mrs Peters?

Mrs Peters. Not—just that way.

Sheriff (chuckling). Married to the law. *(moves toward the other room)* I just want you to come in here a minute, George. We ought to take a look at these windows.

County Attorney (scoffingly). Oh, windows!

Sheriff. We'll be right out, Mr Hale.

(Hale goes outside. The Sheriff follows the County Attorney into the other room. Then Mrs Hale rises, hands tight together, looking intensely at Mrs Peters, whose eyes make a slow turn, finally meeting Mrs Hale's. A moment Mrs Hale holds her, then her own eyes point the way to where the box is concealed. Suddenly Mrs Peters throws back quilt pieces and tries to put the box in the bag she is wearing. It is too big. She opens box, starts to take bird out, cannot touch it, goes to pieces, stands there helpless. Sound of a knob turning in the other room. Mrs Hale snatches the box and puts it in the pocket of her big coat. Enter County Attorney and Sheriff.)

County Attorney (facetiously). Well, Henry, at least we found out that she was not going to quilt it. She was going to—what is it you call it, ladies?

Mrs Hale (her hand against her pocket). We call it—knot it, Mr Henderson.

(CURTAIN)

[1916]

RICHARD WRIGHT
[1908–1960]

Thanks primarily to his first novel and the first half of his autobiography, Richard Wright stands as arguably the most influential African-American fiction writer of the twentieth century. While many scholars might select another novel—such as Ralph Ellison's Invisible Man *(1952) or Toni Morrison's* Beloved *(1987)—as the most important piece of twentieth century African-American fiction, Wright's* Native Son *(1940) so profoundly shaped the direction of the black novel that such later writers as Ellison, James Baldwin, and Morrison have continued to reflect and critique Wright's work more than that of almost any other predecessor. Wright's first novel was surprisingly popular and shockingly unsparing in its portrait of American racial oppression. Applying the naturalistic narrative of Theodore Dreiser or Stephen Crane to black life in the 1930s, Wright launched a long and varied career as a political novelist whose work attacked the American racial system at its deepest levels.*

Wright's career would eventually take him to Chicago, New York, Paris, and Africa, but he began his life in a small Mississippi town, where his father Nathan was a sharecropper and his mother Ella was a teacher. In 1911 the Wrights moved to Memphis, where Nathan abandoned the family. There, Richard became the high scchool valedictorian and moved to Chicago to launch his literary career while his family moved on to Arkansas, and finally returned to Mississippi. After finding work as a Chicago postal clerk, Wright joined the Communist Party in 1933 and published his first story in 1936. American Communists were deeply involved in the "race question," as it was often called; such early socialist publications as New Masses *and* The Liberator *frequently analyzed racism as at bottom a class issue, and Wright became increasingly involved in the Communist movement over the next several years. During this time Wright also began to establish himself as a fiction writer—winning story prizes and publishing the story collection* Uncle Tom's Children *in 1938—and as an insightful literary and social critic, through such essays as "Blueprint for Negro Writing" in 1937. The stories in* Uncle Tom's Children *forcefully portray white mob violence in opposition to isolated black men or, in the case of "Fire and Cloud," in opposition to a more widespread resistance. The volume's republication in 1940 with the addition of the story "Bright and Morning Star" introduces another variant on this narrative structure, though in this case with a more overtly Marxist setting. Wright's first novel, originally titled "Cesspool," went through numerous rejections at this time and was published posthumously as* Lawd Today *in 1965.*

In 1939 Wright married Dhimah Rose Meadman (with Ellison as best man), but the couple separated after a delayed honeymoon, and Wright married his second wife, Ellen Poplar, in 1941. Thanks to a Guggenheim fellowship, Wright was also completing his first novel, Native Son, *at this time.*

Native Son *focuses on Bigger Thomas, a young African-American man who inadvertently murders the daughter of his white employers—in fear that he will be caught alone in her room and therefore accused of rape, a common accusation at the time, especially in the South, that required little or no basis in fact. As Bigger's violence spirals further out of control, he rapes and kills the black woman who discovers his original act. The remainder of the novel takes place during Bigger's trial, which results in his execution.* Native Son *holds nothing back in its portrayal of Bigger as effectively trapped and controlled by the white society around him, a society that, as Dorothy Canfield Fisher observes in her original introduction to the novel, has promised Bigger a series of rights and freedoms and then systematically denied them all. In keeping with his naturalist and Communist analyses of racism, Wright unflinchingly argues through* Native Son *that Bigger's violence is the direct result of a social system designed to produce black men who either submit entirely to oppression or react violently against it, destroying themselves in the process. In contrast to a novel such as James Weldon Johnson's* The Autobiography of an ex-Coloured Man *(1912), or to the tradition of slave narratives,* Native Son *diverges from the story of an individual overcoming racial obstacles, however limited these triumphs may be—and provides no hope for such a story, without a complete overthrow of the racist American social structure first. Comparing* Native Son *to earlier African-American fiction, Alain Locke declared in his review that, "For all its daring and originality, it is significant because it is in step with the advance-guard of contemporary American fiction, and has dared to go a half step farther." Critics have focused more recently on the novel's problematic treatment of African-American women, while still acknowledging Wright's profound effect on the future course of black fiction.*

Native Son *was also a striking commercial success, selling more than two hundred thousand copies in its first month, and becoming a Book-of-the-Month club selection, a distinction no other African-American novel would achieve until Morrison's* Song of Solomon *nearly forty years later. Wright published the pamphlet* How "Bigger" Was Born *on the heels of this success (Harper, his publisher, originally planned to reissue the novel with this essay included for a new "documentary" edition).* Native Son *also appeared for a successful Broadway run with Orson Welles as director, and as a film in 1951, with Wright himself playing Bigger Thomas (though rather awkwardly).*

Wright's next book, Twelve Million Black Voices, *presents a folk history of black America from 1619 to the 1940s as a fundamental element of American cultural identity, concluding that "If we black folk perish, America will perish." Wright also argued against the use of the word "Negro" here, long before the term lost its social acceptability, on the grounds that "Negro" is "not really a name at all," but a white designation "which artificially and arbitrarily defines, regulates, and limits in scope the vital contours of our lives."*

Five years after Native Son *exploded onto the literary scene, Wright had completed an autobiography and secured publication for the first half of his memoir as* Black Boy. *Parts of the second half, published as* American Hunger *thirty-two years later, appeared in the* Atlantic Monthly *as "I Tried to Be a Communist" in 1944, but no complete edition of Wright's autobiography was in print during his lifetime.* Black Boy *recounts Wright's life from age four to nineteen, emphasizing both the literal and figurative hunger that pervaded a childhood spent in poverty and emotional isolation, due both to his father's abandonment of the family and to the cruel racism of Southern whites, which the young Wright finds almost everywhere he looks. There is some note of hope at the book's end, however, as Wright reaches the point at which he leaves the South behind and his literary career will soon begin. (The autobiography's second half, in contrast, closes on a note of profound pessimism for the future of American society and race.)* Black Boy *met with even greater critical and commercial success than* Native Son, *ascending to the top of most bestseller lists and drawing comparisons in the years since its first appearance to the classic American autobiographies of Benjamin Franklin, Frederick Douglass, and Henry Adams.*

As the title of Wright's Atlantic Monthly *"I Tried to Be a Communist" piece suggests, his growing dissatisfaction with the American Communist Party led to his departure from the party in 1944. The Wrights spent most of the next few years traveling abroad, visiting several African nations and making an extended stay in Paris, where Wright befriended Gertrude Stein, Jean Paul Sartre, and Simone de Beauvoir. Following a brief return to America, the Wrights left again for Paris in 1947, where Wright joined Stein as an expatriate American writer. Wright's dissatisfaction with American society and culture was much greater than Stein's, though like her he kept Paris as his home until his death. Wright quickly established himself in the French intellectual scene, incorporating existentialism within his philosophical horizons and beginning to write* The Outsider, *which he termed his "philosophical" novel. Published in 1953, this second novel includes an African-American protagonist, though without the same specifically racial focus that exemplifies his earlier work. Cross Damon, like Bigger Thomas, becomes engaged in a spiralling series of murders, though Damon's killings begin in response to his betrayal by the American Communist Party rather than by Southern white society at large. Taking advantage of a train crash to declare himself dead and assume another identity, Damon becomes engaged and then quickly disillusioned by Communist acquaintances in New York, eventually dying at the Party's hands. Though well received in Europe, most American critics found* The Outsider *too flawed as a narrative to compare it favorably to Wright's earlier work.*

Wright's next novel, Savage Holiday, *applies a Freudian perspective to his only white protagonist, the repressed insurance executive Erskine Fowler. Wright turned increasingly to nonfiction in the latter stages of his career, publishing only one more novel,* The Long Dream, *but writing extensively about international racial issues based on his travels through Africa and Asia. In* White Man, Listen!, *a series of lectures Wright delivered throughout Europe, he returns to some of the themes of intellectual development and constrained freedom that appear via more personal stories in* Black Boy. *The lectures also significantly expand the scope of Wright's autobiography, closing with an exhortation for the African Gold Coast (now Ghana) to expel Western colonial influences in order to establish a new kind of civilization.*

In the years before his death in 1960 from a heart attack brought on by a long bout with dysentery, Wright completed The Long Dream, *the first book of a projected trilogy; the short story collection* Eight Men, *and began writing haiku. The "man" stories span Wright's career in the dates of their original compositions, and each portray in different ways the effects of racism on perceptions of masculinity, as in the desire for guns and violence in such stories as* "The Man Who Was Almost a Man" *and* "The Man Who Lived Underground."

Since his death Wright has remained a major figure in the American canon, with the public's increasing interest in his later work, as well as continued fascination with Native Son *and* Black Boy.

The texts reprinted in The Pearson Custom Library *issue from the sites of original publication: the journal* New Challenge *for* "Blueprint for Negro Writing"; New Masses *for* "Bright and Morning Star"; *and Wright's collection* Eight Men *for* "The Man Who Was Almost a Man."

John Young
Marshall University

For Further Reading

Primary Works

Uncle Tom's Children: Four Novellas (New York & London: Harper, 1938); reissued in an expanded format as *Uncle Tom's Children: Five Long Stories* (New York & London: Harper, 1940); *Native Son (The Biography of a Young American): A Play in Ten Scenes* (New York & London: Harper, 1940); *How "Bigger" Was Born* (New York: Harper, 1940); *Twelve Million Black Voices: A Folk History of the Negro in the United States* (New York: Viking, 1941); *Black Boy: A Record of Childhood and Youth* (New York & London: Harper, 1945); *Native Son* (Classic Films, 1951); *The Outsider* (New York: Harper, 1953); *Black Power: A Record of Reactions in a Land of Pathos* (New York: Harper, 1954); *Savage Holiday* (New York: Avon, 1954); *The Color Curtain: A Report on the Bandung Conference* (Cleveland & New York: World, 1956); *Pagan Spain: A Report of a Journey into the Past* (New York: Harper, 1957); *White Man, Listen!* (Garden City: Doubleday, 1957); *The Long Dream* (Garden City: Doubleday, 1958); *Eight Men* (Cleveland & New York: World, 1960); *Lawd Today* (New York: Walker, 1965); *The Man Who Lived Underground* (Paris: Aubier-Flammarion, 1971); *The Life and Work of Richard Wright, including Haiku and Unpublished Prose*, ed. David Ray (Kansas City: University of Missouri Press, 1971); *American Hunger* (New York: Harper & Row, 1977); *Richard Wright Reader*, eds. Ellen Wright and Michael Fabre (New York: Harper & Row, 1978); *Works*, 2 vols. (New York: Library of America, 1991); *Rite of Passage* (New York: HarperCollins, 1994); *Haiku: This Other World*, eds. Yoshinobu Hakutani and Robert L. Tener (New York: Arcade, 1998).

Secondary Works

David Bakish, *Richard Wright* (New York: Ungar, 1973); Harold Bloom, ed., *Bigger Thomas* (New York: Chelsea House, 1991); Harold Bloom, ed., *Richard Wright* (New York: Chelsea House, 1987); Robert Bone, *Richard Wright* (Minneapolis: University of Minnesota Press, 1969); Russell C. Brignano, *Richard Wright: An Introduction to the Man and His Works* (Pittsburgh: University of Pittsburgh Press, 1970); Robert J. Butler, ed., *The Critical Response to Richard Wright* (Westport, Conn.: Greenwood, 1995); Robert J. Butler, ed., *Native Son: The Emergence of a New Black Hero* (Boston: Twayne, 1991); Michael Fabre, *Richard Wright, Books & Writers* (Jackson: University of Mississippi Press, 1990); Michael Fabre, *The Unfinished Quest of Richard Wright*, trans. Isabel Barzun (New York: Morrow, 1973); Michael Fabre, *The World of Richard Wright* (Jackson: University of Mississippi Press, 1985); Robert Felgar, *Understanding Richard Wright's Black Boy: A Student Casebook to Issues, Sources, and Historical Documents* (Westport, Conn.: Greenwood, 1998); Henry Louis Gates, Jr., and K.A. Appiah, eds., *Richard Wright: Critical Perspectives Past and Present* (New York: Amistad, 1993); Addison Gayle, *Richard Wright: Ordeal of a Native Son* (Garden City: Anchor Press/Doubleday, 1980); Yoshinobu Hakutani,

Richard Wright and Racial Discourse (Columbia: University of Missouri Press, 1996); Joyce Ann Joyce, *Richard Wright's Art of Tragedy* (Iowa City: University of Iowa Press, 1986); Kenneth Kinnamon, ed., *New Essays on* Native Son (Cambridge & New York: Cambridge University Press, 1990); Edward Margolies, *The Art of Richard Wright* (Carbondale: Southern Illinois University Press, 1969); Dan McCall, *The Example of Richard Wright* (New York: Harcourt, Brace, 1969); Eugene E. Miller, *Voice of a Native Son: The Poetics of Richard Wright* (Jackson: University of Mississippi Press, 1990); Arnold Rampersad, *Richard Wright: A Collection of Critical Essays* (Englewood Cliffs, N.J.: Prentice Hall, 1995); David Ray and Robert M. Farnsworth, eds., *Richard Wright: Impressions and Perspectives* (Ann Arbor: University of Michigan Press, 1973); Hazel Rowley, *Richard Wright: The Life and Times* (New York: Henry Holt, 2001); Virginia Watley Smith, ed., *Richard Wright's Travel Writings: New Perspectives* (Jackson: University of Mississippi Press, 2001); Margaret Walker, *Richard Wright, Daemonic Genius: A Portrait of the Man, A Critical Look at His Work* (New York: Warner, 1988); Constance Webb, *Richard Wright: A Biography* (New York: Putnam, 1968); M. Lynn Weiss, *Gertrude Stein and Richard Wright: The Poetics and Politics of Modernism* (Jackson: University of Mississippi Press, 1998); John A. Williams, *The Most Native of Sons: A Biography of Richard Wright* (Garden City: Doubleday, 1970).

The Man Who Was Almost a Man♦

RICHARD WRIGHT

Dave struck out across the fields, looking homeward through paling light. Whut's the use talkin wid em niggers in the field? Anyhow, his mother was putting supper on the table. Them niggers can't understan nothing. One of these days he was going to get a gun and practice shooting, then they couldn't talk to him as though he were a little boy. He slowed, looking at the ground. Shucks, Ah ain scareda them even ef they are biggern me! Aw, Ah know whut Ahma do. Ahm going by ol Joe's sto n git that Sears Roebuck catlog n look at them guns. Mebbe Ma will lemme buy one when she gits mah pay from ol man Hawkins. Ahma beg her t gimme some money. Ahm ol ernough to hava gun. Ahm seventeen. Almost a man. He strode, feeling his long loose-jointed limbs. Shucks, a man oughta hava little gun aftah he done worked hard all day.

He came in sight of Joe's store. A yellow lantern glowed on the front porch. He mounted steps and went through the screen door, hearing it bang behind him. There was a strong smell of coal oil and mackerel fish. He felt very confident until he saw fat Joe walk in through the rear door, then his courage began to ooze.

"Howdy, Dave! Whutcha want?"

"How yuh, Mistah Joe? Aw, Ah don wanna buy nothing. Ah jus wanted t see ef yuhd lemme look at tha catlog erwhile."

"Sure! You wanna see it here?"

"Nawsuh. Ah wants t take it home wid me. Ah'll bring it back termorrow when Ah come in from the fiels."

"You plannin on buying something?"

"Yessuh."

"Your ma lettin you have your own money now?"

"Shucks. Mistah Joe, Ahm gittin t be a man like anybody else!"

From *Eight Men* by Richard Wright. Copyright © 1961 by Richard Wright. Reprinted by permission of Routledge, Inc., part of the Taylor & Francis Group.

♦"The Man Who Was Almost a Man" first appeared as the opening piece in *Eight Men*, a 1961 collection of Wright's "Man" stories. *Harper's Bazaar* published an earlier and shorter version, titled "Almos' a Man," in 1940; it was also selected for the *O. Henry Award Prize Stories* volume for that year. In "Almos' a Man" the main character is Dave, rather than Dan, and he lives with his wife and child, rather than with his parents.

Joe laughed and wiped his greasy white face with a red bandanna.

"Whut you plannin on buyin?"

Dave looked at the floor, scratched his head, scratched his thigh, and smiled. Then he looked up shyly.

"Ah'll tell yuh, Mistah Joe, ef yuh promise yuh won't tell."

"I promise."

"Waal, Ahma buy a gun."

"A gun? What you want with a gun?"

"Ah wanna keep it."

"You ain't nothing but a boy. You don't need a gun."

"Aw, lemme have the catlog, Mistah Joe. Ah'll bring it back."

Joe walked through the rear door. Dave was elated. He looked around at barrels of sugar and flour. He heard Joe coming back. He craned his neck to see if he were bringing the book. Yeah, he's got it. Gawddog, he's got it!

"Here, but be sure you bring it back. It's the only one I got."

"Sho, Mistah Joe."

"Say, if you wanna buy a gun, why don't you buy one from me? I gotta gun to sell."

"Will it shoot?"

"Sure it'll shoot."

"Whut kind is it?"

"Oh, it's kinda old . . . a left-hand Wheeler. A pistol. A big one."

"Is it got bullets in it?"

"It's loaded."

"Kin Ah see it?"

"Where's your money?"

"What yuh wan fer it?"

"I'll let you have it for two dollars."

"Just two dollahs? Shucks, Ah could buy tha when Ah git mah pay."

"I'll have it here when you want it."

"Awright, suh. Ah be in fer it."

He went through the door, hearing it slam again behind him. Ahma git some money from Ma n buy me a gun! Only two dollahs! He tucked the thick catalogue under his arm and hurried.

"Where yuh been, boy?" His mother held a steaming dish of black-eyed peas.

"Aw, Ma, Ah jus stopped down the road t talk wid the boys."

"Yuh know bettah t keep suppah waitin."

He sat down, resting the catalogue on the edge of the table.

"Yuh git up from there and git to the well n wash yosef! Ah ain feedin no hogs in mah house!"

She grabbed his shoulder and pushed him. He stumbled out of the room, then came back to get the catalogue.

"Whut this?"

"Aw, Ma, it's jusa catlog."

"Who yuh git it from?"

"From Joe, down at the sto."

"Waal, thas good. We kin use it in the outhouse."

"Naw, Ma." He grabbed for it. "Gimme ma catlog, Ma."

She held onto it and glared at him.

"Quit hollerin at me! Whut's wrong wid yuh? Yuh crazy?"

"But Ma, please. It ain mine! It's Joe's! He tol me t bring it back t im termorrow."

She gave up the book. He stumbled down the back steps, hugging the thick book under his arm. When he had splashed water on his face and hands, he groped back to the kitchen and fumbled in a corner for the towel. He bumped into a chair; it clattered to the floor. The catalogue sprawled at his feet. When he had dried his eyes he snatched up the book and held it again under his arm. His mother stood watching him.

"Now, ef yuh gonna act a fool over that ol book, Ah'll take it n burn it up."

"Naw, Ma, please."

"Waal, set down n be still!"

He sat down and drew the oil lamp close. He thumbed page after page, unaware of the food his mother set on the table. His father came in. Then his small brother.

"Whutcha got there, Dave?" his father asked.

"Jusa catlog," he answered, not looking up.

"Yeah, here they is!" His eyes glowed at blue-and-black revolvers. He glanced up, feeling sudden guilt. His father was watching him. He eased the book under the table and rested it on his knees. After the blessing was asked, he ate. He scooped up peas and swallowed fat meat without chewing. Buttermilk helped to wash it down. He did not want to mention money before his father. He would do much better by cornering his mother when she was alone. He looked at his father uneasily out of the edge of his eye.

"Boy, how come yuh don quit foolin wid tha book n eat yo suppah?"

"Yessuh."

"How you n ol man Hawkins gitten erlong?"

"Suh?"

"Can't yuh hear? Why don yuh lissen? Ah ast yu how wuz yuh n ol man Hawkins gittin erlong?"

"Oh, swell, Pa. Ah plows mo lan than anybody over there."

"Waal, yuh oughta keep you mind on whut yuh doin."

"Yessuh."

He poured his plate full of molasses and sopped it up slowly with a chunk of cornbread. When his father and brother had left the kitchen, he still sat and looked again at the guns in the catalogue, longing to muster courage enough to present his case to his mother. Lawd, ef Ah only had tha pretty one! He could almost feel the slickness of the weapon with his fingers. If he had a gun like that he would polish it and keep it shining so it would never rust. N Ah'd keep it loaded, by Gawd!

"Ma?" His voice was hesitant.

"Hunh?"

"Ol man Hawkins give yuh mah money yit?"

"Yeah, but ain no usa yuh thinking bout throwin nona it erway. Ahm keeping tha money sos yuh kin have cloes t go to school this winter."

He rose and went to her side with the open catalogue in his palms. She was washing dishes, her head bent low over a pan. Shyly he raised the book. When he spoke, his voice was husky, faint.

"Ma, Gawd knows Ah wans one of these."

"One of whut?" she asked, not raising her eyes.

"One of these," he said again, not daring even to point. She glanced up at the page, then at him with wide eyes.

"Nigger, is yuh gone plumb crazy?"

"Aw, Ma—"

"Git outta here! Don yuh talk t me bout no gun! Yuh a fool!"

"Ma, Ah kin buy one fer two dollahs."

"Not ef Ah knows it, yuh ain!"

"But yuh promised me one—"

"Ah don care what Ah promised! Yuh ain nothing but a boy yit!"

"Ma, ef yuh lemme buy one Ah'll *never* ast yuh fer nothing no mo."

"Ah tol yuh t git outta here! Yuh ain gonna toucha penny of tha money fer no gun! Thas how come Ah has Mistah Hawkins t pay yo wages t me, cause Ah knows yuh ain got no sense."

"But, Ma, we needa gun. Pa ain got no gun. We needa gun in the house. Yuh kin never tell whut might happen."

"Now don yuh try to maka fool outta me, boy! Ef we did hava gun, yuh wouldn't have it!"

He laid the catalogue down and slipped his arm around her waist.

"Aw, Ma, Ah done worked hard alla summer n ain ast yuh fer nothing, is Ah, now?"

"Thas whut yuh spose t do!"

"But Ma, Ah wans a gun. Yuh kin lemme have two dollahs outta mah money. Please, Ma. I kin give it to Pa. . . . Please, Ma! Ah loves yuh, Ma."

When she spoke her voice came soft and low.

"What yu wan wida gun, Dave? Yuh don need no gun. Yuh'll git in trouble. N ef yo pa jus thought Ah let yuh have money t buy a gun he'd hava fit."

"Ah'll hide it, Ma. It ain but two dollahs."

"Lawd, chil, whut's wrong wid yuh?"

"Ain nothin wrong, Ma. Ahm almos a man now. Ah wans a gun."

"Who gonna sell yuh a gun?"

"Ol Joe at the sto."

"N it don cos but two dollahs?"

"Thas all, Ma. Jus two dollahs. Please, Ma."

She was stacking the plates away; her hands moved slowly, reflectively. Dave kept an anxious silence. Finally, she turned to him.

"Ah'll let yuh git tha gun ef yuh promise me one thing."

"What's tha, Ma?"

"Yuh bring it straight back t me, yuh hear? It be fer Pa."

"Yessum! Lemme go now, Ma."

She stooped, turned slightly to one side, raised the hem of her dress, rolled down the top of her stocking, and came up with a slender wad of bills.

"Here," she said. "Lawd knows yuh don need no gun. But yer pa does. Yuh bring it right back t me, yuh hear? Ahma put it up. Now ef yuh don, Ahma have yuh pa lick yuh so hard yuh won fergit it."

"Yessum."

He took the money, ran down the steps, and across the yard.

"Dave! Yuuuuuh Daaaaave!"

He heard, but he was not going to stop now. "Now, Lawd!"

The first movement he made the following morning was to reach under his pillow for the gun. In the gray light of dawn he held it loosely, feeling a sense of power. Could kill a man with a gun like this. Kill anybody, black or white. And if he were holding his gun in his hand, nobody could run over him; they would have to respect him. It was a big gun, with a long barrel and a heavy handle. He raised and lowered it in his hand, marveling at its weight.

He had not come straight home with it as his mother had asked; instead he had stayed out in the fields, holding the weapon in his hand, aiming it now and then at some imaginary foe. But he had not fired it; he had been afraid that his father might hear. Also he was not sure he knew how to fire it.

To avoid surrendering the pistol he had not come into the house until he knew that they were all asleep. When his mother had tiptoed to his bedside late that night and demanded the gun, he had first played possum; then he had told her that the gun was hidden outdoors, that he would bring it to her in the morning. Now he lay turning it slowly in his hands. He broke it, took out the cartridges, felt them, and then put them back.

He slid out of bed, got a long strip of old flannel from a trunk, wrapped the gun in it, and tied it to his naked thigh while it was still loaded. He did not go in to breakfast. Even though it was not yet daylight, he started for Jim Hawkins' plantation. Just as the sun was rising he reached the barns where the mules and plows were kept.

"Hey! That you, Dave?"

He turned. Jim Hawkins stood eying him suspiciously.

"What're yuh doing here so early?"

"Ah didn't know Ah wuz gittin up so early, Mistah Hawkins. Ah was fixin t hitch up ol Jenny n take her t the fiels."

"Good. Since you're so early, how about plowing that stretch down by the woods?"

"Suits me, Mistah Hawkins."

"O.K. Go to it!"

He hitched Jenny to a plow and started across the fields. Hot dog! This was just what he wanted. If he could get down by the woods, he could shoot his gun and nobody would hear. He walked behind the plow, hearing the traces creaking, feeling the gun tied tight to his thigh.

When he reached the woods, he plowed two whole rows before he decided to take out the gun. Finally, he stopped, looked in all directions, then untied the gun and held it in his hand. He turned to the mule and smiled.

"Know whut this is, Jenny? Naw, yuh wouldn know! Yuhs jusa ol mule! Anyhow, this is a gun, n it kin shoot, by Gawd!"

He held the gun at arm's length. Whut t hell, Ahma shoot this thing! He looked at Jenny again.

"Lissen here, Jenny! When Ah pull this ol trigger, Ah don wan yuh t run n acka fool now!"

Jenny stood with head down, her short ears pricked straight. Dave walked off about twenty feet, held the gun far out from him at arm's length, and turned his head. Hell, he told himself, Ah ain afraid. The gun felt loose in his fingers; he waved it wildly for a moment. The he shut his eyes and tightened his forefinger. Bloom! A report half deafened him and he thought his right hand was torn from his arm. He heard Jenny whinnying and galloping over the field, and he found himself on his knees, squeezing his fingers hard between his legs. His hand was numb; he jammed it into his mouth, trying to warm it, trying to stop the pain. The gun lay at his feet. He did not quite know what had happened. He stood up and stared at the gun as though it were a living thing. He gritted his teeth and kicked the gun. Yuh almos broke mah arm! He turned to look for Jenny; she was far over the fields, tossing her head and kicking wildly.

"Hol on there, ol mule!"

When he caught up with her she stood trembling, walling her big white eyes at him. The plow was far away; the traces had broken. Then Dave stopped short, looking, not believing. Jenny was bleeding. Her left side was red and wet with blood. He went closer. Lawd, have mercy! Wondah did Ah shoot this mule? He grabbed for Jenny's mane. She flinched, snorted, whirled, tossing her head.

"Hol on now! Hol on."

Then he saw the hole in Jenny's side, right between the ribs. It was round, wet, red. A crimson stream streaked down the front leg, flowing fast. Good

Gawd! Ah wuzn't shootin at tha mule. He felt panic. He knew he had to stop that blood, or Jenny would bleed to death. He had never seen so much blood in all his life. He chased the mule for half a mile, trying to catch her. Finally she stopped, breathing hard, stumpy tail half arched. He caught her mane and led her back to where the plow and gun lay. Then he stopped and grabbed handfuls of damp black earth and tried to plug the bullet hole. Jenny shuddered, whinnied, and broke from him.

"Hol on! Hol on now!"

He tried to plug it again, but blood came anyhow. His fingers were hot and sticky. He rubbed dirt into his palms, trying to dry them. Then again he attempted to plug the bullet hole, but Jenny shied away, kicking her heels high. He stood helpless. He had to do something. He ran at Jenny; she dodged him. He watched a red stream of blood flow down Jenny's leg and form a bright pool at her feet.

"Jenny . . . Jenny," he called weakly.

His lips trembled. She's bleeding t death! He looked in the direction of home, wanting to go back, wanting to get help. But he saw the pistol lying in the damp black clay. He had a queer feeling that if he only did something, this would not be; Jenny would not be there bleeding to death.

When he went to her this time, she did not move. She stood with sleepy, dreamy eyes; and when he touched her she gave a low-pitched whinny and knelt to the ground, her front knees slopping in blood.

"Jenny . . . Jenny. . ." he whispered.

For a long time she held her neck erect; then her head sank, slowly. Her ribs swelled with a mighty heave and she went over.

Dave's stomach felt empty, very empty. He picked up the gun and held it gingerly between his thumb and forefinger. He buried it at the foot of a tree. He took a stick to cover the pool of blood with dirt—but what was the use? There was Jenny lying with her mouth open and her eyes walled and glassy. He could not tell Jim Hawkins he had shot his mule. But he had to tell something. Yeah, Ah'll tell em Jenny started gittin wil n fell on the joint of the plow. . . . But that would hardly happen to a mule. He walked across the field slowly, head down.

It was sunset. Two of Jim Hawkins' men were over near the edge of the woods digging a hole in which to bury Jenny. Dave was surrounded by a knot of people, all of whom were looking down at the dead mule.

"I don't see how in the world it happened," said Jim Hawkins for the tenth time.

The crowd parted and Dave's mother, father, and small brother pushed into the center.

"Where Dave?" his mother called.

"There he is," said Jim Hawkins.

His mother grabbed him.

"Whut happened, Dave? Whut yuh done?"

"Nothin."

"C mon, boy, talk," his father said.

Dave took a deep breath and told the story he knew nobody believed.

"Waal," he drawled. "Ah brung ol Jenny down here sos Ah could do mah plowin. Ah plowed bout two rows, just like yuh see." He stopped and pointed at the long rows of upturned earth. "Then somethin musta been wrong wid ol Jenny. She wouldn ack right a-tall. She started snortin n kickin her heels. Ah tried t hol her, but she pulled erway, rearin n goin in. Then when the point of the plow was stickin up in the air, she swung erroun n twisted herself back on it. . . . She stuck herself n started t bleed. N fo Ah could do anything, she wuz dead."

"Did you ever hear of anything like that in all your life?" asked Jim Hawkins.

There were white and black standing in the crowd. They murmured. Dave's mother came close to him and looked hard into his face. "Tell the truth, Dave," she said.

"Looks like a bullet hole to me," said one man.

"Dave, whut yuh do wid the gun?" his mother asked.

The crowd surged in, looking at him. He jammed his hands into his pockets, shook his head slowly from left to right, and backed away. His eyes were wide and painful.

"Did he hava gun?" asked Jim Hawkins.

"By Gawd, Ah tol yuh tha wuz a gun wound," said a man, slapping his thigh.

His father caught his shoulders and shook him till his teeth rattled.

"Tell whut happened, yuh rascal! Tell whut . . ."

Dave looked at Jenny's stiff legs and began to cry.

"Whut yuh do wid tha gun?" his mother asked.

"What wuz he doin wida gun?" his father asked.

"Come on and tell the truth," said Hawkins. "Ain't nobody going to hurt you . . ."

His mother crowded close to him.

"Did yuh shoot tha mule, Dave?"

Dave cried, seeing blurred white and black faces.

"Ahh ddinn gggo tt sshooot hher . . . Ah ssswear ffo Gawd Ahh ddin. . . . Ah wuz a-tryin t sssee ef the old gggun would sshoot—"

"Where yuh git the gun from?" his father asked.

"Ah got it from Joe, at the sto."

"Where yuh git the money?"

"Ma give it t me."

"He kept worryin me, Bob. Ah had t. Ah tol im t bring the gun right back t me. . . . It was fer yuh, the gun."

"But how yuh happen to shoot that mule?" asked Jim Hawkins.

"Ah wuzn shootin at the mule, Mistah Hawkins. The gun jumped when Ah pulled the trigger . . . N fo Ah knowed anythin Jenny was there a-bleedin."

Somebody in the crowd laughed. Jim Hawkins walked close to Dave and looked into his face.

"Well, looks like you have bought you a mule, Dave."

"Ah swear fo Gawd, Ah didn go t kill the mule, Mistah Hawkins!"

"But you killed her!"

All the crowd was laughing now. They stood on tiptoe and poked heads over one another's shoulders.

"Well, boy, looks like yuh done bought a dead mule! Hahaha!"

"Ain tha ershame."

"Hohohohoho."

Dave stood, head down, twisting his feet in the dirt.

"Well, you needn't worry about it, Bob," said Jim Hawkins to Dave's father. "Just let the boy keep on working and pay me two dollars a month."

"Whut yuh wan fer yo mule, Mistah Hawkins?"

Jim Hawkins screwed up his eyes.

"Fifty dollars."

"Whut yuh do wid tha gun?" Dave's father demanded.

Dave said nothing.

"Yuh wan me t take a tree n beat yuh till yuh talk!"

"Nawsuh!"

"Whut yuh do wid it?"

"Ah throwed it erway."

"Where?"

"Ah . . . Ah throwed it in the creek."

"Waal, c mon home. N firs thing in the mawnin git to tha creek n fin tha gun."

"Yessuh."

"Whut yuh pay fer it?"

"Two dollahs."

"Take tha gun n git yo money back n carry it to Mistah Hawkins, yuh hear? N don fergit Ahma lam you black bottom good fer this! Now march yosef on home, suh!"

Dave turned and walked slowly. He heard people laughing. Dave glared, his eyes welling with tears. Hot anger bubbled in him. Then he swallowed and stumbled on.

That night Dave did not sleep. He was glad that he had gotten out of killing the mule so easily, but he was hurt. Something hot seemed to turn over inside him each time he remembered how they had laughed. He tossed on his bed, feeling his hard pillow. N Pa says he's gonna beat me . . . He remembered other beatings, and his back quivered. Naw, naw, Ah sho don wan im t beat me tha way no mo. Dam em all! Nobody ever gave him anything. All he did was work. They treat me like a mule, n then they beat me. He gritted his teeth. N Ma had t tell on me.

Well, if he had to, he would take old man Hawkins that two dollars. But that meant selling the gun. And he wanted to keep that gun. Fifty dollars for a dead mule.

He turned over, thinking how he had fired the gun. He had an itch to fire it again. Ef other men kin shoota gun, by Gawd, Ah kin! He was still, listening. Mebbe they all sleepin now. The house was still. He heard the soft breathing of his brother. Yes, now! He would go down and get that gun and see if he could fire it! He eased out of bed and slipped into overalls.

The moon was bright. He ran almost all the way to the edge of the woods. He stumbled over the ground, looking for the spot where he had buried the gun. Yeah, here it is. Like a hungry dog scratching for a bone, he pawed it up. He puffed his black cheeks and blew dirt from the trigger and barrel. He broke it and found four cartridges unshot. He looked around; the fields were filled with silence and moonlight. He clutched the gun stiff and hard in his fingers. But, as soon as he wanted to pull the trigger, he shut his eyes and turned his head. Naw, Ah can't shoot wid mah eyes closed n mah head turned. With effort he held his eyes open; then he squeezed. *Blooooom!* He was stiff, not breathing. The gun was still in his hands. Dammit, he'd done it! He fired again. *Blooooom!* He smiled. *Blooooom! Blooooom! Click, click.* There! It was empty. If anybody could shoot a gun, he could. He put the gun into his hip pocket and started across the fields.

When he reached the top of a ridge he stood straight and proud in the moonlight, looking at Jim Hawkins' big white house, feeling the gun sagging in his pocket. Lawd, ef Ah had just one mo bullet Ah'd taka shot at tha house. Ah'd like t scare ol man Hawkins jusa little. . . . Jusa enough t let im know Dave Saunders is a man.

To his left the road curved, running to the tracks of the Illinois Central. He jerked his head, listening. From far off came a faint *hooooof-hooooof; hooooof-hooooof.* . . . He stood rigid. Two dollahs a mont. Les see now. . . . Tha means it'll take bout two years. Shucks! Ah'll be dam!

He started down the road, toward the tracks. Yeah, here she comes! He stood beside the track and held himself stiffly. Here she comes, erroun the ben . . . C mon, yuh slow poke! C mon! He had his hand on his gun; something quivered in his stomach. Then the train thundered past, the gray and brown box cars rumbling and clinking. He gripped the gun tightly; then he jerked his hand out of his pocket. Ah betcha Bill wouldn't do it! Ah betcha . . . The cars slid past, steel grinding upon steel. Ahm ridin yuh ternight, so hep me Gawd! He was hot all over. He hesitated just a moment; then he grabbed, pulled atop of a car, and lay flat. He felt his pocket; the gun was still there. Ahead the long rails were glinting in the moonlight, stretching away, away to somewhere, somewhere where he could be a man . . . [1961]

Workshop 4: The Scales of Justice and Mercy

ZORA NEALE HURSTON
1891–1960

The daughter of a Baptist Reverend and his intelligent, literate wife, Hurston was born and raised in Eatonville, Florida, a self-governing, all-black rural town that buffered her, in part, from the racist horrors of the Jim Crow South. The death of her mother when Hurston was nine threw her family into turmoil. In the years that followed, Hurston attended school only intermittently. She lived with various relatives, worked as a maid, and became a wardrobe mistress for a traveling Gilbert and Sullivan repertory company. Her work with the theater troupe took her to Baltimore where, determined to gain schooling, she petitioned her way into the Morgan Academy. Armed with only a change of clothes and her scintillating raw intelligence, she soon made up for her lack of formal academic training. Upon leaving high school in 1918, she gained admission to the prestigious "capstone of Negro education," Howard University in Washington, D.C. While working her way part-time through Howard, Hurston began to write fiction and was eventually elected to the campus literary club, the Stylus. The brainchild of Howard's influential young philosophy professor, Alain Locke, a Harvard graduate and the country's first black Rhodes Scholar, the Stylus served to introduce Hurston to a number of the leading African-American thinkers and writers of her day— the luminaries of the New Negro Renaissance. In 1925, Hurston submitted "Spunk," a story based on her Eatonville past, and Color Stuck, *a play about Florida folk life, to a literary competition run by* Opportunity, *the journal of the Urban League edited by Charles S. Johnson. Both pieces won prizes and, encouraged by her success, Hurston packed up her manuscripts and moved to New York City to seek her fortune as a writer.*

Although Hurston came to New York as a writer, she soon found herself deeply engaged in another, related, vocation. Upon arriving in the city, Hurston won a scholarship to Barnard College, the woman's division of Columbia University, where she embarked on the study of anthropology with the renowned German scientist Franz Boas. Fascinated by the African-American folk materials and traditions of her childhood, Hurston began to analyze vernacular African-American culture through the lens of social science. Her transmutations of folk materials into fiction, and her involvement in the intellectual whirl of the New Negro Renaissance coincided with her studies. Hurston's ongoing commitment to her folk heritage ultimately constituted one of her most important contributions to the New Negro movement and literary modernism generally. Dedicated to "race improvement," many New Negro writers and thinkers, W. E. B. DuBois among them, recommended against the literary use of what they considered low-brow images of "common" black life. Locke and others feared that such images would only further reinforce negative African-American stereotypes that whites were predisposed to accept as universal truths. Like Langston Hughes, however, Hurston considered African-American vernacular materials absolutely essential to her art. Unwilling to uphold what she deemed bourgeois standards of "proper" literary subject matter, Hurston insisted on writing what she knew. Hurston understood better than many of her colleagues that folk materials—tall tales, horror stories, sly jokes—constituted shared forms of communication, often subversive, that granted African Americans a sense of group identity apart from white culture. During her two short years in New York, she forged an aesthetic that performed a vital sense of community that reached beyond the circle of New York's black intelligentsia.

In 1927, Hurston left New York to pursue anthropological research in central Florida with the help of a prestigious Columbia fellowship. Working directly for Boas, Hurston set out to collect jokes, stories, and songs from her fellow African-American Floridians. Her collection efforts, however, did not go well and she returned to New York with what she felt were mostly redundant and useless materials. In the midst of her attempts to assemble her data, Hurston met Mrs. Charlotte Mason, a charismatic, wealthy patron of African-American art. Mason, then Langston Hughes's patron, supported Hurston, giving her the resources to return to the South and repair the errors of her previous anthropological expeditions. Between 1927 and 1931, Hurston worked under contract to Mason, collecting a lifetime's worth of vital folk materials that would ultimately make her career when published in the mid-1930s. In the spring of 1930, Hurston coupled her scientific project with a literary one when she and Langston Hughes began to collaborate on the comic folk play, Mule Bone. *Due to a series of misunderstandings, perceived and actual slights, and arguments over the content and ownership of the play, the relationship between Hughes and Hurston deteriorated to the point of legal action and the play was never produced. Hurston turned her full attention to crafting her first book of African-American folklore,* Mules and Men, *which she finished in late 1932.*

Hurston's anthropological book, however, did not find a publisher until she had proved herself a novelist. In 1933, Hurston published her story "The Gilded Six-Bits" in Story *magazine. The piece caught the eye of the publisher Bertram Lippincott, who queried Hurston about her plans in regard to a novel. Lippincott's interest resulted in Hurston's first book of fiction,* Jonah's Gourd Vine (1934). *On the strength of that book Lippincott agreed to publish*

Mules and Men, *which appeared in 1935. Both books, however, ran afoul of criticism from a number of black intellectuals. Hurston, they claimed, fell short of her true potential as a chronicler of African-American experience in that she tended to ignore the harsher aspects of southern black life. The criticism would haunt the course of Hurston's career.*

In 1936, Hurston won a Guggenheim Fellowship to collect folklore in the West Indies. While gathering material for her second book of folklore, Tell My Horse *(1938), Hurston stopped in Haiti. The atmosphere of the country triggered long suppressed memories and she soon found herself working furiously on a second novel,* Their Eyes Were Watching God. *In an astonishing burst of creativity, Hurston completed the book in less than two months and Lippincott published the novel in late 1937. After a brief stint with the Depression-driven Federal Writer's Project in Florida, Hurston took a job teaching drama at North Carolina College. While in Durham, she witnessed the publication of her third novel,* Moses, Man of the Mountain, *in 1939.*

By the 1940s, however, American interest in African-American folk materials had waned. The collections of folklore that had intrigued audiences before the start of World War II seemed dated, insular, and frivolous to many in the light of the rise of global fascism. Following the publication of her successful autobiography, Dust Tracks on a Road, *in 1942, Hurston turned her talents to journalism and began publishing pieces in a number of popular periodicals, many of them concerned with racial issues in America. Her change of genre, however, proved unproductive for her fiction. She published only one more novel in her lifetime,* Seraph on the Suwanee *(1948), her consciously experimental attempt to write a story with white protagonists. The novel confused her most faithful readers while failing to garner the wider audience Hurston hoped to capture. After a subsequent decade-long struggle to make a living with her writing, Hurston died in poverty and relative obscurity in 1960.*

Students encountering Hurston's work for the first time would do well to remember that Hurston considered herself a scientist as well as a fiction writer. Her anthropological work and her creative work frequently intersected. Indeed, one of Hurston's great and enduring themes of her fiction remains the strange blindness that racism breeds in regard to behavior. As an anthropologist, Hurston understood that the African-American cultural rituals that seemed silly or irrational to white outsiders in fact served carefully construed purposes within their respective communities. Throughout her fiction, Hurston frequently challenges her readers to confront her apparently "light" folktales as carefully constructed, complex performances designed to create a special sense of shared experience.

The versions of Hurston's stories printed here issue from The Complete Stories, *introduction by Henry Louis Gates, Jr. and Seiglinde Lemke (HarperCollins, 1995).*

For Further Reading

Primary Works

Jonah's Gourd Vine (Philadelphia & London: Lippincott, 1934); *Mules and Men* (Philadelphia & London: Lippincott, 1935); *Their Eyes Were Watching God* (Philadelphia & London: Lippincott, 1937); *Tell My Horse* (Philadelphia: Lippincott, 1938); republished as *Voodoo Gods* (London: Dent, 1939); *Moses, Man of the Mountain* (Philadelphia: Lippincott, 1939); republished as *The Man of the Mountain* (London: Dent, 1941); *Dust Tracks on a Road* (Philadelphia: Lippincott, 1942; London: Hutchinson, 1944); *Seraph on the Suwanee* (New York: Scribners, 1948); *I Love Myself When I Am Laughing . . . & Then Again When I Am Looking Mean & Impressive,* edited by Alice Walker (Old Westbury, N.Y.: Feminist Press, 1979); *The Sanctified Church* (Berkeley: Turtle Island Foundation, 1981); *Spunk, The Selected Stories of Zora Neale Hurston* (Berkeley: Turtle Island Foundation, 1985); *The Complete Stories* (New York: HarperCollins, 1995).

Secondary Works

Harold Bloom, ed., *Zora Neale Hurston* (New York: Chelsea House, 1986); Trudier Harris, *The Power of the Porch: The Storyteller's Craft in Zora Neale Hurston* (Athens: University of Georgia Press, 1996); Robert E. Hemenway, *Zora Neale Hurston: A Literary Biography* (Urbana: University of Chicago Press, 1977); Karla F. Holloway, *The Character of the Word: The Texts of Zora Neale Hurston* (New York: Greenwood Press, 1987); Susan Edwards Meisenhelder, *Hitting a Straight Lick with a Crooked Stick: Race and Gender in the Work of Zora Neale Hurston* (Tuscaloosa: University of Alabama Press, 1999); Adele S. Newson, *Zora Neale Hurston: A Reference Guide* (Boston: G. K. Hall, 1987); Eric J. Sundquist, *The Hammers of Creation: Folk Culture in Modern African-American Fiction* (Athens: University of Georgia Press, 1992); Alice Walker, "In Search of Zora Neale Hurston," *Ms.,* 3 (March 1975): 74–90.

Sweat[*]

ZORA NEALE HURSTON

It was eleven o'clock of a Spring night in Florida. It was Sunday. Any other night, Delia Jones would have been in bed for two hours by this time. But she was a washwoman, and Monday morning meant a great deal to her. So she collected the soiled clothes on Saturday when she returned the clean things. Sunday night after church, she sorted them and put the white things to soak. It saved her almost a half day's start. A great hamper in the bedroom held the clothes that she brought home. It was so much neater than a number of bundles lying around.

She squatted in the kitchen floor beside the great pile of clothes, sorting them into small heaps according to color, and humming a song in a mournful key, but wondering through it all where Sykes, her husband, had gone with her horse and buckboard.

Just then something long, round, limp, and black fell upon her shoulders and slithered to the floor beside her. A great terror took hold of her. It softened her knees and dried her mouth so that it was a full minute before she could cry out or move. Then she saw that it was the big bull whip her husband liked to carry when he drove.

She lifted her eyes to the door and saw him standing there bent over with laughter at her fright. She screamed at him.

"Sykes, what you throw dat whip on me like dat? You know it would skeer me—looks just like a snake, an' you knows how skeered Ah is of snakes."

"Course Ah knowed it! That's how come Ah done it." He slapped his leg with his hand and almost rolled on the ground in his mirth. "If you such a big fool dat you got to have a fit over a earth worm or a string, Ah don't keer how bad Ah skeer you."

"You ain't got no business doing it. Gawd knows it's a sin. Some day Ah'm gointuh drop dead from some of yo' foolishness. 'Nother thing, where you been wid mah rig? Ah feeds dat pony. He ain't fuh you to be drivin' wid no bull whip."

---

[*]"Sweat" first appeared in *Fire!!* in November 1926.

"You sho' is one aggravatin' nigger woman!" he declared and stepped into the room. She resumed her work and did not answer him at once. "Ah done tole you time and again to keep them white folks' clothes outa dis house."

He picked up the whip and glared down at her. Delia went on with her work. She went out into the yard and returned with a galvanized tub and sat it on the washbench. She saw that Sykes had kicked all of the clothes together again, and now stood in her way truculently, his whole manner hoping, *praying*, for an argument. But she walked calmly around him and commenced to re-sort the things.

"Next time, Ah'm gointer kick 'em outdoors," he threatened as he struck a match along the leg of his corduroy breeches.

Delia never looked up from her work, and her thin, stooped shoulders sagged further.

"Ah ain't for no fuss t'night, Sykes. Ah just come from taking sacrament at the church house."

He snorted scornfully. "Yeah, you just come from de church house on a Sunday night, but heah you is gone to work on them clothes. You ain't nothing but a hypocrite. One of them amen-corner Christians—sing, whoop, and shout, then come home and wash white folks' clothes on the Sabbath."

He stepped roughly upon the whitest pile of things, kicking them helter-skelter as he crossed the room. His wife gave a little scream of dismay, and quickly gathered them together again.

"Sykes, you quit grindin' dirt into these clothes! How can Ah git through by Sat'day if Ah don't start on Sunday?"

"Ah don't keer if you never git through. Anyhow, Ah done promised Gawd and a couple of other men, Ah ain't gointer have it in mah house. Don't gimme no lip neither, else Ah'll throw 'em out and put mah fist up side yo' head to boot."

Delia's habitual meekness seemed to slip from her shoulders like a blown scarf. She was on her feet; her poor little body, her bare knuckly hands bravely defying the strapping hulk before her.

"Looka heah, Sykes, you done gone too fur. Ah been married to you fur fifteen years, and Ah been takin' in washin' fur fifteen years. Sweat, sweat, sweat! Work and sweat, cry and sweat, pray and sweat!"

"What's that got to do with me?" he asked brutally.

"What's it got to do with you, Sykes? Mah tub of suds is filled yo' belly with vittles more times than yo' hands is filled it. Mah sweat is done paid for this house and Ah reckon Ah kin keep on sweatin' in it."

She seized the iron skillet from the stove and struck a defensive pose, which act surprised him greatly, coming from her. It cowed him and he did not strike her as he usually did.

"Naw you won't," she panted, "that ole snaggle-toothed black woman you runnin' with aint comin' heah to pile up on *mah* sweat and blood. You aint paid for nothin' on this place, and Ah'm gointer stay right heah till Ah'm toted out foot foremost."

"Well, you better quit gittin' me riled up, else they'll be totin' you out sooner than you expect. Ah'm so tired of you Ah don't know whut to do. Gawd! How Ah hates skinny wimmen!"

A little awed by this new Delia, he sidled out of the door and slammed the back gate after him. He did not say where he had gone, but she knew too well. She knew very well that he would not return until nearly daybreak also. Her work over, she went on to bed but not to sleep at once. Things had come to a pretty pass!

She lay awake, gazing upon the debris that cluttered their matrimonial trail. Not an image left standing along the way. Anything like flowers had long ago been drowned in the salty stream that had been pressed from her heart. Her tears, her sweat, her blood. She had brought love to the union and he had brought a longing after the flesh. Two months after the wedding, he had given her the first brutal beating. She had the memory of his numerous trips to Orlando with all of his wages when he had returned to her penniless, even before the first year had passed. She was young and soft then, but now she thought of her knotty, muscled limbs, her harsh knuckly hands, and drew herself up into an unhappy little ball in the middle of the big feather bed. Too late now to hope for love, even if it were not Bertha it would be someone else. This case differed from the others only in that she was bolder than the others. Too late for everything except her little home. She had built it for her old days, and planted one by one the trees and flowers there. It was lovely to her, lovely.

Somehow, before sleep came, she found herself saying aloud: "Oh well, whatever goes over the Devil's back, is got to come under his belly. Sometime or ruther, Sykes, like everybody else, is gointer reap his sowing." After that she was able to build a spiritual earthworks against her husband. His shells could no longer reach her. *Amen.* She went to sleep and slept until he announced his presence in bed by kicking her feet and rudely snatching the cover away.

"Gimme some kivah heah, an' git yo' damn foots over on yo' own side! Ah oughter mash you in yo' mouf fuh drawing dat skillet on me."

Delia went clear to the rail without answering him. A triumphant indifference to all that he was or did.

The week was as full of work for Delia as all other weeks, and Saturday found her behind her little pony, collecting and delivering clothes.

It was a hot, hot day near the end of July. The village men on Joe Clarke's porch even chewed cane listlessly. They did not hurl the cane-knots as usual. They let them dribble over the edge of the porch. Even conversation had collapsed under the heat.

"Heah come Delia Jones," Jim Merchant said, as the shaggy pony came 'round the bend of the road toward them. The rusty buckboard was heaped with baskets of crisp, clean laundry.

"Yep," Joe Lindsay agreed. "Hot or col', rain or shine, jes ez reg'lar ez de weeks roll roun' Delia carries 'em an' fetches 'em on Sat'day."

"She better if she wanter eat," said Moss. "Sykes Jones aint wuth de shot an' powder hit would tek tuh kill 'em. Not to *huh* he aint."

"He sho' ain't," Walter Thomas chimed in. "It's too bad, too, cause she wuz a right pretty li'l trick when he got huh. Ah'd uh mah'ied huh mahself if he hadnter beat me to it."

Delia nodded briefly at the men as she drove past.

"Too much knockin' will ruin *any* 'oman. He done beat huh 'nough tuh kill three women, let 'lone change they looks," said Elijah Moseley. "How Syke skin stommuck dat big black greasy Mogul he's layin' roun' wid, gits me. Ah swear dat eight-rock couldn't kiss a sardine can Ah done thowed out de back do' 'way las' yeah."

"Aw, she's fat, thass how come. He's allus been crazy 'bout fat women," put in Merchant. "He'd a' been tied up wid one long time ago if he could a' found one tuh have him. Did Ah tell yuh 'bout him come sidlin' roun' *mah* wife—bringin' her a basket uh pee-cans outa his yard fuh a present? Yessir, mah wife! She tol' him tuh take 'em right straight back home, cause Delia works so hard ovah dat washtub she reckon everything on de place taste lak sweat an' soapsuds. Ah jus' wisht Ah'd a' caught 'im 'roun' dere! Ah'd a' made his hips ketch on fiah down dat shell road."

"Ah know he done it, too. Ah sees 'im grinnin' at every 'oman dat passes," Walter Thomas said. "But even so, he useter eat some mighty big hunks uh humble pie tuh git dat lil' 'oman he got. She wuz ez pritty ez a speckled pup! Dat wuz fifteen yeahs ago. He useter be so skeered uh losin' huh, she could make him do some parts of a husband's duty. Dey never wuz de same in de mind."

"There oughter be a law about him," said Lindsay. "He aint fit tuh carry guts tuh a bear."

Clarke spoke for the first time. "Taint no law on earth dat kin make a man be decent if it ain't in 'im. There's plenty men dat takes a wife lak dey do a joint uh sugar-cane. It's round, juicy, an' sweet when dey gits it. But dey squeeze an' grind, squeeze an' grind an' wring tell dey wring every drop uh pleasure dat's in 'em out. When dey's satisfied dat dey is wrung dry, dey treats 'em jes' lak dey do a cane-chew. Dey thows 'em away. Dey knows whut dey is doin' while dey is at it, an' hates theirselves fuh it but they keeps on hangin' after huh tell she's empty. Den dey hates huh fuh bein' a cane-chew an' in de way."

"We oughter take Sykes an' dat stray 'oman uh his'n down in Lake How-ell swamp an' lay on de rawhide till they cain't say 'Lawd a' mussy.' He allus wuz uh ovahbearin niggah, but since dat white 'oman from up north done teached 'im how to run a automobile, he done got too biggety to live—an' we oughter kill 'im," Old Man Anderson advised.

A grunt of approval went around the porch. But the heat was melting their civic virtue and Elijah Moseley began to bait Joe Clarke.

"Come on, Joe, git a melon outa dere an' slice it up for yo' customers. We'se all sufferin' wid de heat. De bear's done got *me!*"

"Thass right, Joe, a watermelon is jes' whut Ah needs tuh cure de eppizu-dicks." Walter Thomas joined forces with Moseley. "Come on dere, Joe. We all is steady customers an' you aint set us up in a long time. Ah chooses dat long, bowlegged Floridy favorite."

"A god, an' be dough. You all gimme twenty cents and slice away," Clarke retorted. "Ah needs a col' slice m'self. Heah, everybody chip in. Ah'll lend y'all mah meat knife."

The money was all quickly subscribed and the huge melon brought forth. At that moment, Sykes and Bertha arrived. A determined silence fell on the porch and the melon was put away again.

Merchant snapped down the blade of his jack-knife and moved toward the store door.

"Come on in, Joe, an' gimme a slab uh sow belly an' uh pound uh cof-fee—almost fuhgot 'twas Sat'day. Got to git on home." Most of the men left also.

Just then Delia drove past on her way home, as Sykes was ordering mag-nificently for Bertha. It pleased him for Delia to see.

"Git whutsoever yo' heart desires, Honey. Wait a minute, Joe. Give huh two bottles uh strawberry soda-water, uh quart uh parched ground-peas, an' a block uh chewin' gum."

With all this they left the store, with Sykes reminding Bertha that this was his town and she could have it if she wanted it.

The men returned soon after they left, and held their watermelon feast.

"Where did Sykes Jones git da 'oman from nohow?" Lindsay asked.

"Ovah Apopka. Guess dey musta been cleanin' out de town when she lef'. She don't look lak a thing but a hunk uh liver wid hair on it."

"Well, she sho' kin squall," Dave Carter contributed. "When she gits ready tuh laff, she jes' opens huh mouf an' latches it back tuh de las' notch. No ole grandpa alligator down in Lake Bell ain't got nothin' on huh."

Bertha had been in town three months now. Sykes was still paying her room-rent at Della Lewis'—the only house in town that would have taken her in. Sykes took her frequently to Winter Park to "stomps." He still assured her that he was the swellest man in the state.

"Sho' you kin have dat li'l ole house soon's Ah git dat 'oman outa dere. Everything b'longs tuh me an' you sho' kin have it. Ah sho' 'bominates uh skinny 'oman. Lawdy, you sho' is got one portly shape on you! You kin git *anything* you wants. Dis is *mah* town an' you sho' kin have it."

Delia's work-worn knees crawled over the earth in Gethsemane and up the rocks of Calvary many, many times during these months. She avoided the villagers and meeting places in her efforts to be blind and deaf. But Bertha nullified this to a degree, by coming to Delia's house to call Sykes out to her at the gate.

Delia and Sykes fought all the time now with no peaceful interludes. They slept and ate in silence. Two or three times Delia had attempted a timid friendliness, but she was repulsed each time. It was plain that the breaches must remain agape.

The sun had burned July to August. The heat streamed down like a million hot arrows, smiting all things living upon the earth. Grass withered, leaves browned, snakes went blind in shedding, and men and dogs went mad. Dog days!

Delia came home one day and found Sykes there before her. She wondered, but started to go on into the house without speaking, even though he was standing in the kitchen door and she must either stoop under his arm or ask him to move. He made no room for her. She noticed a soap box beside the steps, but paid no particular attention to it, knowing that he must have brought it there. As she was stooping to pass under his outstretched arm, he suddenly pushed her backward, laughingly.

"Look in de box dere Delia, Ah done brung yuh somethin'!"

She nearly fell upon the box in her stumbling, and when she saw what it held, she all but fainted outright.

"Sykes! Sykes, mah Gawd! You take dat rattlesnake 'way from heah! You *gottuh*. Oh, Jesus, have mussy!"

"Ah aint got tuh do nuthin' uh de kin'—fact is Ah aint got tuh do nothin' but die. Taint no use uh you puttin' on airs makin' out lak you skeered uh dat snake—he's gointer stay right heah tell he die. He wouldn't bite me cause Ah knows how tuh handle 'im. Nohow he wouldn't risk breakin' out his fangs 'gin *yo'* skinny laigs."

"Naw, now Sykes, don't keep dat thing 'round heah tuh skeer me tuh death. You knows Ah'm even feared uh earth worms. Thass de biggest snake Ah evah did see. Kill 'im Sykes, please."

"Doan ast me tuh do nothin' fuh yuh. Goin' 'roun' tryin' tuh be so damn astorperious. Naw, Ah ain't gonna kill it. Ah think uh damn sight mo' uh him dan you! Dat's a nice snake an' anybody doan lak 'im kin jes' hit de grit."

The village soon heard that Sykes had the snake, and came to see and ask questions.

"How de hen-fire did you ketch dat six-foot rattler, Sykes?" Thomas asked.

"He's full uh frogs so he cain't hardly move, thass how Ah eased up on 'm. But Ah'm a snake charmer an' knows how tuh handle 'em. Shux, dat ain't nothin'. Ah could ketch one eve'y day if Ah so wanted tuh."

"Whut he needs is a heavy hick'ry club leaned real heavy on his head. Dat's de bes' way tuh charm a rattlesnake."

"Naw, Walt, y'all jes' don't understand dese diamon' backs lak Ah do," said Sykes in a superior tone of voice.

The village agreed with Walter, but the snake stayed on. His box remained by the kitchen door with its screen wire covering. Two or three days later it had digested its meal of frogs and literally came to life. It rattled at every movement in the kitchen or the yard. One day as Delia came down the kitchen steps she saw his chalky-white fangs curved like scimitars hung in the wire meshes. This time she did not run away with averted eyes as usual. She stood for a long time in the doorway in a red fury that grew bloodier for every second that she regarded the creature that was her torment.

That night she broached the subject as soon as Sykes sat down to the table.

"Sykes, Ah wants you tuh take dat snake 'way fum heah. You done starved me an' Ah put up widcher, you done beat me an Ah took dat, but you done kilt all mah insides bringin' dat varmint heah."

Sykes poured out a saucer full of coffee and drank it deliberately before he answered her.

"A whole lot Ah keer 'bout how you feels inside uh out. Dat snake aint goin' no damn wheah till Ah gits ready fuh 'im tuh go. So fur as beatin' is concerned, yuh aint took near all dat you gointer take ef yuh stay 'roun' *me*."

Delia pushed back her plate and got up from the table. "Ah hates you, Sykes," she said calmly. "Ah hates you tuh de same degree dat Ah useter love yuh. Ah done took an' took till mah belly is full up tuh mah neck. Dat's de reason Ah got mah letter fum de church an' moved mah membership tuh Woodbridge—so Ah don't haftuh take no sacrament wid yuh. Ah don't wan- tuh see yuh 'roun' me a-tall. Lay 'roun' wid dat 'oman all yuh wants tuh, but gwan 'way from me an' mah house. Ah hates yuh lak uh suck-egg dog."

Sykes almost let the huge wad of corn bread and collard greens he was chewing fall out of his mouth in amazement. He had a hard time whipping himself up to the proper fury to try to answer Delia.

"Well, Ah'm glad you does hate me. Ah'm sho' tiahed uh you hangin' ontuh me. Ah don't want yuh. Look at yuh stringey ole neck! Yo' rawbony laigs an' arms is enough tuh cut uh man tuh death. You looks jes' lak de devvul's doll-baby tuh *me*. You cain't hate me no worse dan Ah hates you. Ah been hatin' *you* fuh years."

"Yo' ole black hide don't look lak nothin' tuh me, but uh passel uh wrinkled up rubber, wid yo' big ole yeahs flappin' on each side lak uh paih uh buzzard wings. Don't think Ah'm gointuh be run 'way fum mah house neither. Ah'm goin' tuh de white folks 'bout *you*, mah young man, de very nex' time you lay yo' han's on me. Mah cup is done run ovah." Delia said this with no signs of fear and Sykes departed from the house, threatening her, but made not the slightest move to carry out any of them.

That night he did not return at all, and the next day being Sunday, Delia was glad that she did not have to quarrel before she hitched up her pony and drove the four miles to Woodbridge.

She stayed to the night service—"love feast"—which was very warm and full of spirit. In the emotional winds her domestic trials were borne far and wide so that she sang as she drove homeward,

Jurden water, black an' col'
Chills de body, not de soul
An' Ah wantah cross Jurden in uh calm time.

She came from the barn to the kitchen door and stopped.

"Whut's de mattah, ol' satan, you ain't kickin' up yo' racket?" She addressed the snake's box. Complete silence. She went on into the house with a new hope in its birth struggles. Perhaps her threat to go to the white folks had frightened Sykes! Perhaps he was sorry! Fifteen years of misery and suppression had brought Delia to the place where she would hope *anything* that looked towards a way over or through her wall of inhibitions.

She felt in the match-safe behind the stove at once for a match. There was only one there.

"Dat niggah wouldn't fetch nothin' heah tuh save his rotten neck, but he kin run thew whut Ah brings quick enough. Now he done toted off nigh on tuh haff uh box uh matches. He done had dat 'oman heah in mah house, too."

Nobody but a woman could tell how she knew this even before she struck the match. But she did and it put her into a new fury.

Presently she brought in the tubs to put the white things to soak. This time she decided she need not bring the hamper out of the bedroom; she would go in there and do the sorting. She picked up the pot-bellied lamp and went in. The room was small and the hamper stood hard by the foot of the white iron bed. She could sit and reach through the bedposts—resting as she worked.

"Ah wantah cross Jurden in uh calm time." She was singing again. The mood of the "love feast" had returned. She threw back the lid of the basket almost gaily. Then, moved by both horror and terror, she sprung back toward the door. *There lay the snake in the basket!* He moved sluggishly at first, but even as she turned round and round, jumped up and down in an insanity of fear, he began to stir vigorously. She saw him pouring his awful beauty from the basket upon the bed, then she seized the lamp and ran as fast as she could to the kitchen. The wind from the open door blew out the light and the darkness added to her terror. She sped to the darkness of the yard, slamming the door after her before she thought to set down the lamp. She did not feel safe even on the ground, so she climbed up in the hay barn.

There for an hour or more she lay sprawled upon the hay a gibbering wreck.

Finally she grew quiet, and after that coherent thought. With this, stalked through her a cold, bloody rage. Hours of this. A period of introspection, a space of retrospection, then a mixture of both. Out of this an awful calm.

"Well, Ah done de bes' Ah could. If things aint right, Gawd knows taint mah fault."

She went to sleep—a twitchy sleep—and woke up to a faint gray sky. There was a loud hollow sound below. She peered out. Sykes was at the wood-pile, demolishing a wire-covered box.

He hurried to the kitchen door, but hung outside there some minutes before he entered, and stood some minutes more inside before he closed it after him.

The gray in the sky was spreading. Delia descended without fear now, and crouched beneath the low bedroom window. The drawn shade shut out the dawn, shut in the night. But the thin walls held back no sound.

"Dat ol' scratch is woke up now!" She mused at the tremendous whirr inside, which every woodsman knows, is one of the sound illusions. The rattler is a ventriloquist. His whirr sounds to the right, to the left, straight ahead, behind, close under foot—everywhere but where it is. Woe to him who guesses wrong unless he is prepared to hold up his end of the argument! Sometimes he strikes without rattling at all.

Inside, Sykes heard nothing until he knocked a pot lid off the stove while trying to reach the match-safe in the dark. He had emptied his pockets at Bertha's.

The snake seemed to wake up under the stove and Sykes made a quick leap into the bedroom. In spite of the gin he had had, his head was clearing now.

"Mah Gawd!" he chattered, "ef Ah could on'y strack uh light!"

The rattling ceased for a moment as he stood paralyzed. He waited. It seemed that the snake waited also.

"Oh, fuh de light! Ah thought he'd be too sick"—Sykes was muttering to himself when the whirr began again, closer, right underfoot this time. Long before this, Sykes' ability to think had been flattened down to primitive instinct and he leaped—onto the bed.

Outside Delia heard a cry that might have come from a maddened chimpanzee, a stricken gorilla. All the terror, all the horror, all the rage that man possibly could express, without a recognizable human sound.

A tremendous stir inside there, another series of animal screams, the intermittent whirr of the reptile. The shade torn violently down from the window, letting in the red dawn, a huge brown hand seizing the window stick, great dull blows upon the wooden floor punctuating the gibberish of sound long after the rattle of the snake had abruptly subsided. All this Delia could see and hear from her place beneath the window, and it made her ill. She crept over to the four-o'clocks and stretched herself on the cool earth to recover.

She lay there. "Delia, Delia!" She could hear Sykes calling in a most despairing tone as one who expected no answer. The sun crept on up, and he called. Delia could not move—her legs were gone flabby. She never moved, he called, and the sun kept rising.

"Mah Gawd!" She heard him moan, "Mah Gawd fum Heben!" She heard him stumbling about and got up from her flower-bed. The sun was growing warm. As she approached the door she heard him call out hopefully, "Delia, is dat you Ah heah?"

She saw him on his hands and knees as soon as she reached the door. He crept an inch or two toward her—all that he was able, and she saw his horribly swollen neck and his one open eye shining with hope. A surge of pity too strong to support bore her away from that eye that must, could not, fail to see the tubs. He would see the lamp. Orlando with its doctors was too far. She could scarcely reach the chinaberry tree, where she waited in the growing heat while inside she knew the cold river was creeping up and up to extinguish that eye which must know by now that she knew.

[1926]

EMILY DICKINSON
[1830–1886]

The poetry of Emily Dickinson marks both a turning point and a middle point in nineteenth century literature. While it anticipates the concision, skepticism, and formal experimentation of the modernist period, it is also firmly grounded in the concerns, vocabulary, and rhythmic patterns of the middle of her century. Dickinson reacted against both the conservative Calvinist and the progressive transcendental certainties dominating New England during her youth; nevertheless both discourses richly flavor her writing. Few poets have concerned themselves more profoundly with the relation of God to humanity, and few have written with greater tonal variety or intensity about the fluctuations of nature and the human spirit. Outwardly, Dickinson conformed to the restrictions expected of nineteenth-century women, taking some to an extreme. Eventually, she dressed in white (although continued to use brightly colored shawls), confined her movements to house and garden, and presented herself in letters or her occasional meetings with new acquaintances as unusually shy. Yet in her poems and in other letters, or sometimes subtly in the same letters in which she pretended submission, Dickinson rebelled against the culture's definitions of femininity and its most naturalized hierarchies—hierarchies of God to humanity, of man to woman, and generally of "Color—Caste—Denomination," as she puts it in a poem (F 836).

Concern with authority was reasonable for Dickinson. She was the daughter and sister of prominent lawyers in Amherst, Massachusetts, where she spent her life. Her father, Edward, served one term as a national congressman, and was treasurer of Amherst College; her brother Austin became a justice of the peace in 1857 and succeeded his father as treasurer of Amherst. Although her mother, Emily Norcross Dickinson, seems to have been overwhelmed by the strong personalities of her family, she constructed an environment where her talented daughter could feel both at home and independent. After surmounting early financial instability, the Dickinsons lived with ample means to support the continued presence of two single daughters at home: neither the poet nor her younger sister Lavinia ("Vinnie") married or moved beyond their parents' house. The family's closeness is also revealed by their eager assistance in enabling Emily's brother Austin to build his elegant Victorian residence, the "Evergreens," next door to the "Homestead."

The Norcross family of Dickinson's mother had long promoted women's education, and indeed Emily was unusually well-educated, attending both Amherst Academy and, for a year, Mount Holyoke Female Seminary. In the 1840s, there was no expectation for women who entered college to matriculate; Dickinson's leaving Mount Holyoke after a year seems to have been mutually agreed on between the poet and her family: she was homesick, they missed her, and no one saw a point in her further formal education. In 1855, at the age of twenty-five, Dickinson spent several weeks visiting her father in Washington, D. C. during his term in Congress, stopping through Philadelphia on her trip. Later, because of eye problems, she made extended trips to Boston for treatment, living with her Norcross cousins Louise and Frances for seven months in 1864, then again in 1865. Apart from these few prolonged periods away from home, Dickinson remained in Amherst.

Dickinson's reclusiveness has led generations of scholars to read her poems in the light of personal dramas of failed romance, depression or neurosis, pain, and grief. All such stories, however, remain speculative. Few records beyond her own letters describe any aspects of Dickinson's life, and her letters are notoriously metaphorical and elliptical. The poet was vitally connected to friends and to local and national events through the reports of her socially active sister Vinnie, the newspapers and journals subscribed to by the Dickinson household, the high cultural connections of her brother and sister-in-law next door, and her own extensive letter writing. She wrote: "This is my letter to the World / That never wrote to Me" (F 519), but in fact she wrote frequent letters as well as poems to "the world," and it corresponded actively with her. Dickinson's circle of correspondents included relatives, friends, and people of public stature—including Samuel Bowles, editor of the Springfield Republican; Josiah Holland, Bowles's associate at the Republican and later editor of Scribner's; Helen Hunt Jackson, a childhood acquaintance who became a popular poet, novelist, and advocate for Indian Rights, as well as an ardent supporter of Dickinson's poetry; and Thomas Wentworth Higginson, an influential critic, essayist, and poet. Susan Dickinson's salons at the Evergreens also attracted illustrious guests, including Ralph Waldo Emerson—whom Dickinson apparently chose not to cross the lawn to meet, although she admired his poems and even wrote direct responses to a few. The fact that Dickinson composed over half of her poems between 1858 and 1865, the period leading up to and during the Civil War—reaching a highpoint of 295 poems during 1863— suggests the impact of the national tension on her creativity and helps to explain her preoccupation with death, loss, defeat, and theological conflict during this period of extraordinarily bloody battles with both sides claiming divine right for their cause. In short, despite her reclusiveness, Dickinson was intimately aware of the social, political, and cultural events of her times.

When Higginson asked if she "never felt want of employment, never going off the place & never seeing any visitor," she responded (by his report): "'I never thought of conceiving that I could ever have the slightest approach to such a want in all future time' (& added) 'I feel that I have not expressed myself strongly enough'" (L 342a).

Dickinson's correspondence with Higginson provided her with important professional respect and friendly support at a crucial early period of her writing; additionally, in her letters to him, Dickinson pushed herself to articulate a poetics—albeit in her typical, highly metaphorical form. Higginson was a critic and poet but also an ardent abolitionist, naturalist, and supporter of women's education and rights, as Dickinson knew from his frequent essays in The Atlantic Monthly. On April 15, 1862, in her first letter to him, she asked if "my Verse is alive?" and enclosed four poems, as well as a separate envelope containing a card bearing her full name. Later she defined poetry to Higginson as writing that "makes my whole body so cold no fire ever can warm me," or makes her "feel physically as if the top of my head were taken off . . . These are the only way I know it. Is there any other way" (L 342a). While she never attended to Higginson's apparently conventional advice about how to improve her poems, Dickinson continued to write and send him poems often signing her letters "Your scholar" and twice telling him that he had "saved her life" (1869 and 1882).

Speculation remains about whether Dickinson enacted a grand passion and who its object may have been, but there is no doubt that she cherished the woman who became her sister-in-law, Susan Gilbert Dickinson. Dickinson sent "sister Sue" more poems than any other correspondent, and addressed her in terms now associated with erotic romance, longing to see and kiss her—or, for example, writing, "Should I turn in my long night I should murmur 'Sue.'" Such language was relatively common between female friends in the nineteenth century. Nonetheless, its persistence and extremity suggest an unusually powerful attachment. In modern terms, however, Dickinson's sexuality is best understood as "bisexual." Much speculation has centered around three early letters found in draft among her papers and addressed to "Master" and various candidates have been proposed for this figure, including Sue herself. The only firm evidence for a romantic relationship with a man lies in her few surviving late letters to Judge Otis P. Lord, a friend of Edward Dickinson who apparently proposed to the poet around 1878. Dickinson declined, perhaps in part with the words "'No' is the wildest word we consign to Language" (L562). Letters such as these to Lord, the long and intimate correspondence with Sue, and the hundreds of letters Dickinson wrote to other friends reveal that, however secluded her life may have been, it was not void of emotion. As she writes to Elizabeth Holland, "love me if you will, for I had rather be loved than to be called a king in earth, or a lord in Heaven" (L 185).

Only ten of Dickinson's poems were published during her lifetime. She donated three to a newspaper called the Drum Beat *to raise funds for Union troops and evidently did not protest when friends sent others to editors, but she refused all requests to publish. Some poems circulated nonetheless. Dickinson mailed about one-third of her poems to friends, who sometimes read them aloud to other friends or passed them on. More important, she copied nearly two-thirds of her poems into hand-sewn booklets, called "fascicles," and folded booklets, called "sets." Because she did not keep drafts of early poems or date her manuscripts, her poems can be dated only by comparing the handwriting of poems to that of letters, and it can only be ascertained when she copied a poem, not when she composed it. Why Dickinson did not publish is also unknown. Publication was not entirely respectable for women in the mid-nineteenth century, but many women in the United States and England were extremely successful both as poets and novelists—including several Dickinson admired extravagantly, especially Elizabeth Barrett Browning, George Eliot, and the Brontë sisters. Among American authors she also praises Harriet Prescott Spofford and Helen Hunt Jackson. Similarly, many female authors were far more radical than Dickinson in their political stances and feminism; none, however, approached Dickinson in the artistic excellence or innovation of their forms.*

Dickinson began writing poetry seriously in 1858 and wrote until her death, completing around 1,800 poems. No one knew the extent of her writing, however, until her manuscript books and loose pages were found in a cherry wood box in the bottom drawer of her dresser by her sister Lavinia after her death. Vinnie gave the poems to their sister-in-law, Sue. When after two years Sue had taken no steps toward their publication, Vinnie passed a large number of the manuscripts on to Mabel Loomis Todd, Austin's mistress. Todd, with the assistance of Higginson, produced Poems *by Emily Dickinson in 1890. This volume's popularity led her and Higginson to publish a second volume in 1891, and Todd alone edited a third (1896). Heated disagreements between Mabel Todd and Susan Dickinson, who still possessed manuscripts of hundreds of poems, prevented any single editor from having full access to all of the poet's manuscripts until late in the twentieth century. Even Thomas H. Johnson's important 1955 "complete" poems was based on his being allowed to see the manuscripts in Millicent Todd Bingham's possession only twice. Ralph W. Franklin (Poems, 1998) was the first editor to have unrestricted access to all manuscripts of Dickinson's poems.*

Dickinson was a formally experimental poet. Because she did not see her poems through the publication process, however, it is in many cases unclear just how experimental she intended to be. For example, from examination of Dickinson's manuscripts, editors disagree about where line breaks should appear and the significance of her differing length and slant of handwritten dashes. All agree, however, that she typically works from a metrical norm to create complex new rhythms and rhymes: she manipulates simple ballad- or hymn-style meters and stanzas with extraordinary subtlety and variety, and she is one of the great innovators in rhyme, creating multiple "slant" sound echoes—for example, rhyming "me" with the polysyllabic "immortality," or "noon" with "Stone," or "away" with "Poetry." Similarly, her ample substitution of dashes for other marks of punctuation resists normal syntactic and poetic closure. This unconventional punctuation, her frequent capitalizations, and her omission of grammatical connectors, function words (prepositions and articles), and explanatory context for pronoun reference ("He," "it," "I") give her poetry an elliptical, aphoristic quality. Moreover, because her sentences or phrases frequently cross over line and stanza endings, the poems force readers to be sensitive to the play of syntax, sense, and form. Similarly, her brilliantly unconventional metaphors demand thoughtful attention: late summer, for example, appears as "Further in Summer than the Birds" (F 895); a hummingbird is "A Route of Evanescence, / With a revolving Wheel" (F 1489); or the possibility of dying is like "a Face of Steel - / That suddenly looks into our's / With a metallic grin - / The Cordiality of Death - / Who drills his Welcome in -" (F 243).

It is difficult to identify the best or most famous of Dickinson's poems. Moreover, there is a wide range among these poems in topic and levels of conceptual difficulty. Some, such as "This is my letter to the World" (F 519) or "I'm Nobody! Who are you?" (F260) are simple and playful in tone and message. Others are far more difficult. "My Life had stood - a Loaded Gun -" (F 763), about the paradoxically ardent passivity of a life/gun that stood "In Corners - till a Day / The Owner passed - identified - /And carried Me away," raises questions about gender, authority, pleasure, and the relation of the artist to inspiration. Its riddling conclusion has not yet been unraveled: "Though I than He - may longer live / He longer must - than I - / For I have but the power [variant: Art] to kill, / Without - the power to die -." "Because I could not stop for Death -" (F479) tells a simpler story: An individual is courted by a personified Death and accompanies "Him" on a carriage ride to the grave. Yet the fourth stanza of the poem (a stanza omitted by Higginson and Todd, and in all pre-Johnson printings of the poem) uses metrical wordplay to introduce chilling questions about dying. The poem concludes with the speaker in a kind of limbo, remembering "Centuries" that feel shorter "than the Day / I first surmised the Horses' Heads / Were toward Eternity -." Like "Because I could not stop for Death," "The Soul selects her own Society -" suggests the Christian trope whereby each believer is metaphorically a bride of Christ, feminine to God's masculine dominion. Here the feminine "Soul" selects her "Society - / Then - shuts the Door." As the poem insists, however, in its perfect balancing of verbs of choice and exclusion, even the most selective individual admits some companionship, and even the friendliest individual makes some exclusionary choices.

Few poets have expressed as exquisite a sensitivity to pain and loss, as intense an intellectual curiosity or emotional responsiveness, or as profound a *distrust of pious certainties as Emily Dickinson. With astute frankness, this poet insists on what cannot be known—in relation to religious faith but also to epistemological questions generally. Dickinson writes about liminal states of consciousness, uncategorized psychological responses, moments on the cusp of change from one season or feeling to another. Famous for telling "all the Truth" but telling it "slant," Dickinson is one of the great poets of the human condition—philosophically speculative, theologically skeptical, psychologically nuanced far in advance of Freud's theories of consciousness, and attentive to power in multiple manifestations, including the power of daily experience in ordinary life.*

All but a few of the poems in The Pearson Custom Library of American Literature *are taken from Ralph W. Franklin's reading edition of the* Poems of Emily Dickinson *(1999); commentary on the texts is from Franklin's variorum edition of the* Poems *(1998). In his one-volume edition, Franklin prints the text of the last full manuscript for any poem, maintaining the poet's misspellings (e.g., "opon" for "upon," "ancle" for "ankle"), misuse of apostrophes (e.g., "their's"), and unconventional capitalization and punctuation. Although Dickinson frequently altered punctuation and capitalization when copying or revising her poems, this text includes only variant word choices. Because Dickinson did not title her poems they appear without titles here. Franklin has numbered the poems chronologically according to the date of the first handwritten copy of the poem extant (revising Thomas H. Johnson's 1955 numbering and dating of the poems); dates and numbers appear at the bottom right of each poem. The c. indicates approximate dating; the F indicates Franklin's numbering. Franklin also numbers the booklets into which Dickinson copied her poems, sewn (fascicles) and unsewn (sets); an initial note will tell whether any given poem was copied into these booklets. Where Franklin and Johnson choose substantively different manuscript versions of a Dickinson poem for their reader editions,* The Pearson Custom Library of American Literature *also makes the Johnson-edited poem available.*

For Further Reading

Primary Works

The Poems of Emily Dickinson, ed. Thomas H. Johnson, 3 vols., 1951, 1955; *The Letters of Emily Dickinson,* eds. Thomas H. Johnson and Theodora Ward, 3 vols., 1958; Jay Leyda, *The Years and Hours of Emily Dickinson,* 2 vols., 1960; *The Manuscript Books of Emily Dickinson,* ed. Ralph W. Franklin, 2 vols., 1981; *Open Me Carefully: Emily Dickinson's Intimate Letters to Susan Huntington Gilbert,* eds. Ellen Louise Hart and Martha Nell Smith, 1998; *The Poems of Emily Dickinson,* ed. Ralph W. Franklin, 3 vols., 1998 (Reader's Edition, 1 vol., 1999).

Secondary Works

Richard B. Sewall, *The Life of Emily Dickinson*. 2 vols., 1974; Suzanne Juhasz, ed., *Feminist Critics Read Emily Dickinson*, 1983; Vivian Pollak, *Dickinson: The Anxiety of Gender*, 1984; Shira Wolosky, *Emily Dickinson: A Voice of War*, 1984; Jane Donahue Eberwein, *Dickinson: Strategies of Limitation*, 1985; Cynthia Wolff, *Emily Dickinson*, 1986; Cristanne Miller, *Emily Dickinson: A Poet's Grammar*, 1987; Gary Lee Stonum, *The Dickinson Sublime*, 1990; Martha Nell Smith, *Rowing in Eden: Rereading Emily Dickinson*, 1992; Sharon Cameron, *Choosing Not Choosing: Dickinson's Fascicles*, 1992; Marta Werner, *Emily Dickinson's Open Folios: Scenes of Reading, Surfaces of Writing*, 1995; Gudrun Grabher, Roland Hagenbüchle, and Cristanne Miller, eds., *The Emily Dickinson Handbook*, 1998; Jane Donahue Eberwein, ed., *An Emily Dickinson Encyclopedia*, 1998; Domhnall Mitchell, *Emily Dickinson: Monarch of Perception*, 2000; Wendy Martin, ed., *The Cambridge Companion to Emily Dickinson*, 2002.

"The Daisy follows soft the Sun"
Emily Dickinson

The Daisy follows soft the Sun–
And when his golden walk is done–
Sits shyly at his feet–
He–waking–finds the flower there–
Wherefore–Marauder–art thou here?
Because, Sir, love is sweet!

We are the Flower–Thou the Sun!
Forgive us, if as days decline–
We nearer steal to Thee!
Enamored of the parting West–
The peace–the light–the Amethyst—
Night's possibility!

"Tell all the Truth"
Emily Dickinson

Tell all the Truth but tell it slant –
Success in Circuit lies
Too bright for our infirm Delight
the Truth's superb surprise

As Lightning to the Children eased
With explanation kind
The Truth must dazzle gradually
Or every man be blind–

"Essential Oils are wrung"
Emily Dickinson

Essential Oils– are wrung–
The Attar from the Rose
Be not expressed by Suns– alone –
It is the gift of Screws–

The General Rose– decay–
But this– in Lady's Drawer
Make Summer– When the Lady lie
In Ceaseless Rosemary

FLANNERY O'CONNOR
[1925–1964]

Flannery O'Connor's writing was shaped by her life in the rural South, by her strong religious faith, by a debilitating illness that caused her early death, and by her strong sense of irony. These forces contributed to the style and substance of her work: the often troubling but always comic elements of the grotesque convey O'Connor's deeply theological concerns and her vision of modern life. Flannery O'Connor is among the few twentieth century writers who explore from the viewpoint of Catholic orthodoxy the particular anguish of a contemporary society that questions, rejects, or halfheartedly accepts the power of a religious force.

O'Connor, an only child, was born in 1925, in Savannah, Georgia; at twelve, she moved with her family to a farm near Milledgeville. When she was fifteen, her father died of lupus, a progressive and incurable disease that later struck his daughter. She received an A.B. from Georgia State College of Women in 1945 and an M.F.A from the University of Iowa in 1947. Her first short story, "The Geranium," was published in Accent *in 1946, and she received an artists' residency at Yaddo in Saratoga Springs, N.Y. The lasting friendships she formed with other young writers at Iowa and at Yaddo contributed to her artistic growth and, in part, resulted in the remarkable collection of her correspondence, published posthumously as* Letters of Flannery O'Connor: The Habit of Being, *in 1979.*

After brief sojourns in New York and Connecticut in her twenties, she moved back to her mother's farm when she became ill with the lupus. The disease was controlled with medication but limited her energy and led to the use of crutches for the rest of her life. Thus, the farm, Andalusia, became her permanent residence, and the rural life a source for the vividly depicted background and characters of her stories and novels.

Although O'Connor wrote two novels, her artistry is recognized mainly on the strength of her short stories. These appeared regularly in literary journals and formed two collections: A Good Man Is Hard to Find *(1955) and* Everything That Rises Must Converge *(1965). Critical reaction to her novels—* Wise Blood *(1952) and* The Violent Bear It Away *(1960)—was mixed, but even her harshest critics recognized a unique talent and her power as a storyteller.*

In a 1960 letter to a friend, O'Connor comments: "I have the feeling that while many people will read this book in some fashion or other, only a few will really read it, or see anything in it. The reviews prove this, even the favorable ones. The favorable ones are sometimes the worst." Secular critics in praising characters she sees as demonic often misinterpret her intent; Catholic readers, on the other hand, criticize the grotesque or freakish characters, the violence, or a perceived negative depiction of religion. O'Connor, however, in her letters and lectures insists on the need for faith, and posits the reality of the devil.

Writing at a time of general questioning, and in a society where readers often practiced a lukewarm form of Christianity—or were openly hostile to religion—she dramatized the malaise of her bumbling characters through the grotesque. By its nature ambiguous, this mode allows O'Connor to express the tension between horror and humor she perceives in modern life. The depiction of violence or death in her stories and novels is consistent with O'Connor's concept of the grotesque—a use of shock to convey the author's vision: "... to the hard-of-hearing you shout, and for the almost-blind you draw large and startling figures."

O'Connor, of course, is also an unmistakably Southern writer. Although at times she decried such labels, she recognized the value of her heritage—and of the sense of "mystery and manners" the rural South offered for its inhabitants and for her. Upon receiving an award from the Georgia Writers' Association, O'Connor stated: "The best American fiction has always been regional. The ascendancy passed roughly from New England to the Midwest to the South; it has passed to and stayed longest wherever there has been a shared past, a sense of alikeness, and the possibility of reading a small history in a universal light." Her fictional universe is peopled by grotesques: cliché-spouting farmwives, backwoods prophets, physically and emotionally maimed characters, misguided intellectuals. No matter how repulsive or laughable these characters may seem, however, they are offered redemption in the form of grace, a concept very real to the author. Thus the shocking or violent events that many criticize represent an opportunity for the characters to recognize their error, and O'Connor claimed, "there is a moment in every great story in which the presence of grace can be felt as it waits to be accepted or rejected, even though the reader may not recognize this moment." Few of the characters in her fiction accept such grace; O'Connor depicts a materialistic and grotesque world to suggest the need for spiritual awareness and true community.

While an intellectual appears only once in O'Connor's first volume of short stories, intellectual characters are featured in eight of the last eleven stories published before her death. This progression suggests her increasing concern with society's skepticism toward and rejection of the sense of mystery that she associates with faith. Although such characters are more subtly drawn than *her explicitly grotesque freaks, the intellectuals with their capacity for the ideal—a synthesis of reason and intuition—are often more culpable than the earnest but ludicrous seekers. Readers who ignore the complex ironies in her work may thus identify with the cynical one-legged Ph.D., Hulga in "Good Country People"—or with the aspiring writer Julian in "Everything That Rises Must Converge," despite his covert bigotry. O'Connor's sympathies are with the Protestant South, however removed from Catholic orthodoxy its expression of religion may be; the religious writer, she claims, "will feel a good deal more kinship with backwoods prophets and shouting fundamentalists than he will with those politer elements for whom the supernatural is an embarrassment and for whom religion has become a department of sociology or culture or personality development."*

The Collected Stories of Flannery O'Connor *was published in 1971 and received the National Book Award in 1972. Many decades after her death in 1964, O'Connor's stories are widely read; they appear in many anthologies and are taught to students in high school and college. They depict only a brief period in a time and a place, but they probe universal concerns and the always-questioning nature of humans.*

Zita McShane
Frostburg State University

For Further Reading

Primary Works

The Complete Stories. New York: Farrar, Straus and Giroux, 1971; *Everything That Rises Must Converge.* New York: Farrar, Straus and Giroux, 1965; *A Good Man Is Hard to Find.* New York: Harcourt Brace Jovanovich, 1955; *The Habit of Being.* Edited by Sally Fitzgerald. New York: Farrar, Straus and Giroux, 1979; *Mystery and Manners.* Edited by Sally Fitzgerald and Robert Fitzgerald. New York: Farrar, Straus and Giroux, 1969; *The Presence of Grace and Other Book Reviews.* Edited by Carter W. Martin. Athens: University of Georgia Press, 1983; *The Violent Bear It Away.* New York: Farrar, Straus and Giroux, 1960; *Wise Blood.* 2d ed. New York: Farrar, Straus and Giroux, 1962.

Secondary Works

Asals, Frederick. *Flannery O'Connor: The Imagination of Extremity.* Athens: University of Georgia Press, 1982; Coles, Robert. *Flannery O'Connor's South.* Baton Rouge: Louisiana State University Press, 1980; Driskill, Leon V. and Joan T. Brittain. *The Eternal Crossroads: The Art of Flannery O'Connor.* Lexington: University Press of Kentucky, 1971; Farmer, David. *Flannery O'Connor: A Descriptive Bibliography.* New York: Garland, 1981; Friedman, Melvin J. and

Beverly Lyon Clark, eds. *Critical Essays on Flannery O'Connor.* Boston: G. K. Hall, 1985; Gentry, Marshall Bruce. *Flannery O'Connor's Religion of the Grotesque.* Jackson: University Press of Mississippi, 1986; Getz, Lorine M. *Flannery O'Connor, Literary Theologian: The Habits and Discipline of Being.* Lewiston, N.Y.: Mellen, 1999; Giannone, Richard. *Flannery O'Connor and the Mystery of Love.* New York: Fordham University Press, 1999; Hyman, Stanley Edgar. *Flannery O'Connor.* Minneapolis: University of Minnesota Press, 1966; Muller, Gilbert H. *Nightmares and Visions: Flannery O'Connor and the Catholic Grotesque.* Athens: University of Georgia Press, 1972; Walters, Dorothy. *Flannery O'Connor.* New York: Twayne, 1973.

A Good Man Is Hard to Find

FLANNERY O'CONNOR

The grandmother didn't want to go to Florida. She wanted to visit some of her connections in east Tennessee and she was seizing at every chance to change Bailey's mind. Bailey was the son she lived with, her only boy. He was sitting on the edge of his chair at the table, bent over the orange sports section of the *Journal*. "Now look here, Bailey," she said, "see here, read this," and she stood with one hand on her thin hip and the other rattling the newspaper at his bald head. "Here this fellow that calls himself the Misfit is aloose from the Federal Pen and headed toward Florida and you read here what it says he did to these people. Just you read it. I wouldn't take my children in any direction with a criminal like that aloose in it. I couldn't answer to my conscience if I did."

Bailey didn't look up from his reading so she wheeled around then and faced the children's mother, a young woman in slacks, whose face was as broad and innocent as a cabbage and was tied around with a green head-kerchief that had two points on the top like rabbit's ears. She was sitting on the sofa, feeding the baby his apricots out of a jar. "The children have been to Florida before," the old lady said. "You all ought to take them somewhere else for a change so they would see different parts of the world and be broad. They never have been to east Tennessee."

The children's mother didn't seem to hear but the eight-year-old boy, John Wesley, a stocky child with glasses, said, "If you don't want to go to Florida, why dontcha stay at home?" He and the little girl, June Star, were reading the funny papers on the floor.

"She wouldn't stay at home to be queen for a day," June Star said without raising her yellow head.

"Yes and what would you do if this fellow, The Misfit, caught you?" the grandmother asked.

"I'd smack his face," John Wesley said.

"She wouldn't stay at home for a million bucks," June Star said. "Afraid she'd miss something. She has to go everywhere we go."

"All right, Miss," the grandmother said. "Just remember that the next time you want me to curl your hair."

June Star said her hair was naturally curly.

The next morning the grandmother was the first one in the car, ready to go. She had her big black valise that looked like the head of a hippopotamus in one corner, and underneath it she was hiding a basket with Pitty Sing, the cat, in it. She didn't intend for the cat to be left alone in the house for three days because he would miss her too much and she was afraid he might brush against one of the gas burners and accidentally asphyxiate himself. Her son, Bailey, didn't like to arrive at a motel with a cat.

She sat in the middle of the back seat with John Wesley and June Star on either side of her. Bailey and the children's mother and the baby sat in front and they left Atlanta at eight forty-five with the mileage on the car at 55890. The grandmother wrote this down because she thought it would be interesting to say how many miles they had been when they got back. It took them twenty minutes to reach the outskirts of the city.

The old lady settled herself comfortably, removing her white cotton gloves and putting them up with her purse on the shelf in front of the back window. The children's mother still had on slacks and still had her head tied up in a green kerchief, but the grandmother had on a navy blue straw sailor hat with a bunch of white violets on the brim and a navy blue dress with a small white dot in the print. Her collars and cuffs were white organdy trimmed with lace and at her neckline she had pinned a purple spray of cloth violets containing a sachet. In case of an accident, anyone seeing her dead on the highway would know at once that she was a lady.

She said she thought it was going to be a good day for driving, neither too hot nor too cold, and she cautioned Bailey that the speed limit was fifty-five miles an hour and that the patrolmen hid themselves behind billboards and small clumps of trees and sped out after you before you had a chance to slow down. She pointed out interesting details of the scenery: Stone Mountain; the blue granite that in some places came up to both sides of the highway; the brilliant red clay banks slightly streaked with purple; and the various crops that made rows of green lace-work on the ground. The trees were full of silver-white sunlight and the meanest of them sparkled. The children were reading comic magazines and their mother had gone back to sleep.

"Let's go through Georgia fast so we won't have to look at it much," John Wesley said.

"If I were a little boy," said the grandmother, "I wouldn't talk about my native state that way. Tennessee has the mountains and Georgia has the hills."

"Tennessee is just a hillbilly dumping ground," John Wesley said, "and Georgia is a lousy state too."

"You said it," June Star said.

"In my time," said the grandmother, folding her thin veined fingers, "children were more respectful of their native states and their parents and everything else. People did right then. Oh look at the cute little pickaninny!" she said and pointed to a Negro child standing in the door of a shack. "Wouldn't that make a picture, now?" she asked and they all turned and looked at the little Negro out of the back window. He waved.

"He didn't have any britches on," June Star said.

"He probably didn't have any," the grandmother explained. "Little niggers in the country don't have things like we do. If I could paint, I'd paint that picture," she said.

The children exchanged comic books.

The grandmother offered to hold the baby and the children's mother passed him over the front seat to her. She set him on her knee and bounced him and told him about the things they were passing. She rolled her eyes and screwed up her mouth and stuck her leathery thin face into his smooth bland one. Occasionally he gave her a faraway smile. They passed a large cotton field with five or six graves fenced in the middle of it, like a small island. "Look at the graveyard!" the grandmother said, pointing it out. "That was the old family burying ground. That belonged to the plantation."

"Where's the plantation?" John Wesley asked.

"Gone With the Wind," said the grandmother. "Ha. Ha."

When the children finished all the comic books they had brought, they opened the lunch and ate it. The grandmother ate a peanut butter sandwich and an olive and would not let the children throw the box and the paper napkins out the window. When there was nothing else to do they played a game by choosing a cloud and making the other two guess what shape it suggested. John Wesley took one the shape of a cow and June Star guessed a cow and John Wesley said, no, an automobile, and June Star said he didn't play fair, and they began to slap each other over the grandmother.

The grandmother said she would tell them a story if they would keep quiet. When she told a story, she rolled her eyes and waved her head and was very dramatic. She said once when she was a maiden lady she had been courted by a Mr. Edgar Atkins Teagarden from Jasper, Georgia. She said he was a very good-looking man and a gentleman and that he brought her a watermelon every Saturday afternoon with his initials cut in it, E.A.T. Well, one Saturday, she said, Mr. Teagarden brought the watermelon and there was nobody at home and he left it on the front porch and returned in his buggy to Jasper, but she never got the watermelon, she said, because a nigger boy ate it when he saw the initials, E.A.T.! This story tickled John Wesley's funny bone and he giggled and giggled but June Star didn't think it was any good. She said she wouldn't marry a man that just brought her a watermelon on Saturday. The grandmother said she would have done well to marry Mr. Teagarden because he was a gentleman and had bought Coca-Cola stock when it first came out and that he had died only a few years ago, a very wealthy man.

They stopped at The Tower for barbecued sandwiches. The Tower was a part stucco and part wood filling station and dance hall set in a clearing outside of Timothy. A fat man named Red Sammy Butts ran it and there were signs stuck here and there on the building and for miles up and down the highway saying, TRY RED SAMMY'S FAMOUS BARBECUE. NONE LIKE FAMOUS RED SAMMY'S! RED SAM! THE FAT BOY WITH THE HAPPY LAUGH. A VETERAN! RED SAMMY'S YOUR MAN!

Red Sammy was lying on the bare ground outside The Tower with his head under a truck while a gray monkey about a foot high, chained to a small chinaberry tree, chattered nearby. The monkey sprang back into the tree and got on the highest limb as soon as he saw the children jump out of the car and run toward him.

Inside, The Tower was a long dark room with a counter at one end and tables at the other and dancing space in the middle. They all sat down at a board table next to the nickelodeon and Red Sam's wife, a tall burnt-brown woman with hair and eyes lighter than her skin, came and took their order. The children's mother put a dime in the machine and played "The Tennessee Waltz," and the grandmother said that tune always made her want to dance. She asked Bailey if he would like to dance but he only glared at her. He didn't have a naturally sunny disposition like she did and trips made him nervous. The grandmother's brown eyes were very bright. She swayed her head from side to side and pretended she was dancing in her chair. June Star said play something she could tap to so the children's mother put in another dime and played a fast number and June Star stepped out onto the dance floor and did her tap routine.

"Ain't she cute?" Red Sam's wife said, leaning over the counter. "Would you like to come be my little girl?"

"No I certainly wouldn't," June Star said. "I wouldn't live in a broken-down place like this for a million bucks!" and she ran back to the table.

"Ain't she cute?" the woman repeated, stretching her mouth politely.

"Aren't you ashamed?" hissed the grandmother.

Red Sam came in and told his wife to quit lounging on the counter and hurry up with these people's order. His khaki trousers reached just to his hip bones and his stomach hung over them like a sack of meal swaying under his shirt. He came over and sat down at a table nearby and let out a combination sigh and yodel. "You can't win," he said. "You can't win," and he wiped his sweating red face off with a gray handkerchief. "These days you don't know who to trust," he said. "Ain't that the truth?"

"People are certainly not nice like they used to be," said the grandmother.

"Two fellers come in here last week," Red Sammy said, "driving a Chrysler. It was a old beat-up car but it was a good one and these boys looked all right to me. Said they worked at the mill and you know I let them fellers charge the gas they bought? Now why did I do that?"

"Because you're a good man!" the grandmother said at once.

"Yes'm, I suppose so," Red Sam said as if he were struck with this answer.

His wife brought the orders, carrying the five plates all at once without a tray, two in each hand and one balanced on her arm. "It isn't a soul in this green world of God's that you can trust," she said. "And I don't count nobody out of that, not nobody," she repeated, looking at Red Sammy.

"Did you read about that criminal, The Misfit, that's escaped?" asked the grandmother.

"I wouldn't be a bit surprised if he didn't attact this place right here," said the woman. "If he hears about it being here, I wouldn't be none surprised to see him. If he hears it's two cent in the cash register, I wouldn't be a tall surprised if he . . ."

"That'll do," Red Sam said. "Go bring these people their Co'-Colas," and the woman went off to get the rest of the order.

"A good man is hard to find," Red Sammy said. "Everything is getting terrible. I remember the day you could go off and leave your screen door unlatched. Not no more."

He and the grandmother discussed better times. The old lady said that in her opinion Europe was entirely to blame for the way things were now. She said the way Europe acted you would think we were made of money and Red Sam said it was no use talking about it, she was exactly right. The children ran outside into the white sunlight and looked at the monkey in the lacy chinaberry tree. He was busy catching fleas on himself and biting each one carefully between his teeth as if it were a delicacy.

They drove off again into the hot afternoon. The grandmother took cat naps and woke up every few minutes with her own snoring. Outside of Toombsboro she woke up and recalled an old plantation that she had visited in this neighborhood once when she was a young lady. She said the house had six white columns across the front and that there was an avenue of oaks leading up to it and two little wooden trellis arbors on either side in front where you sat down with your suitor after a stroll in the garden. She recalled exactly which road to turn off to get to it. She knew that Bailey would not be willing to lose any time looking at an old house, but the more she talked about it, the more she wanted to see it once again and find out if the little twin arbors were still standing. "There was a secret panel in this house," she said craftily, not telling the truth but wishing that she were, "and the story went that all the family silver was hidden in it when Sherman[1] came through but it was never found . . ."

"Hey!" John Wesley said. "Let's go see it! We'll find it! We'll poke all the woodwork and find it! Who lives there? Where do you turn off at? Hey Pop, can't we turn off there?"

"We never have seen a house with a secret panel!" June Star shrieked. "Let's go to the house with the secret panel! Hey Pop, can't we go see the house with the secret panel!"

"It's not far from here, I know," the grandmother said. "It wouldn't take over twenty minutes."

Bailey was looking straight ahead. His jaw was as rigid as a horseshoe. "No," he said.

The children began to yell and scream that they wanted to see the house with the secret panel. John Wesley kicked the back of the front seat and June Star hung over her mother's shoulder and whined desperately into her ear that they never had any fun even on their vacation, that they could never do what THEY wanted to do. The baby began to scream and John Wesley kicked the back of the seat so hard that his father could feel the blows in his kidney.

"All right!" he shouted and drew the car to a stop at the side of the road. "Will you all shut up? Will you all just shut up for one second? If you don't shut up, we won't go anywhere."

"It would be very educational for them," the grandmother murmured.

"All right," Bailey said, "but get this: this is the only time we're going to stop for anything like this. This is the one and only time."

"The dirt road that you have to turn down is about a mile back," the grandmother directed. "I marked it when we passed."

"A dirt road," Bailey groaned.

After they had turned around and were headed toward the dirt road, the grandmother recalled other points about the house, the beautiful glass over the front doorway and the candle-lamp in the hall. John Wesley said that the secret panel was probably in the fireplace.

"You can't go inside this house," Bailey said. "You don't know who lives there."

"While you all talk to the people in front, I'll run around behind and get in a window," John Wesley suggested.

"We'll all stay in the car," his mother said.

They turned onto the dirt road and the car raced roughly along in a swirl of pink dust. The grandmother recalled the times when there were no paved

---

[1]William Tecumseh Sherman (1820–1891). Northern Civil War general noted for his "March to the Sea" through Georgia in 1864. The march was marked by plundering and destruction of houses and plantations by the Union troops.

roads and thirty miles was a day's journey. The dirt road was hilly and there were sudden washes in it and sharp curves on dangerous embankments. All at once they would be on a hill, looking down over the blue tops of trees for miles around, then the next minute, they would be in a red depression with the dust-coated trees looking down on them.

"This place had better turn up in a minute," Bailey said, "or I'm going to turn around."

The road looked as if no one had traveled on it in months.

"It's not much farther," the grandmother said and just as she said it, a horrible thought came to her. The thought was so embarrassing that she turned red in the face and her eyes dilated and her feet jumped up, upsetting her valise in the corner. The instant the valise moved, the newspaper top she had over the basket under it rose with a snarl and Pitty Sing, the cat, sprang onto Bailey's shoulder.

The children were thrown to the floor and their mother, clutching the baby, was thrown out the door onto the ground; the old lady was thrown into the front seat. The car turned over once and landed right-side-up in a gulch off the side of the road. Bailey remained in the driver's seat with the cat—gray-striped with a broad white face and an orange nose—clinging to his neck like a caterpillar.

As soon as the children saw they could move their arms and legs, they scrambled out of the car, shouting, "We've had an ACCIDENT!" The grandmother was curled up under the dashboard, hoping she was injured so that Bailey's wrath would not come down on her all at once. The horrible thought she had had before the accident was that the house she had remembered so vividly was not in Georgia but in Tennessee.

Bailey removed the cat from his neck with both hands and flung it out the window against the side of a pine tree. Then he got out of the car and started looking for the children's mother. She was sitting against the side of a red gutted ditch, holding the screaming baby, but she only had a cut down her face and a broken shoulder. "We've had an ACCIDENT!" the children screamed in a frenzy of delight.

"But nobody's killed," June Star said with disappointment as the grandmother limped out of the car, her hat still pinned to her head but the broken front brim standing up at a jaunty angle and the violet spray hanging off the side. They all sat down in the ditch, except the children, to recover from the shock. They were all shaking.

"Maybe a car will come along," said the children's mother hoarsely.

"I believe I have injured an organ," said the grandmother, pressing her side, but no one answered her. Bailey's teeth were clattering. He had on a yellow sport shirt with bright blue parrots designed in it and his face was as yellow as the shirt. The grandmother decided that she would not mention that the house was in Tennessee.

The road was about ten feet above and they could see only the tops of the trees on the other side of it. Behind the ditch they were sitting in there were more woods, tall and dark and deep. In a few minutes they saw a car some distance away on top of a hill, coming slowly as if the occupants were watching them. The grandmother stood up and waved both arms dramatically to attract their attention. The car continued to come on slowly, disappeared around a bend and appeared again, moving even slower, on top of the hill they had gone over. It was a big black battered hearse-like automobile. There were three men in it.

It came to a stop just over them and for some minutes, the driver looked down with a steady expressionless gaze to where they were sitting, and didn't speak. Then he turned his head and muttered something to the other two and they got out. One was a fat boy in black trousers and a red sweat shirt with a silver stallion embossed on the front of it. He moved around on the right side of them and stood staring, his mouth partly open in a kind of loose grin. The other had on khaki pants and a blue striped coat and a gray hat pulled down very low, hiding most of his face. He came around slowly on the left side. Neither spoke.

The driver got out of the car and stood by the side of it, looking down at them. He was an older man than the other two. His hair was just beginning to gray and he wore silver-rimmed spectacles that gave him a scholarly look. He had a long creased face and didn't have on any shirt or undershirt. He had on blue jeans that were too tight for him and he was holding a black hat and a gun. The two boys also had guns.

"We've had an ACCIDENT!" the children screamed.

The grandmother had the peculiar feeling that the bespectacled man was someone she knew. His face was as familiar to her as if she had known him all her life but she could not recall who he was. He moved away from the car and began to come down the embankment, placing his feet carefully so that he wouldn't slip. He had on tan and white shoes and no socks, and his ankles were red and thin. "Good afternoon," he said. "I see you all had you a little spill."

"We turned over twice!" said the grandmother.

"Oncet," he corrected. "We seen it happen. Try their car and see will it run, Hiram," he said quietly to the boy with the gray hat.

"What you got that gun for?" John Wesley asked. "Whatcha gonna do with that gun?"

"Lady," the man said to the children's mother, "would you mind calling them children to sit down by you? Children make me nervous. I want all you all to sit down right together there where you're at."

"What are you telling US what to do for?" June Star asked.

Behind them the line of woods gaped like a dark open mouth. "Come here," said the mother.

"Look here now," Bailey began suddenly, "we're in a predicament! We're in . . ."

The grandmother shrieked. She scrambled to her feet and stood staring. "You're The Misfit!" she said. "I recognized you at once!"

"Yes'm," the man said, smiling slightly as if he were pleased in spite of himself to be known, "but it would have been better for all of you, lady, if you hadn't of reckernized me."

Bailey turned his head sharply and said something to his mother that shocked even the children. The old lady began to cry and The Misfit reddened.

"Lady," he said, "don't you get upset. Sometimes a man says things he don't mean. I don't reckon he meant to talk to you thataway."

"You wouldn't shoot a lady, would you?" the grandmother said and removed a clean handkerchief from her cuff and began to slap at her eyes with it.

The Misfit pointed the toe of his shoe into the ground and made a little hole and then covered it up again. "I would hate to have to," he said.

"Listen," the grandmother almost screamed, "I know you're a good man. You don't look a bit like you have common blood. I know you must come from nice people!"

"Yes mam," he said, "finest people in the world." When he smiled he showed a row of strong white teeth. "God never made a finer woman than my mother and my daddy's heart was pure gold," he said. The boy with the red sweat shirt had come around behind them and was standing with his gun at his hip. The Misfit squatted down on the ground. "Watch them children, Bobby Lee," he said. "You know they make me nervous." He looked at the six of them huddled together in front of him and he seemed to be embarrassed as if he couldn't think of anything to say. "Ain't a cloud in the sky," he remarked, looking up at it. "Don't see no sun but don't see no cloud neither."

"Yes, it's a beautiful day," said the grandmother. "Listen," she said, "you shouldn't call yourself The Misfit because I know you're a good man at heart. I can just look at you and tell."

"Hush!" Bailey yelled. "Hush! Everybody shut up and let me handle this!" He was squatting in the position of a runner about to sprint forward but he didn't move.

"I pre-chate that, lady," The Misfit said and drew a little circle in the ground with the butt of his gun.

"It'll take a half a hour to fix this here car," Hiram called, looking over the raised hood of it.

"Well, first you Bobby Lee get him and that little boy to step over yonder with you," The Misfit said, pointing to Bailey and John Wesley. "The boys want to ast you something," he said to Bailey. "Would you mind stepping back in them woods there with them?"

"Listen," Bailey began, "we're in a terrible predicament! Nobody realizes what this is," and his voice cracked. His eyes were as blue and intense as the parrots in his shirt and he remained perfectly still.

The grandmother reached up to adjust her hat brim as if she were going to the woods with him but it came off in her hand. She stood staring at it and after a second she let it fall on the ground. Hiram pulled Bailey up by the arm as if he were assisting an old man. John Wesley caught hold of his father's hand and Bobby Lee followed. They went off toward the woods and just as they reached the dark edge, Bailey turned and supporting himself against a gray naked pine trunk, he shouted, "I'll be back in a minute, Mamma, wait on me!"

"Come back this instant!" his mother shrilled but they all disappeared into the woods.

"Bailey Boy!" the grandmother called in a tragic voice but she found she was looking at The Misfit squatting on the ground in front of her. "I just know you're a good man," she said desperately. "You're not a bit common!"

"Nome, I ain't a good man," The Misfit said after a second as if he had considered her statement carefully, "but I ain't the worst in the world neither. My daddy said I was a different breed of dog from my brothers and sisters. 'You know,' Daddy said, 'it's some that can live their whole life without asking about it and it's others has to know why it is, and this boy is one of the latters. He's going to be into everything!'" He put on his black hat and looked up suddenly and then away deep into the woods as if he were embarrassed again. "I'm sorry I don't have on a shirt before you ladies," he said, hunching his shoulders slightly. "We buried our clothes that we had on when we escaped and we're just making do until we can get better. We borrowed these from some folks we met," he explained.

"That's perfectly all right," the grandmother said. "Maybe Bailey has an extra shirt in his suitcase."

"I'll look and see terrectly," The Misfit said.

"Where are they taking him?" the children's mother screamed.

"Daddy was a card himself," The Misfit said. "You couldn't put anything over on him. He never got in trouble with the Authorities though. Just had the knack of handling them."

"You could be honest too if you'd only try," said the grandmother. "Think how wonderful it would be to settle down and live a comfortable life and not have to think about somebody chasing you all the time."

The Misfit kept scratching in the ground with the butt of his gun as if he were thinking about it. "Yes'm, somebody is always after you," he murmured.

The grandmother noticed how thin his shoulder blades were just behind his hat because she was standing up looking down on him. "Do you ever pray?" she asked.

He shook his head. All she saw was the black hat wiggle between his shoulder blades. "Nome," he said.

There was a pistol shot from the woods, followed closely by another. Then silence. The old lady's head jerked around. She could hear the wind move through the tree tops like a long satisfied insuck of breath. "Bailey Boy!" she called.

"I was a gospel singer for a while," The Misfit said. "I been most everything. Been in the arm service, both land and sea, at home and abroad, been twict married, been an undertaker, been with the railroads, plowed Mother Earth, been in a tornado, seen a man burnt alive oncet," and he looked up at the children's mother and the little girl who were sitting close together, their faces white and their eyes glassy. "I even seen a woman flogged," he said.

"Pray, pray," the grandmother began, "pray, pray . . ."

"I never was a bad boy that I remember of," The Misfit said in an almost dreamy voice, "but somewheres along the line I done something wrong and got sent to the penitentiary. I was buried alive," and he looked up and held her attention to him by a steady stare.

"That's when you should have started to pray," she said, "What did you do to get sent to the penitentiary that first time?"

"Turn to the right, it was a wall," The Misfit said, looking up again at the cloudless sky. "Turn to the left, it was a wall. Look up it was a ceiling, look down it was a floor. I forget what I done, lady. I set there and set there, trying to remember what it was I done and I ain't recalled it to this day. Oncet in a while, I would think it was coming to me, but it never come."

"Maybe they put you in by mistake," the old lady said vaguely.

"Nome," he said. "It wasn't no mistake. They had the papers on me."

"You must have stolen something," she said.

The Misfit sneered slightly. "Nobody had nothing I wanted," he said. "It was a head-doctor at the penitentiary said what I had done was kill my daddy but I known that for a lie. My daddy died in nineteen ought nineteen of the epidemic flu and I never had a thing to do with it. He was buried in the Mount Hopewell Baptist churchyard and you can go there and see for yourself."

"If you would pray," the old lady said, "Jesus would help you."

"That's right," The Misfit said.

"Well then, why don't you pray?" she asked trembling with delight suddenly.

"I don't want no hep," he said. "I'm doing all right by myself."

Bobby Lee and Hiram came ambling back from the woods. Bobby Lee was dragging a yellow shirt with bright blue parrots in it.

"Thow me that shirt, Bobby Lee," The Misfit said. The shirt came flying at him and landed on his shoulder and he put it on. The grandmother couldn't name what the shirt reminded her of. "No, lady," The Misfit said while he was buttoning it up, "I found out the crime don't matter. You can do one thing or you can do another, kill a man or take a tire off his car, because sooner or later you're going to forget what it was you done and just be punished for it."

The children's mother had begun to make heaving noises as if she couldn't get her breath. "Lady," he asked, "would you and that little girl like to step off yonder with Bobby Lee and Hiram and join your husband?"

"Yes, thank you," the mother said faintly. Her left arm dangled helplessly and she was holding the baby, who had gone to sleep, in the other. "Hep that lady up, Hiram," The Misfit said as she struggled to climb out of the ditch, "and Bobby Lee, you hold onto that little girl's hand."

"I don't want to hold hands with him," June Star said. "He reminds me of a pig."

The fat boy blushed and laughed and caught her by the arm and pulled her off into the woods after Hiram and her mother.

Alone with The Misfit, the grandmother found that she had lost her voice. There was not a cloud in the sky nor any sun. There was nothing around her but woods. She wanted to tell him that he must pray. She opened and closed her mouth several times before anything came out. Finally she found herself saying, "Jesus. Jesus," meaning, Jesus will help you, but the way she was saying it, it sounded as if she might be cursing.

"Yes'm," The Misfit said as if he agreed. "Jesus thown everything off balance. It was the same case with Him as with me except He hadn't committed any crime and they could prove I had committed one because they had the papers on me. Of course," he said, "they never shown me my papers. That's why I sign myself now. I said long ago, you get you a signature and sign everything you do and keep a copy of it. Then you'll know what you done and you can hold up the crime to the punishment and see do they match and in the end you'll have something to prove you ain't been treated right. I call myself The Misfit," he said, "because I can't make what all I done wrong fit what all I gone through in punishment."

There was a piercing scream from the woods, followed closely by a pistol report. "Does it seem right to you, lady, that one is punished a heap and another ain't punished at all?"

"Jesus!" the old lady cried. "You've got good blood! I know you wouldn't shoot a lady! I know you come from nice people! Pray! Jesus, you ought not to shoot a lady. I'll give you all the money I've got!"

"Lady," The Misfit said, looking beyond her far into the woods, "there never was a body that give the undertaker a tip."

There were two more pistol reports and the grandmother raised her head like a parched old turkey hen crying for water and called, "Bailey Boy, Bailey Boy!" as if her heart would break.

"Jesus was the only One that ever raised the dead," The Misfit continued, "and He shouldn't have done it. He thown everything off balance. If He did what He said, then it's nothing for you to do but thow away everything and follow Him, and if He didn't, then it's nothing for you to do but enjoy the few minutes you got left the best way you can—by killing somebody or burning down his house or doing some other meanness to him. No pleasure but meanness," he said and his voice had become almost a snarl.

"Maybe He didn't raise the dead," the old lady mumbled, not knowing what she was saying and feeling so dizzy that she sank down in the ditch with her legs twisted under her.

"I wasn't there so I can't say He didn't," The Misfit said. "I wisht I had of been there," he said, hitting the ground with his fist. "It ain't right I wasn't there because if I had of been there I would of known. Listen lady," he said in a high voice, "if I had of been there I would of known and I wouldn't be like I am now." His voice seemed about to crack and the grandmother's head cleared for an instant. She saw the man's face twisted close to her own as if he were going to cry and she murmured, "Why you're one of my babies. You're one of my own children!" She reached out and touched him on the shoulder. The Misfit sprang back as if a snake had bitten him and shot her three times through the chest. Then he put his gun down on the ground and took off his glasses and began to clean them.

Hiram and Bobby Lee returned from the woods and stood over the ditch, looking down at the grandmother who half sat and half lay in a puddle of blood with her legs crossed under her like a child's and her face smiling up at the cloudless sky.

Without his glasses, The Misfit's eyes were red-rimmed and pale and defenseless-looking. "Take her off and thow her where you thown the others," he said, picking up the cat that was rubbing itself against his leg.

"She was a talker, wasn't she?" Bobby Lee said, sliding down the ditch with a yodel.

"She would of been a good woman," The Misfit said, "if it had been somebody there to shoot her every minute of her life."

"Some fun!" Bobby Lee said.

"Shut up, Bobby Lee," The Misfit said. "It's no real pleasure in life."

[1953]

Workshop 5: The Quest for Hope and Redemption

WILLIAM FAULKNER
[1897–1962]

There are many critics who call William Faulkner America's greatest novelist. Faulkner's artistic legacy consists of not only of a large collection of novels and stories, but of an entire fictional world—the rich imaginary landscape he dubbed Yoknapatwapha County, Mississippi, the "little postage stamp of native soil" that formed the basis of some of his most powerful work. Born and raised in Mississippi, Faulkner was obsessed with the South and its past. Throughout his fiction, he explored the effects of slavery and the Civil War on Southern families, both black and white, aristocratic and poor. He also addressed issues of individual identity, responsibility, and honor. Faulkner claimed that he was not interested in ideas, but in people, in man "in conflict with himself, with his fellow man, or with his time and place, his environment." An expert craftsman who experimented with narrative perspective, Faulkner developed what one critic termed "perhaps the most elaborate, intermittently incoherent and ungrammatical, thunderous, polyphonic rhetoric in all American writing." With his own unique and musical prose, Faulkner shaped the rural South and its characters into the stuff of myth.

Born in New Albany, Mississippi, in 1897, Faulkner lived most of his life in Oxford, Mississippi. The oldest of four boys, he spent the better part of his childhood outdoors and, preferring football to his studies, never finished high school. He worked for a while as a bookkeeper in his grandfather's bank but, after America entered World War I in 1917, Faulkner, dreaming of glory, attempted to enlist. At a slim 5' 5" Faulkner failed to meet the U.S. Army's physical requirements. Undaunted, he traveled north to Canada and joined the Royal Air Force in Toronto. The war was over, however, before he had a chance to fight. Disappointed, Faulkner returned to Oxford to find that his girlfriend Estelle had married another man in his absence. He consoled himself by inventing stories of glorious combat that he told throughout his life.

Faulkner attended classes at the University of Mississippi in Oxford from 1919 to 1920 while at the same time holding jobs as a postmaster, carpenter, and house painter. He also began to write verse and short sketches and, in 1924, published a cycle of poems titled The Marble Faun. *Also in 1924,*

Faulkner met and befriended American author Sherwood Anderson. Anderson encouraged Faulkner to try his hand at fiction and to write about what he knew best. In 1925, Faulkner embarked for Europe, and, taking Anderson's advice, wrote his first novel, Soldiers' Pay, *which was published with Anderson's support in 1926.* Soldiers' Pay *depicted a disfigured war hero who discovers he no longer fits into the hypocritical small town society that was once his home. Following* Mosquitoes *(1927), a novel about art and artists, Faulkner wrote* Sartoris, *his first book set in Yoknapatawpha County, that drew heavily on Faulkner's own family history. The character of Col. John Sartoris was based on Faulkner's great-grandfather, Col. William Clark Falkner, while Faulkner's grandfather, John Wesley Thompson Falkner, was the model for the colonel's son, Bayard (these characters reappear in* The Town *and* The Unvanquished*). Heavily edited and published as* Sartoris *in 1929, the novel was republished in its original longer form as* Flags in the Dust *in 1974.*

Although his early works were not embraced by critics or the general public, Faulkner found the voice that would ensure his literary reputation in 1929. In The Sound and the Fury, *Faulkner returned to Yoknapatawpha and revealed a sophisticated and expressive new narrative style based on the exploration of his characters' interior consciousnesses. He began the novel with an image of Caddy Compson, a little girl in muddy drawers who is the daughter of a self-centered aristocratic Southern family in decline. Faulkner chronicled Caddy's story in four narrative sections, each told from the perspective of a different character: Benjy, Caddie's idiot brother, Jason, Caddie's unscrupulous older brother, Quentin, Caddie's sensitive brother, and Dilsey, the Compton's enduring black servant. Capturing each character's consciousness in turn, Faulkner juxtaposed the decay of the loveless Compson clan with the seemingly timeless power of the compassionate Dilsey. Critics still consider* The Sound and the Fury *to be one of Faulkner's greatest works.*

In 1929 Faulkner married his high school sweetheart Estelle, who had divorced her husband, and the couple purchased an old house, Rowan Oak, in Oxford. Faulkner began to make money from the sale of his short stories, but the demands of a large, run-down house and his growing family of three children severely strained his resources. Between 1929 and 1932, he worked the nightshift at the University of Mississippi power plant and struggled to keep writing. Despite the strain, Faulkner remained incredibly productive, publishing a novel a year: As I Lay Dying *(1930),* Sanctuary *(1931), and* Light in August *(1932). A collection of fifty-nine interior monologues by fifteen characters,* As I Lay Dying *told the darkly comic story of a poor white family's journey to bury their mother.* Sanctuary *constituted Faulkner's attempt to write a popular "thriller." The book caused a scandal for its depictions of rape and perversion.* Light in August *presented a psychological study of individual alienation through the character of Joe Christmas, whose possible mixed blood makes him a threat to a Southern community. Faulkner also continued to write short stories to supplement his income, many of which are collected in* These 13 *(1931) and* Doctor Martino and Other Stories *(1934).*

Faulkner traveled to Hollywood in 1932 in search of a steady income as a scriptwriter. Throughout the 1930s, 40s, and 50s, he returned frequently to Hollywood to write screenplays and to "doctor" scripts. Faulkner needed the money, but he always preferred Mississippi to Hollywood. He also continued to write novels and stories. Returning again to Yoknapatawpha County, Faulkner published Absalom, Absalom! *in 1936, the story of "a man who wanted sons and got sons who destroyed him." The novel explored Thomas Sutpen's struggle to rise from poverty to wealth and power. Faulkner depicted Sutpen's rise and fall through four unreliable narrators: the jaded Mr. Compson and his romantic son Quentin, Quentin's Canadian roommate Shreve, and the spinster Miss Rosa. Faulkner also reworked and combined some of his short stories to make* The Unvanquished *(1938), which he considered a trashy romance about the old Civil War South. He was prouder of* The Wild Palms *(1939), which wove together two seemingly unrelated stories: the illicit romance of Charlotte Rittenmeyer and Harry Wilbourne, and the adventure of a convict who rescues a pregnant woman from a flood. Faulkner likened the technique of* The Wild Palms *to musical counterpoint.*

Faulkner's next project was an ambitious Yoknapatawpha trilogy that mapped the spread of Snopes tribe ("like mold over cheese") throughout Jefferson, the county seat of Yoknapatawpha County. The Hamlet *(1940),* The Town *(1957), and* The Mansion *(1959) depict the rise of Flem Snopes, Faulkner's cipher for the debased and materialistic "New South," and the growth of Jefferson. Faulkner depicts Flem as a successful capitalist who sacrifices his family and honor in the pursuit of wealth. While working on the trilogy, Faulkner published* Go Down, Moses *(1942) and* Intruder in the Dust *(1948), which examine the history of the black and white members of the McCaslin family. Despite his prolific career, Faulkner's literary reputation languished until Malcolm Cowley's* The Portable Faulkner *(1946) raised public and critical interest in his work. Cowley's collection marked a turning point in Faulkner's career. Faulkner received the Nobel Prize for Literature in 1949, and his* Collected Stories, *published in 1950, won the National Book Award. He won the Pulitzer Prize for* A Fable *in 1955 and again for* The Reivers *in 1963. In the 1950s he became a well-known public figure, in demand on the lecture circuit. He became writer-in-residence at the University of Virginia in Charlottesville in 1957 and died of a heart attack in 1962.*

"Tell me about the South," the Canadian Shreve commands his Harvard roommate Quentin Compson in Absalom, Absalom! *"What do they do there? Why do they live there? Why do they live at all?" Throughout his fiction, Faulkner struggled to answer these questions in a way that made sense of the Southern past without succumbing to despair. In his 1949 Nobel Prize*

address Faulkner said, "I believe that man will not merely endure: he will prevail." Faulkner's belief in the power of the human spirit still speaks to general readers and critics alike. More critical articles and books have been written on Faulkner than on any other American author.

While Faulkner is perhaps best known for his novels, his stories also exemplify his major themes and characteristic style. "A Rose for Emily," set in Yoknapatawpha County, is the most anthologized of all Faulkner's short stories. Critics have read this Gothic tale of the ancient Miss Emily's loneliness as a commentary on Southern society's inability to let go of its past. Narrated by Quentin Compson, "That Evening Sun" also centers on Yoknapatawpha County and considers the uneasy race relations of the South in relation to the universal human conditions of fear, guilt, and despair. "Wash," first published in Harper's *in 1934, depicts the horrifying effects of the Civil War on ordinary people. Faulkner recycled the story in his 1936 novel* Absalom, Absalom! *"Barn Burning," a story of the Snopes family, won the O. Henry Memorial Award for best short story in 1939. One of the greatest hunting stories ever written, "The Bear" explores the relationship of man to wilderness.*

The versions of "A Rose for Emily," "Barn Burning," "That Evening Son," and "Wash" available in The Pearson Custom Library *issue from* The Collected Stories of William Faulkner *(New York: Random House, 1977). The two vastly different versions of "The Bear," the short magazine version first published in the* Saturday Evening Post *and the expanded version first published in* Go Down, Moses, *issue from* Uncollected Stories of William Faulkner *(New York: Random House, 1979) and* Three Famous Short Novels *(1942) respectively.*

Beth Widmaier Capo
Pennsylvania State University

For Further Reading

Primary Works

The Marble Faun (Boston: Four Seas, 1924); *Soldiers' Pay* (New York: Boni & Liveright, 1926; London: Chatto & Windus, 1930); *Mosquitoes* (New York: Boni and Liveright, 1927; London: Chatto & Windus, 1964); *Sartoris* (New York: Harcourt, Brace, 1929; London: Chatto & Windus, 1932); original, uncut version, edited by Douglas Day as *Flags in the Dust* (New York: Random House, 1974); *The Sound and the Fury* (New York: Cape & Smith, 1929; London: Chatto & Windus, 1931); *As I Lay Dying* (New York: Cape & Smith, 1930; London: Chatto & Windus, 1935); *Sanctuary* (New York: Cape & Smith, 1931; London: Chatto & Windus, 1931); unrevised version, edited by Noel Polk as *Sanctuary: The Original Text* (New York: Random House, 1981); *These 13* (New

York: Cape & Smith, 1931; London: Chatto & Windus, 1933); *Idyll in the Desert* (New York: Random House, 1931); *Miss Zilphia Gant* (Dallas: Book Club of Texas, 1932); *Salmagundi* (Milwaukee: Casanova, 1932); *Light in August* (New York: Smith & Haas, 1932; London: Chatto & Windus, 1933); *A Green Bough* (New York: Smith & Haas, 1933); *Doctor Martino and Other Stories* (New York: Smith and Haas, 1934; London: Chatto & Windus, 1934); *Pylon* (New York: Smith & Haas, 1935; London: Chatto & Windus, 1935); *Absalom, Absalom!* (New York: Random House, 1936; London: Chatto & Windus, 1937); *The Unvanquished* (New York: Random House, 1938; London: Chatto & Windus, 1938); *The Wild Palms* (New York: Random House, 1939; London: Chatto & Windus, 1939; Reprinted as *If I Forget Thee, Jerusalem* (Library of America, 1990); *The Hamlet* (New York: Random House, 1940; London: Chatto & Windus, 1940; revised, New York: Random House, 1964); *Go Down, Moses and Other Stories* (New York: Random House, 1942; London: Chatto & Windus, 1942); *The Portable Faulkner,* edited by Malcolm Cowley (New York: Viking, 1946; revised and enlarged, 1967); republished as *The Essential Faulkner* (London: Chatto & Windus, 1967); *Intruder in the Dust* (New York: Random House, 1948; London: Chatto & Windus, 1949); *Knight's Gambit* (New York: Random House, 1949; London: Chatto & Windus, 1951); *Collected Stories of William Faulkner* (New York: Random House, 1950; London: Chatto & Windus, 1951); *Notes on a Horsethief* (Greenville, Miss.: Levee, 1951); *Requiem for a Nun* (New York: Random House, 1951; London: Chatto & Windus, 1953); *Mirrors of Chartres Street* (Minneapolis: Faulkner Studies, 1953); *A Fable* (New York: Random House, 1954); London: Chatto & Windus, 1955); *Big Woods* (New York: Random House, 1955); *Faulkner's County: Tales of Yoknapatawpha County* (London: Chatto & Windus, 1955); *Jealousy and Episode: Two Stories* (Minneapolis: Faulkner Studies, 1955); *The Town* (New York: Random House, 1957; London: Chatto & Windus, 1958); *New Orleans Sketches,* ed. Carvel Collins (New Brunswick, N.J.: Rutgers University Press, 1958; London: Sidgwick & Jackson, 1959); *The Mansion* (New York: Random House, 1959; London: Chatto & Windus, 1961); *Faulkner's University Pieces,* ed. Collins (Tokyo: Kenkyusha, 1962; Folcroft, Pa.; Folcroft, 1970); *The Reivers* (New York: Random House, 1962; London: Chatto & Windus, 1962); *Early Prose and Poetry,* ed. *Collins* (Boston: Little, Brown, 1962; London: Cape, 1963); *Essays, Speeches & Public Letters,* ed. James B. Meriwether (New York: Random House, 1966; London: Chatto & Windus, 1967); *The Wishing Tree* (New York: Random House, 1967; London: Chatto & Windus, 1967); *The Big Sleep* [screenplay], by Faulkner, Jules Furthman, and Leigh Brackett (New York: Irvington, 1971); *The Marionettes: A Play in One Act* (Charlottesville: Bibliographical Society, University of Virginia, 1975); *Mayday* (South Bend, Ind.: University of Notre Dame Press, 1976); *Mississippi Poems* (Oxford, Miss.: Yoknapatawpha, 1979); *Uncollected Stories of William Faulkner,* ed. Joseph Blotner (New York: Random House, 1979); *To Have and Have Not* [screenplay], by Faulkner and Furthman (Madison: University of Wisconsin Press, 1980); *The Road to Glory* [screenplay], by Faulkner and Joel Sayre (Carbondale & Edwardsville: Southern Illinois University Press, 1981); *Helen: A Courtship* (Oxford, Miss.: Yoknapatawpha, 1981); *Faulkner's MGM Screenplays,* ed. Bruce F. Kawin (Knoxville: University of Tennessee Press, 1982); *Elmer*, ed. Dianne Cox (Northport, Ala: Seajay, 1983); *A Sorority Pledge* (Northport, Ala.: Seajay, 1983); *Father Abraham*, ed. Meriwether (New York: Random House, 1984); *The DeGaulle Story* [screenplay], eds. Louis Daniel Brodsky and Robert W. Hamblin (Jackson: University Press of Mississippi, 1984); *Vision in Spring*, ed. Judith Sensibar (Austin: University of Texas Press, 1984); *Battle Cry* [screenplay], ed. Brodsky and Hamblin (Jackson: University Press of Mississippi, 1985); *William Faulkner Manuscripts*, 25 volumes, eds. Blotner, Thomas L. McHaney, Michael Millgate, and Noel Polk (New York & London: Garland, 1986–1987); *Country Lawyer and Other Stories for the Screen*, ed. Brodsky and Hamblin (Jackson: University Press of Mississippi, 1987); *Stallion Road* [screenplay], ed. Brodsky and Hamblin (Jackson: University Press of Mississippi, 1989); *Snopes: A Trilogy*, 3 volumes—comprises *The Hamlet* (revised edition), *The Town*, and *The Mansion* (New York: Random House, 1964); *Three Famous Short Novels*—comprises *Spotted Horses*, *Old Man*, and *The Bear*.

Secondary Works

Joseph Blotner, *Faulkner: A Biography*, 2 vols. (New York: Random House 1974); Cleanth Brooks, *William Faulkner: Toward Yoknapatawpha and Beyond* (New Haven & London: Yale University Press, 1978); James B. Carothers, *William Faulkner's Short Stories* (Ann Arbor: UMI Research Press, 1985); Deborah Clarke, *Robbing the Mother: Women in Faulkner* (Jackson: University Press of Mississippi, 1994); Thadious M. Davis, *Faulkner's "Negro": Art and the Southern Context* (Baton Rouge: Louisiana State University Press, 1983); James Ferguson, *Faulkner's Short Fiction* (Knoxville: University of Tennessee Press, 1991); Richard J. Gray, *The Life of William Faulkner: A Critical Biography* (Oxford: Blackwell, 1994); Irving Howe, *William Faulkner: A Critical Study*, third edition, revised and enlarged (Chicago: University of Chicago Press, 1975); Evans Harrington and Ann J. Abadie, eds., *Faulkner and the Short Story: Faulkner and Yoknapatawpha, 1990* (Jackson: University of Mississippi Press, 1992); Frederick R. Karl, *William Faulkner: American Writer* (New York: Weidenfeld & Nicolson, 1989); Lewis Leary, *William Faulkner of Yoknapatawpha County* (New York: Crowell, 1973); John Matthews, *The Play of Faulkner's Language* (Ithaca, N.Y.: Cornell University Press, 1982); Michael Millgate, *The Achievement of William Faulkner* (New York: Vintage, 1966); Philip M. Weinstein, ed., *The Cambridge Companion to William Faulkner* (Cambridge, England: Cambridge University Press, 1995); Joel Williamson, *William Faulkner and Southern History* (New York: Oxford University Press, 1993).

Barn Burning[♦]

WILLIAM FAULKNER

The store in which the Justice of the Peace's court was sitting smelled of cheese. The boy, crouched on his nail keg at the back of the crowded room, knew he smelled cheese, and more: from where he sat he could see the ranked shelves close-packed with the solid, squat, dynamic shapes of tin cans whose labels his stomach read, not from the lettering which meant nothing to his mind but from the scarlet devils and the silver curve of fish—this, the cheese which he knew he smelled and the hermetic meat which his intestines believed he smelled coming in intermittent gusts momentary and brief between the other constant one, the smell and sense just a little of fear because mostly of despair and grief, the old fierce pull of blood. He could not see the table where the Justice sat and before which his father and his father's enemy (*our enemy* he thought in that despair; *ourn! mine and hisn both! He's my father!*) stood, but he could hear them, the two of them that is, because his father had said no word yet:

"But what proof have you, Mr. Harris?"

"I told you. The hog got into my corn. I caught it up and sent it back to him. He had no fence that would hold it. I told him so, warned him. The next time I put the hog in my pen. When he came to get it I gave him enough wire to patch up his pen. The next time I put the hog up and kept it. I rode down to his house and saw the wire I gave him still rolled on to the spool in his yard. I told him he could have the hog when he paid me a dollar pound fee. That evening a nigger came with the dollar and got the hog. He was a strange nigger. He said, 'He say to tell you wood and hay kin burn.' I said, 'What?' 'That whut he say to tell you,' the nigger said. 'Wood and hay kin burn.' That night my barn burned. I got the stock out but I lost the barn."

"Where is the nigger? Have you got him?"

"He was a strange nigger, I tell you. I don't know what became of him."

"But that's not proof. Don't you see that's not proof?"

♦"Barn Burning" was first published in *Harper's* magazine in June 1939. It was reprinted in *Collected Stories* (1950). Considered by some critics to be Faulkner's best short story, it was originally written as the opening chapter of *The Hamlet*, only to be edited out of the novel later. The text here is from the 1977 Vintage Books edition of *Collected Stories of William Faulkner*.

"Get that boy up here. He knows." For a moment the boy thought too that the man meant his older brother until Harris said, "Not him. The little one. The boy," and, crouching, small for his age, small and wiry like his father, in patched and faded jeans even too small for him, with straight, uncombed, brown hair and eyes gray and wild as storm scud, he saw the men between himself and the table part and become a lane of grim faces, at the end of which he saw the Justice, a shabby, collarless, graying man in spectacles, beckoning him. He felt no floor under his bare feet; he seemed to walk beneath the palpable weight of the grim turning faces. His father, stiff in his black Sunday coat donned not for the trial but for the moving, did not even look at him. *He aims for me to lie,* he thought, again with that frantic grief and despair. *And I will have to do hit.*

"What's your name, boy?" the Justice said.

"Colonel Sartoris Snopes,"[1] the boy whispered.

"Hey?" the Justice said. "Talk louder. Colonel Sartoris? I reckon anybody named for Colonel Sartoris in this country can't help but tell the truth, can they?" The boy said nothing. *Enemy! Enemy!* he thought; for a moment he could not even see, could not see that the Justice's face was kindly nor discern that his voice was troubled when he spoke to the man named Harris: "Do you want me to question this boy?" But he could hear, and during those subsequent long seconds while there was absolutely no sound in the crowded little room save that of quiet and intent breathing it was as if he had swung outward at the end of a grape vine, over a ravine, and at the top of the swing had been caught in a prolonged instant of mesmerized gravity, weightless in time.

"No!" Harris said violently, explosively. "Damnation! Send him out of here!" Now time, the fluid world, rushed beneath him again, the voices coming to him again through the smell of cheese and sealed meat, the fear and despair and the old grief of blood:

"This case is closed. I can't find against you, Snopes, but I can give you advice. Leave this country and don't come back to it."

His father spoke for the first time, his voice cold and harsh, level, without emphasis: "I aim to. I don't figure to stay in a country among people who . . ." he said something unprintable and vile, addressed to no one.

"That'll do," the Justice said. "Take your wagon and get out of this country before dark. Case dismissed."

His father turned, and he followed the stiff black coat, the wiry figure walking a little stiffly from where a Confederate provost's man's musket ball had taken him in the heel on a stolen horse thirty years ago, followed the two backs now, since his older brother had appeared from somewhere in the

---

[1]The boy, a member of the poor Snopes family, is named for a leading citizen of Jefferson who was a colonel in the Confederate Army. The itinerant Snopes family, the Sartoris family, and Major de Spain are recurring Yoknapatawpha County characters.

crowd, no taller than the father but thicker, chewing tobacco steadily, between the two lines of grim-faced men and out of the store and across the worn gallery and down the sagging steps and among the dogs and half-grown boys in the mild May dust, where as he passed a voice hissed:

"Barn burner!"

Again he could not see, whirling; there was a face in a red haze, moonlike, bigger than the full moon, the owner of it half again his size, he leaping in the red haze toward the face, feeling no blow, feeling no shock when his head struck the earth, scrabbling up and leaping again, feeling no blow this time either and tasting no blood, scrabbling up to see the other boy in full flight and himself already leaping into pursuit as his father's hand jerked him back, the harsh, cold voice speaking above him: "Go get in the wagon."

It stood in a grove of locusts and mulberries across the road. His two hulking sisters in their Sunday dresses and his mother and her sister in calico and sunbonnets were already in it, sitting on and among the sorry residue of the dozen and more movings which even the boy could remember—the battered stove, the broken beds and chairs, the clock inlaid with mother-of-pearl, which would not run, stopped at some fourteen minutes past two o'clock of a dead and forgotten day and time, which had been his mother's dowry. She was crying, though when she saw him she drew her sleeve across her face and began to descend from the wagon. "Get back," the father said.

"He's hurt. I got to get some water and wash his . . ."

"Get back in the wagon," his father said. He got in too, over the tail-gate. His father mounted to the seat where the older brother already sat and struck the gaunt mules two savage blows with the peeled willow, but without heat. It was not even sadistic; it was exactly that same quality which in later years would cause his descendants to over-run the engine before putting a motor car into motion, striking and reining back in the same movement. The wagon went on, the store with its quiet crowd of grimly watching men dropped behind; a curve in the road hid it. *Forever* he thought. *Maybe he's done satisfied now, now that he has . . .* stopping himself, not to say it aloud even to himself. His mother's hand touched his shoulder.

"Does hit hurt?" she said.

"Naw," he said. "Hit don't hurt. Lemme be."

"Can't you wipe some of the blood off before hit dries?"

"I'll wash to-night," he said. "Lemme be, I tell you."

The wagon went on. He did not know where they were going. None of them ever did or ever asked, because it was always somewhere, always a house of sorts waiting for them a day or two days or even three days away. Likely his father had already arranged to make a crop on another farm before he . . . Again he had to stop himself. He (the father) always did. There was something about his wolflike independence and even courage when the advantage was at least neutral which impressed strangers, as if they got from his latent ravening ferocity not so much a sense of dependability as a feeling that his ferocious conviction in the rightness of his own actions would be of advantage to all whose interest lay with his.

That night they camped, in a grove of oaks and beeches where a spring ran. The nights were still cool and they had a fire against it, of a rail lifted from a nearby fence and cut into lengths—a small fire, neat, niggard almost, a shrewd fire; such fires were his father's habit and custom always, even in freezing weather. Older, the boy might have remarked this and wondered why not a big one; why should not a man who had not only seen the waste and extravagance of war, but who had in his blood an inherent voracious prodigality with material not his own, have burned everything in sight? Then he might have gone a step farther and thought that that was the reason: that niggard blaze was the living fruit of nights passed during those four years in the woods hiding from all men, blue or gray, with his strings of horses (captured horses, he called them). And older still, he might have divined the true reason: that the element of fire spoke to some deep mainspring of his father's being, as the element of steel or of powder spoke to other men, as the one weapon for the preservation of integrity, else breath were not worth the breathing, and hence to be regarded with respect and used with discretion.

But he did not think this now and he had seen those same niggard blazes all his life. He merely ate his supper beside it and was already half asleep over his iron plate when his father called him, and once more he followed the stiff back, the stiff and ruthless limp, up the slope and on to the starlit road where, turning, he could see his father against the stars but without face or depth—a shape black, flat, and bloodless as though cut from tin in the iron folds of the frockcoat which had not been made for him, the voice harsh like tin and without heat like tin:

"You were fixing to tell them. You would have told him." He didn't answer. His father struck him with the flat of his hand on the side of the head, hard but without heat, exactly as he had struck the two mules at the store, exactly as he would strike either of them with any stick in order to kill a horse fly, his voice still without heat or anger: "You're getting to be a man. You got to learn. You got to learn to stick to your own blood or you ain't going to have any blood to stick to you. Do you think either of them, any man there this morning, would? Don't you know all they wanted was a chance to get at me because they knew I had them beat? Eh?" Later, twenty years later, he was to tell himself, "If I had said they wanted only truth, justice, he would have hit me again." But now he said nothing. He was not crying. He just stood there. "Answer me," his father said.

"Yes," he whispered. His father turned.

"Get on to bed. We'll be there tomorrow."

To-morrow they were there. In the early afternoon the wagon stopped before a paintless two-room house identical almost with the dozen others it had stopped before even in the boy's ten years, and again, as on the other dozen occasions, his mother and aunt got down and began to unload the wagon, although his two sisters and his father and brother had not moved.

"Likely hit ain't fitten for hawgs," one of the sisters said.

"Nevertheless, fit it will and you'll hog it and like it," his father said. "Get out of them chairs and help your Ma unload."

The two sisters got down, big, bovine, in a flutter of cheap ribbons; one of them drew from the jumbled wagon bed a battered lantern, the other a worn broom. His father handed the reins to the older son and began to climb stiffly over the wheel. "When they get unloaded, take the team to the barn and feed them." Then he said, and at first the boy thought he was still speaking to his brother: "Come with me."

"Me?" he said.

"Yes," his father said. "You."

"Abner," his mother said. His father paused and looked back—the harsh level stare beneath the shaggy, graying, irascible brows.

"I reckon I'll have a word with the man that aims to begin to-morrow owning me body and soul for the next eight months."

They went back up the road. A week ago—or before last night, that is—he would have asked where they were going, but not now. His father had struck him before last night but never before had he paused afterward to explain why; it was as if the blow and the following calm, outrageous voice still rang, repercussed, divulging nothing to him save the terrible handicap of being young, the light weight of his few years, just heavy enough to prevent his soaring free of the world as it seemed to be ordered but not heavy enough to keep him footed solid in it, to resist it and try to change the course of its events.

Presently he could see the grove of oaks and cedars and the other flowering trees and shrubs where the house would be, though not the house yet. They walked beside a fence massed with honeysuckle and Cherokee roses and came to a gate swinging open between two brick pillars, and now, beyond a sweep of drive, he saw the house for the first time and at that instant he forgot his father and the terror and despair both, and even when he remembered his father again (who had not stopped) the terror and despair did not return. Because, for all the twelve movings, they had sojourned until now in a poor country, a land of small farms and fields and houses, and he had never seen a house like this before. *Hit's big as a courthouse* he thought quietly, with a surge of peace and joy whose reason he could not have thought into words, being too young for that: *They are safe from him. People whose lives are a part of this peace and dignity are beyond his touch, he no more to them than a buzzing wasp: capable of stinging for a little moment but that's all; the spell of this peace and dignity rendering even the barns and stable and cribs which belong to it impervious to the puny flames he might contrive . . .* this, the peace and joy, ebbing for an instant, as he looked again at the stiff black back, the stiff and implacable limp of the figure which was not dwarfed by the house, for the reason that it had never looked big anywhere and which now, against the serene columned backdrop, had more than ever that impervious quality of something cut ruthlessly from tin, depthless, as though, sidewise to the sun, it would cast no shadow. Watching him, the boy remarked the absolutely undeviating course which his father held and saw the stiff foot come squarely down in a pile of fresh droppings where a horse had stood in the drive and which his father could have avoided by a simple change of stride. But it ebbed only for a moment, though he could not have thought this into words either, walking on in the spell of the house, which he could ever want but without envy, without sorrow, certainly never with that ravening and jealous rage which unknown to him walked in the ironlike black coat before him: *Maybe he will feel it too. Maybe it will even change him now from what maybe he couldn't help but be.*

They crossed the portico. Now he could hear his father's stiff foot as it came down on the boards with clocklike finality, a sound out of all proportion to the displacement of the body it bore and which was not dwarfed either by the white door before it, as though it had attained to a sort of vicious and ravening minimum not to be dwarfed by anything—the flat, wide, black hat, the formal coat of broadcloth which had once been black but which had now that friction-glazed greenish cast of the bodies of old house flies, the lifted sleeve which was too large, the lifted hand like a curled claw. The door opened so promptly that the boy knew the Negro must have been watching them all the time, an old man with neat grizzled hair, in a linen jacket, who stood barring the door with his body, saying, "Wipe yo foots, white man, fo you come in here. Major ain't home nohow."

"Get out of my way, nigger," his father said, without heat too, flinging the door back and the Negro also and entering, his hat still on his head. And now the boy saw the prints of the stiff foot on the doorjamb and saw them appear on the pale rug behind the machinelike deliberation of the foot which seemed to bear (or transmit) twice the weight which the body compassed. The Negro was shouting "Miss Lula! Miss Lula!" somewhere behind them, then the boy, deluged as though by a warm wave by a suave turn of carpeted stair and a pendant glitter of chandeliers and a mute gleam of gold frames, heard the swift feet and saw her too, a lady—perhaps he had never seen her like before either—in a gray, smooth gown with lace at the throat and an apron tied at the waist and the sleeves turned back, wiping cake or biscuit dough from her hands with a towel as she came up the hall, looking not at his father at all but at the tracks on the blond rug with an expression of incredulous amazement.

"I tried," the Negro cried. "I tole him to . . ."

"Will you please go away?" she said in a shaking voice. "Major de Spain is not at home. Will you please go away?"

His father had not spoken again. He did not speak again. He did not even look at her. He just stood stiff in the center of the rug, in his hat, the shaggy iron-gray brows twitching slightly above the pebble-colored eyes as he appeared to examine the house with brief deliberation. Then with the same deliberation he turned; the boy watched him pivot on the good leg and saw the stiff foot drag round the arc of the turning, leaving a final long and fading smear. His father never looked at it, he never once looked down at the rug. The Negro held the door. It closed behind them, upon the hysteric and indistinguishable woman-wail. His father stopped at the top of the steps and scraped his boot clean on the edge of it. At the gate he stopped again. He stood for a moment, planted stiffly on the stiff foot, looking back at the house. "Pretty and white, ain't it?" he said. "That's sweat. Nigger sweat. Maybe it ain't white enough yet to suit him. Maybe he wants to mix some white sweat with it."

Two hours later the boy was chopping wood behind the house within which his mother and aunt and the two sisters (the mother and aunt, not the two girls, he knew that; even at this distance and muffled by walls the flat loud voices of the two girls emanated an incorrigible idle inertia) were setting up the stove to prepare a meal, when he heard the hooves and saw the linen-clad man on a fine sorrel mare, whom he recognized even before he saw the rolled rug in front of the Negro youth following on a fat bay carriage horse—a suffused, angry face vanishing, still at full gallop, beyond the corner of the house where his father and brother were sitting in the two tilted chairs; and a moment later, almost before he could have put the axe down, he heard the hooves again and watched the sorrel mare go back out of the yard, already galloping again. Then his father began to shout one of the sisters' names, who presently emerged backward from the kitchen door dragging the rolled rug along the ground by one end while the other sister walked behind it.

"If you ain't going to tote, go on and set up the wash pot," the first said.

"You, Sarty!" the second shouted. "Set up the wash pot!" His father appeared at the door, framed against that shabbiness, as he had been against that other bland perfection, impervious to either, the mother's anxious face at his shoulder.

"Go on," the father said. "Pick it up." The two sisters stooped, broad, lethargic; stooping, they presented an incredible expanse of pale cloth and a flutter of tawdry ribbons.

"If I thought enough of a rug to have to git hit all the way from France I wouldn't keep hit where folks coming in would have to tromp on hit," the first said. They raised the rug.

"Abner," the mother said. "Let me do it."

"You go back and git dinner," his father said. "I'll tend to this."

From the woodpile through the rest of the afternoon the boy watched them, the rug spread flat in the dust beside the bubbling wash-pot, the two sisters stooping over it with that profound and lethargic reluctance, while the father stood over them in turn, implacable and grim, driving them though never raising his voice again. He could smell the harsh homemade lye they were using; he saw his mother come to the door once and look toward them with an expression not anxious now but very like despair; he saw his father turn, and he fell to with the axe and saw from the corner of his eye his father raise from the ground a flattish fragment of field stone and examine it and return to the pot, and this time his mother actually spoke: "Abner. Abner. Please don't. Please, Abner."

Then he was done too. It was dusk; the whippoorwills had already begun. He could smell coffee from the room where they would presently eat the cold food remaining from the mid-afternoon meal, though when he entered the house he realized they were having coffee again probably because there was a fire on the hearth, before which the rug now lay spread over the backs of the two chairs. The tracks of his father's foot were gone. Where they had been were now long, water-cloudy scoriations resembling the sporadic course of a lilliputian mowing machine.

It still hung there while they ate the cold food and then went to bed, scattered without order or claim up and down the two rooms, his mother in one bed, where his father would later lie, the older brother in the other, himself, the aunt, and the two sisters on pallets on the floor. But his father was not in bed yet. The last thing the boy remembered was the depthless, harsh silhouette of the hat and coat bending over the rug and it seemed to him that he had not even closed his eyes when the silhouette was standing over him, the fire almost dead behind it, the stiff foot prodding him awake. "Catch up the mule," his father said.

When he returned with the mule his father was standing in the black door, the rolled rug over his shoulder. "Ain't you going to ride?" he said.

"No. Give me your foot."

He bent his knee into his father's hand, the wiry, surprising power flowed smoothly, rising, he rising with it, on to the mule's bare back (they had owned a saddle once; the boy could remember it though not when or where) and with the same effortlessness his father swung the rug up in front of him. Now in the starlight they retraced the afternoon's path, up the dusty road rife with honeysuckle, through the gate and up the black tunnel of the drive to the lightless house, where he sat on the mule and felt the rough warp of the rug drag across his thighs and vanish.

"Don't you want me to help?" he whispered. His father did not answer and now he heard again that stiff foot striking the hollow portico with that wooden and clocklike deliberation, that outrageous overstatement of the weight it carried. The rug, hunched, not flung (the boy could tell that even in the darkness) from his father's shoulder struck the angle of wall and floor with a sound unbelievably loud, thunderous, then the foot again, unhurried and enormous; a light came on in the house and the boy sat, tense, breathing steadily and quietly and just a little fast, though the foot itself did not increase its beat at all, descending the steps now; now the boy could see him.

"Don't you want to ride now?" he whispered. "We kin both ride now," the light within the house altering now, flaring up and sinking. *He's coming down the stairs now,* he thought. He had already ridden the mule up beside the horse block; presently his father was up behind him and he doubled the reins over and slashed the mule across the neck, but before the animal could begin to trot the hard, thin arm came round him, the hard, knotted hand jerking the mule back to a walk.

In the first red rays of the sun they were in the lot, putting plow gear on the mules. This time the sorrel mare was in the lot before he heard it at all, the rider collarless and even bareheaded, trembling, speaking in a shaking voice as the woman in the house had done, his father merely looking up once before stooping again to the hame he was buckling, so that the man on the mare spoke to his stooping back:

"You must realize you have ruined that rug. Wasn't there anybody here, any of your women . . ." he ceased, shaking, the boy watching him, the older brother leaning now in the stable door, chewing, blinking slowly and steadily at nothing apparently. "It cost a hundred dollars. But you never had a hundred dollars. You never will. So I'm going to charge you twenty bushels of corn against your crop. I'll add it in your contract and when you come to the commissary you can sign it. That won't keep Mrs. de Spain quiet but maybe it will teach you to wipe your feet off before you enter her house again."

Then he was gone. The boy looked at his father, who still had not spoken or even looked up again, who was now adjusting the logger-head in the hame.

"Pap," he said. His father looked at him—the inscrutable face, the shaggy brows beneath which the gray eyes glinted coldly. Suddenly the boy went toward him, fast, stopping as suddenly. "You done the best you could!" he cried. "If he wanted hit done different why didn't he wait and tell you how? He won't git no twenty bushels! He won't git none! We'll gether hit and hide hit! I kin watch . . ."

"Did you put the cutter back in that straight stock like I told you?"

"No, sir," he said.

"Then go do it."

That was Wednesday. During the rest of that week he worked steadily, at what was within his scope and some which was beyond it, with an industry that did not need to be driven nor even commanded twice; he had this from his mother, with the difference that some at least of what he did he liked to do, such as splitting wood with the half-size axe which his mother and aunt had earned, or saved money somehow, to present him with at Christmas. In company with the two older women (and on one afternoon, even one of the sisters), he built pens for the shoat and the cow which were a part of his father's contract with the landlord, and one afternoon, his father being absent, gone somewhere on one of the mules, he went to the field.

They were running a middle buster now, his brother holding the plow straight while he handled the reins, and walking beside the straining mule, the rich black soil shearing cool and damp against his bare ankles, he thought *Maybe this is the end of it. Maybe even that twenty bushels that seems hard to have to pay for just a rug will be a cheap price for him to stop forever and always from being what he used to be;* thinking, dreaming now, so that his brother had to speak sharply to him to mind the mule: *Maybe he even won't collect the twenty bushels. May be it will all add up and balance and vanish—corn, rug, fire; the terror and grief, the being pulled two ways like between two teams of horses—gone, done with for ever and ever.*

Then it was Saturday; he looked up from beneath the mule he was harnessing and saw his father in the black coat and hat. "Not that," his father said. "The wagon gear." And then, two hours later, sitting in the wagon bed behind his father and brother on the seat, the wagon accomplished a final curve, and he saw the weathered paintless store with its tattered tobacco- and patent-medicine posters and the tethered wagons and saddle animals below the gallery. He mounted the gnawed steps behind his father and brother, and there again was the lane of quiet, watching faces for the three of them to walk through. He saw the man in spectacles sitting at the plank table and he did not need to be told this was a Justice of the Peace; he sent one glare of fierce, exultant, partisan defiance at the man in collar and cravat now, whom he had seen but twice before in his life, and that on a galloping horse, who now wore on his face an expression not of rage but of amazed unbelief which the boy could not have known was at the incredible circumstance of being sued by one of his own tenants, and came and stood against his father and cried at the Justice: "He ain't done it! He ain't burnt . . ."

"Go back to the wagon," his father said.

"Burnt?" the Justice said. "Do I understand this rug was burned too?"

"Does anybody here claim it was?" his father said. "Go back to the wagon." But he did not, he merely retreated to the rear of the room, crowded as that other had been, but not to sit down this time, instead, to stand pressing among the motionless bodies, listening to the voices:

"And you claim twenty bushels of corn is too high for the damage you did to the rug?"

"He brought the rug to me and said he wanted the tracks washed out of it. I washed the tracks out and took the rug back to him."

"But you didn't carry the rug back to him in the same condition it was in before you made the tracks on it."

His father did not answer, and now for perhaps half a minute there was no sound at all save that of breathing, the faint, steady suspiration of complete and intent listening.

"You decline to answer that, Mr. Snopes?" Again his father did not answer. "I'm going to find against you, Mr. Snopes. I'm going to find that you were responsible for the injury to Major de Spain's rug and hold you liable for it. But twenty bushels of corn seems a little high for a man in your circumstances to have to pay. Major de Spain claims it cost a hundred dollars. October corn will be worth about fifty cents. I figure that if Major de Spain can stand a ninety-five dollar loss on something he paid cash for, you can stand a five-dollar loss you haven't earned yet. I hold you in damages to Major de Spain to the amount of ten bushels of corn over and above your contract with him, to be paid to him out of your crop at gathering time. Court adjourned."

It had taken no time hardly, the morning was but half begun. He thought they would return home and perhaps back to the field, since they were late, far behind all other farmers. But instead his father passed on behind the wagon, merely indicating with his hand for the older brother to follow with it, and crossed the road toward the blacksmith shop opposite, pressing on after his father, overtaking him, speaking, whispering up at the harsh, calm face beneath the weathered hat: "He won't git no ten bushels neither. He won't git one. We'll . . ." until his father glanced for an instant down at him, the face absolutely calm, the grizzled eyebrows tangled above the cold eyes, the voice almost pleasant, almost gentle:

"You think so? Well, we'll wait till October anyway."

The matter of the wagon—the setting of a spoke or two and the tightening of the tires—did not take long either, the business of the tires accomplished by driving the wagon into the spring branch behind the shop and letting it stand there, the mules nuzzling into the water from time to time, and the boy on the seat with the idle reins, looking up the slope and through the sooty tunnel of the shed where the slow hammer rang and where his father sat on an upended cypress bolt, easily, either talking or listening, still sitting there when the boy brought the dripping wagon up out of the branch and halted it before the door.

"Take them on to the shade and hitch," his father said. He did so and returned. His father and the smith and a third man squatting on his heels inside the door were talking, about crops and animals; the boy, squatting too in the ammoniac dust and hoof-parings and scales of rust, heard his father tell a long and unhurried story out of the time before the birth of the older brother even when he had been a professional horsetrader. And then his father came up beside him where he stood before a tattered last year's circus poster on the other side of the store, gazing rapt and quiet at the scarlet horses, the incredible poisings and convolutions of tulle and tights and the painted leers of comedians, and said, "It's time to eat."

But not at home. Squatting beside his brother against the front wall, he watched his father emerge from the store and produce from a paper sack a segment of cheese and divide it carefully and deliberately into three with his pocket knife and produce crackers from the same sack. They all three squatted on the gallery and ate, slowly, without talking; then in the store again, they drank from a tin dipper tepid water smelling of the cedar bucket and of living beech trees. And still they did not go home. It was a horse lot this time, a tall rail fence upon and along which men stood and sat and out of which one by one horses were led, to be walked and trotted and then cantered back and forth along the road while the slow swapping and buying went on and the sun began to slant westward, they—the three of them—watching and listening, the older brother with his muddy eyes and his steady, inevitable tobacco, the father commenting now and then on certain of the animals, to no one in particular.

It was after sundown when they reached home. They ate supper by lamplight, then, sitting on the doorstep, the boy watched the night fully accomplish, listening to the whippoorwills and the frogs, when he heard his mother's voice: "Abner! No! No! Oh, God. Oh, God. Abner!" and he rose, whirled, and saw the altered light through the door where a candle stub now burned in a bottle neck on the table and his father, still in the hat and coat, at once formal and burlesque as though dressed carefully for some shabby and ceremonial violence, emptying the reservoir of the lamp back into the five-gallon kerosene can from which it had been filled, while the mother tugged at his arm until he shifted the lamp to the other hand and flung her back, not savagely or viciously, just hard, into the wall, her hands flung out against the wall for balance, her mouth open and in her face the same quality of hopeless despair as had been in her voice. Then his father saw him standing in the door.

"Go to the barn and get that can of oil we were oiling the wagon with," he said. The boy did not move. Then he could speak.

"What . . ." he cried. "What are you . . ."

"Go get that oil," his father said. "Go."

Then he was moving, running, outside the house, toward the stable: this the old habit, the old blood which he had not been permitted to choose for himself, which had been bequeathed him willy nilly and which had run for so long (and who knew where, battening on what of outrage and savagery and lust) before it came to him. *I could keep on,* he thought. *I could run on and on and never look back, never need to see his face again. Only I can't. I can't,* the rusted can in his hand now, the liquid sploshing in it as he ran back to the house and into it, into the sound of his mother's weeping in the next room, and handed the can to his father.

"Ain't you going to even send a nigger?" he cried. "At least you sent a nigger before!"

This time his father didn't strike him. The hand came even faster than the blow had, the same hand which had set the can on the table with almost excruciating care flashing from the can toward him too quick for him to follow it, gripping him by the back of his shirt and on to tiptoe before he had seen it quit the can, the face stooping at him in breathless and frozen ferocity, the cold, dead voice speaking over him to the older brother who leaned against the table, chewing with that steady, curious, sidewise motion of cows:

"Empty the can into the big one and go on. I'll catch up with you."

"Better tie him up to the bedpost," the brother said.

"Do like I told you," the father said. Then the boy was moving, his bunched shirt and the hard, bony hand between his shoulder-blades, his toes just touching the floor, across the room and into the other one, past the sisters sitting with spread heavy thighs in the two chairs over the cold hearth, and to where his mother and aunt sat side by side on the bed, the aunt's arms about his mother's shoulders.

"Hold him," the father said. The aunt made a startled movement. "Not you," the father said. "Lennie. Take hold of him. I want to see you do it." His mother took him by the wrist. "You'll hold him better than that. If he gets loose don't you know what he is going to do? He will go up yonder." He jerked his head toward the road. "Maybe I'd better tie him."

"I'll hold him," his mother whispered.

"See you do then." Then his father was gone, the stiff foot heavy and measured upon the boards, ceasing at last.

Then he began to struggle. His mother caught him in both arms, he jerking and wrenching at them. He would be stronger in the end, he knew that. But he had no time to wait for it. "Lemme go!" he cried. "I don't want to have to hit you!"

"Let him go!" the aunt said. "If he don't go, before God, I am going up there myself!"

"Don't you see I can't?" his mother cried. "Sarty! Sarty! No! No! Help me, Lizzie!"

Then he was free. His aunt grasped at him but it was too late. He whirled, running, his mother stumbled forward on to her knees behind him, crying to the nearer sister: "Catch him, Net! Catch him!" But that was too late too, the sister (the sisters were twins, born at the same time, yet either of them now gave the impression of being, encompassing as much living meat and volume and weight as any other two of the family) not yet having begun to rise from the chair, her head, face, alone merely turned, presenting to him in the flying instant an astonishing expanse of young female features untroubled by any surprise even, wearing only an expression of bovine interest. Then he was out of the room, out of the house, in the mild dust of the starlit road and the heavy rifeness of honeysuckle, the pale ribbon unspooling with terrific slowness under his running feet, reaching the gate at last and turning in, running, his heart and lungs drumming, on up the drive toward the lighted house, the lighted door. He did not knock, he burst in, sobbing for breath, incapable for the moment of speech; he saw the astonished face of the Negro in the linen jacket without knowing when the Negro had appeared.

"De Spain!" he cried, panted. "Where's . . ." then he saw the white man too emerging from a white door down the hall. "Barn!" he cried. "Barn!"

"What?" the white man said. "Barn?"

"Yes!" the boy cried. "Barn!"

"Catch him!" the white man shouted.

But it was too late this time too. The Negro grasped his shirt, but the entire sleeve, rotten with washing, carried away, and he was out that door too and in the drive again, and had actually never ceased to run even while he was screaming into the white man's face.

Behind him the white man was shouting, "My horse! Fetch my horse!" and he thought for an instant of cutting across the park and climbing the fence into the road, but he did not know the park nor how high the vine-massed fence might be and he dared not risk it. So he ran on down the drive, blood and breath roaring; presently he was in the road again though he could not see it. He could not hear either: the galloping mare was almost upon him before he heard her, and even then he held his course, as if the very urgency of his wild grief and need must in a moment more find him wings, waiting until the ultimate instant to hurl himself aside and into the weed-choked roadside ditch as the horse thundered past and on, for an instant in furious silhouette against the stars, the tranquil early summer night sky which, even before the shape of the horse and rider vanished, stained abruptly and violently upward: a long, swirling roar incredible and soundless, blotting the stars, and he springing up and into the road again, running again, knowing it was too late yet still running even after he heard the shot and, an instant later, two shots, pausing now without knowing he had ceased to run, crying "Pap! Pap!", running again before he knew he had begun to run, stumbling, tripping over something and scrabbling up again without ceasing to run, looking backward over his shoulder at the glare as he got up, running on among the invisible trees, panting, sobbing, "Father! Father!"

At midnight he was sitting on the crest of a hill. He did not know it was midnight and he did not know how far he had come. But there was no glare behind him now and he sat now, his back toward what he had called home for four days anyhow, his face toward the dark woods which he would enter when breath was strong again, small, shaking steadily in the chill darkness, hugging himself into the remainder of his thin, rotten shirt, the grief and despair now no longer terror and fear but just grief and despair. *Father. My father*, he thought. "He was brave!" he cried suddenly, aloud but not loud, no more than a whisper: "He was! He was in the war! He was in Colonel Sartoris' cav'ry!" not knowing that his father had gone to that war a private in the fine old European sense, wearing no uniform, admitting the authority of and giving fidelity to no man or army or flag, going to war as Malbrouck himself did: for booty—it meant nothing and less than nothing to him if it were enemy booty or his own.

The slow constellations wheeled on. It would be dawn and then sun-up after a while and he would be hungry. But that would be to-morrow and now he was only cold, and walking would cure that. His breathing was easier now and he decided to get up and go on, and then he found that he had been asleep because he knew it was almost dawn, the night almost over. He could tell that from the whippoorwills. They were everywhere now among the dark trees below him, constant and inflectioned and ceaseless, so that, as the instant for giving over to the day birds drew nearer and nearer, there was no interval at all between them. He got up. He was a little stiff, but walking would cure that too as it would the cold, and soon there would be the sun. He went on down the hill, toward the dark woods within which the liquid silver voices of the birds called unceasing—the rapid and urgent beating of the urgent and quiring heart of the late spring night. He did not look back.

[1939]

REVEREND MARTIN LUTHER KING, JR.
[1929–1968]

Reverend Martin Luther King, Jr.'s considerable spiritual and oratorical abilities helped galvanize millions of people to protest against legal segregation in the United States. In numerous speeches, interviews, and writings, King interlaced the long tradition of American and African-American political dissent with an African-American Christian faith in and practice of nonviolent action against injustice. In the years before his assassination in 1968, King spoke out against the war in Vietnam and economic injustice against the poor of all races and ethnicities. His efforts received international recognition, including the 1964 Nobel Peace Prize. In 1968, Reverend King was assassinated while appealing for better work conditions for Memphis sanitation workers. Since his death, many have called him a prophet of peace, justice, freedom, and democracy. A statue of Reverend King now sits above the entrance to Westminster Abbey in England.

Born on January 15, 1929, into a prominent black middle class family in Atlanta, Georgia, Martin Luther King, Jr. came of age when legalized segregation had been in place for nearly half a century. King's maternal great-grandfather, grandfather, and his father were all black Baptist preachers. King's father, Reverend Martin Luther King, Sr., was a pastor at Ebenezer Baptist Church. Between 1935 and 1944, King attended David T. Howard Elementary School, Atlanta University Laboratory School, and Booker T. Washington High School. He did not finish high school, opting instead to take a special examination that allowed him to enter Morehouse College at the age of fifteen. Over the next four years, King came in contact with many of the most important liberal and spiritual leaders of the time, including Dr. Benjamin Mays, then president of Morehouse College. In 1947, King's father ordained him as a minister and then licensed him to preach at Ebenezer Baptist Church.

After King graduated from Morehouse at the age of nineteen, he continued his education. He first enrolled in Crozer Theological Seminary in Chester, Pennsylvania, then part of the Northern Baptist Association. After he obtained a bachelor's degree in divinity in 1951, King entered the doctoral program at Boston University School of Theology. While in Boston, he met and soon married Coretta Scott, a graduate student at the New England Conservatory of Music. In 1954, Reverend King accepted the position as pastor of Dexter

Avenue Baptist Church in Montgomery, Alabama, one year before he completed his graduate work.

Later that same year, the landmark Supreme Court case, Brown v. Topeka, *made public school segregation illegal. Despite the 1954 Supreme Court case that called for desegregation in public schools, schools and the federal government made little, if any, effort to do so; de facto and de jure segregation remained firmly intact in other areas of American life. Frustrated by the limited federal and state response to the court's mandate, African Americans turned to boycotts and public protests, forms of dissent long used against racial discrimination. This time, however, these protests became more widespread and the participants encountered violent attacks; many African Americans faced economic intimidation and reprisals. Nonetheless, many persevered and the efforts spread to communities throughout the South. In Montgomery, Alabama, an African-American women's organization, whose members included Rosa Parks and JoAnn Gibson Robinson, decided to protest the city's bus segregation. On December 1, 1955, Rosa Parks was arrested for refusing to give up her seat to a white man. Other members of the women's organization quickly organized a bus boycott. Seeking a minister who could lead the community, but did not have ties to the local white political structure, the community turned to the new minister of Dexter Avenue Baptist Church.*

During the 381 days of the bus boycott, Reverend King emerged as a powerful and eloquent speaker who wove together an African-American Christian vision of a beloved community with an American political belief in the right to full citizenship. King added to these ideas by fitting the nonviolent forms of protest used by Mahatama Gandhi in India to the needs of African-American protest. Reverend King called for a disciplined and loving approach to end discrimination through nonviolent but purposeful marches, sit-ins, and boycotts. Reverend King's challenging call to end injustice and oppression through nonviolent protest was quickly embraced by many African Americans. Other Americans, too, began to support this revolution in U.S. social and political life. This increasingly interracial effort sparked a violent and organized backlash from people committed to maintaining segregation. This new approach to confront racial discrimination along with the frequent violent—and often murderous—efforts to maintain segregation shaped the civil rights movement for the next decade.

Though many other African Americans emerged to plan and lead the civil rights movement, Reverend King's charismatic personality and his eloquent ability to convey the moral and political reasons for ending segregation made him the most recognizable leader. Jailed in 1963 in Birmingham for participating in a boycott against the city's segregation laws and local police brutality, Reverend King wrote his now famous "Letter from Birmingham City Jail," articulating the moral imperative to defy unjust laws. Part theology, part political critique, King swayed a nation still skeptical of the movement's goals and tactics. He always recognized, however, that the movement he led depended on the courage of many. When he won the Nobel Peace Prize in 1964, he noted that he accepted "this award in behalf of a civil rights movement." Over the next years, King and others in the civil rights movement pushed for and ultimately won federal support for legislation that overturned discriminatory laws based on race in housing, voting, employment, transportation, and social services. His criticism of the war in Vietnam and economic discrimination claimed his attention during the last four years of his life. Reverend King was assassinated on April 4, 1968.

Over the course of his short public life, Reverend King left a variety of writing, including books, essays, sermons, and speeches. His "I Have a Dream" speech has become one of the most recognized speeches in American history; it has become one of the most significant orations of the twentieth century. The keynote speaker at the March on Washington, Reverend King delivered the speech in front of the Lincoln Memorial on August 28, 1963. He abandoned the text that he had written and instead gave an extemporaneous speech that masterfully articulated his hope in Americans' ability to create a "beloved community"; he also criticized American society for its failure to extend its democratic promise to all of its citizens. He nonetheless imagined that black and white Americans, together, would bring forth "a bright day of justice." Nearly a quarter of a million people attended the march, first conceived more than twenty years earlier by the labor activist A. Philip Randolph. Broadcast on television, millions more heard the speech in their living rooms. Thirty years after its delivery, the speech is a reminder that ordinary individuals can make extraordinary efforts to bring peace to the world.

Kimberly L. Phillips
The College of William and Mary

For Further Reading

Primary Works

Stride Toward Freedom: The Montgomery Story (New York: Harper and Row, 1958); *Where Do We Go from Here: Chaos or Community* (New York: Harper and Row, 1967); *Why We Can't Wait* (New York: Harper and Row, 1963).

Secondary Works

Fairclough, Adam. *To Redeem the Soul of America: The Southern Christian Leadership Conference and Martin Luther King, Jr.* (Athens, Ga.: University of Georgia Press, 1987); King, Coretta Scott. *My Life with Martin Luther King, Jr.* (New York: Rinehart and Winston, Inc., 1969); Lewis, David L. *King: A Critical Biography* (Baltimore: Penguin Books, Inc., 1970); Washington, James M., ed. *A Testament of Hope: The Essential Writings and Speeches of Martin Luther King, Jr.* (San Francisco: HarperSanFrancisco, 1986).

I Have a Dream

REVEREND MARTIN LUTHER KING, JR.

I am happy to join with you today in what will go down in history as the greatest demonstration for freedom in the history of our nation.

Five score years ago a great American in whose symbolic shadow we stand today signed the Emancipation Proclamation.[1] This momentous decree came as a great beacon light of hope to millions of Negro slaves who had been seared in the flames of withering injustice. It came as a joyous daybreak to end the long night of their captivity. But one hundred years later the Negro still is not free. One hundred years later the life of the Negro is still sadly crippled by the manacles of segregation and the chains of discrimination. One hundred years later the Negro lives on a lonely island of poverty in the midst of a vast ocean of material prosperity. One hundred years later the Negro is still languished in the corners of American society and finds himself in exile in his own land. So we've come here today to dramatize a shameful condition.

In a sense we've come to our nation's capital to cash a check. When the architects of our Republic wrote the magnificent words of the Constitution and the Declaration of Independence, they were signing a promissory note to which every American was to fall heir. This note was a promise that all men—yes, black men as well as white men—would be guaranteed the unalienable rights of life, liberty and the pursuit of happiness.[2] It is obvious today that America has defaulted on this promissory note insofar as her citizens of color are concerned. Instead of honoring this sacred obligation, America has given the Negro people a bad check, a check which has come back marked "insufficient funds."

But we refuse to believe that the bank of justice is bankrupt. We refuse to believe that there are insufficient funds in the great vaults of opportunity of

[1]King delivered his speech on the steps of the Lincoln Memorial, with the marble statue of Abraham Lincoln behind him. He referred to Lincoln's January 1, 1863, Emancipation Proclamation that freed the slaves in the states that were "in rebellion" against the United States.

[2]King quoted a line from the Declaration of Independence written by Thomas Jefferson. The phrase reads: "unalienable rights of life, liberty, and the pursuit of happiness." The Jefferson Memorial stands behind the Lincoln Memorial.

this nation. So we've come to cash this check, a check that will give us upon demand the riches of freedom and the security of justice.

We have also come to this hallowed spot to remind America of the fierce urgency of now. This is no time to engage in the luxury of cooling off or to take the tranquilizing drug of gradualism.[3] Now is the time to make real the promises of democracy. Now is the time to rise from the dark and desolate valley of segregation to the sunlit path of racial justice. Now is the time to lift our nation from the quicksands of racial injustice to the solid rock of brotherhood.

Now is the time to make justice a reality for all of God's children. It would be fatal for the nation to overlook the urgency of the moment. This sweltering summer of the Negro's legitimate discontent will not pass until there is an invigorating autumn of freedom and equality—nineteen sixty-three is not an end but a beginning. Those who hope that the Negro needed to blow off steam and will now be content will have a rude awakening if the nation returns to business as usual.[4]

There will be neither rest nor tranquility in America until the Negro is granted his citizenship rights. The whirlwinds of revolt will continue to shake the foundations of our nation until the bright day of justice emerges.

But there is something that I must say to my people who stand on the worn threshold which leads into the palace of justice. In the process of gaining our rightful place we must not be guilty of wrongful deeds. Let us not seek to satisfy our thirst for freedom by drinking from the cup of bitterness and hatred.

We must forever conduct our struggle on the high plane of dignity and discipline. We must not allow our creative protests to degenerate into physical violence. Again and again we must rise to the majestic heights of meeting physical force with soul force. The marvelous new militancy which has engulfed the Negro community must not lead us to a distrust of all white people, for many of our white brothers, as evidenced by their presence here today, have come to realize that their destiny is tied up with our destiny. They have come to realize that their freedom is inextricably bound to our freedom. We cannot walk alone. And as we walk we must make the pledge that we shall always march ahead. We cannot turn back.

There are those who are asking the devotees of civil rights, "When will you be satisfied?"

---

[3]King paraphrased the central thesis of his April 16, 1963, "Letter from Birmingham City Jail," where he criticized eight white clergymen who suggested that civil rights protesters "wait" for the courts to review segregation laws. King responded: " 'Wait' has almost always meant never."

[4]King inverted Shakespeare's "Now is the winter of our discontent/Made glorious summer by this sun of York . . ." to comment on the riots in Birmingham and Jacksonville. See *Richard III* I. i.

We can never be satisfied as long as the Negro is the victim of the unspeakable horrors of police brutality.

We can never be satisfied as long as our bodies, heavy with the fatigue of travel, cannot gain lodging in the motels of the highways and the hotels of the cities.[5]

We cannot be satisfied as long as the Negro's basic mobility is from a smaller ghetto to a larger one. We can never be satisfied as long as our children are stripped of their selfhood and robbed of their dignity by signs stating "For Whites Only."[6]

We cannot be satisfied as long as the Negro in Mississippi cannot vote and the Negro in New York believes he has nothing for which to vote.[7]

No, no, we are not satisfied, and we will not be satisfied until justice rolls down like waters and righteousness like a mighty stream.[8]

I am not unmindful that some of you have come here out of great trials and tribulations. Some of you have come fresh from narrow jail cells. Some of you have come from areas where your quest for freedom left you battered by the storms of persecution and staggered by the winds of police brutality. You have been the veterans of creative suffering.

Continue to work with the faith that unearned suffering is redemptive. Go back to Mississippi, go back to Alabama, go back to South Carolina, go back to Georgia, go back to Louisiana, go back to the slums and ghettos of our Northern cities, knowing that somehow this situation can and will be changed. Let us not wallow in the valley of despair.

I say to you today, my friends, so even though we face the difficulties of today and tomorrow, I still have a dream. It is a dream deeply rooted in the American dream. I have a dream that one day this nation will rise up, live out the true meaning of its creed: "We hold these truths to be self-evident, that all men are created equal."[9]

I have a dream that one day on the red hills of Georgia sons of former slaves and the sons of former slave-owners will be able to sit down together at the table of brotherhood. I have a dream that one day even the state of Mississippi, a state sweltering with the heat of injustice, sweltering

---

[5]Many hotels, restaurants, and gas stations in the South remained segregated.

[6]In many areas of the South, "For Whites Only" signs maintained segregation in most areas of public life. Throughout the United States, covenants prevented African Americans from purchasing homes.

[7]Between the 1880s and 1908, Southern states passed a variety of laws preventing blacks from voting. Despite concerted legal challenges and local protests by African Americans, these laws remained in effect until the 1965 Voting Rights Act overturned them.

[8]King was first a minister and his speeches often include quotations from the Bible. This statement paraphrases a well-known biblical passage from the Hebrew prophet Amos ("Let Justice roll down . . .)" See Amos 5:24.

[9]another sentence from the Declaration of Independence.

with the heat of oppression, will be transformed into an oasis of freedom and justice.

I have a dream that my four little children will one day live in a nation where they will not be judged by the color of their skin but by the content of their character. I have a dream today. I have a dream that one day down in Alabama, with its vicious racists, with its governor having his lips dripping with the words of interposition and nullification,[10] one day right there in Alabama little black boys and black girls will be able to join hands with little white boys and white girls as sisters and brothers.

I have a dream today. I have a dream that one day every valley shall be exalted, every hill and mountain shall be made low. The rough places will be made plain, and the crooked places will be made straight. And the glory of the Lord shall be revealed, and all flesh shall see it together.[11] This is our hope. This is the faith that I go back to the South with. With this faith we will be able to hew out of the mountain of despair a stone of hope. With this faith we will be able to transform the jangling discords of our nation into a beautiful symphony of brotherhood. With this faith we will be able to work together, to pray together, to struggle together, to go to jail together, to stand up for freedom together, knowing that we will be free one day.

This will be the day, this will be the day when all of God's children will be able to sing with new meaning, "My country, 'tis of thee, sweet land of liberty, of thee I sing. Land where my fathers died, land of the pilgrim's pride, from every mountainside, let freedom ring."[12] And if America is to be a great nation, this must become true. So let freedom ring from the prodigious hilltops of New Hampshire. Let freedom ring from the mighty mountains of New York. Let freedom ring from the heightening Alleghenies of Pennsylvania. Let freedom ring from the snowcapped Rockies of Colorado. Let freedom ring from the curvaceous slopes of California.

But not only that. Let freedom ring from Stone Mountain of Georgia. Let freedom ring from Lookout Mountain of Tennessee. Let freedom ring from every hill and molehill of Mississippi, from every mountainside.[13] Let freedom ring.

---

[10]Governor George Wallace of Alabama attempted to interpose state authority to nullify federal orders to integrate public facilities in the state.

[11]King quoted visionary language from the Hebrew prophet Isaiah ("Every valley shall be exalted...") that reappears in the Christian New Testament ("Every valley shall be filled in..."). See Isaiah 40:04 and Luke 3:05.

[12]These lines come from "My Country 'Tis of Thee," a song that the world-renowned singer Marian Anderson had sung on the steps of the Lincoln Memorial in 1939 after the Daughters of the American Revolution refused to let an African American sing in Constitution Hall.

[13]King borrowed and significantly embellished the "Let freedom ring" passage from a speech given by Archibald J. Carey, an African-American minister, at the 1952 Republican national convention.

And when this happens, when we allow freedom [to] ring—when we let it ring from every village and every hamlet, from every state and every city, we will be able to speed up that day when all of God's children, black men and white men, Jews and Gentiles, Protestants and Catholics, will be able to join hands and sing in the words of the old Negro spiritual, "Free at last, Free at last, Thank God a-mighty, We are free at last."

[1963]

JAMES WELDON JOHNSON
[1871–1938]

Critics often have a hard time describing James Weldon Johnson's work due to the sheer range and versatility of his writing. Indeed, Johnson's literary accomplishments account for only one small part of his wider contributions to the world. Johnson served the public as an attorney, a school principal, a diplomat, a professor of creative writing, and a civil rights activist. Often deemed the "elder statesman" of the New Negro Renaissance, Johnson bridged the nineteenth and twentieth centuries and forged a notion of African-American modernism that his descendents both praised and debated.

Johnson was born in Jacksonville, Florida. His father, a native of New York City, was a self-educated man who worked as a headwaiter; his mother, a native of the Bahamas, was the first African-American public schoolteacher in the state of Florida. The child of a securely middle class household, Johnson attended the Stanton School where his mother taught until the eighth grade. He then moved on to Atlanta University, where, after attending preparatory school, he received his undergraduate degree in 1884. During his college career, Johnson taught at a small rural black school near Hampton, Georgia, for two summers. He also spent much of his free time exploring the Georgia countryside, meeting rural blacks, and expanding his understanding of the varieties of African-American experience beyond his middle class upbringing.

Convinced of the importance of education to the problem of race improvement, Johnson returned to the Stanton School as principal after his graduation from college. While acting as principal, he embarked on the study of the law and was admitted to the Florida bar, despite the racist hostilities of his examiners. He also attempted to raise the level of literacy and awareness in his community through the publication of Jacksonville's first black newspaper, the Daily American, *which was in circulation for eight months between 1895 and 1896. Like many African Americans, however, Johnson began to feel the strain of the increasing racial restrictions that Southern blacks faced with the rise of Jim Crow legislation at the end of the century. He joined the great migration and moved to New York in 1902.*

Johnson's move gave him the opportunity to devote himself full-time to another of his loves: music. Johnson, his brother Rosamond, and Bob Cole formed a successful trio at the turn of the century, writing and performing their own tunes. In honor of Abraham Lincoln's birthday, Johnson and his brother composed "Lift Every Voice and Sing" (1900)—the work that came to be known as the "Negro National Anthem." Throughout the first decade of the century, they penned hits and played gigs, ultimately becoming popular enough on the New York club circuit to secure a six-week booking in London in 1905. Johnson's career as a musician and lyricist inspired him to thoughts of becoming a serious poet. To that end, he began to take graduate classes in his spare time at Columbia University, where he studied with the well-known literary critic Brander Matthews.

Johnson's career, however, took a somewhat unexpected turn in 1906 when, through the agency of powerful political friends, Johnson was appointed the U.S. Consul to Venezuela under Theodore Roosevelt. While in service, Johnson began to write verse and started work on a novel. The Autobiography of an Ex-Colored Man, *Johnson's first book, was published anonymously in 1912 while Johnson was working at his second diplomatic post in Nicaragua. Brander Matthews, keeping Johnson's authorship a secret, tried hard to promote the book, but the volume received little attention until it was re-released by Alfred Knopf in 1927 in the wake of Johnson's other literary successes. In 1913, Johnson resigned from the diplomatic ranks and returned to New York where he supported himself as a journalist and continued to write verse. His first book of poems,* Fifty Years and Other Poems, *a volume of sixty-five verses that ran the gambit from dialect poems, to poems on racial themes, to conventional love lyrics, appeared in 1917.*

The publication of Johnson's volume roughly coincided with his assumption of the role of field secretary for the National Association for the Advancement of Colored People (NAACP). Traveling throughout the country in the 1920s, Johnson proved highly effective at increasing the organization's membership while calling much-needed attention to racial injustice in America. Johnson also became increasingly convinced of the important role that the arts could play in the battle for racial equality. African Americans, he felt, would inevitably be judged as a race by the quality of the art they produced. Throughout the 1920s, Johnson assembled three anthologies to highlight the special cultural contributions of African Americans: The Book of American Negro Poetry *(1922),* The Book of American Negro Spirituals *(1925), and* The Second Book of American Negro Spirituals *(1926). In 1927, his second book of verse,* God's Trombones: Seven Negro Sermons in Verse, *appeared. Inspired by the orations of a black preacher that Johnson witnessed in Kansas City, the poems of* God's Trombones *constituted poetic reconstructions of what Johnson termed "the primitive stuff of the old-time Negro sermon." Together, the verse sermons argued the power and authority of a distinctive*

293

African-American idiom. Like his collections of spirituals, Johnson's book of verse sermons worked to convince readers of the beauty and artistry of vernacular forms of African-American expression.

Following his resignation of the NAACP post in 1930, Johnson joined the faculty of Fisk University as a professor of creative writing. In the wake of God's Trombones, however Johnson's own poetic output slowed significantly as he turned his attention to history, Black Manhattan *(1930), autobiography,* Along This Way *(1933), and political nonfiction,* Negro Americans, What Now? *(1934). In 1930, Johnson privately published his poem* Saint Peter Relates an Incident of the Resurrection *as a pamphlet. In 1935,* Saint Peter Relates an Incident: Selected Poems *appeared. The book contained thirty-seven poems from* Fifty Years and Other Poems, *many of them retitled or revised, along with only five previously uncollected verses.*

Johnson's literary legacy is still much debated. Like other members of the New Negro Renaissance, Johnson believed that black vernacular folk materials should form the basis of black art. Such materials, Johnson felt, offered the black author the best opportunity to express the spirit and life of black people. Unlike Claude McKay and, to a certain extent, Zora Neale Hurston, however, Johnson wished authors to use vernacular materials in such a way that they might reach and move a universal audience. Johnson conceived of black folk materials as the raw stuff of an art that, once crafted, could speak, not only to a particular enclave, but to all peoples. Some critics deem Johnson's use of folk art as a violation of the communal goals of such utterances. Born of separatist impulses, forged of often intentionally subversive languages and images, African-American folk materials, by definition, resist, or at least complicate, attempts to universalize them. Other critics view Johnson's work as a powerful melding of a modernist drive toward poetic experimentation with a committed sense of the enduring uniqueness of black culture. In making folk materials more "universal," the black poet does not weaken them, but rather reconstitutes them in a form that the new age demands.

For Further Reading

Primary Works

The Autobiography of an Ex-Colored Man (Boston: Sherman, French, 1912); republished as *The Autobiography of an Ex-Coloured Man* (New York & London: Knopf, 1927); *Fifty Years and Other Poems* (Boston: Cornhill, 1917); *God's Trombones; Seven Negro Sermons in Verse* (New York: Viking, 1927); *Black Manhattan* (New York: Knopf, 1930); *Saint Peter Relates an Incident of the Resurrection Day* (New York: privately printed, 1930); *Selected Writings of James Weldon Johnson* (New York: Oxford University Press, 1995); *Along This Way; The Autobiography of James Weldon Johnson* (New York: Viking, 1933;

Harmondsworth, U.K., and New York: Penguin, 1941); *Negro Americans, What Now?* (New York: Viking, 1934); *Saint Peter Relates an Incident: Selected Poems* (New York: Viking, 1935); *The Book of American Negro Poetry*, ed. Johnson (New York: Harcourt, Brace, 1922; enlarged, 1931); *The Book of American Negro Spirituals*, ed. Johnson (New York: Viking, 1925); *The Second Book of American Negro Spirituals*, ed. Johnson (New York: Viking, 1926); republished with *The Book of American Negro Spirituals in The Books of American Negro Spirituals* (1940).

Secondary Works

Robert E. Fleming, James Weldon Johnson, and Arna Wendell Bontemps, *A Reference Guide* (Boston: G. K. Hall, 1978); Robert E. Fleming, *James Weldon Johnson* (Boston: Twayne Publishers, 1987); Richard Kostelanetz, *Politics in the African-American Novel: James Weldon Johnson, W.E.B. Du Bois, Richard Wright, and Ralph Ellison* (New York: Greenwood Press, 1991); Eugene Levy, *James Weldon Johnson: Black Leader, Black Voice* (Chicago: University of Chicago Press, 1973); Kenneth Price and Lawrence Oliver, ed., *Critical Essays on James Weldon Johnson* (New York: Simon & Schuster, 1997); Robert B. Stepto, *From Behind the Veil: A Study of Afro-American Narrative* (Urbana: University of Illinois Press, 1979).

O Black and Unknown Bards[*]

JAMES WELDON JOHNSON

O black and unknown bards of long ago,
How came your lips to touch the sacred fire?
How, in your darkness, did you come to know
The power and beauty of the minstrel's lyre?
Who first form midst his bonds lifted his eyes?   5
Who first from out the still watch, lone and long,
Feeling the ancient faith of prophets rise
Within his dark-kept soul, burst into song?

Heart of what slave poured out such melody
As "Steal away to Jesus"?[1] On its strains   10
His spirit must have nightly floated free,
Though still about his hands he felt his chains.
Who heard great "Jordan roll"? Whose starward eye
Saw chariot "swing low"? And who was he
That breathed that comforting, melodic sigh,   15
"Nobody knows de trouble I see"?

What merely living clod, what captive thing,
Could up toward God through all its darkness grope,
And find within its deadened heart to sing
These songs of sorrow, love, and faith, and hope?   20
How did it catch that subtle undertone,
That note in music heard not with the ears?
How sound the elusive reed so seldom blown,
Which stirs the soul or melts the heart to tears.

---

[*]"O Black and Unknown Bards" first appeared in *Century Magazine* in November 1908.
[1]"Steal Away to Jesus," "Roll, Jordan, Roll," "Swing Low, Sweet Chariot," and "Nobody Knows De Trouble I See," and "Go Down, Moses" are all titles of African-American spirituals.

Not that great German master in his dream   25
Of harmonies that thundered amongst the stars
At the creation, ever heard a theme
Nobler than "Go down, Moses." Mark its bars,
How like a mighty trumpet-call they stir
The blood. Such are the notes that men have sung   30
Going to valorous deeds; such tones there were
That helped make history when Time was young.

There is a wide, wide wonder in it all,
That from degraded rest and servile toil
The fiery spirit of the seer should call   35
These simple children of the sun and soil.
O black slave singers, gone, forgot, unfamed,
You—you alone, of all the long, long line
Of those who've sung untaught, unknown, unnamed,
Have stretched out upward, seeking the divine.   40

You sang not deeds of heroes or of kings;
No chant of bloody war, no exulting paean
Of arms-won triumphs; but your humble strings
You touched in chord with music empyrean.
You sang far better than you knew; the songs   45
That for your listeners' hungry hearts sufficed
Still live—but more than this to you belongs:
You sang a race from wood and stone to Christ.

[1908]

The Creation[*]

JAMES WELDON JOHNSON

And God stepped out on space,
And he looked around and said:
I'm lonely—
I'll make me a world.

And far as the eye of God could see   5
Darkness covered everything,
Blacker than a hundred midnights
Down in a cypress swamp.

Then God smiled,
And the light broke,   10
And the darkness rolled up on one side,
And the light stood shining on the other,
And God said: That's good!

Then God reached out and took the light in his hands,
And God rolled the light around in his hands   15
Until he made the sun;
And he set that sun a-blazing in the heavens.
And the light that was left from making the sun
God gathered it up in a shining ball
And flung it against the darkness,   20
Spangling the night with the moon and stars.
Then down between
The darkness and the light
He hurled the world;
And God said: That's good!   25

Then God himself stepped down—
And the sun was on his right hand,

Reprinted by permission of Viking Penguin, a division of Penguin Books USA, Inc.
[*]"The Creation" first appeared in God's Trombones (1927).

And the moon was on his left;
The stars were clustered about his head,
And the earth was under his feet.   30
And God walked, and where he trod
His footsteps hollowed the valleys out
And bulged the mountains up.

Then he stopped and looked and saw
That the earth was hot and barren.   35
So God stepped over to the edge of the world
And he spat out the seven seas—
He batted his eyes, and the lightnings flashed—
He clapped his hands, and the thunders rolled—
And the waters above the earth came down,   40
The cooling waters came down.

Then the green grass sprouted,
And the little red flowers blossomed,
The pine tree pointed his finger to the sky,
And the oak spread out his arms,   45
The lakes cuddled down in the hollows of the ground,
And the rivers ran down to the sea;
And God smiled again,
And the rainbow appeared,
And curled itself around his shoulder.   50

Then God raised his arm and he waved his hand
Over the sea and over the land,
And he said: Bring forth! Bring forth!
And quicker than God could drop his hand,
Fishes and fowls   55
And beasts and birds
Swam the rivers and the seas,
Roamed the forests and the woods,
And split the air with their wings.
And God said: That's good!   60

Then God walked around,
And God looked around
On all that he had made.
He looked at his sun,
And he looked at his moon,   65
And he looked at his little stars;

He looked on his world
With all its living things,
And God said: I'm lonely still.

Then God sat down—   70
On the side of a hill where he could think;
By a deep, wide river he sat down;
With his head in his hands,
God thought and thought,
Till he thought: I'll make me a man!   75

Up from the bed of the river
God scooped the clay;
And by the bank of the river
He kneeled him down;
And there the great God Almighty   80
Who lit the sun and fixed it in the sky,
Who flung the stars to the most far corner of the night,
Who rounded the earth in the middle of his hand;
This Great God,
Like a mammy bending over her baby,   85
Kneeled down in the dust
Toiling over a lump of clay
Till he shaped it in his own image;

Then into it he blew the breath of life,
And man became a living soul.   90
Amen. Amen.

[1927]

Maya Angelou
[1928–   ]

Born Marguerite Johnson in St. Louis, Missouri, MAYA ANGELOU *was reared in rural Arkansas, which she portrays in her autobiography* I Know Why the Caged Bird Sings *(1970). After being violently attacked as a child, she refused to speak for several years, but she eventually found a voice that would influence millions during her lifetime. She grew up with a respected uncle and was a part of a larger Southern community that gave her both a voice and the ambition to change the lives of oppressed children and adults around the world. She married a South African freedom fighter and moved to Cairo, Egypt, where she edited the only English news source, the* Arab Observer. *She also began a career as an actor and dancer at this stage in her life. Next she moved to Ghana where she taught at the University of Ghana and edited the* African Review. *Upon her return to the United States Angelou was persuaded by Dr. Martin Luther King, Jr. to become the Northern leader of the Southern Christian Leadership Conference during the unrest of the sixties. She lent her powerful voice to the American civil rights movement and opened many doors for African Americans through her powerful presence and careful diplomacy. President Carter appointed her to the National Commission on the Observance of International Women's Year, and President Ford appointed her to the Bicentennial Commission so that she used her voice to speak for women around the world. During the seventies she was recipient of the* Ladies Home Journal *Woman of the Year Award. In 1981 she was nominated for the Pulitzer Prize and the National Book award. She received the Golden Eagle award for her PBS series* Afro-Americans in the Arts *and an Emmy for her performance in the acclaimed TV series* Roots. *She wrote the screenplay* Georgia *and was the first black woman to see her play filmed. She also produced, directed, and starred in* Cabaret for Freedom, *a political review.*

Angelou's career has included writing poetry, drama, and prose; acting, producing, and directing drama for both television and the theater; and civil rights activism at home and abroad. At the same time, she has thrilled audiences around the world with her brilliant readings and lectures and has moved many to follow her lead toward a positive advocacy for civil rights for all. She speaks French, Spanish, Italian, and West African Fanti. In 1993 she read at President Clinton's inauguration. She is currently Reynolds Professor of English at Wake Forest University in North Carolina and continues to travel widely, generously giving of her time and energy for political causes, poetry readings, and human rights.

"Still I Rise"
Maya Angelou

You may write me down in history
With your bitter, twisted lies,
You may trod me in the very dirt
But still, like dust, I'll rise.

Does my sassiness upset you?
Why are you beset with gloom?
'Cause I walk like I've got oil wells
Pumping in my living room.

Just like moons and like suns,
With the certainty of tides,
Just like hopes springing high,
Still I'll rise.

Did you want to see me broken?
Bowed head and lowered eyes?
Shoulders falling down like teardrops.
Weakened by my soulful cries.

Does my haughtiness offend you?
Don't you take it awful hard
'Cause I laugh like I've got gold mines
Diggin' in my own back yard.

You may shoot me with your words,
You may cut me with your eyes,
You may kill me with your hatefulness,
But still, like air, I'll rise.

Does my sexiness upset you?
Does it come as a surprise
That I dance like I've got diamonds
At the meeting of my thighs?

Out of the huts of history's shame
I rise
Up from a past that's rooted in pain
I rise
I'm a black ocean, leaping and wide,
Welling and swelling I bear in the tide.
Leaving behind nights of terror and
fear
I rise
Into a daybreak that's wondrously clear
I rise
Bringing the gifts that my ancestors
gave,
I am the dream and the hope of the
slave.
I rise
I rise
I rise

--Published 1978

Additional Stories

STEPHEN CRANE
[1871–1900]

*The range of Stephen Crane's work—from naturalistic fiction of widely dif-
fering geographical regions and urban slums, to psychological studies of war,
to pre-modernist poetry—suggests something of the complexity both of
Crane's imagination and of the period at the end of the nineteenth century.
This era is marked by its rejection of romantic idealism and unquestioned
faith, but only a budding conception of new formal and theological possibilities. Crane might well have become a major modernist writer had he not died
of tuberculosis at the age of twenty-eight. Still, he stands as one of the most
promising and prolific young writers of his era.*

*The fourteenth child of a Methodist minister and a temperance crusader,
Stephen Crane seemed relatively indifferent to everything in his life but writing. After brief enrollment at Pennington Seminary and two and a half years
study at Claverack, a military school in New York, Crane studied mining engi-
neering for a term at Lafayette College. He then entered Syracuse University,
where he spent most of his time working as a stringer for the* New York Tribune, *playing baseball, or writing stories. Crane's stint at Claverack may help
to explain his life-long fascination with the Civil War (concluded six years
before his birth) and the surprising realism of his war fiction—especially* The
Red Badge of Courage, *the novel that catapulted Crane to international fame
in 1895. Crane's most enduring fascination, however, was with writing itself.*

*In 1893, Crane published at his own expense and under the pseudonym
Johnston Smith a story he had begun writing while at Syracuse. "Maggie: A
Girl of the Streets" is now considered to be one of the first naturalistic novellas
or novels by an American. Crane had previously shown a manuscript of the
story to Hamlin Garland, an important realist with whom he played baseball
and talked about literature. After its publication, Crane mailed copies to Garland and several other writers and reformers who might promote the book,
inscribing these copies with words that stand as a kind of manifesto: "It is
inevitable that you be greatly shocked by this book but continue, please[,] with
all possible courage to the end. For it tries to show that environment is a
tremendous thing in the world and frequently shapes lives regardless. If one
proves that theory, one makes room in Heaven for all sorts of souls (notably an*

occasional street girl) who are not confidently expected to be there by many excellent people." Influenced by Jacob Riis's photographic studies of tenement life, Herbert Spencer's environmental ethics, Garland's aesthetic theories, and no doubt by his own mother's lectures on the demoralizing effects of alcohol, in "Maggie" Crane combined colloquial dialogue, broad-stroked psychological portraiture and precisely rendered environmental detail. The story garnered Crane the attention of William Dean Howells, who saw immediately that Crane brought something new to American fiction. By this time, Crane was already preparing The Red Badge of Courage *for abridged publication in several newspapers (December 1894) and writing the nihilistic, experimental poems to be published in his first collection of verse in 1895.*

After leaving Syracuse, Crane worked in New York as a journalist, traveling extensively through the West and to Mexico for feature articles. In 1896, he traveled to Florida, hoping to make it to Cuba in order to write about the Cuban revolution against Spain. While there he both met Cora Taylor, who would later become his life companion, and survived a shipwreck and thirty hours in a dinghy on the open sea—the experience leading to his extraordinary story, "The Open Boat." Taylor nursed Crane back to health, and then traveled with him to Greece, where he had an assignment for William Randolph Hearst's New York Journal *to report on the Greco-Turkish war. In 1897 they returned to England, where their neighbors included Joseph Conrad, Ford Maddox Hueffer, and Henry James. Crane collaborated on a drama with Conrad, James, H. Rider Haggard, H. G. Wells, and others ("The Ghost," performed 1899), and continued to write novels, stories, and poems. By this time he knew of his tuberculosis, but did not slow the pace of his writing or traveling. In 1898 Crane traveled to Florida, Puerto Rico, and finally Cuba to gather information as a war correspondent for the Spanish-American war. After his return to England, Crane suffered two hemorrhages in early 1900. He died in a sanitarium in Badenweiler, Germany, on June 5. Five of his books were published posthumously, between 1900 and 1902.*

Crane has been heralded as one of the great American naturalists, along with Theodore Dreiser—who may have been inspired by Crane's phenomenal success to turn increasingly from his own journalistic career to literature—and Frank Norris. Contradictorily, he is also seen as manipulating astutely psychological, impressionistic description and implied Christian symbolism, showing faith in the ultimate understanding and redemption of humanity. While some have argued that he rejected the idealism of his religious parents, others see him as maintaining the reformer's faith in the possibilities of human change. Similarly, while some have criticized Crane's peripatetic journalism as distracting him from the work of the imagination, others see his journalistic discipline and traveling as providing the basis for some of his finest work. In his fiction, Crane is master of the spare, declarative, deceptively simple style Ernest Hemingway is usually said to have invented. Little attention has been paid to

Crane as poet, but his poems are also groundbreaking for their times. With a compression like Emily Dickinson's and a caustic irony like Ambrose Bierce's, Crane's short-lined, anti-lyrical, formally untraditional verses anticipate the formal experiments of William Carlos Williams. Crane's work, in short, lies on the cusp of modernist form while maintaining a thematic focus representative of the realist aesthetic and naturalistic focus of his own generation. As Crane himself wrote in 1896, "I developed all alone a little creed of art which I thought was a good one. Later I discovered that my creed was identical with the one of Howells and Garland and in this way I became involved in the beautiful war between those who say that art is men's substitute for nature and [that] we are most successful in art when we approach the nearest to nature and truth, and those who say—well, I don't know what they say . . . [but they] keep Garland and I [sic] out of the big magazines." Crane claimed in a letter that he wanted "only to say what I saw." As part of the "beautiful war" of naturalistic expression against romanticism and sentimentalism, Crane reveals "what he saw" through stylistic innovations in fiction and poetry, containing both the spare clarity of pragmatic detail and the larger vistas of human vision.

For Further Reading

Primary Works

Maggie: A Girl of the Streets, 1893; The Black Riders, and Other Lines and The Red Badge of Courage, 1895; George's Mother and The Little Regiment, 1896; The Third Violet, 1897; The Open Boat and Other Tales of Adventure, 1898; War Is Kind, October Service, and The Monster and Other Stories, 1899; Whilomville Stories and Wounds in the Rain, 1900; Great Battles of the World, 1901; Last Words, 1902; The Works of Stephen Crane, 12 vols. Ed. Fredson Bowers, 1969–76; The Correspondence of Stephen Crane, 2 vols. Ed. Stanley Wertheim and Paul Sorrentino, 1987.

Secondary Works

R. W. Stallman, Stephen Crane: A Critical Biography, 1972; Joseph Katz, ed. Stephen Crane in Transition: Centenary Essays, 1972; James Nagel, Stephen Crane and Literary Impressionism, 1980; David Halliburton, The Color of the Sky: A Study of Stephen Crane, 1989; Chester L. Wolford, Stephen Crane: A Study of the Short Fiction, 1989; Christopher Benfey, The Double Life of Stephen Crane, 1992; Patrick K. Dooley, The Pluralistic Philosophy of Stephen Crane, 1993; Stanley Wertheim and Paul Sorrentino, The Crane Log: A Documentary Life of Stephen Crane, 1994; Bill Brown, The Material Unconscious American Amusement: Stephen Crane & The Economies of Play, 1996; Stanley Wertheim, A Stephen Crane Encyclopedia, 1997; Michael Robertson, Stephen Crane, Journalism, and the Making of Modern American Literature, 1997.

The Open Boat[*]

A TALE INTENDED TO BE AFTER THE FACT BEING THE EXPERIENCE OF FOUR MEN FROM THE SUNK STEAMER COMMODORE[1]

STEPHEN CRANE

I

None of them knew the color of the sky. Their eyes glanced level, and were fastened upon the waves that swept toward them. These waves were of the hue of slate, save for the tops, which were of foaming white, and all of the men knew the colors of the sea. The horizon narrowed and widened, and dipped and rose, and at all times its edge was jagged with waves that seemed thrust up in points like rocks.

Many a man ought to have a bath-tub larger than the boat which here rode upon the sea. These waves were most wrongfully and barbarously abrupt and tall, and each froth-top was a problem in small boat navigation.

The cook squatted in the bottom and looked with both eyes at the six inches of gunwale which separated him from the ocean. His sleeves were rolled over his fat forearms, and the two flaps of his unbuttoned vest dangled as he bent to bail out the boat. Often he said: "Gawd! That was a narrow clip." As he remarked it he invariably gazed eastward over the broken sea.

The oiler, steering with one of the two oars in the boat, sometimes raised himself suddenly to keep clear of water that swirled in over the stern. It was a thin little oar and it seemed often ready to snap.

The correspondent, pulling at the other oar, watched the waves and wondered why he was there.

The injured captain, lying in the bow, was at this time buried in that profound dejection and indifference which comes, temporarily at least, to even

---

[*]First published in *Scribner's Magazine* 21 in June, 1897; reprinted in *The Open Boat and Other Stories* published in London by William Heinemann in 1898.

[1]A steamship bound illegally for Cuba in 1897, during the Cuban Revolution and shortly before the Spanish-American war; while the story is fictional, Crane in fact spent thirty hours adrift at sea in a dinghy after the *Commodore* sank, finally landing at Daytona, Florida.

the bravest and most enduring when, willy nilly, the firm fails, the army loses, the ship goes down. The mind of the master of a vessel is rooted deep in the timbers of her, though he command for a day or a decade, and this captain had on him the stern impression of a scene in the grays of dawn of seven turned faces, and later a stump of a top-mast with a white ball on it that slashed to and fro at the waves, went low and lower, and down. Thereafter there was something strange in his voice. Although steady, it was deep with mourning, and of a quality beyond oration or tears.

"Keep'er a little more south, Billie," said he.

"'A little more south,' sir," said the oiler in the stern.

A seat in this boat was not unlike a seat upon a bucking broncho, and, by the same token, a broncho is not much smaller. The craft pranced and reared, and plunged like an animal. As each wave came, and she rose for it, she seemed like a horse making at a fence outrageously high. The manner of her scramble over these walls of water is a mystic thing, and, moreover, at the top of them were ordinarily these problems in white water, the foam racing down from the summit of each wave, requiring a new leap, and a leap from the air. Then, after scornfully bumping a crest, she would slide, and race, and splash down a long incline and arrive bobbing and nodding in front of the next menace.

A singular disadvantage of the sea lies in the fact that after successfully surmounting one wave you discover that there is another behind it just as important and just as nervously anxious to do something effective in the way of swamping boats. In a ten-foot dingey one can get an idea of the resources of the sea in the line of waves that is not probable to the average experience, which is never at sea in a dingey. As each slaty wall of water approached, it shut all else from the view of the men in the boat, and it was not difficult to imagine that this particular wave was the final outburst of the ocean, the last effort of the grim water. There was a terrible grace in the move of the waves, and they came in silence, save for the snarling of the crests.

In the wan light, the faces of the men must have been gray. Their eyes must have glinted in strange ways as they gazed steadily astern. Viewed from a balcony, the whole thing would doubtlessly have been weirdly picturesque. But the men in the boat had no time to see it, and if they had had leisure there were other things to occupy their minds. The sun swung steadily up the sky, and they knew it was broad day because the color of the sea changed from slate to emerald-green, streaked with amber lights, and the foam was like tumbling snow. The process of the breaking day was unknown to them. They were aware only of this effect upon the color of the waves that rolled toward them.

In disjointed sentences the cook and the correspondent argued as to the difference between a life-saving station and a house of refuge. The cook had said: "There's a house of refuge just north of the Mosquito Inlet Light, and as soon as they see us, they'll come off in their boat and pick us up."

"As soon as who see us?" said the correspondent.

"The crew," said the cook.

"Houses of refuge don't have crews," said the correspondent. "As I understand them, they are only places where clothes and grub are stored for the benefit of shipwrecked people. They don't carry crews."

"Oh, yes, they do," said the cook.

"No, they don't," said the correspondent.

"Well, we're not there yet, anyhow," said the oiler, in the stern.

"Well," said the cook, "perhaps it's not a house of refuge that I'm thinking of as being near Mosquito Inlet Light. Perhaps it's a life-saving station."

"We're not there yet," said the oiler, in the stern.

II

As the boat bounced from the top of each wave, the wind tore through the hair of the hatless men, and as the craft plopped her stern down again the spray slashed past them. The crest of each of these waves was a hill, from the top of which the men surveyed, for a moment, a broad tumultuous expanse; shining and wind-riven. It was probably splendid. It was probably glorious, this play of the free sea, wild with lights of emerald and white and amber.

"Bully good thing it's an on-shore wind," said the cook. "If not, where would we be? Wouldn't have a show."

"That's right," said the correspondent.

The busy oiler nodded his assent.

Then the captain, in the bow, chuckled in a way that expressed humor, contempt, tragedy, all in one. "Do you think we've got much of a show, now, boys?" said he.

Whereupon the three were silent, save for a trifle of hemming and hawing. To express any particular optimism at this time they felt to be childish and stupid, but they all doubtless possessed this sense of the situation in their mind. A young man thinks doggedly at such times. On the other hand, the ethics of their condition was decidedly against any open suggestion of hopelessness. So they were silent.

"Oh, well," said the captain, soothing his children, "we'll get ashore all right."

But there was that in his tone which made them think, so the oiler quoth: "Yes! If this wind holds!"

The cook was bailing: "Yes! If we don't catch hell in the surf."

Canton flannel gulls flew near and far. Sometimes they sat down on the sea, near patches of brown sea-weed that rolled over the waves with a movement like carpets on a line in a gale. The birds sat comfortably in groups, and they were envied by some in the dingey, for the wrath of the sea was no more to them than it was to a covey of prairie chickens a thousand miles inland. Often they came very close and stared at the men with black beadlike eyes. At these times they were uncanny and sinister in their unblinking scrutiny, and the men hooted angrily at them, telling them to be gone. One came, and evidently decided to alight on the top of the captain's head. The bird flew parallel to the boat and did not circle, but made short sidelong jumps in the air in chicken-fashion. His black eyes were wistfully fixed upon the captain's head. "Ugly brute," said the oiler to the bird. "You look as if you were made with a jack-knife." The cook and the correspondent swore darkly at the creature. The captain naturally wished to knock it away with the end of the heavy painter,[2] but he did not dare do it, because anything resembling an emphatic gesture would have capsized this freighted boat, and so with his open hand, the captain gently and carefully waved the gull away. After it had been discouraged from the pursuit the captain breathed easier on account of his hair, and others breathed easier because the bird struck their minds at this time as being somehow grewsome and ominous.

In the meantime the oiler and the correspondent rowed. And also they rowed.

They sat together in the same seat, and each rowed an oar. Then the oiler took both oars; then the correspondent took both oars; then the oiler; then the correspondent. They rowed and they rowed. The very ticklish part of the business was when the time came for the reclining one in the stern to take his turn at the oars. By the very last star of truth, it is easier to steal eggs from under a hen than it was to change seats in the dingey. First the man in the stern slid his hand along the thwart and moved with care, as if he were of Sèvres.[3] Then the man in the rowing seat slid his hand along the other thwart. It was all done with the most extraordinary care. As the two sidled past each other, the whole party kept watchful eyes on the coming wave, and the captain cried: "Look out now! Steady there!"

The brown mats of sea-weed that appeared from time to time were like islands, bits of earth. They were travelling, apparently, neither one way nor the other. They were, to all intents, stationary. They informed the men in the boat that it was making progress slowly toward the land.

The captain, rearing cautiously in the bow, after the dingey soared on a great swell, said that he had seen the lighthouse at Mosquito Inlet. Presently the cook remarked that he had seen it. The correspondent was at the oars, then, and for some reason he too wished to look at the lighthouse, but his back was toward the far shore and the waves were important, and for some time he could not seize an opportunity to turn his head. But at last there came a wave more gentle than the others, and when at the crest of it he swiftly scoured the western horizon.

---

[2]A rope attached to the bow, used for tying a boat to the wharf.

[3]A fine porcelain named for the city in France where it is manufactured.

"See it?" said the captain.

"No," said the correspondent, slowly, I didn't see anything."

"Look again," said the captain. He pointed. "It's exactly in that direction."

At the top of another wave, the correspondent did as he was bid, and this time his eyes chanced on a small still thing on the edge of the swaying horizon. It was precisely like the point of a pin. It took an anxious eye to find a lighthouse so tiny.

"Think we'll make it, captain?"

"If this wind holds and the boat don't swamp, we can't do much else," said the captain.

The little boat, lifted by each towering sea, and splashed viciously by the crests, made progress that in the absence of seaweed was not apparent to those in her. She seemed just a wee thing wallowing, miraculously, top-up, at the mercy of five oceans. Occasionally, a great spread of water, like white flames, swarmed into her.

"Bail her, cook," said the captain, serenely.

"All right, captain," said the cheerful cook.

III

It would be difficult to describe the subtle brotherhood of men that was here established on the seas. No one said that it was so. No one mentioned it. But it dwelt in the boat, and each man felt it warm him. They were a captain, an oiler, a cook, and a correspondent, and they were friends, friends in a more curiously ironbound degree than may be common. The hurt captain, lying against the waterjar in the bow, spoke always in a low voice and calmly, but he could never command a more ready and swiftly obedient crew than the motley three of the dingey. It was more than a mere recognition of what was best for the common safety. There was surely in it a quality that was personal and heartfelt. And after this devotion to the commander of the boat there was this comradeship that the correspondent, for instance, who had been taught to be cynical of men, knew even at the time was the best experience of his life. But no one said that it was so. No one mentioned it.

"I wish we had a sail," remarked the captain. "We might try my overcoat on the end of an oar and give you two boys a chance to rest." So the cook and the correspondent held the mast and spread wide the overcoat. The oiler steered, and the little boat made good way with her new rig. Sometimes the oiler had to scull sharply to keep a sea from breaking into the boat, but otherwise sailing was a success.

Meanwhile the light-house had been growing slowly larger. It had now almost assumed color, and appeared like a little gray shadow on the sky. The man at the oars could not be prevented from turning his head rather often to try for a glimpse of this little gray shadow.

At last, from the top of each wave the men in the tossing boat could see land. Even as the light-house was an upright shadow on the sky, this land seemed but a long black shadow on the sea. It certainly was thinner than paper. "We must be about opposite New Smyrna," said the cook, who had coasted this shore often in schooners. "Captain, by the way, I believe they abandoned that life-saving station there about a year ago."

"Did they?" said the captain.

The wind slowly died away. The cook and the correspondent were not now obliged to slave in order to hold high the oar. But the waves continued their old impetuous swooping at the dingey, and the little craft, no longer under way, struggled woundily over them. The oiler or the correspondent took the oars again.

Shipwrecks are *apropos* of nothing. If men could only train for them and have them occur when the men had reached pink condition, there would be less drowning at sea. Of the four in the dingey none had slept any time worth mentioning for two days and two nights previous to embarking in the dingey, and in the excitement of clambering about the deck of a foundering ship they had also forgotten to eat heartily.

For these reasons, and for others, neither the oiler nor the correspondent was fond of rowing at this time. The correspondent wondered ingenuously how in the name of all that was sane could there be people who thought it amusing to row a boat. It was not an amusement; it was a diabolical punishment, and even a genius of mental aberrations could never conclude that it was anything but horror to the muscles and a crime against the back. He mentioned to the boat in general how the amusement of rowing struck him, and the weary-faced oiler smiled in full sympathy. Previously to the foundering, by the way, the oiler had worked doublewatch in the engine-room of the ship.

"Take her easy, now, boys," said the captain. "Don't spend yourselves. If we have to run a surf you'll need all your strength, because we'll sure have to swim for it. Take your time."

Slowly the land arose from the sea. From a black line it became a line of black and a line of white, trees, and sand. Finally, the captain said that he could make out a house on the shore. "That's the house of refuge, sure," said the cook. "They'll see us before long, and come out after us."

The distant light-house reared high. "The keeper ought to be able to make us out now, if he's looking through a glass," said the captain. "He'll notify the life-saving people."

"None of those other boats could have got ashore to give word of the wreck," said the oiler, in a low voice. "Else the life-boat would be out hunting us."

Slowly and beautifully the land loomed out of the sea. The wind came again. It had veered from the northeast to the southeast. Finally, a new sound struck the ears of the men in the boat. It was the low thunder of the surf on the shore. "We'll never be able to make the light-house now," said the captain. "Swing her head a little more north, Billie," said the captain.

"'A little more north,' sir," said the oiler.

Whereupon the little boat turned her nose once more down the wind, and all but the oarsman watched the shore grow. Under the influence of this expansion doubt and direful apprehension was leaving the minds of the men. The management of the boat was still most absorbing, but it could not prevent a quiet cheerfulness. In an hour, perhaps, they would be ashore.

Their back-bones had become thoroughly used to balancing in the boat and they now rode this wild colt of a dingey like circus men. The correspondent thought that he had been drenched to the skin, but happening to feel in the top pocket of his coat, he found therein eight cigars. Four of them were soaked with sea-water; four were perfectly scatheless. After a search, somebody produced three dry matches, and thereupon the four waifs rode in their little boat, and with an assurance of an impending rescue shining in their eyes, puffed at the big cigars and judged well and ill of all men. Everybody took a drink of water.

IV

"Cook," remarked the captain, "there don't seem to be any signs of life about your house of refuge."

"No," replied the cook. "Funny they don't see us!"

A broad stretch of lowly coast lay before the eyes of the men. It was of low dunes topped with dark vegetation. The roar of the surf was plain, and sometimes they could see the white lip of a wave as it spun up the beach. A tiny house was blocked out black upon the sky. Southward, the slim light-house lifted its little gray length.

Tide, wind, and waves were swinging the dingey northward. "Funny they don't see us," said the men.

The surf's roar was here dulled, but its tone was, nevertheless, thunderous and mighty. As the boat swam over the great rollers, the men sat listening to this roar.

"We'll swamp sure," said everybody.

It is fair to say here that there was not a life-saving station within twenty miles in either direction, but the men did not know this fact and in consequence they made dark and opprobrious remarks concerning the eyesight of the nation's life-savers. Four scowling men sat in the dingey and surpassed records in the invention of epithets.

"Funny they don't see us."

The light-heartedness of a former time had completely faded. To their sharpened minds it was easy to conjure pictures of all kinds of incompetency and blindness and, indeed, cowardice. There was the shore of the populous land, and it was bitter and bitter to them that from it came no sign.

"Well," said the captain, ultimately, "I suppose we'll have to make a try for ourselves. If we stay out here too long, we'll none of us have strength left to swim after the boat swamps."

And so the oiler, who was at the oars, turned the boat straight for the shore. There was a sudden tightening of muscles. There was some thinking.

"If we don't all get ashore—" said the captain. "If we don't all get ashore, I suppose you fellows know where to send news of my finish?"

They then briefly exchanged some addresses and admonitions. As for the reflections of the men, there was a great deal of rage in them. Perchance they might be formulated thus: "If I am going to be drowned—if I am going to be drowned—if I am going to be drowned, why, in the name of the seven mad gods who rule the sea, was I allowed to come thus far and contemplate sand and trees? Was I brought here merely to have my nose dragged away as I was about to nibble the sacred cheese of life? It is preposterous. If this old ninny-woman, Fate, cannot do better than this, she should be deprived of the management of men's fortunes. She is an old hen who knows not her intention. If she has decided to drown me, why did she not do it in the beginning and save me all this trouble. The whole affair is absurd. . . . But, no, she cannot mean to drown me. She dare not drown me. She cannot drown me. Not after all this work." Afterward the man might have had an impulse to shake his fist at the clouds: "Just you drown me, now, and then hear what I call you!"

The billows that came at this time were more formidable. They seemed always just about to break and roll over the little boat in a turmoil of foam. There was a preparatory and long growl in the speech of them. No mind unused to the sea would have concluded that the dingey could ascend these sheer heights in time. The shore was still afar. The oiler was a wily surfman. "Boys," he said, swiftly, "she won't live three minutes more and we're too far out to swim. Shall I take her to sea again, captain?"

"Yes! Go ahead!" said the captain.

This oiler, by a series of quick miracles, and fast and steady oarsmanship, turned the boat in the middle of the surf and took her safely to sea again.

There was a considerable silence as the boat bumped over the furrowed sea to deeper water. Then somebody in gloom spoke. "Well, anyhow, they must have seen us from the shore by now."

The gulls went in slanting flight up the wind toward the gray desolate east. A squall, marked by dingy clouds, and clouds brick-red, like smoke from a burning building, appeared from the southeast.

"What do you think of those life-saving people? Ain't they peaches?"

"Funny they haven't seen us."

"Maybe they think we're out here for sport! Maybe they think we're fishin'. Maybe they think we're damned fools."

It was a long afternoon. A changed tide tried to force them southward, but wind and wave said northward. Far ahead, where coast-line, sea, and sky formed their mighty angle, there were little dots which seemed to indicate a city on the shore.

"St. Augustine?"

The captain shook his head. "Too near Mosquito Inlet."

And the oiler rowed, and then the correspondent rowed. Then the oiler rowed. It was a weary business. The human back can become the seat of more aches and pains than are registered in books for the composite anatomy of a regiment. It is a limited area, but it can become the theatre of innumerable muscular conflicts, tangles, wrenches, knots, and other comforts.

"Did you ever like to row, Billie?" asked the correspondent.

"No," said the oiler. "Hang it."

When one exchanged the rowing-seat for a place in the bottom of the boat, he suffered a bodily depression that caused him to be careless of everything save an obligation to wiggle one finger. There was cold sea-water swashing to and fro in the boat, and he lay in it. His head, pillowed on a thwart, was within an inch of the swirl of a wave crest, and sometimes a particularly obstreperous sea came in-board and drenched him once more. But these matters did not annoy him. It is almost certain that if the boat had capsized he would have tumbled comfortably out upon the ocean as if he felt sure that it was a great soft mattress.

"Look! There's a man on the shore!"

"Where?"

"There! See 'im? See 'im?"

"Yes, sure! He's walking along."

"Now he's stopped. Look! He's facing us!"

"He's waving at us!"

"So he is! By thunder!"

"Ah, now, we're all right! Now we're all right! There'll be a boat out here for us in half an hour."

"He's going on. He's running. He's going up to that house there."

The remote beach seemed lower than the sea, and it required a searching glance to discern the little black figure. The captain saw a floating stick and they rowed to it. A bath-towel was by some weird chance in the boat, and, tying this on the stick, the captain waved it. The oarsman did not dare turn his head, so he was obliged to ask questions.

"What's he doing now?"

"He's standing still again. He's looking, I think. . . . There he goes again. Toward the house. . . . Now he's stopped again."

"Is he waving at us?"

"No, not now! he was, though."

"Look! There comes another man!"

"He's running."

"Look at him go, would you."

"Why, he's on a bicycle. Now he's met the other man. They're both waving at us. Look!"

"There comes something up the beach."

"What the devil is that thing?"

"Why, it looks like a boat."

"Why, certainly it's a boat."

"No, it's on wheels."

"Yes, so it is. Well, that must be the life-boat. They drag them along shore on a wagon.

"That's the life-boat, sure."

"No, by—, it's—it's an omnibus."

"I tell you it's a life-boat."

"It is not! It's an omnibus. I can see it plain. See? One of these big hotel omnibuses."

"By thunder, you're right. It's an omnibus, sure as fate. What do you suppose they are doing with an omnibus? Maybe they are going around collecting the life-crew, hey?"

"That's it, likely. Look! There's a fellow waving a little black flag. He's standing on the steps of the omnibus. There come those other two fellows. Now they're all talking together. Look at the fellow with the flag. Maybe he ain't waving it."

"That ain't a flag, is it? That's his coat. Why, certainly, that's his coat."

"So it is. It's his coat. He's taken it off and is waving it around his head. But would you look at him swing it."

"Oh, say, there isn't any life-saving station there. That's just a winter resort hotel omnibus that has brought over some of the boarders to see us drown."

"What's that idiot with the coat mean? What's he signaling, anyhow?"

"It looks as if he were trying to tell us to go north. There must be a life-saving station up there."

"No! He thinks we're fishing. Just giving us a merry hand. See? Ah, there, Willie."

"Well, I wish I could make something out of those signals. What do you suppose he means?"

"He don't mean anything. He's just playing."

"Well, if he'd just signal us to try the surf again, or to go to sea and wait, or go north, or go south, or go to hell—there would be some reason in it. But look at him. He just stands there and keeps his coat revolving like a wheel. The ass!"

"There come more people."

"Now there's quite a mob. Look! Isn't that a boat?"

"Where? Oh, I see where you mean. No, that's no boat."

"That fellow is still waving his coat."

"He must think we like to see him do that. Why don't he quit it. It don't mean anything."

"I don't know. I think he is trying to make us go north. It must be that there's a life-saving station there somewhere."

"Say, he ain't tired yet. Look at 'im wave."

"Wonder how long he can keep that up. He's been revolving his coat ever since he caught sight of us. He's an idiot. Why aren't they getting men to bring a boat out. A fishing boat—one of those big yawls—could come out here all right. Why don't he do something?"

"Oh, it's all right, now."

"They'll have a boat out here for us in less than no time, now that they've seen us."

A faint yellow tone came into the sky over the low land. The shadows on the sea slowly deepened. The wind bore coldness with it, and the men began to shiver.

"Holy smoke!" said one, allowing his voice to express his impious mood, "if we keep on monkeying out here! If we've got to flounder out here all night!"

"Oh, we'll never have to stay here all night! Don't you worry. They've seen us now, and it won't be long before they'll come chasing out after us."

The shore grew dusky. The man waving a coat blended gradually into this gloom, and it swallowed in the same manner the omnibus and the group of people. The spray, when it dashed uproariously over the side, made the voyagers shrink and swear like men who were being branded.

"I'd like to catch the chump who waved the coat. I feel like soaking him one, just for luck."

"Why? What did he do?"

"Oh, nothing, but then he seemed so damned cheerful."

In the meantime the oiler rowed, and then the correspondent rowed, and then the oiler rowed. Gray-faced and bowed forward, they mechanically, turn by turn, plied the leaden oars. The form of the light-house had vanished from the southern horizon, but finally a pale star appeared, just lifting from the sea. The streaked saffron in the west passed before the all-merging darkness, and the sea to the east was black. The land had vanished, and was expressed only by the low and drear thunder of the surf.

"If I am going to be drowned—if I am going to be drowned—if I am going to be drowned, why, in the name of the seven mad gods, who rule the sea, was I allowed to come thus far and contemplate sand and trees? Was I brought here merely to have my nose dragged away as I was about to nibble the sacred cheese of life?"

The patient captain, drooped over the water-jar, was sometimes obliged to speak to the oarsman.

"Keep her head up! Keep her head up!"

"'Keep her head up,' sir." The voices were weary and low.

This was surely a quiet evening. All save the oarsman lay heavily and listlessly in the boat's bottom. As for him, his eyes were just capable of noting the tall black waves that swept forward in a most sinister silence, save for an occasional subdued growl of a crest.

The cook's head was on a thwart, and he looked without interest at the water under his nose. He was deep in other scenes. Finally he spoke. "Billie," he murmured, dreamfully, "what kind of pie do you like best?"

V

"Pie," said the oiler and the correspondent, agitatedly. "Don't talk about those things, blast you!"

"Well," said the cook, "I was just thinking about ham sandwiches, and—"

A night on the sea in an open boat is a long night. As darkness settled finally, the shine of the light, lifting from the sea in the south, changed to full gold. On the northern horizon a new light appeared, a small bluish gleam on the edge of the waters. These two lights were the furniture of the world. Otherwise there was nothing but waves.

Two men huddled in the stern, and distances were so magnificent in the dingey that the rower was enabled to keep his feet partly warmed by thrusting them under his companions. Their legs indeed extended far under the rowing-seat until they touched the feet of the captain forward. Sometimes, despite the efforts of the tired oarsman, a wave came piling into the boat, an icy wave of the night, and the chilling water soaked them anew. They would twist their bodies for a moment and groan, and sleep the dead sleep once more, while the water in the boat gurgled about them as the craft rocked.

The plan of the oiler and the correspondent was for one to row until he lost the ability, and then arouse the other from his sea-water couch in the bottom of the boat.

The oiler plied the oars until his head drooped forward, and the overpowering sleep blinded him. And he rowed yet afterward. Then he touched a man in the bottom of the boat, and called his name. "Will you spell me for a little while?" he said, meekly.

"Sure, Billie," said the correspondent, awakening and dragging himself to a sitting position. They exchanged places carefully, and the oiler, cuddling down in the sea-water at the cook's side, seemed to go to sleep instantly.

The particular violence of the sea had ceased. The waves came without snarling. The obligation of the man at the oars was to keep the boat headed so that the tilt of the rollers would not capsize her, and to preserve her from filling when the crests rushed past. The black waves were silent and hard to be seen in the darkness. Often one was almost upon the boat before the oarsman was aware.

In a low voice the correspondent addressed the captain. He was not sure that the captain was awake, although this iron man seemed to be always awake. "Captain, shall I keep her making for that light north, sir?"

The same steady voice answered him. "Yes. Keep it about two points off the port bow."

The cook had tied a life-belt around himself in order to get even the warmth which this clumsy cork contrivance could donate, and he seemed almost stove-like when a rower, whose teeth invariably chattered wildly as soon as he ceased his labor, dropped down to sleep.

The correspondent, as he rowed, looked down at the two men sleeping under foot. The cook's arm was around the oiler's shoulders, and, with their fragmentary clothing and haggard faces, they were the babes of the sea, a grotesque rendering of the old babes in the wood.

Later he must have grown stupid at his work, for suddenly there was a growling of water, and a crest came with a roar and a swash into the boat, and it was a wonder that it did not set the cook afloat in his life-belt. The cook continued to sleep, but the oiler sat up, blinking his eyes and shaking with the new cold.

"Oh, I'm awful sorry, Billie," said the correspondent, contritely.

"That's all right, old boy," said the oiler, and lay down again and was asleep.

Presently it seemed that even the captain dozed, and the correspondent thought that he was the one man afloat on all the oceans. The wind had a voice as it came over the waves, and it was sadder than the end.

There was a long, loud swishing astern of the boat, and a gleaming trail of phosphorescence, like blue flame, was furrowed on the black waters. It might have been made by a monstrous knife.

Then there came a stillness, while the correspondent breathed with the open mouth and looked at the sea.

Suddenly there was another swish and another long flash of bluish light, and this time it was alongside the boat, and might almost have been reached with an oar. The correspondent saw an enormous fin speed like a shadow through the water, hurling the crystalline spray and leaving the long glowing trail.

The correspondent looked over his shoulder at the captain. His face was hidden, and he seemed to be asleep. He looked at the babes of the sea. They certainly were asleep. So, being bereft of sympathy, he leaned a little way to one side and swore softly into the sea.

But the thing did not then leave the vicinity of the boat. Ahead or astern, on one side or the other, at intervals long or short, fled the long sparkling streak, and there was to be heard the whiroo of the dark fin. The speed and power of the thing was greatly to be admired. It cut the water like a gigantic and keen projectile.

The presence of this biding thing did not affect the man with the same horror that it would if he had been a picnicker. He simply looked at the sea dully and swore in an undertone.

Nevertheless, it is true that he did not wish to be alone with the thing. He wished one of his companions to awaken by chance and keep him company with it. But the captain hung motionless over the water-jar and the oiler and the cook in the bottom of the boat were plunged in slumber.

VI

"If I am going to be drowned—if I am going to be drowned—if I am going to be drowned, why, in the name of the seven mad gods, who rule the sea, was I allowed to come thus far and contemplate sand and trees?"

During this dismal night, it may be remarked that a man would conclude that it was really the intention of the seven mad gods to drown him, despite the abominable injustice of it. For it was certainly an abominable injustice to drown a man who had worked so hard, so hard. The man felt it would be a crime most unnatural. Other people had drowned at sea since galleys swarmed with painted sails, but still—

When it occurs to a man that nature does not regard him as important, and that she feels she would not maim the universe by disposing of him, he at first wishes to throw bricks at the temple, and he hates deeply the fact that there are no bricks and no temples. Any visible expression of nature would surely be pelleted with his jeers.

Then, if there be no tangible thing to hoot he feels, perhaps, the desire to confront a personification and indulge in pleas, bowed to one knee, and with hands supplicant, saying: "Yes, but I love myself."

A high cold star on a winter's night is the word he feels that she says to him. Thereafter he knows the pathos of his situation.

The men in the dingey had not discussed these matters, but each had, no doubt, reflected upon them in silence and according to his mind. There was seldom any expression upon their faces save the general one of complete weariness. Speech was devoted to the business of the boat.

To chime the notes of his emotion, a verse mysteriously entered the correspondent's head. He had even forgotten that he had forgotten this verse, but it suddenly was in his mind.

A soldier of the Legion lay dying in Algiers,
There was lack of woman's nursing, there was dearth of woman's tears;

But a comrade stood beside him, and he took that comrade's hand
And he said: "I shall never see my own, my native land."[4]

In his childhood, the correspondent had been made acquainted with the fact that a soldier of the Legion lay dying in Algiers, but he had never regarded the fact as important. Myriads of his school-fellows had informed him of the soldier's plight, but the dinning had naturally ended by making him perfectly indifferent. He had never considered it his affair that a soldier of the Legion lay dying in Algiers, nor had it appeared to him as a matter for sorrow. It was less to him than breaking of a pencil's point.

Now, however, it quaintly came to him as a human, living thing. It was no longer merely a picture of a few throes in the breast of a poet, meanwhile drinking tea and warming his feet at the grate; it was an actuality—stern, mournful, and fine.

The correspondent plainly saw the soldier. He lay on the sand with his feet out straight and still. While his pale left hand was upon his chest in an attempt to thwart the going of his life, the blood came between his fingers. In the far Algerian distance, a city of low square forms was set against a sky that was faint with the last sunset hues. The correspondent, plying the oars and dreaming of the slow and slower movements of the lips of the soldier, was moved by a profound and perfectly impersonal comprehension. He was sorry for the soldier of the Legion who lay dying in Algiers.

The thing which had followed the boat and waited had evidently grown bored at the delay. There was no longer to be heard the slash of the cut-water, and there was no longer the flame of the long trail. The light in the north still glimmered, but it was apparently no nearer to the boat. Sometimes the boom of the surf rang in the correspondent's ears, and he turned the craft seaward then and rowed harder. Southward, someone had evidently built a watch-fire on the beach. It was too low and too far to be seen, but it made a shimmering, roseate reflection upon the bluff back of it, and this could be discerned from the boat. The wind came stronger, and sometimes a wave suddenly raged out like a mountain-cat and there was to be seen the sheen and sparkle of a broken crest.

The captain, in the bow, moved on his water-jar and sat erect. "Pretty long night," he observed to the correspondent. He looked at the shore. "Those life-saving people take their time."

"Did you see that shark playing around?"

"Yes, I saw him. He was a big fellow, all right."

"Wish I had known you were awake."

Later the correspondent spoke into the bottom of the boat.

---

[4]Condensed and tightened lines from the poem "Bingen on the Rhine" (1883) by Caroline E. S. Norton.

"Billie!" There was a slow and gradual disentanglement. "Billie, will you spell me?"

"Sure," said the oiler.

As soon as the correspondent touched the cold comfortable sea-water in the bottom of the boat, and had huddled close to the cook's life-belt he was deep in sleep, despite the fact that his teeth played all the popular airs. This sleep was so good to him that it was but a moment before he heard a voice call his name in a tone that demonstrated the last stages of exhaustion. "Will you spell me?"

"Sure, Billie."

The light in the north had mysteriously vanished, but the correspondent took his course from the wide-awake captain.

Later in the night they took the boat farther out to sea, and the captain directed the cook to take one oar at the stern and keep the boat facing the seas. He was to call out if he should hear the thunder of the surf. This plan enabled the oiler and the correspondent to get respite together. "We'll give those boys a chance to get into shape again," said the captain. They curled down and, after a few preliminary chatterings and trembles, slept once more the dead sleep. Neither knew they had bequeathed to the cook the company of another shark, or perhaps the same shark.

As the boat caroused on the waves, spray occasionally bumped over the side and gave them a fresh soaking, but this had no power to break their repose. The ominous slash of the wind and the water affected them as it would have affected mummies.

"Boys," said the cook, with the notes of every reluctance in his voice, "she's drifted in pretty close. I guess one of you had better take her to sea again." The correspondent, aroused, heard the crash of the toppled crests.

As he was rowing, the captain gave him some whiskey and water, and this steadied the chills out of him. "If I ever get ashore and anybody shows me even a photograph of an oar—"

At last there was a short conversation.

"Billie. . . . Billie, will you spell me?"

"Sure," said the oiler.

VII

When the correspondent again opened his eyes, the sea and the sky were each of the gray hue of the dawning. Later, carmine and gold was painted upon the waters. The morning appeared finally, in its splendor, with a sky of pure blue, and the sunlight flamed on the tips of the waves.

On the distant dunes were set many little black cottages, and a tall white windmill reared above them. No man, nor dog, nor bicycle appeared on the beach. The cottages might have formed a deserted village.

The voyagers scanned the shore. A conference was held in the boat. "Well," said the captain, "if no help is coming, we might better try to run through the surf right away. If we stay out here much longer we will be too weak to do anything for ourselves at all." The others silently acquiesced in this reasoning. The boat was headed for the beach. The correspondent wondered if none ever ascended the tall wind-tower, and if then they never looked seaward. This tower was a giant, standing with its back to the plight of the ants. It represented in a degree, to the correspondent, the serenity of nature amid the struggles of the individual—nature in the wind, and nature in the vision of men. She did not seem cruel to him then, nor beneficent, nor treacherous, nor wise. But she was indifferent, flatly indifferent. It is, perhaps, plausible that a man in this situation, impressed with the unconcern of the universe, should see the innumerable flaws of his life and have them taste wickedly in his mind and wish for another chance. A distinction between right and wrong seems absurdly clear to him, then, in this new ignorance of the grave-edge, and he understands that if he were given another opportunity he would mend his conduct and his words, and be better and brighter during an introduction, or at a tea.

"Now, boys," said the captain, "she is going to swamp sure. All we can do is to work her in as far as possible, and then when she swamps, pile out and scramble for the beach. Keep cool now and don't jump until she swamps sure."

The oiler took the oars. Over his shoulders he scanned the surf. "Captain," he said, "I think I'd better bring her about, and keep her head-on to the seas and back her in."

"All right, Billie," said the captain. "Back her in." The oiler swung the boat then and, seated in the stern, the cook and the correspondent were obliged to look over their shoulders to contemplate the lonely and indifferent shore.

The monstrous inshore rollers heaved the boat high until the men were again enabled to see the white sheets of water scudding up the slanted beach. "We won't get in very close," said the captain. Each time a man could wrest his attention from the rollers, he turned his glance toward the shore, and in the expression of the eyes during this contemplation there was a singular quality. The correspondent, observing the others, knew that they were not afraid, but the full meaning of their glances was shrouded.

As for himself, he was too tired to grapple fundamentally with the fact. He tried to coerce his mind into thinking of it, but the mind was dominated at this time by the muscles, and the muscles said they did not care. It merely occurred to him that if he should drown it would be a shame.

There were no hurried words, no pallor, no plain agitation. The men simply looked at the shore. "Now, remember to get well clear of the boat when you jump," said the captain.

Seaward the crest of a roller suddenly fell with a thunderous crash, and the long white comber came roaring down upon the boat.

"Steady now," said the captain. The men were silent. They turned their eyes from the shore to the comber and waited. The boat slid up the incline, leaped at the furious top, bounced over it, and swung down the long back of the waves. Some water had been shipped and the cook bailed it out.

But the next crest crashed also. The tumbling boiling flood of white water caught the boat and whirled it almost perpendicular. Water swarmed in from all sides. The correspondent had his hands on the gunwale at this time, and when the water entered at that place he swiftly withdrew his fingers, as if he objected to wetting them.

The little boat, drunken with this weight of water, reeled and snuggled deeper into the sea.

"Bail her out, cook! Bail her out," said the captain.

"All right, captain," said the cook.

"Now, boys, the next one will do for us, sure," said the oiler. "Mind to jump clear of the boat."

The third wave moved forward, huge, furious, implacable. It fairly swallowed the dingey, and almost simultaneously the men tumbled into the sea. A piece of life-belt had lain in the bottom of the boat, and as the correspondent went overboard he held this to his chest with his left hand.

The January water was icy, and he reflected immediately that it was colder than he had expected to find it off the coast of Florida. This appeared to his dazed mind as a fact important enough to be noted at the time. The coldness of the water was sad; it was tragic. This fact was somehow mixed and confused with his opinion of his own situation that it seemed almost a proper reason for tears. The water was cold.

When he came to the surface he was conscious of little but the noisy water. Afterward he saw his companions in the sea. The oiler was ahead in the race. He was swimming strongly and rapidly. Off to the correspondent's left, the cook's great white and corked back bulged out of the water, and in the rear the captain was hanging with his one good hand to the keel of the overturned dingey.

There is a certain immovable quality to a shore, and the correspondent wondered at it amid the confusion of the sea.

It seemed also very attractive, but the correspondent knew that it was a long journey, and he paddled leisurely. The piece of life-preserver lay under him, and sometimes he whirled down the incline of a wave as if he were on a hand-sled.

But finally he arrived at a place in the sea where travel was beset with difficulty. He did not pause swimming to inquire what manner of current had caught him, but there his progress ceased. The shore was set before him like a bit of scenery on a stage, and he looked at it and understood with his eyes each detail of it.

As the cook passed, much farther to the left, the captain was calling to him, "Turn over on your back, cook! Turn over on your back and use the oar."

"All right, sir." The cook turned on his back, and, paddling with an oar, went ahead as if he were a canoe.

Presently the boat also passed to the left of the correspondent with the captain clinging with one hand to the keel. He would have appeared like a man raising himself to look over a board fence, if it were not for the extraordinary gymnastics of the boat. The correspondent marvelled that the captain could still hold to it.

They passed on, nearer to shore—the oiler, the cook, the captain—and following them went the water-jar, bouncing gayly over the seas.

The correspondent remained in the grip of this strange new enemy—a current. The shore, with its white slope of sand and its green bluff, topped with little silent cottages, was spread like a picture before him. It was very near to him then, but he was impressed as one who in a gallery looks at a scene from Brittany or Algiers.

He thought: "I am going to drown? Can it be possible? Can it be possible? Can it be possible?" Perhaps an individual must consider his own death to be the final phenomenon of nature.

But later a wave perhaps whirled him out of this small deadly current, for he found suddenly that he could again make progress toward the shore. Later still, he was aware that the captain, clinging with one hand to the keel of the dingey, had his face turned away from the shore and toward him, and was calling his name. "Come to the boat! Come to the boat!"

In his struggle to reach the captain and the boat, he reflected that when one gets properly wearied, drowning must really be a comfortable arrangement, a cessation of hostilities accompanied by a large degree of relief, and he was glad of it, for the main thing in his mind for some moments had been horror of the temporary agony. He did not wish to be hurt.

Presently he saw a man running along the shore. He was undressing with most remarkable speed. Coat, trousers, shirt, everything flew magically off him.

"Come to the boat," called the captain.

"All right, captain." As the correspondent paddled, he saw the captain let himself down to bottom and leave the boat. Then the correspondent performed his one little marvel of the voyage. A large wave caught him and flung him with ease and supreme speed completely over the boat and far beyond it. It struck him even then as an event in gymnastics, and a true miracle of the sea. An overturned boat in the surf is not a plaything to a swimming man.

The correspondent arrived in water that reached only to his waist, but his condition did not enable him to stand for more than a moment. Each wave knocked him into a heap, and the under-tow pulled at him.

Then he saw the man who had been running and undressing, and undressing and running, come bounding into the water. He dragged ashore the cook, and then waded toward the captain, but the captain waved him away, and sent him to the correspondent. He was naked, naked as a tree in winter, but a halo was about his head, and he shone like a saint. He gave a strong pull, and a long drag, and a bully heave at the correspondent's hand. The correspondent, schooled in the minor formulae, said: "Thanks, old man." But suddenly the man cried: "What's that?" He pointed a swift finger. The correspondent said: "Go."

In the shallows, face downward, lay the oiler. His forehead touched sand that was periodically, between each wave, clear of the sea.

The correspondent did not know all that transpired afterward. When he achieved safe ground he fell, striking the sand with each particular part of his body. It was as if he had dropped from a roof, but the thud was grateful to him.

It seems that instantly the beach was populated with men with blankets, clothes, and flasks, and women with coffee-pots and all the remedies sacred to their minds. The welcome of the land to the men from the sea was warm and generous, but a still and dripping shape was carried slowly up the beach, and the land's welcome for it could only be the different and sinister hospitality of the grave.

When it came night, the white waves paced to and fro in the moonlight, and the wind brought the sound of the great sea's voice to the men on shore, and they felt that they could then be interpreters.

[1897]

F. SCOTT FITZGERALD
[1896–1940]

The career of F. Scott Fitzgerald often elicits a sigh from those who know the story. A brilliantly gifted writer, a "natural" with a keen sense of plot and structure, a prose writer with a poet's ear for language, Fitzgerald, the story goes, squandered his talent. A true genius, he wasted his energies churning out banal and frivolous short stories for the sake of a dollar. Seduced by early fame, he lived too fast and died too young. His carelessness ruined others and himself. Such sighs are justified. Fitzgerald, however, managed to accomplish in his short writing life what few authors ever do—he wrote works that have become, over time, touchstones of American culture.

Fitzgerald was born in St. Paul, Minnesota, in 1896 to a family that existed on the uncertain fringes of midwestern high society. His father was a business man who suffered a series of setbacks during Fitzgerald's childhood that took him from proprietor of his own furniture business to grocery clerk. Determined to keep up appearances and give their son a chance to attend a first-rate college, Fitzgerald's parents sent him east to prep school in 1911. Two years later, he entered Princeton with the help of money inherited from his grandmother. Drawn to the aristocratic, country-club atmosphere of the school, Fitzgerald proved ill-prepared for its academic rigors. Never keen to put responsibilities before pleasures, he spent most of his time socializing and writing and performing musical comedies. In 1917, Fitzgerald left Princeton for health reasons rather than face the humiliation of flunking out.

Unable to fulfill his dream of becoming a "big man on campus" at Princeton, Fitzgerald sought to redeem himself on the battlefields of World War I. He enlisted in the infantry and, because of his education, was awarded an officer's commission. Fitzgerald, however, took his military responsibilities no more seriously than his studies. He spent most of his basic training hours working on a draft of his first novel, "The Romantic Egoist," later retitled This Side of Paradise. *Luckily for Fitzgerald, the Great War ended before he was shipped to Europe. Fitzgerald, however, considered his lack of combat experience a missed opportunity; his aborted military career haunted him for the rest of his days.*

Fitzgerald's stint in the army, however, did change his life. While stationed in Montgomery, Alabama, he met and fell in love with Zelda Sayre, the creative, beautiful daughter of a well-to-do family haunted by a history of mental illness. Zelda was unwilling to commit to Fitzgerald until he could prove his earning power. After his discharge, he headed to New York to seek his fortune in advertising and win his lady. Failing both, he retreated to St. Paul in the summer of 1919 and lived with his parents while he worked hard to revise his novel. Having attracted the attention of the now legendary Scribners editor Max Perkins with his first draft, Fitzgerald reshaped the book and, in a desperate bid for personal and professional success, returned it to the publishers. Scribners accepted This Side of Paradise. *Released in the spring of 1920, the novel's portrayal of restless and reckless Princeton youth struck a chord with the post-war generation. The book sold an astonishing 49,000 copies by the end of 1921. Critics deemed the work sloppy but vital, and welcomed Fitzgerald as a writer of great potential. The novel made the young writer an instant celebrity and guaranteed him a ready market for the short stories that became the staple of his literary income and, many argue, the drain and ruin of his talent. (His first collection of short stories,* Flappers and Philosophers, *appeared in September 1920). Christened the golden boy of American letters, Fitzgerald found himself wealthy and famous. He also got the girl. He and Zelda were married in 1920.*

Fitzgerald's life, however, was destined to be anything but a fairy tale. Young, beautiful, charming, and unconventional, Scott and Zelda took up residence in New York's posh Plaza Hotel and embarked on a chaotic life of people, parties, and alcohol that left Fitzgerald little time for his art. Fitzgerald alternated periods of dissipation with stretches of hard work, financing his lifestyle by publishing lighthearted, clever stories about young men and women negotiating a sophisticated world of changing social manners and mores. In 1921, Zelda became pregnant and the couple, after a whirlwind trip to Europe, retreated to St. Paul to await the birth of their only child, their daughter Frances Scott, nicknamed "Scottie." The move gave Fitzgerald the opportunity to concentrate on finishing his second novel, The Beautiful and the Damned, *which appeared in 1922. A much darker book than* This Side of Paradise, The Beautiful and the Damned *convinced critics of Fitzgerald's increasing maturity as a writer. The book was also a financial success, selling 50,000 copies in its first few months.* Tales of the Jazz Age, *Fitzgerald's second collection of short stories, appeared the same year.*

With baby in tow, the Fitzgeralds returned to New York and took a house on Long Island. There they became members of an elite artistic circle that included John Dos Passos, H. L. Mencken, Van Wyck Brooks, Edmund Wilson, and Carl Van Vechten. Although Fitzgerald now commanded incredible sums for his stories, he had difficulty making ends meet due to the lavishness of his spending. In an attempt to make a big score financially, he turned his talents to writing a political play with the unlikely title The Vegetable. *When the production flopped, the Fitzgeralds retreated to France ostensibly to live more cheaply. Rather than settle in a garret in Paris, however, Scott and Zelda chose an expensive villa on the French Riviera. Constantly strapped for cash, in debt to his editor and his agent, Fitzgerald began work on* The Great Gatsby. *Published in 1925,* Gatsby *sold only half as many copies of* The Beautiful and the Damned *and barely covered the cost of Fitzgerald's advance from the publishers. The relative financial failure of Fitzgerald's extraordinary novel ensured that he would never be free from the short story market that demanded so much of his energies.*

Gatsby *turned out to be personally costly as well. During Fitzgerald's long hours of crafting the novel, Zelda fell in love with a French aviator and asked Fitzgerald for a divorce. Shocked and hurt, he retreated further into alcoholism. When Zelda's lover abandoned her, the couple reconciled, but their relationship was never the same and deteriorated into one of mutual psychological abuse. The years immediately following the publication of* Gatsby *were those of rootless and stressful wandering for the Fitzgeralds. They moved from England, to France, to Hollywood (where Fitzgerald made his first run at screenwriting) to New York, to Delaware, to France, to Delaware, and back to Paris in March 1929. In 1926, Fitzgerald published his third collection of short stories,* All the Sad Young Men. *The rest of the time he spent struggling to write* Tender Is the Night, *the book that would ultimately become his final completed novel. In 1927, Zelda, in an attempt to create an outlet for her own considerable talents, decided to pursue a career as a professional ballerina. At the age of twenty-six, she began studying, pushing herself hard to make up for lost years. By the beginning of 1929, Zelda's behavior had become increasingly erratic until, in the spring of 1930, she suffered a nervous breakdown from which she never fully recovered. For the next few years, Zelda moved in and out of various mental institutions, making tentative progress only to relapse into madness. Blind-sided by her illness, Fitzgerald scrambled to secure good treatment for Zelda and to pay for it. Just when Fitzgerald needed money most, however, his fees began to plummet in the wake of the Great Depression. As a result, he had to churn out even more stories to secure the same income. In 1931, he traveled for a second time to Hollywood in the hopes of making money as a screenwriter. The experience, an unmitigated failure, resulted in the short story "Crazy Sunday."*

The year 1934 marked the apex of both Fitzgerald's literary triumph and personal tragedy. That year his final novel, the painfully autobiographical Tender Is the Night, *was published. That same year, Zelda suffered a catastrophic mental breakdown that dashed hopes of her ultimate recovery and resulted in her institutionalization for the duration of Fitzgerald's life. In 1935, Fitzgerald succeeded in publishing another collection of short stories,* Taps at Reveille, *but his health began to fail. Diagnosed with the beginning* signs of tuberculosis, struggling to sell his work, and drinking himself to death, Fitzgerald suffered a nervous breakdown of his own that he immortalized in a series of three essays, the "Crack Up" essays, in Esquire Magazine.

While Fitzgerald's final years in Hollywood often strike critics as the absolute low point of his career, the call he received from MGM studios in 1937 did help to abate his financial problems. MGM initially offered Fitzgerald a six-month contract at $1000 a week. Although his 1937–39 stint with the studio resulted in endless frustration and only one screen credit, Fitzgerald was able to pay off his debts and fund Zelda's treatment. Fitzgerald also mined his Hollywood experience for the stuff of his final novel, The Last Tycoon. Unfortunately, Fitzgerald did not have time to complete the book. His body ravaged by years of hard drinking, he died of heart failure in 1940 at the age of forty-four.

While critics favor Fitzgerald's novels, the best of his stories stand up well beside the longer fiction. His early tales lay bare the poignant distances between his characters' romantic dreams and the banal, often sordid stuff of their everyday lives. Those who believe in the fictions of sentimental romance are as damned for their innocence as those without illusions are damned for their emptiness. In a clever twist on the Pygmalion story, Marjorie in "Bernice Bobs Her Hair" strips Bernice of her girlish fantasies by wising her up to the frank "economy" of adolescent female popularity. The more successful Bernice becomes in her manipulations of the opposite sex, however, the less sense she has of her true self and desires. Edith Bradin in "May Day" harbors romantic memories of her first love, the artist Gordon Sterrett. When she finds herself back in Sterrett's arms, however, she is repulsed by the broken man he has become. Like Gatsby and his Daisy, Dexter Edge in "Winter Dreams" gives his life to the memory of his lost love, Judy Jones. When Dexter learns years later that the shining girl of his youth has become a beleaguered, aging, abused wife trapped in an unhappy marriage, he loses all sense of the possibility of beauty in the world. Like Gatsby with Daisy, he loses not Judy, but the memory of Judy, and with it all hope of recapturing the youth, passion, and freshness of his past. The pastoral green world of the country club golf course, the place where Dexter first lays eyes on Judy, proves as untenable as the green light at the end of Daisy's dock. Such stories interlace knowing comments about class, and about haves and have nots, with subtle critiques of American postwar materialism. Fitzgerald's two great late stories, "Babylon Revisited" and "Crazy Sunday" are both deeply personal tales of guilt and absolution. In "Babylon Revisited," Charles Wales discovers that, despite his efforts to redeem the horrors and his drunken former life, he can never escape his past. Fitzgerald, too, was haunted by his personal mistakes and his ghosts often form the basis of his prose.

The texts of the stories in The Pearson Custom Library of American Literature issue from The Stories of F. Scott Fitzgerald, edited by Malcolm Cowley

(New York: Scribners, 1951). Fitzgerald revised many of his stories after their first presentation in periodicals; the versions that Cowley selected sometimes differ from those first printed.

For Further Reading

Primary Works

This Side of Paradise (New York: Scribners, 1920; London: Collins, 1921); *Flappers and Philosophers* (New York: Scribners, 1920; London: Collins, 1922); *The Beautiful and the Damned* (New York: Scribners, 1922; London: Collins, 1922); *Tales of the Jazz Age* (New York: Scribners, 1922; London: Collins, 1923); *The Vegetable* (New York: Scribners, 1923); *The Great Gatsby* (New York: Scribners, 1925; London: Chatto & Windus, 1926); *All the Sad Young Men* (New York: Scribners, 1926); *Tender Is the Night* (New York: Scribners, 1934; London: Chatto & Windus, 1934); *Taps at Reveille* (New York: Scribners, 1935); *The Last Tycoon,* edited by Edmund Wilson (New York: Scribners, 1941; London: Grey Walls, 1949); republished as *The Love of the Last Tycoon: A Western,* edited by Matthew J. Bruccoli (Cambridge & New York: Cambridge University Press, 1993; New York: Scribner, 1994); *The Crack-Up,* edited by Wilson (New York: New Directions, 1945; Harmondsworth, U.K.: Penguin, 1965); *The Stories of F. Scott Fitzgerald,* edited by Malcolm Cowley (New York: Scribners, 1951).

Secondary Works

Matthew J. Bruccoli, *F. Scott Fitzgerald: A Descriptive Bibliography,* revised edition (Pittsburgh: University of Pittsburgh Press, 1987); Matthew J. Bruccoli, *Some Sort of Epic Grandeur: The Life of F. Scott Fitzgerald* (New York: Carroll & Graf, 1993, 1991); Ronald Berman, *Fitzgerald, Hemingway, and the Twenties* (Tuscaloosa: University of Alabama Press, 2001); Jackson R. Bryer, *The Critical Reputation of F. Scott Fitzgerald: A Bibliographical Study* (Hamden, Conn.: Archon Books, 1967; supplement, 1984); Jackson R. Bryer and J. Gerald Kennedy, eds., *French Connections: Hemingway and Fitzgerald Abroad* (New York: St. Martin's Press, 1998); Jackson R. Bryer, Alan Margolies, and Ruth Prigozy, eds., *F. Scott Fitzgerald: New Perspectives* (Athens, Ga.: University of Georgia Press, 2000); Robert L. Gale, *An F. Scott Fitzgerald Encyclopedia* (Westport, Conn.: Greenwood Press, 1998); John A. Higgins, *F. Scott Fitzgerald: A Study of the Stories* (Jamaica, N.Y.: St. John's University Press, 1971); John Kuehl, *F. Scott Fitzgerald: A Study of the Short Fiction* (Boston: Twayne Publishers, 1991); Richard D. Lehan, *F. Scott Fitzgerald and the Craft of Fiction* (Carbondale: Southern Illinois University Press, 1966); Bryant Mangum, *A Fortune Yet: Money in the Art of F. Scott Fitzgerald's Short Stories* (New York: Garland, 1991); Jeffrey Meyers, *Scott Fitzgerald: A Biography* (New York: HarperCollins, 1994); Linda C. Pelzer, *Student Companion to F. Scott Fitzgerald* (Westport, Conn.: Greenwood Press, 2000).

Winter Dreams[1]

F. SCOTT FITZGERALD

Some of the caddies were poor as sin and lived in one-room houses with a neurasthenic cow in the front yard, but Dexter Green's father owned the second best grocery-store in Black Bear—the best one was "The Hub," patronized by the wealthy people from Sherry Island—and Dexter caddied only for pocket-money.

In the fall when the days became crisp and gray, and the long Minnesota winter shut down like the white lid of a box, Dexter's skis moved over the snow that hid the fairways of the golf course. At these times the country gave him a feeling of profound melancholy—it offended him that the links should lie in enforced fallowness, haunted by ragged sparrows for the long season. It was dreary, too, that on the tees where the gay colors fluttered in summer there were now only the desolate sand-boxes knee-deep in crusted ice. When he crossed the hills the wind blew cold as misery, and if the sun was out he tramped with his eyes squinted up against the hard dimensionless glare.

In April the winter ceased abruptly. The snow ran down into Black Bear Lake scarcely tarrying for the early golfers to brave the season with red and black balls. Without elation, without an interval of moist glory, the cold was gone.

Dexter knew that there was something dismal about this Northern spring, just as he knew there was something gorgeous about the fall. Fall made him clinch his hands and tremble and repeat idiotic sentences to himself, and make brisk abrupt gestures of command to imaginary audiences and armies. October filled him with hope which November raised to a sort of ecstatic triumph, and in this mood the fleeting brilliant impressions of the summer at Sherry Island were ready grist to his mill. He became a golf champion and defeated Mr. T. A. Hedrick in a marvellous match played a hundred times over the fairways of his imagination, a match each detail of which he changed about untiringly—sometimes he won with almost laughable ease, sometimes he came up magnificently from behind. Again, stepping from a Pierce-Arrow automobile,

---

[1]"Winter Dreams" first appeared in *Metropolitan Magazine* in December 1922. Fitzgerald first collected the story in *All the Sad Young Men* (1926).

like Mr. Mortimer Jones, he strolled frigidly into the lounge of the Sherry Island Golf Club—or perhaps, surrounded by an admiring crowd, he gave an exhibition of fancy diving from the spring-board of the club raft. . . . Among those who watched him in open-mouthed wonder was Mr. Mortimer Jones.

And one day it came to pass that Mr. Jones—himself and not his ghost—came up to Dexter with tears in his eyes and said that Dexter was the——best caddy in the club, and wouldn't he decide not to quit if Mr. Jones made it worth his while, because every other——caddy in the club lost one ball a hole for him—regularly——

"No, sir," said Dexter decisively, "I don't want to caddy any more." Then, after a pause: "I'm too old."

"You're not more than fourteen. Why the devil did you decide just this morning that you wanted to quit? You promised that next week you'd go over to the State tournament with me."

"I decided I was too old."

Dexter handed in his "A Class" badge, collected what money was due him from the caddy master, and walked home to Black Bear Village.

"The best——caddy I ever saw," shouted Mr. Mortimer Jones over a drink that afternoon. "Never lost a ball! Willing! Intelligent! Quiet! Honest! Grateful!"

The little girl who had done this was eleven—beautifully ugly as little girls are apt to be who are destined after a few years to be inexpressibly lovely and bring no end of misery to a great number of men. The spark, however, was perceptible. There was a general ungodliness in the way her lips twisted down at the corners when she smiled, and in the—Heaven help us!—in the almost passionate quality of her eyes. Vitality is born early in such women. It was utterly in evidence now, shining through her thin frame in a sort of glow.

She had come eagerly out on to the course at nine o'clock with a white linen nurse and five small new golf-clubs in a white canvas bag which the nurse was carrying. When Dexter first saw her she was standing by the caddy house, rather ill at ease and trying to conceal the fact by engaging her nurse in an obviously unnatural conversation graced by startling and irrelevant grimaces from herself.

"Well, it's certainly a nice day, Hilda," Dexter heard her say. She drew down the corners of her mouth, smiled, and glanced furtively around, her eyes in transit falling for an instant on Dexter.

Then to the nurse:

"Well, I guess there aren't very many people out here this morning, are there?"

The smile again—radiant, blatantly artificial—convincing.

"I don't know what we're supposed to do now," said the nurse looking nowhere in particular.

"Oh, that's all right. I'll fix it up."

Dexter stood perfectly still, his mouth slightly ajar. He knew that if he moved forward a step his stare would be in her line of vision—if he moved backward he would lose his full view of her face. For a moment he had not realized how young she was. Now he remembered having seen her several times the year before—in bloomers.

Suddenly, involuntarily, he laughed, a short abrupt laugh—then, startled by himself, he turned and began to walk quickly away.

"Boy!"

Dexter stopped.

"Boy——"

Beyond question he was addressed. Not only that, but he was treated to that absurd smile, that preposterous smile—the memory of which at least a dozen men were to carry into middle age.

"Boy, do you know where the golf teacher is?"

"He's giving a lesson."

"Well, do you know where the caddy-master is?"

"He isn't here yet this morning."

"Oh." For a moment this baffled her. She stood alternately on her right and left foot.

"We'd like to get a caddy," said the nurse. "Mrs. Mortimer Jones sent us out to play golf, and we don't know how without we get a caddy."

Here she was stopped by an ominous glance from Miss Jones, followed immediately by the smile.

"There aren't any caddies here except me," said Dexter to the nurse, "and I got to stay here in charge until the caddy-master gets here."

"Oh."

Miss Jones and her retinue now withdrew, and at a proper distance from Dexter became involved in a heated conversation, which was concluded by Miss Jones taking one of the clubs and hitting it on the ground with violence. For further emphasis she raised it again and was about to bring it down smartly upon the nurse's bosom, when the nurse seized the club and twisted it from her hands.

"You damn little mean old *thing*!" cried Miss Jones wildly.

Another argument ensued. Realizing that the elements of comedy were implied in the scene, Dexter several times began to laugh, but each time restrained the laugh before it reached audibility. He could not resist the monstrous conviction that the little girl was justified in beating the nurse.

The situation was resolved by the fortuitous appearance of the caddy-master, who was appealed to immediately by the nurse.

"Miss Jones is to have a little caddy, and this one says he can't go."

"Mr. McKenna said I was to wait here till you came," said Dexter quickly.

"Well, he's here now." Miss Jones smiled cheerfully at the caddy-master. Then she dropped her bag and set off at a haughty mince toward the first tee.

"Well?" The caddy-master turned to Dexter. "What you standing there like a dummy for? Go pick up the young lady's clubs."

"I don't think I'll go out to-day," said Dexter.

"You don't— —"

"I think I'll quit."

The enormity of his decision frightened him. He was a favorite caddy, and the thirty dollars a month he earned through the summer were not to be made elsewhere around the lake. But he had received a strong emotional shock, and his perturbation required a violent and immediate outlet.

It is not so simple as that, either. As so frequently would be the case in the future, Dexter was unconsciously dictated to by his winter dreams.

II

Now, of course, the quality and the seasonability of these winter dreams varied, but the stuff of them remained. They persuaded Dexter several years later to pass up a business course at the State university—his father, prospering now, would have paid his way—for the precarious advantage of attending an older and more famous university in the East, where he was bothered by his scanty funds. But do not get the impression, because his winter dreams happened to be concerned at first with musings on the rich, that there was anything merely snobbish in the boy. He wanted not association with glittering things and glittering people—he wanted the glittering things themselves. Often he reached out for the best without knowing why he wanted it—and sometimes he ran up against the mysterious denials and prohibitions in which life indulges. It is with one of those denials and not with his career as a whole that this story deals.

He made money. It was rather amazing. After college he went to the city from which Black Bear Lake draws its wealthy patrons. When he was only twenty-three and had been there not quite two years, there were already people who liked to say: "Now *there's* a boy— " All about him rich men's sons were peddling bonds precariously, or investing patrimonies precariously, or plodding through the two dozen volumes of the "George Washington Commercial Course," but Dexter borrowed a thousand dollars on his college degree and his confident mouth, and bought a partnership in a laundry.

It was a small laundry when he went into it, but Dexter made a specialty of learning how the English washed fine woolen golf-stockings without shrinking them, and within a year he was catering to the trade that wore knickerbockers. Men were insisting that their Shetland hose and sweaters go to his laundry, just as they had insisted on a caddy who could find golf-balls. A little later he was doing their wives' lingerie as well—and running five branches in different parts of the city. Before he was twenty-seven he owned the largest string of laundries in his section of the country. It was then that he sold out and went to New York. But the part of his story that concerns us goes back to the days when he was making his first big success.

When he was twenty-three Mr. Hart—one of the gray-haired men who liked to say "Now there's a boy"—gave him a guest card to the Sherry Island Golf Club for a week-end. So he signed his name one day on the register, and that afternoon played golf in a foursome with Mr. Hart and Mr. Sandwood and Mr. T. A. Hedrick. He did not consider it necessary to remark that he had once carried Mr. Hart's bag over this same links, and that he knew every trap and gully with his eyes shut—but he found himself glancing at the four caddies who trailed them, trying to catch a gleam or gesture that would remind him of himself, that would lessen the gap which lay between his present and his past.

It was a curious day, slashed abruptly with fleeting, familiar impressions. One minute he had the sense of being a trespasser—in the next he was impressed by the tremendous superiority he felt toward Mr. T. A. Hedrick, who was a bore and not even a good golfer any more.

Then, because of a ball Mr. Hart lost near the fifteenth green, an enormous thing happened. While they were searching the stiff grasses of the rough there was a clear call of "Fore!" from behind a hill in their rear. And as they all turned abruptly from their search a bright new ball sliced abruptly over the hill and caught Mr. T. A. Hedrick in the abdomen.

"By Gad!" cried Mr. T. A. Hedrick, "they ought to put some of these crazy women off the course. It's getting to be outrageous."

A head and a voice came up together over the hill:

"Do you mind if we go through?"

"You hit me in the stomach!" declared Mr. Hedrick wildly.

"Did I?" The girl approached the group of men. "I'm sorry. I yelled 'Fore!'"

Her glance fell casually on each of the men—then scanned the fairway for her ball.

"Did I bounce into the rough?"

It was impossible to determine whether this question was ingenuous or malicious. In a moment, however, she left no doubt, for as her partner came up over the hill she called cheerfully:

"Here I am! I'd have gone on the green except that I hit something."

As she took her stance for a short mashie shot, Dexter looked at her closely. She wore a blue gingham dress, rimmed at throat and shoulders with a white edging that accentuated her tan. The quality of exaggeration, of thinness, which had made her passionate eyes and down-turning mouth absurd at eleven, was gone now. She was arrestingly beautiful. The color in her cheeks was centred like the color in a picture—it was not a "high" color, but a sort of fluctuating and feverish warmth, so shaded that it seemed at any moment it would recede and disappear. This color and the mobility of her mouth gave a continual impression of flux, of intense life, of passionate vitality—balanced only partially by the sad luxury of her eyes.

She swung her mashie impatiently and without interest, pitching the ball into a sand-pit on the other side of the green. With a quick, insincere smile and a careless "Thank you!" she went on after it.

"That Judy Jones!" remarked Mr. Hedrick on the next tee, as they waited—some moments—for her to play on ahead. "All she needs is to be turned up and spanked for six months and then to be married off to an old-fashioned cavalry captain."

"My God, she's good-looking!" said Mr. Sandwood, who was just over thirty.

"Good-looking!" cried Mr. Hedrick contemptuously, "she always looks as if she wanted to be kissed! Turning those big cow-eyes on every calf in town!"

It was doubtful if Mr. Hedrick intended a reference to the maternal instinct.

"She'd play pretty good golf if she'd try," said Mr. Sandwood.

"She has no form," said Mr. Hedrick solemnly.

"She has a nice figure," said Mr. Sandwood.

"Better thank the Lord she doesn't drive a swifter ball," said Mr. Hart, winking at Dexter.

Later in the afternoon the sun went down with a riotous swirl of gold and varying blues and scarlets, and left the dry, rustling night of Western summer. Dexter watched from the veranda of the Golf Club, watched the even overlap of the waters in the little wind, silver molasses under the harvest-moon. Then the moon held a finger to her lips and the lake became a clear pool, pale and quiet. Dexter put on his bathing-suit and swam out to the farthest raft, where he stretched dripping on the wet canvas of the springboard.

There was a fish jumping and a star shining and the lights around the lake were gleaming. Over on a dark peninsula a piano was playing the songs of last summer and of summers before that—songs from "Chin-Chin" and "The Count of Luxemburg" and "The Chocolate Soldier"—and because the sound of a piano over a stretch of water had always seemed beautiful to Dexter he lay perfectly quiet and listened.

The tune the piano was playing at that moment had been gay and new five years before when Dexter was a sophomore at college. They had played it at a prom once when he could not afford the luxury of proms, and he had stood outside the gymnasium and listened. The sound of the tune precipitated in him a sort of ecstasy and it was with that ecstasy he viewed what happened to him now. It was a mood of intense appreciation, a sense that, for once, he was magnificently attuned to life and that everything about him was radiating a brightness and a glamour he might never know again.

A low, pale oblong detached itself suddenly from the darkness of the Island, spitting forth the reverberated sound of a racing motorboat. Two white streamers of cleft water rolled themselves out behind it and almost immediately the boat was beside him, drowning out the hot tinkle of the piano in the drone of its spray. Dexter raising himself on his arms was aware of a figure standing at the wheel, of two dark eyes regarding him over the lengthening space of water—then the boat had gone by and was sweeping in an immense and purposeless circle of spray round and round in the middle of the lake. With equal eccentricity one of the circles flattened out and headed back toward the raft.

"Who's that?" she called, shutting off her motor. She was so near now that Dexter could see her bathing-suit, which consisted apparently of pink rompers.

The nose of the boat bumped the raft, and as the latter tilted rakishly he was precipitated toward her. With different degrees of interest they recognized each other.

"Aren't you one of those men we played through this afternoon?" she demanded.

He was.

"Well, do you know how to drive a motor-boat? Because if you do I wish you'd drive this one so I can ride on the surf-board behind. My name is Judy Jones"—she favored him with an absurd smirk—rather, what tried to be a smirk, for, twist her mouth as she might, it was not grotesque, it was merely beautiful—"and I live in a house over there on the Island, and in that house there is a man waiting for me. When he drove up at the door I drove out of the dock because he says I'm his ideal."

There was a fish jumping and a star shining and the lights around the lake were gleaming. Dexter sat beside Judy Jones and she explained how her boat was driven. Then she was in the water, swimming to the floating surf-board with a sinuous crawl. Watching her was without effort to the eye, watching a branch waving or a sea-gull flying. Her arms, burned to butternut, moved sinuously among the dull platinum ripples, elbow appearing first, casting the forearm back with a cadence of falling water, then reaching out and down, stabbing a path ahead.

They moved out into the lake; turning, Dexter saw that she was kneeling on the low rear of the now uptilted surf-board.

"Go faster," she called, "fast as it'll go."

Obediently he jammed the lever forward and the white spray mounted at the bow. When he looked around again the girl was standing up on the rushing board, her arms spread wide, her eyes lifted toward the moon.

"It's awful cold," she shouted. "What's your name?"

He told her.

"Well, why don't you come to dinner to-morrow night?"

His heart turned over like the fly-wheel of the boat, and, for the second time, her casual whim gave a new direction to his life.

III

Next evening while he waited for her to come down-stairs, Dexter peopled the soft deep summer room and the sun-porch that opened from it with the men who had already loved Judy Jones. He knew the sort of men they were—the men who when he first went to college had entered from the great prep schools with graceful clothes and the deep tan of healthy summers. He had seen that, in one sense, he was better than these men. He was newer and stronger. Yet in acknowledging to himself that he wished his children to be like them he was admitting that he was but the rough, strong stuff from which they eternally sprang.

When the time had come for him to wear good clothes, he had known who were the best tailors in America, and the best tailors in America had made him the suit he wore this evening. He had acquired that particular reserve peculiar to his university, that set it off from other universities. He recognized the value to him of such a mannerism and he had adopted it; he knew that to be careless in dress and manner required more confidence than to be careful. But carelessness was for his children. His mother's name had been Krimelich. She was a Bohemian of the peasant class and she had talked broken English to the end of her days. Her son must keep to the set patterns.

At a little after seven Judy Jones came down-stairs. She wore a blue silk afternoon dress, and he was disappointed at first that she had not put on something more elaborate. This feeling was accentuated when, after a brief greeting, she went to the door of a butler's pantry and pushing it open called: "You can serve dinner, Martha." He had rather expected that a butler would announce dinner, that there would be a cocktail. Then he put these thoughts behind him as they sat down side by side on a lounge and looked at each other.

"Father and mother won't be here," she said thoughtfully.

He remembered the last time he had seen her father, and he was glad the parents were not to be here to-night—they might wonder who he was. He had been born in Keeble, a Minnesota village fifty miles farther north, and he always gave Keeble as his home instead of Black Bear Village. Country towns were well enough to come from if they weren't inconveniently in sight and used as footstools by fashionable lakes.

They talked of his university, which she had visited frequently during the past two years, and of the near-by city which supplied Sherry Island with its patrons, and whither Dexter would return next day to his prospering laundries.

During dinner she slipped into a moody depression which gave Dexter a feeling of uneasiness. Whatever petulance she uttered in her throaty voice worried him. Whatever she smiled at—at him, at a chicken liver, at nothing—it disturbed him that her smile could have no root in mirth, or even in amusement. When the scarlet corners of her lips curved down, it was less a smile than an invitation to a kiss.

Then, after dinner, she led him out on the dark sun-porch and deliberately changed the atmosphere.

"Do you mind if I weep a little?" she said.

"I'm afraid I'm boring you," he responded quickly.

"You're not. I like you. But I've just had a terrible afternoon, There was a man I cared about, and this afternoon he told me out of a clear sky that he was poor as a church-mouse. He'd never even hinted it before. Does this sound horribly mundane?"

"Perhaps he was afraid to tell you."

"Suppose he was," she answered. "He didn't start right. You see, if I'd thought of him as poor—well, I've been mad about loads of poor men, and fully intended to marry them all. But in this case, I hadn't thought of him that way, and my interest in him wasn't strong enough to survive the shock. As if a girl calmly informed her fiancé that she was a widow. He might not object to widows, but—

"Let's start right," she interrupted herself suddenly. "Who are you, anyhow?"

For a moment Dexter hesitated. Then:

"I'm nobody," he announced. "My career is largely a matter of futures."

"Are you poor?"

"No," he said frankly, "I'm probably making more money than any man my age in the Northwest. I know that's an obnoxious remark, but you advised me to start right."

There was a pause. Then she smiled and the corners of her mouth drooped and an almost imperceptible sway brought her closer to him, looking up into his eyes. A lump rose in Dexter's throat, and he waited breathless for the experiment, facing the unpredictable compound that would form mysteriously from the elements of their lips. Then he saw—she communicated her excitement to him, lavishly, deeply, with kisses that were not a promise but a fulfilment. They aroused in him not hunger demanding renewal but surfeit that would demand more surfeit . . . kisses that were like charity, creating want by holding back nothing at all.

It did not take him many hours to decide that he had wanted Judy Jones ever since he was a proud, desirous little boy.

IV

It began like that—and continued, with varying shades of intensity, on such a note right up to the dénouement. Dexter surrendered a part of himself to the most direct and unprincipled personality with which he had ever come in contact. Whatever Judy wanted, she went after with the full pressure of her charm. There was no divergence of method, no jockeying for position or premeditation of effects—there was a very little mental side to any of her affairs. She simply made men conscious to the highest degree of her physical loveliness. Dexter had no desire to change her. Her deficiencies were knit up with a passionate energy that transcended and justified them.

When, as Judy's head lay against his shoulder that first night, she whispered, "I don't know what's the matter with me. Last night I thought I was in love with a man and to-night I think I'm in love with you— —"—it seemed to him a beautiful and romantic thing to say. It was the exquisite excitability that for the moment he controlled and owned. But a week later he was compelled to view this same quality in a different light. She took him in her roadster to a picnic supper, and after supper she disappeared, likewise in her roadster, with another man. Dexter became enormously upset and was scarcely able to be decently civil to the other people present. When she assured him that she had not kissed the other man, he knew she was lying—yet he was glad that she had taken the trouble to lie to him.

He was, as he found before the summer ended, one of a varying dozen who circulated about her. Each of them had at one time been favored above all others—about half of them still basked in the solace of occasional sentimental revivals. Whenever one showed signs of dropping out through long neglect, she granted him a brief honeyed hour, which encouraged him to tag along for a year or so longer. Judy made these forays upon the helpless and defeated without malice, indeed half unconscious that there was anything mischievous in what she did.

When a new man came to town every one dropped out—dates were automatically cancelled.

The helpless part of trying to do anything about it was that she did it all herself. She was not a girl who could be "won" in the kinetic sense—she was proof against cleverness, she was proof against charm; if any of these assailed her too strongly she would immediately resolve the affair to a physical basis, and under the magic of her physical splendor the strong as well as the brilliant played her game and not their own. She was entertained only by the gratification of her desires and by the direct exercise of her own charm. Perhaps from so much youthful love, so many youthful lovers, she had come, in self-defense, to nourish herself wholly from within.

Succeeding Dexter's first exhilaration came restlessness and dissatisfaction. The helpless ecstasy of losing himself in her was opiate rather than tonic. It was fortunate for his work during the winter that those moments of ecstasy came infrequently. Early in their acquaintance it had seemed for a while that there was a deep and spontaneous mutual attraction—that first August, for example—three days of long evenings on her dusky veranda, of strange wan kisses through the late afternoon, in shadowy alcoves or behind the protecting trellises of the garden arbors, of mornings when she was fresh as a dream and almost shy at meeting him in the clarity of the rising day. There was all the ecstasy of an engagement about it, sharpened by his realization that there was no engagement. It was during those three days that, for the first time, he had asked her to marry him. She said "maybe some day," she said "kiss me," she said "I'd like to marry you," she said "I love you"— she said—nothing.

The three days were interrupted by the arrival of a New York man who visited at her house for half September. To Dexter's agony, rumor engaged them. The man was the son of the president of a great trust company. But at the end of a month it was reported that Judy was yawning. At a dance one night she sat all evening in a motor-boat with a local beau, while the New Yorker searched the club for her frantically. She told the local beau that she was bored with her visitor, and two days later he left. She was seen with him at the station, and it was reported that he looked very mournful indeed.

On this note the summer ended. Dexter was twenty-four, and he found himself increasingly in a position to do as he wished. He joined two clubs in the city and lived at one of them. Though he was by no means an integral part of the stag-lines at these clubs, he managed to be on hand at dances where Judy Jones was likely to appear. He could have gone out socially as much as he liked—he was an eligible young man, now, and popular with down-town fathers. His confessed devotion to Judy Jones had rather solidified his position. But he had no social aspirations and rather despised the dancing men who were always on tap for the Thursday or Saturday parties and who filled in at dinners with the younger married set. Already he was playing with the idea of going East to New York. He wanted to take Judy Jones with him. No disillusion as to the world in which she had grown up could cure his illusion as to her desirability.

Remember that—for only in the light of it can what he did for her be understood.

Eighteen months after he first met Judy Jones he became engaged to another girl. Her name was Irene Scheerer, and her father was one of the men who had always believed in Dexter. Irene was light-haired and sweet and honorable, and a little stout, and she had two suitors whom she pleasantly relinquished when Dexter formally asked her to marry him.

Summer, fall, winter, spring, another summer, another fall—so much he had given of his active life to the incorrigible lips of Judy Jones. She had treated him with interest, with encouragement, with malice, with indifference, with contempt. She had inflicted on him the innumerable little slights and indignities possible in such a case—as if in revenge for having ever cared for him at all. She had beckoned him and yawned at him and beckoned him again and he had responded often with bitterness and narrowed eyes. She had brought him ecstatic happiness and intolerable agony of spirit. She had caused him untold inconvenience and not a little trouble. She had insulted him, and she had ridden over him, and she had played his interest in her against his interest in his work—for fun. She had done everything to him except to criticise him—this she had not done—it seemed to him only because it might have sullied the utter indifference she manifested and sincerely felt toward him.

When autumn had come and gone again it occurred to him that he could not have Judy Jones. He had to beat this into his mind but he convinced himself at last. He lay awake at night for a while and argued it over. He told himself the trouble and the pain she had caused him, he enumerated her glaring deficiencies as a wife. Then he said to himself that he loved her, and after a while he fell asleep. For a week, lest he imagined her husky voice over the telephone or her eyes opposite him at lunch, he worked hard and late, and at night he went to his office and plotted out his years.

At the end of a week he went to a dance and cut in on her once. For almost the first time since they had met he did not ask her to sit out with him or tell her that she was lovely. It hurt him that she did not miss these things— that was all. He was not jealous when he saw that there was a new man tonight. He had been hardened against jealousy long before.

He stayed late at the dance. He sat for an hour with Irene Scheerer and talked about books and about music. He knew very little about either. But he was beginning to be master of his own time now, and he had a rather priggish notion that he—the young and already fabulously successful Dexter Green—should know more about such things.

That was in October, when he was twenty-five. In January, Dexter and Irene became engaged. It was to be announced in June, and they were to be married three months later.

The Minnesota winter prolonged itself interminably, and it was almost May when the winds came soft and the snow ran down into Black Bear Lake at last. For the first time in over a year Dexter was enjoying a certain tranquillity of spirit. Judy Jones had been in Florida, and afterward in Hot Springs, and somewhere she had been engaged, and somewhere she had broken it off. At first, when Dexter had definitely given her up, it had made him sad that people still linked them together and asked for news of her, but when he began to be placed at dinner next to Irene Scheerer people didn't ask him about her any more—they told him about her. He ceased to be an authority on her.

May at last. Dexter walked the streets at night when the darkness was damp as rain, wondering that so soon, with so little done, so much of ecstasy had gone from him. May one year back had been marked by Judy's poignant, unforgivable, yet forgiven turbulence—it had been one of those rare times when he fancied she had grown to care for him. That old penny's worth of happiness he had spent for this bushel of content. He knew that Irene would be no more than a curtain spread behind him, a hand moving among gleaming teacups, a voice calling to children . . . fire and loveliness were gone, the magic of nights and the wonder of the varying hours and seasons . . . slender lips, down-turning, dropping to his lips and bearing him up into a heaven of eyes. . . . The thing was deep in him. He was too strong and alive for it to die lightly.

In the middle of May when the weather balanced for a few days on the thin bridge that led to deep summer he turned in one night at Irene's house. Their engagement was to be announced in a week now—no one would be surprised at it. And to-night they would sit together on the lounge at the University Club and look on for an hour at the dancers. It gave him a sense of solidity to go with her—she was so sturdily popular, so intensely "great."

He mounted the steps of the brownstone house and stepped inside.

"Irene," he called.

Mrs. Scheerer came out of the living-room to meet him.

"Dexter," she said, "Irene's gone up-stairs with a splitting headache. She wanted to go with you but I made her go to bed."

"Nothing serious, I——"

"Oh, no. She's going to play golf with you in the morning. You can spare her for just one night, can't you, Dexter?"

Her smile was kind. She and Dexter liked each other. In the living-room he talked for a moment before he said good-night.

Returning to the University Club, where he had rooms, he stood in the doorway for a moment and watched the dancers. He leaned against the door-post, nodded at a man or two—yawned.

"Hello, darling."

The familiar voice at his elbow startled him. Judy Jones had left a man and crossed the room to him—Judy Jones, a slender enamelled doll in cloth of gold: gold in a band at her head, gold in two slipper points at her dress's hem. The fragile glow of her face seemed to blossom as she smiled at him. A breeze of warmth and light blew through the room. His hands in the pockets of his dinner-jacket tightened spasmodically. He was filled with a sudden excitement.

"When did you get back?" he asked casually.

"Come here and I'll tell you about it."

She turned and he followed her. She had been away—he could have wept at the wonder of her return. She had passed through enchanted streets, doing things that were like provocative music. All mysterious happenings, all fresh and quickening hopes, had gone away with her, come back with her now.

She turned in the doorway.

"Have you a car here? If you haven't, I have."

"I have a coupé."

In then, with a rustle of golden cloth. He slammed the door. Into so many cars she had stepped—like this—like that—her back against the leather, so—her elbow resting on the door—waiting. She would have been soiled long since had there been anything to soil her—except herself—but this was her own self outpouring.

With an effort he forced himself to start the car and back into the street. This was nothing, he must remember. She had done this before, and he had put her behind him, as he would have crossed a bad account from his books.

He drove slowly down-town and, affecting abstraction, traversed the deserted streets of the business section, peopled here and there where a movie was giving out its crowd or where consumptive or pugilistic youth lounged in front of pool halls. The clink of glasses and the slap of hands on the bars issued from saloons, cloisters of glazed glass and dirty yellow light.

She was watching him closely and the silence was embarrassing, yet in this crisis he could find no casual word with which to profane the hour. At a convenient turning he began to zigzag back toward the University Club.

"Have you missed me?" she asked suddenly.

"Everybody missed you."

He wondered if she knew of Irene Scheerer. She had been back only a day—her absence had been almost contemporaneous with his engagement.

"What a remark!" Judy laughed sadly—without sadness. She looked at him searchingly. He became absorbed in the dashboard.

"You're handsomer than you used to be," she said thoughtfully. "Dexter, you have the most rememberable eyes."

He could have laughed at this, but he did not laugh. It was the sort of thing that was said to sophomores. Yet it stabbed at him.

"I'm awfully tired of everything, darling." She called every one darling, endowing the endearment with careless, individual comraderie. "I wish you'd marry me."

The directness of this confused him. He should have told her now that he was going to marry another girl, but he could not tell her. He could as easily have sworn that he had never loved her.

"I think we'd get along," she continued, on the same note, "unless probably you've forgotten me and fallen in love with another girl."

Her confidence was obviously enormous. She had said, in effect, that she found such a thing impossible to believe, that if it were true he had merely committed a childish indiscretion—and probably to show off. She would forgive him, because it was not a matter of any moment but rather something to be brushed aside lightly.

"Of course you could never love anybody but me," she continued, "I like the way you love me. Oh, Dexter, have you forgotten last year?"

"No, I haven't forgotten."

"Neither have I!"

Was she sincerely moved—or was she carried along by the wave of her own acting?

"I wish we could be like that again," she said, and he forced himself to answer:

"I don't think we can."

"I suppose not. . . . I hear you're giving Irene Scheerer a violent rush."

There was not the faintest emphasis on the name, yet Dexter was suddenly ashamed.

"Oh, take me home," cried Judy suddenly; "I don't want to go back to that idiotic dance—with those children."

Then, as he turned up the street that led to the residence district, Judy began to cry quietly to herself. He had never seen her cry before.

The dark street lightened, the dwellings of the rich loomed up around them, he stopped his coupé in front of the great white bulk of the Mortimer Joneses' house, somnolent, gorgeous, drenched with the splendor of the damp moonlight. Its solidity startled him. The strong walls, the steel of the girders, the breadth and beam and pomp of it were there only to bring out the contrast with the young beauty beside him. It was sturdy to accentuate her slightness—as if to show what a breeze could be generated by a butterfly's wing.

He sat perfectly quiet, his nerves in wild clamor, afraid that if he moved he would find her irresistibly in his arms. Two tears had rolled down her wet face and trembled on her upper lip.

"I'm more beautiful than anybody else," she said brokenly, "why can't I be happy?" Her moist eyes tore at his stability—her mouth turned slowly downward with an exquisite sadness: "I'd like to marry you if you'll have me, Dexter. I suppose you think I'm not worth having, but I'll be so beautiful for you, Dexter."

A million phrases of anger, pride, passion, hatred, tenderness fought on his lips. Then a perfect wave of emotion washed over him, carrying off with it a sediment of wisdom, of convention, of doubt, of honor. This was his girl who was speaking, his own, his beautiful, his pride.

"Won't you come in?" He heard her draw in her breath sharply.

Waiting.

"All right," his voice was trembling, "I'll come in."

V

It was strange that neither when it was over nor a long time afterward did he regret that night. Looking at it from the perspective of ten years, the fact that Judy's flare for him endured just one month seemed of little importance. Nor did it matter that by his yielding he subjected himself to a deeper agony in the end and gave serious hurt to Irene Scheerer and to Irene's parents, who had befriended him. There was nothing sufficiently pictorial about Irene's grief to stamp itself on his mind.

Dexter was at bottom hard-minded. The attitude of the city on his action was of no importance to him, not because he was going to leave the city, but because any outside attitude on the situation seemed superficial. He was completely indifferent to popular opinion. Nor, when he had seen that it was no use, that he did not possess in himself the power to move fundamentally or to hold Judy Jones, did he bear any malice toward her. He loved her, and he would love her until the day he was too old for loving—but he could not have her. So he tasted the deep pain that is reserved only for the strong, just as he had tasted for a little while the deep happiness.

Even the ultimate falsity of the grounds upon which Judy terminated the engagement that she did not want to "take him away" from Irene—Judy, who had wanted nothing else—did not revolt him. He was beyond any revulsion or any amusement.

He went East in February with the intention of selling out his laundries and settling in New York—but the war came to America in March and changed his plans. He returned to the West, handed over the management of the business to his partner, and went into the first officers' training-camp in late April. He was one of those young thousands who greeted the war with a certain amount of relief, welcoming the liberation from webs of tangled emotion.

VI

This story is not his biography, remember, although things creep into it which have nothing to do with those dreams he had when he was young. We are almost done with them and with him now. There is only one more incident to be related here, and it happens seven years farther on.

It took place in New York, where he had done well—so well that there were no barriers too high for him. He was thirty-two years old, and, except for one flying trip immediately after the war, he had not been West in seven years. A man named Devlin from Detroit came into his office to see him in a business way, and then and there this incident occurred, and closed out, so to speak, this particular side of his life.

"So you're from the Middle West," said the man Devlin with careless curiosity. "That's funny—I thought men like you were probably born and raised on Wall Street. You know—wife of one of my best friends in Detroit came from your city. I was an usher at the wedding."

Dexter waited with no apprehension of what was coming.

"Judy Simms," said Devlin with no particular interest; "Judy Jones she was once."

"Yes, I knew her." A dull impatience spread over him. He had heard, of course, that she was married—perhaps deliberately he had heard no more.

"Awfully nice girl," brooded Devlin meaninglessly, "I'm sort of sorry for her."

"Why?" Something in Dexter was alert, receptive, at once.

"Oh, Lud Simms has gone to pieces in a way. I don't mean he ill-uses her, but he drinks and runs around——"

"Doesn't she run around?"

"No. Stays at home with her kids."

"Oh."

"She's a little too old for him," said Devlin.

"Too old!" cried Dexter. "Why, man, she's only twenty-seven."

He was possessed with a wild notion of rushing out into the streets and taking a train to Detroit. He rose to his feet spasmodically.

"I guess you're busy," Devlin apologized quickly. "I didn't realize—"

"No, I'm not busy," said Dexter, steadying his voice. "I'm not busy at all. Not busy at all. Did you say she was—twenty-seven? No, I said she was twenty-seven."

"Yes, you did," agreed Devlin dryly.

"Go on, then. Go on."

"What do you mean?"

"About Judy Jones."

Devlin looked at him helplessly.

"Well, that's—I told you all there is to it. He treats her like the devil. Oh, they're not going to get divorced or anything. When he's particularly outrageous she forgives him. In fact, I'm inclined to think she loves him. She was a pretty girl when she first came to Detroit."

A pretty girl! The phrase struck Dexter as ludicrous.

"Isn't she—a pretty girl, any more?"

"Oh, she's all right."

"Look here," said Dexter, sitting down suddenly. "I don't understand. You say she was a 'pretty girl' and now you say she's 'all right.' I don't understand what you mean—Judy Jones wasn't a pretty girl, at all. She was a great beauty. Why, I knew her, I knew her. She was——"

Devlin laughed pleasantly.

"I'm not trying to start a row," he said. "I think Judy's a nice girl and I like her. I can't understand how a man like Lud Simms could fall madly in love with her, but he did." Then he added: "Most of the women like her."

Dexter looked closely at Devlin, thinking wildly that there must be a reason for this, some insensitivity in the man or some private malice.

"Lots of women fade just like *that,*" Devlin snapped his fingers. "You must have seen it happen. Perhaps I've forgotten how pretty she was at her wedding. I've seen her so much since then, you see. She has nice eyes."

A sort of dullness settled down upon Dexter. For the first time in his life he felt like getting very drunk. He knew that he was laughing loudly at something Devlin had said, but he did not know what it was or why it was funny. When, in a few minutes, Devlin went he lay down on his lounge and looked out the window at the New York sky-line into which the sun was sinking in dull lovely shades of pink and gold.

He had thought that having nothing else to lose he was invulnerable at last—but he knew that he had just lost something more, as surely as if he had married Judy Jones and seen her fade away before his eyes.

The dream was gone. Something had been taken from him. In a sort of panic he pushed the palms of his hands into his eyes and tried to bring up a picture of the waters lapping on Sherry Island and the moonlit veranda, and gingham on the golf-links and the dry sun and the gold color of her neck's soft down. And her mouth damp to his kisses and her eyes plaintive with melancholy and her freshness like new fine linen in the morning. Why, these things were no longer in the world! They had existed and they existed no longer.

For the first time in years the tears were streaming down his face. But they were for himself now. He did not care about mouth and eyes and moving hands. He wanted to care, and he could not care. For he had gone away and he could never go back any more. The gates were closed, the sun was gone down, and there was no beauty but the gray beauty of steel that withstands all time. Even the grief he could have borne was left behind in the country of illusion, of youth, of the richness of life, where his winter dreams had flourished.

"Long ago," he said, "long ago, there was something in me, but now that thing is gone. Now that thing is gone, that thing is gone. I cannot cry. I cannot care. That thing will come back no more."

[1922]

The Birth-mark

NATHANIEL HAWTHORNE

In the latter part of the last century, there lived a man of science—an eminent proficient in every branch of natural philosophy—who, not long before our story opens, had made experience of a spiritual affinity, more attractive than any chemical one. He had left his laboratory to the care of an assistant, cleared his fine countenance from the furnace-smoke, washed the stain of acids from his fingers, and persuaded a beautiful woman to become his wife. In those days, when the comparatively recent discovery of electricity, and other kindred mysteries of nature, seemed to open paths into the region of miracle, it was not unusual for the love of science to rival the love of woman, in its depth and absorbing energy. The higher intellect, the imagination, the spirit, and even the heart, might all find their congenial aliment in pursuits which, as some of their ardent votaries believed, would ascend from one step of powerful intelligence to another, until the philosopher should lay his hand on the secret of creative force, and perhaps make new worlds for himself. We know not whether Aylmer possessed this degree of faith in man's ultimate control over nature. He had devoted himself, however, too unreservedly to scientific studies, ever to be weaned from them by any second passion. His love for his young wife might prove the stronger of the two; but it could only be by intertwining itself with his love of science, and uniting the strength of the latter to its own.

Such a union accordingly took place, and was attended with truly remarkable consequences, and a deeply impressive moral. One day, very soon after their marriage, Aylmer sat gazing at his wife, with a trouble in his countenance that grew stronger, until he spoke.

"Georgiana," said he, "has it never occurred to you that the mark upon your cheek might be removed?"

"No, indeed," said she, smiling; but perceiving the seriousness of his manner, she blushed deeply. "To tell you the truth, it has been so often called a charm, that I was simple enough to imagine it might be so."

First published in *The Pioneer* (March, 1843); collected in *Mosses from an Old Manse* (1846). This text is from vol. 10 of *The Centenary Edition of the Works of Nathaniel Hawthorne* (1974).

"Ah, upon another face, perhaps it might," replied her husband. "But never on yours! No, dearest Georgiana, you came so nearly perfect from the hand of Nature, that this slightest possible defect—which we hesitate whether to term a defect or a beauty—shocks me, as being the visible mark of earthly imperfection."

"Shocks you, my husband!" cried Georgiana, deeply hurt; at first reddening with momentary anger, but then bursting into tears. "Then why did you take me from my mother's side? You cannot love what shocks you!"

To explain this conversation, it must be mentioned, that, in the centre of Georgiana's left cheek, there was a singular mark, deeply interwoven, as it were, with the texture and substance of her face. In the usual state of her complexion,—a healthy, though delicate bloom,—the mark wore a tint of deeper crimson, which imperfectly defined its shape amid the surrounding rosiness. When she blushed, it gradually became more indistinct, and finally vanished amid the triumphant rush of blood, that bathed the whole cheek with its brilliant glow. But, if any shifting emotion caused her to turn pale, there was the mark again, a crimson stain upon the snow, in what Aylmer sometimes deemed an almost fearful distinctness. Its shape bore not a little similarity to the human hand, though of the smallest pigmy size. Georgiana's lovers were wont to say, that some fairy, at her birth-hour, had laid her tiny hand upon the infant's cheek, and left this impress there, in token of the magic endowments that were to give her such sway over all hearts. Many a desperate swain would have risked life for the privilege of pressing his lips to the mysterious hand. It must not be concealed, however, that the impression wrought by this fairy sign-manual varied exceedingly, according to the difference of temperament in the beholders. Some fastidious persons—but they were exclusively of her own sex—affirmed that the Bloody Hand, as they chose to call it, quite destroyed the effect of Georgiana's beauty, and rendered her countenance even hideous. But it would be as reasonable to say, that one of those small blue stains, which sometimes occur in the purest statuary marble, would convert the Eve of Powers[1] to a monster. Masculine observers, if the birth-mark did not heighten their admiration, contented themselves with wishing it away, that the world might possess one living specimen of ideal loveliness, without the semblance of a flaw. After his marriage—for he thought little or nothing of the matter before—Aylmer discovered that this was the case with himself.

Had she been less beautiful—if Envy's self could have found aught else to sneer at—he might have felt his affection heightened by the prettiness of this mimic hand, now vaguely portrayed, now lost, now stealing forth again, and glimmering to-and-fro with every pulse of emotion that throbbed within her

---

[1] "Eve Before the Fall," an idealized marble statue (1842) by the American sculptor Hiram Powers (1805–1873).

heart. But, seeing her otherwise so perfect, he found this one defect grow more and more intolerable, with every moment of their united lives. It was the fatal flaw of humanity, which Nature, in one shape or another, stamps ineffaceably on all her productions, either to imply that they are temporary and finite, or that their perfection must be wrought by toil and pain. The Crimson Hand expressed the ineludible gripe, in which mortality clutches the highest and purest of earthly mould, degrading them into kindred with the lowest, and even with the very brutes, like whom their visible frames return to dust. In this manner, selecting it as the symbol of his wife's liability to sin, sorrow, decay, and death, Aylmer's sombre imagination was not long in rendering the birth-mark a frightful object, causing him more trouble and horror than ever Georgiana's beauty, whether of soul or sense, had given him delight.

At all the seasons which should have been their happiest, he invariably, and without intending it—nay, in spite of a purpose to the contrary—reverted to this one disastrous topic. Trifling as it at first appeared, it so connected itself with innumerable trains of thought, and modes of feeling, that it became the central point of all. With the morning twilight, Aylmer opened his eyes upon his wife's face, and recognized the symbol of imperfection; and when they sat together at the evening hearth, his eyes wandered stealthily to her cheek, and beheld, flickering with the blaze of the wood fire, the spectral Hand that wrote mortality, where he would fain have worshipped. Georgiana soon learned to shudder at his gaze. It needed but a glance, with the peculiar expression that his face often wore, to change the roses of her cheek into a deathlike paleness, amid which the Crimson Hand was brought strongly out, like a bas-relief of ruby on the whitest marble.

Late, one night, when the lights were growing dim, so as hardly to betray the stain on the poor wife's cheek, she herself, for the first time, voluntarily took up the subject.

"Do you remember, my dear Aylmer," said she, with a feeble attempt at a smile—"have you any recollection of a dream, last night, about this odious Hand?"

"None!—none whatever!" replied Aylmer, starting; but then he added in a dry, cold tone, affected for the sake of concealing the real depth of his emotion:—"I might well dream of it; for before I fell asleep, it had taken a pretty firm hold of my fancy."

"And you did dream of it," continued Georgiana, hastily; for she dreaded lest a gush of tears should interrupt what she had to say—"A terrible dream! I wonder that you can forget it. Is it possible to forget this one expression?—'It is in her heart now—we must have it out!'—Reflect, my husband; for by all means I would have you recall that dream."

The mind is in a sad note, when Sleep, the all-involving, cannot confine her spectres within the dim region of her sway, but suffers them to break forth, affrighting this actual life with secrets that perchance belong to a deeper one. Aylmer now remembered his dream. He had fancied himself, with his servant Aminadab, attempting an operation for the removal of the birthmark. But the deeper went the knife, the deeper sank the Hand, until at length its tiny grasp appeared to have caught hold of Georgiana's heart; whence, however, her husband was inexorably resolved to cut or wrench it away.

When the dream had shaped itself perfectly in his memory, Aylmer sat in his wife's presence with a guilty feeling. Truth often finds its way to the mind close-muffled in robes of sleep, and then speaks with uncompromising directness of matters in regard to which we practise an unconscious self-deception, during our waking moments. Until now, he had not been aware of the tyrannizing influence acquired by one idea over his mind, and of the lengths which he might find in his heart to go, for the sake of giving himself peace.

"Aylmer," resumed Georgiana, solemnly, "I know not what may be the cost to both of us, to rid me of this fatal birth-mark. Perhaps its removal may cause cureless deformity. Or, it may be, the stain goes as deep as life itself. Again, do we know that there is a possibility, on any terms, of unclasping the firm gripe of this little Hand, which was laid upon me before I came into the world?"

"Dearest Georgiana, I have spent much thought upon the subject," I hastily interrupted Aylmer—"I am convinced of the perfect practicability of its removal."

"If there be the remotest possibility of it," continued Georgiana, "let the attempt be made, at whatever risk. Danger is nothing to me; for life—while this hateful mark makes me the object of your horror and disgust—life is a burthen which I would fling down with joy. Either remove this dreadful Hand, or take my wretched life! You have deep science! All the world bears witness of it. You have achieved great wonders! Cannot you remove this little, little mark, which I cover with the tips of two small fingers? Is this beyond your power, for the sake of your own peace, and to save your poor wife from madness?"

"Noblest—dearest—tenderest wife!" cried Aylmer, rapturously. "Doubt not my power. I have already given this matter the deepest thought—thought which might almost have enlightened me to create a being less perfect than yourself. Georgiana, you have led me deeper than ever into the heart of science. I feel myself fully competent to render this dear cheek as faultless as its fellow; and then, most beloved, what will be my triumph, when I shall have corrected what Nature left imperfect, in her fairest work! Even Pygmalion, when his sculptured woman assumed life, felt not greater ecstasy than mine will be."[2]

---

[2]A sculptor from Greek myth who fell in love with his own statue of a beautiful woman. He prayed to Aphrodite to bring the statue to life, a wish the goddess granted.

"It is resolved, then," said Georgiana, faintly smiling, — "And, Aylmer, spare me not, though you should find the birth-mark take refuge in my heart at last."

Her husband tenderly kissed her cheek — her right cheek — not that which bore the impress of the Crimson Hand.

The next day, Aylmer apprized his wife of a plan that he had formed, whereby he might have opportunity for the intense thought and constant watchfulness, which the proposed operation would require; while Georgiana, likewise, would enjoy the perfect repose essential to its success. They were to seclude themselves in the extensive apartments occupied by Aylmer as a laboratory, and where, during his toilsome youth, he had made discoveries in the elemental powers of nature, that had roused the admiration of all the learned societies in Europe. Seated calmly in this laboratory, the pale philosopher had investigated the secrets of the highest cloud-region, and of the profoundest mines; he had satisfied himself of the causes that kindled and kept alive the fires of the volcano; and had explained the mystery of fountains, and how it is that they gush forth, some so bright and pure, and others with such rich medicinal virtues, from the dark bosom of the earth. Here, too, at an earlier period, he had studied the wonders of the human frame, and attempted to fathom the very process by which Nature assimilates all her precious influences from earth and air, and from the spiritual world, to create and foster Man, her masterpiece. The latter pursuit, however, Aylmer had long laid aside, in unwilling recognition of the truth, against which all seekers sooner or later stumble, that our great creative Mother, while she amuses us with apparently working in the broadest sunshine, is yet severely careful to keep her own secrets, and, in spite of her pretended openness, shows us nothing but results. She permits us indeed, to mar, but seldom to mend, and, like a jealous patentee, on no account to make. Now, however, Aylmer resumed these half-forgotten investigations; not, of course, with such hopes or wishes as first suggested them; but because they involved much physiological truth, and lay in the path of his proposed scheme for the treatment of Georgiana.

As he led her over the threshold of the laboratory, Georgiana was cold and tremulous. Aylmer looked cheerfully into her face, with intent to reassure her, but was so startled with the intense glow of the birth-mark upon the whiteness of her cheek, that he could not restrain a strong convulsive shudder. His wife fainted.

"Aminadab! Aminadab!" shouted Aylmer, stamping violently on the floor.

Forthwith, there issued from an inner apartment a man of low stature, but bulky frame, with shaggy hair hanging about his visage, which was grimed with the vapors of the furnace. This personage had been Aylmer's underworker during his whole scientific career, and was admirably fitted for that office by his great mechanical readiness, and the skill with which, while incapable of comprehending a single principle, he executed all the practical details of his master's experiments. With his vast strength, his shaggy hair, his smoky aspect, and the indescribable earthiness that incrusted him, he seemed to represent man's physical nature; while Aylmer's slender figure, and pale, intellectual face, were no less apt a type of the spiritual element.

"Throw open the door of the boudoir, Aminadab," said Aylmer, "and burn a pastille."

"Yes, master," answered Aminadab, looking intently at the lifeless form of Georgiana; and then he muttered to himself: — "If she were my wife, I'd never part with that birth-mark."

When Georgiana recovered consciousness, she found herself breathing an atmosphere of penetrating fragrance, the gentle potency of which had recalled her from her deathlike faintness. The scene around her looked like enchantment. Aylmer had converted those smoky, dingy, sombre rooms, where he had spent his brightest years in recondite pursuits, into a series of beautiful apartments, not unfit to be the secluded abode of a lovely woman. The walls were hung with gorgeous curtains, which imparted the combination of grandeur and grace, that no other species of adornment can achieve; and as they fell from the ceiling to the floor, their rich and ponderous folds, concealing all angles and straight lines, appeared to shut in the scene from infinite space. For aught Georgiana knew, it might be a pavilion among the clouds. And Aylmer, excluding the sunshine, which would have interfered with his chemical processes, had supplied its place with perfumed lamps, emitting flames of various hue, but all uniting in a soft, empurpled radiance. He now knelt by his wife's side, watching her earnestly, but without alarm; for he was confident in his science, and felt that he could draw a magic circle round her, within which no evil might intrude.

"Where am I? — Ah, I remember!" said Georgiana, faintly; and she placed her hand over her cheek, to hide the terrible mark from her husband's eyes.

"Fear not, dearest!" exclaimed he. "Do not shrink from me! Believe me, Georgiana, I even rejoice in this single imperfection, since it will be such rapture to remove it."

"Oh, spare me!" sadly replied his wife — "Pray do not look at it again. I never can forget that convulsive shudder."

In order to soothe Georgiana, and, as it were, to release her mind from the burthen of actual things, Aylmer now put in practice some of the light and playful secrets, which science had taught him among its profounder lore. Airy figures, absolutely bodiless ideas, and forms of unsubstantial beauty, came and danced before her, imprinting their momentary footsteps on beams of light. Though she had some indistinct idea of the method of these optical phenomena, still the illusion was almost perfect enough to warrant the belief, that her husband possessed sway over the spiritual world. Then again, when she felt a wish to look forth from her seclusion, immediately, as if her thoughts were answered, the procession of external existence flitted across a screen. The scenery and the figures of actual life were perfectly represented, but with that bewitching, yet indescribable difference, which always makes a picture, an image, or a shadow, so much more attractive than the original. When wearied of this, Aylmer bade her cast her eyes upon a vessel, containing a quantity of earth. She did so, with little interest at first, but was soon startled, to perceive the germ of a plant, shooting upward from the soil. Then came the slender stalk-—the leaves gradually unfolded themselves—and amid them was a perfect and lovely flower.

"It is magical!" cried Georgiana, "I dare not touch it."

"Nay, pluck it," answered Aylmer, "pluck it, and inhale its brief perfume while you may. The flower will wither in a few moments, and leave nothing save its brown seed-vessels—but thence may be perpetuated a race as ephemeral as itself."

But Georgiana had no sooner touched the flower than the whole plant suffered a blight, its leaves turning coal-black, as if by the agency of fire.

"There was too powerful a stimulus," said Aylmer thoughtfully.

To make up for this abortive experiment, he proposed to take her portrait by a scientific process of his own invention. It was to be effected by rays of light striking upon a polished plate of metal. Georgiana assented—but, on looking at the result, was affrighted to find the features of the portrait blurred and indefinable, while the minute figure of a hand appeared where the cheek should have been. Aylmer snatched the metallic plate, and threw it into a jar of corrosive acid.

Soon, however, he forgot these mortifying failures. In the intervals of study and chemical experiment, he came to her, flushed and exhausted, but seemed invigorated by her presence, and spoke in glowing language of the resources of his art. He gave a history of the long dynasty of the Alchemists, who spent so many ages in quest of the universal solvent, by which the Golden Principle might be elicited from all things vile and base. Aylmer appeared to believe, that, by the plainest scientific logic, it was altogether within the limits of possibility to discover this long-sought medium; but, he added, a philosopher who should go deep enough to acquire the power, would attain too lofty a wisdom to stoop to the exercise of it. Not less singular were his opinions in regard to the Elixir Vitæ.[3] He more than intimated, that it was his option to concoct a liquid that should prolong life for years— perhaps interminably—but that it would produce a discord in nature, which all the world, and chiefly the quaffer of the immortal nostrum, would find cause to curse.

---

[3]Elixir of life, a mythical substance thought to prolong life indefinitely.

"Aylmer, are you in earnest?" asked Georgiana, looking at him with amazement and fear; "it is terrible to possess such power, or even to dream of possessing it!"

"Oh, do not tremble, my love!" said her husband, "I would not wrong either you or myself by working such inharmonious effects upon our lives. But I would have you consider how trifling, in comparison, is the skill requisite to remove this little Hand."

At the mention of the birth-mark, Georgiana, as usual, shrank, as if a red-hot iron had touched her cheek.

Again Aylmer applied himself to his labors. She could hear his voice in the distant furnace-room, giving directions to Aminadab, whose harsh, uncouth, misshapen tones were audible in response, more like the grunt or growl of a brute than human speech. After hours of absence, Aylmer reappeared, and proposed that she should now examine his cabinet of chemical products, and natural treasures of the earth. Among the former he showed her a small vial, in which, he remarked, was contained a gentle yet most powerful fragrance, capable of impregnating all the breezes that blow across a kingdom. They were of inestimable value, the contents of that little vial; and, as he said so, he threw some of the perfume into the air, and filled the room with piercing and invigorating delight.

"And what is this?" asked Georgiana, pointing to a small crystal globe, containing a gold-colored liquid. "It is so beautiful to the eye, that I could imagine it the Elixir of Life."

"In one sense it is," replied Aylmer, "or rather the Elixir of Immortality. It is the most precious poison that ever was concocted in this world. By its aid, I could apportion the lifetime of any mortal at whom you might point your finger. The strength of the dose would determine whether he were to linger out years, or drop dead in the midst of a breath. No king, on his guarded throne, could keep his life, if I, in my private station, should deem that the welfare of millions justified me in depriving him of it."

"Why do you keep such a terrific drug?" inquired Georgiana in horror.

"Do not mistrust me, dearest!" said her husband, smiling; "its virtuous potency is yet greater than its harmful one. But, see! here is a powerful cosmetic. With a few drops of this, in a vase of water, freckles may be washed away as easily as the hands are cleansed. A stronger infusion would take the blood out of the cheek, and leave the rosiest beauty a pale ghost."

"Is it with this lotion that you intend to bathe my cheek?" asked Georgiana anxiously.

"Oh, no!" hastily replied her husband—"this is merely superficial. Your case demands a remedy that shall go deeper."

In his interviews with Georgiana, Aylmer generally made minute inquiries as to her sensations, and whether the confinement of the rooms, and the temperature of the atmosphere, agreed with her. These questions had such a particular drift, that Georgiana began to conjecture that she was already subjected to certain physical influences, either breathed in with the fragrant air, or taken with her food. She fancied, likewise—but it might be altogether fancy—that there was a stirring up of her system,—a strange indefinite sensation creeping through her veins, and tingling, half painfully, half pleasurably, at her heart. Still, whenever she dared to look into the mirror, there she beheld herself, pale as a white rose, and with the crimson birth-mark stamped upon her cheek. Not even Aylmer now hated it so much as she.

To dispel the tedium of the hours which her husband found it necessary to devote to the processes of combination and analysis, Georgiana turned over the volumes of his scientific library. In many dark old tomes, she met with chapters full of romance and poetry. They were the works of the philosophers of the middle ages, such as Albertus Magnus, Cornelius Agrippa, Paracelsus, and the famous friar who created the prophetic Brazen Head.[4] All these antique naturalists stood in advance of their centuries, yet were imbued with some of their credulity, and therefore were believed, and perhaps imagined themselves, to have acquired from the investigation of nature a power above nature, and from physics a sway over the spiritual world. Hardly less curious and imaginative were the early volumes of the Transactions of the Royal Society,[5] in which the members, knowing little of the limits of natural possibility, were continually recording wonders, or proposing methods whereby wonders might be wrought.

But, to Georgiana, the most engrossing volume was a large folio from her husband's own hand, in which he had recorded every experiment of his scientific career, with its original aim, the methods adopted for its development, and its final success or failure, with the circumstances to which either event was attributable. The book, in truth, was both the history and emblem of his ardent, ambitious, imaginative, yet practical and laborious, life. He handled physical details, as if there were nothing beyond them; yet spiritualized them all, and redeemed himself from materialism, by his strong and eager aspiration towards the infinite. In his grasp, the veriest clod of earth assumed a soul. Georgiana, as she read, reverenced Aylmer, and loved him more profoundly than ever, but with a less entire dependence on his judgment than heretofore. Much as he had accomplished, she could not but observe that his most splendid successes were almost invariably failures, if compared with the ideal at which he aimed. His brightest diamonds were the merest pebbles, and felt to be so by himself, in comparison with the inestimable gems which lay hidden beyond his reach. The volume, rich with achievements that had

---

[4]Albertus Magnus (1193?–1280), Cornelius Agrippa (1486?–1535), and Philippus Aureolus Paracelsus (1493–1541) were early scientists associated with magic and alchemy. Friar Roger Bacon (1214?–1294) allegedly created a brass head that made strange prophecies.

[5]The British Royal Society was founded in London in 1662 to promote scientific inquiry.

won renown for its author, was yet as melancholy a record as ever mortal hand had penned. It was the sad confession, and continual exemplification, of the short-comings of the composite man—the spirit burthened with clay and working in matter—and of the despair that assails the higher nature, at finding itself so miserably thwarted by the earthly part. Perhaps every man of genius, in whatever sphere, might recognize the image of his own experience in Aylmer's journal.

So deeply did these reflections affect Georgiana, that she laid her face upon the open volume, and burst into tears. In this situation she was found by her husband.

"It is dangerous to read in a sorcerer's books," said he, with a smile, though his countenance was uneasy and displeased. "Georgiana, there are pages in that volume, which I can scarcely glance over and keep my senses. Take heed lest it prove as detrimental to you!"

"It has made me worship you more than ever," said she.

"Ah! wait for this one success," rejoined he, "then worship me if you will. I shall deem myself hardly unworthy of it. But, come! I have sought you for the luxury of your voice. Sing to me, dearest!"

So she poured out the liquid music of her voice to quench the thirst of his spirit. He then took his leave, with a boyish exuberance of gaiety, assuring her that her seclusion would endure but a little longer, and that the result was already certain. Scarcely had he departed, when Georgiana felt irresistibly impelled to follow him. She had forgotten to inform Aylmer of a symptom, which, for two or three hours past, had begun to excite her attention. It was a sensation in the fatal birth-mark, not painful, but which induced a restlessness throughout her system. Hastening after her husband, she intruded, for the first time, into the laboratory.

The first thing that struck her eye was the furnace, that hot and feverish worker, with the intense glow of its fire, which, by the quantities of soot clustered above it, seemed to have been burning for ages. There was a distilling apparatus in full operation. Around the room were retorts, tubes, cylinders, crucibles, and other apparatus of chemical research. An electrical machine stood ready for immediate use. The atmosphere felt oppressively close, and was tainted with gaseous odors, which had been tormented forth by the processes of science. The severe and homely simplicity of the apartment, with its naked walls and brick pavement, looked strange, accustomed as Georgiana had become to the fantastic elegance of her boudoir. But what chiefly, indeed almost solely, drew her attention, was the aspect of Aylmer himself.

He was pale as death, anxious, and absorbed, and hung over the furnace as if it depended upon his utmost watchfulness whether the liquid, which it was distilling, should be the draught of immortal happiness or misery. How different from the sanguine and joyous mien that he had assumed for Georgiana's encouragement!

"Carefully now, Aminadab! Carefully, thou human machine! Carefully, thou man of clay!" muttered Aylmer, more to himself than his assistant. "Now, if there be a thought too much or too little, it is all over!"

"Hoh! hoh!" mumbled Aminadab—"look, master, look!"

Aylmer raised his eyes hastily, and at first reddened, then grew paler than ever, on beholding Georgiana. He rushed towards her, and seized her arm with a gripe that left the print of his fingers upon it.

"Why do you come hither? Have you no trust in your husband?" cried he impetuously. "Would you throw the blight of that fatal birth-mark over my labors? It is not well done. Go, prying woman, go!"

"Nay, Aylmer," said Georgiana, with the firmness of which she possessed no stinted endowment, "it is not you that have a right to complain. You mistrust your wife! You have concealed the anxiety with which you watch the development of this experiment. Think not so unworthily of me, my husband! Tell me all the risk we run; and fear not that I shall shrink, for my share in it is far less than your own!"

"No, no, Georgiana!" said Aylmer impatiently, "it must not be."

"I submit," replied she calmly. "And, Aylmer, I shall quaff whatever draught you bring me; but it will be on the same principle that would induce me to take a dose of poison, if offered by your hand."

"My noble wife," said Aylmer, deeply moved, "I knew not the height and depth of your nature, until now. Nothing shall be concealed. Know, then, that this Crimson Hand, superficial as it seems, has clutched its grasp into your being, with a strength of which I had no previous conception. I have already administered agents powerful enough to do aught except to change your entire physical system. Only one thing remains to be tried. If that fail us, we are ruined!"

"Why did you hesitate to tell me this?" asked she.

"Because, Georgiana," said Aylmer, in a low voice, "there is danger!"

"Danger? There is but one danger—that this horrible stigma shall be left upon my cheek!" cried Georgiana. "Remove it! remove it!—whatever be the cost—or we shall both go mad!"

"Heaven knows, your words are too true," said Aylmer, sadly. "And now, dearest, return to your boudoir. In a little while, all will be tested."

He conducted her back, and took leave of her with a solemn tenderness, which spoke far more than his words how much was now at stake. After his departure, Georgiana became wrapt in musings. She considered the character of Aylmer, and did it completer justice than at any previous moment. Her heart exulted, while it trembled, at his honorable love, so pure and lofty that it would accept nothing less than perfection, nor miserably make itself contented with an earthlier nature than he had dreamed of. She felt how much more precious was such a sentiment, than that meaner kind which would have borne with the imperfection for her sake, and have been guilty of treason to holy love, by degrading its perfect idea to the level of the actual. And, with her whole spirit, she prayed, that, for a single moment, she might satisfy his highest and deepest conception. Longer than one moment, she well knew, it could not be; for his spirit was ever on the march—ever ascending—and each instant required something that was beyond the scope of the instant before.

The sound of her husband's footsteps aroused her. He bore a crystal goblet, containing a liquor colorless as water, but bright enough to be the draught of immortality. Aylmer was pale; but it seemed rather the consequence of a highly wrought state of mind, and tension of spirit, than of fear or doubt.

"The concoction of the draught has been perfect," said he, in answer to Georgiana's look. "Unless all my science have deceived me, it cannot fail."

"Save on your account, my dearest Aylmer," observed his wife, "I might wish to put off this birth-mark of mortality by relinquishing mortality itself, in preference to any other mode. Life is but a sad possession to those who have attained precisely the degree of moral advancement at which I stand. Were I weaker and blinder, it might be happiness. Were I stronger, it might be endured hopefully. But, being what I find myself, methinks I am of all mortals the most fit to die."

"You are fit for heaven without tasting death!" replied her husband. "But why do we speak of dying? The draught cannot fail. Behold its effect upon this plant!"

On the window-seat there stood a geranium, diseased with yellow blotches, which had overspread all its leaves. Aylmer poured a small quantity of the liquid upon the soil in which it grew. In a little time, when the roots of the plant had taken up the moisture, the unsightly blotches began to be extinguished in a living verdure.

"There needed no proof," said Georgiana, quietly. "Give me the goblet. I joyfully stake all upon your word."

"Drink, then, thou lofty creature!" exclaimed Aylmer, with fervid admiration. "There is no taint of imperfection on thy spirit. Thy sensible frame, too, shall soon be all perfect!"

She quaffed the liquid, and returned the goblet to his hand.

"It is grateful," said she, with a placid smile. "Methinks it is like water from a heavenly fountain; for it contains I know not what of unobtrusive fragrance and deliciousness. It allays a feverish thirst, that had parched me for many days. Now, dearest, let me sleep. My earthly senses are closing over my spirit, like the leaves round the heart of a rose, at sunset."

She spoke the last words with a gentle reluctance, as if it required almost more energy than she could command to pronounce the faint and lingering syllables. Scarcely had they loitered through her lips, ere she was lost in slumber. Aylmer sat by her side, watching her aspect with the emotions proper to a man, the whole value of whose existence was involved in the process now to be tested. Mingled with this mood, however, was the philosophic investigation, characteristic of the man of science. Not the minutest symptom escaped him. A heightened flush of the cheek—a slight irregularity of breath—a quiver of the eyelid—a hardly perceptible tremor through the frame—such were the details which, as the moments passed, he wrote down in his folio volume. Intense thought had set its stamp upon every previous page of that volume; but the thoughts of years were all concentrated upon the last.

While thus employed, he failed not to gaze often at the fatal Hand, and not without a shudder. Yet once, by a strange and unaccountable impulse, he pressed it with his lips. His spirit recoiled, however, in the very act, and Georgiana, out of the midst of her deep sleep, moved uneasily and murmured, as if in remonstrance. Again, Aylmer resumed his watch. Nor was it without avail. The Crimson Hand, which at first had been strongly visible upon the marble paleness of Georgiana's cheek now grew more faintly outlined. She remained not less pale than ever; but the birth-mark, with every breath that came and went, lost somewhat of its former distinctness. Its presence had been awful; its departure was more awful still. Watch the stain of the rainbow fading out of the sky; and you will know how that mysterious symbol passed away.

"By Heaven, it is well nigh gone!" said Aylmer to himself, in almost irrepressible ecstasy. "I can scarcely trace it now. Success! Success! And now it is like the faintest rose-color. The slightest flush of blood across her cheek would overcome it. But she is so pale!"

He drew aside the window-curtain, and suffered the light of natural day to fall into the room, and rest upon her cheek. At the same time, he heard a gross, hoarse chuckle, which he had long known as his servant Aminadab's expression of delight.

" Ah, clod! Ah, earthly mass!" cried Aylmer, laughing in a sort of frenzy. "You have served me well! Matter and Spirit—Earth and Heaven—have both done their part in this! Laugh, thing of senses! You have earned the right to laugh."

These exclamations broke Georgiana's sleep. She slowly unclosed her eyes, and gazed into the mirror, which her husband had arranged for that purpose. A faint smile flitted over her lips, when she recognized how barely perceptible was now that Crimson Hand, which had once blazed forth with such disastrous brilliancy as to scare away all their happiness. But then her eyes sought Aylmer's face, with a trouble and anxiety that he could by no means account for.

"My poor Aylmer!" murmured she.

"Poor? Nay, richest! Happiest! Most favored!" exclaimed he. "My peerless bride, it is successful! You are perfect!"

"My poor Aylmer!" she repeated, with a more than human tenderness. "You have aimed loftily!—you have done nobly! Do not repent, that, with so high and pure a feeling, you have rejected the best that earth could offer. Aylmer—dearest Aylmer—I am dying!"

Alas, it was too true! The fatal Hand had grappled with the mystery of life, and was the bond by which an angelic spirit kept itself in union with a mortal frame. As the last crimson tint of the birth-mark—that sole token of human imperfection—faded from her cheek, the parting breath of the now perfect woman passed into the atmosphere, and her soul, lingering a moment near her husband, took its heavenward flight. Then a hoarse, chuckling laugh was heard again! Thus ever does the gross Fatality of Earth exult in its invariable triumph over the immortal essence, which, in this dim sphere of half-development, demands the completeness of a higher state. Yet, had Aylmer reached a profounder wisdom, he need not thus have flung away the happiness, which would have woven his mortal life of the self-same texture with the celestial. The momentary circumstance was too strong for him; he failed to look beyond the shadowy scope of Time, and living once for all in Eternity, to find the perfect Future in the present.

[1843]

Shirley Jackson
[1919–1965]

At once a doting mother who wrote humorous accounts of her family life and a self-described witch who penned incisive studies of psychologic aberration and unsettling tales of the supernatural, SHIRLEY JACKSON *explored the unstable boundary between domesticity and horror. Considered one of the finest American fiction writers of the 1950s and 1960s, Jackson is now best known for the widely anthologized short story "The Lottery" (1948).*

Jackson was born in 1919 in San Francisco, the first child of an affluent and conservative family. During childhood and adolescence and well into adulthood, this unruly and overweight daughter struggled against her mother Geraldine's firmly held standards of propriety and femininity. As she resisted the conventions of class and gender, Jackson developed her gift of seeing beneath the decorous surface of middle-class life into its vicious core. In the sunny and seemingly placid northern California suburb of Burlingame, where she attended high school and began writing poetry and short stories, Jackson discerned her neighbors' intolerance and cruelty—traits that later characterized the suburbanites of her fiction.

In 1933 Jackson's family moved to Rochester, New York. After attending the University of Rochester from 1934 to 1936, Jackson withdrew from school and spent a year at home, writing a thousand words a day. In 1937 she entered Syracuse University, where she edited the campus humor magazine, won second prize in a poetry contest, and founded the literary magazine Spectre. *She married the magazine's managing editor, Stanley Edgar Hyman, immediately after her graduation in 1940. The couple moved to New York City, where Jackson held a variety of unsatisfying jobs while continuing to write. In 1941 her experience selling books at Macy's formed the basis for "My Life with R. H. Macy," published in the* New Republic. *This success was followed by the birth of her first child and the publication of many stories in the New Yorker. Her reputation as a writer of short fiction grew, and in 1944 "Come Dance with Me in Ireland" was the first of her four stories chosen for* Best American Short Stories.

Jackson's family continued to grow, and her body of writing continued to expand after she moved to North Bennington, Vermont. She had three more children and published short stories, novels, family chronicles, a one-act play, a children's book, and a nonfictional account of witchcraft in Salem. Her works were made into plays, films, and television shows. "The Lottery" appeared as a short play, a television drama, a radio show, an opera, and a ballet. The family chronicles Life Among the Savages *(1953) and* Raising Demons *(1957) were bestsellers, and Jackson's popular success was matched by critical acclaim for her short fiction and novels alike. These latter include* The Road Through the Wall *(1948), a look at the dark side of suburban life inspired by Jackson's years in Burlingame;* Hangsaman *(1951) and* The Bird's Nest *(1954), two penetrating depictions of mental illness; and* The Sundial *(1958), a Gothic fantasy about the end of the world. Jackson's last two novels,* The Haunting of Hill House *(1959) and* We Have Always Lived in the Castle *(1962), are her best. At once chilling and tender, these haunted-house stories transcend their genre, portraying the often-strained relationship between mother and daughter with consummate sympathy and skill. Three years after* We Have Always Lived in the Castle *appeared on the bestseller list and was named one of the year's best novels by* Time *magazine, Shirley Jackson died of heart failure on August 8, 1965.*

—Jamil Musstafa, *Lewis University*

The Lottery

SHIRLEY JACKSON

THE MORNING OF JUNE 27TH was clear and sunny, with the fresh warmth of a full-summer day; the flowers were blossoming profusely and the grass was richly green. The people of the village began to gather in the square, between the post office and the bank, around ten o'clock; in some towns there were so many people that the lottery took two days and had to be started on June 26th, but in this village, where there were only about three hundred people, the whole lottery took less than two hours, so it could begin at ten o'clock in the morning and still be through in time to allow the villagers to get home for noon dinner.

The children assembled first, of course. School was recently over for the summer, and the feeling of liberty sat uneasily on most of them; they tended to gather together quietly for a while before they broke into boisterous play, and their talk was still of the classroom and the teacher, of books and reprimands. Bobby Martin had already stuffed his pockets full of stones, and the other boys soon followed his example, selecting the smoothest and roundest stones; Bobby and Harry Jones and Dickie Delacroix—the villagers pronounced this name "Dellacroy"—eventually made a great pile of stones in one corner of the square and guarded it against the raids of the other boys. The girls stood aside, talking among themselves, looking over their shoulders at the boys, and the very small children rolled in the dust or clung to the hands of their older brothers or sisters.

Soon the men began to gather, surveying their own children, speaking of planting and rain, tractors and taxes. They stood together, away from the pile of stones in the corner, and their jokes were quiet and they smiled rather than laughed. The women, wearing faded house dresses and sweaters, came shortly after their menfolk. They greeted one another and exchanged bits of gossip as they went to join their husbands. Soon the women, standing by their husbands, began to call to their children, and the children came reluctantly, having to be called four or five times. Bobby Martin ducked under his mother's grasping hand and ran, laughing, back to the pile of stones. His father spoke up sharply, and Bobby came quickly and took his place between his father and his oldest brother.

Reprinted from *The Lottery and Other Stories,* by permission of Farrar, Straus & Giroux, LLC. Copyright © 1976, 1977 by Laurence Hyman, Barry Hyman, Mrs. Sarah Webster and Mrs. Joanne Schnurer.

The lottery was conducted—as were the square dances, the teenage club, the Halloween program—by Mr. Summers, who had time and energy to devote to civic activities. He was a round-faced, jovial man and he ran the coal business, and people were sorry for him, because he had no children and his wife was a scold. When he arrived in the square, carrying the black wooden box, there was a murmur of conversation among the villagers, and he waved and called, "Little late today, folks." The postmaster, Mr. Graves, followed him, carrying a three-legged stool, and the stool was put in the center of the square and Mr. Summers set the black box down on it. The villagers kept their distance, leaving a space between themselves and the stool, and when Mr. Summers said, "Some of you fellows want to give me a hand?" there was a hesitation before two men, Mr. Martin and his oldest son, Baxter, came forward to hold the box steady on the stool while Mr. Summers stirred up the papers inside it.

The original paraphernalia for the lottery had been lost long ago, and the black box now resting on the stool had been put into use even before Old Man Warner, the oldest man in town, was born. Mr. Summers spoke frequently to the villagers about making a new box, but no one liked to upset even as much tradition as was represented by the black box. There was a story that the present box had been made with some pieces of the box that had preceded it, the one that had been constructed when the first people settled down to make a village here. Every year, after the lottery, Mr. Summers began talking again about a new box, but every year the subject was allowed to fade off without anything's being done. The black box grew shabbier each year; by now it was no longer completely black but splintered badly along one side to show the original wood color, and in some places faded or stained.

Mr. Martin and his oldest son, Baxter, held the black box securely on the stool until Mr. Summers had stirred the papers thoroughly with his hand. Because so much of the ritual had been forgotten or discarded, Mr. Summers had been successful in having slips of paper substituted for the chips of wood that had been used for generations. Chips of wood, Mr. Summers had argued, had been all very well when the village was tiny, but now that the population was more than three hundred and likely to keep on growing, it was necessary to use something that would fit more easily into the black box. The night before the lottery, Mr. Summers and Mr. Graves made up the slips of paper and put them in the box, and it was then taken to the safe of Mr. Summers' coal company and locked up until Mr. Summers was ready to take it to the square next morning. The rest of the year, the box was put away, sometimes one place, sometimes another; it had spent one year in Mr. Graves's barn and another year underfoot in the post office, and sometimes it was set on a shelf in the Martin grocery and left there.

There was a great deal of fussing to be done before Mr. Summers declared the lottery open. There were the lists to make up—of heads of families, heads of households in each family, members of each household in each family. There was the proper swearing-in of Mr. Summers by the postmaster, as the official of the lottery; at one time, some people remembered, there had been a recital of some sort, performed by the official of the lottery, a perfunctory, tuneless chant that had been rattled off duly each year; some people believed that the official of the lottery used to stand just so when he said or sang it, others believed that he was supposed to walk among the people, but years and years ago this part of the ritual had been allowed to lapse. There had been, also, a ritual salute, which the official of the lottery had had to use in addressing each person who came up to draw from the box, but this also had changed with time, until now it was felt necessary only for the official to speak to each person approaching. Mr. Summers was very good at all this; in his clean white shirt and blue jeans, with one hand resting carelessly on the black box, he seemed very proper and important as he talked interminably to Mr. Graves and the Martins.

Just as Mr. Summers finally left off talking and turned to the assembled villagers, Mrs. Hutchinson came hurriedly along the path to the square, her sweater thrown over her shoulders, and slid into place in the back of the crowd. "Clean forgot what day it was," she said to Mrs. Delacroix, who stood next to her, and they both laughed softly. "Thought my old man was out back stacking wood," Mrs. Hutchinson went on, "and then I looked out the window and the kids were gone, and then I remembered it was the twentyseventh and came a-running." She dried her hands on her apron, and Mrs. Delacroix said, "You're in time, though. They're still talking away up there."

Mrs. Hutchinson craned her neck to see through the crowd and found her husband and children standing near the front. She tapped Mrs. Delacroix on the arm as a farewell and began to make her way through the crowd. The people separated good-humoredly to let her through; two or three people said, in voices just loud enough to be heard across the crowd, "Here comes your Missus, Hutchinson," and "Bill, she made it after all." Mrs. Hutchinson reached her husband, and Mr. Summers, who had been waiting, said cheerfully, "Thought we were going to have to get on without you, Tessie." Mrs. Hutchinson said, grinning, "Wouldn't have me leave m'dishes in the sink, now, would you, Joe?" and soft laughter ran through the crowd as the people stirred back into position after Mrs. Hutchinson's arrival.

"Well, now," Mr. Summers said soberly, "guess we better get started, get this over with, so's we can go back to work. Anybody ain't here?"

"Dunbar," several people said. "Dunbar, Dunbar."

Mr. Summers consulted his list. "Clyde Dunbar," he said. "That's right. He's broke his leg, hasn't he? Who's drawing for him?"

"Me, I guess," a woman said, and Mr. Summers turned to look at her. "Wife draws for her husband," Mr. Summers said. "Don't you have a grown boy to do it for you, Janey?" Although Mr. Summers and everyone else in the village knew the answer perfectly well, it was the business of the official of the lottery to ask such questions formally. Mr. Summers waited with an expression of polite interest while Mrs. Dunbar answered.

"Horace's not but sixteen yet," Mrs. Dunbar said regretfully. "Guess I gotta fill in for the old man this year."

"Right," Mr. Summers said. He made a note on the list he was holding. Then he asked, "Watson boy drawing this year?"

A tall boy in the crowd raised his hand. "Here," he said. "I'm drawing for m'mother and me." He blinked his eyes nervously and ducked his head as several voices in the crowd said things like "Good fellow, Jack," and "Glad to see your mother's got a man to do it."

"Well," Mr. Summers said, "guess that's everyone. Old Man Warner make it?"

"Here," a voice said, and Mr. Summers nodded.

A sudden hush fell on the crowd as Mr. Summers cleared his throat and looked at the list. "All ready?" he called. "Now, I'll read the names—heads of families first—and the men come up and take a paper out of the box. Keep the paper folded in your hand without looking at it until everyone has had a turn. Everything clear?"

The people had done it so many times that they only half listened to the directions; most of them were quiet, wetting their lips, not looking around. Then Mr. Summers raised one hand high and said, "Adams." A man disengaged himself from the crowd and came forward. "Hi, Steve," Mr. Summers said, and Mr. Adams said, "Hi, Joe." They grinned at one another humorlessly and nervously. Then Mr. Adams reached into the black box and took out a folded paper. He held it firmly by one corner as he turned and went hastily back to his place in the crowd, where he stood a little apart from his family, not looking down at his hand.

"Allen," Mr. Summers said. "Anderson . . . Bentham."

"Seems like there's no time at all between lotteries any more," Mrs. Delacroix said to Mrs. Graves in the back row. "Seems like we got through with the last one only last week."

"Time sure goes fast," Mrs. Graves said.

"Clark . . . Delacroix."

"There goes my old man," Mrs. Delacroix said. She held her breath while her husband went forward.

"Dunbar," Mr. Summers said, and Mrs. Dunbar went steadily to the box while one of the women said, "Go on, Janey," and another said, "There she goes."

"We're next," Mrs. Graves said. She watched while Mr. Graves came around from the side of the box, greeted Mr. Summers gravely, and selected a slip of paper from the box. By now, all through the crowd there were men holding the small folded papers in their large hands, turning them over and over nervously. Mrs. Dunbar and her two sons stood together, Mrs. Dunbar holding the slip of paper.

"Harburt . . . Hutchinson."

"Get up there, Bill," Mrs. Hutchinson said, and the people near her laughed.

"Jones."

"They do say," Mr. Adams said to Old Man Warner, who stood next to him, "that over in the north village they're talking of giving up the lottery."

Old Man Warner snorted. "Pack of crazy fools," he said. "Listening to the young folks, nothing's good enough for *them*. Next thing you know, they'll be wanting to go back to living in caves, nobody work any more, live *that* way for a while. Used to be a saying about 'Lottery in June, corn be heavy soon.' First thing you know, we'd all be eating stewed chickweed and acorns. There's *always* been a lottery," he added petulantly. "Bad enough to see young Joe Summers up there joking with everybody."

"Some places have already quit lotteries," Mrs. Adams said.

"Nothing but trouble in *that*," Old Man Warner said stoutly. "Pack of young fools."

"Martin." And Bobby Martin watched his father go forward. "Overdyke . . . Percy."

"I wish they'd hurry," Mrs. Dunbar said to her older son. "I wish they'd hurry."

"They're almost through," her son said.

"You get ready to run tell Dad," Mrs. Dunbar said.

Mr. Summers called his own name and then stepped forward precisely and selected a slip from the box. Then he called, "Warner."

"Seventy-seventh year I been in the lottery," Old Man Warner said as he went through the crowd. "Seventy-seventh time."

"Watson." The tall boy came awkwardly through the crowd. Someone said, "Don't be nervous, Jack," and Mr. Summers said, "Take your time, son."

"Zanini."

After that, there was a long pause, a breathless pause, until Mr. Summers, holding his slip of paper in the air, said, "All right, fellows." For a minute, no one moved, and then all the slips of paper were opened. Suddenly, all the women began to speak at once, saying, "Who is it?" "Who's got it?" "Is it the Dunbars?" "Is it the Watsons?" Then the voices began to say, "It's Hutchinson. It's Bill," "Bill Hutchinson's got it."

"Go tell your father," Mrs. Dunbar said to her older son.

People began to look around to see the Hutchinsons. Bill Hutchinson was standing quiet, staring down at the paper in his hand. Suddenly, Tessie Hutchinson shouted to Mr. Summers, "You didn't give him time enough to take any paper he wanted. I saw you. It wasn't fair."

"Be a good sport, Tessie," Mrs. Delacroix called, and Mrs. Graves said, "All of us took the same chance."

"Shut up, Tessie," Bill Hutchinson said.

"Well, everyone," Mr. Summers said, "that was done pretty fast, and now we've got to be hurrying a little more to get done in time." He consulted his next list. "Bill," he said, "you draw for the Hutchinson family. You got any other households in the Hutchinsons?"

"There's Don and Eva," Mrs. Hutchinson yelled. "Make them take their chance!"

"Daughters draw with their husbands' families, Tessie," Mr. Summers said gently. "You know that as well as anyone else."

"It wasn't *fair*," Tessie said.

"I guess not, Joe," Bill Hutchinson said regretfully. "My daughter draws with her husband's family, that's only fair. And I've got no other family except the kids."

"Then, as far as drawing for families is concerned, it's you." Mr. Summers said in explanation, "and as far as drawing for households is concerned, that's you, too. Right?"

"Right," Bill Hutchinson said.

"How many kids, Bill?" Mr. Summers asked formally.

"Three," Bill Hutchinson said. "There's Bill, Jr., and Nancy, and little Dave. And Tessie and me."

"All right, then," Mr. Summers said. "Harry, you got their tickets back?"

Mr. Graves nodded and held up the slips of paper. "Put them in the box, then," Mr. Summers directed. "Take Bill's and put it in."

"I think we ought to start over," Mrs. Hutchinson said, as quietly as she could. "I tell you it wasn't *fair*. You didn't give him time enough to choose. *Every*body saw that."

Mr. Graves had selected the five slips and put them in the box, and he dropped all the papers but those onto the ground, where the breeze caught them and lifted them off.

"Listen, everybody," Mrs. Hutchinson was saying to the people around her.

"Ready, Bill?" Mr. Summers asked, and Bill Hutchinson, with one quick glance around at his wife and children, nodded.

"Remember," Mr. Summers said, "take the slips and keep them folded until each person has taken one. Harry, you help little Dave." Mr. Graves took the hand of the little boy, who came willingly with him up to the box. "Take a paper out of the box, Davy," Mr. Summers said. Davy put his hand into the box and laughed. "Take just *one* paper," Mr. Summers said. "Harry, you hold it for him." Mr. Graves took the child's hand and removed the folded paper from the tight fist and held it while little Dave stood next to him and looked up at him wonderingly.

"Nancy next," Mr. Summers said. Nancy was twelve, and her school friends breathed heavily as she went forward, switching her skirt, and took a slip daintily from the box. "Bill, Jr.," Mr. Summers said, and Billy, his face red and his feet over-large, nearly knocked the box over as he got a paper out. "Tessie," Mr. Summers said. She hesitated for a minute, looking around defiantly, and then set her lips and went up to the box. She snatched a paper out and held it behind her.

"Bill," Mr. Summers said, and Bill Hutchinson reached into the box and felt around, bringing his hand out at last with the slip of paper in it.

The crowd was quiet. A girl whispered, "I hope it's not Nancy," and the sound of the whisper reached the edges of the crowd.

"It's not the way it used to be," Old Man Warner said clearly. "People ain't the way they used to be."

"All right," Mr. Summers said. "Open the papers. Harry, you open little Dave's."

Mr. Graves opened the slip of paper and there was a general sigh through the crowd as he held it up and everyone could see that it was blank. Nancy and Bill, Jr., opened theirs at the same time, and both beamed and laughed, turning around to the crowd and holding their slips of paper above their heads.

"Tessie," Mr. Summers said. There was a pause, and then Mr. Summers looked at Bill Hutchinson, and Bill unfolded his paper and showed it. It was blank.

"It's Tessie," Mr. Summers said, and his voice was hushed. "Show us her paper, Bill."

Bill Hutchinson went over to his wife and forced the slip of paper out of her hand. It had a black spot on it, the black spot Mr. Summers had made the night before with the heavy pencil in the coal-company office. Bill Hutchinson held it up, and there was a stir in the crowd.

"All right, folks," Mr. Summers said. "Let's finish quickly."

Although the villagers had forgotten the ritual and lost the original black box, they still remembered to use stones. The pile of stones the boys had made earlier was ready; there were stones on the ground with the blowing scraps of paper that had come out of the box. Mrs. Delacroix selected a stone so large she had to pick it up with both hands and turned, to Mrs. Dunbar. "Come on," she said. "Hurry up."

Mrs. Dunbar had small stones in both hands, and she said, gasping for breath, "I can't run at all. You'll have to go ahead and I'll catch up with you."

The children had stones already, and someone gave little Davy Hutchinson a few pebbles.

Tessie Hutchinson was in the center of a cleared space by now, and she held her hands out desperately as the villagers moved in on her. "It isn't fair," she said. A stone hit her on the side of the head.

Old Man Warner was saying, "Come on, come on, everyone." Steve Adams was in the front of the crowd of villagers, with Mrs. Graves beside him.

"It isn't fair, it isn't right," Mrs. Hutchinson screamed, and then they were upon her.

[1949]

HENRY JAMES
[1843–1916]

Henry James occupies a unique place in the history of American literature because of the ambition and achievement of his art. His focus on the art of the novel has sometimes obscured the range of his social vision, particularly in the eyes of readers who find his elaborate style unnecessarily difficult. In his own time, his insistence that the novel be a form of art that must have structure and not be "a loose and baggy monster" was a reaction to the common belief that the novelist's only obligation was to serve the moral interests of the conventional public. James's early novel Daisy Miller *(1878) scandalized readers who thought he was un-American to portray so critically the naïve girl adrift in the intricacies of European society. This notoriety made the novel one of his bestselling books and established his reputation as a writer of great promise with a distinctive style and a subject that lent itself to much exploration. Although James has never had a large popular audience, most of his twenty-two novels and more than one hundred short stories remain in print; his critical reputation continues to grow even as disagreements about his value and values flourish; a wider public has come to know his work though its recent translations into film* (The Portrait of a Lady, Washington Square, The Wings of the Dove, *and* The Golden Bowl); *and a narrower public enjoys the operas based on his fictions* The Aspern Papers *and* The Turn of the Screw, *which is perhaps the best ghost story every written.*

Henry James was born in 1843 near Washington Square in New York City, the city that he always considered his home even as his family jaunted in his early years to various capitals of Europe and north to Newport, Rhode Island and Cambridge, Massachusetts. His father, Henry James, Sr., was an heir to an upstate New York real estate fortune that left him free to pursue his own philosophical and religious interests. He was influenced by the great theologian Emmanuel Swedenborg but he was not orthodox in any sense and has been frequently puzzling to readers unsympathetic to the validity of religious experience. As distinguished a philosopher as Charles Sanders Peirce, whose own father was a Swedenborgian scholar as well as a Harvard mathematician, found Henry James, Sr. to be a supremely subtle moralist. Indeed, as Henry "Junior" recalls in his autobiographical memoir, A Small Boy and

Others, *the lesson his father taught most consistently was "that we need never fear to be good enough if we are only social enough: a splendid meaning indeed being attached to the latter term." This pre-eminent value of the social, of the relations between people in the most intimate ways and with the most far-reaching consequences, is at the core of James's work.*

James's childhood travels to Europe with his family may or may not have given him the "sensuous education" that his father intended for his children, but both Henry and his older brother William, who distinguished himself as a professor at Harvard by formulating psychology as an academic discipline, profited by the exposure to cultures other than that of the United States. Though neither of them fought in the Civil War, as did their two younger brothers, they both had a sense of the way that conflicting beliefs profoundly shaped one's understanding of experience and actions. This can be seen in works as different as The Variety of Religious Experience *(1902), one of William's most popular and influential works, and* The American *(1877), an early novel of Henry's in which the differences between American and European courtship rules lead to much sorrow and heartbreak.*

The "international theme" became James's signature topic. He explored how what Thorstein Veblen dubbed "the leisure class" negotiated exchanges between New World money, Old World prestige, and the needs for intimacy, mutual understanding, and creativity and the effect of class differences and these needs. The Portrait of a Lady *(1881), in which a young, poor, intelligent woman is courted both by an English lord and an impoverished American expatriate aesthete, is his most successful examination of these issues in this early phase of his career, and for many readers it remains his best novel. James has often been characterized as focusing on exclusively and even defending the lives of the economically privileged, but a brief survey of his novels and stories—for example,* The Bostonians *(1886),* The Princess Casamassima *(1886), and* In the Cage *(1898)—shows his awareness of the difficult position of working-class characters, even if his representation of their conversational skills is implausible. This awareness of the ways in which emerging capitalism, or "business" as he would have called it, was putting pressure on human relations informs all his writing, but it becomes more explicit in some of the nonfiction texts that have recently been of interest to critics, especially* The American Scene *(1907).*

This record of his return to the United States in 1904 after an absence of nearly two decades has become the focus of much recent interest. James's reactions to the many social and material changes that took place during the "gilded age" are often very mixed. He admires the energy of the people and natural beauty of the country while lamenting the way that wealth is being used to conceal, if not destroy, any living sense of the past, whether it be in the customs and language of the new immigrants, or the architecture of Fifth Avenue. Although this text has sometimes been read as expressing nostalgia for the world of his youth, it is more ambivalent than that about develop-

ments in American society. James's last novel, The Ivory Tower, was unfinished at the time of his death in 1916, but it records vividly how he felt that the concentration of great wealth in the hands of few crippled even the people it seemed intended to benefit.

James returned to his native land after an extended residence in Europe, mostly London, that had begin in 1876. He had gone to Europe because he felt that his writing needed a different and denser social fabric than existed for him in the States. In his biography of Nathaniel Hawthorne, the American writer he most admired, he lamented the absence of many things that could be taken for granted in Europe: "No sovereign, no court, no personal loyalty . . . no palaces, no castles, nor manors, nor old country houses, nor parsonages, nor thatched cottages nor ivied ruins; no cathedrals, nor abbeys, nor little Norman churches; no great Universities nor public schools" and, more importantly for his own ambitions, "no literature, no novels, no museums, no pictures. . . ." When James went to Paris he could see plenty of pictures, and he also frequented the literary salon of Gustave Flaubert and became friendly with the Russian writer, Ivan Turgenev. He even met George Eliot on a trip to England. These writers set a model for him of what could be done with the novel if it was treated as a piece of fine art rather than a kind of journalism. The influence of Flaubert's Madame Bovary might be seen in the attention to style in James's writing, in the care for the individual sentence as well as the structure of the plot, but the influence of Turgenev's Virgin Soil is more conspicuous in The Princess Casamassima. As in Turgenev's novel, James's characters are involved in radical social movements that want to redistribute power and wealth. James's more explicit criticism of the status quo in this novel and in The Bostonians, whose characters are working for women's rights, was not, however, as warmly received by critics or his readers as his previous works. Until recently some critics have pointed to James's sister Alice not only as a possible model for one of the characters in The Bostonians but also as the member of the family who, in a diary that was unpublished in her lifetime, was most acute about politics. She was, however, also the most disabled by a family tendency toward psychosomatic illness and depression. Henry contributed his inherited wealth to her support until her death in 1892. For the next decade James's many short stories and novellas focused again on the meeting of American and European leisure class characters and the conflicts in their manners and values. He also tried to write for the theater, but his plays had no success, however well his texts seem to serve now as the basis for screenplays. In 1895 he gave up this theatrical effort and wrote a series of relatively short experimental novels, including The Spoils of Poynton (1897), What Maisie Knew (1897), The Awkward Age (1899), and The Turn of the Screw (1898). His control of the character's limited point of view, which James believed intensified the drama of the situation, has the effect in this great ghost story of creating so much uncertainty about what is real that readers remain haunted long after *the story is done. James explores and produces ambiguity in all his writing, but here it is coupled with terror. The reader might well wonder about the state of mind of the narrator in* "The Figure in the Carpet" *(1896) or* "The Beast in the Jungle" *(1903) or* "The Jolly Corner" *(1908), but his audience does not suffer because of this doubt, as does the reader of* The Turn of the Screw.

The next phase of James's career has been called "the major phase" by readers who believe that the three novels he wrote from 1901–03 represent a supreme achievement in the art of the novel. Regardless of a reader's taste for the intricacies of syntax that characterize these late works, they are by any standard the works of a literary master who has developed his own style and moral perspective on life. The Wings of the Dove *(1902),* The Ambassadors *(1903), and* The Golden Bowl *(1904) continue to examine the relations between American innocence and European experience, but the nuances of perception and the ambiguity of interpretation that characterize these novels are thrilling to the reader for whom the drama of understanding one's experience is of paramount interest. After the extraordinary production of these three masterpieces, James felt the need for a change of scene and returned to visit his family in his native country, the journey recorded in* The American Scene.

Although James continued to write short stories, his next major literary achievement was the compilation of his life's work into what has become known as The New York Edition *(1907–09). James took the opportunity when making this 24-volume collection (which was modeled after the collection,* La Comédie Humaine, *of his other great predecessor, Balzac), not only to revise the works included, but to write Prefaces to each volume that have become classics of literary criticism. James's reflections on his art of composition are entwined with his recollections of the circumstances of his composition in ways that illustrate his claim in* The Art of Fiction *(1884) that "the deepest quality of a work of art will always be the quality of the mind of the producer."*

Although James did not complete another novel after The Golden Bowl, *he continued to produce criticism as well as stories and wrote two volumes of his memoirs,* A Small Boy and Others *(1913) and* Notes of a Son and Brother *(1914). This is not to mention his collected travel writings, which comprise several volumes, and the tens of thousands of letters that he wrote over his lifetime and which have been only partially published in a four-volume edition to date. When war broke out in Europe in 1914, James put aside* The Ivory Tower, *a novel about the Newport he had visited in 1904, and returned to* The Sense of the Past, *a novel he had abandoned in 1901. In this story of time travel, James explores what it means to lose connection to the living past, which was one of the consequences of this war that he most feared. He wrote several essays about the war that were collected in* Within the Rim and Other Essays, 1914–1915 *(1918). He also began working on a third volume of his autobiography,* The Middle Years. *James's decision to become a British subject in 1915 has allowed some critics to question his loyalty to his native land,* but it can also be read as a sign of his sense of a debt to his adopted country, which had nourished his artistic sensibility for most of his adult life. He was awarded the British Order of Merit shortly before his death in 1916.

James's reputation has taken many turns in the last century. He has represented the Artist, the Aesthete, and the Decadent, among other roles. Some readers, including his older brother William, make the challenge of his style a reason to miss the opportunity to appreciate the representation of some of the most subtle and complex activity of which the human mind is capable under the pressure of a moral dilemma. Recent critical interest has focused on the social and cultural dimensions of his writings, as the recognition that art cannot be separated from its context (except in theory) has become more common. Also of interest has been the reevaluation of James's sexuality. Earlier biographers read his bachelorhood as a sign of devotion to his art, but a changed social context has allowed critics to address the issue of James's sexuality more openly. Although there is disagreement about whether he did, indeed, remain celibate all his life, there are few critics who would now deny that James was well aware of the discourses and issues surrounding homosexuality in his day. Several of the young men with whom he was friendly in his later years were as openly homosexual as was thinkable under the laws that sent Oscar Wilde to prison. Certainly James's views on the power of sex to affect human relations as they are represented in his fiction, however discreetly, make it clear that he knew how much could be lost and gained by acting on one's sexual desires. James's greatest passion was, however, for his art and if it did not provide him with great financial success, it did allow him to live a life devoted to the creation of a body of work that changed the range of possibilities for the American artist. Both T. S. Eliot and Ezra Pound looked to him as a model in his belief in the significance of literature. Less predictably, writers such as Richard Wright, James Baldwin, Ralph Ellison, and Cynthia Ozick have cited James as the most important influence on their work. His effect on contemporary literature may well be mediated through the films based on his novels, but for those who turn to James for the pleasure of his text, there will never be a substitute for the nuances and complexities of his long and marvelous sentences.

Beverly Haviland,
Brown University

For Further Reading

Primary Works

Transatlantic Sketches, 1875; *Roderick Hudson*, 1876; *The American*, 1877; *The Europeans*, 1878; *Daisy Miller*, 1878; *An International Episode*, 1879; *Washington Square*, 1881; *The Portrait of a Lady*, 1881; *The Point of View*, 1883; *Tales of Three Cities*, 1884; *The Bostonians*, 1886; *The Princess Casamassima*, 1886; *The Aspern Papers*, 1888; *A London Life*, 1889; *The Lesson of the Master*, 1892; *The Real Thing and Other Tales*, 1893; *Picture and Text*, 1893; *The Spoils of Poynton*, 1897; *What Maisie Knew*, 1897; *The Turn of the Screw*, 1898; *The Awkward Age*, 1899; *The Sacred Fount*, 1901; *The Wings of the Dove*, 1902; *The Ambassadors*, 1903; *The Golden Bowl*, 1904; *The Lesson of Balzac*, 1905; *English Hours*, 1905; *The American Scene*, 1907; *Views and Reviews*, 1908; *Italian Hours*, 1909; *A Small Boy and Others*, 1913; *Notes of a Son and Brother*, 1914; *The Ivory Tower*, 1917; *The Middle Years*, 1917; *The Sense of the Past*, 1917; *Within the Rim and Other Essays, 1914–1915*, 1918; *Collected Works: The Novels and Tales of Henry James*, 1907–1917 (known as The New York Edition).

Secondary Works

F. O. Matthiessen, *Henry James: The Major Phase*, 1944; D. Crook, *The Ordeal of Consciousness in Henry James*, 1962; L. Holland, *The Expense of Vision: Essays on the Craft of Henry James*, 1964, 1982; W. Veeder, *Henry James: the Lesson of the Master: Popular Fiction and Personal Style in the Nineteenth Century*, 1975; R. Yeazell, *Language and Knowledge in the Late Novels of Henry James*, 1976; P. Armstrong, *The Phenomenology of Henry James*, 1983; J. Rowe, *The Theoretical Dimensions of Henry James*, 1984; L. Edel, *Henry James A Life*, 1985; R. Hocks, *Henry James*, 1990; M. Bell, *Meaning in Henry James*, 1990; J. Freedman, *Professions of Taste: Henry James, British Aestheticism and Commodity Culture*, 1990; P. Horne, *Henry James and Revision*, 1991; R. Posnock, *The Trial of Curiosity: Henry James, William James, and the Challenge of Modernity*, 1991; S. Teahan, *The Rhetorical Logic of Henry James*, 1995; S. Blair, *Henry James and The Writing of Race and Nation*, 1996; B. Haviland, *Henry James's Last Romance: Making Sense of the Past and The American Scene*, 1997; J. Rowe, *The Other Henry James*, 1998; H. Stevens, *Henry James and Sexuality*, 1998; P. Horne, *Henry James: A Life in Letters*, 1999; W. Graham, *Henry James's Thwarted Love*, 1999; R. Pippen, *Henry James and Modern Moral Life*, 2000.

Daisy Miller: A Study[*]

HENRY JAMES

I

At the little town of Vevey, in Switzerland, there is a particularly comfort-able hotel. There are, indeed, many hotels; for the entertainment of tourists is the business of the place, which, as many travellers will remember, is seated upon the edge of a remarkably blue lake—a lake that it behoves every tourist to visit. The shore of the lake presents an unbroken array of establish-ments of this order, of every category, from the "grand hotel" of the newest fashion, with a chalk-white front, a hundred balconies, and a dozen flags flying from its roof, to the little Swiss *pension*[1] of an elder day, with its name inscribed in German-looking lettering upon a pink or yellow wall, and an awkward summer-house in the angle of the garden. One of the hotels at Vevey, however, is famous, even classical, being distinguished from many of its upstart neigh-bours by an air both of luxury and of maturity. In this region, in the month of June, American travellers are extremely numerous; it may be said, indeed, that Vevey assumes at this period some of the characteristics of an American watering-place. There are sights and sounds which evoke a vision, an echo, of Newport and Saratoga.[2] There is a flitting hither and thither of "stylish" young girls, a rustling of muslin flounces, a rattle of dance-music in the morning hours, a sound of high-pitched voices at all times. You receive an impression of these things at the excellent inn of the "Trois Couronnes," and are transported in fancy to the Ocean House or to Congress Hall.[3] But at the "Trois Couronnes," it must be added, there are other features that are much at vari-ance with these suggestions: neat German waiters, who look like secretaries of

---

[*]First published in *Cornhill Magazine,* June/July 1878; republished as *Daisy Miller: A Study,* (N.Y.: Harper & Brothers, 1879).

[1]French: modest hotel; Vevey is in the French-speaking part of Switzerland.

[2]Newport, Rhode Island, and Saratoga, New York—the sites of popular resorts.

[3]Hotels in Newport and Saratoga; *Trois Couronnes,* French: three crowns.

legation; Russian princesses sitting in the garden; little Polish boys walking about, held by the hand, with their governors; a view of the snowy crest of the Dent du Midi[4] and the picturesque towers of the Castle of Chillon.

I hardly know whether it was the analogies or the differences that were uppermost in the mind of a young American, who, two or three years ago, sat in the garden of the "Trois Couronnes," looking about him, rather idly, at some of the graceful objects I have mentioned. It was a beautiful summer morning, and in whatever fashion the young American looked at things, they must have seemed to him charming. He had come from Geneva the day before, by the little steamer, to see his aunt, who was staying at the hotel— Geneva having been for a long time his place of residence. But his aunt had a headache—his aunt had almost always a headache—and now she was shut up in her room, smelling camphor, so that he was at liberty to wander about. He was some seven-and-twenty years of age; when his friends spoke of him, they usually said that he was at Geneva, "studying." When his enemies spoke of him they said—but, after all, he had no enemies; he was an extremely amiable fellow, and universally liked. What I should say is, simply, that when certain persons spoke of him they affirmed that the reason of his spending so much time at Geneva was that he was extremely devoted to a lady who lived there—a foreign lady—a person older than himself. Very few Americans— indeed I think none—had ever seen this lady, about whom there were some singular stories. But Winterbourne had an old attachment for the little metropolis of Calvinism;[5] he had been put to school there as a boy, and he had afterwards gone to college there—circumstances which had led to his forming a great many youthful friendships. Many of these he had kept, and they were a source of great satisfaction to him.

After knocking at his aunt's door and learning that she was indisposed, he had taken a walk about the town, and then he had come in to his breakfast. He had now finished his breakfast; but he was drinking a small cup of coffee, which had been served to him on a little table in the garden by one of the waiters who looked like an *attaché*.[6] At last he finished his coffee and lit a cigarette. Presently a small boy came walking along the path—an urchin of nine or ten. The child, who was diminutive for his years, had an aged expression of countenance, a pale complexion, and sharp little features. He was dressed in knickerbockers, with red stockings, which displayed his poor little spindleshanks; he also wore a brilliant red cravat. He carried in his hand

---

[4]Swiss mountain.

[5]John Calvin (1509–1564) led the Protestant reformation of the Roman Catholic church in Switzerland, primarily from Geneva, where he published his *Articuli de Regimine Ecclesiae* in 1536 and developed the doctrines founding the theological system that became known as Calvinism.

[6]Diplomatic staff member.

a long alpenstock, the sharp point of which he thrust into everything that he approached—the flower-beds, the garden-benches, the trains of the ladies' dresses. In front of Winterbourne he paused, looking at him with a pair of bright, penetrating little eyes.

"Will you give me a lump of sugar?" he asked, in a sharp, hard little voice—a voice immature, and yet, somehow, not young.

Winterbourne glanced at the small table near him, on which his coffee-service rested, and saw that several morsels of sugar remained. "Yes, you may take one," he answered; "but I don't think sugar is good for little boys."

This little boy stepped forward and carefully selected three of the coveted fragments, two of which he buried in the pocket of his knickerbockers, depositing the other as promptly in another place. He poked his alpenstock, lance-fashion, into Winterbourne's bench, and tried to crack the lump of sugar with his teeth.

"Oh, blazes; it's har-r-d!" he exclaimed, pronouncing the adjective in a peculiar manner.

Winterbourne had immediately perceived that he might have the honour of claiming him as a fellow-countryman. "Take care you don't hurt your teeth," he said, paternally.

"I haven't got any teeth to hurt. They have all come out. I have only got seven teeth. My mother counted them last night, and one came out right afterwards. She said she'd slap me if any more came out. I can't help it. It's this old Europe. It's the climate that makes them come out. In America they didn't come out. It's these hotels."

Winterbourne was much amused. "If you eat three lumps of sugar, your mother will certainly slap you," he said.

"She's got to give me some candy, then," rejoined his young interlocutor. "I can't get any candy here—any American candy. American candy's the best candy."

"And are American little boys the best little boys?" asked Winterbourne.

"I don't know. I'm an American boy," said the child.

"I see you are one of the best!" laughed Winterbourne.

"Are you an American man?" pursued this vivacious infant. And then, on Winterbourne's affirmative reply—"American men are the best," he declared.

His companion thanked him for the compliment; and the child, who had now got astride of his alpenstock, stood looking about him, while he attacked a second lump of sugar. Winterbourne wondered if he himself had been like this in his infancy, for he had been brought to Europe at about this age.

"Here comes my sister!" cried the child, in a moment. "She's an American girl."

Winterbourne looked along the path and saw a beautiful young lady advancing. "American girls are the best girls," he said, cheerfully, to his young companion.

"My sister ain't the best!" the child declared. "She's always blowing at me."

"I imagine that is your fault, not hers," said Winterbourne. The young lady meanwhile had drawn near. She was dressed in white muslin, with a hundred frills and flounces, and knots of pale-coloured ribbon. She was bare-headed; but she balanced in her hand a large parasol, with a deep border of embroidery; and she was strikingly, admirably pretty. "How pretty they are!" thought Winterbourne, straightening himself in his seat, as if he were prepared to rise.

The young lady paused in front of his bench, near the parapet of the garden, which overlooked the lake. The little boy had now converted his alpenstock into a vaulting-pole, by the aid of which he was springing about in the gravel, and kicking it up not a little.

"Randolph," said the young lady, "what *are* you doing?"

"I'm going up the Alps," replied Randolph. "This is the way!" And he gave another little jump, scattering the pebbles about Winterbourne's ears.

"That's the way they come down," said Winterbourne.

"He's an American man!" cried Randolph, in his little hard voice.

The young lady gave no heed to this announcement, but looked straight at her brother. "Well, I guess you had better be quiet," she simply observed.

It seemed to Winterbourne that he had been in a manner presented. He got up and stepped slowly towards the young girl, throwing away his cigarette. "This little boy and I have made acquaintance," he said, with great civility. In Geneva, as he had been perfectly aware, a young man was not at liberty to speak to a young unmarried lady except under certain rarely-occurring conditions; but here at Vevey, what conditions could be better than these?—a pretty American girl coming and standing in front of you in a garden. This pretty American girl, however, on hearing Winterbourne's observation, simply glanced at him; she then turned her head and looked over the parapet, at the lake and the opposite mountains. He wondered whether he had gone too far; but he decided that he must advance farther, rather than retreat. While he was thinking of something else to say, the young lady turned to the little boy again.

"I should like to know where you got that pole," she said.

"I bought it!" responded Randolph.

"You don't mean to say you're going to take it to Italy."

"Yes, I am going to take it to Italy!" the child declared.

The young girl glanced over the front of her dress, and smoothed out a knot or two of ribbon. Then she rested her eyes upon the prospect again. "Well, I guess you had better leave it somewhere," she said, after a moment.

"Are you going to Italy?" Winterbourne inquired, in a tone of great respect.

The young lady glanced at him again. "Yes, sir," she replied. And she said nothing more.

"Are you—a—going over the Simplon?"[7] Winterbourne pursued, a little embarrassed.

"I don't know," she said. "I suppose it's some mountain. Randolph, what mountain are we going over?"

"Going where?" the child demanded.

"To Italy," Winterbourne explained.

"I don't know," said Randolph. "I don't want to go to Italy. I want to go to America."

"Oh, Italy is a beautiful place!" rejoined the young man.

"Can you get candy there?" Randolph loudly inquired.

"I hope not," said his sister. "I guess you have had enough candy, and mother thinks so too."

"I haven't had any for ever so long—for a hundred weeks!" cried the boy, still jumping about.

The young lady inspected her flounces and smoothed her ribbons again; and Winterbourne presently risked an observation upon the beauty of the view. He was ceasing to be embarrassed, for he had begun to perceive that she was not in the least embarrassed herself. There had not been the slightest alteration in her charming complexion; she was evidently neither offended nor fluttered. If she looked another way when he spoke to her, and seemed not particularly to hear him, this was simply her habit, her manner. Yet, as he talked a little more, and pointed out some of the objects of interest in the view, with which she appeared quite unacquainted, she gradually gave him more of the benefit of her glance; and then he saw that this glance was perfectly direct and unshrinking. It was not, however, what would have been called an immodest glance, for the young girl's eyes were singularly honest and fresh. They were wonderfully pretty eyes; and, indeed, Winterbourne had not seen for a long time anything prettier than his fair countrywoman's various features—her complexion, her nose, her ears, her teeth. He had a great relish for feminine beauty; he was addicted to observing and analysing it; and as regards this young lady's face he made several observations. It was not at all insipid, but it was not exactly expressive; and though it was eminently delicate Winterbourne mentally accused it—very forgivingly—of a want of finish. He thought it very possible that Master Randolph's sister was a coquette; he was sure she had a spirit of her own; but in her bright, sweet, superficial little visage there was no mockery, no irony. Before long it became obvious that she was much disposed towards conversation. She told him that they were going to Rome for the winter—she and her mother and Randolph. She asked him if he was a "real American;" she wouldn't have taken him for one; he seemed more like a German—this was said after a little hesitation, especially when he

---

[7]Mountain pass between Switzerland and Italy.

spoke. Winterbourne, laughing, answered that he had met Germans who spoke like Americans; but that he had not, so far as he remembered, met an American who spoke like a German. Then he asked her if she would not be more comfortable in sitting upon the bench which he had just quitted. She answered that she liked standing up and walking about; but she presently sat down. She told him she was from New York State—"if you know where that is." Winterbourne learned more about her by catching hold of her small, slippery brother and making him stand a few minutes by his side.

"Tell me your name, my boy," he said.

"Randolph C. Miller," said the boy, sharply. "And I'll tell you her name;" and he levelled his alpenstock at his sister.

"You had better wait till you are asked!" said this young lady, calmly.

"I should like very much to know your name," said Winterbourne.

"Her name is Daisy Miller!" cried the child. "But that isn't her real name; that isn't her name on her cards."

"It's a pity you haven't got one of my cards!" said Miss Miller.

"Her real name is Annie P. Miller," the boy went on.

"Ask him *his* name," said his sister, indicating Winterbourne.

But on this point Randolph seemed perfectly indifferent; he continued to supply information with regard to his own family. "My father's name is Ezra B. Miller," he announced. "My father ain't in Europe; my father's in a better place than Europe."

Winterbourne imagined for a moment that this was the manner in which the child had been taught to intimate that Mr. Miller had been removed to the sphere of celestial rewards. But Randolph immediately added, "My father's in Schenectady. He's got a big business. My father's rich, you bet."

"Well!" ejaculated Miss Miller, lowering her parasol and looking at the embroidered border. Winterbourne presently released the child, who departed, dragging his alpenstock along the path. "He doesn't like Europe," said the young girl. "He wants to go back."

"To Schenectady, you mean?"

"Yes; he wants to go right home. He hasn't got any boys here. There is one boy here, but he always goes round with a teacher; they won't let him play."

"And your brother hasn't any teacher?" Winterbourne inquired.

"Mother thought of getting him one, to travel round with us. There was a lady told her of a very good teacher; an American lady—perhaps you know her—Mrs. Sanders. I think she came from Boston. She told her of this teacher, and we thought of getting him to travel round with us. But Randolph said he didn't want a teacher travelling round with us. He said he wouldn't have lessons when he was in the cars.[8] And we *are* in the cars about

---

[8]Railroad cars.

half the time. There was an English lady we met in the cars—I think her name was Miss Featherstone; perhaps you know her. She wanted to know why I didn't give Randolph lessons—give him "instruction," she called it. I guess he could give me more instruction than I could give him. He's very smart."

"Yes," said Winterbourne; "he seems very smart."

"Mother's going to get a teacher for him as soon as we get to Italy. Can you get good teachers in Italy?"

"Very good, I should think," said Winterbourne.

"Or else she's going to find some school. He ought to learn some more. He's only nine. He's going to college." And in this way Miss Miller continued to converse upon the affairs of her family, and upon other topics. She sat there with her extremely pretty hands, ornamented with very brilliant rings, folded in her lap, and with her pretty eyes now resting upon those of Winterbourne, now wandering over the garden, the people who passed by, and the beautiful view. She talked to Winterbourne as if she had known him a long time. He found it very pleasant. It was many years since he had heard a young girl talk so much. It might have been said of this unknown young lady, who had come and sat down beside him upon a bench, that she chattered. She was very quiet, she sat in a charming tranquil attitude; but her lips and her eyes were constantly moving. She had a soft, slender, agreeable voice, and her tone was decidedly sociable. She gave Winterbourne a history of her movements and intentions, and those of her mother and brother, in Europe, and enumerated, in particular, the various hotels at which they had stopped. "That English lady in the cars," she said—"Miss Featherstone—asked me if we didn't all live in hotels in America. I told her I had never been in so many hotels in my life as since I came to Europe. I have never seen so many—it's nothing but hotels." But Miss Miller did not make this remark with a querulous accent; she appeared to be in the best humour with everything. She declared that the hotels were very good, when once you got used to their ways, and that Europe was perfectly sweet. She was not disappointed—not a bit. Perhaps it was because she had heard so much about it before. She had ever so many intimate friends that had been there ever so many times. And then she had had ever so many dresses and things from Paris. Whenever she put on a Paris dress she felt as if she were in Europe.

"It was a kind of a wishing-cap," said Winterbourne.

"Yes," said Miss Miller, without examining this analogy; "it always made me wish I was here. But I needn't have done that for dresses. I am sure they send all the pretty ones to America; you see the most frightful things here. The only thing I don't like," she proceeded, "is the society. There isn't any society; or, if there is, I don't know where it keeps itself. Do you? I suppose there is some society somewhere, but I haven't seen anything of it. I'm very fond of society, and I have always had a great deal of it. I don't mean only in

Schenectady, but in New York. I used to go to New York every winter. In New York I had lots of society. Last winter I had seventeen dinners given me; and three of them were by gentlemen," added Daisy Miller. "I have more friends in New York than in Schenectady—more gentlemen friends; and more young lady friends too," she resumed in a moment. She paused again for an instant; she was looking at Winterbourne with all her prettiness in her lively eyes and in her light, slightly monotonous smile. "I have always had," she said, "a great deal of gentlemen's society."

Poor Winterbourne was amused, perplexed, and decidedly charmed. He had never yet heard a young girl express herself in just this fashion; never, at least, save in cases where to say such things seemed a kind of demonstrative evidence of a certain laxity of deportment. And yet was he to accuse Miss Daisy Miller of actual or potential *inconduite*,[9] as they said at Geneva? He felt that he had lived at Geneva so long that he had lost a good deal; he had become dishabituated to the American tone. Never, indeed, since he had grown old enough to appreciate things, had he encountered a young American girl of so pronounced a type as this. Certainly she was very charming; but how deucedly sociable! Was she simply a pretty girl from New York State—were they all like that, the pretty girls who had a good deal of gentlemen's society? Or was she also a designing, an audacious, an unscrupulous young person? Winterbourne had lost his instinct in this matter, and his reason could not help him. Miss Daisy Miller looked extremely innocent. Some people had told him that, after all, American girls were exceedingly innocent; and others had told him that, after all, they were not. He was inclined to think Miss Daisy Miller was a flirt—a pretty American flirt. He had never, as yet, had any relations with young ladies of this category. He had known, here in Europe, two or three women—persons older than Miss Daisy Miller, and provided, for respectability's sake, with husbands—who were great coquettes—dangerous, terrible women, with whom one's relations were liable to take a serious turn. But this young girl was not a coquette in that sense; she was very unsophisticated; she was only a pretty American flirt. Winterbourne was almost grateful for having found the formula that applied to Miss Daisy Miller. He leaned back in his seat; he remarked to himself that she had the most charming nose he had ever seen; he wondered what were the regular conditions and limitations of one's intercourse with a pretty American flirt. It presently became apparent that he was on the way to learn.

"Have you been to that old castle?" asked the young girl, pointing with her parasol to the far-gleaming walls of the Château de Chillon.

"Yes, formerly, more than once," said Winterbourne. "You too, I suppose, have seen it?"

---

[9]French: misconduct.

"No; we haven't been there. I want to go there dreadfully. Of course I mean to go there. I wouldn't go away from here without having seen that old castle."

"It's a very pretty excursion," said Winterbourne, "and very easy to make. You can drive, you know, or you can go by the little steamer."

"You can go in the cars," said Miss Miller.

"Yes; you can go in the cars," Winterbourne assented.

"Our courier says they take you right up to the castle," the young girl continued. "We were going last week; but my mother gave out. She suffers dreadfully from dyspepsia. She said she couldn't go. Randolph wouldn't go either; he says he doesn't think much of old castles. But I guess we'll go this week, if we can get Randolph."

"Your brother is not interested in ancient monuments?" Winterbourne inquired, smiling.

"He says he don't care much about old castles. He's only nine. He wants to stay at the hotel. Mother's afraid to leave him alone, and the courier won't stay with him; so we haven't been to many places. But it will be too bad if we don't go up there." And Miss Miller pointed again at the Château de Chillon.

"I should think it might be arranged," said Winterbourne. "Couldn't you get some one to stay—for the afternoon—with Randolph?"

Miss Miller looked at him a moment; and then, very placidly—"I wish you would stay with him!" she said.

Winterbourne hesitated a moment. "I would much rather go to Chillon with you."

"With me?" asked the young girl, with the same placidity.

She didn't rise, blushing, as a young girl at Geneva would have done; and yet Winterbourne, conscious that he had been very bold, thought it possible she was offended. "With your mother," he answered very respectfully.

But it seemed that both his audacity and his respect were lost upon Miss Daisy Miller. "I guess my mother won't go, after all," she said. "She don't like to ride round in the afternoon. But did you really mean what you said just now; that you would like to go up there?"

"Most earnestly," Winterbourne declared.

"Then we may arrange it. If mother will stay with Randolph, I guess Eugenio will."

"Eugenio?" the young man inquired.

"Eugenio's our courier.[10] He doesn't like to stay with Randolph; he's the most fastidious man I ever saw. But he's a splendid courier. I guess he'll stay at home with Randolph if mother does, and then we can go to the castle."

---

[10]A personal attendant hired to make travel and other arrangements, especially when traveling in foreign countries.

Winterbourne reflected for an instant as lucidly as possible—"we" could only mean Miss Daisy Miller and himself. This programme seemed almost too agreeable for credence; he felt as if he ought to kiss the young lady's hand. Possibly he would have done so—and quite spoiled the project; but at this moment another person—presumably Eugenio—appeared. A tall, handsome man, with superb whiskers, wearing a velvet morning-coat and a brilliant watch-chain, approached Miss Miller, looking sharply at her companion. "Oh, Eugenio!" said Miss Miller, with the friendliest accent.

Eugenio had looked at Winterbourne from head to foot; he now bowed gravely to the young lady. "I have the honour to inform mademoiselle that luncheon is upon the table."

Miss Miller slowly rose. "See here, Eugenio," she said. "I'm going to that old castle, any way."

"To the Château de Chillon, mademoiselle?" the courier inquired. "Mademoiselle has made arrangements?" he added, in a tone which struck Winterbourne as very impertinent.

Eugenio's tone apparently threw, even to Miss Miller's own apprehension, a slightly ironical light upon the young girl's situation. She turned to Winterbourne, blushing a little—a very little. "You won't back out?" she said.

"I shall not be happy till we go!" he protested.

"And you are staying in this hotel?" she went on. "And you are really an American?"

The courier stood looking at Winterbourne, offensively. The young man, at least, thought his manner of looking an offence to Miss Miller; it conveyed an imputation that she "picked up" acquaintances. "I shall have the honour of presenting to you a person who will tell you all about me," he said smiling, and referring to his aunt.

"Oh, well, we'll go some day," said Miss Miller. And she gave him a smile and turned away. She put up her parasol and walked back to the inn beside Eugenio. Winterbourne stood looking after her; and as she moved away, drawing her muslin furbelows over the gravel, said to himself that she had the *tournure*[11] of a princess.

II

He had, however, engaged to do more than proved feasible, in promising to present his aunt, Mrs. Costello, to Miss Daisy Miller. As soon as the former lady had got better of her headache he waited upon her in her apartment; and, after the proper inquiries in regard to her health, he asked her if she had

---

[11]Bearing, manner.

observed, in the hotel, an American family—a mamma, a daughter, and a little boy.

"And a courier?" said Mrs. Costello. "Oh, yes, I have observed them. Seen them—heard them—and kept out of their way." Mrs. Costello was a widow with a fortune; a person of much distinction, who frequently intimated that, if she were not so dreadfully liable to sick-headaches, she would probably have left a deeper impress upon her time. She had a long pale face, a high nose, and a great deal of very striking white hair, which she wore in large puffs and *rouleaux*[12] over the top of her head. She had two sons married in New York, and another who was now in Europe. This young man was amusing himself at Homburg,[13] and, though he was on his travels, was rarely perceived to visit any particular city at the moment selected by his mother for her own appearance there. Her nephew, who had come up to Vevey expressly to see her, was therefore more attentive than those who, as she said, were nearer to her. He had imbibed at Geneva the idea that one must always be attentive to one's aunt. Mrs. Costello had not seen him for many years, and she was greatly pleased with him, manifesting her approbation by initiating him into many of the secrets of that social sway which, as she gave him to understand, she exerted in the American capital. She admitted that she was very exclusive; but, if he were acquainted with New York, he would see that one had to be. And her picture of the minutely hierarchical constitution of the society of that city, which she presented to him in many different lights, was, to Winterbourne's imagination, almost oppressively striking.

He immediately perceived, from her tone, that Miss Daisy Miller's place in the social scale was low. "I am afraid you don't approve of them," he said.

"They are very common," Mrs. Costello declared. "They are the sort of Americans that one does one's duty by not—not accepting."

"Ah, you don't accept them?" said the young man.

"I can't, my dear Frederick. I would if I could, but I can't."

"The young girl is very pretty," said Winterbourne, in a moment.

"Of course she's pretty. But she is very common."

"I see what you mean, of course," said Winterbourne, after another pause.

"She has that charming look that they all have," his aunt resumed. "I can't think where they pick it up; and she dresses in perfection—no, you don't know how well she dresses. I can't think where they get their taste."

"But, my dear aunt, she is not, after all, a Comanche savage."

"She is a young lady," said Mrs. Costello, "who has an intimacy with her mamma's courier?"

"An intimacy with the courier?" the young man demanded.

---

[12]French: rolls.

[13]German town famous for its health spa and resort.

"Oh, the mother is just as bad! They treat the courier like a familiar friend—like a gentleman. I shouldn't wonder if he dines with them. Very likely they have never seen a man with such good manners, such fine clothes, so like a gentleman. He probably corresponds to the young lady's idea of a Count. He sits with them in the garden, in the evening. I think he smokes."

Winterbourne listened with interest to these disclosures; they helped him to make up his mind about Miss Daisy. Evidently she was rather wild. "Well," he said, "I am not a courier, and yet she was very charming to me."

"You had better have said at first," said Mrs. Costello with dignity, "that you had made her acquaintance."

"We simply met in the garden, and we talked a bit."

"*Tout bonnement!*[14] And pray what did you say?"

"I said I should take the liberty of introducing her to my admirable aunt."

"I am much obliged to you."

"It was to guarantee my respectability," said Winterbourne.

"And pray who is to guarantee hers?"

"Ah, you are cruel!" said the young man. "She's a very nice girl."

"You don't say that as if you believed it," Mrs. Costello observed.

"She is completely uncultivated," Winterbourne went on. "But she is wonderfully pretty, and, in short, she is very nice. To prove that I believe it, I am going to take her to the Château de Chillon."

"You two are going off there together? I should say it proved just the contrary. How long had you known her, may I ask, when this interesting project was formed? You haven't been twenty-four hours in the house."

"I had known her half-an-hour!" said Winterbourne, smiling.

"Dear me!" cried Mrs. Costello. "What a dreadful girl!"

Her nephew was silent for some moments. "You really think, then," he began, earnestly, and with a desire for trustworthy information—"you really think that——" But he paused again.

"Think what, sir?" said his aunt.

"That she is the sort of young lady who expects a man—sooner or later—to carry her off?"

"I haven't the least idea what such young ladies expect a man to do. But I really think that you had better not meddle with little American girls that are uncultivated, as you call them. You have lived too long out of the country. You will be sure to make some great mistake. You are too innocent."

"My dear aunt, I am not so innocent," said Winterbourne, smiling and curling his moustache.

"You are too guilty, then!"

---

[14]French: As simply as that!

Winterbourne continued to curl his moustache, meditatively. "You won't let the poor girl know you then?" he asked at last.

"Is it literally true that she is going to the Château de Chillon with you?"

"I think that she fully intends it."

"Then, my dear Frederick," said Mrs. Costello, "I must decline the honour of her acquaintance. I am an old woman, but I am not too old—thank Heaven—to be shocked!"

"But don't they all do these things—the young girls in America?" Winterbourne inquired.

Mrs. Costello stared a moment. "I should like to see my granddaughters do them!" she declared, grimly.

This seemed to throw some light upon the matter, for Winterbourne remembered to have heard that his pretty cousins in New York were "tremendous flirts." If, therefore, Miss Daisy Miller exceeded the liberal license allowed to these young ladies, it was probable that anything might be expected of her. Winterbourne was impatient to see her again, and he was vexed with himself that, by instinct, he should not appreciate her justly.

Though he was impatient to see her, he hardly knew what he should say to her about his aunt's refusal to become acquainted with her; but he discovered, promptly enough, that with Miss Daisy Miller there was no great need of walking on tiptoe. He found her that evening in the garden, wandering about in the warm starlight, like an indolent sylph, and swinging to and fro the largest fan he had ever beheld. It was ten o'clock. He had dined with his aunt, had been sitting with her since dinner, and had just taken leave of her till the morrow. Miss Daisy Miller seemed very glad to see him; she declared it was the longest evening she had ever passed.

"Have you been all alone?" he asked.

"I have been walking round with mother. But mother gets tired walking round," she answered.

"Has she gone to bed?"

"No; she doesn't like to go to bed," said the young girl. "She doesn't sleep—not three hours. She says she doesn't know how she lives. She's dreadfully nervous. I guess she sleeps more than she thinks. She's gone somewhere after Randolph; she wants to try to get him to go to bed. He doesn't like to go to bed."

"Let us hope she will persuade him," observed Winterbourne.

"She will talk to him all she can; but he doesn't like her to talk to him," said Miss Daisy, opening her fan. "She's going to try to get Eugenio to talk to him. But he isn't afraid of Eugenio. Eugenio's a splendid courier, but he can't make much impression on Randolph! I don't believe he'll go to bed before eleven." It appeared that Randolph's vigil was in fact triumphantly prolonged, for Winterbourne strolled about with the young girl for some time without meeting her mother. "I have been looking round for that lady you want to introduce me to," his companion resumed. "She's your aunt." Then, on Winterbourne's admitting the fact, and expressing some curiosity as to how she had learned it, she said she had heard all about Mrs. Costello from the chambermaid. She was very quiet and very *comme il faut*;[15] she wore white puffs; she spoke to no one, and she never dined at the *table d'hôte*.[16] Every two days she had a headache. "I think that's a lovely description, headache and all!" said Miss Daisy, chattering along in her thin, gay voice. "I want to know her ever so much. I know just what *your* aunt would be; I know I should like her. She would be very exclusive. I like a lady to be exclusive; I'm dying to be exclusive myself. Well, we *are* exclusive, mother and I. We don't speak to every one—or they don't speak to us. I suppose it's about the same thing. Any way, I shall be ever so glad to know your aunt."

Winterbourne was embarrassed. "She would be most happy," he said; "but I am afraid those headaches will interfere."

The young girl looked at him through the dusk. "But I suppose she doesn't have a headache every day," she said, sympathetically.

Winterbourne was silent a moment. "She tells me she does," he answered at last—not knowing what to say.

Miss Daisy Miller stopped and stood looking at him. Her prettiness was still visible in the darkness; she was opening and closing her enormous fan. "She doesn't want to know me!" she said, suddenly. "Why don't you say so? You needn't be afraid. I'm not afraid!" And she gave a little laugh.

Winterbourne fancied there was a tremor in her voice; he was touched, shocked, mortified by it. "My dear young lady," he protested, "she knows no one. It's her wretched health."

The young girl walked on a few steps, laughing still. "You needn't be afraid," she repeated. "Why should she want to know me?" Then she paused again; she was close to the parapet of the garden, and in front of her was the starlit lake. There was a vague sheen upon its surface, and in the distance were dimly-seen mountain forms. Daisy Miller looked out upon the mysterious prospect, and then she gave another little laugh. "Gracious! she *is* exclusive!" she said. Winterbourne wondered whether she was seriously wounded, and for a moment almost wished that her sense of injury might be such as to make it becoming in him to attempt to reassure and comfort her. He had a pleasant sense that she would be very approachable for consolatory purposes. He felt then, for the instant, quite ready to sacrifice his aunt, conversationally; to admit that she was a proud, rude woman, and to declare that they needn't mind her. But before he had time to commit himself to this perilous mixture of gallantry and impiety, the young lady, resuming her walk,

[15]French: proper, correct.
[16]French: common dining table or room in a hotel.

gave an exclamation in quite another tone. "Well; here's mother! I guess she hasn't got Randolph to go to bed." The figure of a lady appeared, at a distance, very indistinct in the darkness, and advancing with a slow and wavering movement. Suddenly it seemed to pause.

"Are you sure it is your mother? Can you distinguish her in this thick dusk?" Winterbourne asked.

"Well!" cried Miss Daisy Miller, with a laugh, "I guess I know my own mother. And when she has got on my shawl, too! She is always wearing my things."

The lady in question, ceasing to advance, hovered vaguely about the spot at which she had checked her steps.

"I am afraid your mother doesn't see you," said Winterbourne. "Or perhaps," he added—thinking, with Miss Miller, the joke permissible—"perhaps she feels guilty about your shawl."

"Oh, it's a fearful old thing!" the young girl replied, serenely. "I told her she could wear it. She won't come here, because she sees you."

"Ah, then," said Winterbourne, "I had better leave you."

"Oh no; come on!" urged Miss Daisy Miller.

"I'm afraid your mother doesn't approve of my walking with you."

Miss Miller gave him a serious glance. "It isn't for me; it's for you—that is, it's for *her*. Well; I don't know who it's for! But mother doesn't like any of my gentlemen friends. She's right down timid. She always makes a fuss if I introduce a gentleman. But I *do* introduce them—almost always. If I didn't introduce my gentlemen friends to mother," the young girl added, in her little soft, flat monotone, "I shouldn't think I was natural."

"To introduce me," said Winterbourne, "you must know my name." And he proceeded to pronounce it.

"Oh, dear; I can't say all that!" said his companion, with a laugh. But by this time they had come up to Mrs. Miller, who, as they drew near, walked to the parapet of the garden and leaned upon it, looking intently at the lake and turning her back upon them. "Mother!" said the young girl, in a tone of decision. Upon this the elder lady turned round. "Mr. Winterbourne," said Miss Daisy Miller, introducing the young man very frankly and prettily. "Common," she was, as Mrs. Costello had pronounced her; yet it was a wonder to Winterbourne that, with her commonness, she had a singularly delicate grace.

Her mother was a small, spare, light person, with a wandering eye, a very exiguous nose, and a large forehead, decorated with a certain amount of thin, much-frizzled hair. Like her daughter, Mrs. Miller was dressed with extreme elegance; she had enormous diamonds in her ears. So far as Winterbourne could observe, she gave him no greeting—she certainly was not looking at him. Daisy was near her, pulling her shawl straight. "What are you doing, poking round here?" this young lady inquired; but by no means with that harshness of accent which her choice of words may imply.

"I don't know," said her mother, turning towards the lake again.

"I shouldn't think you'd want that shawl!" Daisy exclaimed.

"Well—I do!" her mother answered, with a little laugh.

"Did you get Randolph to go to bed?" asked the young girl.

"No; I couldn't induce him," said Mrs. Miller, very gently. "He wants to talk to the waiter. He likes to talk to that waiter."

"I was telling Mr. Winterbourne," the young girl went on; and to the young man's ear her tone might have indicated that she had been uttering his name all her life.

"Oh, yes!" said Winterbourne; "I have the pleasure of knowing your son."

Randolph's mamma was silent; she turned her attention to the lake. But at last she spoke. "Well, I don't see how he lives!"

"Anyhow, it isn't so bad as it was at Dover,"[17] said Daisy Miller.

"And what occurred at Dover?" Winterbourne asked.

"He wouldn't go to bed at all. I guess he sat up all night—in the public parlour. He wasn't in bed at twelve o'clock: I know that."

"It was half-past twelve," declared Mrs. Miller, with mild emphasis.

"Does he sleep much during the day?" Winterbourne demanded.

"I guess he doesn't sleep much," Daisy rejoined.

"I wish he would!" said her mother. "It seems as if he couldn't."

"I think he's real tiresome," Daisy pursued.

Then, for some moments, there was silence. "Well, Daisy Miller," said the elder lady, presently, "I shouldn't think you'd want to talk against your own brother!"

"Well, he is tiresome, mother," said Daisy, quite without the asperity of a retort.

"He's only nine," urged Mrs. Miller.

"Well, he wouldn't go to that castle," said the young girl. "I'm going there with Mr. Winterbourne."

To this announcement, very placidly made, Daisy's mamma offered no response. Winterbourne took for granted that she deeply disapproved of the projected excursion; but he said to himself that she was a simple, easily-managed person, and that a few deferential protestations would take the edge from her displeasure. "Yes," he began; "your daughter has kindly allowed me the honour of being her guide."

Mrs. Miller's wandering eyes attached themselves, with a sort of appealing air, to Daisy, who, however, strolled a few steps farther, gently humming to herself. "I presume you will go in the cars," said her mother.

"Yes; or in the boat," said Winterbourne.

---

[17]Port town on the English side of the English channel.

"Well, of course, I don't know," Mrs. Miller rejoined. "I have never been to that castle."

"It is a pity you shouldn't go," said Winterbourne, beginning to feel reassured as to her opposition. And yet he was quite prepared to find that, as a matter of course, she meant to accompany her daughter.

"We've been thinking ever so much about going," she pursued; "but it seems as if we couldn't. Of course Daisy—she wants to go round. But there's a lady here—I don't know her name—she says she shouldn't think we'd want to go to see castles *here;* she should think we'd want to wait till we got to Italy. It seems as if there would be so many there," continued Mrs. Miller, with an air of increasing confidence. "Of course, we only want to see the principal ones. We visited several in England," she presently added.

"Ah, yes! in England there are beautiful castles," said Winterbourne. "But Chillon, here, is very well worth seeing."

"Well, if Daisy feels up to it——," said Mrs. Miller, in a tone impregnated with a sense of the magnitude of the enterprise. "It seems as if there was nothing she wouldn't undertake."

"Oh, I think she'll enjoy it!" Winterbourne declared. And he desired more and more to make it a certainty that he was to have the privilege of a *tête-à-tête*[18] with the young lady, who was still strolling along in front of them, softly vocalising. "You are not disposed, madam," he inquired, "to undertake it yourself?"

Daisy's mother looked at him, an instant, askance, and then walked forward in silence. Then—"I guess she had better go alone," she said, simply.

Winterbourne observed to himself that this was a very different type of maternity from that of the vigilant matrons who massed themselves in the forefront of social intercourse in the dark old city at the other end of the lake. But his meditations were interrupted by hearing his name very distinctly pronounced by Mrs. Miller's unprotected daughter.

"Mr. Winterbourne!" murmured Daisy.

"Mademoiselle!" said the young man.

"Don't you want to take me out in a boat?"

"At present?" he asked.

"Of course!" said Daisy.

"Well, Annie Miller!" exclaimed her mother.

"I beg you, madam, to let her go," said Winterbourne, ardently; for he had never yet enjoyed the sensation of guiding through the summer starlight a skiff freighted with a fresh and beautiful young girl.

"I shouldn't think she'd want to," said her mother. "I should think she'd rather go indoors."

---

[18]Private encounter, literally "head to head."

"I'm sure Mr. Winterbourne wants to take me," Daisy declared. "He's so awfully devoted!"

"I will row you over to Chillon, in the starlight."

"I don't believe it!" said Daisy.

"Well!" ejaculated the elder lady again.

"You haven't spoken to me for half-an-hour," her daughter went on.

"I have been having some very pleasant conversation with your mother," said Winterbourne.

"Well; I want you to take me out in a boat!" Daisy repeated. They had all stopped, and she had turned round and was looking at Winterbourne. Her face wore a charming smile, her pretty eyes were gleaming, she was swinging her great fan about. No; it's impossible to be prettier than that; thought Winterbourne.

"There are half-a-dozen boats moored at that landing-place," he said, pointing to certain steps which descended from the garden to the lake. "If you will do me the honour to accept my arm, we will go and select one of them."

Daisy stood there smiling; she threw back her head and gave a little light laugh. "I like a gentleman to be formal!" she declared.

"I assure you it's a formal offer."

"I was bound I would make you say something," Daisy went on.

"You see it's not very difficult," said Winterbourne. "But I am afraid you are chaffing me."

"I think not, sir," remarked Mrs. Miller, very gently.

"Do, then, let me give you a row," he said to the young girl.

"It's quite lovely, the way you say that!" cried Daisy.

"It will be still more lovely to do it."

"Yes, it would be lovely!" said Daisy. But she made no movement to accompany him; she only stood there laughing.

"I should think you had better find out what time it is," interposed her mother.

"It is eleven o'clock, madam," said a voice, with a foreign accent, out of the neighbouring darkness; and Winterbourne, turning, perceived the florid personage who was in attendance upon the two ladies. He had apparently just approached.

"Oh, Eugenio," said Daisy, "I am going out in a boat!"

Eugenio bowed. "At eleven o'clock, mademoiselle?"

"I am going with Mr. Winterbourne. This very minute."

"Do tell her she can't," said Mrs. Miller to the courier.

"I think you had better not go out in a boat, mademoiselle," Eugenio declared.

Winterbourne wished to Heaven this pretty girl were not so familiar with her courier; but he said nothing.

"I suppose you don't think it's proper!" Daisy exclaimed. "Eugenio doesn't think anything's proper."

"I am at your service," said Winterbourne.

"Does mademoiselle propose to go alone?" asked Eugenio of Mrs. Miller.

"Oh, no; with this gentleman!" answered Daisy's mamma.

The courier looked for a moment at Winterbourne—the latter thought he was smiling—and then, solemnly, with a bow, "As mademoiselle pleases!" he said.

"Oh, I hoped you would make a fuss!" said Daisy. "I don't care to go now."

"I myself shall make a fuss if you don't go," said Winterbourne.

"That's all I want—a little fuss!" And the young girl began to laugh again.

"Mr. Randolph has gone to bed!" the courier announced, frigidly.

"Oh, Daisy; now we can go!" said Mrs. Miller.

Daisy turned away from Winterbourne, looking at him, smiling and fanning herself. "Good night," she said; "I hope you are disappointed, or disgusted, or something!"

He looked at her, taking the hand she offered him. "I am puzzled," he answered.

"Well; I hope it won't keep you awake!" she said, very smartly; and, under the escort of the privileged Eugenio, the two ladies passed towards the house.

Winterbourne stood looking after them; he was indeed puzzled. He lingered beside the lake for a quarter of an hour, turning over the mystery of the young girl's sudden familiarities and caprices. But the only very definite conclusion he came to was that he should enjoy deucedly "going off" with her somewhere.

Two days afterwards he went off with her to the Castle of Chillon. He waited for her in the large hall of the hotel, where the couriers, the servants, the foreign tourists were lounging about and staring. It was not the place he would have chosen, but she had appointed it. She came tripping downstairs, buttoning her long gloves, squeezing her folded parasol against her pretty figure, dressed in the perfection of a soberly elegant travelling-costume. Winterbourne was a man of imagination and, as our ancestors used to say, of sensibility; as he looked at her dress and, on the great staircase, her little rapid, confiding step, he felt as if there were something romantic going forward. He could have believed he was going to elope with her. He passed out with her among all the idle people that were assembled there; they were all looking at her very hard; she had begun to chatter as soon as she joined him. Winterbourne's preference had been that they should be conveyed to Chillon in a carriage; but she expressed a lively wish to go in the little steamer; she declared that she had a passion for steamboats. There was always such a lovely breeze upon the water, and you saw such lots of people.

The sail was not long, but Winterbourne's companion found time to say a great many things. To the young man himself their little excursion was so much of an escapade—an adventure—that, even allowing for her habitual sense of freedom, he had some expectation of seeing her regard it in the same way. But it must be confessed that, in this particular, he was disappointed. Daisy Miller was extremely animated, she was in charming spirits; but she was apparently not at all excited; she was not fluttered; she avoided neither his eyes nor those of any one else; she blushed neither when she looked at him nor when she saw that people were looking at her. People continued to look at her a great deal, and Winterbourne took much satisfaction in his pretty companion's distinguished air. He had been a little afraid that she would talk loud, laugh overmuch, and even, perhaps, desire to move about the boat a good deal. But he quite forgot his fears; he sat smiling, with his eyes upon her face, while, without moving from her place, she delivered herself of a great number of original reflections. It was the most charming garrulity he had ever heard. He had assented to the idea that she was "common;" but was she so, after all, or was he simply getting used to her commonness? Her conversation was chiefly of what metaphysicians term the objective cast; but every now and then it took a subjective turn.

"What on *earth* are you so grave about?" she suddenly demanded, fixing her agreeable eyes upon Winterbourne's.

"Am I grave?" he asked. "I had an idea I was grinning from ear to ear."

"You look as if you were taking me to a funeral. If that's a grin, your ears are very near together."

"Should you like me to dance a hornpipe on the deck?"

"Pray do, and I'll carry round your hat. It will pay the expenses of our journey."

"I never was better pleased in my life," murmured Winterbourne.

She looked at him a moment, and then burst into a little laugh. "I like to make you say those things! You're a queer mixture!"

In the castle, after they had landed, the subjective element decidedly prevailed. Daisy tripped about the vaulted chambers, rustled her skirts in the corkscrew staircases, flirted back with a pretty little cry and a shudder from the edge of the *oubliettes*,[19] and turned a singularly well-shaped ear to everything that Winterbourne told her about the place. But he saw that she cared very little for feudal antiquities, and that the dusky traditions of Chillon made but a slight impression upon her. They had the good fortune to have been able to walk about without other companionship than that of the custodian; and Winterbourne arranged with this functionary that they should not be hurried—that they should linger and pause wherever they chose. The custodian

---

[19]Dungeons.

interpreted the bargain generously—Winterbourne, on his side, had been generous—and ended by leaving them quite to themselves. Miss Miller's observations were not remarkable for logical consistency; for anything she wanted to say she was sure to find a pretext. She found a great many pretexts in the rugged embrasures of Chillon for asking Winterbourne sudden questions about himself—his family, his previous history, his tastes, his habits, his intentions—and for supplying information upon corresponding points in her own personality. Of her own tastes, habits and intentions Miss Miller was prepared to give the most definite, and indeed the most favourable, account.

"Well; I hope you know enough!" she said to her companion, after he had told her the history of the unhappy Bonivard.[20] "I never saw a man that knew so much!" The history of Bonivard had evidently, as they say, gone into one ear and out of the other. But Daisy went on to say that she wished Winterbourne would travel with them and "go round" with them; they might know something, in that case. "Don't you want to come and teach Randolph?" she asked. Winterbourne said that nothing could possibly please him so much; but that he had unfortunately other occupations. "Other occupations? I don't believe it!" said Miss Daisy. "What do you mean? You are not in business." The young man admitted that he was not in business; but he had engagements which, even within a day or two, would force him to go back to Geneva. "Oh, bother!" she said, "I don't believe it!" and she began to talk about something else. But a few moments later, when he was pointing out to her the pretty design of an antique fireplace, she broke out irrelevantly, "You don't mean to say you are going back to Geneva?"

"It is a melancholy fact that I shall have to return to Geneva to-morrow."

"Well, Mr. Winterbourne," said Daisy; "I think you're horrid!"

"Oh, don't say such dreadful things!" said Winterbourne—"just at the last."

"The last!" cried the young girl; "I call it the first. I have half a mind to leave you here and go straight back to the hotel alone." And for the next ten minutes she did nothing but call him horrid. Poor Winterbourne was fairly bewildered; no young lady had as yet done him the honour to be so agitated by the announcement of his movements. His companion, after this, ceased to pay any attention to the curiosities of Chillon or the beauties of the lake; she opened fire upon the mysterious charmer in Geneva, whom she appeared to have instantly taken it for granted that he was hurrying back to see. How did Miss Daisy Miller know that there was a charmer in Geneva? Winterbourne, who denied the existence of such a person, was quite unable to discover; and he was divided between amazement at the rapidity of her induction and

---

[20]François de Bonivard: Leader of the Genevan resistance, imprisoned in the castle 1532–1536 and made famous by Lord George Gordon Byron's poem "The Prisoner of Chillon" (1816).

amusement at the frankness of her *persiflage*.[21] She seemed to him, in all this, an extraordinary mixture of innocence and crudity. "Does she never allow you more than three days at a time?" asked Daisy, ironically. "Doesn't she give you a vacation in summer? There's no one so hard worked but they can get leave to go off somewhere at this season. I suppose, if you stay another day, she'll come after you in the boat. Do wait over till Friday, and I will go down to the landing to see her arrive!" Winterbourne began to think he had been wrong to feel disappointed in the temper in which the young lady had embarked. If he had missed the personal accent, the personal accent was now making its appearance. It sounded very distinctly, at last, in her telling him she would stop "teasing" him if he would promise her solemnly to come down to Rome in the winter.

"That's not a difficult promise to make," said Winterbourne. "My aunt has taken an apartment in Rome for the winter, and has already asked me to come and see her."

"I don't want you to come for your aunt," said Daisy; "I want you to come for me." And this was the only allusion that the young man was ever to hear her make to his invidious kinswoman. He declared that, at any rate, he would certainly come. After this Daisy stopped teasing. Winterbourne took a carriage, and they drove back to Vevey in the dusk; the young girl was very quiet.

In the evening Winterbourne mentioned to Mrs. Costello that he had spent the afternoon at Chillon, with Miss Daisy Miller.

"The Americans—of the courier?" asked this lady.

"Ah, happily," said Winterbourne, "the courier stayed at home."

"She went with you all alone?"

"All alone."

Mrs. Costello sniffed a little at her smelling-bottle. "And that," she exclaimed, "is the young person you wanted me to know!"

III

Winterbourne, who had returned to Geneva the day after his excursion to Chillon, went to Rome towards the end of January. His aunt had been established there for several weeks, and he had received a couple of letters from her. "Those people you were so devoted to last summer at Vevey have turned up here, courier and all," she wrote. "They seem to have made several acquaintances, but the courier continues to be the most *intime*.[22] The young

---

[21]French: mockery, banter.
[22]French: intimate, familiar.

lady, however, is also very intimate with some third-rate Italians, with whom she rackets about in a way that makes much talk. Bring me that pretty novel of Cherbuliez's—'Paule Méré'[23]—and don't come later than the 23rd."

In the natural course of events, Winterbourne, on arriving in Rome, would presently have ascertained Mrs. Miller's address at the American banker's and have gone to pay his compliments to Miss Daisy. "After what happened at Vevey I certainly think I may call upon them," he said to Mrs. Costello.

"If, after what happens—at Vevey and everywhere—you desire to keep up the acquaintance, you are very welcome. Of course a man may know every one. Men are welcome to the privilege!"

"Pray what is it that happens—here, for instance?" Winterbourne demanded.

"The girl goes about alone with her foreigners. As to what happens farther, you must apply elsewhere for information. She has picked up half-a-dozen of the regular Roman fortune-hunters, and she takes them about to people's houses. When she comes to a party she brings with her a gentleman with a good deal of manner and a wonderful moustache."

"And where is the mother?"

"I haven't the least idea. They are very dreadful people."

Winterbourne meditated a moment. "They are very ignorant—very innocent only. Depend upon it they are not bad."

"They are hopelessly vulgar," said Mrs. Costello. "Whether or not being hopelessly vulgar is being 'bad' is a question for the metaphysicians. They are bad enough to dislike, at any rate; and for this short life that is quite enough."

The news that Daisy Miller was surrounded by half-a-dozen wonderful moustaches checked Winterbourne's impulse to go straightway to see her. He had perhaps not definitely flattered himself that he had made an ineffaceable impression upon her heart, but he was annoyed at hearing of a state of affairs so little in harmony with an image that had lately flitted in and out of his own meditations; the image of a very pretty girl looking out of an old Roman window and asking herself urgently when Mr. Winterbourne would arrive. If, however, he determined to wait a little before reminding Miss Miller of his claims to her consideration, he went very soon to call upon two or three other friends. One of these friends was an American lady who had spent several winters at Geneva, where she had placed her children at school. She was a very accomplished woman and she lived in the Via Gregoriana. Winterbourne found her in a little crimson drawing-room, on a third-floor; the room was filled with southern sunshine. He had not been there ten minutes when the

---

[23]1864 novel by Victor Cherbuliez about a young woman who maintains the strict social codes required of women in Geneva.

servant came in, announcing "Madame Mila!" This announcement was presently followed by the entrance of little Randolph Miller, who stopped in the middle of the room and stood staring at Winterbourne. An instant later his pretty sister crossed the threshold; and then, after a considerable interval, Mrs. Miller slowly advanced.

"I know you!" said Randolph.

"I'm sure you know a great many things," exclaimed Winterbourne, taking him by the hand. "How is your education coming on?"

Daisy was exchanging greetings very prettily with her hostess; but when she heard Winterbourne's voice she quickly turned her head. "Well, I declare!" she said.

"I told you I should come, you know," Winterbourne rejoined, smiling.

"Well—I didn't believe it," said Miss Daisy.

"I am much obliged to you," laughed the young man.

"You might have come to see me!" said Daisy.

"I arrived only yesterday."

"I don't believe that!" the young girl declared.

Winterbourne turned with a protesting smile to her mother; but this lady evaded his glance, and seating herself, fixed her eyes upon her son. "We've got a bigger place than this," said Randolph. "It's all gold on the walls."

Mrs. Miller turned uneasily in her chair. "I told you if I were to bring you, you would say something!" she murmured.

"I told *you*!" Randolph exclaimed. "I tell *you,* sir!" he added jocosely, giving Winterbourne a thump on the knee. "It *is* bigger, too!"

Daisy had entered upon a lively conversation with her hostess; Winterbourne judged it becoming to address a few words to her mother. "I hope you have been well since we parted at Vevey," he said.

Mrs. Miller now certainly looked at him—at his chin. "Not very well, sir," she answered.

"She's got the dyspepsia," said Randolph. "I've got it too. Father's got it. I've got it worst!"

This announcement, instead of embarrassing Mrs. Miller, seemed to relieve her. "I suffer from the liver," she said. "I think it's this climate; it's less bracing than Schenectady, especially in the winter season. I don't know whether you know we reside at Schenectady. I was saying to Daisy that I certainly hadn't found any one like Dr. Davis, and I didn't believe I should. Oh, at Schenectady, he stands first; they think everything of him. He has so much to do, and yet there was nothing he wouldn't do for me. He said he never saw anything like my dyspepsia, but he was bound to cure it. I'm sure there was nothing he wouldn't try. He was just going to try something new when we came off. Mr. Miller wanted Daisy to see Europe for herself. But I wrote to Mr. Miller that it seems as if I couldn't get on without Dr. Davis. At Schenectady he stands at the very top; and there's a great deal of sickness there, too. It affects my sleep."

Winterbourne had a good deal of pathological gossip with Dr. Davis's patient, during which Daisy chattered unremittingly to her own companion. The young man asked Mrs. Miller how she was pleased with Rome. "Well, I must say I am disappointed," she answered. "We had heard so much about it; I suppose we had heard too much. But we couldn't help that. We had been led to expect something different."

"Ah, wait a little, and you will become very fond of it," said Winterbourne.

"I hate it worse and worse every day!" cried Randolph.

"You are like the infant Hannibal,"[24] said Winterbourne.

"No, I ain't!" Randolph declared, at a venture.

"You are not much like an infant," said his mother. "But we have seen places," she resumed, "that I should put a long way before Rome." And in reply to Winterbourne's interrogation, "There's Zurich," she observed; "I think Zurich is lovely; and we hadn't heard half so much about it."

"The best place we've seen is the City of Richmond!" said Randolph.

"He means the ship," his mother explained. "We crossed in that ship. Randolph had a good time on the City of Richmond."

"It's the best place I've seen," the child repeated. "Only it was turned the wrong way."

"Well, we've got to turn the right way some time," said Mrs. Miller, with a little laugh. Winterbourne expressed the hope that her daughter at least found some gratification in Rome, and she declared that Daisy was quite carried away. "It's on account of the society—the society's splendid. She goes round everywhere; she has made a great number of acquaintances. Of course she goes round more than I do. I must say they have been very sociable; they have taken her right in. And then she knows a great many gentlemen. Oh, she thinks there's nothing like Rome. Of course, it's a great deal pleasanter for a young lady if she knows plenty of gentlemen."

By this time Daisy had turned her attention again to Winterbourne. "I've been telling Mrs. Walker how mean you were!" the young girl announced.

"And what is the evidence you have offered?" asked Winterbourne, rather annoyed at Miss Miller's want of appreciation of the zeal of an admirer who on his way down to Rome had stopped neither at Bologna nor at Florence, simply because of a certain sentimental impatience. He remembered that a cynical compatriot had once told him that American women—the pretty ones, and this gave a largeness to the axiom—were at once the most exacting in the world and the least endowed with a sense of indebtedness.

"Why, you were awfully mean at Vevey," said Daisy. "You wouldn't do anything. You wouldn't stay there when I asked you."

---

[24]Carthaginian general 247–183 B.C.E.

"My dearest young lady," cried Winterbourne, with eloquence, "have I come all the way to Rome to encounter your reproaches?"

"Just hear him say that!" said Daisy to her hostess, giving a twist to a bow on this lady's dress. "Did you ever hear anything so quaint?"

"So quaint, my dear?" murmured Mrs. Walker, in the tone of a partisan of Winterbourne.

"Well, I don't know," said Daisy, fingering Mrs. Walker's ribbons. "Mrs. Walker, I want to tell you something."

"Motherr," interposed Randolph, with his rough ends to his words, "I tell you you've got to go. Eugenio'll raise something!"[25]

"I'm not afraid of Eugenio," said Daisy, with a toss of her head. "Look here, Mrs. Walker," she went on, "you know I'm coming to your party."

"I am delighted to hear it."

"I've got a lovely dress."

"I am very sure of that."

"But I want to ask a favour—permission to bring a friend."

"I shall be happy to see any of your friends," said Mrs. Walker, turning with a smile to Mrs. Miller.

"Oh, they are not my friends," answered Daisy's mamma, smiling shyly, in her own fashion. "I never spoke to them!"

"It's an intimate friend of mine—Mr. Giovanelli," said Daisy, without a tremor in her clear little voice or a shadow on her brilliant little face.

Mrs. Walker was silent a moment, she gave a rapid glance at Winterbourne. "I shall be glad to see Mr. Giovanelli," she then said.

"He's an Italian," Daisy pursued, with the prettiest serenity. "He's a great friend of mine—he's the handsomest man in the world—except Mr. Winterbourne! He knows plenty of Italians, but he wants to know some Americans. He thinks ever so much of Americans. He's tremendously clever. He's perfectly lovely!"

It was settled that this brilliant personage should be brought to Mrs. Walker's party, and then Mrs. Miller prepared to take her leave. "I guess we'll go back to the hotel," she said.

"You may go back to the hotel, mother, but I'm going to take a walk," said Daisy.

"She's going to walk with Mr. Giovanelli," Randolph proclaimed.

"I am going to the Pincio,"[26] said Daisy, smiling.

"Alone, my dear—at this hour?" Mrs. Walker asked. The afternoon was drawing to a close—it was the hour for the throng of carriages and of contemplative pedestrians. "I don't think it's safe, my dear," said Mrs. Walker.

---

[25]Implying "be angry," raise Cain.

[26]Elevated terrace popular for afternoon walks and drives.

"Neither do I," subjoined Mrs. Miller. "You'll get the fever[27] as sure as you live. Remember what Dr. Davis told you!"

"Give her some medicine before she goes," said Randolph.

The company had risen to its feet; Daisy, still showing her pretty teeth, bent over and kissed her hostess. "Mrs. Walker, you are too perfect," she said. "I'm not going alone; I am going to meet a friend."

"Your friend won't keep you from getting the fever," Mrs. Miller observed.

"Is it Mr. Giovanelli?" asked the hostess.

Winterbourne was watching the young girl; at this question his attention quickened. She stood there smiling and smoothing her bonnet-ribbons; she glanced at Winterbourne. Then, while she glanced and smiled, she answered without a shade of hesitation, "Mr. Giovanelli—the beautiful Giovanelli."

"My dear young friend," said Mrs. Walker, taking her hand, pleadingly, "don't walk off to the Pincio at this hour to meet a beautiful Italian."

"Well, he speaks English," said Mrs. Miller.

"Gracious me!" Daisy exclaimed, "I don't want to do anything improper. There's an easy way to settle it." She continued to glance at Winterbourne. "The Pincio is only a hundred yards distant, and if Mr. Winterbourne were as polite as he pretends he would offer to walk with me!"

Winterbourne's politeness hastened to affirm itself, and the young girl gave him gracious leave to accompany her. They passed down-stairs before her mother, and at the door Winterbourne perceived Mrs. Miller's carriage drawn up, with the ornamental courier whose acquaintance he had made at Vevey seated within. "Good-bye, Eugenio!" cried Daisy, "I'm going to take a walk." The distance from the Via Gregoriana to the beautiful garden at the other end of the Pincian Hill is, in fact, rapidly traversed. As the day was splendid, however, and the concourse of vehicles, walkers, and loungers numerous, the young Americans found their progress much delayed. This fact was highly agreeable to Winterbourne, in spite of his consciousness of his singular situation. The slow-moving, idly-gazing Roman crowd bestowed much attention upon the extremely pretty young foreign lady who was passing through it upon his arm; and he wondered what on earth had been in Daisy's mind when she proposed to expose herself, unattended, to its appreciation. His own mission, to her sense, apparently, was to consign her to the hands of Mr. Giovanelli; but Winterbourne, at once annoyed and gratified, resolved that he would do no such thing.

"Why haven't you been to see me?" asked Daisy. "You can't get out of that."

"I have had the honour of telling you that I have only just stepped out of the train."

---

[27]Malaria, also called Roman fever.

"You must have stayed in the train a good while after it stopped!" cried the young girl, with her little laugh. "I suppose you were asleep. You have had time to go to see Mrs. Walker."

"I knew Mrs. Walker—" Winterbourne began to explain.

"I knew where you knew her. You knew her at Geneva. She told me so. Well, you knew me at Vevey. That's just as good. So you ought to have come." She asked him no other question than this; she began to prattle about her own affairs. "We've got splendid rooms at the hotel; Eugenio says they're the best rooms in Rome. We are going to stay all winter—if we don't die of the fever; and I guess we'll stay then. It's a great deal nicer than I thought; I thought it would be fearfully quiet; I was sure it would be awfully poky. I was sure we should be going round all the time with one of those dreadful old men that explain about the pictures and things. But we only had about a week of that, and now I'm enjoying myself. I know ever so many people, and they are all so charming. The society's extremely select. There are all kinds—English, and Germans, and Italians. I think I like the English best. I like their style of conversation. But there are some lovely Americans. I never saw anything so hospitable. There's something or other every day. There's not much dancing; but I must say I never thought dancing was everything. I was always fond of conversation. I guess I shall have plenty at Mrs. Walker's—her rooms are so small." When they had passed the gate of the Pincian Gardens, Miss Miller began to wonder where Mr. Giovanelli might be. "We had better go straight to that place in front," she said, "where you look at the view."

"I certainly shall not help you to find him," Winterbourne declared.

"Then I shall find him without you," said Miss Daisy.

"You certainly won't leave me!" cried Winterbourne.

She burst into her little laugh. "Are you afraid you'll get lost—or run over? But there's Giovanelli, leaning against that tree. He's staring at the women in the carriages: did you ever see anything so cool?"

Winterbourne perceived at some distance a little man standing with folded arms, nursing his cane. He had a handsome face, an artfully poised hat, a glass in one eye and a nosegay in his button-hole. Winterbourne looked at him a moment and then said, "Do you mean to speak to that man?"

"Do I mean to speak to him? Why, you don't suppose I mean to communicate by signs?"

"Pray understand, then," said Winterbourne, "that I intend to remain with you."

Daisy stopped and looked at him, without a sign of troubled consciousness in her face; with nothing but the presence of her charming eyes and her happy dimples. "Well, she's a cool one!" thought the young man.

"I don't like the way you say that," said Daisy. "It's too imperious."

"I beg your pardon if I say it wrong. The main point is to give you an idea of my meaning."

The young girl looked at him more gravely, but with eyes that were prettier than ever. "I have never allowed a gentleman to dictate to me, or to interfere with anything I do."

"I think you have made a mistake," said Winterbourne. "You should sometimes listen to a gentleman—the right one?"

Daisy began to laugh again. "I do nothing but listen to gentlemen!" she exclaimed. "Tell me if Mr. Giovanelli is the right one?"

The gentleman with the nosegay in his bosom had now perceived our two friends, and was approaching the young girl with obsequious rapidity. He bowed to Winterbourne as well as to the latter's companion; he had a brilliant smile, an intelligent eye; Winterbourne thought him not a bad-looking fellow. But he nevertheless said to Daisy—"No, he's not the right one."

Daisy evidently had a natural talent for performing introductions; she mentioned the name of each of her companions to the other. She strolled along with one of them on each side of her; Mr. Giovanelli, who spoke English very cleverly—Winterbourne afterwards learned that he had practised the idiom upon a great many American heiresses—addressed her a great deal of very polite nonsense; he was extremely urbane, and the young American, who said nothing, reflected upon that profundity of Italian cleverness which enables people to appear more gracious in proportion as they are more acutely disappointed. Giovanelli, of course, had counted upon something more intimate; he had not bargained for a party of three. But he kept his temper in a manner which suggested far-stretching intentions. Winterbourne flattered himself that he had taken his measure. "He is not a gentleman," said the young American; "he is only a clever imitation of one. He is a music-master, or a penny-a-liner,[28] or a third-rate artist. Damn his good looks!" Mr. Giovanelli had certainly a very pretty face; but Winterbourne felt a superior indignation at his own lovely fellow-country-woman's not knowing the difference between a spurious gentleman and a real one. Giovanelli chattered and jested and made himself wonderfully agreeable. It was true that if he was an imitation the imitation was very skilful. "Nevertheless," Winterbourne said to himself, "a nice girl ought to know!" And then he came back to the question whether this was in fact a nice girl. Would a nice girl—even allowing for her being a little American flirt—make a rendezvous with a presumably low-lived foreigner? The rendezvous in this case, indeed, had been in broad daylight, and in the most crowded corner of Rome; but was it not impossible to regard the choice of these circumstances as a proof of extreme cynicism? Singular though it may seem, Winterbourne was vexed that the young girl, in joining her *amoroso*,[29] should not appear more impatient of his own company, and he

---

[28]Hack writer, like those paid for their prose by the line.
[29]Italian: admirer, suitor.

was vexed because of his inclination. It was impossible to regard her as a perfectly well-conducted young lady; she was wanting in a certain indispensable delicacy. It would therefore simplify matters greatly to be able to treat her as the object of one of those sentiments which are called by romancers "lawless passions." That she should seem to wish to get rid of him would help him to think more lightly of her, and to be able to think more lightly of her would make her much less perplexing. But Daisy, on this occasion, continued to present herself as an inscrutable combination of audacity and innocence.

She had been walking some quarter of an hour, attended by her two cavaliers, and responding in a tone of very childish gaiety, as it seemed to Winterbourne, to the pretty speeches of Mr. Giovanelli, when a carriage that had detached itself from the revolving train drew up beside the path. At the same moment Winterbourne perceived that his friend Mrs. Walker—the lady whose house he had lately left—was seated in the vehicle and was beckoning to him. Leaving Miss Miller's side, he hastened to obey her summons. Mrs. Walker was flushed; she wore an excited air. "It is really too dreadful," she said. "That girl must not do this sort of thing. She must not walk here with you two men. Fifty people have noticed her."

Winterbourne raised his eyebrows. "I think it's a pity to make too much fuss about it."

"It's a pity to let the girl ruin herself!"

"She is very innocent," said Winterbourne.

"She's very crazy!" cried Mrs. Walker. "Did you ever see anything so imbecile as her mother? After you had all left me, just now, I could not sit still for thinking of it. It seemed too pitiful, not even to attempt to save her. I ordered the carriage and put on my bonnet, and came here as quickly as possible. Thank heaven I have found you!"

"What do you propose to do with us?" asked Winterbourne, smiling.

"To ask her to get in, to drive her about here for half-an-hour, so that the world may see she is not running absolutely wild, and then to take her safely home."

"I don't think it's a very happy thought," said Winterbourne; "but you can try."

Mrs. Walker tried. The young man went in pursuit of Miss Miller, who had simply nodded and smiled at his interlocutrix in the carriage and had gone her way with her own companion. Daisy, on learning that Mrs. Walker wished to speak to her, retraced her steps with a perfect good grace and with Mr. Giovanelli at her side. She declared that she was delighted to have a chance to present this gentleman to Mrs. Walker. She immediately achieved the introduction, and declared that she had never in her life seen anything so lovely as Mrs. Walker's carriage-rug.

"I am glad you admire it," said this lady, smiling sweetly. "Will you get in and let me put it over you?"

"Oh, no, thank you," said Daisy. "I shall admire it much more as I see you driving round with it."

"Do get in and drive with me," said Mrs. Walker.

"That would be charming, but it's so enchanting just as I am!" and Daisy gave a brilliant glance at the gentlemen on either side of her.

"It may be enchanting, dear child, but it is not the custom here," urged Mrs. Walker, leaning forward in her victoria[30] with her hands devoutly clasped.

"Well, it ought to be, then!" said Daisy. "If I didn't walk I should expire."

"You should walk with your mother, dear," cried the lady from Geneva, losing patience.

"With my mother dear!" exclaimed the young girl. Winterbourne saw that she scented interference. "My mother never walked ten steps in her life. And then, you know," she added with a laugh, "I am more than five years old."

"You are old enough to be more reasonable. You are old enough, dear Miss Miller, to be talked about."

Daisy looked at Mrs. Walker, smiling intensely. "Talked about? What do you mean?"

"Come into my carriage and I will tell you."

Daisy turned her quickened glance again from one of the gentlemen beside her to the other. Mr. Giovanelli was bowing to and fro, rubbing down his gloves and laughing very agreeably; Winterbourne thought it a most unpleasant scene. "I don't think I want to know what you mean," said Daisy presently. "I don't think I should like it."

Winterbourne wished that Mrs. Walker would tuck in her carriage-rug and drive away; but this lady did not enjoy being defied, as she afterwards told him. "Should you prefer being thought a very reckless girl?" she demanded.

"Gracious me!" exclaimed Daisy. She looked again at Mr. Giovanelli, then she turned to Winterbourne. There was a little pink flush in her cheek; she was tremendously pretty. "Does Mr. Winterbourne think," she asked slowly, smiling, throwing back her head and glancing at him from head to foot, "that—to save my reputation—I ought to get into the carriage?"

Winterbourne coloured; for an instant he hesitated greatly. It seemed so strange to hear her speak that way of her "reputation." But he himself, in fact, must speak in accordance with gallantry. The finest gallantry, here, was simply to tell her the truth; and the truth, for Winterbourne, as the few indications I have been able to give have made him known to the reader, was that Daisy Miller should take Mrs. Walker's advice. He looked at her exquisite prettiness; and then he said very gently, "I think you should get into the carriage."

---

[30]Carriage for two.

Daisy gave a violent laugh. "I never heard anything so stiff! If this is improper, Mrs. Walker," she pursued, "then I am all improper, and you must give me up. Good-bye; I hope you'll have a lovely ride!" and, with Mr. Giovanelli, who made a triumphantly obsequious salute, she turned away.

Mrs. Walker sat looking after her, and there were tears in Mrs. Walker's eyes. "Get in here, sir," she said to Winterbourne, indicating the place beside her. The young man answered that he felt bound to accompany Miss Miller; whereupon Mrs. Walker declared that if he refused her this favour she would never speak to him again. She was evidently in earnest. Winterbourne overtook Daisy and her companion and, offering the young girl his hand, told her that Mrs. Walker had made an imperious claim upon his society. He expected that in answer she would say something rather free, something to commit herself still farther to that "recklessness" from which Mrs. Walker had so charitably endeavoured to dissuade her. But she only shook his hand, hardly looking at him, while Mr. Giovanelli bade him farewell with a too emphatic flourish of the hat.

Winterbourne was not in the best possible humour as he took his seat in Mrs. Walker's victoria. "That was not clever of you," he said candidly, while the vehicle mingled again with the throng of carriages.

"In such a case," his companion answered, "I don't wish to be clever, I wish to be *earnest*!"

"Well, your earnestness has only offended her and put her off."

"It has happened very well," said Mrs. Walker. "If she is so perfectly determined to compromise herself, the sooner one knows it the better; one can act accordingly."

"I suspect she meant no harm," Winterbourne rejoined.

"So I thought a month ago. But she has been going too far."

"What has she been doing?"

"Everything that is not done here. Flirting with any man she could pick up; sitting in corners with mysterious Italians; dancing all the evening with the same partners; receiving visits at eleven o'clock at night. Her mother goes away when visitors come."

"But her brother," said Winterbourne, laughing, "sits up till midnight."

"He must be edified by what he sees. I'm told that at their hotel every one is talking about her, and that a smile goes round among the servants when a gentleman comes and asks for Miss Miller."

"The servants be hanged!" said Winterbourne angrily. "The poor girl's only fault," he presently added, "is that she is very uncultivated."

"She is naturally indelicate," Mrs. Walker declared. "Take that example this morning. How long had you known her at Vevey?"

"A couple of days."

"Fancy, then, her making it a personal matter that you should have left the place!"

Winterbourne was silent for some moments; then he said, "I suspect, Mrs. Walker, that you and I have lived too long at Geneva!" And he added a request that she should inform him with what particular design she had made him enter her carriage.

"I wished to beg you to cease your relations with Miss Miller—not to flirt with her—to give her no farther opportunity to expose herself—to let her alone, in short."

"I'm afraid I can't do that," said Winterbourne. "I like her extremely."

"All the more reason that you shouldn't help her to make a scandal."

"There shall be nothing scandalous in my attentions to her."

"There certainly will be in the way she takes them. But I have said what I had on my conscience," Mrs. Walker pursued. "If you wish to rejoin the young lady I will put you down. Here, by-the-way, you have a chance."

The carriage was traversing that part of the Pincian Garden which over-hangs the wall of Rome and overlooks the beautiful Villa Borghese.[31] It is bordered by a large parapet, near which there are several seats. One of the seats, at a distance, was occupied by a gentleman and a lady, towards whom Mrs. Walker gave a toss of her head. At the same moment these persons rose and walked towards the parapet. Winterbourne had asked the coachman to stop; he now descended from the carriage. His companion looked at him a moment in silence; then, while he raised his hat, she drove majestically away. Winterbourne stood there; he had turned his eyes towards Daisy and her cavalier. They evidently saw no one; they were too deeply occupied with each other. When they reached the low garden-wall they stood a moment looking off at the great flat-topped pine-clusters of the Villa Borghese; then Giovanelli seated himself familiarly upon the broad ledge of the wall. The western sun in the opposite sky sent out a brilliant shaft through a couple of cloud-bars; whereupon Daisy's companion took her parasol out of her hands and opened it. She came a little nearer and he held the parasol over her; then, still holding it, he let it rest upon her shoulder, so that both of their heads were hidden from Winterbourne. This young man lingered a moment, then he began to walk. But he walked—not towards the couple with the parasol; towards the residence of his aunt, Mrs. Costello.

IV

He flattered himself on the following day that there was no smiling among the servants when he, at least, asked for Mrs. Miller at her hotel. This lady and her daughter, however, were not at home; and on the next day after,

---

[31]A famed Roman mansion and museum with a large wooded park.

repeating his visit, Winterbourne again had the misfortune not to find them. Mrs. Walker's party took place on the evening of the third day, and in spite of the frigidity of his last interview with the hostess Winterbourne was among the guests. Mrs. Walker was one of those American ladies who, while residing abroad, make a point, in their own phrase, of studying European society; and she had on this occasion collected several specimens of her diversely-born fellow-mortals to serve, as it were, as text-books. When Winterbourne arrived Daisy Miller was not there; but in a few moments he saw her mother come in alone, very shyly and ruefully. Mrs. Miller's hair, above her exposed-looking temples, was more frizzled than ever. As she approached Mrs. Walker, Winterbourne also drew near.

"You see I've come all alone," said poor Mrs. Miller. "I'm so frightened; I don't know what to do; it's the first time I've ever been to a party alone—especially in this country. I wanted to bring Randolph or Eugenio, or some one, but Daisy just pushed me off by myself. I ain't used to going round alone."

"And does not your daughter intend to favour us with her society?" demanded Mrs. Walker, impressively.

"Well, Daisy's all dressed," said Mrs. Miller, with that accent of the dispassionate, if not of the philosophic, historian with which she always recorded the current incidents of her daughter's career. "She got dressed on purpose before dinner. But she's got a friend of hers there; that gentleman—the Italian—that she wanted to bring. They've got going at the piano; it seems as if they couldn't leave off. Mr. Giovanelli sings splendidly. But I guess they'll come before very long," concluded Mrs. Miller hopefully.

"I'm sorry she should come—in that way," said Mrs. Walker.

"Well, I told her that there was no use in her getting dressed before dinner if she was going to wait three hours," responded Daisy's mamma. "I didn't see the use of her putting on such a dress as that to sit round with Mr. Giovanelli."

"This is most horrible!" said Mrs. Walker, turning away and addressing herself to Winterbourne. "*Elle s'affiche.*[32] It's her revenge for my having ventured to remonstrate with her. When she comes I shall not speak to her."

Daisy came after eleven o'clock, but she was not, on such an occasion, a young lady to wait to be spoken to. She rustled forward in radiant loveliness, smiling and chattering, carrying a large bouquet and attended by Mr. Giovanelli. Every one stopped talking, and turned and looked at her. She came straight to Mrs. Walker. "I'm afraid you thought I never was coming, so I sent mother off to tell you. I wanted to make Mr. Giovanelli practise some things before he came; you know he sings beautifully, and I want you to ask

---

[32]French: she is making a spectacle of herself.

him to sing. This is Mr. Giovanelli; you know I introduced him to you; he's got the most lovely voice and he knows the most charming set of songs. I made him go over them this evening, on purpose; we had the greatest time at the hotel." Of all this Daisy delivered herself with the sweetest, brightest audibleness, looking now at her hostess and now round the room, while she gave a series of little pats, round her shoulders, to the edges of her dress. "Is there any one I know?" she asked.

"I think every one knows you!" said Mrs. Walker pregnantly, and she gave a very cursory greeting to Mr. Giovanelli. This gentleman bore himself gallantly. He smiled and bowed and showed his white teeth, he curled his moustaches and rolled his eyes, and performed all the proper functions of a handsome Italian at an evening party. He sang, very prettily, half-a-dozen songs, though Mrs. Walker afterwards declared that she had been quite unable to find out who asked him. It was apparently not Daisy who had given him his orders. Daisy sat at a distance from the piano, and though she had publicly, as it were, professed a high admiration for his singing, talked, not inaudibly, while it was going on.

"It's a pity these rooms are so small; we can't dance," she said to Winterbourne, as if she had seen him five minutes before.

"I am not sorry we can't dance," Winterbourne answered; "I don't dance."

"Of course you don't dance; you're too stiff," said Miss Daisy. "I hope you enjoyed your drive with Mrs. Walker."

"No, I didn't enjoy it; I preferred walking with you."

"We paired off, that was much better," said Daisy. "But did you ever hear anything so cool as Mrs. Walker's wanting me to get into her carriage and drop poor Mr. Giovanelli; and under the pretext that it was proper? People have different ideas! It would have been most unkind; he had been talking about that walk for ten days."

"He should not have talked about it at all," said Winterbourne; "he would never have proposed to a young lady of this country to walk about the streets with him."

"About the streets?" cried Daisy, with her pretty stare. "Where then would he have proposed to her to walk? The Pincio is not the streets, either; and I, thank goodness, am not a young lady of this country. The young ladies of this country have a dreadfully poky time of it, so far as I can learn; I don't see why I should change my habits for *them*."

"I am afraid your habits are those of a flirt," said Winterbourne gravely.

"Of course they are," she cried, giving him her little smiling stare again. "I'm a fearful, frightful flirt! Did you ever hear of a nice girl that was not? But I suppose you will tell me now that I am not a nice girl."

"You're a very nice girl, but I wish you would flirt with me, and me only," said Winterbourne.

"Ah! thank you, thank you very much; you are the last man I should think of flirting with. As I have had the pleasure of informing you, you are too stiff."

"You say that too often," said Winterbourne.

Daisy gave a delighted laugh. "If I could have the sweet hope of making you angry, I would say it again."

"Don't do that; when I am angry I'm stiffer than ever. But if you won't flirt with me, do cease at least to flirt with your friend at the piano; they don't understand that sort of thing here."

"I thought they understood nothing else!" exclaimed Daisy.

"Not in young unmarried women."

"It seems to me much more proper in young unmarried women than in old married ones," Daisy declared.

"Well," said Winterbourne, "when you deal with natives you must go by the custom of the place. Flirting is a purely American custom; it doesn't exist here. So when you show yourself in public with Mr. Giovanelli and without your mother— —."

"Gracious! poor mother!" interposed Daisy.

"Though you may be flirting, Mr. Giovanelli is not; he means something else."

"He isn't preaching, at any rate," said Daisy with vivacity. "And if you want very much to know, we are neither of us flirting; we are too good friends for that; we are very intimate friends."

"Ah!" rejoined Winterbourne, "if you are in love with each other it is another affair."

She had allowed him up to this point to talk so frankly that he had no expectation of shocking her by this ejaculation; but she immediately got up, blushing visibly, and leaving him to exclaim mentally that little American flirts were the queerest creatures in the world. "Mr. Giovanelli, at least," she said, giving her interlocutor a single glance, "never says such very disagreeable things to me."

Winterbourne was bewildered; he stood staring. Mr. Giovanelli had finished singing; he left the piano and came over to Daisy. "Won't you come into the other room and have some tea?" he asked, bending before her with his decorative smile.

Daisy turned to Winterbourne, beginning to smile again. He was still more perplexed, for this inconsequent smile made nothing clear, though it seemed to prove, indeed, that she had a sweetness and softness that reverted instinctively to the pardon of offences. "It has never occurred to Mr. Winterbourne to offer me any tea," she said, with her little tormenting manner.

"I have offered you advice," Winterbourne rejoined.

"I prefer weak tea!" cried Daisy, and she went off with the brilliant Giovanelli. She sat with him in the adjoining room, in the embrasure of the window, for the rest of the evening. There was an interesting performance at the piano, but neither of these young people gave heed to it. When Daisy came to take leave of Mrs. Walker, this lady conscientiously repaired the weakness of which she had been guilty at the moment of the young girl's arrival. She turned her back straight upon Miss Miller and left her to depart with what grace she might. Winterbourne was standing near the door; he saw it all. Daisy turned very pale and looked at her mother, but Mrs. Miller was humbly unconscious of any violation of the usual social forms. She appeared, indeed, to have felt an incongruous impulse to draw attention to her own striking observance of them. "Good night, Mrs. Walker," she said; "we've had a beautiful evening. You see if I let Daisy come to parties without me, I don't want her to go away without me." Daisy turned away, looking with a pale, grave face at the circle near the door; Winterbourne saw that, for the first moment, she was too much shocked and puzzled even for indignation. He on his side was greatly touched.

"That was very cruel," he said to Mrs. Walker.

"She never enters my drawing-room again," replied his hostess.

Since Winterbourne was not to meet her in Mrs. Walker's drawing-room, he went as often as possible to Mrs. Miller's hotel. The ladies were rarely at home, but when he found them the devoted Giovanelli was always present. Very often the polished little Roman was in the drawing-room with Daisy alone, Mrs. Miller being apparently constantly of the opinion that discretion is the better part of surveillance.[33] Winterbourne noted, at first with surprise, that Daisy on these occasions was never embarrassed or annoyed by his own entrance; but he very presently began to feel that she had no more surprises for him; the unexpected in her behaviour was the only thing to expect. She showed no displeasure at her *tête-à-tête* with Giovanelli being interrupted; she could chatter as freshly and freely with two gentlemen as with one; there was always in her conversation, the same odd mixture of audacity and puerility. Winterbourne remarked to himself that if she was seriously interested in Giovanelli it was very singular that she should not take more trouble to preserve the sanctity of their interviews, and he liked her the more for her innocent-looking indifference and her apparently inexhaustible good humour. He could hardly have said why, but she seemed to him a girl who would never be jealous. At the risk of exciting a somewhat derisive smile on the reader's part, I may affirm that with regard to the women who had hitherto interested him it very often seemed to Winterbourne among the possibilities that, given certain contingencies, he should be afraid — literally afraid — of these ladies. He had a pleasant sense that he should never be afraid of Daisy Miller. It must be added that this sentiment was not altogether

---

[33]In Shakespeare's *Henry IV, Part I,* Falstaff says "the better part of valour is discretion."

flattering to Daisy; it was part of his conviction, or rather of his apprehension, that she would prove a very light young person.

But she was evidently very much interested in Giovanelli. She looked at him whenever he spoke; she was perpetually telling him to do this and to do that; she was constantly "chaffing" and abusing him. She appeared completely to have forgotten that Winterbourne had said anything to displease her at Mrs. Walker's little party. One Sunday afternoon, having gone to St. Peter's[34] with his aunt, Winterbourne perceived Daisy strolling about the great church in company with the inevitable Giovanelli. Presently he pointed out the young girl and her cavalier to Mrs. Costello. This lady looked at them a moment through her eyeglass, and then she said:

"That's what makes you so pensive in these days, eh?"

"I had not the least idea I was pensive," said the young man.

"You are very much pre-occupied, you are thinking of something."

"And what is it," he asked, "that you accuse me of thinking of?"

"Of that young lady's—Miss Baker's, Miss Chandler's—what's her name?—Miss Miller's intrigue with that little barber's block."

"Do you call it an intrigue," Winterbourne asked—"an affair that goes on with such peculiar publicity?"

"That's their folly," said Mrs. Costello, "it's not their merit."

"No," rejoined Winterbourne, with something of that pensiveness to which his aunt had alluded. "I don't believe that there is anything to be called an intrigue."

"I have heard a dozen people speak of it; they say she is quite carried away by him."

"They are certainly very intimate," said Winterbourne.

Mrs. Costello inspected the young couple again with her optical instrument. "He is very handsome. One easily sees how it is. She thinks him the most elegant man in the world, the finest gentleman. She has never seen anything like him; he is better even than the courier. It was the courier probably who introduced him, and if he succeeds in marrying the young lady, the courier will come in for a magnificent commission."

"I don't believe she thinks of marrying him," said Winterbourne, "and I don't believe he hopes to marry her."

"You may be very sure she thinks of nothing. She goes on from day to day, from hour to hour, as they did in the Golden Age. I can imagine nothing more vulgar. And at the same time," added Mrs. Costello, "depend upon it that she may tell you any moment that she is 'engaged.'"

"I think that is more than Giovanelli expects," said Winterbourne.

"Who is Giovanelli?"

---

[34]The Papal cathedral.

"The little Italian. I have asked questions about him and learned something. He is apparently a perfectly respectable little man. I believe he is in a small way a *cavaliere avvocato*.[35] But he doesn't move in what are called the first circles. I think it is really not absolutely impossible that the courier introduced him. He is evidently immensely charmed with Miss Miller. If she thinks him the finest gentleman in the world, he, on his side, has never found himself in personal contact with such splendour, such opulence, such expensiveness, as this young lady's. And then she must seem to him wonderfully pretty and interesting. I rather doubt whether he dreams of marrying her. That must appear to him too impossible a piece of luck. He has nothing but his handsome face to offer, and there is a substantial Mr. Miller in that mysterious land of dollars. Giovanelli knows that he hasn't a title to offer. If he were only a count or a *marchese*![36] He must wonder at his luck at the way they have taken him up."

"He accounts for it by his handsome face, and thinks Miss Miller a young lady *qui se passe ses fantaisies*![37] said Mrs. Costello.

"It is very true," Winterbourne pursued, "that Daisy and her mamma have not yet risen to that stage of—what shall I call it?—of culture, at which the idea of catching a count or a *marchese* begins. I believe that they are intellectually incapable of that conception."

"Ah! but the *cavaliere* can't believe it," said Mrs. Costello.

Of the observation excited by Daisy's "intrigue," Winterbourne gathered that day at St. Peter's sufficient evidence. A dozen of the American colonists in Rome came to talk with Mrs. Costello, who sat on a little portable stool at the base of one of the great pilasters. The vesper-service was going forward in splendid chants and organ-tones in the adjacent choir, and meanwhile, between Mrs. Costello and her friends, there was a great deal said about poor little Miss Miller's going really "too far." Winterbourne was not pleased with what he heard; but when, coming out upon the great steps of the church, he saw Daisy, who had emerged before him, get into an open cab with her accomplice and roll away through the cynical streets of Rome, he could not deny to himself that she was going very far indeed. He felt very sorry for her—not exactly that he believed that she had completely lost her head, but because it was painful to hear so much that was pretty and undefended and natural assigned to a vulgar place among the categories of disorder. He made an attempt after this to give a hint to Mrs. Miller. He met one day in the Corso a friend—a tourist like himself—who had just come out of the Doria Palace,[38] where he had been walking through the beautiful gallery. His friend

---

[35]Italian honorary knighthood conferred on a lawyer by the government; the lowest noble rank.
[36]Italian: marquis—rank below a duke and above an earl or count.
[37]French: who follows her fantasies or whims.
[38]Famed museum; the Corso is one of Rome's primary ancient streets.

talked for a moment about the superb portrait of Innocent X. by Velasquez, which hangs in one of the cabinets of the palace, and then said, "And in the same cabinet, by-the-way, I had the pleasure of contemplating a picture of a different kind — that pretty American girl whom you pointed out to me last week." In answer to Winterbourne's inquiries, his friend narrated that the pretty American girl — prettier than ever — was seated with a companion in the secluded nook in which the great papal portrait is enshrined.

"Who was her companion?" asked Winterbourne.

"A little Italian with a bouquet in his button-hole. The girl is delightfully pretty, but I thought I understood from you the other day that she was a young lady *du meilleur monde*."[39]

"So she is!" answered Winterbourne; and having assured himself that his informant had seen Daisy and her companion but five minutes before, he jumped into a cab and went to call on Mrs. Miller. She was at home; but she apologised to him for receiving him in Daisy's absence.

"She's gone out somewhere with Mr. Giovanelli," said Mrs. Miller. "She's always going round with Mr. Giovanelli."

"I have noticed that they are very intimate," Winterbourne observed.

"Oh! it seems as if they couldn't live without each other!" said Mrs. Miller. "Well, he's a real gentleman, anyhow. I keep telling Daisy she's engaged!"

"And what does Daisy say?"

"Oh, she says she isn't engaged. But she might as well be!" this impartial parent resumed. "She goes on as if she was. But I've made Mr. Giovanelli promise to tell me, if *she* doesn't. I should want to write to Mr. Miller about it — shouldn't you?"

Winterbourne replied that he certainly should; and the state of mind of Daisy's mamma struck him as so unprecedented in the annals of parental vigilance that he gave up as utterly irrelevant the attempt to place her upon her guard.

After this Daisy was never at home, and Winterbourne ceased to meet her at the houses of their common acquaintance, because, as he perceived, these shrewd people had quite made up their minds that she was going too far. They ceased to invite her, and they intimated that they desired to express to observant Europeans the great truth that, though Miss Daisy Miller was a young American lady, her behaviour was not representative — was regarded by her compatriots as abnormal. Winterbourne wondered how she felt about all the cold shoulders that were turned towards her, and sometimes it annoyed him to suspect that she did not feel at all. He said to himself that she was too light and childish, too uncultivated and unreasoning, too provincial,

---

[39]French: of good society.

to have reflected upon her ostracism or even to have perceived it. Then at other moments he believed that she carried about in her elegant and irresponsible little organism a defiant, passionate, perfectly observant consciousness of the impression she produced. He asked himself whether Daisy's defiance came from the consciousness of innocence or from her being, essentially, a young person of the reckless class. It must be admitted that holding oneself to a belief in Daisy's "innocence" came to seem to Winterbourne more and more a matter of fine-spun gallantry. As I have already had occasion to relate, he was angry at finding himself reduced to chopping logic about this young lady; he was vexed at his want of instinctive certitude as to how far her eccentricities were generic, national, and how far they were personal. From either view of them he had somehow missed her, and now it was too late. She was "carried away" by Mr. Giovanelli.

A few days after his brief interview with her mother, he encountered her in that beautiful abode of flowering desolation known as the Palace of the Caesars. The early Roman spring had filled the air with bloom and perfume, and the rugged surface of the Palatine was muffled with tender verdure. Daisy was strolling along the top of one of those great mounds of ruin that are embanked with mossy marble and paved with monumental inscriptions. It seemed to him that Rome had never been so lovely as just then. He stood looking off at the enchanting harmony of line and colour that remotely encircles the city, inhaling the softly humid odours and feeling the freshness of the year and the antiquity of the place reaffirm themselves in mysterious interfusion. It seemed to him also that Daisy had never looked so pretty; but this had been an observation of his whenever he met her. Giovanelli was at her side, and Giovanelli, too, wore an aspect of even unwonted brilliancy.

"Well," said Daisy, "I should think you would be lonesome!"

"Lonesome?" asked Winterbourne.

"You are always going round by yourself. Can't you get any one to walk with you?"

"I am not so fortunate," said Winterbourne, "as your companion."

Giovanelli, from the first, had treated Winterbourne with distinguished politeness; he listened with a deferential air to his remarks; he laughed, punctiliously, at his pleasantries; he seemed disposed to testify to his belief that Winterbourne was a superior young man. He carried himself in no degree like a jealous wooer; he had obviously a great deal of tact; he had no objection to your expecting a little humility of him. It even seemed to Winterbourne at times that Giovanelli would find a certain mental relief in being able to have a private understanding with him—to say to him, as an intelligent man, that, bless you, *he* knew how extraordinary was this young lady, and didn't flatter himself with delusive—or at least *too* delusive—hopes of matrimony and dollars. On this occasion he strolled away from his companion to pluck a sprig of almond blossom, which he carefully arranged in his button-hole.

"I know why you say that," said Daisy, watching Giovanelli. "Because you think I go round too much with *him*!" And she nodded at her attendant.

"Every one thinks so—if you care to know," said Winterbourne.

"Of course I care to know!" Daisy exclaimed seriously. "But I don't believe it. They are only pretending to be shocked. They don't really care a straw what I do. Besides, I don't go round so much."

"I think you will find they do care. They will show it—disagreeably."

Daisy looked at him a moment. "How—disagreeably?"

"Haven't you noticed anything?" Winterbourne asked.

"I have noticed you. But I noticed you were as stiff as an umbrella the first time I saw you."

"You will find I am not so stiff as several others," said Winterbourne, smiling.

"How shall I find it?"

"By going to see the others."

"What will they do to me?"

"They will give you the cold shoulder. Do you know what that means?"

Daisy was looking at him intently; she began to colour. "Do you mean as Mrs. Walker did the other night?"

"Exactly!" said Winterbourne.

She looked away at Giovanelli, who was decorating himself with his almond-blossom. Then looking back at Winterbourne—"I shouldn't think you would let people be so unkind!" she said.

"How can I help it?" he asked.

"I should think you would say something."

"I do say something;" and he paused a moment. "I say that your mother tells me that she believes you are engaged."

"Well, she does," said Daisy very simply.

Winterbourne began to laugh. "And does Randolph believe it?" he asked.

"I guess Randolph doesn't believe anything," said Daisy. Randolph's scepticism excited Winterbourne to farther hilarity, and he observed that Giovanelli was coming back to them. Daisy, observing it too, addressed herself again to her countryman. "Since you have mentioned it," she said, "I *am* engaged." . . . Winterbourne looked at her; he had stopped laughing. "You don't believe it!" she added.

He was silent a moment; and then, "Yes, I believe it!" he said.

"Oh, no, you don't," she answered. "Well, then—I am not!"

The young girl and her cicerone[40] were on their way to the gate of the enclosure, so that Winterbourne, who had but lately entered, presently took leave of them. A week afterwards he went to dine at a beautiful villa on the

---

[40]Italian: a guide who conducts sightseers, as in a museum.

Cælian Hill, and, on arriving, dismissed his hired vehicle. The evening was charming, and he promised himself the satisfaction of walking home beneath the Arch of Constantine and past the vaguely-lighted monuments of the Forum.[41] There was a waning moon in the sky, and her radiance was not brilliant, but she was veiled in a thin cloud-curtain which seemed to diffuse and equalise it. When, on his return from the villa (it was eleven o'clock), Winterbourne approached the dusky circle of the Colosseum, it occurred to him, as a lover of the picturesque, that the interior, in the pale moonshine, would be well worth a glance. He turned aside and walked to one of the empty arches, near which, as he observed, an open carriage—one of the little Roman street-cabs—was stationed. Then he passed in among the cavernous shadows of the great structure, and emerged upon the clear and silent arena. The place had never seemed to him more impressive. One-half of the gigantic circus was in deep shade; the other was sleeping in the luminous dusk. As he stood there he began to murmur Byron's famous lines, out of "Manfred;"[42] but before he had finished his quotation he remembered that if nocturnal meditations in the Colosseum are recommended by the poets, they are deprecated by the doctors. The historic atmosphere was there, certainly; but the historic atmosphere, scientifically considered, was no better than a villainous miasma. Winterbourne walked to the middle of the arena, to take a more general glance, intending thereafter to make a hasty retreat. The great cross in the centre was covered with shadow; it was only as he drew near it that he made it out distinctly. Then he saw that two persons were stationed upon the low steps which formed its base. One of these was a woman, seated; her companion was standing in front of her.

Presently the sound of the woman's voice came to him distinctly in the warm night-air. "Well, he looks at us as one of the old lions or tigers may have looked at the Christian martyrs!" These were the words he heard, in the familiar accent of Miss Daisy Miller.

"Let us hope he is not very hungry," responded the ingenious Giovanelli. "He will have to take me first; you will serve for dessert!"

Winterbourne stopped, with a sort of horror; and, it must be added, with a sort of relief. It was as if a sudden illumination had been flashed upon the ambiguity of Daisy's behaviour and the riddle had become easy to read. She was a young lady whom a gentleman need no longer be at pains to respect. He stood there looking at her—looking at her companion, and not reflecting that though he saw them vaguely, he himself must have been more brightly

---

[41]The center of ancient Rome, site of the senate and several temples, near the arch celebrating a military victory of the Emperor Constantine (306–377); the Colosseum is the ancient Roman amphitheater where gladiators fought and Christians were martyred.

[42]1817 poetic drama by Lord Byron: ". . . upon such a night / I stood within the Coliseum's wall, / Midst the chief relics of almighty Rome." *Manfred* III, iv, 9–11.

visible. He felt angry with himself that he had bothered so much about the right way of regarding Miss Daisy Miller. Then, as he was going to advance again, he checked himself; not from the fear that he was doing her injustice, but from a sense of the danger of appearing unbecomingly exhilarated by this sudden revulsion from cautious criticism. He turned away towards the entrance of the place; but as he did so he heard Daisy speak again.

"Why, it was Mr. Winterbourne! He saw me—and he cuts me!"

What a clever little reprobate she was, and how smartly she played an injured innocence! But he wouldn't cut her. Winterbourne came forward again, and went towards the great cross. Daisy had got up; Giovanelli lifted his hat. Winterbourne had now begun to think simply of the craziness, from a sanitary point of view, of a delicate young girl lounging away the evening in this nest of malaria. What if she *were* a clever little reprobate? that was no reason for her dying of the *perniciosa*.[43] "How long have you been here?" he asked, almost brutally.

Daisy, lovely in the flattering moonlight, looked at him a moment. Then—"All the evening," she answered gently.... "I never saw anything so pretty."

"I am afraid," said Winterbourne, "that you will not think Roman fever very pretty. This is the way people catch it. I wonder," he added, turning to Giovanelli, "that you, a native Roman, should countenance such a terrible indiscretion."

"Ah," said the handsome native, "for myself, I am not afraid."

"Neither am I—for you! I am speaking for this young lady."

Giovanelli lifted his well-shaped eyebrows and showed his brilliant teeth. But he took Winterbourne's rebuke with docility. "I told the Signorina[44] it was a grave indiscretion; but when was the Signorina ever prudent?"

"I never was sick, and I don't mean to be!" the Signorina declared. "I don't look like much, but I'm healthy! I was bound to see the Colosseum by moonlight; I shouldn't have wanted to go home without that; and we have had the most beautiful time, haven't we, Mr. Giovanelli? If there has been any danger, Eugenio can give me some pills. He has got some splendid pills."

"I should advise you," said Winterbourne, "to drive home as fast as possible and take one!"

"What you say is very wise," Giovanelli rejoined. "I will go and make sure the carriage is at hand." And he went forward rapidly.

Daisy followed with Winterbourne. He kept looking at her; she seemed not in the least embarrassed. Winterbourne said nothing; Daisy chattered about the beauty of the place. "Well, I *have* seen the Colosseum by moonlight!" she

---

[43]Italian: something dangerous; in this case, malaria.

[44]Italian: unmarried young woman, young lady.

exclaimed. "That's one good thing." Then, noticing Winterbourne's silence, she asked him why he didn't speak. He made no answer; he only began to laugh. They passed under one of the dark archways; Giovanelli was in front with the carriage. Here Daisy stopped a moment, looking at the young American. "*Did* you believe I was engaged the other day?" she asked.

"It doesn't matter what I believed the other day," said Winterbourne, still laughing.

"Well, what do you believe now?"

"I believe that it makes very little difference whether you are engaged or not!"

He felt the young girl's pretty eyes fixed upon him through the thick gloom of the archway; she was apparently going to answer. But Giovanelli hurried her forward. "Quick, quick," he said; "if we get in by midnight we are quite safe."

Daisy took her seat in the carriage, and the fortunate Italian placed himself beside her. "Don't forget Eugenio's pills!" said Winterbourne, as he lifted his hat.

"I don't care," said Daisy, in a little strange tone, "whether I have Roman fever or not!" Upon this the cab-driver cracked his whip, and they rolled away over the desultory patches of the antique pavement.

Winterbourne—to do him justice, as it were—mentioned to no one that he had encountered Miss Miller, at midnight, in the Colosseum with a gentleman; but nevertheless, a couple of days later, the fact of her having been there under these circumstances was known to every member of the little American circle, and commented accordingly. Winterbourne reflected that they had of course known it at the hotel, and that, after Daisy's return, there had been an exchange of jokes between the porter and the cab-driver. But the young man was conscious at the same moment that it had ceased to be a matter of serious regret to him that the little American flirt should be "talked about" by low-minded menials. These people, a day or two later, had serious information to give: the little American flirt was alarmingly ill. Winterbourne, when the rumour came to him, immediately went to the hotel for more news. He found that two or three charitable friends had preceded him, and that they were being entertained in Mrs. Miller's salon by Randolph.

"It's going round at night," said Randolph—"that's what made her sick. She's always going round at night. I shouldn't think she'd want to—it's so plaguey dark. You can't see anything here at night, except when there's a moon. In America there's always a moon!" Mrs. Miller was invisible; she was now, at least, giving her daughter the advantage of her society. It was evident that Daisy was dangerously ill.

Winterbourne went often to ask for news of her, and once he saw Mrs. Miller, who, though deeply alarmed, was—rather to his surprise—perfectly composed, and, as it appeared, a most efficient and judicious nurse. She talked a good deal about Dr. Davis, but Winterbourne paid her the compliment of saying to himself that she was not, after all, such a monstrous goose. "Daisy spoke of you the other day," she said to him. "Half the time she doesn't know what she's saying, but that time I think she did. She gave me a message; she told me to tell you. She told me to tell you that she never was engaged to that handsome Italian. I am sure I am very glad; Mr. Giovanelli hasn't been near us since she was taken ill. I thought he was so much of a gentleman; but I don't call that very polite! A lady told me that he was afraid I was angry with him for taking Daisy round at night. Well, so I am; but I suppose he knows I'm a lady. I would scorn to scold him. Any way, she says she's not engaged. I don't know why she wanted you to know; but she said to me three times—'Mind you tell Mr. Winterbourne.' And then she told me to ask if you remembered the time you went to that castle, in Switzerland. But I said I wouldn't give any such messages as that. Only, if she is not engaged, I'm sure I'm glad to know it."

But, as Winterbourne had said, it mattered very little. A week after this the poor girl died; it had been a terrible case of the fever. Daisy's grave was in the little Protestant cemetery, in an angle of the wall of imperial Rome, beneath the cypresses and the thick spring-flowers. Winterbourne stood there beside it, with a number of other mourners; a number larger than the scandal excited by the young lady's career would have led you to expect. Near him stood Giovanelli, who came nearer still before Winterbourne turned away. Giovanelli was very pale; on this occasion he had no flower in his button-hole; he seemed to wish to say something. At last he said, "She was the most beautiful young lady I ever saw, and the most amiable." And then he added in a moment, "And she was the most innocent."

Winterbourne looked at him, and presently repeated his words, "And the most innocent?"

"The most innocent!"

Winterbourne felt sore and angry. "Why the devil," he asked, "did you take her to that fatal place?"

Mr. Giovanelli's urbanity was apparently imperturbable. He looked on the ground a moment, and then he said, "For myself, I had no fear; and she wanted to go."

"That was no reason!" Winterbourne declared.

The subtle Roman again dropped his eyes. "If she had lived, I should have got nothing. She would never have married me, I am sure."

"She would never have married you?"

"For a moment I hoped so. But no. I am sure."

Winterbourne listened to him; he stood staring at the raw protuberance among the April daisies. When he turned away again Mr. Giovanelli, with his light slow step, had retired.

Winterbourne almost immediately left Rome; but the following summer he again met his aunt, Mrs. Costello, at Vevey. Mrs. Costello was fond of

Vevey. In the interval Winterbourne had often thought of Daisy Miller and her mystifying manners. One day he spoke of her to his aunt—said it was on his conscience that he had done her injustice.

"I am sure I don't know," said Mrs. Costello. "How did your injustice affect her?"

"She sent me a message before her death which I didn't understand at the time. But I have understood it since. She would have appreciated one's esteem."

"Is that a modest way," asked Mrs. Costello, "of saying that she would have reciprocated one's affection?"

Winterbourne offered no answer to this question; but he presently said, "You were right in that remark that you made last summer. I was booked to make a mistake. I have lived too long in foreign parts."

Nevertheless, he went back to live at Geneva, whence there continue to come the most contradictory accounts of his motives of sojourn: a report that he is "studying" hard—an intimation that he is much interested in a very clever foreign lady.

[1878]

SARAH ORNE JEWETT
[1849–1909]

In 1908, Sarah Orne Jewett wrote to her young admirer Willa Cather, advising her to write from her "own quiet center of life." This is certainly advice Jewett herself followed. The empathetic and realistically detailed stories, sketches, and articles she wrote about the New England countryside and its people have a firm basis in her own experience and memories of such places and lives. Born in South Berwick, Maine, in 1849, Jewett frequently accompanied her father on his medical rounds as a practicing obstetrician. "Write about things just as they are," her father would say, and Jewett both honed her descriptive skills in talking to him and learned from his longer memory of the region. Also a professor of medicine at Bowdoin College, her father encouraged the young Sarah to read extensively in the family library—horticulture, theology, history, and philosophy, as well as poetry and fiction. Jewett's childhood bouts of rheumatoid arthritis further contributed to her early education, insofar as the treatment was to send her outdoors on long walks through the countryside. By the end of the Civil War, however, the rural Maine of her childhood had been largely transformed: textile mills and a cannery replaced the earlier agricultural and shipbuilding economic base for the region, and with the factories came French-Canadian and Irish immigration. In her youth, Jewett read Harriet Beecher Stowe's novel of the Maine seacoast, Pearl of Orr's Island *(1862). Together, Stowe's text and the changing conditions of her environment stimulated her own interest in writing about Maine. Jewett published her first poems and stories in 1863, when she was fourteen; later, she became famous for memorializing with acute sensitivity and realism a fast-disappearing world.*

By the age of twenty-two Jewett had developed her mature subject and style—detailed, freshly original, unsentimental reflections on the strengths of the human spirit in a changing social and rugged natural landscape. Focusing especially on the lives of older women living alone or among other women—as large numbers of women did, following the war—Jewett wrote in a regional dialect, describing particular towns or seacoasts to explore problems faced by people throughout the nation. Regarded as a leader of the "local color" or regional writing movement, Jewett was never limited in her ideas by the narrowness of her geographical focus. Without great drama and often even without a strong plot, her stories present the lives of women and men caring for each other, enduring their own losses, and finding humor and pleasure in straitened circumstances. As she emphasizes through repeated comparison, these people manifest courage, endurance, and ethical resolution resembling those of Greek drama or Biblical tales—qualities Jewett depicted without agrandizement in the impoverished settings of rural New England. While primarily concerned with classic character types (sea captains, seamen's widows), she also wrote at length about the response of these "natives" to Irish and other immigrants to the region, and those immigrants' own experiences of the grudging acceptance they found—as in "The Foreigner," where a Catholic Frenchwoman from the West Indies must negotiate a social climate almost as harsh as Maine weather. Critics repeatedly hailed her stories as "fresh," "delicate," "simple," and "true." William Dean Howells wrote of Jewett's "uncommon feeling for talk," *and Henry James praised the "beautiful quantum" of her achievement.*

Jewett's first important publication was the story "Mr. Bruce," in the prestigious Atlantic Monthly. *In 1873, with the encouragement of Howells and the* Atlantic's *editor James Fields, Jewett began developing another story into a series of sketches on Maine, later collected as* Deephaven *(1877). With the publication of* A White Heron and Other Stories *in 1886, her reputation was firmly established. By that time, Jewett had written two novels—*A Country Doctor *(1884) and* A Marsh Island *(1885)—and was spending as much, or more, of her time in Boston as in Maine. Most of this time was spent living with Annie Fields, hostess of one of Boston's most prominent literary salons and collaborator with her husband James in editing the* Atlantic Monthly *until his death in 1881. Shortly thereafter, Annie Fields and Jewett developed an intense and intimate relationship that would end only with Jewett's death in 1909. The two women moved between Fields's houses in Boston and Manchester-by-the-Sea and Jewett's home in South Berwick, traveled together in Europe, and encouraged each others' literary ambitions and talents. By the mid-1880s Jewett's friends included several of Boston's most influential writers—Howells, Henry Wadsworth Longfellow, James Russell Lowell, John Greenleaf Whittier—as well as a number of female artists and writers, including Sarah Wyman Whitman, Cecilia Thaxter, and Julia Ward Howe. The utter normalcy with which this society regarded the intimacy of Jewett and Fields, and other women choosing to live their lives together, reveals itself in the term "Boston Marriage," an informal arrangement relatively common in New England during the period, especially for feminist, educated women, financially independent of men, like Jewett and Fields.*

Jewett's most famous and best work is The Country of the Pointed Firs *(1896), a series of sketches about a small seacoast town in Maine unified by the perspective of a visiting older woman who spends her summer there. This series has the impact of a novel, developing both ongoing thematic concerns and depth of character through the narrator's meditations and exquisite eye for detail. Here, as in her best stories, Jewett uses the specificity of local idiom, natural setting, and almost comic regional idiosyncrasy of profession and character to ground her larger concerns with the ravages of social metamorphosis and human pettiness or passions, and the moral steadfastness and good-humored endurance of individual survivors. These qualities are also present in other of her collections of sketches and stories:* The King of Folly Island *(1888),* A Native of Winby *(1893),* The Life of Nancy *(1893), and* The Queen's Twin *(1899). By the time of her death in 1909, Jewett had published more than twenty volumes, including sketches, short stories, poems, children's books, and novels. Never seeing her characters as doomed by the harsh conditions depicted in her fiction, Jewett combined the descriptive toughness of naturalism with the sympathies of memoir or romance. While her work achieved neither bestseller status nor the peaks of highest critical acclaim during her lifetime, it has continued to be admired for its fineness and, with the increased attention of feminist criticism to narrative modes eschewing the adventurous, action-packed, or suspenseful, has come into new prominence in recent decades.*

For Further Reading

Primary Works

Deephaven, 1877; *Old Friends and New,* 1879; *Country By-Ways,* 1881; *A Country Doctor,* 1884; *A Marsh Island,* 1885; *The King of Folly Island, and Other People,* 1888; *Betty Leicester,* 1890; *A Native of Winby, and Other Tales,* 1893; *The Life of Nancy,* 1895; *The Country of the Pointed Firs,* 1896; *The Queen's Twin, and Other Stories,* 1899; *Stories and Tales,* 7 vols., 1910; Annie Fields, ed., *Letters of Sarah Orne Jewett,* 1911; Richard Cary, ed., *Sarah Orne Jewett Letters,* 1956, revised 1967; Michael Davitt Bell, ed., *Novels and Stories,* 1994.

Secondary Works

Gwen L. Nagel and James Nagel, *Sarah Orne Jewett: A Reference Guide,*1978; Josephine Donovan, *Sarah Orne Jewett,* 1973; Gwen Nagel, ed., *Critical Essays on Sarah Orne Jewett,* 1984; Louis A. Renzer, *"A White Heron" and the Question of Minor Literature,* 1984; Sarah Way Sherman, *Sarah Orne Jewett: An American Persephone,* 1989; M. Mobley, *Folk Roots and Mythic Wings in Sarah Orne Jewett and Toni Morrison,* 1991; Margaret Roman, *Sarah Orne Jewett: Reconstructing Gender,* 1992; June Howard, ed., *New Essays on "The Country of the Pointed Firs,"* 1994; P. Blanchard, *Sarah Orne Jewett, Her World and Her Work,* 1994; Karen L. Kilcup and Thomas S. Edwards, eds., *Jewett and her Contemporaries: Reshaping the Canon,* 1999.

A White Heron[*]

SARAH ORNE JEWETT

I

The woods were already filled with shadows one June evening, just before eight o'clock, though a bright sunset still glimmered faintly among the trunks of the trees. A little girl was driving home her cow, a plodding, dilatory, provoking creature in her behavior, but a valued companion for all that. They were going away from whatever light there was, and striking deep into the woods, but their feet were familiar with the path, and it was no matter whether their eyes could see it or not.

There was hardly a night the summer through when the old cow could be found waiting at the pasture bars; on the contrary, it was her greatest pleasure to hide herself away among the huckleberry bushes, and though she wore a loud bell she had made the discovery that if one stood perfectly still it would not ring. So Sylvia had to hunt for her until she found her, and call Co'! Co'! with never an answering Moo, until her childish patience was quite spent. If the creature had not given good milk and plenty of it, the case would have seemed very different to her owners. Besides, Sylvia had all the time there was, and very little use to make of it. Sometimes in pleasant weather it was a consolation to look upon the cow's pranks as an intelligent attempt to play hide and seek, and as the child had no playmates she lent herself to this amusement with a good deal of zest. Though this chase had been so long that the wary animal herself had given an unusual signal of her whereabouts, Sylvia had only laughed when she came upon Mistress Moolly at the swampside, and urged her affectionately homeward with a twig of birch leaves. The old cow was not inclined to wander farther, she even turned in the right direction for once as they left the pasture, and stepped along the road at a good pace. She was quite ready to be milked now, and seldom stopped to browse. Sylvia wondered what her grandmother would say because they were so late. It was a great while since she had left home at half-past five o'clock, but everybody knew the difficulty of making this errand a short one.

---

[*]First published in *A White Heron and Other Stories*, 1886, the source of this text.

Mrs. Tilley had chased the hornéd torment too many summer evenings her-self to blame any one else for lingering, and was only thankful as she waited that she had Sylvia, nowadays, to give such valuable assistance. The good woman suspected that Sylvia loitered occasionally on her own account; there never was such a child for straying about out-of-doors since the world was made! Everybody said that it was a good change for a little maid who had tried to grow for eight years in a crowded manufacturing town, but, as for Sylvia herself, it seemed as if she never had been alive at all before she came to live at the farm. She thought often with wistful compassion of a wretched geranium that belonged to a town neighbor.

"'Afraid of folks,'" old Mrs. Tilley said to herself, with a smile, after she had made the unlikely choice of Sylvia from her daughter's houseful of chil-dren, and was returning to the farm. "'Afraid of folks,' they said! I guess she won't be troubled no great with 'em up to the old place!" When they reached the door of the lonely house and stopped to unlock it, and the cat came to purr loudly, and rub against them, a deserted pussy, indeed, but fat with young robins, Sylvia whispered that this was a beautiful place to live in, and she never should wish to go home.

The companions followed the shady woodroad, the cow taking slow steps and the child very fast ones. The cow stopped long at the brook to drink, as if the pasture were not half a swamp, and Sylvia stood still and waited, letting her bare feet cool themselves in the shoal water, while the great twilight moths struck softly against her. She waded on through the brook as the cow moved away, and listened to the thrushes with a heart that beat fast with pleasure. There was a stirring in the great boughs overhead. They were full of little birds and beasts that seemed to be wide awake, and going about their world, or else saying good-night to each other in sleepy twitters. Sylvia her-self felt sleepy as she walked along. However, it was not much farther to the house, and the air was soft and sweet. She was not often in the woods so late as this, and it made her feel as if she were a part of the gray shadows and the moving leaves. She was just thinking how long it seemed since she first came to the farm a year ago, and wondering if everything went on in the noisy town just the same as when she was there; the thought of the great red-faced boy who used to chase and frighten her made her hurry along the path to escape from the shadow of the trees.

Suddenly this little woods-girl is horror-stricken to hear a clear whistle not very far away. Not a bird's-whistle, which would have a sort of friendliness, but a boy's whistle, determined, and somewhat aggressive. Sylvia left the cow to whatever sad fate might await her, and stepped discreetly aside into the bushes, but she was just too late. The enemy had discovered her, and called out in a very cheerful and persuasive tone, "Halloa, little girl, how far is it to the road?" and trembling Sylvia answered almost inaudibly, "A good ways."

She did not dare to look boldly at the tall young man, who carried a gun over his shoulder, but she came out of her bush and again followed the cow, while he walked alongside.

"I have been hunting for some birds," the stranger said kindly, "and I have lost my way, and need a friend very much. Don't be afraid," he added gallantly. "Speak up and tell me what your name is, and whether you think I can spend the night at your house, and go out gunning early in the morning."

Sylvia was more alarmed than before. Would not her grandmother consider her much to blame? But who could have foreseen such an accident as this? It did not seem to be her fault, and she hung her head as if the stem of it were broken, but managed to answer "Sylvy," with much effort when her companion again asked her name.

Mrs. Tilley was standing in the doorway when the trio came into view. The cow gave a loud moo by way of explanation.

"Yes, you'd better speak up for yourself, you old trial! Where'd she tucked herself away this time, Sylvy?" But Sylvia kept an awed silence; she knew by instinct that her grandmother did not comprehend the gravity of the situation. She must be mistaking the stranger for one of the farmer-lads of the region.

The young man stood his gun beside the door, and dropped a lumpy game-bag beside it; then he bade Mrs. Tilley good-evening, and repeated his wayfarer's story, and asked if he could have a night's lodging.

"Put me anywhere you like," he said. "I must be off early in the morning, before day; but I am very hungry, indeed. You can give me some milk at any rate, that's plain."

"Dear sakes, yes," responded the hostess, whose long slumbering hospitality seemed to be easily awakened. "You might fare better if you went out to the main road a mile or so, but you're welcome to what we've got. I'll milk right off, and you make yourself at home. You can sleep on husks or feathers," she proffered graciously. "I raised them all myself. There's good pasturing for geese just below here towards the ma'sh. Now step round and set a plate for the gentleman, Sylvy!" And Sylvia promptly stepped. She was glad to have something to do, and she was hungry herself.

It was a surprise to find so clean and comfortable a little dwelling in this New England wilderness. The young man had known the horrors of its most primitive housekeeping, and the dreary squalor of that level of society which does not rebel at the companionship of hens. This was the best thrift of an old-fashioned farmstead, though on such a small scale that it seemed like a hermitage. He listened eagerly to the old woman's quaint talk, he watched Sylvia's pale face and shining gray eyes with ever growing enthusiasm, and insisted that this was the best supper he had eaten for a month, and afterward the new-made friends sat down in the door-way together while the moon came up.

431

Soon it would be berry-time, and Sylvia was a great help at picking. The cow was a good milker, though a plaguy thing to keep track of, the hostess gossiped frankly, adding presently that she had buried four children, so Sylvia's mother, and a son (who might be dead) in California were all the children she had left. "Dan, my boy, was a great hand to go gunning," she explained sadly. "I never wanted for pa'tridges or gray squer'ls while he was to home. He's been a great wand'rer, I expect, and he's no hand to write letters. There, I don't blame him, I'd ha' seen the world myself if it had been so I could."

"Sylvy takes after him," the grandmother continued affectionately, after a minute's pause. "There ain't a foot o' ground she don't know her way over, and the wild creaturs counts her one o' themselves. Squer'ls she'll tame to come an' feed right out o' her hands, and all sorts o' birds. Last winter she got the jaybirds to bangeing[1] here, and I believe she'd 'a' scanted herself of her own meals to have plenty to throw out amongst 'em, if I had n't kep' watch. Anything but crows, I tell her, I'm willin' to help support—though Dan he had a tamed one o' them that did seem to have reason same as folks. It was round here a good spell after he went away. Dan an' his father they did n't hitch,—but he never held up his head ag'in after Dan had dared him an' gone off."

The guest did not notice this hint of family sorrows in his eager interest in something else.

"So Sylvy knows all about birds, does she?" he exclaimed, as he looked round at the little girl who sat, very demure but increasingly sleepy, in the moonlight. "I am making a collection of birds myself. I have been at it ever since I was a boy." (Mrs. Tilley smiled.) "There are two or three very rare ones I have been hunting for these five years. I mean to get them on my own ground if they can be found."

"Do you cage 'em up?" asked Mrs. Tilley doubtfully, in response to this enthusiastic announcement.

"Oh no, they're stuffed and preserved, dozens and dozens of them," said the ornithologist, "and I have shot or snared every one myself. I caught a glimpse of a white heron a few miles from here on Saturday, and I have followed it in this direction. They have never been found in this district at all. The little white heron, it is," and he turned again to look at Sylvia with the hope of discovering that the rare bird was one of her acquaintances.

But Sylvia was watching a hop-toad in the narrow footpath.

"You would know the heron if you saw it," the stranger continued eagerly. "A queer tall white bird with soft feathers and long thin legs. And it would have a nest perhaps in the top of a high tree, made of sticks, something like a hawk's nest."

---

[1]Gathering, hanging around.

Sylvia's heart gave a wild beat; she knew that strange white bird, and had once stolen softly near where it stood in some bright green swamp grass, away over at the other side of the woods. There was an open place where the sunshine always seemed strangely yellow and hot, where tall, nodding rushes grew, and her grandmother had warned her that she might sink in the soft black mud underneath and never be heard of more. Not far beyond were the salt marshes just this side the sea itself, which Sylvia wondered and dreamed much about, but never had seen, whose great voice could sometimes be heard above the noise of the woods on stormy nights.

"I can't think of anything I should like so much as to find that heron's nest," the handsome stranger was saying. "I would give ten dollars to anybody who could show it to me," he added desperately, "and I mean to spend my whole vacation hunting for it if need be. Perhaps it was only migrating, or had been chased out of its own region by some bird of prey."

Mrs. Tilley gave amazed attention to all this, but Sylvia still watched the toad, not divining, as she might have done at some calmer time, that the creature wished to get to its hole under the door-step, and was much hindered by the unusual spectators at that hour of the evening. No amount of thought, that night, could decide how many wished-for treasures the ten dollars, so lightly spoken of, would buy.

The next day the young sportsman hovered about the woods, and Sylvia kept him company, having lost her first fear of the friendly lad, who proved to be most kind and sympathetic. He told her many things about the birds and what they knew and where they lived and what they did with themselves. And he gave her a jackknife, which she thought as great a treasure as if she were a desert-islander. All day long he did not once make her troubled or afraid except when he brought down some unsuspecting singing creature from its bough. Sylvia would have liked him vastly better without his gun; she could not understand why he killed the very birds he seemed to like so much. But as the day waned, Sylvia still watched the young man with loving admiration. She had never seen anybody so charming and delightful; the woman's heart, asleep in the child, was vaguely thrilled by a dream of love. Some premonition of that great power stirred and swayed these young creatures who traversed the solemn woodlands with soft-footed silent care. They stopped to listen to a bird's song; they pressed forward again eagerly, parting the branches—speaking to each other rarely and in whispers; the young man going first and Sylvia following, fascinated, a few steps behind, with her gray eyes dark with excitement.

She grieved because the longed-for white heron was elusive, but she did not lead the guest, she only followed, and there was no such thing as speaking first. The sound of her own unquestioned voice would have terrified her—it was hard enough to answer yes or no when there was need of that. At last evening began to fall, and they drove the cow home together, and Sylvia smiled with pleasure when they came to the place where she heard the whistle and was afraid only the night before.

II

Half a mile from home, at the farther edge of the woods, where the land was highest, a great pine-tree stood, the last of its generation. Whether it was left for a boundary mark, or for what reason, no one could say; the wood-choppers who had felled its mates were dead and gone long ago, and a whole forest of sturdy trees, pines and oaks and maples, had grown again. But the stately head of this old pine towered above them all and made a landmark for sea and shore miles and miles away. Sylvia knew it well. She had always believed that whoever climbed to the top of it could see the ocean; and the little girl had often laid her hand on the great rough trunk and looked up wistfully at those dark boughs that the wind always stirred, no matter how hot and still the air might be below. Now she thought of the tree with a new excitement, for why, if one climbed it at break of day could not one see all the world, and easily discover from whence the white heron flew, and mark the place, and find the hidden nest?

What a spirit of adventure, what wild ambition! What fancied triumph and delight and glory for the later morning when she could make known the secret! It was almost too real and too great for the childish heart to bear.

All night the door of the little house stood open and the whippoorwills came and sang upon the very step. The young sportsman and his old hostess were sound asleep, but Sylvia's great design kept her broad awake and watching. She forgot to think of sleep. The short summer night seemed as long as the winter darkness, and at last when the whippoorwills ceased, and she was afraid the morning would after all come too soon, she stole out of the house and followed the pasture path through the woods, hastening toward the open ground beyond, listening with a sense of comfort and companionship to the drowsy twitter of a half-awakened bird, whose perch she had jarred in passing. Alas, if the great wave of human interest which flooded for the first time this dull little life should sweep away the satisfactions of an existence heart to heart with nature and the dumb life of the forest!

There was the huge tree asleep yet in the paling moonlight, and small and silly Sylvia began with utmost bravery to mount to the top of it, with tingling, eager blood coursing the channels of her whole frame, with her bare feet and fingers, that pinched and held like bird's claws to the monstrous ladder reaching up, up, almost to the sky itself. First she must mount the white oak tree that grew alongside, where she was almost lost among the dark branches and the green leaves heavy and wet with dew; a bird fluttered off its nest, and a red squirrel ran to and fro and scolded pettishly at the harmless housebreaker. Sylvia felt her way easily. She had often climbed there, and knew that higher still one of the oak's upper branches chafed against the pine trunk, just where its lower boughs were set close together. There, when she made the dangerous pass from one tree to the other, the great enterprise would really begin.

She crept out along the swaying oak limb at last, and took the daring step across into the old pine-tree. The way was harder than she thought; she must reach far and hold fast, the sharp dry twigs caught and held her and scratched her like angry talons, the pitch made her thin little fingers clumsy and stiff as she went round and round the tree's great stem, higher and higher upward. The sparrows and robins in the woods below were beginning to wake and twitter to the dawn, yet it seemed much lighter there aloft in the pine-tree, and the child knew she must hurry if her project were to be of any use.

The tree seemed to lengthen itself out as she went up, and to reach farther and farther upward. It was like a great main-mast to the voyaging earth; it must truly have been amazed that morning through all its ponderous frame as it felt this determined spark of human spirit wending its way from higher branch to branch. Who knows how steadily the least twigs held themselves to advantage this light, weak creature on her way! The old pine must have loved his new dependent. More than all the hawks, and bats, and moths, and even the sweet voiced thrushes, was the brave, beating heart of the solitary gray-eyed child. And the tree stood still and frowned away the winds that June morning while the dawn grew bright in the east.

Sylvia's face was like a pale star, if one had seen it from the ground, when the last thorny bough was past, and she stood trembling and tired but wholly triumphant, high in the treetop. Yes, there was the sea with the dawning sun making a golden dazzle over it, and toward that glorious east flew two hawks with slow-moving pinions. How low they looked in the air from that height when one had only seen them before far up, and dark against the blue sky. Their gray feathers were as soft as moths; they seemed only a little way from the tree, and Sylvia felt as if she too could go flying away among the clouds. Westward, the woodlands and farms reached miles and miles into the distance; here and there were church steeples, and white villages, truly it was a vast and awesome world!

The birds sang louder and louder. At last the sun came up bewilderingly bright. Sylvia could see the white sails of ships out at sea, and the clouds that were purple and rose-colored and yellow at first began to fade away. Where was the white heron's nest in the sea of green branches, and was this wonderful sight and pageant of the world the only reward for having climbed to such a giddy height? Now look down again, Sylvia, where the green marsh is set among the shining birches and dark hemlocks; there where you saw the white heron once you will see him again; look, look! a white spot of him like a single floating feather comes up from the dead hemlock and grows larger, and rises, and comes close at last, and goes by the landmark pine with steady sweep of wing and outstretched slender neck and crested head. And wait! wait! do not move a foot or a finger, little girl, do not send an arrow of light and consciousness from your two eager eyes, for the heron has perched on a pine bough not far beyond yours, and cries back to his mate on the nest and plumes his feathers for the new day!

The child gives a long sigh a minute later when a company of shouting cat-birds comes also to the tree, and vexed by their fluttering and lawlessness the solemn heron goes away. She knows his secret now, the wild, light, slender bird that floats and wavers, and goes back like an arrow presently to his home in the green world beneath. Then Sylvia, well satisfied, makes her perilous way down again, not daring to look far below the branch she stands on, ready to cry sometimes because her fingers ache and her lamed feet slip. Wondering over and over again what the stranger would say to her, and what he would think when she told him how to find his way straight to the heron's nest.

"Sylvy, Sylvy!" called the busy old grandmother again and again, but nobody answered, and the small husk bed was empty and Sylvia had disappeared.

The guest waked from a dream, and remembering his day's pleasure hurried to dress himself that might it sooner begin. He was sure from the way the shy little girl looked once or twice yesterday that she had at least seen the white heron, and now she must really be made to tell. Here she comes now, paler than ever, and her worn old frock is torn and tattered, and smeared with pine pitch. The grandmother and the sportsman stand in the door together and question her, and the splendid moment has come to speak of the dead hemlock-tree by the green marsh.

But Sylvia does not speak after all, though the old grandmother fretfully rebukes her, and the young man's kind, appealing eyes are looking straight in her own. He can make them rich with money; he has promised it, and they are poor now. He is so well worth making happy, and he waits to hear the story she can tell.

No, she must keep silence! What is it that suddenly forbids her and makes her dumb? Has she been nine years growing and now, when the great world for the first time puts out a hand to her, must she thrust it aside for a bird's sake? The murmur of the pine's green branches is in her ears, she remembers how the white heron came flying through the golden air and how they watched the sea and the morning together, and Sylvia cannot speak; she cannot tell the heron's secret and give its life away.

Dear loyalty, that suffered a sharp pang as the guest went away disappointed later in the day, that could have served and followed him and loved him as a dog loves! Many a night Sylvia heard the echo of his whistle haunting the pasture path as she came home with the loitering cow. She forgot even her sorrow at the sharp report of his gun and the sight of thrushes and sparrows dropping silent to the ground, their songs hushed and their pretty feathers stained and wet with blood. Were the birds better friends than their hunter might have been,—who can tell? Whatever treasures were lost to her, woodlands and summer-time, remember! Bring your gifts and graces and tell your secrets to this lonely country child!

[1886]

EDGAR ALLAN POE
[1809–1849]

Edgar Allan Poe has the reputation of being the "bad boy" of early American literature: an alcoholic, drug-addicted cradle-robber who lived wild and died young. Most of this is legend based on slanders created by Poe's enemies and perpetuated by the reader's tendency to confuse a writer with his characters and by the general desire to have "bad boys" among literary heroes. Of course, there is some truth amid the falsity: Poe drank too much and married his thirteen-year-old cousin. But his worst sin was his ability to irritate his peers with his insistence upon intellectual integrity and literary brilliance in them, and in himself.

Poe resists easy classification; he was a literary movement of his own, always rubbing against the establishment despite his own establishment views. He inclined toward idealism yet disdained the New England transcendentalists. He was a poet, (not a moralizer) striving for beauty and "suggestiveness," and yet he was a hoaxer who indulged in gross fantasies. He had no desire to promote a national literature; for him, literature existed beyond nationality. Thus, he rarely indulged in the culture's standard themes of individualism, race, revolution, domesticity, and nature, but pursued deeper problems of the mind, science, creation, and the supernatural.

Born in Boston into a family of minor actors, Poe was orphaned at the age of two but immediately taken under the wing of John and Frances Allan of Richmond, Virginia. Frances doted over Edgar as if he were her own, and John, a merchant of substantial wealth, treated this only child as the heir to his fortune. In 1815, business took the Allans and Edgar to England, where for five formative years, the boy excelled in Latin and French. Back home Edgar continued to read and translate. However, his adolescence was shaped by a troubling relationship to his foster father. John Allan, who never legally adopted Poe, was a parent in every sense of the word: by turns loving and exasperating to his trying ward. As a family man, he was decidedly flawed; he cheated on his wife (producing several illegitimate children) and thereby scarred the teenage boy. Up to the day of Allan's death, Edgar's dealings with his foster father would be a tumultuous history of self-destructive screw-ups and reconciliations, ending sadly with an estrangement between the two that left Edgar without an inheritance.

In 1826, Poe attended the University of Virginia where, apparently, matriculation was his license to gamble and outspend his father's allowance. Gone by the following spring, he joined the U.S. Army under the name Edgar A. Perry and was stationed in Boston where he published his long poem "Tamerlane," about an ambitious world conqueror who deserts the girl he loves and dies regretting his pursuit of fame and power. Transferred to Charleston and then back to Virginia, Sergeant Major Poe produced a second, more widely received volume of poetry, Al Aaraaf, Tamerlane, and Minor Poems, which includes some of Poe's best works, not only the tough and lengthy title poems but also "Sonnet—To Science," which pairs off the seemingly contradictory worlds of thought and creativity. The more ambitious "Al Aaraaf" is the first (and perhaps best) of several cosmological works (including his last treatise Eureka) that create a celestial world symbolic of human passions and the inherent nothingness of existence.

Three years in the Army disciplined Poe. With renewed support from his father he enrolled at West Point in 1830. Just prior to this, his mother died, freeing John Allan to re-marry one woman despite having just fathered twins with another. Perhaps with this exemplary father figure in mind, Poe began to sabotage his West Point career before it even started. He charmed officers and students, but drinking got him dismissed before the end of the year. In the spring of 1831, he published Poems by Edgar A. Poe. Second Edition, which he dedicated to "the U.S. corps of cadets." Featured in this new volume are poems about creativity and ruin prefaced by the essay "Letter to B—" and including the memorable poem "Israfel"; Poe's paeon to female beauty in "To Helen"; his facetious "Fairy-Land"; and the haunting "The City in the Sea."

Now thoroughly estranged from his father, Poe moved to Baltimore. Living with his aunt, he supported himself, barely, with short comic and gothic fictions published in Philadelphia and Baltimore magazines. By 1833 Poe proposed to include these dozen or so mostly forgettable pieces into "The Tales of the Folio Club." The organizing principle of the collection is that each month a member of the Folio Club—they have ridiculous names such as Convolvulus Gondola and Solomon Seadrift—composes a tale that parodies contemporary writing and writers. Poe never managed to convince a publisher to accept the Folio Club project, and its exact contents is still a matter of conjecture. The best of these tales—"Metzengerstein" and "MS Found in a Bottle"—are gothic tales that play effortlessly and concisely upon the thin line separating the supernatural and bunkum. Others, such as "The Duke de L'Omlette" and "Loss of Breath," take on familiar situations (betting against the devil or losing one's breath) and run them into the ground. Poe's aim was to make his mark in the growing American literary scene through satires on the worst of European sensationalism, as found in Blackwood's Magazine and the worst of America's scribblers, such as Nathaniel Parker Willis. But his joking in these tales is too obvious to be an effective hoax, the wit too strained to be effective *parody. The more lasting and resilient comic mode of Washington Irving's nostalgic humor, as opposed to his own brand of satiric attack, was what American culture rewarded, and Poe seemed constitutionally unable to engage in such sentiment; he preferred excess and "the ludicrous heightened to the grotesque."*

While publishers were not convinced the public needed a volume of Poe's obscure satire, they recognized his talent, and in 1835 the Southern Literary Messenger, *Richmond's newest journal, hired him as editor. This was the beginning of Poe's career as a man of letters, and as a man given to drink. In that year, his grandmother died, leaving his Aunt Marie and thirteen-year-old cousin Virginia Clemm without income. Rather than have this small remnant of his original family dissolve any further, he quickly married Virginia and brought both aunt and wife under his roof. The marriage to the girl thirteen years his junior lasted until Virginia's death twelve years later but, according to Poe, it was never consummated. Poe drank heavily at this time; however, the need to support a family forced him to moderate, and he produced a prodigious amount of writing for the* Messenger—*reviews (treating his most important critical ideas concerning the emotional intensity and unity of literary works), filler (such as "Autography" and "Pinakidia"), an unfinished play* (Politian), *and more tales, including "Berenice" (concerning one man's experiments in dental extraction), and "Hans Phaal" (a science fiction hoax concerning space travel).*

Under Poe's two-year editorship, the Southern Literary Messenger *grew from a local rag to a national journal, but Poe's drinking got him fired. In 1837 he moved to New York City where he completed his only novel,* The Narrative of Arthur Gordon Pym *(1838). This sea-gothic relates young Pym's survival in a wild storm, entombment in a dark hold, defeat of a mutinous crew, and encounter with a plague-ridden ghost ship. Rescued, his new ship is pulled to the Antarctic, which oddly enough is rather hot and populated by black natives. The novel ends in riot with the apocalyptic emergence of a great white god. The novel's racialized ending contains a political allegory of various meanings. Given Poe's ardent anti-Jacksonian views against "the mob," the conclusion may warn against the extension of freedom to the masses and in particular African-Americans, or more liberally articulate America's precarious racial condition.*

After less than a year in New York, Poe moved to Philadelphia where in 1839 he signed on as editor for Burton's Gentleman's Magazine, *and published (in various journals) some of his best short fiction: "The Fall of the House of Usher," "Ligeia," and "William Wilson." The first two deal with the will to conquer death. In "Usher" the narrator witnesses the actual disintegration of Usher castle as its occupants (the family's last brother and sister about whom there are vague hints of incest) sicken and die, but not before the premature burial of the sister. In "Ligeia" a less reliable narrator tells of the death of his first, transcendently beautiful wife and her apparent return from the dead through the possession of his second, also deceased, wife's body. But here the narrator's intentions may be to hoax the reader into believing his rather convenient transcendental wishes. "William Wilson" is a* doppelgänger *tale in which a young con man is plagued by his double who represents his conscience. In these three works, Poe moved his gothic art from the entertainingly grotesque to the deeply psychological, or what in symbolic terms Poe called "the arabesque," and in 1840 his* Tales of the Grotesque and Arabesque *finally found a willing publisher.*

In 1840 Burton's changed hands and combined with another journal to become Graham's Magazine, *and Poe, whose reputation as an audacious but effective editor had continued to grow, stayed on. In the following years, he invented a new form of fiction, the tale of ratiocination or detective story. In "The Murders in the Rue Morgue" (1841), "The Mystery of Marie Roget" (1843), and "The Purloined Letter" (1845), Poe's sleuth, C. Auguste Dupin, makes a creative art out of his masterful analytical skills. He not only deduces but imagines in creative ways the solution to his mystery, playing upon a sharp sense of human nature. Of course, in writing these "mysteries," Poe had the advantage of knowing the mystery in advance and was always amused by dull readers who praised his skill in uncovering the very mysteries he had invented and purposefully concealed in order to achieve an effect of sublime ratiocination. In short, his detective tales were another form of hoax.*

By 1842 Poe had lifted Graham's *circulation to 20,000. But the self-destructive behavior that would come to characterize his life was about to begin. In this year, Virginia burst a blood vessel while singing, exhibiting the ghastly symptoms of tuberculosis. Moving her and the family into the countryside, Poe began drinking more heavily. He was dismissed from* Graham's *but made ends meet by publishing new tales, including "The Masque of the Red Death" about the insinuation of disease (the plague) into a castle despite the king's attempt to block its entry, no doubt a response to Virginia's condition. Despite this kind of allegorical writing, he made cogent arguments against this overly determined symbolic form, but did so by castigating (in separate reviews) Longfellow's and Hawthorne's use of allegory, thus bringing to a higher pitch his antagonisms against the literary establishment.*

For years, Poe had wanted to head a journal of his own; his first proposal had been for a periodical he wanted to call Penn Magazine *and then* Stylus, *but few wanted to invest in the brainchild of such an erratic personality. However, in 1845 with the instant and remarkable success of his best-known poem "The Raven" (about a student tormented by the memory of his dead lover), Poe's notoriety was tempered with admiration; he was asked to recite the poem and lecture on it. Later that year Wiley and Putnam published* The Raven and Other Poems *as well as a volume of* Tales. *With his career at its highest point, Poe's dream of magazine ownership was finally realized when he joined novelist Charles F. Briggs, in New York City, as co-owner of Broadway Journal; within a year, he was its sole proprietor. In it, he revised and reprinted many of his tales and poems, but he also published in other journals such new works as "The Imp of the Perverse" (about the death wish) and the overlooked classic "The System of Dr. Tarr and Prof. Fether" (about the inability to distinguish madness and sanity). Poe also engaged at this time in a wreckless attack upon Longfellow (charging the popular poet professor with plagiarism) that created a minor sensation in both Boston and New York. The so-called "Longfellow War" increased circulation for the Broadway Journal but only underscored Poe's edgy personality. In one episode, his anger became physical when he got in a brawl with the minor poet Thomas Dunn English. The more substantial James Russell Lowell had admired Poe during these years and had earlier published "The Tell-Tale Heart" (about a murderer's inability to keep his perfect crime a secret), but when Lowell finally met Poe in 1845, he found him drunk, and Poe's relationship with one of the nation's more influential writers ended. Nor did it help his reputation when he began overly praising the poetry of Frances Sargent Osgood, and then dating the woman, even as his wife Virginia was slowly dying at home.*

Poe fell quickly. Although he was creating some of his best tales — "The Black Cat" and "The Cask of Amontillado"—he could not pay his bills, and in 1846 the Broadway Journal folded. A year later, Virginia died at their Fordham (The Bronx) cottage. Devastated, Poe considered suicide but instead wrote "Ulalume," a moving musical poem about a lost love and the separation of body and soul. He also composed a grim fairy tale, "Hop-Frog," about a jester (himself) and a dancer (Virginia) who dress the king and courtiers (critics) as monkeys and burn them to death. Despite his desperate condition or perhaps because of it, Poe's lectures drew large crowds, and out of one of them he composed his last semi-scientific, semi-hoax treatise on being and nothingness, Eureka. Poe's final months were wrenching. He frantically sought female companions while desperately trying to curb his drinking. Death came in the streets. One theory holds that his drinking coupled with undiagnosed diabetes (Type II) led to a series of strokes that left him disoriented and seemingly deranged. He was found dying in a Baltimore gutter, on Election Day, 1849.

Poe grabs young readers (with his lurid tales and rhythmic poems) and holds them into adulthood (with his fierce penetrations into darkness). Poe's enemies, in particular his own literary executor Rufus Griswold, reviled his memory and lied about his life. But the lies only fed his popularity, first among French symbolists and now universally. In his poems, gothic tales, hoaxes, mysteries, and essays, Poe used language to trick his readers into fear and wonder; he used language like music to suggest what can never be spoken directly. In this regard, "bad boy" Poe has survived into the modern age.

For Further Reading

Primary Works

Tamerlane and Other Poems. By a Bostonian (1827); *Al Aaraaf, Tamerlane, and Minor Poems* (1829); *Poems by Edgar A. Poe. Second Edition* (1831); *The Narrative of Arthur Gordon Pym of Nantucket* (1838); *Tales of the Grotesque and Arabesque* (1840); *The Prose Romances of Edgar A. Poe* (1843); *Tales by Edgar A. Poe* (1845); *The Raven and Other Poems* (1845); *Eureka: A Prose Poem by Edgar A. Poe* (1848); *Works of Edgar Allan Poe, with a Memoir by Rufus Wilmot Griswold and Notices of his Life and Genius by N. P. Willis and J. R. Lowell* (ed. Griswold, 1850–1856); *The Complete Works of Edgar Allan Poe* (ed. James A. Harrison, 1902); *The Letters of Edgar Allan Poe* (ed. John Ward Ostrom,1948); *Collected Works of Edgar Allan Poe* (ed. Thomas Ollive Mabbott, 1969–78); *Collected Writings of Edgar Allan Poe* (ed. Burton R. Pollin, 1981 and 1985); *Edgar Allan Poe: Poetry and Tales* (ed. Patrick F. Quinn, 1984); *Edgar Allan Poe: Essays and Reviews* (ed. G. R. Thompson, 1984).

Secondary Works

Arthur Hobson Quinn, *Edgar Allan Poe: A Critical Biography* (1941); Daniel Hoffman, *Poe Poe Poe Poe Poe Poe Poe* (1973); G. R. Thompson, *Poe's Fiction: Romantic Irony in the Gothic Tales* (1973); Esther F. Hyneman, *Edgar Allan Poe: An Annotated Bibliography* (1974); David Ketterer, *The Rationale of Deception in Poe* (1979); *The Poe Log: A Documentary Life* (ed. Dwight Thomas and David K. Jackson, 1987); John Bryant, "Poe's Ape of Unreason: Humor, Ritual, and Culture," in *Nineteenth-Century Literature* 51 (June 1996); *A Companion to Poe Studies* (ed. Eric W. Carlson, 1996); Kenneth Silverman, *Edgar A. Poe: A Biography* (1991).

The Tell-Tale Heart[*]

EDGAR ALLAN POE

True!—nervous—very, very dreadfully nervous I had been and am; but why *will* you say that I am mad? The disease had sharpened my senses— not destroyed—not dulled them. Above all was the sense of hearing acute. I heard all things in the heaven and in the earth. I heard many things in hell. How, then, am I mad? Hearken! and observe how healthily—how calmly I can tell you the whole story.

It is impossible to say how first the idea entered my brain; but once conceived, it haunted me day and night. Object there was none. Passion there was none. I loved the old man. He had never wronged me. He had never given me insult. For his gold I had no desire. I think it was his eye! yes, it was this! He had the eye of a vulture—a pale blue eye, with a film over it. Whenever it fell upon me, my blood ran cold; and so by degrees—very gradually— I made up my mind to take the life of the old man, and thus rid myself of the eye forever.

Now this is the point. You fancy me mad. Madmen know nothing. But you should have seen *me*. You should have seen how wisely I proceeded— with what caution—with what foresight—with what dissimulation[1] I went to work! I was never kinder to the old man than during the whole week before I killed him. And every night, about midnight, I turned the latch of his door and opened it—oh so gently! And then, when I had made an opening sufficient for my head, I put in a dark lantern,[2] all closed, closed, so that no light shone out, and then I thrust in my head. Oh, you would have laughed

---

[*]First published in January 1843 in James Russell Lowell's magazine *The Pioneer*, the tale at that time began with an epigraph, the fourth stanza of Henry Wadsworth Longfellow's "A Psalm of Life," subtitled "What the Heart of the Young Man Said to the Psalmist." The stanza Poe quotes is:

> Art is long and Time is fleeting,
> And our hearts, though stout and brave,
> Still, like muffled drums, are beating
> Funeral marches to the grave.

The text is derived from Poe's *Works* (1850) with annotations on selected revisions.

[1]Deception

[2]A lantern with perforated metal covering to give minimal light.

to see how cunningly I thrust it in! I moved it slowly—very, very slowly, so that I might not disturb the old man's sleep. It took me an hour to place my whole head within the opening so far that I could see him[3] as he lay upon his bed. Ha!—would a madman have been so wise as this? And then, when my head was well in the room, I undid the lantern cautiously—oh, so cautiously—cautiously (for the hinges creaked)—I undid it just so much that a single thin ray fell upon the vulture eye. And this I did for seven long nights—every night just at midnight—but I found the eye always closed; and so it was impossible to do the work; for it was not the old man who vexed me, but his Evil Eye. And every morning, when the day broke, I went boldly into the chamber, and spoke courageously to him, calling him by name in a hearty tone and inquiring how he had passed the night. So you see he would have been a very profound old man, indeed, to suspect that every night, just at twelve, I looked in upon him while he slept.

Upon the eighth night I was more than usually cautious in opening the door. A watch's minute hand moves more quickly than did mine. Never, before that night, had I *felt* the extent of my own powers—of my sagacity. I could scarcely contain my feelings of triumph. To think that there I was, opening the door, little by little, and he not even to dream of my secret deeds or thoughts. I fairly chuckled at the idea; and perhaps he heard me; for he moved on the bed suddenly, as if startled. Now you may think that I drew back—but no. His room was as black as pitch with the thick darkness, (for the shutters were close fastened, through fear of robbers,) and so I knew that he could not see the opening of the door, and I kept pushing it on steadily, steadily.

I had my head in, and was about to open the lantern, when my thumb slipped upon the tin fastening, and the old man sprang up in bed, crying out—"Who's there?"

I kept quite still and said nothing. For a whole hour I did not move a muscle, and in the meantime I did not hear him lie down. He was still sitting up in the bed listening;—just as I have done, night after night, hearkening to the death watches[4] in the wall.

Presently I heard a slight groan, and I knew it was the groan of mortal terror. It was not a groan of pain or of grief—oh, no!—it was the low stifled sound that arises from the bottom of the soul when overcharged with awe. I knew the sound well. Many a night, just at midnight, when all the world slept, it had welled up from my own bosom, deepening, with its dreadful echo, the terrors that distracted me. I say I knew it well. I knew what the old man felt, and pitied him, although I chuckled at heart. I knew that he had

---

[3]In 1843, Poe originally printed here and elsewhere "the old man" for he or him.

[4]Small beetles that live in wood whose chewing makes a ticking sound that supposedly foretells death.

been lying awake ever since the first slight noise, when he had turned in the bed. His fears had been ever since growing upon him. He had been trying to fancy them causeless, but could not. He had been saying to himself—"It is nothing but the wind in the chimney—it is only a mouse crossing the floor," or "it is merely a cricket which has made a single chirp." Yes, he had been trying to comfort himself with these suppositions: but he had found all in vain. *All in vain;* because Death, in approaching him, had stalked with his black shadow before him, and enveloped the victim.[5] And it was the mournful influence of the perceived shadow that caused him to feel—although he neither saw nor heard—to *feel* the presence of my head within the room.

When I had waited a long time, very patiently, without hearing him lie down, I resolved to open a little—a very, very little crevice in the lantern. So I opened it—you cannot imagine how stealthily, stealthily—until, at length, a simple dim ray, like the thread of the spider, shot from out the crevice and fell full upon the vulture eye.

It was open—wide, wide open—and I grew furious as I gazed upon it. I saw it with perfect distinctness—all a dull blue, with a hideous veil over it that chilled the very marrow in my bones; but I could see nothing else of the old man's face or person: for I had directed the ray as if by instinct, precisely upon the damned spot.

And have I not told you that what you mistake for madness is but over acuteness of the senses?—now, I say, there came to my ears a low, dull quick sound, such as a watch makes when enveloped in cotton. I knew *that* sound well, too. It was the beating of the old man's heart. It increased my fury, as the beating of a drum stimulates the soldier into courage.

But even yet I refrained and kept still. I scarcely breathed. I held the lantern motionless. I tried how steadily I could maintain the ray upon the eye. Meantime the hellish tattoo[6] of the heart increased. It grew quicker and quicker, and louder and louder every instant. The old man's terror *must* have been extreme! It grew louder, I say, louder every moment!—do you mark me well? I have told you that I am nervous: so I am. And now at the dead hour of the night, amid the dreadful silence of that old house, so strange a noise as this excited me to uncontrollable terror.[7] Yet, for some minutes longer I refrained and stood still. But the beating grew louder, louder! I thought the heart must burst. And now a new anxiety seized me—the sound would be heard by a neighbour! The old man's hour had come! With a loud yell, I threw open the lantern and leaped into the room. He shrieked once—once only. In an instant I dragged him to the floor, and pulled the heavy bed over

[5]In 1843, Poe originally printed "and the shadow had now reached, and enveloped the victim" for "and enveloped the victim."
[6]Drumbeat
[7]In 1843, Poe printed "wrath" for "terror."

him. I then smiled gaily,[8] to find the deed so far done. But, for many minutes, the heart beat on with a muffled sound. This, however, did not vex me; it would not be heard through the wall. At length it ceased. The old man was dead. I removed the bed and examined the corpse. Yes, he was stone, stone dead. I placed my hand upon the heart and held it there many minutes. There was no pulsation. He was stone dead. His eye would trouble me no more.

If still you think me mad, you will think so no longer when I describe the wise precautions I took for the concealment of the body. The night waned, and I worked hastily, but in silence. First of all I dismembered the corpse. I cut off the head and the arms and the legs.

I then took up three planks from the flooring of the chamber, and deposited all between the scantlings.[9] I then replaced the boards so cleverly, so cunningly, that no human eye—not even *his*—could have detected anything wrong. There was nothing to wash out—no stain of any kind—no blood-spot whatever. I had been too wary for that. A tub had caught all—ha! ha!

When I had made an end of these labors, it was four o'clock—still dark as midnight. As the bell sounded the hour, there came a knocking at the street door. I went down to open it with a light heart,—for what had I *now* to fear? There entered three men, who introduced themselves, with perfect suavity, as officers of the police. A shriek had been heard by a neighbour during the night; suspicion of foul play had been aroused; information had been lodged at the police office, and they (the officers) had been deputed to search the premises.

I smiled,—for *what* had I to fear? I bade the gentlemen welcome. The shriek, I said, was my own in a dream. The old man, I mentioned, was absent in the country. I took my visitors all over the house. I bade them search— search *well*. I led them, at length, to *his* chamber. I showed them his treasures, secure, undisturbed. In the enthusiasm of my confidence, I brought chairs into the room and desired them *here* to rest from their fatigues, while I myself, in the wild audacity of my perfect triumph, placed my own seat upon the very spot beneath which reposed the corpse of the victim.

The officers were satisfied. My *manner* had convinced them. I was singularly at ease. They sat, and while I answered cheerily, they chatted of familiar things. But, ere long, I felt myself getting pale and wished them gone. My head ached, and I fancied a ringing in my ears: but still they sat and still chatted. The ringing became more distinct:—it continued and became more distinct: I talked more freely to get rid of the feeling: but it continued and gained definiteness—until, at length, I found that the noise was *not* within my ears.

No doubt I now grew *very* pale;—but I talked more fluently, and with a heightened voice. Yet the sound increased—and what could I do? It was

---

[8] In 1843, Poe printed "I then sat upon the bed and smiled gaily" for "I then smiled gaily."
[9] Upright beam in a house frame.

a low, dull, quick sound—much such as a watch makes when enveloped in cotton. I gasped for breath—and yet the officers heard it not. I talked more quickly—more vehemently; but the noise steadily increased. I arose and argued about trifles, in a high key and with violent gesticulations; but the noise steadily increased. Why *would* they not be gone? I paced the floor to and fro with heavy strides, as if excited to fury by the observations of the men—but the noise steadily increased. Oh God! what *could* I do? I foamed—I raved—I swore! I swung the chair upon which I had been sitting, and grated it upon the boards, but the noise arose over all and continually increased. It grew louder—louder—*louder!* And still the men chatted pleasantly, and smiled. Was it possible they heard not? Almighty God!—no, no! They heard!—they suspected!—they *knew!*—they were making a mockery of my horror!—this I thought, and this I think. But anything was better than this agony! Anything was more tolerable than this derision! I could bear those hypocritical smiles no longer! I felt that I must scream or die! and now—again!—hark! louder! louder! louder! *louder!*

"Villains!" I shrieked, "dissemble[10] no more! I admit the deed!—tear up the planks! here, here!—it is the beating of his hideous heart!"

[1843]

---

[10]Pretend

KATHERINE ANNE PORTER
[1890–1980]

Katherine Anne Porter was a consummate storyteller, a gift she frequently used to shape the substance of her own life. Throughout her career, she told those who asked that she was a wealthy, aristocratic daughter of the Old South, descended from a long line of prominent statesmen. Porter, in fact, grew up in poverty, received little formal education, and witnessed firsthand the sufferings of rural life in some of the most desolate parts of the Southwest. While the life she created for herself was, for the most part, a fiction, her writing often reflected the hard, gritty stuff of her actual existence.

Porter was the fourth of five children born to a poor farming family in Indian Creek, Texas. Porter's mother died when Porter was only two. Devastated by his wife's death and unable to support his children, Porter's father, Harrison Porter, took his four surviving children to live with his mother in Kyle, Texas. Porter was raised by her stoic, indomitable grandmother who managed to provide for the family until her death in 1901. His mother gone, Harrison uprooted the family again to San Antonio where Porter ultimately convinced her father to borrow money to send her to private school. At the Thomas School in San Antonio, Porter, a dismal student academically, set about training for a life on the stage. She took drama classes as well as singing and dancing lessons and, in two years, gained enough training to support her father as a teacher of dramatic arts when the family moved again to Victoria, Texas.

In 1906, at the age of sixteen, Porter married the son of a well-to-do German ranching family. In 1914, she abruptly left her husband and made her way to Chicago (then the home of many successful movie studios) to make a name for herself as a movie actress. Porter was a popular player, but the work proved too strenuous for Porter's always frail health. At the end of the year, she traveled to Louisiana to help support her ailing sister and then to Dallas, Texas, to rebuild her life. By the time she arrived in Dallas, however, she was suffering from tuberculosis. After a brief and horrible stay in a public asylum in Dallas, Porter was rescued by her brother who provided her with funds to move to a good hospital, Carlsbad Sanatorium, for treatment. Her trip to

Carlsbad changed her life. While recovering from her illness, she met Kitty Barry Crawford, a well-known Texas journalist who inspired Porter to make her living in words. After their release, the two women went together to Fort Worth where Porter began to work for the Fort Worth newspaper, the Critic. *When Kitty's health necessitated a further remove to Denver, Porter followed her and succeeded in landing a job with the* Rocky Mountain News. *After nearly dying a second time in the worldwide flu epidemic of 1918, Porter decided to move to New York City and pursue her true goal of becoming a fiction writer.*

Porter settled in Greenwich Village, the acknowledged literary Mecca for young Americans, and began to circulate among a host of writers and artists. In particular, Porter was drawn to a small group of Mexican artists, among them Adolpho Best-Maugard, a fine artist who drew his inspiration from ancient Mayan and Aztec designs. In 1920, Porter parlayed her interest in Mexican culture into a job with the Magazine of Mexico *and left on assignment to the country that so intrigued her. Porter arrived in Mexico City just as the country was emerging from ten years of bloody civil war during which the longstanding dictator, Porfirio Diaz, lost power. In his wake, several factions vied for control of the country. Alvaro Obregón assumed the presidency in a free election in 1920 and, although he was cautiously progressive, radical socialists soon found his policies unsatisfactory and began to rebel. Through her friend Mary Louise Doherty, a communist sympathizer who taught English to Indian children in Xochimilco, Porter met many of Mexico City's radical Marxists. In the spring of 1921, Porter came under government suspicion because of her leftist contacts and returned to the United States. By 1922, she was back in Greenwich Village where, in a burst of creativity, she crafted her first published short story, "María Concepción," which appeared in* Century Magazine *that same year.*

Following one additional short trip to Mexico to help arrange an exhibition of art to tour the United States, Porter spent the rest of the 1920s in New York and New England starting many stories, but completing few. In 1927, in part to cure her writer's block, Porter contracted to write a biography of seventeenth century theologian Cotton Mather. Porter's work on the book stalled, but her thoughts about Mather, whose sanctimoniousness she despised, allowed her to crystallize her own sense of moral and ethical values and strengthen her art. The great sin of many of Porter's fictional characters lies in their inability to feel passion and act on it. Some are indifferent to the world at large. Their cynicism and passivity, far from being neutral, destroys all those who come into their orbit. Others are bound by cold, principled visions of the universe. They unwittingly do evil to others under the guise of doing good. During her work on the biography, she wrote "The Jilting of Granny Weatherall," her first serious attempt to make the stuff of her childhood into art. Her attempt to come to grips with Mather also led to her to pen "Flower-

ing Judas," the tale that made her literary career. In 1930, Porter finally succeeded in publishing a small book of six stories named for her most recent effort, Flowering Judas.

In 1931, Porter sailed for Europe and, after a brief stay in Germany on a Guggenheim grant, settled in Paris in 1933. The next three years were productive for Porter. She published an expanded edition of Flowering Judas in 1935, as well as a steady stream of stories in the Southern Review and the Virginia Quarterly. Upon her return to the United States in 1936, Porter visited her family in Texas for the first time in fifteen years. She then settled in Doylestown, Pennsylvania, and set to work bringing into shape the three great stories drawn from her own early experience— "Old Mortality," "Noon Wine," and "Pale Horse, Pale Rider." The three long stories appeared together in her 1939 collection, Pale Horse, Pale Rider. The book was hailed as a tour de force and Porter found herself, for the first time, truly at the center of the literary limelight.

Her rise in fame, however, was accompanied by another collapse in her creativity. Moving from place to place around the United States, Porter found herself unable to write. As her stories dried up (she published only two new stories between 1939 and 1944) so did her income. Her current publisher, Harcourt Brace, expected a novel from Porter, but assuming her career at an end, published a third and last collection of her stories, The Leaning Tower, and Other Stories (1944). The book consisted primarily of stories that Porter had written and published during her years in Paris. Throughout the 1940s and 1950s Porter supported herself by script writing, speaking, and teaching at a variety of universities. In 1962, she shocked the literary world by publishing her only novel, Ship of Fools. The book was an immediate bestseller. Porter sold the movie rights and finally achieved the financial security she had longed for her entire life. In 1964, she cemented her literary reputation by receiving both the National Book Award and the Pulitzer Prize for her Collected Stories.

Like many women of her generation, Porter was rarely comfortable with the personal sacrifices she made for the sake of her art. Throughout her stories, she portrays women and men who float free from domestic attachments as oddly obsessed. In "Noon Wine," the mysterious, silent, unattached Mr. Helton kills for the sake of his music. In "Flowering Judas," the unattached Laura lives a life of principled denial and gives herself to a movement rather than a person. She understands the corruption that surrounds her and the hopelessness of her missions, but cannot bring herself to love. In "The Jilting of Granny Weatherall," Porter portrays death itself as a horrible denial of domestic bliss.

The texts presented in the Library are from Porter's Collected Stories (New York: Harcourt Brace, 1965; reprint 1979).

For Further Reading

Primary Works

Flowering Judas (New York: Harcourt, Brace, 1930); enlarged as *Flowering Judas and Other Stories* (New York: Harcourt, Brace, 1935; London: Cape, 1936); *Hacienda* (New York: Harrison of Paris, 1934); *Noon Wine* (Detroit: Schuman's, 1937); *Pale Horse, Pale Rider: Three Short Novels* (New York: Harcourt, Brace, 1939); republished as *Pale Horse, Pale Rider and Other Stories* (London: Cape, 1939); *The Leaning Tower, and Other Stories* (New York: Harcourt, Brace, 1944; London: Cape, 1945); *The Days Before* (New York: Harcourt, Brace, 1952; London: Secker & Warburg, 1953); *The Old Order: Stories of the South* (New York: Harcourt, Brace, 1955); *A Christmas Story* (limited edition, New York: *Mademoiselle*, 1955; trade edition, New York: Seymour Lawrence, 1967); *Ship of Fools* (Boston & Toronto: *Atlantic Monthly*/Little, Brown, 1962; London: Secker & Warburg, 1962); *Collected Stories* (London: Cape, 1964; New York: Harcourt, Brace, 1965; enlarged edition, London: Cape, 1967); *The Collected Essays and Occasional Writings of Katherine Anne Porter* (New York: Delacorte, 1970); *The Never-Ending Wrong* (Boston: Little, Brown, 1977; London: Secker & Warburg, 1977).

Secondary Works

Harold Bloom, ed., *Katherine Anne Porter* (New York, New Haven & Philadelphia: Chelsea House, 1986); Robert H. Brinkmeyer, *Katherine Anne Porter's Artistic Development: Primitivism, Traditionalism, and Totalitarianism* (Baton Rouge: Louisiana State University Press, 1993); Joan Givner, *Katherine Anne Porter: A Life* (New York: Simon and Schuster, 1982; revised edition, Athens: Brown Thrasher, 1991); Kathryn Hilt, *Katherine Anne Porter: An Annotated Bibliography* (New York: Garland, 1990); Jane Krause DeMouy, *Katherine Anne Porter's Women: The Eye of Her Fiction* (Austin: University of Texas Press, 1983); Janis P. Stout, *Katherine Anne Porter: A Sense of the Times* (Charlottesville: University of Virginia Press, 1995); Louise Waldrip and Shirley Ann Bauer, *A Bibliography of the Works of Katherine Anne Porter and A Bibliography of the Criticism of the Works of Katherine Anne Porter* (Metuchen, N.J.: Scarecrow Press, 1969).

The Jilting of Granny Weatherall[*]

KATHERINE ANNE PORTER

She flicked her wrist neatly out of Doctor Harry's pudgy careful fingers and pulled the sheet up to her chin. The brat ought to be in knee breeches. Doctoring around the country with spectacles on his nose! "Get along now, take your schoolbooks and go. There's nothing wrong with me."

Doctor Harry spread a warm paw like a cushion on her forehead where the forked green vein danced and made her eyelids twitch. "Now, now, be a good girl, and we'll have you up in no time."

"That's no way to speak to a woman nearly eighty years old just because she's down. I'd have you respect your elders, young man."

"Well, Missy, excuse me." Doctor Harry patted her cheek. "But I've got to warn you, haven't I? You're a marvel, but you must be careful or you're going to be good and sorry."

"Don't tell me what I'm going to be. I'm on my feet now, morally speaking. It's Cornelia. I had to go to bed to get rid of her."

Her bones felt loose, and floated around in her skin, and Doctor Harry floated like a balloon around the foot of the bed. He floated and pulled down his waistcoat and swung his glasses on a cord. "Well, stay where you are, it certainly can't hurt you."

"Get along and doctor your sick," said Granny Weatherall. "Leave a well woman alone. I'll call for you when I want you. . . . Where were you forty years ago when I pulled through milk-leg and double pneumonia? You weren't even born. Don't let Cornelia lead you on," she shouted, because Doctor Harry appeared to float up to the ceiling and out. "I pay my own bills, and I don't throw my money away on nonsense!"

She meant to wave good-by, but it was too much trouble. Her eyes closed of themselves, it was like a dark curtain drawn around the bed. The pillow rose and floated under her, pleasant as a hammock in a light wind. She listened to the leaves rustling outside the window. No, somebody was swishing

---

[*]"The Jilting of Granny Weatherall" first appeared in *transition* in February 1929.

newspapers: no, Cornelia and Doctor Harry were whispering together. She leaped broad awake, thinking they whispered in her ear.

"She was never like this, *never* like this!" "Well, what can we expect?" "Yes, eighty years old. . . ."

Well, and what if she was? She still had ears. It was like Cornelia to whisper around doors. She always kept things secret in such a public way. She was always being tactful and kind. Cornelia was dutiful; that was the trouble with her. Dutiful and good: "So good and dutiful," said Granny, "that I'd like to spank her." She saw herself spanking Cornelia and making a fine job of it.

"What'd you say, Mother?"

Granny felt her face tying up in hard knots.

"Can't a body think, I'd like to know?"

"I thought you might want something."

"I do. I want a lot of things. First off, go away and don't whisper."

She lay and drowsed, hoping in her sleep that the children would keep out and let her rest a minute. It had been a long day. Not that she was tired. It was always pleasant to snatch a minute now and then. There was always so much to be done, let me see: tomorrow.

Tomorrow was far away and there was nothing to trouble about. Things were finished somehow when the time came; thank God there was always a little margin over for peace: then a person could spread out the plan of life and tuck in the edges orderly. It was good to have everything clean and folded away, with the hair brushes and tonic bottles sitting straight on the white embroidered linen: the day started without fuss and the pantry shelves laid out with rows of jelly glasses and brown jugs and white stone-china jars with blue whirligigs and words painted on them: coffee, tea, sugar, ginger, cinnamon, allspice: and the bronze clock with the lion on top nicely dusted off. The dust that lion could collect in twenty-four hours! The box in the attic with all those letters tied up, well, she'd have to go through that tomorrow. All those letters—George's letters and John's letters and her letters to them both—lying around for the children to find afterwards made her uneasy. Yes, that would be tomorrow's business. No use to let them know how silly she had been once.

While she was rummaging around she found death in her mind and it felt clammy and unfamiliar. She had spent so much time preparing for death there was no need for bringing it up again. Let it take care of itself now. When she was sixty she had felt very old, finished, and went around making farewell trips to see her children and grandchildren, with a secret in her mind: This is the very last of your mother, children! Then she made her will and came down with a long fever. That was all just a notion like a lot of other things, but it was lucky too, for she had once for all got over the idea of dying for a long time. Now she couldn't be worried. She hoped she had better sense now. Her father had lived to be one hundred and two years old and had drunk a noggin of strong hot toddy on his last birthday. He told the reporters it was his daily habit, and he owed his long life to that. He had made quite a scandal and was very pleased about it. She believed she'd just plague Cornelia a little.

"Cornelia! Cornelia!" No footsteps, but a sudden hand on her cheek. "Bless you, where have you been?"

"Here, Mother."

"Well, Cornelia, I want a noggin of hot toddy."

"Are you cold, darling?"

"I'm chilly, Cornelia. Lying in bed stops the circulation. I must have told you that a thousand times."

Well, she could just hear Cornelia telling her husband that Mother was getting a little childish and they'd have to humor her. The thing that most annoyed her was that Cornelia thought she was deaf, dumb, and blind. Little hasty glances and tiny gestures tossed around her and over her head saying, "Don't cross her, let her have her way, she's eighty years old," and she sitting there as if she lived in a thin glass cage. Sometimes Granny almost made up her mind to pack up and move back to her own house where nobody could remind her every minute that she was old. Wait, wait, Cornelia, till your own children whisper behind your back!

In her day she had kept a better house and had got more work done. She wasn't too old yet for Lydia to be driving eighty miles for advice when one of the children jumped the track, and Jimmy still dropped in and talked things over: "Now, Mammy, you've a good business head, I want to know what you think of this? . . ." Old. Cornelia couldn't change the furniture around without asking. Little things, little things! They had been so sweet when they were little. Granny wished the old days were back again with the children young and everything to be done over. It had been a hard pull, but not too much for her. When she thought of all the food she had cooked, and all the clothes she had cut and sewed, and all the gardens she had made—well, the children showed it. There they were, made out of her, and they couldn't get away from that. Sometimes she wanted to see John again and point to them and say, Well, I didn't do so badly, did I? But that would have to wait. That was for tomorrow. She used to think of him as a man, but now all the children were older than their father, and he would be a child beside her if she saw him now. It seemed strange and there was something wrong in the idea. Why, he couldn't possibly recognize her. She had fenced in a hundred acres once, digging the post holes herself and clamping the wires with just a negro boy to help. That changed a woman. John would be looking for a young woman with the peaked Spanish comb in her hair and the painted fan. Digging post holes changed a woman. Riding country roads in the winter when women had their babies was another thing: sitting up nights with sick horses and sick negroes and sick children and hardly ever losing one. John, I hardly ever lost one of them! John would see that in a minute, that would be something he could understand, she wouldn't have to explain anything!

It made her feel like rolling up her sleeves and putting the whole place to rights again. No matter if Cornelia was determined to be everywhere at once, there were a great many things left undone on this place. She would start tomorrow and do them. It was good to be strong enough for everything, even if all you made melted and changed and slipped under your hands, so that by the time you finished you almost forgot what you were working for. What was it I set out to do? she asked herself intently, but she could not remember. A fog rose over the valley, she saw it marching across the creek swallowing the trees and moving up the hill like an army of ghosts. Soon it would be at the near edge of the orchard, and then it was time to go in and light the lamps. Come in, children, don't stay out in the night air.

Lighting the lamps had been beautiful. The children huddled up to her and breathed like little calves waiting at the bars in the twilight. Their eyes followed the match and watched the flame rise and settle in a blue curve, then they moved away from her. The lamp was lit, they didn't have to be scared and hang on to mother any more. Never, never, never more. God, for all my life I thank Thee. Without Thee, my God, I could never have done it. Hail, Mary, full of grace.

I want you to pick all the fruit this year and see that nothing is wasted. There's always someone who can use it. Don't let good things rot for want of using. You waste life when you waste good food. Don't let things get lost. It's bitter to lose things. Now, don't let me get to thinking, not when I am tired and taking a little nap before supper. . . .

The pillow rose about her shoulders and pressed against her heart and the memory was being squeezed out of it: oh, push down the pillow, somebody: it would smother her if she tried to hold it. Such a fresh breeze blowing and such a green day with no threats in it. But he had not come, just the same. What does a woman do when she has put on the white veil and set out the white cake for a man and he doesn't come? She tried to remember. No, I swear he never harmed me but in that. He never harmed me but in that . . . and what if he did? There was the day, the day, but a whirl of dark smoke rose and covered it, crept up and over into the bright field where everything was planted so carefully in orderly rows. That was hell, she knew hell when she saw it. For sixty years she had prayed against remembering him and against losing her soul in the deep pit of hell, and now the two things were mingled in one and the thought of him was a smoky cloud from hell that moved and crept in her head when she had just got rid of Doctor Harry and was trying to rest a minute. Wounded vanity, Ellen, said a sharp voice in the top of her mind. Don't let your wounded vanity get the upper hand of you. Plenty of girls get jilted. You were jilted, weren't you? Then stand up to it. Her eyelids wavered and let in streamers of blue-gray light like tissue paper over her eyes. She must get up and pull the shades down or she'd never sleep. She was in bed again and the shades were not down. How could that happen? Better turn over, hide from the light, sleeping in the light gave you nightmares. "Mother, how do you feel now?" and a stinging wetness on her forehead. But I don't like having my face washed in cold water!

Hapsy? George? Lydia? Jimmy? No, Cornelia, and her features were swollen and full of little puddles. "They're coming, darling, they'll all be here soon." Go wash your face, child, you look funny.

Instead of obeying, Cornelia knelt down and put her head on the pillow. She seemed to be talking but there was no sound. "Well, are you tongue-tied? Whose birthday is it? Are you going to give a party?"

Cornelia's mouth moved urgently in strange shapes. "Don't do that, you bother me, daughter."

"Oh, no, Mother. Oh, no. . . ."

Nonsense. It was strange about children. They disputed your every word. "No what, Cornelia?"

"Here's Doctor Harry."

"I won't see that boy again. He just left five minutes ago."

"That was this morning, Mother. It's night now. Here's the nurse."

"This is Doctor Harry, Mrs. Weatherall. I never saw you look so young and happy!"

"Ah, I'll never be young again—but I'd be happy if they'd let me lie in peace and get rested."

She thought she spoke up loudly, but no one answered. A warm weight on her forehead, a warm bracelet on her wrist, and a breeze went on whispering, trying to tell her something. A shuffle of leaves in the everlasting hand of God, He blew on them and they danced and rattled. "Mother, don't mind, we're going to give you a little hypodermic." "Look here, daughter, how do ants get in this bed? I saw sugar ants yesterday." Did you send for Hapsy too?

It was Hapsy she really wanted. She had to go a long way back through a great many rooms to find Hapsy standing with a baby on her arm. She seemed to herself to be Hapsy also, and the baby on Hapsy's arm was Hapsy and himself and herself, all at once, and there was no surprise in the meeting. Then Hapsy melted from within and turned flimsy as gray gauze and the baby was a gauzy shadow, and Hapsy came up close and said, "I thought you'd never come," and looked at her very searchingly and said, "You haven't changed a bit!" They leaned forward to kiss, when Cornelia began whispering from a long way off, "Oh, is there anything you want to tell me? Is there anything I can do for you?"

Yes, she had changed her mind after sixty years and she would like to see George. I want you to find George. Find him and be sure to tell him I forgot him. I want him to know I had my husband just the same and my children and my house like any other woman. A good house too and a good husband that I loved and fine children out of him. Better than I hoped for even. Tell him I was given back everything he took away and more. Oh, no, oh, God, no, there was something else besides the house and the man and the children. Oh, surely they were not all? What was it? Something not given back.... Her breath crowded down under her ribs and grew into a monstrous frightening shape with cutting edges; it bored up into her head, and the agony was unbelievable: Yes, John, get the Doctor now, no more talk my time has come.

When this one was born it should be the last. The last. It should have been born first, for it was the one she had truly wanted. Everything came in good time. Nothing left out, left over. She was strong, in three days she would be as well as ever. Better. A woman needed milk in her to have her full health.

"Mother, do you hear me?"

"I've been telling you—"

"Mother, Father Connolly's here."

"I went to Holy Communion only last week. Tell him I'm not so sinful as all that."

"Father just wants to speak to you."

He could speak as much as he pleased. It was like him to drop in and inquire about her soul as if it were a teething baby, and then stay on for a cup of tea and a round of cards and gossip. He always had a funny story of some sort, usually about an Irishman who made his little mistakes and confessed them, and the point lay in some absurd thing he would blurt out in the confessional showing his struggles between native piety and original sin. Granny felt easy about her soul. Cornelia, where are your manners? Give Father Connolly a chair. She had her secret comfortable understanding with a few favorite saints who cleared a straight road to God for her. All as surely signed and sealed as the papers for the new Forty Acres. Forever... heirs and assigns forever. Since the day the wedding cake was not cut, but thrown out and wasted. The whole bottom dropped out of the world, and there she was blind and sweating with nothing under her feet and the walls falling away. His hand had caught her under the breast, she had not fallen, there was the freshly polished floor with the green rug on it, just as before. He had cursed like a sailor's parrot and said, "I'll kill him for you." Don't lay a hand on him, for my sake leave something to God. "Now, Ellen, you must believe what I tell you...."

So there was nothing, nothing to worry about any more, except sometimes in the night one of the children screamed in a nightmare, and they both hustled out shaking and hunting for the matches and calling, "There, wait a minute, here we are!" John, get the doctor now, Hapsy's time has come. But there was Hapsy standing by the bed in a white cap. "Cornelia, tell Hapsy to take off her cap. I can't see her plain."

Her eyes opened very wide and the room stood out like a picture she had seen somewhere. Dark colors with the shadows rising towards the ceiling in long angles. The tall black dresser gleamed with nothing on it but John's picture, enlarged from a little one, with John's eyes very black when they should have been blue. You never saw him, so how do you know how he looked? But the man insisted the copy was perfect, it was very rich and handsome. For a picture, yes, but it's not my husband. The table by the bed had a linen cover and a candle and a crucifix. The light was blue from Cornelia's silk lampshades. No sort of light at all, just frippery. You had to live forty years with kerosene lamps to appreciate honest electricity. She felt very strong and she saw Doctor Harry with a rosy nimbus around him.

"You look like a saint, Doctor Harry, and I vow that's as near as you'll ever come to it."

"She's saying something."

"I heard you, Cornelia. What's all this carrying-on?"

"Father Connolly's saying—"

Cornelia's voice staggered and bumped like a cart in a bad road. It rounded corners and turned back again and arrived nowhere. Granny stepped up in the cart very lightly and reached for the reins, but a man sat beside her and she knew him by his hands, driving the cart. She did not look in his face, for she knew without seeing, but looked instead down the road where the trees leaned over and bowed to each other and a thousand birds were singing a Mass. She felt like singing too, but she put her hand in the bosom of her dress and pulled out a rosary, and Father Connolly murmured Latin in a very solemn voice and tickled her feet. My God, will you stop that nonsense? I'm a married woman. What if he did run away and leave me to face the priest by myself? I found another a whole world better. I wouldn't have exchanged my husband for anybody except St. Michael himself, and you may tell him that for me with a thank you in the bargain.

Light flashed on her closed eyelids, and a deep roaring shook her. Cornelia, is that lightning? I hear thunder. There's going to be a storm. Close all the windows. Call the children in. . . . "Mother, here we are, all of us." "Is that you, Hapsy?" "Oh, no, I'm Lydia. We drove as fast as we could." Their faces drifted above her, drifted away. The rosary fell out of her hands and Lydia put it back. Jimmy tried to help, their hands fumbled together, and Granny closed two fingers around Jimmy's thumb. Beads wouldn't do, it must be something alive. She was so amazed her thoughts ran round and round. So, my dear Lord, this is my death and I wasn't even thinking about it. My children have come to see me die. But I can't, it's not time. Oh, I always hated surprises. I wanted to give Cornelia the amethyst set—Cornelia, you're to have the amethyst set, but Hapsy's to wear it when she wants, and, Doctor Harry, do shut up. Nobody sent for you. Oh, my dear Lord, do wait a minute. I meant to do something about the Forty Acres, Jimmy doesn't need it and Lydia will later on, with that worthless husband of hers. I meant to finish the altar cloth and send six bottles of wine to Sister Borgia for her dyspepsia. I want to send six bottles of wine to Sister Borgia, Father Connolly, now don't let me forget.

Cornelia's voice made short turns and tilted over and crashed. "Oh, Mother, oh, Mother, oh, Mother. . . ."

"I'm not going, Cornelia. I'm taken by surprise. I can't go."

You'll see Hapsy again. What about her? "I thought you'd never come." Granny made a long journey outward, looking for Hapsy. What if I don't find her? What then? Her heart sank down and down, there was no bottom to death, she couldn't come to the end of it. The blue light from Cornelia's lampshade drew into a tiny point in the center of her brain, it flickered and winked like an eye, quietly it fluttered and dwindled. Granny lay curled down within herself, amazed and watchful, staring at the point of light that was herself; her body was now only a deeper mass of shadow in an endless darkness and this darkness would curl around the light and swallow it up. God, give a sign!

For a second time there was no sign. Again no bridegroom and the priest in the house. She could not remember any other sorrow because this grief wiped them all away. Oh, no, there's nothing more cruel than this—I'll never forgive it. She stretched herself with a deep breath and blew out the light.

[1929]

MARK TWAIN
[1835–1910]

On October 19, 1865, about one month shy of his thirtieth birthday, Mark Twain wrote to his brother that he had finally, after at least four false starts, decided on a career: "I have had a 'call' to literature, of a low order—i.e., humorous. It is nothing to be proud of, but it is my strongest suit, & if I were to listen to that maxim of stern duty which says that to do right you <u>must</u> multiply the one or the two or the three talents which the Almighty entrust to your keeping, I would long ago have ceased to meddle with things for which I was by nature unfitted & turned my attention to seriously scribbling to excite the <u>laughter</u> of God's creatures." Forty years later, in a passage written for his autobiography, he described his career as a humorist in a different way: "Humor is only a fragrance, a decoration. . . . Humor must not professedly teach, and it must not professedly preach, but it must do both if it would live forever. . . . I have always preached. That is the reason that I have lasted thirty years. If the humor came of its own accord and uninvited, I have allowed it a place in my sermon, but I was not writing the sermon for the sake of the humor. I should have written the sermon just the same, whether any humor applied for admission or not" (July 31, 1906). As befits a man who was known for his exaggerations, both statements stretch the truth, and as equally befits a man who gave himself the pen name Mark Twain, each is essentially true to one of Twain's two main poses. On the one hand, he set himself up as mischievous iconoclast bent on having and provoking fun. In this pose, Twain provided much-needed comic relief from Victorian seriousness. On the other hand, much of his greatest work is profoundly serious, participating in the Victorian obsession with morality and character, chastising hypocrisy wherever he found it—including in himself.

In a sense, Twain's doubleness is a pure product of America, stemming from the variety of experiences a chaotic and turbulent life brought his way. Born Samuel Langhorn Clemens on November 30, 1835, in the recently founded rural hamlet of Florida, Missouri, and raised in the Mississippi riverfront town of Hannibal, Missouri, Twain began his life on the edge of American culture. Though his father was a fairly well-read, free-thinking, self-styled aristocrat, Twain's main social context was the crude culture of the Old Southwest, with its peculiar mix of working-class democracy and slavery, of practical morality and revival religion, of grog shops and temperance movements. The next to last of seven children and one of three to live to adulthood, Samuel Clemens was born into a family of declining fortunes. His family tried to maintain a stance of gentility in the face of adversity, but they could afford no more than a haphazard education for Sam up to the age of twelve, when, a year after his father's death, he was apprenticed to the printing trade.

Printing appealed to the family not simply because it was practical, but also because it was one of few manual trades that had an aura of gentility. With the honorable precedent of Benjamin Franklin to vouch for its value, the print shop was seen by many Americans as an alternative education for ambitious bright young men who could not afford college. And so it served for Clemens. Already an avid reader, he found in the print shop as heterogeneous a mix of written material as any person could hope for. Beyond the usual doses of politics and opinion, which were the bread and butter of early American journalism, a rural Western paper of the day printed fine poetry, doggerel verse, humorous sketches, speeches, travel correspondence, and just about anything else that might interest its audience. The crucial thing was that the copy would be either very cheap or free, and in a day of weak copyright law, that meant that every tiny local newspaper could—and usually did—steal almost any short piece of writing that came across its path.

In this context, Clemens learned both the rough rhythms of vernacular expression and the complex cadences of formal rhetoric. In the rambunctious context of the print shop, he also learned much about practical joking, irreverence, and the spirit of satire. In June of 1853, aged seventeen, he left home to begin life as an itinerant journeyman printer. Over the next four years, he worked in St. Louis, New York City, Philadelphia, Muscatine and Keokuk Iowa, and Cincinnati, and looked for work in Washington, D.C. His letters home suggest that he was hard working, averse to drinking, and devoted to self-cultivation by taking his recreation in the fine libraries established by the printer's guilds in New York and Philadelphia. By twenty-one, Clemens had lived in the East and West, North and South, big city and small town, and had already begun to write travel letters describing his experiences.

In the spring of 1857, tired of printing's long hours and limited prospects, Clemens sought a change. He first planned to go to Brazil to participate in the then legal trade in coca, but on his way down the Mississippi River, changed his mind again. Borrowing money from his brother-in-law in St. Louis to pay for another apprenticeship, he began the onerous process of learning to be a riverboat pilot, described in loving detail in "Old Times on the Mississippi," serialized in the Atlantic Monthly *in 1875. Riverboats were the lifeblood of Western commerce, but the reputation of boatmen was not high. As much as piloting was difficult and lucrative, it was a job suspect in the eyes of the genteel, in part because it brought the boat-worker into contact with gamblers, prostitutes, slave-traders, business sharks, frontiersmen, and various other opportunists who were drawn to this turbulent conduit between frontier and city. From an environment steeped in literature, Clemens stepped into a different world. For the first time in his life, he had money and the prestige money could bring, and began a habit of conspicuous consumption and terrible investments. His interest in cultivating gentility waned, and he learned the rougher accomplishments that his mother had warned him against. Nonetheless, he maintained an interest in writing, publishing occasional satires and travel letters.*

As a man whose livelihood was based on North-South commerce and on an economy based on slavery, Clemens was opposed to the Republican Party and to secessionists. When the Civil War began in 1861, he first hid out so as not to be conscripted as a Union riverboat pilot; when it was clear that river commerce had ceased until war's end, he left his career as a pilot and enlisted in a Missouri militia supporting states' rights, an experience he described later in "A Private History of a Campaign that Failed" (1885). Within weeks, he abandoned military service to travel West with his brother Orion, an ardent abolitionist Republican who had just been appointed by the new Lincoln Administration to serve as secretary to the new Territorial government of Nevada. Like many Americans, Clemens could not reconcile his divided loyalties; he left Missouri in July of 1861 for what he thought would be a brief vacation and some desultory silver mining while the war passed. The war turned out to be more substantial than anyone expected, and Clemens's exile turned out to be longer yet. He spent over five years in Nevada and California, with a trip to Hawaii—described in a rich mix of autobiography and fiction in Roughing It *(1872). In the far West, the former printer and pilot became a professional writer.*

The transition was not an easy one. Bitten with mining fever, Clemens spent himself into debt. Desperate for money, he took an offer from the Virginia City (Nevada) Territorial Enterprise *to work as a reporter. There, he learned much about writing from Joe Goodman, the paper's editor and proprietor, who had Clemens write regular news and gave him free reign for creative work. Goodman was the first in a series of editors and colleagues who understood that Clemens's talents and experiences gave him the unique opportunity to create an important literature in an American vernacular.*

It was in Nevada that Clemens adopted the pen name Mark Twain, which was variously interpreted as the leadsman's call on a riverboat for "two fathoms," or as the number of drinks Clemens habitually added to his bar tab. This second interpretation says much about the kind of life Clemens led out West, where he participated energetically in the rough-and-tumble world of frontier journalism. He made many enemies, but the wit and wildness of his style also won him a wide audience in the West. After leaving his staff position on the Enterprise *in 1864 and after a brief stint as a staff reporter for the San Francisco* Call, *he worked as a traveling corespondent for several newspapers and as a writer for San Francisco's literary journal,* The Golden Era, *publishing literary sketches in magazines and travel correspondence, usually first in newspapers and then collected in books. At about the same time, he developed another of his talents, that of a humorist on the lecture circuit. His stage performances kept him in touch with the spoken quality of American English, preventing him from imitating the British literary forms usually preferred by American writers.*

His life experiences to this point enabled him to see much of the richness and many of the contradictions of American culture. Without usually working too deeply into the substance of those contradictions, his early sketches tend to play on the surface, exploiting incongruities in manners and language. The exception may be the "Jumping Frog" story he published in 1865, which rises to an iconographic level in depicting the development of American culture. Still, Clemens had not yet developed the habit of pushing incongruity to great depth, nor had he conjoined his ability to see through public shams with self-reflection. At this stage in his career, Mark Twain came across as a cocky, ebullient humorist and satirist. At the same time, the serious side of Clemens was far from satisfied with what he saw as the financial, moral, and intellectual shortcomings in his life. As he put it in a letter to his mother when he was on the verge of the first of many trips to Europe:

> *Curse the endless delays! They always kill me—they make me neglect every duty & then I have a conscience that tears me like a wild beast. I wish I never had to stop anywhere a month. I do more mean things, the moment I get a chance to fold my hands & sit down than ever I can get forgiveness for. (June 1, 1867)*

As much as Clemens mocked the rest of the world in his pose as Mark Twain, he privately reviled his participation in that world.

In running away, he found two things that provided material for his writing and the strength to develop it. While touring Europe and the Middle East, he struck on a typically American refrain about history, suggesting in the letters that would be collected into the extraordinary bestseller The Innocents Abroad *(1869) that Europe is dead, trapped by the burden of its own past. But in seeing America's relationship to that history, he began a lifelong meditation on the power of the past to shape the present. Twain found support to develop these ideas in personal relationships, most importantly that with Olivia Langdon, whom he met in 1867. Olivia Langdon was one of three children of a wealthy Elmira, New York, couple that was politically well connected, had been active abolitionists and members of the Underground Railroad, and who vigorously supported radical Republican efforts to secure equal rights for African Americans. They were also quite religious, strong temperance advocates, and were* among the founders of Elmira College. To Clemens, they represented the respectability he had once been encouraged to pursue but that he had left behind, and they exposed him to social attitudes toward African Americans that were radically different from those of his youth. In almost every way, his connections with the Langdon family stretched him.

After an intense courtship that is well documented in their letters, Olivia Langdon married Samuel Clemens, and thus began a literary collaboration that lasted until her death in 1904. Clemens turned over to his wife the task of "taming" him, suggesting how completely he accepted Victorian attitudes toward gender roles. But over the course of a marriage, their prescribed roles became less rigid. Olivia became Twain's most important literary adviser. She edited his manuscripts and, while she often pushed him toward propriety, she as often pushed him away from ironic bitterness and toward humor. Thus, she encouraged that aspect of Twain's work that was imbued with serious moral purpose, but she also encouraged his more extravagant humor, and encouraged him to use his humor to develop his moral vision.

About the same time that Clemens found his marriage helping him to reconcile two very different sides of his personality, he developed a number of friendships with scholars, writers, and artists. Most important of these was his friendship with William Dean Howells. Along with Olivia Langdon and Joseph Goodman, Howells had the greatest influence on Clemens's career. And like both Goodman and Langdon, Howells shared a deep knowledge of conventional culture with an appreciation for the power and potential depth of Twain's unconventional gifts. In various ways, all three connected the once provincial Twain to a larger world of letters, helped him to discipline himself as a writer and encouraged him to look into himself and his world to create a deep humor. With their advice, guidance, and frequently, editing, Twain learned to turn simple social incongruity into a way of interrogating human ethics. As much as he began his career seeing himself torn between old and new, East and West, gentility and barbarism, his experiences with both sides of those ostensible divides showed commonalities, for both good and evil, and helped him develop a moral sensitivity that turned him into America's conscience by the end of his career. No longer a trivial funny fellow, no longer a self-loathing clown, Twain came to accept the power of humor to find depth and solace.

Beginning in the 1870s, then, came a series of books that drew on Twain's personal experiences and on his continuing study of history. These converged in his most famous books, The Adventures of Tom Sawyer (1876) and Adventures of Huckleberry Finn (1884), both of which address the American experience from personal and historical points of view. The shift in tone between the two—with the first being what Twain called a "hymn to boyhood," and the second a much darker and thematically richer book—suggests something of the serious turn his studies and self-reflection had given his writing. His *sense of humor had become an incisive tool for challenging America's growing nostalgia for the antebellum days. With a broader eye on the English-speaking world, Twain then published* A Connecticut Yankee in King Arthur's Court *(1889) taking late Victorian medievalism on both sides of the Atlantic to task. At the same time, the twisting incongruities Twain's ironic imagination kept uncovering, led him to doubt whether material progress made much difference in human moral development. By this time, his writings presented a counter-voice both to elitist longing for an orderly and hierarchical world and to simplistic American faith in progress. In this way, his humor threatened to turn into a deeply pessimistic irony, and much of Twain's late work has a bitter tone. But as much as many readers have thus drawn the conclusion that Twain's career described a trajectory toward nihilism and despair, many of his later works, most particularly the innovative "Chapters from My Autobiography" (1906–07) show that his humor was equally capable of finding joy out of sorrow.*

In finding through humor a way to bridge his internal divides, Twain became one of America's most influential writers. At first, most Americans held him to be little more than a popular favorite, but influential figures of his own generation, such as Annie Fields, John Hay, and William Dean Howells, supported his work, and many writers of the next generation saw him as a significant model to follow in creating a truly American literature in both form and substance. Substantially because he created new ways of treating American materials through American voices, he provided a model for such widely different kinds of writers as Ernest Hemingway, T. S. Eliot, Ralph Ellison, and Kurt Vonnegut. His work endures in part because it looks at the fundamental paradoxes of American life, and as such, his writings have generated as much antipathy as praise. Indeed, the unease Twain's writings inspires is perhaps more important than the emulation. Toni Morrson, describing the anxiety and pleasure Huck Finn *has given both to her and to today's culture, says, "For a hundred years, the argument about what this novel is has been identified, reidentified, examined, waged, and advanced. What it cannot be is dismissed. It is classic literature, which is to say it heaves, manifests, and lasts." These words could easily apply to any number of Twain's works.*

Gregg Camfield
University of the Pacific

For Further Reading

Primary Works:

The Celebrated Jumping Frog of Calaveras County, and Other Sketches, 1867; *The Innocents Abroad,* 1869; *Roughing It,* 1872; *The Gilded Age* (with Charles Dudley Warner), 1873; *Old Times on the Mississippi,* 1875, 1883; "The Facts Concerning the Recent Carnival of Crime in Connecticut," 1876; *The Adventures of Tom Sawyer,* 1876; *A Tramp Abroad,* 1880; *The Prince and the Pauper,* 1881; *Life on the Mississippi,* 1883; *Adventures of Huckleberry Finn,* 1884; "The Private History of a Campaign that Failed," 1885; *A Connecticut Yankee in King Arthur's Court,* 1889; *Pudd'nhead Wilson,* 1894; "How to Tell a Story," 1895; *Personal Recollections of Joan of Arc,* 1896; *Following the Equator,* 1897; "The Man That Corrupted Hadleyburg," 1899; "To the Person Sitting in Darkness," 1901; "Chapters from My Autobiography," 1906–07; *Mark Twain's Speeches,* 1910; *The Mysterious Stranger and Other Stories,* 1922; *Mark Twain's Autobiography,* ed. A. B. Paine, 1924; *Mark Twain's Notebooks and Journals,* 3 vols., ed. Frederick Anderson, et al., 1975; *Mark Twain's Letters,* 5 vols., ed. Edgar Marquess Branch, 1988–97; *Mark Twain: Collected Tales, Sketches, Speeches, and Essays,* ed. Louis J. Budd, 1992; *Oxford Mark Twain,* 29 vols., series ed. Shelley Fisher Fishkin, 1997.

Secondary Works:

Kenneth Lynn, *Mark Twain and Southwestern Humor,* 1959; Henry Nash Smith, *Mark Twain: The Development of a Writer,* 1962; James M. Cox, *Mark Twain: The Fate of Humor,* 1966; Alan Gribben, *Mark Twain's Library,* 1980; Louis J. Budd, *Our Mark Twain: The Making of His Public Personality,* 1983; Robert Sattelmeyer and J. Donald Crowley, eds., *One Hundred Years of Huckleberry Finn,* 1985; James S Leonard and Thomas A. Tenney, *Satire or Evasion? Black Perspectives on Huckleberry Finn,* 1992; Shelley Fisher Fishkin, *Was Huck Black? Mark Twain and African-American Voices,* 1994; Gregg Camfield, *Sentimental Twain: Samuel Clemens in the Maze of Moral Philosophy,* 1994; Laura Skandera-Trombley, *Mark Twain in the Company of Women,* 1995; Bruce Michelson, *Mark Twain on the Loose,* 1995; Susan K. Harris, *The Courtship of Olivia Langdon and Mark Twain,* 1996; Everett Emerson, *Mark Twain: A Literary Life,* 2000.

The Man That Corrupted Hadleyburg

MARK TWAIN

I

IT WAS MANY YEARS ago. Hadleyburg was the most honest and upright town in all the region round about. It had kept that reputation unsmirched during three generations, and was prouder of it than of any other of its possessions. It was so proud of it, and so anxious to insure its perpetuation, that it began to teach the principles of honest dealing to its babies in the cradle, and made the like teachings the staple of their culture thenceforward through all the years devoted to their education. Also, throughout the formative years temptations were kept out of the way of the young people, so that their honesty could have every chance to harden and solidify, and become a part of their very bone. The neighboring towns were jealous of this honorable supremacy, and affected to sneer at Hadleyburg's pride in it and call it vanity; but all the same they were obliged to acknowledge that Hadleyburg was in reality an incorruptible town; and if pressed they would also acknowledge that the mere fact that a young man hailed from Hadleyburg was all the recommendation he needed when he went forth from his natal town to seek for responsible employment.

But at last, in the drift of time, Hadleyburg had the ill luck to offend a passing stranger—possibly without knowing it, certainly without caring, for Hadleyburg was sufficient unto itself, and cared not a rap for strangers or their opinions. Still, it would have been well to make an exception in this one's case, for he was a bitter man and revengeful. All through his wanderings during a whole year he kept his injury in mind, and gave all his leisure moments to trying to invent a compensating satisfaction for it. He contrived many plans, and all of them were good, but none of them was quite sweeping enough; the poorest of them would hurt a great many individuals, but what he wanted was a plan which would comprehend the entire town, and not let so much as one person escape unhurt. At last he had a fortunate idea,

Reprinted from *Mark Twain: Collected Tales, Sketches, Speeches, & Essays 1891–1910*, edited by Louis J Budd (1899).

and when it fell into his brain it lit up his whole head with an evil joy. He began to form a plan at once, saying to himself, "That is the thing to do—I will corrupt the town."

Six months later he went to Hadleyburg, and arrived in a buggy at the house of the old cashier of the bank about ten at night. He got a sack out of the buggy, shouldered it, and staggered with it through the cottage yard, and knocked at the door. A woman's voice said "Come in," and he entered, and set his sack behind the stove in the parlor, saying politely to the old lady who sat reading the *Missionary Herald* by the lamp:

"Pray keep your seat, madam, I will not disturb you. There—now it is pretty well concealed; one would hardly know it was there. Can I see your husband a moment, madam?"

No, he was gone to Brixton, and might not return before morning.

"Very well, madam, it is no matter. I merely wanted to leave that sack in his care, to be delivered to the rightful owner when he shall be found. I am a stranger; he does not know me; I am merely passing through the town to-night to discharge a matter which has been long in my mind. My errand is now completed, and I go pleased and a little proud, and you will never see me again. There is a paper attached to the sack which will explain everything. Good-night, madam."

The old lady was afraid of the mysterious big stranger, and was glad to see him go. But her curiosity was roused, and she went straight to the sack and brought away the paper. It began as follows:

"TO BE PUBLISHED; or, the right man sought out by private inquiry—either will answer. This sack contains gold coin weighing a hundred and sixty pounds four ounces—"

"Mercy on us, and the door not locked!"

Mrs. Richards flew to it all in a tremble and locked it, then pulled down the window-shades and stood frightened, worried, and wondering if there was anything else she could do toward making herself and the money more safe. She listened awhile for burglars, then surrendered to curiosity and went back to the lamp and finished reading the paper:

"I am a foreigner, and am presently going back to my own country, to remain there permanently. I am grateful to America for what I have received at her hands during my long stay under her flag; and to one of her citizens—a citizen of Hadleyburg—I am especially grateful for a great kindness done me a year or two ago. Two great kindnesses, in fact. I will explain. I was a gambler. I say I *was*. I was a ruined gambler. I arrived in this village at night, hungry and without a penny. I asked for help—in the dark; I was ashamed to beg in the light. I begged of the right man. He gave me twenty dollars—that is to say, he gave me life, as I considered it. He also gave me fortune; for out of that money I have made myself rich at the gaming-table. And finally, a remark which he made to me has remained with me to this day, and has at last conquered me; and in conquering has saved the remnant of my morals: I shall gamble no more. Now I have no idea who that man was, but I want him found, and I want him to have this money, to give away, throw away, or keep, as he pleases. It is merely my way of testifying my gratitude to him. If I could stay, I would find him myself; but no matter, he will be found. This is an honest town, an incorruptible town, and I know I can trust it without fear. This man can be identified by the remark which he made to me; I feel persuaded that he will remember it.

"And now my plan is this: If you prefer to conduct the inquiry privately, do so. Tell the contents of this present writing to any one who is likely to be the right man. If he shall answer, 'I am the man; the remark I made was so-and-so,' apply the test— to wit: open the sack, and in it you will find a sealed envelope containing that remark. If the remark mentioned by the candidate tallies with it, give him the money, and ask no further questions, for he is certainly the right man.

"But if you shall prefer a public inquiry, then publish this present writing in the local paper—with these instructions added, to wit: Thirty days from now, let the candidate appear at the town-hall at eight in the evening (Friday), and hand his remark, in a sealed envelope, to the Rev. Mr. Burgess (if he will be kind enough to act); and let Mr. Burgess there and then destroy the seals of the sack, open it, and see if the remark is correct; if correct, let the money be delivered, with my sincere gratitude, to my benefactor thus identified."

Mrs. Richards sat down, gently quivering with excitement, and was soon lost in thinkings—after this pattern: "What a strange thing it is!. . . . And what a fortune for that kind man who set his bread afloat upon the waters!. . . . If it had only been my husband that did it!—for we are so poor, so old and poor!. . . ." Then, with a sigh—"But it was not my Edward; no, it was not he that gave a stranger twenty dollars. It is a pity too; I see it now. . . ." Then, with a shudder—"But it is *gambler's* money! the wages of sin; we couldn't take it; we couldn't touch it. I don't like to be near it; it seems a defilement." She moved to a farther chair. . . . "I wish Edward would come, and take it to the bank; a burglar might come at any moment; it is dreadful to be here all alone with it."

At eleven Mr. Richards arrived, and while his wife was saying, "I am *so* glad you've come!" he was saying, "I'm so tired—tired clear out; it is dreadful to be poor, and have to make these dismal journeys at my time of life. Always at the grind, grind, grind, on a salary—another man's slave, and he sitting at home in his slippers, rich and comfortable."

"I am so sorry for you, Edward, you know that; but be comforted; we have our livelihood; we have our good name—"

"Yes, Mary, and that is everything. Don't mind my talk—it's just a moment's irritation and doesn't mean anything. Kiss me—there, it's all gone now, and I am not complaining any more. What have you been getting? What's in the sack?".

Then his wife told him the great secret. It dazed him for a moment; then he said:

"It weighs a hundred and sixty pounds? Why, Mary, it's for-ty thou-sand dollars—think of it—a whole fortune! Not ten men in this village are worth that much. Give me the paper."

He skimmed through it and said:

"Isn't it an adventure! Why, it's a romance; it's like the impossible things one reads about in books, and never sees in life." He was well stirred up now; cheerful, even gleeful. He tapped his old wife on the cheek, and said, humorously, "Why, we're rich, Mary, rich; all we've got to do is to bury the money and burn the papers. If the gambler ever comes to inquire, we'll merely look coldly upon him and say: 'What is this nonsense you are talking? We have never heard of you and your sack of gold before;' and then he would look foolish, and—"

"And in the mean time, while you are running on with your jokes, the money is still here, and it is fast getting along toward burglar-time."

"True. Very well, what shall we do—make the inquiry private? No, not that; it would spoil the romance. The public method is better. Think what a noise it will make! And it will make all the other towns jealous; for no stranger would trust such a thing to any town but Hadleyburg, and they know it. It's a great card for us. I must get to the printing-office now, or I shall be too late."

"But stop—stop—don't leave me here alone with it, Edward!"

But he was gone. For only a little while, however. Not far from his own house he met the editor-proprietor of the paper, and gave him the document, and said, "Here is a good thing for you, Cox—put it in."

"It may be too late, Mr. Richards, but I'll see."

At home again he and his wife sat down to talk the charming mystery over; they were in no condition for sleep. The first question was, Who could the citizen have been who gave the stranger the twenty dollars? It seemed a simple one; both answered it in the same breath—

"Barclay Goodson."

"Yes," said Richards, "he could have done it, and it would have been like him, but there's not another in the town."

"Everybody will grant that, Edward—grant it privately, anyway. For six months, now, the village has been its own proper self once more—honest, narrow, self-righteous, and stingy."

"It is what he always called it, to the day of his death—said it right out publicly, too."

"Yes, and he was hated for it."

"Oh, of course; but he didn't care. I reckon he was the best-hated man among us, except the Reverend Burgess."

"Well, Burgess deserves it—he will never get another congregation here. Mean as the town is, it knows how to estimate *him*. Edward, doesn't it seem odd that the stranger should appoint Burgess to deliver the money?"

"Well, yes—it does. That is—that is—"

"Why so much that-*is*-ing? Would *you* select him?"

"Mary, maybe the stranger knows him better than this village does."

"Much *that* would help Burgess!"

The husband seemed perplexed for an answer; the wife kept a steady eye upon him, and waited. Finally Richards said, with the hesitancy of one who is making a statement which is likely to encounter doubt,

"Mary, Burgess is not a bad man."

His wife was certainly surprised.

"Nonsense!" she exclaimed.

"He is not a bad man. I know. The whole of his unpopularity had its foundation in that one thing—the thing that made so much noise."

"That 'one thing,' indeed! As if that 'one thing' wasn't enough, all by itself."

"Plenty. Plenty. Only he wasn't guilty of it."

"How you talk! Not guilty of it! Everybody knows he *was* guilty."

"Mary, I give you my word—he was innocent."

"I can't believe it, and I don't. How do you know?"

"It is a confession. I am ashamed, but I will make it. I was the only man who knew he was innocent. I could have saved him, and—and—well, you know how the town was wrought up—I hadn't the pluck to do it. It would have turned everybody against me. I felt mean, ever so mean; but I didn't dare; I hadn't the manliness to face that."

Mary looked troubled, and for a while was silent. Then she said, stammeringly:

"I—I don't think it would have done for you to—to—One mustn't—er—public opinion—one has to be so careful—so—" It was a difficult road, and she got mired; but after a little she got started again. "It was a great pity, but—Why, we couldn't afford it, Edward—we couldn't indeed. Oh, I wouldn't have had you do it for anything!"

"It would have lost us the good-will of so many people, Mary; and then—and then—"

"What troubles me now is, what *he* thinks of us, Edward."

"He? *He* doesn't suspect that I could have saved him."

"Oh," exclaimed the wife, in a tone of relief, "I am glad of that. As long as he doesn't know that you could have saved him, he—he—well, that makes it a great deal better. Why, I might have known he didn't know, because he is always trying to be friendly with us, as little encouragement as we give him. More than once people have twitted me with it. There's the Wilsons, and the Wilcoxes, and the Harknesses, they take a mean pleasure in saying, '*Your friend* Burgess,' because they know it pesters me. I wish he wouldn't persist in liking us so; I can't think why he keeps it up."

"I can explain it. It's another confession. When the thing was new and hot, and the town made a plan to ride him on a rail, my conscience hurt me so that I couldn't stand it, and I went privately and gave him notice, and he got out of the town and staid out till it was safe to come back."

"Edward! If the town had found it out—"

"*Don't!* It scares me yet, to think of it. I repented of it the minute it was done; and I was even afraid to tell you, lest your face might betray it to somebody. I didn't sleep any that night, for worrying. But after a few days I saw that no one was going to suspect me, and after that I got to feeling glad I did it. And I feel glad yet, Mary—glad through and through."

"So do I, now, for it would have been a dreadful way to treat him. Yes, I'm glad; for really you did owe him that, you know. But, Edward, suppose it should come out yet, some day!"

"It won't."

"Why?"

"Because everybody thinks it was Goodson."

"Of course they would!"

"Certainly. And of course *he* didn't care. They persuaded poor old Sawlsberry to go and charge it on him, and he went blustering over there and did it. Goodson looked him over, like as if he was hunting for a place on him that he could despise the most, then he says, 'So you are the Committee of Inquiry, are you?' Sawlsberry said that was about what he was. 'Hm. Do they require particulars, or do you reckon a kind of a *general* answer will do?' 'If they require particulars, I will come back, Mr. Goodson; I will take the general answer first.' 'Very well, then, tell them to go to hell—I reckon that's general enough. And I'll give you some advice, Sawlsberry: when you come back for the particulars, fetch a basket to carry the relics of yourself home in.' "

"Just like Goodson; it's got all the marks. He had only one vanity; he thought he could give advice better than any other person."

"It settled the business, and saved us, Mary. The subject was dropped."

"Bless you, I'm not doubting *that*."

Then they took up the gold-sack mystery again, with strong interest. Soon the conversation began to suffer breaks—interruptions caused by absorbed thinkings. The breaks grew more and more frequent. At last Richards lost himself wholly in thought. He sat long, gazing vacantly at the floor, and by-and-by he began to punctuate his thoughts with little nervous movements of his hands that seemed to indicate vexation. Meantime his wife too had relapsed into a thoughtful silence, and her movements were beginning to show a troubled discomfort. Finally Richards got up and strode aimlessly about the room, ploughing his hands through his hair, much as a somnambulist might do who was having a bad dream. Then he seemed to arrive at a definite purpose; and without a word he put on his hat and passed quickly out of the house. His wife sat brooding, with a drawn face, and did not seem to be aware that she was alone. Now and then she murmured, "Lead us not into t. . . . but—but—we are so poor, so poor!. . . . Lead us not into. . . . Ah, who would be hurt by it?— and no one would ever know. . . . Lead us. . . ." The voice died out in mumblings. After a little she glanced up and muttered in a half-frightened, half-glad way—

"He is gone! But, oh dear, he may be too late—too late. . . . Maybe not— maybe there is still time." She rose and stood thinking, nervously clasping and unclasping her hands. A slight shudder shook her frame, and she said, out of a dry throat, "God forgive me—it's awful to think such things—but. . . . Lord, how we are made—how strangely we are made!"

She turned the light low, and slipped stealthily over and kneeled down by the sack and felt of its ridgy sides with her hands, and fondled them lovingly; and there was a gloating light in her poor old eyes. She fell into fits of absence; and came half out of them at times to mutter, "If we had only waited!—oh, if we had only waited a little, and not been in such a hurry!"

Meantime Cox had gone home from his office and told his wife all about the strange thing that had happened, and they had talked it over eagerly, and guessed that the late Goodson was the only man in the town who could have helped a suffering stranger with so noble a sum as twenty dollars. Then there was a pause, and the two became thoughtful and silent. And by-and-by nervous and fidgety. At last the wife said, as if to herself,

"Nobody knows this secret but the Richardses. . . . and us. . . . nobody."

The husband came out of his thinkings with a slight start, and gazed wistfully at his wife, whose face was become very pale; then he hesitatingly rose, and glanced furtively at his hat, then at his wife—a sort of mute inquiry. Mrs. Cox swallowed once or twice, with her hand at her throat, then in place of speech she nodded her head. In a moment she was alone, and mumbling to herself.

And now Richards and Cox were hurrying through the deserted streets, from opposite directions. They met, panting, at the foot of the printing-office stairs; by the night-light there they read each other's face. Cox whispered,

"Nobody knows about this but us?"

The whispered answer was,

"Not a soul—on honor, not a soul!"

"If it isn't too late to—"

The men were starting up stairs; at this moment they were overtaken by a boy, and Cox asked,

"Is that you, Johnny?"

"Yes, sir."

"You needn't ship the early mail—nor *any* mail; wait till I tell you."

"It's already gone, sir."

"Gone?" It had the sound of an unspeakable disappointment in it.

"Yes, sir. Time-table for Brixton and all the towns beyond changed to-day, sir—had to get the papers in twenty minutes earlier than common. I had to rush; if I had been two minutes later—"

The men turned and walked slowly away, not waiting to hear the rest. Neither of them spoke during ten minutes; then Cox said, in a vexed tone,

"What possessed you to be in such a hurry, *I* can't make out."

The answer was humble enough:

"I see it now, but somehow I never thought, you know, until it was too late. But the next time—"

"Next time be hanged! It won't come in a thousand years."

Then the friends separated without a good-night, and dragged themselves home with the gait of mortally stricken men. At their homes their wives sprang up with an eager "Well?"—then saw the answer with their eyes and sank down sorrowing, without waiting for it to come in words. In both houses a discussion followed of a heated sort—a new thing; there had been discussions before, but not heated ones, not ungentle ones. The discussions to-night were a sort of seeming plagiarisms of each other. Mrs. Richards said,

"If you had only waited, Edward—if you had only stopped to think; but no, you must run straight to the printing-office and spread it all over the world."

"It *said* publish it."

"That is nothing; it also said do it privately, if you liked. There, now—is that true, or not?"

"Why, yes—yes, it is true; but when I thought what a stir it would make, and what a compliment it was to Hadleyburg that a stranger should trust it so—"

"Oh, certainly, I know all that; but if you had only stopped to think, you would have seen that you *couldn't* find the right man, because he is in his grave, and hasn't left chick nor child nor relation behind him; and as long as the money went to somebody that awfully needed it, and nobody would be hurt by it, and—and—"

She broke down, crying. Her husband tried to think of some comforting thing to say, and presently came out with this:

"But after all, Mary, it must be for the best—it *must* be; we know that. And we must remember that it was so ordered—"

"Ordered! Oh, everything's *ordered*, when a person has to find some way out when he has been stupid. Just the same, it was *ordered* that the money should come to us in this special way, and it was you that must take it on yourself to go meddling with the designs of Providence—and who gave you the right. It was wicked, that is what it was—just blasphemous presumption, and no more becoming to a meek and humble professor of—"

"But, Mary, you know how we have been trained all our lives long, like the whole village, till it is absolutely second nature to us to stop not a single moment to think when there's an honest thing to be done—"

"Oh, I know it, I know it—it's been one everlasting training and training and training in honesty—honesty shielded, from the very cradle, against every possible temptation, and so it's *artificial* honesty, and weak as water when temptation comes, as we have seen this night. God knows I never had shade nor shadow of a doubt of my petrified and indestructible honesty until now—and now, under the very first big and real temptation, I— Edward, it is my belief that this town's honesty is as rotten as mine is; as rotten as yours is. It is a mean town, a hard, stingy town, and hasn't a virtue in the world but this honesty it is so celebrated for and so conceited about; and so help me, I do believe that if ever the day comes that its honesty falls under great temptation, its grand reputation will go to ruin like a house of cards. There, now, I've made confession, and I feel better; I am a humbug, and I've been one all my life, without knowing it. Let no man call me honest again— I will not have it."

"I—Well, Mary, I feel a good deal as you do; I certainly do. It seems strange, too, so strange. I never could have believed it—never."

A long silence followed; both were sunk in thought. At last the wife looked up and said,

"I know what you are thinking, Edward."

Richards had the embarrassed look of a person who is caught.

"I am ashamed to confess it, Mary, but—"

"It's no matter, Edward, I was thinking the same question myself."

"I hope so. State it."

"You were thinking, if a body could only guess out *what the remark was* that Goodson made to the stranger."

"It's perfectly true. I feel guilty and ashamed. And you?"

"I'm past it. Let us make a pallet here; we've got to stand watch till the bank vault opens in the morning and admits the sack. . . . Oh, dear, oh, dear— if we hadn't made the mistake!"

The pallet was made, and Mary said:

"The open sesame—what could it have been? I do wonder what that remark could have been? But come; we will get to bed now."

"And sleep?"

"No; think."

"Yes, think."

By this time the Coxes too had completed their spat and their reconciliation, and were turning in—to think, to think, and toss, and fret, and worry over what the remark could possibly have been which Goodson made to the stranded derelict: that golden remark; that remark worth forty thousand dollars, cash.

The reason that the village telegraph-office was open later than usual that night was this: The foreman of Cox's paper was the local representative of the Associated Press. One might say its honorary representative, for it wasn't four times a year that he could furnish thirty words that would be accepted. But this time it was different. His despatch stating what he had caught got an instant answer:

"Send the whole thing—all the details—twelve hundred words."

A colossal order! The foreman filled the bill; and he was the proudest man in the State. By breakfast-time the next morning the name of Hadleyburg the Incorruptible was on every lip in America, from Montreal to the Gulf, from the glaciers of Alaska to the orange-groves of Florida; and millions and millions of people were discussing the stranger and his money-sack, and wondering if the right man would be found, and hoping some more news about the matter would come soon—right away.

II

Hadleyburg village woke up world-celebrated—astonished—happy—vain. Vain beyond imagination. Its nineteen principal citizens and their wives went about shaking hands with each other, and beaming, and smiling, and congratulating, and saying *this* thing adds a new word to the dictionary—*Hadleyburg*, synonym for *incorruptible*—destined to live in dictionaries forever! And the minor and unimportant citizens and their wives went around acting in much the same way. Everybody ran to the bank to see the gold-sack; and before noon grieved and envious crowds began to flock in from Brixton and all neighboring towns; and that afternoon and next day reporters began to arrive from everywhere to verify the sack and its history and write the whole thing up anew, and make dashing free-hand pictures of the sack, and of Richards's house, and the bank, and the Presbyterian church, and the Baptist church, and the public square, and the town-hall where the test would be applied and the money delivered; and damnable portraits of the Richardses, and Pinkerton the banker, and Cox, and the foreman, and Reverend Burgess, and the postmaster—and even of Jack Halliday, who was the loafing, good-natured, no-account, irreverent fisherman, hunter, boys' friend, stray-dogs' friend, typical "Sam Lawson" of the town. The little mean, smirking, oily Pinkerton showed the sack to all comers, and rubbed his sleek palms together pleasantly, and enlarged upon the town's fine old reputation for honesty and upon this wonderful endorsement of it, and hoped and believed that the example would now spread far and wide over the American world, and be epoch-making in the matter of moral regeneration. And so on, and so on.

By the end of a week things had quieted down again; the wild intoxication of pride and joy had sobered to a soft, sweet, silent delight—a sort of deep, nameless, unutterable content. All faces bore a look of peaceful, holy happiness.

Then a change came. It was a gradual change: so gradual that its beginnings were hardly noticed; maybe were not noticed at all, except by Jack Halliday, who always noticed everything; and always made fun of it, too, no matter what it was. He began to throw out chaffing remarks about people not looking quite so happy as they did a day or two ago; and next he claimed that the new aspect was deepening to positive sadness; next, that it was taking on a sick look; and finally he said that everybody was become so moody, thoughtful, and absent-minded that he could rob the meanest man in town of a cent out of the bottom of his breeches pocket and not disturb his revery.

At this stage—or at about this stage—a saying like this was dropped at bedtime—with a sigh, usually—by the head of each of the nineteen principal households:

"Ah, what *could* have been the remark that Goodson made!"

And straightway—with a shudder—came this, from the man's wife:

"Oh, *don't!* What horrible thing are you mulling in your mind? Put it away from you, for God's sake!"

But that question was wrung from those men again the next night—and got the same retort. But weaker.

And the third night the men uttered the question yet again—with anguish, and absently. This time—and the following night—the wives fidgeted feebly, and tried to say something. But didn't.

And the night after that they found their tongues and responded—longingly,

"Oh, if we *could* only guess!"

Halliday's comments grew daily more and more sparklingly disagreeable and disparaging. He went diligently about, laughing at the town, individually and in mass. But his laugh was the only one left in the village: it fell upon a hollow and mournful vacancy and emptiness. Not even a smile was findable anywhere. Halliday carried a cigar-box around on a tripod, playing that it was a camera, and halted all passers and aimed the thing and said, "Ready!—now look pleasant, please," but not even this capital joke could surprise the dreary faces into any softening.

So three weeks passed—one week was left. It was Saturday evening—after supper. Instead of the aforetime Saturday-evening flutter and bustle and shopping and larking, the streets were empty and desolate. Richards and his old wife sat apart in their little parlor—miserable and thinking. This was become their evening habit now: the life-long habit which had preceded it, of reading, knitting, and contented chat, or receiving or paying neighborly calls, was dead and gone and forgotten, ages ago—two or three weeks ago; nobody talked now, nobody read, nobody visited—the whole village sat at home, sighing, worrying, silent. Trying to guess out that remark.

The postman left a letter. Richards glanced listlessly at the superscription and the post-mark—unfamiliar, both—and tossed the letter on the table and resumed his might-have-beens and his hopeless dull miseries where he had left them off. Two or three hours later his wife got wearily up and was going away to bed without a good-night—custom now—but she stopped near the letter and eyed it awhile with a dead interest, then broke it open, and began to skim it over. Richards, sitting there with his chair tilted back against the wall and his chin between his knees, heard something fall. It was his wife. He sprang to her side, but she cried out:

"Leave me alone, I am too happy. Read the letter—read it!"

He did. He devoured it, his brain reeling. The letter was from a distant State, and it said:

"I am a stranger to you, but no matter: I have something to tell. I have just arrived home from Mexico, and learned about that episode. Of course you do not know who made that remark, but I know, and I am the only person living who does know. It was *Goodson*. I knew him well, many years ago. I passed through your village that very night, and was his guest till the midnight train came along. I over-heard him make that remark to the stranger in the dark—it was in Hale Alley. He and I talked of it the rest of the way home, and while smoking in his house. He mentioned many of your villagers in the course of his talk—most of them in a very uncomplimentary way, but two or three favorably: among these latter yourself. I say 'favorably'— nothing stronger. I remember his saying he did not actually *like* any person in the town—not one; but that you—I *think* he said you—am almost sure—had done him a very great service once, possibly without knowing the full value of it, and he wished he had a fortune, he would leave it to you when he died, and a curse apiece for the rest of the citizens. Now, then, if it was you that did him that service, you are his legitimate heir, and entitled to the sack of gold. I know that I can trust to your honor and honesty, for in a citizen of Hadleyburg these virtues are an unfailing inheritance, and so I am going to reveal to you the remark, well satisfied that if you are not the right man you will seek and find the right one and see that poor

Goodson's debt of gratitude for the service referred to is paid. This is the remark: *'You are far from being a bad man: go, and reform.'*

HOWARD L. STEPHENSON."

"Oh, Edward, the money is ours, and I am so grateful, *oh*, so grateful—kiss me, dear, it's forever since we kissed—and we needed it so—the money—and now you are free of Pinkerton and his bank, and nobody's slave any more; it seems to me I could fly for joy."

It was a happy half-hour that the couple spent there on the settee caressing each other; it was the old days come again—days that had begun with their courtship and lasted without a break till the stranger brought the deadly money. By-and-by the wife said:

"Oh, Edward, how lucky it was you did him that grand service, poor Goodson! I never liked him, but I love him now. And it was fine and beautiful of you never to mention it or brag about it." Then, with a touch of reproach, "But you ought to have told *me*, Edward, you ought to have told your wife, you know."

"Well, I—er—well, Mary, you see—"

"Now stop hemming and hawing, and tell me about it, Edward. I always loved you, and now I'm proud of you. Everybody believes there was only one good generous soul in this village, and now it turns out that you—Edward, why don't you tell me?"

"Well—er—er—Why, Mary, I can't!"

"You *can't? Why* can't you?"

"You see, he—well, he—he made me promise I wouldn't."

The wife looked him over, and said, very slowly,

"Made—you—promise? Edward, what do you tell me that for?"

"Mary, do you think I would lie?"

She was troubled and silent for a moment, then she laid her hand within his and said:

"No. . . . no. We have wandered far enough from our bearings—God spare us that! In all your life you have never uttered a lie. But now—now that the foundations of things seem to be crumbling from under us, we—we—" She lost her voice for a moment, then said, brokenly, "Lead us not into temptation. . . . I think you made the promise, Edward. Let it rest so. Let us keep away from that ground. Now—that is all gone by; let us be happy again; it is no time for clouds."

Edward found it something of an effort to comply, for his mind kept wandering—trying to remember what the service was that he had done Goodson.

The couple lay awake the most of the night, Mary happy and busy, Edward busy, but not so happy. Mary was planning what she would do with the money. Edward was trying to recall that service. At first his conscience was sore on account of the lie he had told Mary—if it was a lie. After much reflection—suppose it *was* a lie? What then? Was it such a great matter? Aren't we always *acting* lies? Then why not *tell* them? Look at Mary—look what she had done. While he was hurrying off on his honest errand, what was she doing? Lamenting because the papers hadn't been destroyed and the money kept! Is theft better than lying?

That point lost its sting—the lie dropped into the background and left comfort behind it. The next point came to the front: *had* he rendered that service? Well, here was Goodson's own evidence as reported in Stephenson's letter; there could be no better evidence than that—it was even *proof* that he had rendered it. Of course. So that point was settled. . . . No, not quite. He recalled with a wince that this unknown Mr. Stephenson was just a trifle unsure as to whether the performer of it was Richards or some other—and, oh dear, he had put Richards on his honor! He must himself decide whither that money must go—and Mr. Stephenson was not doubting that if he was the wrong man he would go honorably and find the right one. Oh, it was odious to put a man in such a situation—ah, why couldn't Stephenson have left out that doubt! What did he want to intrude that for?

Further reflection. How did it happen that *Richards's* name remained in Stephenson's mind as indicating the right man, and not some other man's name? That looked good. Yes, that looked very good. In fact, it went on looking better and better, straight along—until by-and-by it grew into positive *proof*. And then Richards put the matter at once out of his mind, for he had a private instinct that a proof once established is better left so.

He was feeling reasonably comfortable now, but there was still one other detail that kept pushing itself on his notice: of course he had done that service—that was settled; but what *was* that service? He must recall it—he would not go to sleep till he had recalled it; it would make his peace of mind perfect. And so he thought and thought. He thought of a dozen things—possible services, even probable services—but none of them seemed adequate, none of them seemed large enough, none of them seemed worth the money—worth the fortune Goodson had wished he could leave in his will. And besides, he couldn't remember having done them, anyway. Now, then—now, then—what *kind* of a service would it be that would make a man so inordinately grateful? Ah— the saving of his soul! That must be it. Yes, he could remember, now, how he once set himself the task of converting Goodson, and labored at it as much as—he was going to say three months; but upon closer examination it shrunk to a month, then to a week, then to a day, then to nothing. Yes, he remembered, now, and with unwelcome vividness, that Goodson had told him to go to thunder and mind his own business—*he* wasn't hankering to follow Hadleyburg to heaven!

So that solution was a failure—he hadn't saved Goodson's soul. Richards was discouraged. Then after a little came another idea: had he saved Goodson's property? No, that wouldn't do—he hadn't any. His life? That is it! Of course. Why, he might have thought of it before. This time he was on the right track, sure. His imagination-mill was hard at work in a minute, now.

Thereafter during a stretch of two exhausting hours he was busy saving Goodson's life. He saved it in all kinds of difficult and perilous ways. In every case he got it saved satisfactorily up to a certain point; then, just as he was beginning to get well persuaded that it had really happened, a troublesome detail would turn up which made the whole thing impossible. As in the matter of drowning, for instance. In that case he had swum out and tugged Goodson ashore in an unconscious state with a great crowd looking on and applauding, but when he had got it all thought out and was just beginning to remember all about it a whole swarm of disqualifying details arrived on the ground: the town would have known of the circumstance, Mary would have known of it, it would glare like a limelight in his own memory instead of being an inconspicuous service which he had possibly rendered "without knowing its full value." And at this point he remembered that he couldn't swim, anyway.

Ah—*there* was a point which he had been overlooking from the start: it had to be a service which he had rendered "possibly without knowing the full value of it." Why, really, that ought to be an easy hunt—much easier than those others. And sure enough, by-and-by he found it. Goodson, years and years ago, came near marrying a very sweet and pretty girl, named Nancy Hewitt, but in some way or other the match had been broken off; the girl died, Goodson remained a bachelor, and by-and-by became a soured one and a frank despiser of the human species. Soon after the girl's death the village found out, or thought it had found out, that she carried a spoonful of negro blood in her veins. Richards worked at these details a good while, and in the end he thought he remembered things concerning them which must have gotten mislaid in his memory through long neglect. He seemed to dimly remember that it was *he* that found out about the negro blood; that it was he that told the village; that the village told Goodson where they got it; that he thus saved Goodson from marrying the tainted girl; that he had done him this great service "without knowing the full value of it," in fact without knowing that he *was* doing it; but that Goodson knew the value of it, and what a narrow escape he had had, and so went to his grave grateful to his benefactor and wishing he had a fortune to leave him. It was all clear and simple now, and the more he went over it the more luminous and certain it grew; and at last, when he nestled to sleep satisfied and happy, he remembered the whole thing just as if it had been yesterday. In fact, he dimly remembered Goodson's *telling* him his gratitude once. Meantime Mary had spent six thousand dollars on a new house for herself and a pair of slippers for her pastor, and then had fallen peacefully to rest.

That same Saturday evening the postman had delivered a letter to each of the other principal citizens—nineteen letters in all. No two of the envelopes were alike, and no two of the superscriptions were in the same hand, but the letters inside were just like each other in every detail but one. They were exact copies of the letter received by Richards—handwriting and all—and were all signed by Stephenson, but in place of Richards's name each receiver's own name appeared.

All night long eighteen principal citizens did what their caste-brother Richards was doing at the same time—they put in their energies trying to remember what notable service it was that they had unconsciously done Barclay Goodson. In no case was it a holiday job; still they succeeded.

And while they were at this work, which was difficult, their wives put in the night spending the money, which was easy. During that one night the nineteen wives spent an average of seven thousand dollars each out of the forty thousand in the sack—a hundred and thirty-three thousand altogether.

Next day there was a surprise for Jack Halliday. He noticed that the faces of the nineteen chief citizens and their wives bore that expression of peaceful and holy happiness again. He could not understand it, neither was he able to invent any remarks about it that could damage it or disturb it. And so it was his turn to be dissatisfied with life. His private guesses at the reasons for the happiness failed in all instances, upon examination. When he met Mrs. Wilcox and noticed the placid ecstasy in her face, he said to himself, "Her cat has had kittens"—and went and asked the cook; it was not so; the cook had detected the happiness, but did not know the cause. When Halliday found the duplicate ecstasy in the face of "Shadbelly" Billson (village nickname), he was sure some neighbor of Billson's had broken his leg, but inquiry showed that this had not happened. The subdued ecstasy in Gregory Yates's face could mean but one thing—he was a mother-in-law short; it was another mistake. "And Pinkerton—Pinkerton—he has collected ten cents that he thought he was going to lose." And so on, and so on. In some cases the guesses had to remain in doubt, in the others they proved distinct errors. In the end Halliday said to himself, "Anyway it foots up that there's nineteen Hadleyburg families temporarily in heaven; I don't know how it happened; I only know Providence is off duty to-day."

An architect and builder from the next State had lately ventured to set up a small business in this unpromising village, and his sign had now been hanging out a week. Not a customer yet; he was a discouraged man, and sorry he had come. But his weather changed suddenly now. First one and then another chief citizen's wife said to him privately:

"Come to my house Monday week—but say nothing about it for the present. We think of building."

He got eleven invitations that day. That night he wrote his daughter and broke off her match with her student. He said she could marry a mile higher than that.

Pinkerton the banker and two or three other well-to-do men planned country-seats—but waited. That kind don't count their chickens until they are hatched.

The Wilsons devised a grand new thing—a fancy-dress ball. They made no actual promises, but told all their acquaintanceship in confidence that they were thinking the matter over and thought they should give it—"and if we do, you will be invited, of course." People were surprised, and said, one to another, "Why, they are crazy, those poor Wilsons, they can't afford it." Several among the nineteen said privately to their husbands, "It is a good idea; we will keep still till their cheap thing is over, then *we* will give one that will make it sick."

The days drifted along, and the bill of future squanderings rose higher and higher, wilder and wilder, more and more foolish and reckless. It began to look as if every member of the nineteen would not only spend his whole forty thousand dollars before receiving-day, but be actually in debt by the time he got the money. In some cases light-headed people did not stop with planning to spend, they really spent—on credit. They bought land, mortgages, farms, speculative stocks, fine clothes, horses, and various other things, paid down the bonus, and made themselves liable for the rest—at ten days. Presently the sober second thought came, and Halliday noticed that a ghastly anxiety was beginning to show up in a good many faces. Again he was puzzled, and didn't know what to make of it. "The Wilcox kittens aren't dead, for they weren't born; nobody's broken a leg; there's no shrinkage in mother-in-laws; *nothing* has happened—it is an insolvable mystery."

There was another puzzled man, too—the Rev. Mr. Burgess. For days, wherever he went, people seemed to follow him or to be watching out for him; and if he ever found himself in a retired spot, a member of the nineteen would be sure to appear, thrust an envelope privately into his hand, whisper "To be opened at the town-hall Friday evening," then vanish away like a guilty thing. He was expecting that there might be one claimant for the sack—doubtful, however, Goodson being dead—but it never occurred to him that all this crowd might be claimants. When the great Friday came at last, he found that he had nineteen envelopes.

III

The town-hall had never looked finer. The platform at the end of it was backed by a showy draping of flags; at intervals along the walls were festoons of flags; the gallery fronts were clothed in flags; the supporting columns were swathed in flags; all this was to impress the stranger, for he would be there in considerable force, and in a large degree he would be connected with the press. The house was full. The 412 fixed seats were occupied; also the 68 extra chairs which had been packed into the aisles; the steps of the platform were occupied; some distinguished strangers were given seats on the platform; at the horseshoe of tables which fenced the front and sides of the platform sat a strong force of special correspondents who had come from everywhere. It was the best-dressed house the town had ever produced. There were some tolerably expensive toilets there, and in several cases the ladies who wore them had the look of being unfamiliar with that kind of clothes. At least the town thought they had that look, but the notion could have arisen from the town's knowledge of the fact that these ladies had never inhabited such clothes before.

The gold-sack stood on a little table at the front of the platform where all the house could see it. The bulk of the house gazed at it with a burning interest, a mouth-watering interest, a wistful and pathetic interest; a minority of nineteen couples gazed at it tenderly, lovingly, proprietarily, and the male half of this minority kept saying over to themselves the moving little impromptu speeches of thankfulness for the audience's applause and congratulations which they were presently going to get up and deliver. Every now and then one of these got a piece of paper out of his vest pocket and privately glanced at it to refresh his memory.

Of course there was a buzz of conversation going on—there always is; but at last when the Rev. Mr. Burgess rose and laid his hand on the sack he could hear his microbes gnaw, the place was so still. He related the curious history of the sack, then went on to speak in warm terms of Hadleyburg's old and well-earned reputation for spotless honesty, and of the town's just pride in this reputation. He said that this reputation was a treasure of priceless value; that under Providence its value had now become inestimably enhanced, for the recent episode had spread this fame far and wide, and thus had focussed the eyes of the American world upon this village, and made its name for all time, as he hoped and believed, a synonym for commercial incorruptibility. (*Applause.*) "And who is to be the guardian of this noble treasure—the community as a whole? No! The responsibility is individual, not communal. From this day forth each and every one of you is in his own person its special guardian, and individually responsible that no harm shall come to it. Do you—does each of you—accept this great trust? [*Tumultuous assent.*] Then all is well. Transmit it to your children and to your children's children. To-day your purity is beyond reproach—see to it that it shall remain so. To-day there is not a person in your community who could be beguiled to touch a penny not his own—see to it that you abide in this grace. ["*We will! we will!*"] This is not the place to make comparisons between ourselves and other communities—some of them ungracious toward us; they have their ways, we have ours; let us be content. [*Applause.*] I am done. Under my hand, my friends, rests a stranger's eloquent recognition of what we are; through him the world will always henceforth know what we are. We do not know who he is, but in your name I utter your gratitude, and ask you to raise your voices in indorsement."

The house rose in a body and made the walls quake with the thunders of its thankfulness for the space of a long minute. Then it sat down, and Mr. Burgess took an envelope out of his pocket. The house held its breath while he slit the envelope open and took from it a slip of paper. He read its contents—slowly and impressively—the audience listening with tranced attention to this magic document, each of whose words stood for an ingot of gold:

" '*The remark which I made to the distressed stranger was this: "You are very far from being a bad man; go, and reform."* ' " Then he continued: "We shall know in a moment now whether the remark here quoted corresponds with the one concealed in the sack; and if that shall prove to be so—and it undoubtedly will—this sack of gold belongs to a fellow-citizen who will henceforth stand before the nation as the symbol of the special virtue which has made our town famous throughout the land—Mr. Billson!"

The house had gotten itself all ready to burst into the proper tornado of applause; but instead of doing it, it seemed stricken with a paralysis; there was a deep hush for a moment or two, then a wave of whispered murmurs swept the place—of about this tenor: "*Billson!* oh, come, this is *too* thin! Twenty dollars to a stranger—or *anybody—Billson!* Tell it to the marines!" And now at this point the house caught its breath all of a sudden in a new access of astonishment, for it discovered that whereas in one part of the hall Deacon Billson was standing up with his head meekly bowed, in another part of it Lawyer Wilson was doing the same. There was a wondering silence now for a while. Everybody was puzzled, and nineteen couples were surprised and indignant.

Billson and Wilson turned and stared at each other. Billson asked, bitingly,

"Why do *you* rise, Mr. Wilson?"

"Because I have a right to. Perhaps you will be good enough to explain to the house why *you* rise?"

"With great pleasure. Because I wrote that paper."

"It is an impudent falsity! I wrote it myself."

It was Burgess's turn to be paralyzed. He stood looking vacantly at first one of the men and then the other, and did not seem to know what to do. The house was stupefied. Lawyer Wilson spoke up, now, and said,

"I ask the Chair to read the name signed to that paper."

That brought the Chair to itself, and it read out the name,

"'John Wharton *Billson.*'"

"There!" shouted Billson, "what have you got to say for yourself, now? And what kind of apology are you going to make to me and to this insulted house for the imposture which you have attempted to play here?"

"No apologies are due, sir; and as for the rest of it, I publicly charge you with pilfering my note from Mr. Burgess and substituting a copy of it signed with your own name. There is no other way by which you could have gotten hold of the test-remark; I alone, of living men, possessed the secret of its wording."

There was likely to be a scandalous state of things if this went on; everybody noticed with distress that the short-hand scribes were scribbling like mad; many people were crying "Chair, Chair! Order! order!" Burgess rapped with his gavel, and said:

"Let us not forget the proprieties due. There has evidently been a mistake somewhere, but surely that is all. If Mr. Wilson gave me an envelope—and I remember now that he did—I still have it."

He took one out of his pocket, opened it, glanced at it, looked surprised and worried, and stood silent a few moments. Then he waved his hand in a wandering and mechanical way, and made an effort or two to say something, then gave it up, despondently. Several voices cried out:

"Read it! read it! What is it?"

So he began in a dazed and sleep-walker fashion:

" 'The remark which I made to the unhappy stranger was this: "You are far from being a bad man. [The house gazed at him, marvelling.] *Go, and reform.*" ' [*Murmurs:* "Amazing! what can this mean?"] This one," said the Chair, "is signed Thurlow G. Wilson."

"There!" cried Wilson, "I reckon that settles it! I knew perfectly well my note was purloined."

"Purloined!" retorted Billson. "I'll let you know that neither you nor any man of your kidney must venture to—"

The Chair. "Order, gentlemen, order! Take your seats, both of you, please."

They obeyed, shaking their heads and grumbling angrily. The house was profoundly puzzled; it did not know what to do with this curious emergency. Presently Thompson got up. Thompson was the hatter. He would have liked to be a Nineteener; but such was not for him; his stock of hats was not considerable enough for the position. He said:

"Mr. Chairman, if I may be permitted to make a suggestion, can both of these gentlemen be right? I put it to you, sir, can both have happened to say the very same words to the stranger? It seems to me—"

The tanner got up and interrupted him. The tanner was a disgruntled man; he believed himself entitled to be a Nineteener, but he couldn't get recognition. It made him a little unpleasant in his ways and speech. Said he:

"Sho, *that's* not the point! *That* could happen—twice in a hundred years—but not the other thing. *Neither* of them gave the twenty dollars!" (*A ripple of applause.*)

Billson. "*I* did!"

Wilson. "*I* did!"

Then each accused the other of pilfering.

The Chair. "Order! Sit down, if you please—both of you. Neither of the notes has been out of my possession at any moment."

A Voice. "Good—that settles *that!*"

The Tanner. "Mr. Chairman, one thing is now plain: one of these men has been eavesdropping under the other one's bed, and filching family secrets. If it is not unparliamentary to suggest it, I will remark that both are equal to it. [*The Chair.* "Order! order!"] I withdraw the remark, sir, and will confine myself to suggesting that *if* one of them has overheard the other reveal the test-remark to his wife, we shall catch him now."

A Voice. "How?"

The Tanner. "Easily. The two have not quoted the remark in exactly the same words. You would have noticed that, if there hadn't been a considerable stretch of time and an exciting quarrel inserted between the two readings."

A Voice. "Name the difference."

The Tanner. "The word *very* is in Billson's note, and not in the other."

Many Voices. "That's so—he's right!"

The Tanner. "And so, if the Chair will examine the test-remark in the sack, we shall know which of these two frauds—[*The Chair.* "Order!"]—which of these two adventurers—[*The Chair.* "Order! order!"]—which of these two gentlemen—[*laughter and applause*]—is entitled to wear the belt as being the first dishonest blatherskite ever bred in this town—which he has dishonored, and which will be a sultry place for him from now out!" (*Vigorous applause.*)

Many Voices. "Open it!—open the sack!"

Mr. Burgess made a slit in the sack, slid his hand in and brought out an envelope. In it were a couple of folded notes. He said:

"One of these is marked, 'Not to be examined until all written communications which have been addressed to the Chair—if any—shall have been read.' The other is marked 'The Test.' Allow me. It is worded—to wit:

" 'I do not require that the first half of the remark which was made to me by my benefactor shall be quoted with exactness, for it was not striking, and could be forgotten; but its closing fifteen words are quite striking, and I think easily rememberable; unless *these* shall be accurately reproduced, let the applicant be regarded as an impostor. My benefactor began by saying he seldom gave advice to any one, but that it always bore the hall-mark of high value when he did give it. Then he said this—and it has never faded from my memory: *"You are far from being a bad man—"*'"

Fifty Voices. "That settles it—the money's Wilson's! Wilson! Wilson! Speech! Speech!"

People jumped up and crowded around Wilson, wringing his hand and congratulating fervently—meantime the Chair was hammering with the gavel and shouting:

"Order, gentlemen! Order! Order! Let me finish reading, please." When quiet was restored, the reading was resumed—as follows:

"'"Go, and reform—or, mark my words—some day, for your sins, you will die and go to hell or Hadleyburg—TRY AND MAKE IT THE FORMER."'"

A ghastly silence followed. First an angry cloud began to settle darkly upon the faces of the citizenship; after a pause the cloud began to rise, and a tickled expression tried to take its place; tried so hard that it was only kept under with great and painful difficulty; the reporters, the Brixtonites, and other strangers bent their heads down and shielded their faces with their hands, and managed to hold in by main strength and heroic courtesy. At this most inopportune time burst upon the stillness the roar of a solitary voice—Jack Halliday's:

"That's got the hall-mark on it!"

Then the house let go, strangers and all. Even Mr. Burgess's gravity broke down presently, then the audience considered itself officially absolved from all restraint, and it made the most of its privilege. It was a good long laugh, and a tempestuously whole-hearted one, but it ceased at last—long enough for Mr. Burgess to try to resume, and for the people to get their eyes partially wiped; then it broke out again; and afterward yet again; then at last Burgess was able to get out these serious words:

"It is useless to try to disguise the fact—we find ourselves in the presence of a matter of grave import. It involves the honor of your town, it strikes at the town's good name. The difference of a single word between the test-remarks offered by Mr. Wilson and Mr. Billson was itself a serious thing, since it indicated that one or the other of these gentlemen had committed a theft—"

The two men were sitting limp, nerveless, crushed; but at these words both were electrified into movement, and started to get up—

"Sit down!" said the Chair, sharply, and they obeyed. "That, as I have said, was a serious thing. And it was—but for only one of them. But the matter has become graver; for the honor of *both* is now in formidable peril. Shall I go even further, and say in inextricable peril? *Both* left out the crucial fifteen words." He paused. During several moments he allowed the pervading stillness to gather and deepen its impressive effects, then added: "There would seem to be but one way whereby this could happen. I ask these gentlemen— Was there *collusion?—agreement?"*

A low murmur sifted through the house; its import was, "He's got them both."

Billson was not used to emergencies; he sat in a helpless collapse. But Wilson was a lawyer. He struggled to his feet, pale and worried, and said:

"I ask the indulgence of the house while I explain this most painful matter. I am sorry to say what I am about to say, since it must inflict irreparable injury upon Mr. Billson, whom I have always esteemed and respected until now, and in whose invulnerability to temptation I entirely believed—as did you all. But for the preservation of my own honor I must speak—and with frankness. I confess with shame—and I now beseech your pardon for it—that I said to the ruined stranger all of the words contained in the test-remark, including the disparaging fifteen. [*Sensation.*] When the late publication was made I recalled them, and I resolved to claim the sack of coin, for by every right I was entitled to it. Now I will ask you to consider this point, and weigh it well: that stranger's gratitude to me that night knew no bounds; he said himself that he could find no words for it that were adequate, and that if he should ever be able he would repay me a thousandfold. Now, then, I ask you this: could I expect—could I believe—could I even remotely imagine—that, feeling as he did, he would do so ungrateful a thing as to add those quite unnecessary fifteen words to his test?—set a trap for me?—expose me as a slanderer of my own town before my own people assembled in a public hall? It was preposterous; it was impossible. His test would contain only the kindly opening clause of my remark. Of that I had no shadow of doubt. You would have thought as I did. You would not have expected a base betrayal from one whom you had befriended and against whom you had committed no offence. And so, with perfect confidence, perfect trust, I wrote on a piece of paper the opening words—ending with 'Go, and reform,'—and signed it. When I was about to put it in an envelope I was called into my back office, and without thinking I left the paper lying open on my desk." He stopped, turned his head slowly toward Billson, waited a moment, then added: "I ask you to note this: when I returned, a little later, Mr. Billson was retiring by my street door." (*Sensation.*)

In a moment Billson was on his feet and shouting:

"It's a lie!" It's an infamous lie!"

The Chair. "Be seated, sir! Mr. Wilson has the floor."

Billson's friends pulled him into his seat and quieted him, and Wilson went on:

"Those are the simple facts. My note was now lying in a different place on the table from where I had left it. I noticed that, but attached no importance to it, thinking a draught had blown it there. That Mr. Billson would read a private paper was a thing which could not occur to me; he was an honorable man, and he would be above that. If you will allow me to say it, I think his extra word 'very' stands explained; it is attributable to a defect of memory. I was the only man in the world who could furnish here any detail of the test-mark—by *honorable* means. I have finished."

There is nothing in the world like a persuasive speech to fuddle the mental apparatus and upset the convictions and debauch the emotions of an audience not practised in the tricks and delusions of oratory. Wilson sat down victorious. The house submerged him in tides of approving applause; friends swarmed to him and shook him by the hand and congratulated him, and Billson was shouted down and not allowed to say a word. The Chair hammered and hammered with its gavel, and kept shouting,

"But let us proceed, gentlemen, let us proceed!"

At last there was a measurable degree of quiet, and the hatter said,

"But what is there to proceed with, sir, but to deliver the money?"

Voices. "That's it! That's it! Come forward, Wilson!"

The Hatter. "I move three cheers for Mr. Wilson, Symbol of the special virtue which—"

The cheers burst forth before he could finish; and in the midst of them— and in the midst of the clamor of the gavel also—some enthusiasts mounted Wilson on a big friend's shoulder and were going to fetch him in triumph to the platform. The Chair's voice now rose above the noise—

"Order! To your places! You forget that there is still a document to be read." When quiet had been restored he took up the document, and was going to read it, but laid it down again, saying, "I forgot; this is not to be read until all written communications received by me have first been read." He took an envelope out of his pocket, removed its enclosure, glanced at it—seemed astonished—held it out and gazed at it—stared at it.

Twenty or thirty voices cried out:

"What is it? Read it! read it!"

And he did—slowly, and wondering:

"'The remark which I made to the stranger—[*Voices.* "Hello! how's this?"]—was this: "You are far from being a bad man. [*Voices.* "Great Scott!"] Go, and reform."' [*Voices.* "Oh, saw my leg off!"] Signed by Mr. Pinkerton the banker."

The pandemonium of delight which turned itself loose now was of a sort to make the judicious weep. Those whose withers were unwrung laughed till the tears ran down; the reporters, in throes of laughter, set down disordered pothooks which would never in the world be decipherable; and a sleeping dog jumped up, scared out of its wits, and barked itself crazy at the turmoil. All manner of cries were scattered through the din: "We're getting rich—*two* Symbols of Incorruptibility!—without counting Billson!" "*Three!*—count

Shadbelly in—we can't have too many!" "All right—Billson's elected!" "Alas, poor Wilson—victim of *two* thieves!"

A Powerful Voice. "Silence! The Chair's fished up something more out of its pocket."

Voices. "Hurrah! Is it something fresh? Read it! read! read!"

The Chair (reading). " 'The remark which I made,' etc. 'You are far from being a bad man. Go,' etc. Signed, 'Gregory Yates.'"

Tornado of Voices. "Four Symbols!" " 'Rah for Yates!" "Fish again!"

The house was in a roaring humor now, and ready to get all the fun out of the occasion that might be in it. Several Nineteeners, looking pale and distressed, got up and began to work their way toward the aisles, but a score of shouts went up:

"The doors, the doors—close the doors; no Incorruptible shall leave this place! Sit down, everybody!"

The mandate was obeyed.

"Fish again! Read! read!"

The Chair fished again, and once more the familiar words began to fall from its lips—" 'You are far from being a bad man—' "

"Name! name! What's his name?"

" 'L. Ingoldsby Sargent.' "

"Five elected! Pile up the Symbols! Go on, go on!"

" 'You are far from being a bad—' "

"Name! name!"

" 'Nicholas Whitworth.'"

"Hooray! hooray! it's a symbolical day!"

Somebody wailed in, and began to sing this rhyme (leaving out "it's") to the lovely *Mikado*[1] tune of "When a man's afraid of a beautiful maid"; the audience joined in, with joy; then, just in time, somebody contributed another line—

"And don't you this forget—"

The house roared it out. A third line was at once furnished—

"Corruptibles far from Hadleyburg are—"

The house roared that one too. As the last note died, Jack Halliday's voice rose high and clear, freighted with a final line—

"But the Symbols are here, you bet!"

---

[1] *The Mikado, or The Town of Titipu* (1885), a light comic opera by William Schwenck Gilbert (1836–1911) and Arthur Sullivan (1842–1900).

That was sung, with booming enthusiasm. Then the happy house started in at the beginning and sang the four lines through twice, with immense swing and dash, and finished up with a crashing three-times-three and a tiger for "Hadleyburg the Incorruptible and all Symbols of it which we shall find worthy to receive the hall-mark to-night."

Then the shoutings at the Chair began again, all over the place:

"Go on! go on! Read! read some more! Read all you've got!"

"That's it—go on! We are winning eternal celebrity!"

A dozen men got up now and began to protest. They said that this farce was the work of some abandoned joker, and was an insult to the whole community. Without a doubt these signatures were all forgeries—

"Sit down! sit down! Shut up! You are confessing. We'll find *your* names in the lot."

"Mr. Chairman, how many of those envelopes have you got?"

The Chair counted.

"Together with those that have been already examined, there are nineteen."

A storm of derisive applause broke out.

"Perhaps they all contain the secret. I move that you open them all and read every signature that is attached to a note of that sort—and read also the first eight words of the note."

"Second the motion!"

It was put and carried—uproariously. Then poor old Richards got up, and his wife rose and stood at his side. Her head was bent down, so that none might see that she was crying. Her husband gave her his arm, and so supporting her, he began to speak in a quavering voice:

"My friends, you have known us two—Mary and me—all our lives, and I think you have liked us and respected us—"

The Chair interrupted him:

"Allow me. It is quite true—that which you are saying, Mr. Richards; this town *does* know you two; it *does* like you; it *does* respect you; more—it honors you and *loves* you—"

Halliday's voice rang out:

"That's the hall-marked truth, too! If the Chair is right, let the house speak up and say it. Rise! Now, then—hip! hip! hip!—all together!"

The house rose in mass, faced toward the old couple eagerly, filled the air with a snow-storm of waving handkerchiefs, and delivered the cheers with all its affectionate heart.

The Chair then continued:

"What I was going to say is this: We know your good heart, Mr. Richards, but this is not a time for the exercise of charity toward offenders. [Shouts of

"Right! right!"] I see your generous purpose in your face, but I cannot allow you to plead for these men—"

"But I was going to—"

"Please take your seat, Mr. Richards. We must examine the rest of these notes—simple fairness to the men who have already been exposed requires this. As soon as that has been done—I give you my word for this—you shall be heard."

Many Voices. "Right!—the Chair is right—no interruption can be permitted at this stage! Go on!—the names! the names!—according to the terms of the motion!"

The old couple sat reluctantly down, and the husband whispered to the wife, "It is pitifully hard to have to wait; the shame will be greater than ever when they find we were only going to plead for *ourselves.*"

Straightway the jollity broke loose again with the reading of the names.

" 'You are far from being a bad man—' Signature, 'Robert J. Titmarsh.'

" 'You are far from being a bad man—' Signature, 'Eliphalet Weeks.'

" 'You are far from being a bad man—' Signature, 'Oscar B. Wilder.' "

At this point the house lit upon the idea of taking the eight words out of the Chairman's hands. He was not unthankful for that. Thenceforward he held up each note in its turn, and waited. The house droned out the eight words in a massed and measured and musical deep volume of sound (with a daringly close resemblance to a well-known church chant)—" 'You are f-a-r from being a b-a-a-a-d man.' " Then the Chair said, "Signature, 'Archibald Wilcox.' " And so on, and so on, name after name, and everybody had an increasingly and gloriously good time except the wretched Nineteen. Now and then, when a particularly shining name was called, the house made the Chair wait while it chanted the whole of the test-remark from the beginning to the closing words, "And go to hell or Hadleyburg—try and make it the for-or-m-e-r!" and in these special cases they added a grand and agonized and imposing "A-a-a-a-*men!*"

The list dwindled, dwindled, dwindled, poor old Richards keeping tally of the count, wincing when a name resembling his own was pronounced, and waiting in miserable suspense for the time to come when it would be his humiliating privilege to rise with Mary and finish his plea, which he was intending to word thus: " . . . for until now we have never done any wrong thing, but have gone our humble way unreproached. We are very poor, we are old, and have no chick nor child to help us; we were sorely tempted, and we fell. It was my purpose when I got up before to make confession and beg that my name might not be read out in this public place, for it seemed to us that we could not bear it; but I was prevented. It was just; it was our place to suffer with the rest. It has been hard for us. It is the first time we have ever heard our name fall from any one's lips—sullied. Be merciful—for the sake of the better days; make our shame as light to bear as in your charity you can." At this point in his revery Mary nudged him, perceiving that his mind was absent. The house was chanting, "You are f-a-r," etc.

"Be ready," Mary whispered. "Your name comes now; he has read eighteen."

The chant ended.

"Next! next! next!" came volleying from all over the house.

Burgess put his hand into his pocket. The old couple, trembling, began to rise. Burgess fumbled a moment, then said,

"I find I have read them all."

Faint with joy and surprise, the couple sank into their seats, and Mary whispered,

"Oh, bless God, we are saved!—he has lost ours—I wouldn't give this for a hundred of those sacks!"

The house burst out with its *Mikado* travesty, and sang it three times with ever-increasing enthusiasm, rising to its feet when it reached for the third time the closing line—

"But the Symbols are here, you bet!"

and finishing up with cheers and a tiger for "Hadleyburg purity and our eighteen immortal representatives of it."

Then Wingate, the saddler, got up and proposed cheers "for the cleanest man in town, the one solitary important citizen in it who didn't try to steal that money—Edward Richards."

They were given with great and moving heartiness; then somebody proposed that Richards be elected sole Guardian and Symbol of the now Sacred Hadleyburg Tradition, with power and right to stand up and look the whole sarcastic world in the face.

Passed, by acclamation; then they sang the *Mikado* again, and ended it with,

"And there's *one* Symbol left, you bet!"

There was a pause; then—

A Voice. "Now, then, who's to get the sack?"

The Tanner (with bitter sarcasm). "That's easy. The money has to be divided among the eighteen Incorruptibles. They gave the suffering stranger twenty dollars apiece—and that remark—each in his turn—it took twenty-two minutes for the procession to move past. Staked the stranger—total contribution, $360. All they want is just the loan back—and interest—forty thousand dollars altogether."

Many Voices (derisively). "That's it! Divvy! divvy! Be kind to the poor—don't keep them waiting!"

The Chair. "Order! I now offer the stranger's remaining document. It says: 'If no claimant shall appear [*grand chorus of groans*], I desire that you open the sack and count out the money to the principal citizens of your town, they to take it in trust [*Cries of "Oh! Oh! Oh!"*], and use it in such ways as to them shall seem best for the propagation and preservation of your community's noble reputation for incorruptible honesty [*more cries*]—a reputation to which their names and their efforts will add a new and far-reaching lustre.' [*Enthusiastic outburst of sarcastic applause.*] That seems to be all. No—here is a postscript:

" 'P. S.—CITIZENS OF HADLEYBURG: There *is* no test-remark—nobody made one. [*Great sensation.*] There wasn't any pauper stranger, nor any twenty-dollar contribution, nor any accompanying benediction and compliment—these are all inventions. [*General buzz and hum of astonishment and delight.*] Allow me to tell my story—it will take but a word or two. I passed through your town at a certain time, and received a deep offence which I had not earned. Any other man would have been content to kill one or two of you and call it square, but to me that would have been a trivial revenge, and inadequate; for the dead do not *suffer*. Besides, I could not kill you all—and, anyway, made as I am, even that would not have satisfied me. I wanted to damage every man in the place, and every woman—and not in their bodies or in their estate, but in their vanity—the place where feeble and foolish people are most vulnerable. So I disguised myself, and came back and studied you. You were easy game. You had an old and lofty reputation for honesty, and naturally you were proud of it—it was your treasure of treasures, the very apple of your eye. As soon as I found out that you carefully and vigilantly kept yourselves and your children *out of temptation*, I knew how to proceed. Why, you simple creatures, the weakest of all weak things is a virtue which has not been tested in the fire. I laid a plan, and gathered a list of names. My project was to corrupt Hadleyburg the Incorruptible. My idea was to make liars and thieves of nearly half a hundred smirchless men and women who had never in their lives uttered a lie or stolen a penny. I was afraid of Goodson. He was neither born nor reared in Hadleyburg. I was afraid that if I started to operate my scheme by getting my letter laid before you, you would say to yourselves, "Goodson is the only man among us who would give away twenty dollars to a poor devil"—and then you might not bite at my bait. But Heaven took Goodson; then I knew I was safe, and I set my trap and baited it. It may be that I shall not catch all the men to whom I mailed the pretended test secret, but I shall catch the most of them, if I know Hadleyburg nature. [*Voices.* "Right—he got every last one of them."] I believe they will even steal ostensible *gamble*-money, rather than miss, poor, tempted, and mistrained fellows. I am hoping to eternally and everlastingly squelch your vanity and give Hadleyburg a new renown—one that will *stick*—and spread far. If I have succeeded, open the sack and summon the Committee on Propagation and Preservation of the Hadleyburg Reputation.' "

A Cyclone of Voices. "Open it! Open it! The Eighteen to the front! Committee on Propagation of the Tradition! Forward—the Incorruptibles!"

The Chair ripped the sack wide, and gathered up a handful of bright, broad, yellow coins, shook them together, then examined them—

"Friends, they are only gilded disks of lead!"

There was a crashing outbreak of delight over this news, and when the noise had subsided, the tanner called out:

"By right of apparent seniority in this business, Mr. Wilson is Chairman of the Committee on Propagation of the Tradition. I suggest that he step forward on behalf of his pals, and receive in trust the money."

A Hundred Voices. "Wilson! Wilson! Wilson! Speech! Speech!"

Wilson (in a voice trembling with anger). "You will allow me to say, and without apologies for my language, *damn* the money!"

A Voice. "Oh, and him a Baptist!"

A Voice. "Seventeen Symbols left! Step up, gentlemen, and assume your trust!"

There was a pause—no response.

The Saddler. "Mr. Chairman, we've got *one* clean man left, anyway, out of the late aristocracy; and he needs money, and deserves it. I move that you appoint Jack Halliday to get up there and auction off that sack of gilt twenty-dollar pieces, and give the result to the right man—the man whom Hadleyburg delights to honor—Edward Richards."

This was received with great enthusiasm, the dog taking a hand again; the saddler started the bids at a dollar, the Brixton folk and Barnum's representative fought hard for it, the people cheered every jump that the bids made, the excitement climbed moment by moment higher and higher, the bidders got on their mettle and grew steadily more and more daring, more and more determined, the jumps went from a dollar up to five, then to ten, then to twenty, then fifty, then to a hundred, then—

At the beginning of the auction Richards whispered in distress to his wife: "Oh, Mary, can we allow it? It—it—you see, it is an honor-reward, a testimonial to purity of character, and—and—can we allow it? Hadn't I better get up and—Oh, Mary, what ought we to do?—what do you think we—" (*Halliday's voice. "Fifteen I'm bid!—fifteen for the sack!—twenty!—ah, thanks!—thirty—thanks again! Thirty, thirty, thirty!—do I hear forty?—forty it is! Keep the ball rolling, gentlemen, keep it rolling!—fifty!—thanks, noble Roman!—going at fifty, fifty, fifty!—seventy!—ninety!—splendid!—a hundred!—pile it up, pile it up!—hundred and twenty—forty!—just in time!—hundred and fifty!—TWO hundred!—superb! Do I hear two h—thanks!—two hundred and fifty!—"*)

"It is another temptation, Edward—I'm all in a tremble—but, oh, we've escaped *one* temptation, and that ought to warn us, to—[*"Six did I hear?— thanks!—six fifty, six f—*SEVEN *hundred!"*] And yet, Edward, when you think— nobody susp—[*"Eight hundred dollars!—hurrah!—make it nine!—Mr. Parsons, did I hear you say—thanks!—nine!—this noble sack of virgin lead going at only nine hundred dollars, gilding and all—come! do I hear—a thousand!— gratefully yours!—did some one say eleven?—a sack which is going to be the most celebrated in the whole Uni—"*] Oh, Edward" (beginning to sob), "we are *so* poor!—but—but—do as you think best—do as you think best."

Edward fell—that is, he sat still; sat with a conscience which was not sat- isfied, but which was overpowered by circumstances.

Meantime a stranger, who looked like an amateur detective gotten up as an impossible English earl, had been watching the evening's proceedings with manifest interest, and with a contented expression in his face; and he had been privately commenting to himself. He was now soliloquizing somewhat like this: "None of the Eighteen are bidding; that is not satisfactory; I must change that—the dramatic unities require it; they must buy the sack they tried to steal; they must pay a heavy price, too—some of them are rich. And another thing, when I make a mistake in Hadleyburg nature the man that puts that error upon me is entitled to a high honorarium, and some one must pay it. This poor old Richards has brought my judgment to shame; he is an honest man:—I don't understand it, but I acknowledge it. Yes, he saw my deuces-*and* with a straight flush, and by rights the pot is his. And it shall be a jack-pot, too, if I can manage it. He disappointed me, but let that pass."

He was watching the bidding. At a thousand, the market broke; the prices tumbled swiftly. He waited—and still watched. One competitor dropped out; then another, and another. He put in a bid or two, now. When the bids had sunk to ten dollars, he added a five; some one raised him a three; he waited a moment, then flung in a fifty-dollar jump, and the sack was his—at $1282. The house broke out in cheers—then stopped; for he was on his feet, and had lifted his hand. He began to speak.

"I desire to say a word, and ask a favor. I am a speculator in rarities, and I have dealings with persons interested in numismatics all over the world. I can make a profit on this purchase, just as it stands; but there is a way, if I can get your approval, whereby I can make every one of these leaden twenty-dollar pieces worth its face in gold, and perhaps more. Grant me that approval, and I will give part of my gains to your Mr. Richards, whose invulnerable probity you have so justly and so cordially recognized to-night; his share shall be ten thousand dollars, and I will hand him the money tomorrow. [*Great applause from the house.* But the "invulnerable probity" made the Richardses blush prettily; however, it went for modesty, and did no harm.] If you will pass my proposition by a good majority—I would like a two-thirds vote—I will regard that as the town's consent, and that is all I ask. Rarities are always helped by any device which will rouse curiosity and compel remark. Now if I may have your permission to stamp upon the faces of each of these ostensible coins the names of the eighteen gentlemen who—"

Nine-tenths of the audience were on their feet in a moment—dog and all—and the proposition was carried with a whirlwind of approving applause and laughter.

They sat down, and all the Symbols except "Dr." Clay Harkness got up, violently protesting against the proposed outrage, and threatening to—

"I beg you not to threaten me," said the stranger, calmly. "I know my legal rights, and am not accustomed to being frightened at bluster." (*Applause.*) He sat down. "Dr." Harkness saw an opportunity here. He was one of the two very rich men of the place, and Pinkerton was the other. Harkness was proprietor of a mint; that is to say, a popular patent medicine. He was running for the Legislature on one ticket, and Pinkerton on the other. It was a close race and a hot one, and getting hotter every day. Both had strong appetites for money; each had bought a great tract of land, with a purpose: there was going to be a new railway, and each wanted to be in the Legislature and help locate the route to his own advantage; a single vote might make the decision, and with it two or three fortunes. The stake was large, and Harkness was a daring speculator. He was sitting close to the stranger. He leaned over while one or another of the other Symbols was entertaining the house with protests and appeals, and asked, in a whisper,

"What is your price for the sack?"

"Forty thousand dollars."

"I'll give you twenty."

"No."

"Twenty-five."

"No."

"Say thirty."

"The price is forty thousand dollars; not a penny less."

"All right, I'll give it. I will come to the hotel at ten in the morning. I don't want it known; will see you privately."

"Very good." Then the stranger got up and said to the house:

"I find it late. The speeches of these gentlemen are not without merit, not without interest, not without grace; yet if I may be excused I will take my leave. I thank you for the great favor which you have shown me in granting my petition. I ask the Chair to keep the sack for me until tomorrow, and to hand these three five-hundred dollar notes to Mr. Richards." They were passed up to the Chair. "At nine I will call for the sack, and at eleven will deliver the rest of the ten thousand to Mr. Richards in person, at his home. Goodnight."

Then he slipped out, and left the audience making a vast noise, which was composed of a mixture of cheers, the *Mikado* song, dog-disapproval, and the chant, "You are f-a-r from being a b-a-a-d man—a-a-a-a-men!"

IV

At home the Richardses had to endure congratulations and compliments until midnight. Then they were left to themselves. They looked a little sad, and they sat silent and thinking. Finally Mary sighed and said,

"Do you think we are to blame, Edward—*much* to blame?" and her eyes wandered to the accusing triplet of big bank-notes lying on the table, where the congratulators had been gloating over them and reverently fingering them. Edward did not answer at once; then he brought out a sigh and said, hesitatingly:

"We—we couldn't help it, Mary. It—well, it was ordered. *All* things are."

Mary glanced up and looked at him steadily, but he didn't return the look. Presently she said:

"I thought congratulations and praises always tasted good. But—it seems to me, now—Edward?"

"Well?"

"Are you going to stay in the bank?"

"N-no."

"Resign?"

"In the morning—by note."

"It does seem best."

Richards bowed his head in his hands and muttered:

"Before, I was not afraid to let oceans of people's money pour through my hands, but—Mary, I am so tired, so tired—"

"We will go to bed."

At nine in the morning the stranger called for the sack and took it to the hotel in a cab. At ten Harkness had a talk with him privately. The stranger asked for and got five checks on a metropolitan bank—drawn to "Bearer,"—four for $1500 each, and one for $34,000. He put one of the former in his pocket-book, and the remainder, representing $38,500, he put in an envelope, and with these he added a note, which he wrote after Harkness was gone. At eleven he called at the Richards house and knocked. Mrs. Richards peeped through the shutters, then went and received the envelope, and the stranger disappeared without a word. She came back flushed and a little unsteady on her legs, and gasped out:

"I am sure I recognized him! Last night it seemed to me that maybe I had seen him somewhere before."

"He is the man that brought the sack here?"

"I am almost sure of it."

"Then he is the ostensible Stephenson too, and sold every important citizen in this town with his bogus secret. Now if he has sent checks instead of money, we are sold too, after we thought we had escaped. I was beginning to feel fairly comfortable once more, after my night's rest, but the look of that envelope makes me sick. It isn't fat enough; $8500 in even the largest banknotes makes more bulk than that."

"Edward, why do you object to checks?"

"Checks signed by Stephenson! I am resigned to take the $8500 if it could come in bank-notes—for it does seem that it was so ordered, Mary—but I have never had much courage, and I have not the pluck to try to market a check signed with that disastrous name. It would be a trap. That man tried to catch me; we escaped somehow or other; and now he is trying a new way. If it is checks—"

"Oh, Edward, it is *too* bad!" and she held up the checks and began to cry.

"Put them in the fire! quick! we mustn't be tempted. It is a trick to make the world laugh at *us*, along with the rest, and—Give them to *me*, since you can't do it!" He snatched them and tried to hold his grip till he could get to the stove; but he was human, he was a cashier, and he stopped a moment to make sure of the signature. Then he came near to fainting.

"Fan me, Mary, fan me! They are the same as gold!"

"Oh, how lovely, Edward! Why?"

"Signed by Harkness. What can the mystery of that be, Mary?"

"Edward, do you think—"

"Look here—look at this! Fifteen—fifteen—fifteen—thirty-four. Thirty-eight thousand five hundred! Mary, the sack isn't worth twelve dollars, and Harkness—apparently—has paid about par for it."

"And does it all come to us, do you think—instead of the ten thousand?"

"Why, it looks like it. And the checks are made to 'Bearer,' too."

"Is that good, Edward? What is it for?"

"A hint to collect them at some distant bank, I reckon. Perhaps Harkness doesn't want the matter known. What is that—a note?"

"Yes. It was with the checks."

It was in the "Stephenson" handwriting, but there was no signature. It said:

"I am a disappointed man. Your honesty is beyond the reach of temptation. I had a different idea about it, but I wronged you in that, and I beg pardon, and do it sincerely. I honor you—and that is sincere, too. This town is not worthy to kiss the hem of your garment. Dear sir, I made a square bet with myself that there were nineteen debauchable men in your self-righteous community. I have lost. Take the whole pot, you are entitled to it."

Richards drew a deep sigh, and said:

"It seems written with fire—it burns so. Mary—I am miserable again."

"I, too. Ah, dear, I wish—"

"To think, Mary—he *believes* in me."

"Oh, don't, Edward—I can't bear it."

"If those beautiful words were deserved, Mary—and God knows I believed I deserved them once—I think I could give the forty thousand dollars for them. And I would put that paper away, as representing more than gold and jewels, and keep it always. But now—We could not live in the shadow of its accusing presence, Mary."

He put it in the fire.

A messenger arrived and delivered an envelope. Richards took from it a note and read it; it was from Burgess.

> "You saved me, in a difficult time. I saved you last night. It was at cost of a lie, but I made the sacrifice freely, and out of a grateful heart. None in this village knows so well as I know how brave and good and noble you are. At bottom you cannot respect me, knowing as you do of that matter of which I am accused, and by the general voice condemned; but I beg that you will at least believe that I am a grateful man; it will help me to bear my burden.
>
> [Signed] BURGESS."

"Saved, once more. And on such terms!" He put the note in the fire. "I—I wish I were dead, Mary, I wish I were out of it all."

"Oh, these are bitter, bitter days, Edward. The stabs, through their very generosity, are so deep—and they come so fast!"

Three days before the election each of two thousand voters suddenly found himself in possession of a prized memento—one of the renowned bogus double-eagles. Around one of its faces was stamped these words: "THE REMARK I MADE TO THE POOR STRANGER WAS—" Around the other face was stamped these: "GO, AND REFORM. (SIGNED) PINKERTON." Thus the entire remaining refuse of the renowned joke was emptied upon a single head, and with calamitous effect. It revived the recent vast laugh and concentrated it upon Pinkerton; and Harkness's election was a walk-over.

Within twenty-four hours after the Richardses had received their checks their consciences were quieting down, discouraged; the old couple were learning to reconcile themselves to the sin which they had committed. But they were to learn, now, that a sin takes on new and real terrors when there seems a chance that it is going to be found out. This gives it a fresh and most substantial and important aspect. At church the morning sermon was of the usual pattern; it was the same old things said in the same old way; they had heard them a thousand times and found them innocuous, next to meaningless, and easy to sleep under; but now it was different: the sermon seemed to bristle with accusations; it seemed aimed straight and specially at people who were concealing deadly sins. After church they got away from the mob of congratulators as soon as they could, and hurried homeward, chilled to the bone at they did not know what— vague, shadowy, indefinite fears. And by chance they caught a glimpse of Mr. Burgess as he turned a corner. He paid no attention to their nod of recognition! He hadn't seen it; but they did not know that. What could his conduct mean? It might mean—it might mean—oh, a dozen dreadful things. Was it possible that he knew that Richards could have cleared him of guilt in that bygone time, and had been silently waiting for a chance to even up accounts? At home, in their distress they got to imagining that their servant might have been in the next room listening when Richards revealed the secret to his wife that he knew of Burgess's innocence; next, Richards began to imagine that he had heard the swish of a gown in there at that time; next, he was sure he *had* heard it. They would call Sarah in, on a pretext, and watch her face; if she had been betraying them to Mr. Burgess, it would show in her manner. They asked her some questions—questions which were so random and incoherent and seemingly purposeless that the girl felt sure that the old people's minds had been affected by their sudden good fortune; the sharp and watchful gaze which they bent upon her frightened her, and that completed the business. She blushed, she became nervous and confused, and to the old people these were plain signs of guilt—guilt of some fearful sort or other—without doubt she was a spy and a traitor. When they were alone again they began to piece many unrelated things together and get horrible results out of the combination. When things had got about to the worst, Richards was delivered of a sudden gasp, and his wife asked,

"Oh, what is it?—what is it?"

"The note—Burgess's note! Its language was sarcastic, I see it now." He quoted: "'At bottom you cannot respect me, *knowing*, as you do, of *that matter* of which I am accused'—oh, it is perfectly plain, now, God help me! He knows that I know! You see the ingenuity of the phrasing. It was a trap—and like a fool, I walked into it. And Mary—?"

"Oh, it is dreadful—I know what you are going to say—he didn't return your transcript of the pretended test-remark."

"No—kept it to destroy us with. Mary, he has exposed us to some already. I know it—I know it well. I saw it in a dozen faces after church. Ah, he wouldn't answer our nod of recognition—*he* knew what he had been doing!"

In the night the doctor was called. The news went around in the morning that the old couple were rather seriously ill—prostrated by the exhausting excitement growing out of their great windfall, the congratulations, and the late hours, the doctor said. The town was sincerely distressed; for these old people were about all it had left to be proud of, now.

Two days later the news was worse. The old couple were delirious, and were doing strange things. By witness of the nurses, Richards had exhibited checks—for $8500? No—for an amazing sum—$38,500! What could be the explanation of this gigantic piece of luck?

The following day the nurses had more news—and wonderful. They had concluded to hide the checks, lest harm come to them; but when they searched they were gone from under the patient's pillow—vanished away. The patient said:

"Let the pillow alone; what do you want?"

"We thought it best that the checks—"

"You will never see them again—they are destroyed. They came from Satan. I saw the hell-brand on them, and I knew they were sent to betray me to sin." Then he fell to gabbling strange and dreadful things which were not clearly understandable, and which the doctor admonished them to keep to themselves.

Richards was right; the checks were never seen again.

A nurse must have talked in her sleep, for within two days the forbidden gabblings were the property of the town; and they were of a surprising sort. They seemed to indicate that Richards had been a claimant for the sack himself, and that Burgess had concealed that fact and then maliciously betrayed it.

Burgess was taxed with this and stoutly denied it. And he said it was not fair to attach weight to the chatter of a sick old man who was out of his mind. Still, suspicion was in the air, and there was much talk.

After a day or two it was reported that Mrs. Richards's delirious deliveries were getting to be duplicates of her husband's. Suspicion flamed up into conviction, now, and the town's pride in the purity of its one undiscredited important citizen began to dim down and flicker toward extinction.

Six days passed, then came more news. The old couple were dying. Richards's mind cleared in his latest hour, and he sent for Burgess. Burgess said:

"Let the room be cleared. I think he wishes to say something in privacy."

"No!" said Richards; "I want witnesses. I want you all to hear my confession, so that I may die a man, and not a dog. I was clean—artificially—like the rest; and like the rest I fell when temptation came. I signed a lie, and claimed the miserable sack. Mr. Burgess remembered that I had done him a service, and in gratitude (and ignorance) he suppressed my claim and saved me. You know the thing that was charged against Burgess years ago. My testimony, and mine alone, could have cleared him, and I was a coward, and left him to suffer disgrace—"

"No—no—Mr. Richards, you—"

"My servant betrayed my secret to him—"

"No one has betrayed anything to me—"

—"and then he did a natural and justifiable thing; he repented of the saving kindness which he had done me, and he *exposed* me—as I deserved—"

"Never!—I make oath—"

"Out of my heart I forgive him."

Burgess's impassioned protestations fell upon deaf ears; the dying man passed away without knowing that once more he had done poor Burgess a wrong. The old wife died that night.

The last of the sacred Nineteen had fallen a prey to the fiendish sack; the town was stripped of the last rag of its ancient glory. Its mourning was not showy, but it was deep.

By act of the Legislature—upon prayer and petition—Hadleyburg was allowed to change its name to (never mind what—I will not give it away), and leave one word out of the motto that for many generations had graced the town's official seal.

It is an honest town once more, and the man will have to rise early that catches it napping again.

[1899]

EDITH WHARTON
[1862–1937]

In her 1934 autobiography, A Backward Glance, *Edith Wharton advised readers to be "unafraid of change, insatiable in intellectual curiosity, interested in big things, and happy in small ways." These qualities define her work, which spans a vast range of genres and displays both her international awareness and her sensitivity to detail. Along with more than thirty volumes of prose fiction, Wharton's works include three collections of poetry, five travel books, an astute study of French culture, a co-authored treatise on* The Decoration of Houses, *personal and professional memoirs, and numerous essays and reviews. During Wharton's lifetime, her fiction enjoyed both popular appeal and critical acclaim. Her 1905* The House of Mirth *was an unexpected bestseller, her 1920* The Age of Innocence *received the Pulitzer Prize, and in 1930, Wharton became the first woman writer to be honored with a gold medal by the National Institute of Arts and Letters.*

Such novels as The House of Mirth, The Custom of the Country *(1913), and* The Age of Innocence *have positioned Wharton within the tradition of the novel of manners, a genre popularized by Jane Austen and characterized by its focus on social customs and often by its depiction of conflicts between the individual and social conventions. Wharton's psychologically complex characters struggle both to come to terms with personal longings silenced by societal influences and to reconcile these longings with social allegiances. As in the case of* Mirth's *Lily Bart, who halfheartedly pursues expected social goals yet "despises the things she's trying for," these psychological and social struggles often culminate in tragedy. Blending the influences of classical drama, nineteenth-century fiction, and turn-of-the-century social and economic theory, Wharton crafted narratives that present both stark images of suffering and fierce indictments of cultural hypocrisy.*

Wharton's earliest memory was of her "awakening to the importance of dress, and to herself as an object for adornment." Born into one of Old New York's wealthiest and most elite families, Wharton was aware of her social position's benefits and burdens virtually "since infancy." Her parents, George Frederic and Lucretia Rhinelander Jones, were descendants of Dutch and English colonists who had established family fortunes. Along with wealth, Wharton's parents had inherited their ancestors' elite social status—something that, in Old New York society, newcomers and those born in lower social classes could never purchase or achieve. Old New York's leisure class viewed the newly wealthy as ostentatious, ill-mannered, and threatening to established social conventions. More broadly, as portrayed in Wharton's society novels, these elite families distrusted innovation and ambition, even—and in some cases, especially—when displayed by members of their own circle. Throughout Wharton's childhood and adolescence, her mother adorned the family's drawing room with numerous figurines and oil paintings of her daughter—constant reminders of the upperclass woman's role as an aesthetic object whose value was determined by her image in others' eyes. Ironically, in The Decoration of Houses (1897), co-authored with architect Ogden Codman, Wharton criticized such elaborate displays in both American interior design and upperclass family life. Overfurnished and difficult to navigate, cluttered with ornamental objects, and shrouded with thick curtains, the Victorian American drawing room symbolized disturbing trends in upperclass society—its pursuit of frivolous activities and objects to distract attention from interpersonal conflicts, its paranoid exclusivity, and its obsessive maintenance of familial privacy at the expense of domestic comfort.

Although Wharton received private tutoring and read widely from her father's library, her parents discouraged her imaginative tendencies and desire to write. Within the family's social circle, writing was viewed as "something between a black art and a form of manual labor," and Wharton's mother feared that her daughter's literary ambitions might jeopardize her social position. As Wharton matured, the conflict between her authorial aspirations and her expected career as a socialite wife intensified. When her first engagement was broken, The New York Daily News reported that Wharton's fiancé disapproved of her creative inclinations. Shortly thereafter, in 1885, she married Edward "Teddy" Wharton. Although the couple's frequent European sojourns provided material for Wharton's travel writings, Teddy never shared his wife's intellectual and artistic interests. This problem, along with Teddy's mental illness, contributed to the marriage's decline and the couple's eventual divorce. Teddy, whose father had committed suicide in 1891, began exhibiting severe psychological symptoms around 1900. While Teddy grew more socially withdrawn, Wharton's success and her deepening involvement in American expatriate and European literary communities exacerbated tensions within the marriage.

Edith Wharton's work quickly attained popularity, but critical recognition came slowly. Early critics tended to cast her as the disciple of her good friend, the more celebrated novelist Henry James. Indeed, there are important thematic and stylistic similarities between the two authors' works. Yet

Wharton's work has its own distinction, in part for its perceptive critique of Victorian models of American womanhood. Such critique is perhaps most evident in her portrayal of The House of Mirth's *Lily, the marriage market commodity who is ultimately consumed by the society that produced her. A victim of sexual hypocrisy, Lily is exiled from her social circle by scandalous gossip. Reduced to menial work in a hat-making factory, Lily labors to produce the very trappings with which she herself was once adorned. In New York society's eyes, Lily has failed to fulfill her assigned role. Yet, as her demise demonstrates, she can sustain no role beyond the one her society has cast.*

Along with dramatizing sexual hypocrisy's destructive effects, Wharton explored the hidden power of female sexuality itself. Her brief affair with the journalist Morton Fullerton, which began in Paris in 1908, inspired her most explicitly erotic writings—a private journal of the relationship, as well as the poetic pieces "The Mortal Lease" and "Colophon to 'The Mortal Lease'" (1909). In turn, her fiction—most notably The Age of Innocence, Summer *(1917), and the short story "Roman Fever" (1934)—portrays women's covert rebellions against sexual repression and hypocrisy. In these works, female figures outwardly conform to cultural expectations while concealing crucial knowledge about sexual matters or secrets regarding their own sexuality. At the end of each work, a shrewd plot twist exposes the inaccuracy of other characters' or society's perceptions of women, revealing women to be more complex, intelligent, and artful than others—especially men—typically recognize.*

Although Wharton's narratives frequently center on the urban leisure class and women, her portrayals of small-town and working-class subjects demonstrate the range of Wharton's insight into the tyranny of rigid traditionalism and social hierarchy in American society. Much as her detailed descriptions of drawing rooms and evening dresses contribute to her portraits of Old New York, the bleak landscapes of Ethan Frome *(1911) evoke the economic stagnation and social desolation pervading the aptly named Starkfield, a rural New England village. In this novel, often considered Wharton's darkest work and the best example of classical tragedy's influence on her fiction, the Starkfield landscape fuses with the terrain of the title character's consciousness. From his hometown soil spring ominous markers of his ancestors' inability to escape the town's literal and psychological confines. Ultimately, Ethan's imaginative fancies reinforce his environment's constraints, and the Starkfield landscape figures prominently in the tragedy that condemns the text's three major figures to a dismal fate. Here, as in much of her fiction, Wharton portrays her characters both as creations of and in rebellion against their social and physical environments.*

Edith Wharton's short stories brilliantly illustrate this complex relationship between her characters and their surroundings. In ghost stories such as "The

Eyes" (1910) and "Mr. Jones" (1928), the interplay between supernatural forces and genteel settings reveals the characters' repressed psychic torments and unspoken interpersonal conflicts. Similarly, in "Souls Belated" (1899), a married woman, Lydia, who has traveled to Europe with her lover, must choose between the "respectability" of her former life in America and the freedom of fleeing to Paris with her beloved. The resort hotel where the couple settles temporarily and pretends to be married provides a middle ground between these two symbolic destinations, a catalyst for Lydia's ruminations, and a vehicle for the text's explorations of cultural convention's role in defining romantic relationships.

The 1910s initiated major changes in Wharton's own cultural allegiances and her ties to marital "respectability." After twenty-eight largely unhappy years of marriage, she finally sought a divorce from Teddy in 1913 and settled in Europe. During World War I, she repaid France, the country that had given her psychic refuge and creative stimulation, by becoming one of the nation's most dynamic social reformers. She founded the American Hostels for Refugees, which offered housing and provisions to the many who had fled Belgium, and collaborated with other humanitarian activists to create workrooms for impoverished female laborers. She was especially concerned with the plight of Europe's children, and, largely for her efforts on their behalf, Wharton was named a Chevalier of the Legion of Honor by the French government. She shaped her extensive observations of French culture into French Ways and Their Meaning (1914). In Fighting France: From Dunkerque to Belfort (1915), she presented a compelling portrait of the relief effort, which motivated many to contribute to the cause. In fact, although she continued writing fiction, many consider her nonfiction pieces the strongest products of her late career. Her treatise on The Writing of Fiction (1925) has led many scholars to reevaluate Wharton's contribution to literary criticism. During the last twenty-five years of her life, she returned to her homeland only once—in 1923—to accept the first honorary doctorate that Yale University had ever awarded to a woman.

The tensions in Wharton's own life shaped both her fiction and her career in social reform. She helped to rebuild war-torn France, reviving interest in its history and traditions, and she portended the fall of Gilded Age New York, vividly capturing its luxuries and facades. Yet even as she critically examined American society within an international context, she sympathetically portrayed the psychic conflicts of individual Americans. Through Edith Wharton's work, readers may relish luxuries forever lost, gain perspective on the historical context surrounding these social fixtures, and experience some of American literature's most memorable and evocative scenes.

Lucinda M. Kriete
Washington University

509

For Further Reading

Primary Works

The Decoration of Houses, 1897; *The House of Mirth*, 1905; *Madame de Treymes*, 1907; *Artemis to Actaeon and Other Verse*, 1909; *Ethan Frome*, 1911; *The Reef*, 1912; *The Custom of the Country*, 1913; *Fighting France: From Dunkerque to Belfort*, 1915; *Summer*, 1917; *The Marne*, 1918; *French Ways and Their Meaning*, 1919; *The Age of Innocence*, 1920; *Old New York*, 1924; *The Mother's Recompense*, 1925; *The Writing of Fiction*, 1925; *A Backward Glance*, 1934; *The Collected Short Stories of Edith Wharton*, 2 vols., ed. R. W. B. Lewis, 1968; *The Letters of Edith Wharton*, eds. R. W. B. Lewis and Nancy Lewis, 1989; *Edith Wharton: The Uncollected Critical Writings*, ed. Frederick Wegener, 1996; *Edith Wharton Abroad: Selected Travel Writings*, 1888–1920, ed. Sarah Bird Wright, 1996.

Secondary Works

Irving Howe, ed., *Edith Wharton*, 1962; R. W. B. Lewis, *Edith Wharton: A Biography*, 1975; Elizabeth Ammons, *Edith Wharton's Argument with America*, 1980; Carol Wershoven, *The Female Intruder in the Novels of Edith Wharton*, 1982; Linda Wagner-Martin, *The House of Mirth: A Novel of Admonition*, 1990; Susan Goodman, *Edith Wharton's Women: Friends and Rivals*, 1990; David Holbrook, *Edith Wharton and the Unsatisfactory Man*, 1991; Barbara A. White, *Edith Wharton: A Study of the Short Fiction*, 1991; Gloria C. Erlich, *The Sexual Education of Edith Wharton*, 1992; Kristin Lauer and James Tuttleton, eds., *Edith Wharton: The Contemporary Reviews*, 1992; Alan Price and Katherine Joslin, eds., *Wretched Exotic: Essays on Edith Wharton in Europe*, 1993; Dale M. Bauer, *Edith Wharton's Brave New Politics*, 1994; Shari Benstock, *No Gifts from Chance: A Biography of Edith Wharton*, 1994; Carol Singley, *Edith Wharton: Matters of Mind and Spirit*, 1995; Millicent Bell, ed., *The Cambridge Companion to Edith Wharton*, 1995; Linda Wagner-Martin, *The Age of Innocence: A Novel of Ironic Nostalgia*, 1996; Sarah Bird Wright, *Edith Wharton A to Z: The Essential Guide to the Life and Work*, 1998; Clare Colquitt, Susan Goodman, and Candace Waid, eds., *A Forward Glance: New Essays on Edith Wharton*, 1999; Hildegard Hoeller, *Edith Wharton's Dialogue with Realism and Sentimental Fiction*, 2000.

The Other Two

EDITH WHARTON

I

WAYTHORN, ON THE DRAWING-ROOM HEARTH, waited for his wife to come down to dinner.

It was their first night under his own roof, and he was surprised at his thrill of boyish agitation. He was not so old, to be sure—his glass gave him little more than the five-and-thirty years to which his wife confessed—but he had fancied himself already in the temperate zone; yet here he was listening for her step with a tender sense of all it symbolised, with some old trail of verse about the garlanded nuptial door-posts floating through his enjoyment of the pleasant room and the good dinner just beyond it.

They had been hastily recalled from their honey-moon by the illness of Lily Haskett, the child of Mrs. Waythorn's first marriage. The little girl, at Waythorn's desire, had been transferred to his house on the day of her mother's wedding, and the doctor, on their arrival, broke the news that she was ill with typhoid, but declared that all the symptoms were favourable. Lily could show twelve years of unblemished health, and the case promised to be a light one. The nurse spoke as reassuringly, and after a moment of alarm Mrs. Waythorn had adjusted herself to the situation. She was very fond of Lily— her affection for the child had perhaps been her decisive charm in Waythorn's eyes—but she had the perfectly balanced nerves which her little girl had inherited, and no woman ever wasted less tissue in unproductive worry. Waythorn was therefore quite prepared to see her come in presently, a little late because of a last look at Lily, but as serene and well-appointed as if her goodnight kiss had been laid on the brow of health. Her composure was restful to him; it acted as ballast to his somewhat unstable sensibilities. As he pictured her bending over the child's bed he thought how soothing her presence must be in illness: her very step would prognosticate recovery.

His own life had been a gray one, from temperament rather than circumstance, and he had been drawn to her by the unperturbed gaiety which kept

First published in *Colliers Weekly* in 1904. Also collected in *The Descent of Man, and Other Stories*, the same year.

her fresh and elastic at an age when most women's activities are growing either slack or febrile. He knew what was said about her; for, popular as she was, there had always been a faint undercurrent of detraction. When she had appeared in New York, nine or ten years earlier, as the pretty Mrs. Haskett whom Gus Varick had unearthed somewhere—was it in Pittsburgh or Utica?—society, while promptly accepting her, had reserved the right to cast a doubt on its own indiscrimination. Enquiry, however, established her undoubted connection with a socially reigning family, and explained her recent divorce as the natural result of a runaway match at seventeen; and as nothing was known of Mr. Haskett it was easy to believe the worst of him.

Alice Haskett's remarriage with Gus Varick was a passport to the set whose recognition she coveted, and for a few years the Varicks were the most popular couple in town. Unfortunately, the alliance was brief and stormy, and this time the husband had his champions. Still, even Varick's staunchest supporters admitted that he was not meant for matrimony, and Mrs. Varick's grievances were of a nature to bear the inspection of the New York courts. A New York divorce is in itself a diploma of virtue, and in the semi-widowhood of this second separation Mrs. Varick took on an air of sanctity, and was allowed to confide her wrongs to some of the most scrupulous ears in town. But when it was known that she was to marry Waythorn there was a momentary reaction. Her best friends would have preferred to see her remain in the rôle of the injured wife, which was as becoming to her as crape to a rosy complexion. True, a decent time had elapsed, and it was not even suggested that Waythorn had supplanted his predecessor. People shook their heads over him, however, and one grudging friend, to whom he affirmed that he took the step with his eyes open, replied oracularly: "Yes—and with your ears shut."

Waythorn could afford to smile at these innuendoes. In the Wall Street phrase, he had "discounted" them. He knew that society has not yet adapted itself to the consequences of divorce, and that till the adaptation takes place every woman who uses the freedom the law accords her must be her own social justification. Waythorn had an amused confidence in his wife's ability to justify herself. His expectations were fulfilled, and before the wedding took place Alice Varick's group had rallied openly to her support. She took it all imperturbably: she had a way of surmounting obstacles without seeming to be aware of them, and Waythorn looked back with wonder at the trivialities over which he had worn his nerves thin. He had the sense of having found refuge in a richer, warmer nature than his own, and his satisfaction, at the moment, was humorously summed up in the thought that his wife, when she had done all she could for Lily, would not be ashamed to come down and enjoy a good dinner.

The anticipation of such enjoyment was not, however, the sentiment expressed by Mrs. Waythorn's charming face when she presently joined him. Though she had put on her most engaging teagown she had neglected to assume the smile that went with it, and Waythorn thought he had never seen her look so nearly worried.

"What is it?" he asked. "Is anything wrong with Lily?"

"No; I've just been in and she's still sleeping." Mrs. Waythorn hesitated. "But something tiresome has happened."

He had taken her two hands, and now perceived that he was crushing a paper between them.

"This letter?"

"Yes—Mr. Haskett has written—I mean his lawyer has written."

Waythorn felt himself flush uncomfortably. He dropped his wife's hands.

"What about?"

"About seeing Lily. You know the courts—"

"Yes, yes," he interrupted nervously.

Nothing was known about Haskett in New York. He was vaguely supposed to have remained in the outer darkness from which his wife had been rescued, and Waythorn was one of the few who were aware that he had given up his business in Utica and followed her to New York in order to be near his little girl. In the days of his wooing, Waythorn had often met Lily on the doorstep, rosy and smiling, on her way "to see papa."

"I am so sorry," Mrs. Waythorn murmured.

He roused himself. "What does he want?"

"He wants to see her. You know she goes to him once a week."

"Well—he doesn't expect her to go to him now, does he?"

"No—he has heard of her illness; but he expects to come here."

"*Here?*"

Mrs. Waythorn reddened under his gaze. They looked away from each other.

"I'm afraid he has the right. . . . You'll see. . . ." She made a proffer of the letter.

Waythorn moved away with a gesture of refusal. He stood staring about the softly lighted room, which a moment before had seemed so full of bridal intimacy.

"I'm so sorry," she repeated. "If Lily could have been moved—"

"That's out of the question," he returned impatiently.

"I suppose so."

Her lip was beginning to tremble, and he felt himself a brute.

"He must come, of course," he said. "When is—his day?"

"I'm afraid—to-morrow."

"Very well. Send a note in the morning."

The butler entered to announce dinner.

Waythorn turned to his wife. "Come—you must be tired. It's beastly, but try to forget about it," he said, drawing her hand through his arm.

"You're so good, dear. I'll try," she whispered back.

Her face cleared at once, and as she looked at him across the flowers, between the rosy candle-shades, he saw her lips waver back into a smile.

"How pretty everything is!" she sighed luxuriously.

He turned to the butler. "The champagne at once, please. Mrs. Waythorn is tired."

In a moment or two their eyes met above the sparkling glasses. Her own were quite clear and untroubled: he saw that she had obeyed his injunction and forgotten.

II

Waythorn, the next morning, went down town earlier than usual. Haskett was not likely to come till the afternoon, but the instinct of flight drove him forth. He meant to stay away all day—he had thoughts of dining at his club. As his door closed behind him he reflected that before he opened it again it would have admitted another man who had as much right to enter it as himself, and the thought filled him with a physical repugnance.

He caught the "elevated" at the employees' hour, and found himself crushed between two layers of pendulous humanity. At Eighth Street the man facing him wriggled out, and another took his place. Waythorn glanced up and saw that it was Gus Varick. The men were so close together that it was impossible to ignore the smile of recognition on Varick's handsome over-blown face. And after all—why not? They had always been on good terms, and Varick had been divorced before Waythorn's attentions to his wife began. The two exchanged a word on the perennial grievance of the congested trains, and when a seat at their side was miraculously left empty the instinct of self-preservation made Waythorn slip into it after Varick.

The latter drew the stout man's breath of relief. "Lord—I was beginning to feel like a pressed flower." He leaned back, looking unconcernedly at Waythorn. "Sorry to hear that Sellers is knocked out again."

"Sellers?" echoed Waythorn, starting at his partner's name.

Varick looked surprised. "You didn't know he was laid up with the gout?"

"No. I've been away—I only got back last night." Waythorn felt himself reddening in anticipation of the other's smile.

"Ah—yes; to be sure. And Sellers's attack came on two days ago. I'm afraid he's pretty bad. Very awkward for me, as it happens, because he was just putting through a rather important thing for me."

"Ah?" Waythorn wondered vaguely since when Varick had been dealing in "important things." Hitherto he had dabbled only in the shallow pools of speculation, with which Waythorn's office did not usually concern itself.

It occurred to him that Varick might be talking at random, to relieve the strain of their propinquity. That strain was becoming momentarily more apparent to Waythorn, and when, at Cortlandt Street, he caught sight of an acquaintance and had a sudden vision of the picture he and Varick must present to an initiated eye, he jumped up with a muttered excuse.

"I hope you'll find Sellers better," said Varick civilly, and he stammered back: "If I can be of any use to you—" and let the departing crowd sweep him to the platform.

At his office he heard that Sellers was in fact ill with the gout, and would probably not be able to leave the house for some weeks.

"I'm sorry it should have happened so, Mr. Waythorn," the senior clerk said with affable significance. "Mr. Sellers was very much upset at the idea of giving you such a lot of extra work just now."

"Oh, that's no matter," said Waythorn hastily. He secretly welcomed the pressure of additional business, and was glad to think that, when the day's work was over, he would have to call at his partner's on the way home.

He was late for luncheon, and turned in at the nearest restaurant instead of going to his club. The place was full, and the waiter hurried him to the back of the room to capture the only vacant table. In the cloud of cigar-smoke Waythorn did not at once distinguish his neighbours; but presently, looking about him, he saw Varick seated a few feet off. This time, luckily, they were too far apart for conversation, and Varick, who faced another way, had probably not even seen him; but there was an irony in their renewed nearness.

Varick was said to be fond of good living, and as Waythorn sat despatching his hurried luncheon he looked across half enviously at the other's leisurely degustation of his meal. When Waythorn first saw him he had been helping himself with critical deliberation to a bit of Camembert at the ideal point of liquefaction, and now, the cheese removed, he was just pouring his *café double* from its little two-storied earthen pot. He poured slowly, his ruddy profile bent above the task, and one beringed white hand steadying the lid of the coffee-pot; then he stretched his other hand to the decanter of cognac at his elbow, filled a liqueur-glass, took a tentative sip, and poured the brandy into his coffee-cup.

Waythorn watched him in a kind of fascination. What was he thinking of—only of the flavour of the coffee and the liqueur? Had the morning's meeting left no more trace in his thoughts than on his face? Had his wife so completely passed out of his life that even this odd encounter with her present husband, within a week after her remarriage, was no more than an incident in his day? And as Waythorn mused, another idea struck him: had Haskett ever met Varick as Varick and he had just met? The recollection of Haskett perturbed him, and he rose and left the restaurant, taking a circuitous way out to escape the placid irony of Varick's nod.

It was after seven when Waythorn reached home. He thought the footman who opened the door looked at him oddly.

"How is Miss Lily?" he asked in haste.

"Doing very well, sir. A gentleman—"

"Tell Barlow to put off dinner for half an hour," Waythorn cut him off, hurrying upstairs.

He went straight to his room and dressed without seeing his wife. When he reached the drawing-room she was there, fresh and radiant. Lily's day had been good; the doctor was not coming back that evening.

At dinner Waythorn told her of Seller's illness and of the resulting complications. She listened sympathetically, adjuring him not to let himself be overworked, and asking vague feminine questions about the routine of the office. Then she gave him the chronicle of Lily's day; quoted the nurse and doctor, and told him who had called to inquire. He had never seen her more serene and unruffled. It struck him, with a curious pang, that she was very happy in being with him, so happy that she found a childish pleasure in rehearsing the trivial incidents of her day.

After dinner they went to the library, and the servant put the coffee and liqueurs on a low table before her and left the room. She looked singularly soft and girlish in her rosy pale dress, against the dark leather of one of his bachelor armchairs. A day earlier the contrast would have charmed him.

He turned away now, choosing a cigar with affected deliberation.

"Did Haskett come?" he asked, with his back to her.

"Oh, yes—he came."

"You didn't see him, of course?"

She hesitated a moment. "I let the nurse see him."

That was all. There was nothing more to ask. He swung round toward her, applying a match to his cigar. Well, the thing was over for a week, at any rate. He would try not to think of it. She looked up at him, a trifle rosier than usual, with a smile in her eyes.

"Ready for your coffee, dear?"

He leaned against the mantelpiece, watching her as she lifted the coffeepot. The lamplight struck a gleam from her bracelets and tipped her soft hair with brightness. How light and slender she was, and how each gesture flowed into the next! She seemed a creature all compact of harmonies. As the thought of Haskett receded, Waythorn felt himself yielding again to the joy of possessorship. They were his, those white hands with their flitting motions, his the light haze of hair, the lips and eyes. . . .

She set down the coffee-pot, and reaching for the decanter of cognac, measured off a liqueur-glass and poured it into his cup.

Waythorn uttered a sudden exclamation.

"What is the matter?" she said, startled.

"Nothing; only—I don't take cognac in my coffee."

"Oh, how stupid of me," she cried.

Their eyes met, and she blushed a sudden agonised red.

III

Ten days later, Mr. Sellers, still house-bound, asked Waythorn to call on his way down town.

The senior partner, with his swaddled foot propped up by the fire, greeted his associate with an air of embarrassment.

"I'm sorry, my dear fellow; I've got to ask you to do an awkward thing for me."

Waythorn waited, and the other went on, after a pause apparently given to the arrangement of his phrases: "The fact is, when I was knocked out I had just gone into a rather complicated piece of business for—Gus Varick."

"Well?" said Waythorn, with an attempt to put him at his ease.

"Well—it's this way: Varick came to me the day before my attack. He had evidently had an inside tip from somebody, and had made about a hundred thousand. He came to me for advice, and I suggested his going in with Vanderlyn."

"Oh, the deuce!" Waythorn exclaimed. He saw in a flash what had happened. The investment was an alluring one, but required negotiation. He listened quietly while Sellers put the case before him, and, the statement ended, he said: "You think I ought to see Varick?"

"I'm afraid I can't as yet. The doctor is obdurate. And this thing can't wait. I hate to ask you, but no one else in the office knows the ins and outs of it."

Waythorn stood silent. He did not care a farthing for the success of Varick's venture, but the honour of the office was to be considered, and he could hardly refuse to oblige his partner.

"Very well," he said, "I'll do it."

That afternoon, apprised by telephone, Varick called at the office. Waythorn, waiting in his private room, wondered what the others thought of it. The newspapers, at the time of Mrs. Waythorn's marriage, had acquainted their readers with every detail of her previous matrimonial ventures, and Waythorn could fancy the clerks smiling behind Varick's back as he was ushered in.

517

Varick bore himself admirably. He was easy without being undignified, and Waythorn was conscious of cutting a much less impressive figure. Varick had no experience of business, and the talk prolonged itself for nearly an hour while Waythorn set forth with scrupulous precision the details of the proposed transaction.

"I'm awfully obliged to you," Varick said as he rose. "The fact is I'm not used to having much money to look after, and I don't want to make an ass of myself—" He smiled, and Waythorn could not help noticing that there was something pleasant about his smile. "It feels uncommonly queer to have enough cash to pay one's bills. I'd have sold my soul for it a few years ago!"

Waythorn winced at the allusion. He had heard it rumoured that a lack of funds had been one of the determining causes of the Varick separation, but it did not occur to him that Varick's words were intentional. It seemed more likely that the desire to keep clear of embarrassing topics had fatally drawn him into one. Waythorn did not wish to be outdone in civility.

"We'll do the best we can for you," he said. "I think this is a good thing you're in."

"Oh, I'm sure it's immense. It's awfully good of you—" Varick broke off, embarrassed. "I suppose the thing's settled now—but if—"

"If anything happens before Sellers is about, I'll see you again," said Waythorn quietly. He was glad, in the end, to appear the more self-possessed of the two.

The course of Lily's illness ran smooth, and as the days passed Waythorn grew used to the idea of Haskett's weekly visit. The first time the day came round, he stayed out late, and questioned his wife as to the visit on his return. She replied at once that Haskett had merely seen the nurse downstairs, as the doctor did not wish any one in the child's sick-room till after the crisis.

The following week Waythorn was again conscious of the recurrence of the day, but had forgotten it by the time he came home to dinner. The crisis of the disease came a few days later, with a rapid decline of fever, and the little girl was pronounced out of danger. In the rejoicing which ensued the thought of Haskett passed out of Waythorn's mind, and one afternoon, letting himself into the house with a latchkey, he went straight to his library without noticing a shabby hat and umbrella in the hall.

In the library he found a small effaced-looking man with a thinnish gray beard sitting on the edge of a chair. The stranger might have been a piano-tuner, or one of those mysteriously efficient persons who are summoned in emergencies to adjust some detail of the domestic machinery. He blinked at Waythorn through a pair of gold-rimmed spectacles and said mildly: "Mr. Waythorn, I presume? I am Lily's father."

Waythorn flushed. "Oh—" he stammered uncomfortably. He broke off, disliking to appear rude. Inwardly he was trying to adjust the actual Haskett to the image of him projected by his wife's reminiscences. Waythorn had been allowed to infer that Alice's first husband was a brute.

"I am sorry to intrude," said Haskett, with his over-the-counter politeness.

"Don't mention it," returned Waythorn, collecting himself. "I suppose the nurse has been told?"

"I presume so. I can wait," said Haskett. He had a resigned way of speaking, as though life had worn down his natural powers of resistance.

Waythorn stood on the threshold, nervously pulling off his gloves.

"I'm sorry you've been detained. I will send for the nurse," he said; and as he opened the door he added with an effort: "I'm glad we can give you a good report of Lily." He winced as the *we* slipped out, but Haskett seemed not to notice it.

"Thank you, Mr. Waythorn. It's been an anxious time for me."

"Ah, well, that's past. Soon she'll be able to go to you." Waythorn nodded and passed out.

In his own room he flung himself down with a groan. He hated the womanish sensibility which made him suffer so acutely from the grosteque chances of life. He had known when he married that his wife's former husbands were both living, and that amid the multiplied contact of modern existence there were a thousand chances to one that he would run against one or the other, yet he found himself as much disturbed by his brief encounter with Haskett as though the law had not obligingly removed all difficulties in the way of their meeting.

Waythorn sprang up and began to pace the room nervously. He had not suffered half as much from his two meetings with Varick. It was Haskett's presence in his own house that made the situation so intolerable. He stood still, hearing steps in the passage.

"This way, please," he heard the nurse say. Haskett was being taken upstairs, then: not a corner of the house but was open to him. Waythorn dropped into another chair, staring vaguely ahead of him. On his dressing-table stood a photograph of Alice, taken when he had first known her. She was Alice Varick then—how fine and exquisite he had thought her! Those were Varick's pearls about her neck. At Waythorn's instance they had been returned before her marriage. Had Haskett ever given her any trinkets—and what had become of them, Waythorn wondered? He realised suddenly that he knew very little of Haskett's past or present situation; but from the man's appearance and manner of speech he could reconstruct with curious precision the surroundings of Alice's first marriage. And it startled him to think that she had, in the background of her life, a phase of existence so different from any-thing with which he had connected her. Varick, whatever his faults, was a gen-tleman, in the conventional, traditional sense of the term: the sense which at that moment seemed, oddly enough, to have most meaning to Waythorn. He and Varick had the same social habits, spoke the same language, understood the same allusions. But this other man . . . it was grotesquely uppermost in Waythorn's mind that Haskett had worn a made-up tie attached with an elas-tic. Why should that ridiculous detail symbolise the whole man? Waythorn was exasperated by his own paltriness, but the fact of the tie expanded, forced itself on him, became as it were the key to Alice's past. He could see her, as Mrs. Haskett, sitting in a "front parlour" furnished in plush, with a pianola, and a copy of "Ben Hur" on the centre-table. He could see her going to the theatre with Haskett—or perhaps even to a "Church Sociable"—she in a "pic-ture hat" and Haskett in a black frock-coat, a little creased, with the made-up tie on an elastic. On the way home they would stop and look at the illumi-nated shopwindows, lingering over the photographs of New York actresses. On Sunday afternoons Haskett would take her for a walk, pushing Lily ahead of them in a white enamelled perambulator, and Waythorn had a vision of the people they would stop and talk to. He could fancy how pretty Alice must have looked, in a dress adroitly constructed from the hints of a New York fashion-paper, and how she must have looked down on the other women, chafing at her life, and secretly feeling that she belonged in a bigger place.

For the moment his foremost thought was one of wonder at the way in which she had shed the phase of existence which her marriage with Haskett implied. It was as if her whole aspect, every gesture, every inflection, every allusion, were a studied negation of that period of her life. If she had denied being married to Haskett she could hardly have stood more convicted of duplicity than in this obliteration of the self which had been his wife.

Waythorn started up, checking himelf in the analysis of her motives. What right had he to create a fantastic effigy of her and then pass judgment on it? She had spoken vaguely of her first marriage as unhappy, had hinted, with becoming reticence, that Haskett had wrought havoc among her young illu-sions. . . . It was a pity for Waythorn's peace of mind that Haskett's very inof-fensiveness shed a new light on the nature of those illusions. A man would rather think that his wife has been brutalised by her first husband than that the process has been reversed.

IV

"Mr. Waythorn, I don't like that French governess of Lily's."

Haskett, subdued and apologetic, stood before Waythorn in the library, revolving his shabby hat in his hand.

Waythorn, surprised in his armchair over the evening paper, stared back perplexedly at his visitor.

"You'll excuse my asking to see you," Haskett continued. "But this is my last visit, and I thought if I could have a word with you it would be a better way than writing to Mrs. Waythorn's lawyer."

Waythorn rose uneasily. He did not like the French governess either; but that was irrelevant.

"I am not so sure of that," he returned stiffly; "but since you wish it I will give your message to—my wife." He always hesitated over the possessive pronoun in addressing Haskett.

The latter sighed. "I don't know as that will help much. She didn't like it when I spoke to her."

Waythorn turned red. "When did you see her?" he asked.

"Not since the first day I came to see Lily—right after she was taken sick. I remarked to her then that I didn't like the governess."

Waythorn made no answer. He remembered distinctly that, after that first visit, he had asked his wife if she had seen Haskett. She had lied to him then, but she had respected his wishes since; and the incident cast a curious light on her characer. He was sure she would not have seen Haskett that first day if she had divined that Waythorn would object, and the fact that she did not divine it was almost as disagreeable to the latter as the discovery that she had lied to him.

"I don't like the woman," Haskett was repeating with mild persistency. "She ain't straight, Mr. Waythorn—she'll teach the child to be underhand, I've noticed a change in Lily—she's too anxious to please—and she don't always tell the truth. She used to be the straightest child, Mr. Waythorn—" He broke off, his voice a little thick. "Not but what I want her to have a stylish education," he ended.

Waythorn was touched. "I'm sorry, Mr. Haskett; but frankly, I don't quite see what I can do."

Haskett hesitated. Then he laid his hat on the table, and advanced to the hearthrug, on which Waythorn was standing. There was nothing aggressive in his manner, but he had the solemnity of a timid man resolved on a decisive measure.

"There's just one thing you can do, Mr. Waythorn," he said. "You can remind Mrs. Waythorn that, by the decree of the courts, I am entitled to have a voice in Lily's bringing-up." He paused, and went on more deprecatingly: "I'm not the kind to talk about enforcing my rights, Mr. Waythorn. I don't know as I think a man is entitled to rights he hasn't known how to hold on to; but this business of the child is different. I've never let go there—and I never mean to."

The scene left Waythorn deeply shaken. Shamefacedly, in indirect ways, he had been finding out about Haskett; and all that he had learned was favorable. The little man, in order to be near his daughter, had sold out his share in a profitable business in Utica, and accepted a modest clerkship in a New York manufacturing house. He boarded in a shabby street and had few acquaintances. His passion for Lily filled his life. Waythorn felt that this exploration of Haskett was like groping about with a dark lantern in his wife's past; but he saw now that there were recesses his lantern had not explored. He had never inquired into the exact circumstances of his wife's first matrimonial rupture. On the surface all had been fair. It was she who had obtained the divorce, and the court had given her the child. But Waythorn knew how many ambiguities such a verdict might cover. The mere fact that Haskett retained a right over his daughter implied an unsuspected compromise. Waythorn was an idealist. He always refused to recognize unpleasant contingencies till he found himself confronted with them, and then he saw them followed by a spectral train of consequences. His next days were thus haunted, and he determined to try to lay the ghosts by conjuring them up in his wife's presence.

When he repeated Haskett's request a flame of anger passed over her face; but she subdued it instantly and spoke with a slight quiver of outraged motherhood.

"It is very ungentlemanly of him," she said.

The word grated on Waythorn. "That is neither here nor there. It's a bare question of rights."

She murmured: "It's not as if he could ever be a help to Lily—"

Waythorn flushed. This was even less to his taste. "The question is," he repeated "what authority has he over her?"

She looked downward, twisting herself a little in her seat. "I am willing to see him—I thought you objected," she faltered.

In a flash he understood that she knew the extent of Haskett's claims. Perhaps it was not the first time she had resisted them.

"My objecting has nothing to do with it," he said coldly; "if Haskett has a right to be consulted you must consult him."

She burst into tears, and he saw that she expected him to regard her as a victim.

Haskett did not abuse his rights. Waythorn had felt miserably sure that he would not. But the governess was dismissed, and from time to time the little man demanded an interview with Alice. After the first outburst she accepted the situation with her usual adaptability. Haskett had once reminded Waythorn of the piano tuner, and Mrs. Waythorn, after a month or two, appeared to class him with that domestic familiar. Waythorn could not but respect the father's tenacity. At first he had tried to cultivate the suspicion that

Haskett might be "up to" something, that he had an object in securing a foothold in the house. But in his heart Waythorn was sure of Haskett's single-mindedness; he even guessed in the latter a mild contempt for such advantages as his relation with the Waythorns might offer. Haskett's sincerity of purpose made him invulnerable, and his successor had to accept him as a lien on the property.

Mr. Sellers was sent to Europe to recover from his gout, and Varick's affairs hung on Waythorn's hands. The negotiations were prolonged and complicated; they necessitated frequent conferences between the two men, and the interests of the firm forbade Waythorn's suggesting that his client should transfer his business to another office.

Varick appeared well in the transaction. In moments of relaxation his coarse streak appeared, and Waythorn dreaded his geniality; but in the office he was concise and clear-headed, with a flattering deference to Waythorn's judgment. Their business relations being so affably established, it would have been absurd for the two men to ignore each other in society. The first time they met in a drawing room, Varick took up their intercourse in the same easy key, and his hostess' grateful glance obliged Waythorn to respond to it. After that they ran across each other frequently, and one evening at a ball Waythorn, wandering through the remoter rooms, came upon Varick seated beside his wife. She colored a little, and faltered in what she was saying; but Varick nodded to Waythorn without rising, and the latter strolled on.

In the carriage, on the way home, he broke out nervously: "I didn't know you spoke to Varick."

Her voice trembled a little. "It's the first time—he happened to be standing near me; I didn't know what to do. It's so awkward, meeting everywhere—and he said you had been very kind about some business."

"That's different," said Waythorn.

She paused a moment. "I'll do just as you wish," she returned pliantly. "I thought it would be less awkward to speak to him when we meet."

Her pliancy was beginning to sicken him. Had she really no will of her own—no theory about her relation to these men? She had accepted Haskett—did she mean to accept Varick? It was "less awkward," as she had said, and her instinct was to evade difficulties or to circumvent them. With sudden vividness Waythorn saw how the instinct had developed. She was "as easy as an old shoe"—a shoe that too many feet had worn. Her elasticity was the result of tension in too many different directions. Alice Haskett—Alice Varick—Alice Waythorn—she had been each in turn, and had left hanging to each name a little of her privacy, a little of her personality, a little of the inmost self where the unknown god abides.

"Yes—it's better to speak to Varick," said Waythorn wearily.

V

The winter wore on, and society took advantage of the Waythorns' acceptance of Varick. Harassed hostesses were grateful to them for bridging over a social difficulty, and Mrs. Waythorn was held up as a miracle of good taste. Some experimental spirits could not resist the diversion of throwing Varick and his former wife together, and there were those who thought he found a zest in the propinquity. But Mrs. Waythorn's conduct remained irreproachable. She neither avoided Varick nor sought him out. Even Waythorn could not but admit that she had discovered the solution of the newest social problem.

He had married her without giving much thought to that problem. He had fancied that a woman can shed her past like a man. But now he saw that Alice was bound to hers both by the circumstances which forced her into continued relation with it, and by the traces it had left on her nature. With grim irony Waythorn compared himself to a member of a syndicate. He held so many shares in his wife's personality and his predecessors were his partners in the business. If there had been any element of passion in the transaction he would have felt less deteriorated by it. The fact that Alice took her change of husbands like a change of weather reduced the situation to mediocrity. He could have forgiven her for blunders, for excesses; for resisting Haskett, for yielding to Varick; for anything but her acquiescence and her tact. She reminded him of a juggler tossing knives; but the knives were blunt and she knew they would never cut her.

And then, gradually, habit formed a protecting surface for his sensibilities. If he paid for each day's comfort with the small change of his illusions, he grew daily to value the comfort more and set less store upon the coin. He had drifted into a dulling propinquity with Haskett and Varick and he took refuge in the cheap revenge of satirizing the situation. He even began to reckon up the advantages which accrued from it, to ask himself if it were not better to own a third of a wife who knew how to make a man happy than a whole one who had lacked opportunity to acquire the art. For it *was* an art, and made up, like all others, of concessions, eliminations and embellishments; of lights judiciously thrown and shadows skillfully softened. His wife knew exactly how to manage the lights, and he knew exactly to what training she owed her skill. He even tried to trace the source of his obligations, to discriminate between the influences which had combined to produce his domestic happiness: he perceived that Haskett's commonness had made Alice worship good breeding, while Varick's liberal construction of the marriage bond had taught her to value the conjugal virtues; so that he was directly indebted to his predecessors for the devotion which made his life easy if not inspiring.

From this phase he passed into that of complete acceptance. He ceased to satirize himself because time dulled the irony of the situation and the joke lost its humor with its sting. Even the sight of Haskett's hat on the hall table had ceased to touch the springs of epigram. The hat was often seen there now, for it had been decided that it was better for Lily's father to visit her than for the little girl to go to his boardinghouse. Waythorn, having acquiesced in this arrangement, had been surprised to find how little difference it made. Haskett was never obtrusive, and the few visitors who met him on the stairs were unaware of his identity. Waythorn did not know how often he saw Alice, but with himself Haskett was seldom in contact.

One afternoon, however, he learned on entering that Lily's father was waiting to see him. In the library he found Haskett occupying a chair in his usual provisional way. Waythorn always felt grateful to him for not leaning back.

"I hope you'll excuse me, Mr. Waythorn," he said rising. "I wanted to see Mrs. Waythorn about Lily, and your man asked me to wait here till she came in."

"Of course," said Waythorn, remembering that a sudden leak had that morning given over the drawing room to the plumbers.

He opened his cigar case and held it out to his visitor, and Haskett's acceptance seemed to mark a fresh stage in their intercourse. The spring evening was chilly, and Waythorn invited his guest to draw up his chair to the fire. He meant to find an excuse to leave Haskett in a moment; but he was tired and cold, and after all the little man no longer jarred on him.

The two were enclosed in the intimacy of their blended cigar smoke when the door opened and Varick walked into the room. Waythorn rose abruptly. It was the first time that Varick had come to the house, and the surprise of seeing him, combined with the singular inopportuneness of his arrival, gave a new edge to Waythorn's blunted sensibilities. He stared at his visitor without speaking.

Varick seemed too preoccupied to notice his host's embarrassment.

"My dear fellow," he exclaimed in his most expansive tone, "I must apologize for tumbling in on you in this way, but I was too late to catch you downtown, and so I thought—"

He stopped short, catching sight of Haskett, and his sanguine color deepened to a flush which spread vividly under his scant blond hair. But in a moment he recovered himself and nodded slightly. Haskett returned the bow in silence, and Waythorn was still groping for speech when the footman came in carrying a tea table.

The intrusion offered a welcome vent to Waythorn's nerves. "What the deuce are you bringing this here for?" he said sharply.

"I beg your pardon, sir, but the plumbers are still in the drawing room, and Mrs. Waythorn said she would have tea in the library." The footman's perfectly respectful tone implied a reflection on Waythorn's reasonableness.

"Oh, very well," said the latter resignedly, and the footman proceeded to open the folding tea table and set out its complicated appointments. While this interminable process continued the three men stood motionless, watching it with a fascinated stare, till Waythorn, to break the silence, said to Varick, "Won't you have a cigar?"

He held out the case he had just tendered to Haskett, and Varick helped himself with a smile. Waythorn looked about for a match, and finding none, proffered a light from his own cigar. Haskett, in the background held his ground mildly, examining his cigar tip now and then, and stepping forward at the right moment to knock its ashes into the fire.

The footman at last withdrew, and Varick immediately began: "If I could just say half a word to you about this business—"

"Certainly," stammered Waythorn; "in the dining room—"

But as he placed his hand on the door it opened from without, and his wife appeared on the threshold.

She came in fresh and smiling, in her street dress and hat, shedding a fragrance from the boa which she loosened in advancing.

"Shall we have tea in here, dear?" she began; and then she caught sight of Varick. Her smile deepened, veiling a slight tremor of surprise.

"Why, how do you do?" she said with a distinct note of pleasure.

As she shook hands with Varick she saw Haskett standing behind him. Her smile faded for a moment, but she recalled it quickly, with a scarcely perceptible side glance at Waythorn.

"How do you do, Mr. Haskett?" she said, and shook hands with him a shade less cordially.

The three men stood awkwardly before her, till Varick, always the most self-possessed, dashed into an explanatory phrase.

"We—I had to see Waythorn a moment on business," he stammered, brick-red from chin to nape.

Haskett stepped forward with his air of mild obstinacy. "I am sorry to intrude; but you appointed five o'clock—" he directed his resigned glance to the timepiece on the mantel.

She swept aside their embarrassment with a charming gesture of hospitality.

"I'm so sorry—I'm always late; but the afternoon was so lovely." She stood drawing off her gloves, propitiatory and graceful, diffusing about her a sense of ease and familiarity in which the situation lost its grotesqueness. "But before talking business," she added brightly, "I'm sure everyone wants a cup of tea."

She dropped into her low chair by the tea table, and the two visitors, as if drawn by her smile, advanced to receive the cups she held out.

She glanced about for Waythorn, and he took the third cup with a laugh.

[1904]

Additional Poems

ANNE BRADSTREET
[1612–1672]

The poet Anne Bradstreet was born into a family notable for talent and ambition. Her father, Thomas Dudley, a Puritan intellectual who soldiered under Queen Elizabeth and managed the affairs of the Earl of Lincoln, was one of the principal figures in the Puritan migration to Massachusetts Bay. He would eventually become governor of the colony. Her husband, the Cambridge-educated Simon Bradstreet, would also become governor of the colony, as would her brother Joseph. Anne was educated in an English country estate in the years after Queen Elizabeth had made the woman of letters a powerful image in English culture. Her parents permitted her the sort of extensive education that only women in aristocratic families with dynastic ambitions or daughters of radical Reformed Christians were allowed. She mastered the classical and Biblical languages, French, theology, bookkeeping, and history. By the time of her 1630 voyage to New England on the flagship of the Puritan migration, the Arabella, she was an accomplished scholar and devout Christian. Her first glimpse of the wilds of New England inspired intense homesickness. She was eighteen years old, two years married. The Bradstreets lived briefly in several new towns, until they secured a tract of land in Ipswich. There she set up household, gave birth to and educated eight children. She enjoyed a loving marriage with a man who recognized her superlative talents. Sometime in the 1640s her husband secured a large parcel of land in the frontier and the family resettled in what would become Andover. There in the wilds of mid-Massachusetts she wrote poetry.

Bradstreet's verse, like much poetry composed in the England and America during the seventeenth century, was circulated in manuscript. Its readership was an elite literati connected to her influential family. Indeed, her brother-in-law Rev. John Woodbridge conveyed one manuscript collection to England and had it published as The Tenth Muse Lately Sprung Up in America *(London: Stephen Bowtell, 1650). His reasons for having the book printed may have been political. The establishment of Oliver Cromwell's Puritan Commonwealth in England had put into question the need for Massachusetts Bay. Believers in the Puritan errand in New England sought during the late 1640s and 1650s to promote reasons why the Massachusetts venture was worth continuing. Since they* could no longer present it as a haven for persecuted Puritans, they devised new reasons for the colony's existence—to convert Native Americans to the Reformed Christian faith—to spread civility into the wild. What better way to demonstrate the latter than by publicizing the literary accomplishment of an orthodox Puritan woman writing on the verge of the wilderness?

That Bradstreet's poetry was orthodox was important. The mid-century saw the emergence of a number of women (Quakers and antinomians such as Anne Hutchinson and Mary Dyer) who claimed prophetic power and the authority of the spirit to speak about whatever they felt to be important. Their revelations and testimonies often stood at odds with scripture and Christian teaching, and the speakers reveled in their marginal status. Anne's sister, Sarah Cain would suffer divorce and rejection for her prophesying. Anne Bradstreet's adherence to the conventions of Christian Reformed poetry—to the philosophical poetry of Guilleme Du Bartas, to the meditations of Bishop Joseph Hall, and to the emblem tradition of George Wither—and her symbolic alignment with women of learning and authority—from Queen Elizabeth to Mary Sydney—revealed her to be a self-conscious agent of Christian civilization. The poetry collected in The Tenth Muse was predominantly public: "The Foure Elements," "Of the Foure Humours," "Man's Constitution," "The Four Ages of Man," "The Four Seasons of the Yeare," "A Dialogue between Old England and New," "The Foure Monarchie." As the repeated figuration of the number four in the titles of the major poems suggests, Bradstreet viewed the world as a structured entity, inscribed with a divine design that framed nature and history. Much as an early scientist or a philosopher, Bradstreet attempted to comprehend the whole design of nature, man, and history. Rev. Woodbridge's intuition that there would be an audience for Bradstreet's work proved accurate. The book sold well. In 1678, six years after Bradstreet's death, a second collection, Several Poems (Boston: John Foster, 1678) claiming to be "Corrected by the Author, and enlarged by an Addition of several other Poems found amongst her Papers after her Death" appeared. Among these works were two long poems, "The Flesh and the Spirit" and "Contemplations," regarded as her most accomplished pieces. Certain poems of a more private nature collected in the "Andover Manuscript Book" were not printed.

While Bradstreet won fame in her lifetime as a poet in the public and philosophical mode, her current reputation lies in her private poetry—in reflections addressed to family members and to herself upon suffering and disease, her fear at the dangers of childbirth, in her expressions of love for her husband. Puritanism put a great premium on the importance of individual life, for each person was understood to experience the ultimate spiritual drama—the war between sin and redemption, life and death. The world that surrounded each individual contained spiritual messages and moral instructions. Meditative poetry—such as her "Contemplations"—attempted to decode the meaning of *nature and experience, discovering the eternal laws of life that God had inscribed in them.*

Throughout her life, Bradstreet composed verse in a range of public and private forms. Only Edward Taylor of seventeenth century Anglo-American poets approached her interest in the variety of poetic forms. No American poet of that century was better known in the republic of letters than Anne Bradstreet.

For Further Reading

Primary Works

The Tenth Muse (1650), and, from the Manuscripts, Meditations Divine and Morall Together with Letters and Occasional Pieces. Josephine K. Piercy, ed. (Gainesville, Florida: Scholars' Facsimiles and Reprints, 1965); *The Complete Works of Anne Bradstreet.* Joseph R. McElrath, Jr., and Allan P. Robb, eds. (Boston: Twayne, 1981).

Secondary Works

Caldwell, Patricia. "Why Our First Poet Was a Woman: Bradstreet and the Birth of an American Poetic Voice." *Prospects* 13 (1988): 1–35. Cowell, Pattie, and Ann Stanford, eds. *Critical Essays on Anne Bradstreet.* (Boston: G. K. Hall, 1983); Rosenmeier, Rosamond. *Anne Bradstreet Revisited.* (Boston: Twayne Publishers, 1991). Schweitzer, Ivy. "Anne Bradstreet Wrestles with the Renaissance." *Early American Literature* 23 (1988): 291–312. Stanford, Ann. *Anne Bradstreet, the Worldly Puritan.* (New York: B. Franklin, 1975). White, Elizabeth Wade. *Anne Bradstreet, the "Tenth Muse."* (Oxford and New York: Oxford University Press, 1971).

Upon the Burning of Our House July 10th, 1666◆

ANNE BRADSTREET

In silent night when rest I took
For sorrow near I did not look
I wakened was with thund'ring noise
And piteous shrieks of dreadful voice.
That fearful sound of "Fire!" and "Fire!"   5
Let no man know is my desire.
I, starting up, the light did spy,
And to my God my heart did cry
To strengthen me in my distress
And not to leave me succorless.   10
Then, coming out, beheld a space
The flame consume my dwelling place.
And when I could no longer look,
I blest His name that gave and took,
That laid my goods now in the dust.   15
Yea, so it was, and so 'twas just.
It was His own, it was not mine,
Far be it that I should repine;
He might of all justly bereft
But yet sufficient for us left.   20
When by the ruins oft I past
My sorrowing eyes aside did cast,
And here and there the places spy
Where oft I sat and long did lie:
Here stood that trunk, and there that chest,   25
There lay that store I counted best.
My pleasant things in ashes lie,
And them behold no more shall I.
Under thy roof no guest shall sit,
Nor at thy table eat a bit.   30

◆The Bradstreets were living in Andover at the time of the fire. Text from Andover manuscript.

No pleasant tale shall e'er be told,
Nor things recounted done of old.
No candle e'er shall shine in thee,
Nor bridegroom's voice e'er heard shall be.
In silence ever shall thou lie,   35
Adieu, Adieu, all's vanity.
Then straight I 'gin my heart to chide,
And did thy wealth on earth abide?
Didst fix thy hope on mold'ring dust?
The arm of flesh didst make thy trust?   40
Raise up thy thoughts above the sky
That dunghill mists away may fly.
Thou hast an house on high erect,
Framed by that mighty Architect,
With glory richly furnished,   45
Stands permanent though this be fled.
It's purchased and paid for too
By Him who hath enough to do.
A price so vast as is unknown
Yet by His gift is made thine own;   50
There's wealth enough, I need no more,
Farewell, my pelf,[1] farewell my store.
The world no longer let me love,
My hope and treasure lies above.

[1666]

---

[1]Material possessions

ROBERT FROST
[1874–1963]

No other modern American poet can match the staying power of Robert Frost. Even so, Frost remains the poet that critics love to hate. Words like "egocentric," "manipulative," "ambitious," and "vindictive" have dominated the discussion of Frost's personality for decades. Frost, however, never felt that being a nice guy constituted his primary mission in life. A poet and a teacher, he was willing to shock, annoy, anger, and abuse in his efforts to instruct and create. He could be belligerent and paranoid, but his pen gave him time and space to transmute his harsher lessons and insights into the poems Americans still find poignant and prophetic.

When Frost's father, a hard-drinking, hard-living journalist died in 1885, Frost's mother moved her eleven-year-old back East to Lawrence, Massachusetts. Between 1885 and 1892, Frost held a succession of blue collar jobs, including shoe factory worker, farm worker, leather worker, messenger, and bobbin boy in a woolen factory. He wrote for the Lawrence High School Bulletin, earned the rank of "class poet," and fell in love with his co-valedictorian, Elinor White. Before finishing school Frost proposed, but Elinor wanted a college education and pursued a three-year bachelor's degree at St. Lawrence University. Frost enrolled at Dartmouth, but did not last a term. He returned to Lawrence and factory work and finally convinced (some say badgered) Elinor to marry him in 1895.

His family intact, Frost enrolled for two years at Harvard and absorbed the gentile, erudite, slightly bored flavor of the school at the time. Frost read the works of the psychologist and philosopher William James, and listened to the pronouncements of poet and philosopher George Santayana. Never quite comfortable in the Ivy League, Frost abandoned college for good in 1899 and soon after suffered two personal tragedies that would change his life. In 1900, Frost and Elinor lost their three-year-old first-born son to cholera, and Frost's mother died of cancer. Desperate to escape painful memories, Frost moved to a poultry farm in Derry, New Hampshire. The farm would be Frost's home for the next nine years.

Amidst the chickens, the children (Elinor gave birth to four children between 1899 and 1905), and the deep New Hampshire woods, Frost began to write in earnest. Supported by a small allowance from his grandfather, he struggled to provide for his growing family with the proceeds of the never successful farm. In 1906, he took a full-time teaching job at the Pinkerton Academy in Derry, a move that coincided with his first post-Harvard attempts to publish his verse. In 1906, Frost published "The Tuft of Flowers" in the local Derry Enterprise. *That same year he placed "Ghost House" in* The Youth's Companion *and "Trial by Existence" in* The Independent. *Between 1905 and 1911, he crafted most of the poems that would constitute his first volume of verse,* A Boy's Will.

Having amassed enough poems to make a book, Frost sold the Derry farm, uprooted his family, and followed American poets Ezra Pound and Hilda Doolittle to London, the early twentieth century center of modernist literature. Frost's first book of verse, A Boy's Will *(David Nutt, 1913), did not cause much of a stir, but it did attract the attention of two influential reviewers, both American expatriates: poets F. S. Flint and Ezra Pound. Flint and Pound were marketing the new verse form they called "Imagism," a type of poetry designed to rid verse of hackneyed diction and "emotional slither." The central tenants of Imagism were the "direct treatment of the 'thing,'" the use of "absolutely no word" that did not contribute to the presentation, and the need to compose "in the sequence of the musical phrase, not in sequence of the metronome." Both Pound and Flint heard a simplicity and freedom from "sham and affectation" in Frost's early verse that seemed to identify him as a fellow Imagist. But Pound overlooked Frost's artistry, the careful craft that held the verses together. In truth, Frost felt more at home with the more formally traditional English poets of the period, the Georgians Wilfred Gibson, Lascelles Abercrombie, W. H. Davies, and Edward Thomas.*

Reacting in part against Pound's attempts to colonize his art, Frost formulated his own theory of verse while assembling the poems for the book that would launch his career in earnest, North of Boston *(1914). Always a poet of the ear rather than the eye, Frost developed what he termed "sentence sounds" or "the sound of sense." In Frost's view, speech utterances had a vital power apart from the literal meaning of the words. The "sound" of a sentence, the tones or inflections of words when strung together, carried a "sense" all its own, an instinctual musical current that always threatened to capsize what the words seemed to be saying. A good poet, Frost argued, would never lose track of the current of spoken speech sounds in the formalities of poetic meter or the urgencies of subject matter. Frost's commitment to the sound of sentences made him one of the great poets of idiomatic and colloquial speech, the seeming throw-away lines that pepper talk and hold both riches and horrors for those who dare to go behind the words. What does it really mean to say, for instance, "I see?" What does it mean to be "just far from home?"* North of Boston *places such questions front and center.*

North of Boston *(1914) was positively received by the critics. Filled with extended dramatic monologues and dialogues, poems in which Frost captured the rural inflections that formed the backdrop for his art,* North of Boston *marked a distinct departure from the more personal ruminations of* A Boy's Will. *The poems in* North of Boston *often present confrontations over the way things should be said and show the reader that the ways people speak and argue inevitably shape events. Buoyed by his success, Frost looked forward to releasing another book in England, but England went to war and turned its attention to matters other than poetry; Frost headed back to the United States.*

Frost left America in 1912 as a school teacher with a suitcase full of poems. In 1915, he returned as an established poet. Having accomplished his primary mission abroad, he solidified his position by courting Ellery Sedgwick, editor of the Atlantic Monthly, *and American publisher Henry Holt, who introduced Frost to the progressive American periodical, the* New Republic. *Frost also met the influential poet and critic Louis Untermeyer who became his lifelong champion. Purchasing a farm in Franconia, New Hampshire, Frost assembled a third volume,* Mountain Interval *(1916), containing several poems that Frost composed during the Derry years. In 1917, Frost accepted a post as an English teacher at Amherst College. The experience brought out the worst in Frost. He despised the regimentation of academic life, fought with his colleagues, and quit in a huff in 1920. After retreating to Franconia, Frost accepted a two-year term fellowship at the University of Michigan. In 1923, Frost published his fourth book of verse,* New Hampshire, *for which he won the Pulitzer Prize.*

Frost also surprised everyone by heading back to Amherst, where he would teach until 1938. The 1930s, however, were not kind to Frost. Following the publication of West-Running Brook *in 1928 and the* Collected Poems of Robert Frost *(1930), for which he won a second Pulitzer, Frost faced the fate of many of his modernist peers in light of a changing world. With the onset of the Great Depression, American poets and critics clamored for socially relevant verse. Frost, however, remained skeptical of mass political movements and refused, as critic William Pritchard put it, to write about "grievances" rather than "grief."* A Further Range *(1936) won Frost yet another Pulitzer, but critics attacked its naive detachment from economic circumstances and socialist priorities. The fading popularity of Frost's poetry coincided with a string of personal tragedies. Frost's beloved daughter Marjorie died horribly of an infection contracted while giving birth in 1934. Four years later Elinor died after a heart attack. Finally, his adult son Carol committed suicide in 1940, leaving behind a wife and children.*

Frost collapsed under these blows, but, with the help of his secretary Kathleen Morrison, a married woman some twenty years his junior, Frost completed A Witness Tree *in 1942. The book garnered Frost his fourth Pulitzer.*

During the final two decades of his life, Frost turned his attention primarily to the cultivation of his role as a public figure and cultural ambassador. Two final collections, The Steeple Bush *and* In the Clearing, *appeared in 1947 and 1962 respectively. In 1961, he capped his career with his reading of "The Gift Outright" at the inauguration of President John F. Kennedy. Frost died from complications following prostate surgery in 1963 at the age of eighty-eight.*

Those embarking on a first reading of Frost will be happily surprised by the simplicity of his language. Frost's simple speech, however, does not imply simple thoughts. Frost's poems often take on the difficult questions of just how we know what we know. The ways in which we read the world around us, Frost believes, depend upon the preexisting, often traditional ideas that we have about how things work ("Good fences make good neighbors"). If we abandon our preexisting notions, we open ourselves up to new ideas and experiences. At the same time, however, we leave ourselves vulnerable to the potential horrors and confusions of the unknown. Frost's poems are filled with characters determined to test the boundaries of what they know. They leave the comforts of home, wander beyond the constraints of human contracts, rules, and promises, and peer into the depths of experience unordered by such understandings. The results of such adventures are both ecstasies and agonies, the best that verse can offer.

Frost revised his poems throughout his career. The versions of his poems presented in the library issue from his volumes: A Boy's Will *(1913),* North of Boston *(1914),* Mountain Interval *(1916),* New Hampshire *(1923),* West-Running Brook *(1928),* A Further Range *(1936),* A Witness Tree *(1942), and* Steeple Bush *(1947). Significant variants are noted in the annotations to the poems.*

For Further Reading

Primary Works

Twilight (Lawrence, Mass.: American Printing House [?], 1894; Charlottesville: Clifton Waller Barrett Library, University of Virginia, 1966); *A Boy's Will* (London: David Nutt, 1913; New York: Holt, 1915); *North of Boston* (London: David Nutt, 1914; New York: Holt, 1914); *Mountain Interval* (New York: Holt, 1916); *Selected Poems* (New York: Holt, 1923; London: Heinemann/New York: Holt, 1923); *New Hampshire* (New York: Holt, 1923; London: Grant Richards, 1924); *Several Short Poems* (New York: Holt, 1924); *Selected Poems* (New York: Holt, 1928); *West-Running Brook* (New York: Holt, 1928); *Collected Poems of Robert Frost* (New York: Holt, 1930; London: Longmans, Green, 1930); *Selected Poems: Third Edition* (New York: Holt, 1934); *A Further Range* (New York: Holt, 1936; London: Cape, 1937); *Selected Poems* (London: Cape, 1936); *Collected Poems of Robert Frost* (New York: Holt, 1939; London: Longmans, Green, 1939); *A Witness Tree* (New York: Holt, 1942; London: Cape, 1943); *Steeple Bush* (New

York: Holt, 1947); *Complete Poems of Robert Frost, 1949* (New York: Holt, 1949; London: Cape, 1951); *Robert Frost: Selected Poems* (Harmondsworth, U.K.: Penguin, 1955); *In the Clearing* (New York: Holt, Rinehart & Winston, 1962; London: Holt, Rinehart & Winston, 1962).

Secondary Works

Karen L. Kilcup, *Robert Frost and Feminine Literary Tradition* (Ann Arbor: University of Michigan Press, 1998); Frank Lentricchia, *Robert Frost: Modern Poetics and the Landscapes of Self* (Durham: Duke University Press, 1975); Frank Lentricchia, *Modernist Quartet* (Cambridge: Cambridge University Press, 1994); Jay Parini, *Robert Frost: A Life* (New York: H. Holt and Co., 1999); Richard Poirier, *Robert Frost: The Work of Knowing*, (New York: Oxford University Press, 1977); William H. Pritchard, *Frost: A Literary Life Reconsidered* (New York: Oxford University Press, 1984); Lawrance Thompson, *Fire and Ice: The Art and Thought of Robert Frost* (New York: Holt, 1942); Lawrance Thompson, *Robert Frost: The Early Years, 1874–1915* (New York, Chicago & San Francisco: Holt, Rinehart & Winston, 1966); *Robert Frost: The Years of Triumph, 1915–1938* (New York, Chicago & San Francisco: Holt, Rinehart & Winston, 1970); Thompson and R. H. Winnick, *Robert Frost: The Later Years, 1938–1963* (New York: Holt, Rinehart & Winston, 1976); these three volumes abridged by Edward Connery Lathem, with Winnick, as *Robert Frost: A Biography* (New York: Holt, Rinehart & Winston, 1982); Linda W. Wagner, ed., *Robert Frost: The Critical Reception* (New York: Burt Franklin, 1977).

The Road Not Taken[1]

ROBERT FROST

Two roads diverged in a yellow wood,
And sorry I could not travel both
And be one traveler, long I stood
And looked down one as far as I could
To where it bent in the undergrowth;   5

Then took the other, as just as fair,
And having perhaps the better claim,
Because it was grassy and wanted wear;
Though as for that the passing there
Had worn them really about the same,   10

And both that morning equally lay
In leaves no step had trodden black.
Oh, I kept the first for another day!
Yet knowing how way leads on to way,
I doubted if I should ever come back.   15

I shall be telling this with a sigh
Somewhere ages and ages hence:
Two roads diverged in a wood, and I—
I took the one less traveled by,
And that has made all the difference.   20

[1915]

---

[1]"The Road Not Taken" first appeared in the *Atlantic Monthly* in August 1915. Frost first collected the poem in *Mountain Interval* (1916).

Mending Wall[1]

ROBERT FROST

Something there is that doesn't love a wall,
That sends the frozen-ground-swell under it,
And spills the upper boulders in the sun;
And makes gaps even two can pass abreast.
The work of hunters is another thing: 5
I have come after them and made repair
Where they have left not one stone on a stone,
But they would have the rabbit out of hiding,
To please the yelping dogs. The gaps I mean,
No one has seen them made or heard them made,   10
But at spring mending-time we find them there.
I let my neighbor know beyond the hill;
And on a day we meet to walk the line
And set the wall between us once again.
We keep the wall between us as we go.   15
To each the boulders that have fallen to each.
And some are loaves and some so nearly balls
We have to use a spell to make them balance:
"Stay where you are until our backs are turned!"
We wear our fingers rough with handling them.   20
Oh, just another kind of outdoor game,
One on a side. It comes to little more:
There where it is we do not need the wall:
He is all pine and I am apple orchard.
My apple trees will never get across   25
And eat the cones under his pines, I tell him.
He only says, "Good fences make good neighbors."
Spring is the mischief in me, and I wonder
If I could put a notion in his head:
"*Why* do they make good neighbors? Isn't it   30
Where there are cows? But here there are no cows.

---

[1]"Mending Wall" first appeared in Frost's second book of poems, *North of Boston* (1914).

Before I built a wall I'd ask to know
What I was walling in or walling out,
And to whom I was like to give offense.
Something there is that doesn't love a wall,   35
That wants it down." I could say "Elves" to him,
But it's not elves exactly, and I'd rather
He said it for himself. I see him there
Bringing a stone grasped firmly by the top
In each hand, like an old-stone savage armed.   40
He moves in darkness as it seems to me,
Not of woods only and the shade of trees.
He will not go behind his father's saying,
And he likes having thought of it so well
He says again, "Good fences make good neighbors."   45

[1914]

The Raven

EDGAR ALLAN POE

Once upon a midnight dreary, while I pondered, weak and
   weary,
Over many a quaint and curious volume of forgotten lore—
While I nodded, nearly napping, suddenly there came a tapping,
As of some one gently rapping, rapping at my chamber door.
"'Tis some visiter," I muttered, "tapping at my chamber door—   5
        Only this and nothing more."

Ah, distinctly I remember it was in the bleak December;
And each separate dying ember wrought its ghost upon the floor.
Eagerly I wished the morrow;—vainly I had sought to borrow
From my books surcease of sorrow—sorrow for the lost
   Lenore—   10
For the rare and radiant maiden whom the angels name
   Lenore—
        Nameless *here* for evermore.

And the silken, sad, uncertain rustling of each purple curtain
Thrilled me—filled me with fantastic terrors never felt before;
So that now, to still the beating of my heart, I stood repeating   15
"'Tis some visiter entreating entrance at my chamber door—
Some late visiter entreating entrance at my chamber door;—
        This it is and nothing more."

Presently my soul grew stronger; hesitating then no longer,
"Sir," said I, "or Madam, truly your forgiveness I implore;   20
But the fact is I was napping, and so gently you came rapping,
And so faintly you came tapping, tapping at my chamber door,
That I scarce was sure I heard you"—here I opened wide the
   door;——
        Darkness there and nothing more.

Deep into that darkness peering, long I stood there wondering,
    fearing,   25
Doubting, dreaming dreams no mortal ever dared to dream
    before;
But the silence was unbroken, and the stillness gave no token,
And the only word there spoken was the whispered word,
    "Lenore?"
This I whispered, and an echo murmured back the word,
    "Lenore!"
              Merely this and nothing more.   30

Back into the chamber turning, all my soul within me burning,
Soon again I heard a tapping somewhat louder than before.
"Surely," said I, "surely that is something at my window lattice;
Let me see, then, what thereat is, and this mystery explore—
Let my heart be still a moment and this mystery explore;—   35
             'Tis the wind and nothing more!"

Open here I flung the shutter, when, with many a flirt and
    flutter,
In there stepped a stately Raven of the saintly days of yore;
Not the least obeisance made he; not a minute stopped or
    stayed he;
But, with mien of lord or lady, perched above my chamber
    door—   40
Perched upon a bust of Pallas[1] just above my chamber door—
             Perched, and sat, and nothing more.

Then this ebony bird beguiling my sad fancy into smiling,
By the grave and stern decorum of the countenance it wore,
"Though thy crest be shorn and shaven, thou," I said, "art sure no
    craven,   45
Ghastly grim and ancient Raven wandering from the Nightly
    shore—
Tell me what thy lordly name is on the Night's Plutonian shore!"[2]
             Quoth the Raven "Nevermore."

---

[1] Pallas: Pallas Athene, Greek goddess of wisdom, arts, and war.
[2] Poe's speaker here associates the raven with Pluto, Roman god of death and the underworld.

Much I marvelled this ungainly fowl to hear discourse so plainly,
Though its answer little meaning—little relevancy bore;   *50*
For we cannot help agreeing that no living human being
Ever yet was blessed with seeing bird above his chamber door—
Bird or beast upon the sculptured bust above his chamber door,
            With such name as "Nevermore."

But the Raven, sitting lonely on the placid bust, spoke only   *55*
That one word, as if his soul in that one word he did outpour.
Nothing farther then he uttered—not a feather then he
    fluttered—
Till I scarcely more than muttered "Other friends have flown
    before—
On the morrow *he* will leave me, as my Hopes have flown
    before."
            Then the bird said "Nevermore."   *60*

Startled at the stillness broken by reply so aptly spoken,
"Doubtless," said I, "what it utters is its only stock and store
Caught from some unhappy master whom unmerciful Disaster
Followed fast and followed faster till his songs one burden
    bore—
Till the dirges of his Hope that melancholy burden bore   *65*
            Of 'Never—nevermore.'"

But the Raven still beguiling my sad fancy into smiling,
Straight I wheeled a cushioned seat in front of bird, and bust
    and door;
Then, upon the velvet sinking, I betook myself to linking
Fancy unto fancy, thinking what this ominous bird of yore—   *70*
What this grim, ungainly, ghastly, gaunt, and ominous bird of
    yore
            Meant in croaking "Nevermore."

This I sat engaged in guessing, but no syllable expressing
To the fowl whose fiery eyes now burned into my bosom's core;
This and more I sat divining, with my head at ease reclining   *75*
On the cushion's velvet lining that the lamp-light gloated o'er,
But whose velvet-violet lining with the lamp-light gloating o'er,
          She shall press, ah, nevermore!

Then, methought, the air grew denser, perfumed from an unseen
   censer
Swung by seraphim[3] whose foot-falls tinkled on the tufted
   floor.   80
"Wretch," I cried, "thy God hath lent thee—by these angels he
   hath sent thee
Respite—respite and nepenthe[4] from thy memories of Lenore;
Quaff, oh quaff this kind nepenthe and forget this lost Lenore!"
            Quoth the Raven "Nevermore."

"Prophet!" said I, "thing of evil!—prophet still, if bird or
   devil!—   85
Whether Tempter sent, or whether tempest tossed thee here
   ashore,
Desolate yet all undaunted, on this desert land enchanted—
On this home by Horror haunted—tell me truly, I implore—
Is there—*is* there balm in Gilead?[5]—tell me—tell me, I implore!"
            Quoth the Raven "Nevermore."   90

"Prophet!" said I, "thing of evil!—prophet still, if bird or devil!
By that Heaven that bends above us—by that God we both
   adore—
Tell this soul with sorrow laden if, within the distant Aidenn,[6]
It shall clasp a sainted maiden whom the angels name Lenore—
Clasp a rare and radiant maiden whom the angels name
   Lenore."   95
            Quoth the Raven "Nevermore."

"Be that word our sign of parting, bird or fiend!" I shrieked,
   upstarting—
"Get thee back into the tempest and the Night's Plutonian shore!
Leave no black plume as a token of that lie thy soul hath spoken!
Leave my loneliness unbroken!—quit the bust above my door!   100
Take thy beak from out my heart, and take thy form from off my
   door!"
            Quoth the Raven "Nevermore."

---

[3] Seraphim: in Judeo-Christian tradition, seraphim are the highest order of angels; these beings are known to inspire prophecy.

[4] Nepenthe: an ancient potion reputed to cure grief and sorrow.

[5] In the Hebrew Bible, the "balm of Gilead" is a healing ointment suggestive of God's power to restore the soul.

[6] Aidenn: this is an alternate spelling for the biblical Garden of Eden.

And the Raven, never flitting, still is sitting, *still* is sitting
On the pallid bust of Pallas just above my chamber door;
And his eyes have all the seeming of a demon's that is dreaming,　105
And the lamp-light o'er him streaming throws his shadow on the
　floor;
And my soul from out that shadow that lies floating on the floor
　　　　Shall be lifted—nevermore!

　　　　　　　　　　　　　　　　　　[1845]